EDUCATION 98/99

Twenty-Fifth Edition

W9-BTQ-485

Editor

Fred Schultz

University of Akron

Fred Schultz, professor of education at the University of Akron, attended Indiana University
to earn a B.S. in social science education in 1962, an M.S. in the history and philosophy
of education in 1966, and a Ph.D. in the history and philosophy of education and American
studies in 1969. His B.A. in Spanish was conferred from the University of Akron in May 1985.
He is actively involved in researching the development and history of American education
with a primary focus on the history of ideas and social philosophy of education.
He also likes to study languages.

Annual Editions
A Library of Information from the Public Press
Dushkin/McGraw·Hill
Sluice Dock, Guilford, Connecticut 06437

Visit us on the Internet—http://www.dushkin.com/

The Annual Editions Series

ANNUAL EDITIONS, including GLOBAL STUDIES, consist of over 70 volumes designed to provide the reader with convenient, low-cost access to a wide range of current, carefully selected articles from some of the most important magazines, newspapers, and journals published today. ANNUAL EDITIONS are updated on an annual basis through a continuous monitoring of over 300 periodical sources. All ANNUAL EDITIONS have a number of features that are designed to make them particularly useful, including topic guides, annotated tables of contents, unit overviews, and indexes. For the teacher using ANNUAL EDITIONS in the classroom, an Instructor's Resource Guide with test questions is available for each volume. GLOBAL STUDIES titles provide comprehensive background information and selected world press articles on the regions and countries of the world.

VOLUMES AVAILABLE

ANNUAL EDITIONS

Abnormal Psychology
Accounting
Adolescent Psychology
Aging
American Foreign Policy
American Government
American History, Pre-Civil War
American History, Post-Civil War
American Public Policy
Anthropology
Archaeology
Astronomy
Biopsychology
Business Ethics
Canadian Politics
Child Growth and Development
Comparative Politics
Computers in Education
Computers in Society
Criminal Justice
Criminology
Developing World
Deviant Behavior
Drugs, Society, and Behavior
Dying, Death, and Bereavement

Early Childhood Education
Economics
Educating Exceptional Children
Education
Educational Psychology
Environment
Geography
Geology
Global Issues
Health
Human Development
Human Resources
Human Sexuality
International Business
Macroeconomics
Management
Marketing
Marriage and Family
Mass Media
Microeconomics
Multicultural Education
Nutrition
Personal Growth and Behavior
Physical Anthropology
Psychology
Public Administration
Race and Ethnic Relations

Social Problems
Social Psychology
Sociology
State and Local Government
Teaching English as a Second
    Language
Urban Society
Violence and Terrorism
Western Civilization, Pre-Reformation
Western Civilization, Post-Reformation
Women's Health
World History, Pre-Modern
World History, Modern
World Politics

GLOBAL STUDIES

Africa
China
India and South Asia
Japan and the Pacific Rim
Latin America
Middle East
Russia, the Eurasian Republics, and
    Central/Eastern Europe
Western Europe

Cataloging in Publication Data
Main entry under title: Annual editions: Education. 1998/99.
    1. Education—Periodicals. I. Schultz, Fred, comp. II. Title: Education.
    ISBN 0–697–41280–6   ISSN 0272–5010   370'.5   73-78580

Twenty-Fifth Edition

Cover image © 1998 PhotoDisc, Inc.

Printed in the United States of America

Printed on Recycled Paper

Editors/Advisory Board

Members of the Advisory Board are instrumental in the final selection of articles for each edition of ANNUAL EDITIONS. Their review of articles for content, level, currentness, and appropriateness provides critical direction to the editor and staff. We think that you will find their careful consideration well reflected in this volume.

EDITOR

Fred Schultz
University of Akron

ADVISORY BOARD

Staff

Ian A. Nielsen, Publisher

To the Reader

In publishing ANNUAL EDITIONS we recognize the enormous role played by the magazines, newspapers, and journals of the *public press* in providing current, first-rate educational information in a broad spectrum of interest areas. Many of these articles are appropriate for students, researchers, and professionals seeking accurate, current material to help bridge the gap between principles and theories and the real world. These articles, however, become more useful for study when those of lasting value are carefully *collected, organized, indexed,* and *reproduced* in a *low-cost format,* which provides easy and permanent access when the material is needed. That is the role played by ANNUAL EDITIONS. Under the direction of each volume's *academic editor,* who is an expert in the subject area, and with the guidance of an *Advisory Board,* each year we seek to provide in each ANNUAL EDITION a current, well-balanced, carefully selected collection of the best of the public press for your study and enjoyment. We think that you will find this volume useful, and we hope that you will take a moment to let us know what you think.

The public conversation on the purposes and future directions of education is lively as ever. Alternative visions and voices regarding the broad social aims of schools and the preparation of teachers continue to be presented. *Annual Editions: Education 98/99* attempts to reflect current mainstream as well as alternative visions as to what education ought to be. Equity issues regarding what constitutes equal treatment of students in the schools continue to be addressed. This year's edition contains articles on the remaining gender issues in the field and on the application of research in multicultural education to the areas of teacher preparation and the staff development of teachers already in the schools. The debate over whether all public monies for education should go to the public schools or whether these funds should follow the student into either public or private schools has again intensified.

Communities are deeply interested in local school politics and school funding issues. "The 29th Annual Phi Delta Kappa/Gallup Poll of the Public's Attitudes toward the Public Schools" as well as other essays in this edition reflect these interests and concerns as well. There continues to be healthy dialogue about and competition for the support of the various "publics" involved in public schooling.

The articles reflect spirited critique as well as spirited defense of our public schools. There are competing, and very differing, school reform agendas being discussed, as has been the case for years now. Democratic publics tend to debate and disagree on important issues affecting public institutions and resources. All of this occurs as the United States continues to experience fundamentally important demographic shifts in its cultural makeup. By the year 2000, it is estimated that 43 percent of the overall student body will comprise students from minority cultural backgrounds. Minority student populations are growing at a much faster rate than traditional Caucasian populations.

Many scholars argue that the distinction between majority and minority school populations is being steadily eroded and will become relatively meaningless by the year 2030.

Dialogue and compromise continue to be the order of the day. The many interest groups within the educational field reflect a broad spectrum of viewpoints ranging from various behaviorist and cognitive developmental perspectives to humanistic, postmodernist, and critical theoretical ones.

In assembling this volume, we make every effort to stay in touch with movements in educational studies and with the social forces at work in schools. Members of the advisory board contribute valuable insights, and the production and editorial staffs at the publisher, Dushkin/McGraw-Hill, coordinate our efforts. Through this process we collect a wide range of articles on a variety of topics relevant to education in North America.

New to this edition are *World Wide Web* sites that can be used to further explore topics addressed in the article. These sites are cross-referenced by number in the *topic guide.*

The readings in *Annual Editions: Education 98/99* explore the social and academic goals of education, the current condition of the nation's educational systems, the teaching profession, and the future of American education. In addition, these selections address the issues of change and the moral and ethical foundations of schooling. As always, we would like you to help us improve this volume. Please rate the material in this edition on the postage-paid form provided at the back of this book and send it to us. We care about what you think. Give us the public feedback that we need.

Fred Schultz

Fred Schultz
Editor

Contents

UNIT 1

How Others See Us and How We See Ourselves

Six articles examine today's most significant educational issues: the debate over privatization, the equality of schools, and the current public opinion about U.S. schools.

The concepts in bold italics are developed in the article. For further expansion please refer to the Topic Guide and the Index.

UNIT 2

Rethinking and Changing the Educative Effort

Five articles discuss the tension between ideals and socioeconomic reality at work in today's educational system.

UNIT 3

Striving for Excellence: The Drive for Quality

Five selections examine the debate over achieving excellence in education by addressing issues relating to questions of how best to teach and how best to test.

The concepts in bold italics are developed in the article. For further expansion please refer to the Topic Guide and the Index.

UNIT 4

Morality and Values in Education

Four articles examine the role of American schools in teaching morality and social values.

The concepts in bold italics are developed in the article. For further expansion please refer to the Topic Guide and the Index.

UNIT 5

Managing Life in Classrooms

Five selections consider the importance of building effective teacher-student and student-student relationships in the classroom.

UNIT 6

Equal Opportunity in Education

Seven articles discuss issues relating to fairness and justice for students from all cultural backgrounds and how curricula should respond to culturally pluralistic student populations.

The concepts in bold italics are developed in the article. For further expansion please refer to the Topic Guide and the Index.

UNIT 7

Serving Special Needs and Concerns

Seven articles examine some of the important aspects of special educational needs and building cooperative learning communities in the classroom setting.

The concepts in bold italics are developed in the article. For further expansion please refer to the Topic Guide and the Index.

ix

UNIT 8

The Profession of Teaching Today

Four articles assess the current state of teaching in U.S. schools and how well today's teachers approach subject matter learning.

The concepts in bold italics are developed in the article. For further expansion please refer to the Topic Guide and the Index.

UNIT 9

A Look to the Future

Three articles look at new forms of schooling that break from traditional conceptions of education in America.

The concepts in bold italics are developed in the article. For further expansion please refer to the Topic Guide and the Index.

Topic Guide

This topic guide suggests how the selections in this book relate to topics of traditional concern to students and professionals involved with the study of education. It is useful for locating articles that relate to each other for reading and research. The guide is arranged alphabetically according to topic. Articles may, of course, treat topics that do not appear in the topic guide. In turn, entries in the topic guide do not necessarily constitute a comprehensive listing of all the contents of each selection. **In addition, relevant Web sites, which are annotated on pages 4 and 5, are noted in bold italics under the topic articles.**

TOPIC AREA	TREATED IN	TOPIC AREA	TREATED IN
Affirmative Action	26. Challenge of Affirmative Action *(1, 2, 3, 23, 24)*	**Effective Schools (cont.)**	10. Learning Curve 11. It Takes a School 12. What Matters Most *(5, 6, 7, 8, 9, 13)*
Change and Education	7. Reforming the Wannabe Reformers 8. Sweeping Decentralization of Educational Decision-Making Authority 9. Teaching Teachers 10. Learning Curve 11. It Takes a School *(8, 9, 10, 11, 26, 32, 33, 34)*	**Equality of Educational Opportunity**	5. Voucher Advocates Step Up Attack 26. Challenge of Affirmative Action 27. Social Class Issues in Family Life Education 28. Accommodating Cultural Differences 29. Children's Views of Social Poverty 30. Early Childhood Education 31. Race and Class Consciousness 32. One Drop of Blood 33. Invincible Kids 34. Family and Cultural Context 39. Seventy-Five Years Later . . . Gender-Based Harassment *(3, 5, 6, 16, 21, 23, 24, 25)*
Classroom Climate	21. Creating School and Classroom Cultures That Value Learning 22. Converting Peer Pressure 23. Changing the Way Kids Settle Conflicts 24. Six Surefire Strategies 25. Classroom Climate and First-Year Teachers *(19, 20, 21, 22)*		
Classroom Management	21. Creating School and Classroom Cultures That Value Learning 22. Converting Peer Pressure 23. Changing the Way Kids Settle Conflicts 24. Six Surefire Strategies 25. Classroom Climate and First-Year Teachers *(3, 19, 20, 21, 22)*	**Equity Issues in Schooling**	26. Challenge of Affirmative Action 27. Social Class Issues in Family Life Education 28. Accommodating Cultural Differences 29. Children's Views of Poverty 30. Early Childhood Education 31. Race and Class Consciousness 32. One Drop of Blood 33. Invincible Kids 34. Family and Cultural Context 39. Seventy-Five Years Later . . . Gender-Based Harassment *(3, 5, 6, 16, 21, 23, 24, 25)*
Columbus and the Curriculum	37. Columbus in the Curriculum *(23)*		
Computers and Schools	36. Computer Delusion 44. Silicon Classroom *(26, 34)*	**Ethics and Teaching**	17. Professional Ethics and the Education of Professionals 18. Last Freedom 19. Moral Dimensions of Schools 20. Public Schools, Religion, and Public Responsibility *(15, 16, 17, 18)*
Cultural Diversity	26. Challenge of Affirmative Action 27. Social Class Issues in Family Life Education 28. Accommodating Cultural Differences 29. Children's Views of Poverty 30. Early Childhood Education 31. Race and Class Consciousness 32. One Drop of Blood 33. Invincible Kids *(3, 4, 6, 21, 23, 24)*	**Excellence and Education**	12. What Matters Most 13. Using Standards to Make a Difference 14. Challenges of National Standards in a Multicultural Society 15. Case for National Standards and Assessments 16. Teachers Favor Standards, Consequences *(1, 2, 3, 12, 13, 14)*
Discipline	21. Creating School and Classroom Cultures That Value Learning 22. Converting Peer Pressure 24. Six Surefire Strategies 25. Classroom Climate and First-Year Teachers *(1, 3, 19, 20, 21, 22)*	**First-Year Teachers**	24. Six Surefire Strategies 25. Classroom Climate and First-Year Teachers *(19, 21, 22)*
Education in England and New Zealand	8. Sweeping Decentralization of Educational Decision-Making Authority	**Future of Education**	44. Silicon Classroom 45. Revisiting Tomorrow's Classrooms 46. Philosophy of Education for the Year 2000 *(32, 33, 34)*
Effective Schools	1. Schools That Work 2. Education: More Reform, Please 3. Can the Schools Be Saved? 7. Reforming the Wannabe Reformers 8. Sweeping Decentralization of Educational Decision-Making Authority	**Gallup Poll**	6. 29th Annual Phi Delta Kappa/Gallup Poll

TOPIC AREA	TREATED IN	TOPIC AREA	TREATED IN
Gender and Schooling	39. Seventy-Five Years Later . . . Gender-Based Harassment	**Public Perceptions of Public Schools**	1. Schools That Work 2. Education: More Reform, Please 3. Can the Schools Be Saved? 4. Republicans and the Education Debate 5. Voucher Advocates Step Up Attack 6. 29th Annual Phi Delta Kappa/Gallup Poll 35. Pomp and Promises 36. Computer Delusion *(1, 2, 3, 5, 6, 7, 26)*
Home/School Relations	11. It Takes a School *(8, 9)*		
Morality and Schooling	17. Professional Ethics and the Education of Professionals 18. Last Freedom 19. Moral Dimensions of Schools 20. Public Schools, Religion, and Public Responsibility *(15, 16, 17, 18)*	**Race and Education**	31. Race and Class Consciousness 32. One Drop of Blood *(23, 24)*
Multicultural Education	14. Challenges of National Standards in a Multicultural Society 26. Challenge of Affirmative Action 27. Social Class Issues in Family Life Education 28. Accommodating Cultural Differences 29. Children's Views of Poverty 30. Early Childhood Education 31. Race and Class Consciousness 32. One Drop of Blood 33. Invincible Kids 34. Family and Cultural Context *(3, 4, 6, 21, 23, 24)*	**Reform and Schooling**	7. Reforming the Wannabe Reformers 8. Sweeping Decentralization of Educational Decision-Making Authority 9. Teaching Teachers 10. Learning Curve 11. It Takes a School 12. What Matters Most 13. Using Standards to Make a Difference 14. Challenges of National Standards in a Multicultural Society 15. Case for National Standards and Assessments 16. Teachers Favor Standards, Consequences *(1, 3, 8, 9, 10, 11, 12, 13, 14, 23, 24, 25)*
National Education Association (NEA)	42. NEA's Teacher Education Initiative *(3)*		
National Educational Standards	13. Using Standards to Make a Difference 14. Challenges of National Standards in a Multicultural Society 15. Case for National Standards and Assessments 16. Teachers Favor Standards, Consequences *(1, 2, 3, 12, 13, 14)*	**Religion and Schools**	18. Last Freedom 20. Public Schools, Religion, and Public Responsibility *(15, 18)*
		School Failure and Success	41. New Look at School Failure and School Success 43. Paying Attention to Relationships *(29, 30)*
Nonviolent Conflict Resolution	22. Converting Peer Pressure 23. Changing the Way Kids Settle Conflicts *(19, 20, 22)*	**Social Class and Schooling**	27. Social Class Issues in Family Life Education 29. Children's Views of Social Inequality 31. Race and Class Consciousness *(21, 23, 24)*
Peer Pressure in School	22. Converting Peer Pressure 39. Seventy-Five Years Later . . . Gender-Based Harassment	**Student Self-Esteem**	33. Invincible Kids *(25)*
Philosophy of Education	46. Philosophy of Education for the Year 2000 *(32)*	**Teacher Education**	8. Sweeping Decentralization of Educational Decision-Making Authority 9. Teaching Teachers 12. What Matters Most *(8, 9, 10, 11, 12, 13, 14)*
Profession of Teaching	40. Quiet Revolution: Rethinking Teacher Development 41. New Look at School Failure and School Success 42. NEA's Teacher Education Initiative 43. Paying Attention to Relationships *(27, 28, 29, 30, 31)*	**Teachers' Success or Failure**	12. What Matters Most 40. Quiet Revolution: Rethinking Teacher Development 41. New Look at School Failure and School Success 43. Paying Attention to Relationships *(10, 11, 12, 13, 14, 29, 30, 31)*
Professional Development for Teachers	40. Quiet Revolution: Rethinking Teacher Development 41. New Look at School Failure and School Success 42. NEA's Teacher Education Initiative 43. Paying Attention to Relationships *(27, 28, 29, 30, 31)*	**Values in Education**	17. Professional Ethics and the Education of Professionals 18. Last Freedom 19. Moral Dimensions of Schools 20. Public Schools, Religion, and Public Responsibility *(15, 16, 17, 18)*
Professional Relationships	41. New Look at School Failure and School Success 43. Paying Attention to Relationships *(27, 29, 30)*	**Work and Schooling**	38. When Is Work a Learning Experience? *(21, 23, 24)*

Selected World Wide Web Sites for Annual Editions: Education

All of these Web sites are hot-linked through the *Annual Editions* home page: *http://www.dushkin.com/annualeditions* (just click on a book). In addition, these sites are referenced by number and appear where relevant in the Topic Guide on the previous two pages.

Some Web sites are continually changing their structure and content, so the information listed may not always be available.

General Sources

1. Educational Resources Information Center—*http://www.aspensys.com/eric/index.html*—This invaluable site provides links to all ERIC sites: clearinghouses, support components, and publishers of ERIC materials. You can search the ERIC database, find out what is new, and ask questions about ERIC.

2. Education Week on the Web—*http://www.edweek.org/*—At this *Education Week* home page, you will be able to open its archives, read special reports on education, keep up on current events in education, look at job opportunities, and access a variety of articles of relevance to educators today.

3. National Education Association—*http://www.nea.org/*—Something—and often quite a lot—about virtually every education-related topic can be accessed at or through this site of the 2.3-million-strong National Education Association.

4. National Parent Information Network/ERIC—*http://ericps.ed.uiuc.edu/npin/npinhome.html*—This is a clearinghouse of information on elementary and early childhood education as well as urban education. Browse through its links for information for parents and for people who work with parents.

How Others See Us and How We See Ourselves

5. Charter School Research—*http://csr.syr.edu/index.html/*—Open this site for news about charter schools. It provides information about charter schools and special education, a first-year report of the National Charter Schools Study, links to the U.S. Charter Schools Web site, and a database of state and school profiles.

6. PREPnet—*http://prep.net/*—This Pennsylvania site contains Web sites for educators. It covers a wide range of topics dealing with government, science, environment, literature, history, and K–12 resources and curricula. Its links will prove useful for examining issues ranging from school reform to values in education.

7. World Education Exchange/Hamline University—*http://www.hamline.edu/~kjmaier/*—This site, which aims for "educational collaboration," takes you around the world to examine virtual classrooms, trends, policy, and infrastructure development. It leads to information about school reform, multiculturalism, technology in education, and much more.

Rethinking and Changing the Educative Effort

8. The Center for Innovation in Education—*http://www.educenter.org/*—The Center for Innovation in Education, self-described as a "not-for-profit, non-partisan research organization" focuses on K–12 education reform strategies. Click on its links for information

about and varying perspectives on school privatization and other reform initiatives.

9. Colorado Department of Education—*http://www.cde.state.co.us/*—This site's links will lead you to information about education-reform efforts, technology in education initiatives, and many documents of interest to educators, parents, and students.

10. National Council for Accreditation of Teacher Education—*http://ncate.westlake.com/*—The NCATE is the professional accrediting organization for schools, colleges, and departments of education in the United States. Accessing this page will lead to information about teacher and school standards, state relations, and developmental projects.

11. Phi Delta Kappa International—*http://www.pdkintl.org/*—This important organization publishes articles about all facets of education. By clicking on the links at this site, for example, you can learn "FastFacts About Vouchers" and information about "The Seventh Bracey Report on the Condition of Public Education."

Striving for Excellence: The Drive for Quality

12. Education World—*http://www.education-world.com/*—Education World provides a database of literally thousands of sites that can be searched by grade level, plus education news, lesson plans, and professional-development resources.

13. EdWeb/Andy Carvin—*http://edweb.cnidr.org/*—The purpose of Ed-Web is to explore the worlds of educational reform and information technology. Access educational resources around the world, learn about trends in education policy and information infrastructure development, examine success stories of computers in the classroom, and much more.

14. Teacher's Guide to the U.S. Department of Education—*http://www.ed.gov/pubs/TeachersGuide/*—Government goals, projects, grants, and other educational programs are listed here as well as many links to teacher services and resources.

Morality and Values in Education

15. Carfax—*http://www.carfax.co.uk/subjeduc.htm*—Look through this superb index for links to education publications such as *Journal of Beliefs and Values, Educational Philosophy and Theory,* and *Assessment in Education.* The site also provides links to articles and research.

16. Child Welfare League of America—*http://www.cwla.org/*—The CWLA is the United States' oldest and largest organization devoted entirely to the well-being of vulnerable children and their families. This site provides links to information about issues related to morality and values in education.

17. The National Academy for Child Development—*http://www.nacd.org/*—This international organization is dedicated to helping children and adults reach their full potential. Its home page presents links to various programs, research, and resources into such topics as ADD.

18. Ethics Updates—*http://ethics.acusd.edu/*—This is Professor Lawrence Hinman's consummate learning tool. The site provides both simple concept definition and complex analysis of ethics, original treatises, and sophisticated search engine capability. Subject matter covers the gamut, from ethical theory to applied ethical venues. There are many opportunities for user input.

Managing Life in Classrooms

19. Classroom Connect—*http://www.classroom.net/*—This is a major Web site for K–12 teachers and students, with links to schools, teachers, and resources online. It includes discussion of the use of technology in the classroom.

20. Early Intervention Solutions—*http://www.earlyintervention.com/library4.htm*—EIS presents this site to address concerns about child stress and reinforcement. It suggests ways to deal with negative behaviors that may result from stress and anxiety among children.

21. Global SchoolNet Foundation—*http://www.gsn.org/*—Access this site for multicultural educational information. The site includes news for teachers, students, and parents, as well as chat rooms, links to educational resources, programs, and contests and competitions.

22. Teacher Talk Forum—*http://education.indiana.edu/cas/tt/tthmpg.html*—Visit this site for access to a variety of articles discussing life in the classroom. Clicking on the various links will lead you to electronic lesson plans covering a variety of topic areas from Indiana University's Center for Adolescent Studies.

Equal Opportunity in Education

23. Multicultural Publishing and Education Council—*http://www.mpec.org/*—This is the home page of the MPEC, a networking and support organization for independent publishers, authors, educators, and librarians fostering authentic multicultural books and materials. It has excellent links to a vast array of resources related to multicultural education.

24. Prospects: The Congressionally Mandated Study of Educational Growth and Opportunity—*http://www.ed.gov/pubs/Prospects/index.html*—This report analyzes cross-sectional data on language-minority and LEP students in the United States and outlines what actions are needed to improve their educational performance. Family and economic situations are addressed. Information on related reports and sites is provided.

Serving Special Needs and Concerns

25. National Institute on the Education of At-Risk Students—*http://www.ed.gov.offices/OERI/At-Risk/*—The At-risk Institute, created by OERI (Office of Educational Research and Improvement) supports a range of research and development activities designed to improve the education of students at risk of educational failure due to limited english proficiency, poverty, race, geographic location, or economic disadvantage. Access their work at this site.

26. Teaching with Electronic Technology—*http://www.wam.umd.edu/~mlhall/teaching.html*—This collection of World Wide Web sites ad-

dresses the use of electronic technologies in the classroom, which range from general and theoretical resources to instructive samples of specific applications to teaching and learning.

The Profession of Teaching Today

27. Canada's SchoolNet Staff Room—*http://www.schoolnet.ca/adm/staff/*—Here is a resource and link site for anyone involved in education, including special-needs educators, teachers, parents, volunteers, and administrators.

28. National Network for Family Resiliency—*http://www.nnfr.org/nnfr/*—This organization's home page will lead you to a number of resource areas of interest in learning about resiliency, including General Family Resiliency, Violence Prevention, and Family Economics.

29. Teachers Helping Teachers—*http://www.pacificnet.net/~mandel/*—This site provides basic teaching tips, new teaching methodology ideas, and forums for teachers to share their experiences. Download software and participate in chat sessions. It features educational resources on the Web, with new ones added each week.

30. The Teachers' Network—*http://www.teachnet.org/*—Bulletin boards, classroom projects, online forums, and Web mentors are featured on this site, as well as the book *Teachers' Guide to Cyberspace* and an online, 4-week course on how to use the Internet.

31. Michael's Website—*http://www.wam.umd.edu/~mlhall/teaching.html*—This site leads to many resources of values to those contemplating the future of education, particularly as regards the role of technology in the classroom and beyond.

A Look to the Future

32. Goals 2000: A Progress Report—*http://www.ed.gov/pubs/goals/progrpt/index.html*—Open this site to survey a progress report by the U.S. Department of Education on the Goals 2000 reform initiative. It provides a sense of what goals educators are reaching for as they look toward the future.

33. Mighty Media—*http://www.mightymedia.com/*—The mission of this privately funded consortium is to empower youth, teachers, and organizations through the use of interactive communications technology. The site provides links to teacher talk forums, educator resources, networks for students, and more.

34. Online Internet Institute—*http://www.oii.org/*—A collaborative project among Internet-using educators, proponents of systemic reform, content-area experts, and teachers who desire professional growth, this site provides a learning environment for integrating the Internet into educators' individual teaching styles.

We highly recommend that you review our Web site for expanded information and our other product lines. We are continually updating and adding links to our Web site in order to offer you the most usable and useful information that will support and expand the value of your Annual Editions. You can reach us at: *http://www. dushkin.com/annualeditions/.*

How Others See Us and How We See Ourselves

The United States has great interest in policy issues related to increased accountability to the public for what goes on in schools. Also, we are possibly the most culturally pluralistic nation in the world, and we are becoming even more diverse.

In addition, we may be approaching a historic moment in our national history regarding the public funding of education and the options parents might be given for the education of their children. Some of these options and the lines of reasoning for them are explored in this volume. Financial as well as qualitative options are being debated. Scholars in many fields of study as well as journalists and legislators are asking how we can make our nation's schools more effective as well as how we might optimize parents' sense of control over how their children are to be educated.

Democratic societies have always enjoyed spirited dialogue and debate over the purposes of their public institutions. Aristotle noted in his *Politics* that citizens of Athens could not seem to agree as to the purposes of education. He noted further that many of Athens' youth questioned traditional values. So has it been wherever people have been free. Yet this reality of democratic life in no way excuses us from our continuing civic duty to address directly, and with our best resources, the intellectual and social well-being of our youth. Young people "read" certain adult behaviors well; they see it as hypocrisy when the adult community wants certain standards and values to be taught in schools but rewards other, often opposite behaviors in society. Dialogue regarding what it means to speak of "literacy" in democratic communities continues. Our students read much from our daily activities and our many information sources, and they form their own shrewd analyses of what social values actually do prevail in society. How to help young people develop their intellectual potential and become perceptive students of and participants in democratic traditions are major public concerns. These have always been primary concerns to democratic educators.

Concerns regarding the quality of public schooling can also be seen in the social context of the dramatic demographic changes currently taking place in the United States. Over the past 12 years, cuts in federal government funding of such important early educational programs as

Head Start have created a situation in some areas of the nation (such as West Virginia) where only about one in three eligible children from poverty-level homes can have a place in Head Start programs. In addition, school drop-out rates, adult and youth illiteracy, the increasing rate of teenage pregnancy, and several interrelated health and security issues in schools cause continued public concern.

There is public uncertainty as well regarding whether state and provincial legislators will or should accept a greater state government role in funding needed changes in the schools. Intense controversy continues among citizens about the quality and adequacy of our schools. Meanwhile, the plight of many children is getting worse, not better. Some have estimated that a child is molested or neglected in the United States every 47 seconds; a student drops out of school every 8 seconds. More than a third of the children have no health insurance coverage. Our litany of tragedies affecting our nation's children and teenagers could be extended; however, the message is clear. There is serious business yet to be attended to by the social service and educational agencies that try to serve youth. People are impatient to see some fundamental efforts made to meet the basic educational needs of young people. The problems are the greatest in major cities and in more isolated rural areas. Public perceptions of the schools are affected by high levels of economic deprivation among large sectors of the population and by the economic pressures that our interdependent world economy produces as a result of international competition for the world's markets.

Studies conducted in the past few years, particularly the Carnegie Corporation's studies of adolescents in the United States, document the plight of millions of young persons in the United States. Some authors point out that although there was much talk about educational change in the 1990s, those changes were only marginal and cosmetic at best. States responded by demanding more course work and tougher exit standards from schools. With still more than 25 percent of schoolchildren in the United States living at or below the poverty level, and almost a third of them in more economically and socially vulnerable nontraditional family settings, the overall social situation for many young persons continues to be difficult. The public wants more effective responses to public needs.

Alternative approaches to attracting new and talented teachers have received sympathetic support among some sectors of the public, but these alternative teacher certification approaches have met with stiff opposition from large segments of the incumbent school staffs. Many states are exploring and experimenting with such programs at the urging of government and business leaders. Yet many of these alternative programs appear to be superficial and are failing to teach the candidates the new knowledge base on teaching and learning that has been developed in recent years.

So, in the face of major demographic shifts and of the persistence of many long-term social problems, the public watches how schools respond to new as well as old challenges. In recent years, these challenges have aggravated rather than allayed much public concern about the efficacy of public schooling. Various political, cultural, corporate, and philanthropic interests continue to articulate alternative educational agendas. At the same time the incumbents in the system respond with their own educational agendas, which reflect their views from the inside. Overall, it is surely the well-being and the academic progress of students that are the chief motivating forces behind the recommendations of all well-meaning interest groups in this dialogue.

Looking Ahead: Challenge Questions

What educational issues are of greatest concern to citizens today?

What ought to be the policy directions of national and state governments regarding educational reform?

What are the most important problems blocking efforts to improve educational standards? How can we best build a national public consensus regarding the structure and purposes of schooling?

What are the differences between the myth and the reality of U.S. schooling? Have the schools done anything right?

How can we most accurately assess public perceptions of the educational system?

What is the functional effect of public opinion on national public policy regarding educational development?

What generalizations concerning public schools in the United States can be drawn from the Phi Delta Kappa/Gallup poll data?

SCHOOLS THAT WORK

Two titans of education square off on school reform.
But both have important lessons to impart to the nation's troubled schools

They are two guys in tweed jackets. Ivy Leaguers. Professors. Grandfathers. They are also vocal critics of America's schools, in a year when education looms as one of the largest issues in the presidential race. Both are convinced that public school performance is lagging because many schools are, to put it bluntly, miseducating kids. And both have spent more than a decade trying to help schools out of the wilderness.

But E. D. Hirsch, Jr. and Theodore Sizer, each weighing in this fall with a new book on education, take strikingly different routes to reform. Hirsch is an educational traditionalist, Sizer a progressive. To Hirsch, knowledge is education's brass ring. The sorts of classroom strategies best suited to knowledge building are often old-fashioned ones: a tough course of study, book learning, in-charge teachers and lots of testing. To Sizer, schools ought to be about teaching students mental skills, like independent and creative thinking. Students' curiosity should drive the curriculum. In-depth projects should replace standardized testing. And single-subject teaching ought to be abandoned in favor of interdisciplinary study.

At schools Hirsch has nurtured, like Roland Park Elementary and Middle School on Baltimore's West Side, his philosophy is on display. Students in Regina White's fifth-grade classroom perform a scene, theater-in-the-round style, from *Don Quixote*. Elizabeth Aliberti's sixth-grade pupils practice songs from the musical version of *Oliver Twist*. Each day is an expedition into core

E. D. HIRSCH JR.
Knowledge is education's brass ring; WHAT students learn is most important.

knowledge, from Bach to Michelangelo to the science of rainbows.

The atmosphere at Hope Essential High School in Providence, R.I., where Sizer's ideas flourish, reflects his emphasis on developing students' minds. Housed on the top floor of an inner-city building, the 370 mostly African-American and Latino students of this school-within-a-school move through their day in 90-minute sessions. There are few textbooks. Teachers rarely lecture. The curriculum is divided into four large blocks—math, science, English and so-

THEODORE SIZER
Education ought to stress thinking skills; HOW students learn is key.

cial studies. In many courses, students study only a few topics intensively.

Two blueprints for reform. Two visions of what the basics of education should be. While Bob Dole and Bill Clinton tantalize voters with pledges of billions of dollars for new tuition plans, new schools and new technology, Hirsch and Sizer address the most fundamental questions facing the nation's classrooms: What should teachers teach, and how should they teach it? Smart answers to these questions are a sure way to improve schools, with or without infusions of money or machines.

For decades, schooling battles have been fought along progressive and traditionalist lines, and today the two camps are locked in opposition on major issues ranging from national standards to the teaching of reading. Yet school reform doesn't have to be an either-or proposition. In fact, it shouldn't be. Both Hirsch, with his traditionalist allies, and Sizer, with his progressive followers, have valuable contributions to make.

Plato, not Play-Doh. "Vermouth. Half dry. Half sweet. Straight up. Chill it," says Hirsch, Linden Kent Memorial Professor of English at the University of Virginia, red half glasses dangling on his chest. He's sitting in a Washington, D.C., restaurant, talking about education and battling a nasty cold. "Medicinal," he explains, as the waiter leaves.

Nearly a decade ago, the Yale University-trained expert on the English Romantic poets vaulted into the leadership of the traditionalist movement when he published a bestselling—and controversial—book, *Cultural Literacy:*

What Every American Needs to Know. In it, he argued that the nation's democratic institutions were threatened by a citizenry lacking a shared cultural vocabulary. The schools' "holiday curriculum"—cutting out paper turkeys at Thanksgiving and the like—wasn't doing the job.

In his new book, *The Schools We Need & Why We Don't Have Them,* Hirsch, 68, blasts the progressive teaching methods he says stand in the way of the wide-ranging cultural knowledge he advocates. Schools rely too much on progressive techniques like interdisciplinary instruction, ungraded work, "hands on" units and "cooperative" learning, he asserts, and such techniques are often used badly. Instead, Hirsch stresses the value of recitation, memorization, standardized tests and other traditional devices. Verbal instruction, he says, should be an "essential and even dominant focus of schooling."

Hirsch supports national education standards because he believes that to give kids the knowledge they need, a school's curriculum has to be prescribed. "What kids should know each year should be engraved in stone because the year is the unit of accountability." Able to navigate through Latin (as well as German, French and Italian) and always ready to take a computer apart, Hirsch rejects the notion of the "child centered" curriculum, in which subjects like ancient history and science are withheld from kids in early grades in favor of material focused on the students' world. "The presumption that the affairs of one's neighborhood are more interesting than those of faraway times and places is contradicted in every classroom that studies dinosaurs and fairy tales," he writes.

In 1986, Hirsch created the Core Knowledge Foundation to help schools implement his theories. The foundation, funded in part with the educator's book royalties, is now working with 350 schools in 40 states, including Baltimore's Roland Park. At such "Hirsch" schools, teaching cultural knowledge is indistinguishable from teaching basic skills like reading, writing and speaking. A culture-rich curriculum is crucial, Hirsch argues, because a shared cultural vocabulary is a cornerstone of literacy. "To grasp the words on a page we have to know a lot of information that isn't set down on the page," he writes. That knowledge then serves as a kind of intellectual Velcro, to which new learning can cling.

Cultural Literacy landed Hirsch in the middle of the then raging culture wars, with multiculturalists and others on the left denouncing the book as elitist and authoritarian. But it was in reality a product of Hirsch's long interest in the theory of writing, a polemic less about the shape of the cultural canon than about how kids learn to read and write. In fact, Hirsch says, a traditionally taught core curriculum helps disadvantaged students the most: "Kids from affluent backgrounds get knowledge from outside school; those who rely on school to give it to them—disadvantaged students don't get it" because schools aren't teaching it.

Habits of mind. Ted Sizer, 64, has been called an elitist nearly as often as has Hirsch. Like Hirsch, he believes all kids should get a demanding intellectual education. But Sizer, a Yalie who was dean of Harvard's graduate school of education in the 1960s and headmaster of prestigious Phillips Academy in Andover, Mass., in the '70s, thinks the way to a good education lies in progressive reforms. In a blistering 1984 study of the nation's public schools, Sizer deemed the typical high school "a place of friendly, orderly, uncontentious wasteful triviality," notable mostly for "the docility of students' minds." In classroom after classroom, he found a "conspiracy of the least"—an unspoken pledge by students and teachers to demand little of one another.

Like Hirsch, Sizer sought a way to help schools reform themselves. Backed by major foundations, he launched the Coalition of Essential Schools, an organization housed at Brown University, where Sizer served as education department chairman. Twelve years and $60 million later, Sizer's coalition has grown to 238 schools, including Hope Essential.

In his new book, *Horace's Hope: What Works for the American High School,* the educator reflects on his years in the school reform trenches. He again takes aim at educational traditionalism in public high schools, attacking the "lecture-drill-and-test systems" of many schools, "with their swift march over lists of topics and unconnected material." The average school, he charges, is "stuck with the notion that a curriculum is primarily a list." To Sizer, true education means students who exhibit the right "habits of mind," ask inquiring questions and utilize knowledge in thoughtful ways.

Crucial to such thoughtfulness, he says, is interdisciplinary instruction. Grasping the complexities of a topic like immigration, for example, requires investigating a host of other seemingly unconnected subjects, such as history, economics, statistics, geography, even ecology. To encourage such probing, he urges schools to reorganize each day into longer blocks of time and to increase team teaching.

High on Sizer's list of educational crimes is the reliance on standardized testing, a practice he dismisses as "giving at best snippets of knowledge about a student and at worst a profoundly distorted view of that child." He calls instead for measuring students' achievement by having them present "exhibitions" to their classmates. He strongly opposes national and state education standards, arguing that parents should control what their kids learn through local school boards. To impose nonlocal standards, he says, is a form of intellec-

CREATIVE SOLUTIONS

Cette école est publique

Madame DaSilva asks a math question, surveys her first-grade class and finally points to Caroline. *"Trois?"* the student answers tentatively. *"Qui, c'est ça,"* beams DaSilva.

Caroline is not a French exchange student, and this is not your average first-grade math lesson. Instead, DaSilva's pupils are part of a bold experiment: a language "immersion" program at Mary A. Cunningham Elementary School in Milton, Mass., where students are taught entirely in French during the first and second grades, and partly in French through high school.

Launched in the 1980s to attract students to a new school, Milton's French program is a striking example of the results typical public school systems can achieve when classroom rigor becomes a community priority. The program started in two classrooms and steadily won converts within the Milton commu-

nity. Today, it enrolls almost half of Milton's incoming first graders.

Milton is not a posh suburban school system: It spends less per student than the average Massachusetts district, and the immersion program includes as many kids from the city's housing projects as hail from the million-dollar homes in Milton Hills. The French program has drawn its share of controversy, largely over the issue of resources. Opponents say students in traditional classrooms have been neglected. When parents whose kids were not in the immersion program thought that a student exchange to Grenoble, France, was limited to program students, they protested. Milton spends equally on both programs, Superintendent of Schools Mary Grassa O'Neill says. But the resentment has nonetheless spilled into school politics, with candidates running on "pro" and "anti" immersion platforms in last year's school board

election. (Pro-immersion candidates prevailed, garnering about 70 percent of the vote.) In response to favoritism protests, Grassa O'Neill says, French, Spanish and Latin have been introduced in Milton's middle schools, and the school system is contemplating adding such classes in elementary schools, too.

The French program seems to have given Milton kids a general academic edge. The school system now shines in state performance tests in subjects from reading to science. Tellingly, Milton's French program has also lured students from area private schools. "We believe the schools are offering our children something special and unique," says Bella English, parent of a fifth grader in the program. "It's great for those of us who still believe in a public school education."

BY ROBIN M. BENNEFIELD
IN MILTON

---

tual censorship, "a dangerous and potentially undemocratic road."

Common ground. School reform is a difficult road, as Sizer and Hirsch readily acknowledge. Sizer's book is far less sanguine than its title suggests. "We are sobered by how hard it is to accomplish change," he writes. With Sizer's reform measures come new classroom roles for students and teachers, and the task of battling union rules and school regulations. Faculty turf battles, tradition and simple cynicism have slowed the "Sizerization" of many coalition schools: Only a fraction have introduced his entire plan. Not by accident, a portrait of Don Quixote hangs in the coalition's offices. Hirsch's curriculum, for its part, demands a far greater grasp of subjects like ancient history than the typical elementary teacher possesses, and it often runs head-on into local curriculum edicts.

Where the educators' efforts have been successful, however, the results have been impressive, suggesting that reform is not an either-or proposition, not a matter of selecting one philosophy over the other. To be convinced by Hirsch's argument for a core curriculum, one need look no further than schools like Roland Park, with its diverse student body. Classroom life in such

schools is hardly the drudgery Hirsch's critics claim, nor is the course material "Eurocentric" or otherwise elitist. There are units on African-American scientists, African and Norse myths, Maya culture and more. Diversity rules even in gym class, where students perform American Indian dances.

Roland Park's curriculum is a far cry from the school's pre-Hirsch version, which was essentially a fat list of skills the Baltimore school system wanted students to master, such as identifying the main idea in a story or locating a body of water on a map—in other words, a curriculum built on the belief that skills mattered more than what kids studied. The new curriculum is far more demanding, but students rise to the challenge. "I never thought of teaching astronomy or the Roman Empire in the third grade," says teacher Pat Wolff. "Originally, I said the kids are not going to read this," adds fifth-grade teacher Regina White, whose students read abridged versions of classics such as *Julius Caesar* and the *Iliad.* "Now I know differently. Even in remedial classes, there's a lot of enthusiasm."

Test scores suggest as much. In the two years since the core-knowledge curriculum began, the proportion of fifth graders passing Maryland's state social

studies test has jumped from 27 percent to 44 percent; passing grades in science have risen from 34 percent to 47 percent and in language usage from 18 percent to 49 percent. Other core-knowledge schools with large populations of disadvantaged students report similar gains.

Attendance up. But if Hirsch's schools prove that traditionalism doesn't equal mind-numbing learning, Sizer is right to make the culture of schools a priority. Too many schools are large, impersonal places; too many students are alienated and apathetic. In many classrooms, the instruction is as dry and lifeless as Sizer paints it; students are

TEACHING

HIRSCH

Old-fashioned methods such as recitation work. And in the hands of innovative teachers, they are fun.

SIZER

Frequent "hands on" projects, with teachers acting as "coaches," are a good way to help students learn.

required merely to parrot surface facts and figures, and many never learn how to put their minds to good use. Sizer's assessment of standardized testing also has merit: Tests drive down the level of instruction in many classrooms as teachers match their teaching to the low-level skills often being measured.

At Hope Essential, breaking the school day into large blocks makes relationships between students and teachers more personal. In turn, student attendance is up, discipline problems are down. Interdisciplinary instruction gives students a richer understanding of what they are learning, exemplified in the student exhibitions so important to Sizer as alternatives to standardized tests. Last year, with the O.J. Simpson trial in the news, a month's study of Shakespeare's *Othello* in an 11th-grade English class at Hope Essential culminated not in a multiple-choice test but in a mock trial of the Moor for Desdemona's murder. Students explored the tragedy's insights into marriage, jealousy and responsibility. Their tasks included reciting por-

tions of the play, writing papers in the form of opening and closing legal arguments and a host of other activities.

Such intensive study pays off: Nearly 90 percent of Hope Essential's students are admitted to college, up from 18 percent at Hope High School before Sizer arrived. Hirsch himself is not opposed per se to exhibitions or other Sizeresque methods—if they deliver enough of the right content.

Even Hirsch's conviction that knowledge building is schools' primary task can be partly reconciled with Sizer's view that knowledge is secondary to the teaching of mental skills, or "habits of mind." Hirsch's focus is elementary school; Sizer's is high school. Indeed, when he talks about high school, Hirsch moves closer to Sizer's stance, suggesting that older students, secure in a broad knowledge base, be encouraged to "focus more narrowly and probe more deeply."

Nowhere is the value of merging the best of traditional and progressive strategies better illustrated than in the thorny

question of how best to teach kids to read. Overwhelmingly, studies suggest that kids need to learn phonics, the building blocks of sound-letter relationships, as traditionalists argue. But equally compelling evidence exists that kids learn such skills faster and more thoroughly when teachers use progressive techniques to teach phonics, such as asking students to write stories using phonetic or "invented" spelling.

In the reading debate, as in other school reform issues, many progressives and traditionalists seem more eager to fight than to find common ground, routinely misrepresenting each other's views and needlessly polarizing debates at students' expense. It is left to the rest of us to break through the overheated rhetoric, finding in both sides important pieces of a national solution.

———

By Thomas Toch with Missy Daniel in Providence

EDUCATION: MORE REFORM, PLEASE

Public schools in the U.S. are improving—but far too slowly

Nineteen ninety-six will go down as the year education finally achieved mass-market political appeal. Republicans, warning of wholesale failure in the nation's schools, called for radical restructuring; President Clinton and other Democrats, their assessment of the crisis no less dire, pushed somewhat more moderate solutions. The message resonated with an electorate that consistently ranked education as a top-of-mind issue.

Was the rhetoric justified? Are schools that bad? By most measures, yes. A study of students in 41 countries, released on Nov. 20, found that American eighth-graders ranked smack in the middle of the international pack—between Romania and Bulgaria—in math and science. The U.S. is laughably behind schedule in meeting the standards for graduation rates and science and math prowess specified in 1990 by the Education Dept.'s Goals 2000 task force. Business executives complain less about global rivals or the price of raw materials than about the millions they are spending on remedial education for new hires—if they can find them.

Amid the distressing news, though, there is hope: Public schools are getting better. The nation was jolted awake 13 years ago by the Education Dept.'s report, *A Nation at Risk,* which warned that schools were pro-

America needs both broad national standards and plenty of flexibility for local school districts

ducing a vast legion of mediocre students. Since then, education reform has produced signs of slow but consistent progress. National test scores, especially in math and science, are up over the past decade; more students are taking advanced placement courses; and the gap between graduation rates of blacks and whites has narrowed dramatically.

The achievements are modest—but remarkable, say many educators and analysts, given schools' resources and the deteriorating qualifications of many students entering the system. More than 40% of kids attending urban schools come from families in poverty, according to the National Center for Education Statistics. Single-parent families, teen pregnancies, and higher drug use all have created barriers to learning. City teachers typically wrestle with larger classes, more immigrants with limited English proficiency, and fewer resources than their suburban counterparts. Yet two-thirds of the city kids graduate on time.

That's encouraging. So, too, is the commitment the nation seems to be making to create change. Over the past decade, Americans have witnessed a boom in educational experimentation, from self-directed charter schools to voucher systems that encourage competition for students. Elementary-school teachers in Caspar, Wyo., for example, recently won permission

It's essential to reach kids early. That means expanding preschool programs while getting parents more involved

to eliminate their principal's job and spend the money on more teachers; the school is run by committee now. Even teachers' unions, long opponents of such efforts, have cautiously joined the parade.

For all the reforming, though, there's little consensus on what works when it comes to schooling our children. Only now are officials starting to rigorously assess the patchwork of projects into which states, cities, and school districts have variously sunk many millions of dollars over the past decade. In lieu of evidence, "the traditional debate is one guy saying, 'Charter schools work,' and another saying, 'No they don't,'" complains Frank Newman, president of the Education Commission of the States.

TURNAROUND. The evidence will come from places such as Oriole Park Elementary School, serving a largely poor, racially mixed population on Chicago's northwest side. Six years ago, Oriole Park was slated for closure, so dismal were its results; since then, the school has moved from 224 out of 472 schools in Chicago to 67th, based on test scores. Principal Gail Szulc urges teams of teachers, parents, and social workers to meet high standards, providing preschool and full-day kindergarten, a full-time tutor in all classrooms, and heavy teacher training. She insists: "We will not make any excuse for poor performance—or take any."

The nation must embrace reformers such as Szulc, and it must encourage experimentation. "There is no simple solution—there are many roads to success," says Commissioner of Education Statistics Pascal D. Forgione. Increasingly, too, schools will have to demonstrate better results to compete for government funding, notes Duke University economist Helen F. Ladd. At the same time, there must be a national blueprint—some

central oversight to ensure that schools adopt best practices without constantly reinventing wheels. As schools brace for the next decade, here is a strategy to keep reform thriving.

Broad national standards. The U.S. is the only industrial nation without math and science standards. Many states are trying to establish their own, with chaotic, if creative, results. Virginia is writing standards for fourth- and fifth-graders that emphasize grammar and organization; Delaware's focus is on reflection and reasoning. Science teachers and scientists are teaming up to write standards for their discipline. While encouraging all these disparate flowers to bloom, Washington should help evaluate what works and provide the information to all states.

Loosen the system. Tighten standards and hold teachers and administrators accountable. But allow local districts—or, better, individual schools—flexibility in figuring out how to meet the goals. Charter schools—performance-based and legally freed of many regulations—are sprouting across the nation. According to Joseph Nathan of the University of Minnesota's Center for School Change, early results show higher parental satisfaction and student achievement. Consider, too, the striking results of a back-to-basics mathematics effort aimed at minority students in Prince George's County, Md. The combination of newly trained teachers, afterschool tutors, and a Saturday "Math Academy" for additional help has helped lift enrollment of minority ninth-graders in advanced algebra from 53% to 90% since 1991.

Early intervention and parental involvement. Carnegie Corp. researchers point to a direct link between reaching kids early and later achievement. So expand preschool and full-day kindergarten to the half of all students not now attending. Also, seek imaginative ways to tune in parents as

U.S. SCHOOLS: MIRED IN MEDIOCRITY...		...BUT SHOWING SIGNS OF LIFE			
Combined average scores on math and science tests (1995)		Average scale scores on standardized tests			
		AGE 9		AGE 17	
		1970	1994	1970	1994
JAPAN	1176				
KOREA	1172				
CZECH REPUBLIC	1138	225	231	305	294
BULGARIA	1105	219	231	304	306
RUSSIA	1073	208	211	285	288
GERMANY	1040	204	205	290	285
U.S.	1034				
AVERAGE	1029				
ROMANIA	968				
IRAN	898				
SOUTH AFRICA	680				

DATA: EDUCATION DEPARTMENT; NATIONAL ASSESSMENT OF EDUCATIONAL PROGRESS

coaches. At the Richard Yzaguirre School for Success, a charter school in Houston's barrio, parents are required to sign a contract to volunteer in the school, binding them to their kids' education.

Expand teacher training. A growing number of teachers lack either certification or sufficient time for training and planning. By some estimates, U.S. schools spend less than 2% of their budgets on training. Spend more, and teachers can overcome some of the problems kids bring to the classroom. "We don't have to change the social and economic background of every parent in the country to have better schools," says Michigan State University Professor William H. Schmidt.

Put it all together, and the results can be striking. A few years ago, the 1,200-student Vaughn Next Century Learning Center in northeast Los Angeles was be-

ing shunned by students and teachers. Now, there's a waiting list to get in, attendance is near perfect, and test scores are up sharply.

What happened? Vaughn became a charter school, giving "chief education officer" Yvonne Chan control over budget, curriculum, even length of the school year. Chan redirected funds from administrative overhead to teacher training and computers. She started a career-training center for parents. Parents, teachers, and students alike quickly responded.

It's a powerful lesson. Set high standards but allow flexibility in determining solutions. Invest in teachers. Involve parents. Hold everyone, including students, accountable. "We've got the opportunity to get out of the box," Chan says. "The handcuffs are off."

By Richard A. Melcher in Chicago and Paul Magnusson in Washington

IS THE NEA GETTING ON THE REFORM TRAIN?

See any horns?" Robert F. Chase asks. Nope—nothing obvious, anyway. Just a graying former Danbury (Conn.) junior high school social studies teacher—soft-spoken and rather unassuming.

Yet Chase now sits atop the National Education Assn., the organization most conservatives indict as the single greatest obstructor of education reform in America. Bob Dole demonized the NEA throughout his failed Presidential campaign: "If education were a business, [teachers' unions] would be driving it into bankruptcy," he warned.

True, the NEA still backs off many changes that would threaten the security of its 2.2 million members. But it quietly is opening the door to reform. Chase has no problem, for example, with requiring higher standards for teachers and for student achievement. He backs school choice—as long as it is limited to a choice among public schools, a position adopted by President Clinton. And now, the NEA is spending $1.5 million to plan charter schools—institutions freed from most district and state rules. Next September, the NEA will be a partner in chartered schools in Atlanta, Phoenix, and four other cities.

ON BOARD. Such movement, however tentative, contradicts decades of NEA opposition to change—a rigidity that has undermined many reform efforts. In fact, the NEA comes late to the party: The much smaller American

Federation of Teachers has espoused support of reform experiments for a decade. The AFT local in Boston, for example, last year co-sponsored five pilot schools that circumvent many provisions of its contract.

So why is the more powerful NEA buying in now? In part, it recognizes

The NEA's president backs school reform—as long as the choice is limited to public schools

that the reform train was leaving with the NEA still on the platform— and that participating in charter schools allows it to help shape the result. What the union wants to avoid, after all, are charters that completely bypass collective bargaining. "I don't think teacher salaries ought to be low-

ered in order to create a charter school," Chase says.

"FRUSTRATED." Critics say such a shift doesn't amount to much. "The essential difference between the days gone by and now is that [the NEA] recognizes that people are frustrated," says Jeanne Allen, president of the Washington-based Center for Education Reform. "But [the NEA] doesn't agree with the vast majority of real reforms." Charlene Haar, president of the Education Policy Institute, says the NEA, while trying to appease teachers who want less regulation, "still has an anticompetitive mentality."

Indeed, the NEA hasn't abandoned many of its traditional positions. Merit pay, for one, remains anathema. The union won't embrace the reformist notion of encouraging private schools to seek public tuition vouchers, either. And in Milwaukee, where NEA-backed school board members precipitated the resignation in 1995 of reformist superintendent Howard Fuller, the union local has agreed to loosen the rules for firing underperforming teachers—but it is taking the school board to court over charter legislation. Still, national leader Chase acknowledges that the NEA must start doing more than just resist change. Says Chase: "We're all in this together." Teachers surely want a piece of the solution—not just the blame.

By Paul Magnusson in Washington

Can the Schools Be Saved?

Chester E. Finn, Jr.

CHESTER E. FINN, JR., *a former Assistant Secretary of Education, is John M. Olin fellow at the Hudson Institute in Washington, D.C.*

PUBLIC EDUCATION in the United States is a vast enterprise, involving some 45 million young people, or three-fifths of all Americans under the age of nineteen; 85,000 schools; 5 million employees; and a cost to taxpayers of more than a quarter-trillion dollars annually. Vast as this enterprise is, it is also increasingly precarious. The evidence is by now so familiar as hardly to bear repeating:

- In 1994, according to the National Assessment of Educational Progress (NAEP), six out of seven eighth-graders were not "proficient" in American history, and 57 percent of high-school seniors registered "below basic" in this subject.

- In the same year, three out of four seniors were less than "proficient" in geography; 30 percent lacked even rudimentary understanding.

- Two out of five fourth-graders, including two out of every three black and Hispanic youngsters, can hardly read at all. Among high-school seniors in 1994, only 36 percent were "proficient" in this most basic skill.

- Almost half the entering freshmen in the California state-university system in 1994 required remedial instruction in reading or math or both—the fifth straight year in which this number has increased.

This ever-expanding catalogue of inadequacy and outright failure has led to a development full of significance for the future: a broad cross-section of America is losing faith in public education itself. In one 1995 survey, 72 percent of respondents voiced concern about drugs and violence in local schools, 61 percent complained of low standards, 60 percent of a lack of attention to "basics." In the words of the report summarizing the data, "support for public education is fragile and porous." Even Albert Shanker, president of the American Federation of Teachers, has declared that "time is running out on public education. . . . The dissatisfaction that people feel is very basic." Or, in the recent words of David Mathews, a former secretary of the Department of Health, Education, and Welfare, "Americans today seem to be halfway out the schoolhouse door."

Indeed they do. Hundreds of thousands of families are already paying private firms to tutor their children in skills and branches of knowledge they are not acquiring in school. Others have increasingly begun to opt out altogether. Private-school enrollment, though still below the "market share" it attained in the 60's and early 70's, has risen faster than public enrollment for the past five years; Catholic schools have arrested their long-term slippage; and home schooling is on the rise.

CAN THE institution of public education be saved? Should it be?

However one answers these questions, there can be no doubt that the *principle* of public education runs deep in our society. The American Founders clearly believed that some general provision of education was necessary if democracy was to prosper. Though the word "education" appears nowhere in the Constitution—it was a responsibility reserved for the states—the writings of the Founders are replete with references to the need, as

Thomas Jefferson put it, to "enlighten the people generally [so that] tyranny and oppressions of body and mind will vanish. . . ."

By the mid-19th-century, the rationale for public education had become very ambitious: universal schooling would not only equip the poor as well as the rich with skills that would enable all to succeed economically, but it would also foster and reinforce American civic ideals, in particular by easing the assimilation of immigrants and thus strengthening national unity. Horace Mann (1796–1859), the foremost educational thinker of his day, conceived of schooling as "the great equalizer of the conditions of men—the balance-wheel of the social machinery."

In fulfillment of these ideas, government gradually but inexorably became involved with the delivery of education. By the 1840's, Massachusetts, under Mann's leadership (and borrowing heavily from the Prussian model), had established the elements of a universal system of government-financed and government-run elementary schools. By the 1850's, New York City had a semblance of public schooling. And as newer territories joined the union, their constitutions all embraced a state obligation to furnish education to the citizenry.

But no sooner was the mid-19th-century model established than it began to change under the pressure of various movements of "reform." The cumulative effect of these waves of reform has much to do with where we are today.

Perhaps the earliest such wave was romantic progressivism, which introduced into the schools Rousseauian notions of "natural" learning. Rather than imposing the judgment of adults about what was worth learning and how it should be taught, classroom activity, it was held, should center on the interests and proclivities of the young. By the 1920's, progressivism was joined and extended by the "mental-hygiene" movement, whose thrust, as the psychiatrist Yale Kramer has written, "was to transform the goals of the public school from education to therapy. The schools were to produce not informed and skilled students but students with healthy personalities."

Progressivism had its undeniable virtues, especially when contrasted with the exclusive reliance on rote memorization of some 19th-century classrooms: children do learn best when the material they study is interesting, the teacher is encouraging, and their minds are engaged. But progressivism was nevertheless in tension with the notion of externally set standards and vigorous, teacher-led instruction. In many schools today it has been carried farther still. There is no punishment, no confining rows of desks, no wearying homework, no prescribed program of study, little respect for authority, and less discipline. In contributing to this state of affairs, progressivism and the various contemporary incarnations of the mental-hygiene movement have been a calamity, depriving children of basic skills while providing an amplitude of activity designed to augment empty concepts like self-esteem.

A different fruit of the progressive movement in American history was civil-service reform. The changes it brought had less impact on what went on in the classroom and more on how schools were governed. Reacting against the widespread practice of reserving educational slots for patronage, reformers lobbied for the creation of nonpartisan structures. In localities across the country, they succeeded in establishing elected or appointed boards consisting of eminent, public-spirited citizens who in turn entrusted their executive duties to certified professionals.

This had the beneficial effect of putting public schools beyond the sometimes avaricious grasp of mayors, aldermen, and party bosses. But it also had the less than desirable consequence of sealing off the whole arena of educational policy from the self-correcting mechanisms of democratic politics. Today, public schools may not be at the mercy of patronage machines; instead, they operate in an anaerobic environment in which interest-group self-dealing flourishes away from the public eye.

Even as civil-service reforms were insulating the schools from politics, the disciples of Frederick Winslow Taylor (1856–1915), the "management-science" genius, began to apply his precepts to education. A heightened emphasis came to be placed on credentialed expertise, disinterested professionalism, orderly management, and uniformity. By the thousands, small school systems were consolidated into districts in which only state-licensed teachers could be hired; principals and superintendents were also required to obtain professional certificates. Once again there were some benefits, and once again there were costs: colleges of education gained a stranglehold on entry into the profession; the priorities of parents and communities receded beneath the theories and dogmas of professors of education; and villages and towns lost direct control of their children's schools.

The most damaging changes to public education came after World War II. One source of trouble was the expanding role of the federal government, which made its debut in this arena in the 1950's in the name of combating racial segregation. In the 60's, Washington came to play an even greater role on behalf of the poor. In the 70's and 80's, it extended its reach dramatically to feed a growing army of special interests. Thus dawned the era of 1,000-page federal-education statutes and a 5,000-person federal Education Department managing hundreds of distinct programs, each with its stakeholders, state and local bureaucratic counterparts, and a bewildering array of regulatory requirements.

Of course, many of the problems the federal government stepped in to tackle were genuine, beginning with the shame of the "dual" school system for white and blacks. But federal expansion also meant that schools came to be enveloped in red tape, and many policy disputes that had formerly been settled at the local level were now drawn into national politics.

The growth of Washington's role was mirrored by a process that had equally far-reaching implications: the conversion of teachers' professional organizations into the two giant unions known today as the National Education Association and the American Federation of Teachers. As with most union movements, workers with bona-fide grievances—wretched pay, bans on marriage for female teachers, race-based hiring—joined together to win better terms of employment. With the passage of time, however, the unions came to push onto the bargaining table all manner of policy and management decisions. By generously funding the political campaigns of friendly candidates at every level of government, they gained immense power within the public-education system. Today the teachers' unions have become a formidable bulwark against any true reform of our educational mess.

As if all this were not enough, perhaps the greatest harm befalling public education over the last few decades has come from the intellectuals. The currents of deconstructionism, relativism, and multiculturalism that gained force in the nation's universities in the 1960's and 70's, and then spilled over into the broader society in the 1980's, have left a deep imprint on the schools. It is visible in the pervasive teaching of revisionist anti-American accounts of history, in separatist literature seemingly designed to heighten ethnic discontent, and in the growth of bilingual education, which has turned the traditional mission of the schools on its head by *slowing* the pace at which immigrants assimilate and thus contributing not to the unity but to the further balkanization of American culture and society.

PARENTS, THEN, are right to be up in arms about the schools; politicians are right to be exercised; and professionals like Albert Shanker are right to be alarmed. Indeed, ever since the United States was labeled a "nation at risk" in 1983 by the National Commission on Excellence in Education, a new movement of school reform has taken root. Today, it is a whole industry, staffed by thousands of experts and funded by generous federal and private grants. In a manner characteristic of all such undertakings, its primary output appears to be innumerable conferences, journals, books, studies, and—considering the magnitude of the problem—precious little else.

The most common approach of the school-reform industry has amounted to piecemeal tinkering with the countless gears and levers of the existing educational machinery: upgrading teacher-training programs, stiffening graduation requirements, installing modern technology, revamping reading programs, shrinking class size, adding a period to the school day, and on and on through hundreds of variations and permutations.

Certainly, many such changes are worth making. Ample evidence exists, for example, that tougher graduation requirements impel students to take more challenging courses. Better training for teachers and modern information technology help, too, in their own ways. But piecemeal reform will not fundamentally alter the working of a system in such serious disarray. As Steve Jobs, the full-time computer pioneer and part-time school reformer, wrote earlier this year:

> I've probably spearheaded giving away more computer equipment to schools than anybody else on the planet. But I've had to come to the inevitable conclusion that the problem is not one that technology can hope to solve. . . . It's a political problem. . . . The problems are unions. . . . The problem is bureaucracy.

And Jobs is hardly alone.

A more ambitious reform strategy concentrates on redesigning individual schools. Its proponents would devolve management authority away from the central bureaucracy; empower principals; and experiment with novel designs for school structure and curriculum. Examples include Chicago's local school councils, the fast-spreading charter-school movement, and the seven competing school-design "teams" underwritten by the New American Schools Development Corporation.

Many of the reforms proposed under this rubric make considerable sense, creating a variety of possibilities within school districts and, ideally, enabling parents to choose among them. But in the end this approach, too, faces severe constraints. Resistance from entrenched interest groups has already been great, and seldom has much real power—like the right to hire and fire teachers—actually devolved. Innovative governance schemes have often deteriorated into bickering or paralysis. Finally, in a country with tens of thousands of schools, the proportion of educators with truly fresh ideas and the courage to take risks is too small for an approach like this to transform the entire enterprise.

A different and still more far-reaching tack concentrates less on structure than on substance, bringing academic standards, curriculum, textbooks, tests, and teacher training into national or statewide alignment. This strategy underlies President Clinton's "Goals 2000" program and the efforts by many educators, business leaders, and governors to impose uniform standards on entire states and communities. Here, again, there is much to praise in principle, but there are also pitfalls that have been well-illustrated in practice. For one thing, standards are easily hijacked by ideologues—as we have seen in the recent uproar over national history standards.* For another thing, to press so many divergent elements into true alignment would require additional layers of bureaucratic regulation and the kind of top-down control that has created so much difficulty in the past.

The most radical solution of all is perhaps better characterized as an abandonment of the public-school model than as a reform. Voucher and privatization advocates believe that the market (fueled by the tax revenues that are now directed exclusively to public schools) can rise to the challenge of educating America's young. A number of Wall Street firms have already sponsored conferences for

---

* See Walter A. McDougall's "Whose History? Whose Standards?" in COMMENTARY, May 1995 and "What Johnny Still Won't Know About History," July 1996.

investors eager to play in this emerging field, and several corporations are launching ambitious schemes for privatizing education much in the way security services have been privatized in neighborhoods weary of inadequate police protection. The grass-roots have also become engaged: at one end of the movement, a lobbying organization called the Separation of School and State Alliance is agitating for a complete halt to "government-compelled attendance, financing, curriculum, testing, credentializing, and accreditation."

Would thrusting the schools into the rigors of the marketplace have a beneficial effect? It would certainly free some youngsters from the dead hand of awful schools, and it would crack the government's near-monopoly that now protects such schools. It should also foster innovation and flexibility, although only if a degree of entrepreneurship arises which private schools have thus far rarely demonstrated. But such a move faces intense political opposition from the entire public-education establishment. Nor is it yet clear that for-profit schools can yield a competitive return to investors while providing solid skills to those children whom the public schools have failed most notoriously: namely, the inner city poor. Finally, the scheme might well conduce to the creation of separatist schools that reject the American civic culture even more forcefully than conventional public schools, under the spell of multiculturalism, are already doing.

D o I have a better way? What I have is not so much a blueprint as a set of principles, and a concept of what an American public education worthy of the name should look like. In other words, I would start from where we want to get to, not from where we are, although I would also borrow freely from the reform strategies already being tried.

To begin with structure: public education ought not mean government-run schools. Society's obligation is to see that instruction is provided and that learning occurs. It is not to operate a bureaucratic system of uniform institutions staffed by government employees.

As I envision them, public schools would continue to be open to all, financed by tax revenues, and accountable to elected authorities; they would thus remain public in every significant sense of the term. But—and here I side with the advocates of vouchers and other such schemes—the schools would also be accountable to their clients, who would be free to select among them and never forced against their will to attend a bad one. The management of the schools would be "out-sourced," "chartered," "contracted," or "co-oped." This means that schools might be directed by groups of parents or teachers, by private firms, or by nonprofit organizations.

Ending the present monopoly of the bureaucrats and unions would liberate thousands of capable educators to break with the orthodoxies of their profession and create schools that parents might actually want their children to attend. Such schools would differ in dozens of ways: style of pedagogy, form of organization and governance, mode of discipline, hours of operations, and so on, up to and including curriculum, at least those elements of curriculum that fall outside the common core.

Where would that core come from? We have had enough sorry experience with standards to have learned that academic experts are not to be trusted with writing a curriculum designed either to inculcate basic skills or to foster civic culture; nor can this task be left entirely to individual teachers and schools, much less to the federal government. Although I am as allergic as the next person to Rockefeller-type commissions, they are not all bad—the one that produced the *Nation at Risk* report in 1983 had much to commend it—and a panel of respected civic, business, and intellectual leaders, *privately* constituted, might be able to frame a core "curriculum of national unity" for states and communities (and textbook writers and test-makers) to adopt if they find it meritorious, and to suggest the performance standards that would denote student mastery of such a curriculum. That, at least, would be a beginning.

Most critically, the schools I have in mind would be built not around intentions, expenditures, or credentials, but around academic results. Examinations, devised and administered from without, would assess whether and how well the curriculum is learned. Students, teachers, and principals would be held accountable for performance, and real consequences would follow from failure and success.

I N SHORT, what I would do is to encourage freedom and rigor at once: freedom of structure, rigor of substance. Above all, however, by means of that substance I would restore to the schools their vital role in fostering, reinforcing, and transmitting the sense of a common civic culture.

Here perhaps is where I differ most fundamentally with recent reform strategies, virtually all of which focus on useful skills and enhanced productivity. If that were all we wanted from our schools, we might well stick with the efforts of the privatizers, standard-setters, and tinkerers. They have shown signs of modest progress and, particularly with greater political support, would likely make more.

But the narrowly utilitarian function of public education was only part of Horace Mann's vision, and should be the lesser part of our own. Simply put, the great project of public education in America should not be the creation of skilled workers but the formation of Americans. If our children do not assimilate a common body of knowledge and values, a shared set of customs and institutional arrangements, there will be little to prevent us from falling even farther apart as a nation.

Yet there, precisely, is the rub. National cultural transmission may be the most pressing task before public education today, but it is also the one task rejected out of hand both by many of the staunchest defenders of the public schools and by many of their most ardent reformers. Worse: although it is a task which seems to have fallen by default to the schools alone, they can hardly be expected to perform it alone.

For reasons having little to do with education *per se*, the base on which the old model of public education was originally constructed—namely, the assumption of an already existing common culture, sustained by home, church, media, and national political institutions, not to mention a wide network of consensual ideas and social habits—has broken down. It would be foolish to suggest that the schools, which all too faithfully reflect the condition in which we find ourselves, can single-handedly mend it. Although I believe that a full-fledged revolution from within could indeed recreate a worthy form of public education, even the best of schools cannot recreate a sound civic culture—and that, alas, not only is the more urgent, but may be the prior, task.

COMMENTARY

Republicans and the Education Debate

by Charles L. Heatherly

In his State of the Union address and the budget message that followed, President Clinton chose education policy as one of the major initiatives for his second term. This may or may not be good news for the country, but it is surely bad news for the Republicans because they have no education agenda of their own.

Public education in America is a disaster zone, and a healthy national debate on education policy would be good for the country. Perhaps Clinton's proposals will stimulate that much-needed debate but probably not.

It appears that Republicans will not engage the president on the issue at the level of principle. The most likely response will be the generic answer Republicans give to a Democratic initiative: They will modify it here and there, reduce its cost, and then adopt it as their own in the spirit of bipartisan compromise that is fashionable in Washington today.

This has been the pattern of Republican behavior in education matters for the past 40 years. Unfortunately, many in the "Party of Lincoln" do not see a principled reason to oppose Clinton's 10-point plan for expanding the federal role in American education.

A Republican policy agenda in education would build on the lessons of failed liberal experiments. It would aim to create new models of educational excellence, fueled not by new federal spending but by the power of competition. This is language Republicans understand and use across the policy spectrum but have never applied to education.

Perhaps if Republicans started calling our public schools by the right name—government schools—they would gain the confidence they need to examine education failures as problems of government monopolies, not the result of inadequate funding. Republicans have yet to take the first steps toward such a winning strategy. In fact, they have no strategy whatsoever.

CLINTON'S CRAFT AND REPUBLICAN DRIFT

Clinton's 1998 budget proposals in education should not surprise anyone. The disastrous health-care battle of 1993–94 taught him a lesson: Massive or expensive proposals will be "dead on arrival" on Capitol Hill. New Clinton initiatives will be relatively small and incremental, and they will be proposed only in areas where there is a broad public consensus that "something must be done."

Clinton's strategy is simple and smart, but what is more interesting is the hollowness and halfheartedness of the Republican response. In education, this timidity follows the pattern set in the Republican handling of the issue in 1996. House conservatives did an about-face on education matters that was embarrassing in its abject surrender to the education lobby.

The education budget passed by the 104th Congress gave more money to the federal education bureaucracy than Clinton had requested, and it did nothing to devolve any federal program to the states. The House Republican Task Force on the Department of Education, launched with great fanfare in 1995 with the paramount goal of abolishing that agency, is now seeking a new mission.

In the wake of this Republican disarray, the national education policy debate is drifting back toward business as usual—more federal funding as a substitute for education reform and a corresponding decline of state and local initiative. And why not? Why should President Clinton or Secretary of Education Richard Riley pursue serious restructuring or downsizing if the conservatives in Congress have given up? Take the money and run!

Why can't Republicans come up with a serious alternative to the bureaucratic fraud that passes for public education today? There is a serious disconnect between the importance of education policy in national politics and the lack of

This article originally appeared in *The World & I*, May 1997, pp. 66-77. Reprinted by permission of *The World & I*, a publication of The Washington Times Corporation. © 1997.

attention to education by Republican leaders.

The reasons for Republican timidity and ambivalence on education policy can be found in three places—philosophy, economics, and the confluence of those two forces in what we call the survival instinct. The sad history of Republican education philosophy since the Nixon administration is the story of policy pragmatism unguided by any coherent plan or principle. Never has the old saying been more appropriate: "The trouble with pragmatism is, it doesn't work."

A major reason for conservatives' default on education policy is their preoccupation with budgets and taxes. The federal budget outlay on education is comparatively small, though not as small as many believe. The budget of the Department of Education is only slightly over 2 percent of total federal spending at $34 billion. But if you add the education spending of other federal agencies, including the research funds going to education institutions from the National Science Foundation and the Defense and Energy Departments, federal education spending approaches $50 billion.

Another reason for Republican reticence on education policy may well be the most important one: the perceived power of teachers unions to intimidate and punish politicians who stray from the party line. This is an argument not from principle but from self-interest, so we do not hear it made explicitly in public debates. But public officials do tend to think that their continuation in office is more important than the pursuit of any single policy goal, and the Republican reluctance to take on the teachers unions is well known.

Conservatives have ignored federal education policy because they believe it shouldn't be necessary to have a federal education policy. Since education is not a federal matter under our Constitution, it is therefore not a proper focus of national politics.

Even in the Reagan years, conservatives did not take on education reform as a priority. In 1981, conservatives in the White House and Congress stood by while Reagan's first secretary of education, Terrell H. Bell, successfully stalled the administration's dismantlement plan for the department. The proposal was not sent up to Capitol Hill until after the window of opportunity had closed.

Bell also obstructed any significant reduction in the federal role in elementary and secondary education. But the important point is that he could not have succeeded in this sabotage without the tacit cooperation of conservatives in the White House and Congress. His successor, William Bennett, was blocked by Congress from making major changes in the federal programs he administered.

So Republican timidity and ambivalence on federal education policy are not new. The federal role keeps growing even under Republican presidents and now under a Republican-controlled Congress.

For every other area of federal policy, conservatives have a detailed and ambitious long-term policy agenda—the flat tax, cost-benefit analysis in environmental regulations, international free trade, and so on. Why is there no comparable conservative agenda on education?

FEDERALISM AND EDUCATION REFORM

Conservatives tend to relegate education to a "second tier" status, mutable for state policy innovation but not a priority for national politics. In the traditional view, education is best understood as a matter for energetic reform at the state level, not a subject for bold federal initiatives.

This position, no matter how sound in theory, raises a number of questions about strategies for policy development. Does this mean there is nothing to be done about the in-

ertia of federal education policy? Are federal programs a help or hindrance to state and local innovation? Are state innovations to take place entirely outside the federal framework? Do conservatives running for national office keep silent on education issues?

The solution to this dilemma is to be found by first recovering and renewing the federal principle, which is sound advice in many policy areas, not just education. The second step is to give new content to the education-policy agenda. The "return to federalism" is hardly a winning platform for education renewal.

Citizens must not be left to wonder if conservatives are arguing over the "who" and not the "what" of education issues. There must be a new paradigm behind education reform, and that new paradigm will be competition among providers and choice for consumers. The way to open the door to public recognition and acceptance of that new paradigm is by opening the window on the scandalous cost of government schooling. The truth shall indeed set us free.

The recovery of federalism and the pursuit of competition and choice as the engine of change are twin policy goals, compatible and mutually reinforcing, and they can be pursued simultaneously. But in practical terms, the case for federalism must be made and that argument won before competition can become the centerpiece of radical reform.

To win these battles, conservatives first will have to understand the federal principle and adopt it as their own. This task is more difficult and complicated than it appears, because the federal principle has been all but abandoned in American politics over the past 60 years. Adopting it seriously would entail a commitment to a radical dismantlement of federal government programs not only in education but in housing, transportation, agriculture, and commerce. That is not to say it is not the right course, but it *is* a radical one.

Practical Solutions on the Local Level

☞ Use parent vouchers to enable disadvantaged students to go to better schools.

☞ Have state governors cooperate with congressional conservatives to prepare oversight hearings on bilingual education.

☞ Give block grants to states to meet the needs of students with serious handicaps.

☞ Seek measures to return control of the classroom to teachers and local school boards.

☞ Reject federal funding for student testing. Show that each state can and should handle this responsibility as part of its constitutional obligation to public education.

FEDERALISM AND THE LIMITS OF LOCAL CONTROL

A return to the federal principle in education, however, may not be quite so radical because our nation still believes in neighborhood schools and local control of education. All politicians at least pay lip service to the importance of local control of the curriculum, and federal bureaucrats still see the political necessity of denying any intention of imposing a national curriculum on local schools.

Thus, devolution of federal programs to the states has a strong appeal across the political spectrum. It must be clearly understood, however, that under the Constitution the federal principle (or devolution) cannot mean the abandonment of federal responsibility for basic constitutional protections. All local schools must meet certain minimum standards under the equal protection clause of the Fourteenth Amendment. Thus, conservatives must recognize that while federalism remains a necessary cornerstone of education policy, it is not synonymous with local control.

Local control in many communities is more myth than reality even without the federal regulatory overlay. There are three factors that have led to the decline of local control in the last 25 years. The first is the change in school finance. Real decisions on curriculum, standards, and budget priorities come from the same place most of the money comes from—the state government, not the local school board. In California, about 75 percent of per-pupil spending statewide comes from the state, not from local taxes.

A second reason for this eclipse of local authority is the growing clout of teachers unions in local school-board elections. The union local indeed has a local membership comprising the teachers in that district, but it is part of a very powerful statewide and national organization that assists union-endorsed slates of candidates in numerous ways. The state organization can target key school-board races and import professional managers as well as dollars for campaign expenses.

Finally, local control in any meaningful sense is made impossible by the sheer size of large urban districts. Does the parent in a district the size of six congressional districts feel "empowered" by the election of school-board members? The larger the district, the lower the voter participation. Is it surprising that teachers unions have supported this consolidation of local school districts into megadistricts?

Counties, cities, and school districts are legal fictions, mere creatures of the state constitution. This means that state governments of necessity have ultimate authority over local agencies, including schools. Therefore, they also have responsibility, through constitutionally defined processes, over school-funding formulas and mechanisms. Thus, the increased state centralization of school funding is not a usurpation of local authority, and it has nothing to do with federalism. Whether it is sound policy is another matter.

Shifting more authority from the bureaucracy in Washington to state governments will not by itself energize local school boards, improve parental access to curriculum decisions, or recover revenue sources now controlled by politicians in the state capital.

These issues are best debated and resolved within each state, and states will differ in the answers they find. The recovery of federalism would allow the *possibility* that these issues can be resolved in local communities instead of a centralized federal bureaucracy. Federalism assures greater diversity and experimentation, but it guarantees nothing. It demands more of citizens and parents, not less.

THE REPUBLICAN OPPORTUNITY

The main obstacle to progress in meeting the education crisis is not, as liberals claim, either racism or inequality of financial resources. These may be legitimate issues in isolated cases, but they are not the main problem in education today. The main obstacle is lack of clarity about the nature of the crisis. It is not a battle over public moneys; it is a battle over the uses of that money. This is another way of saying that our policy confusion and indecision are derived from the breakdown of a national consensus over the goals of education.

This confusion is the by-product of the liberal crusade to use schools for a more grandiose purpose then merely teaching children the traditional skills with which people begin to acquire knowledge and learn vocational skills. That is what most parents and most citizens assume education is all about. But for liberals and the educational bureaucracy now controlled by liberals, public education is the principal vehicle for an agenda that Hillary Clinton has described most succinctly: It aims "to change what it means to be a human being in the twenty-first century."

It so happens that the teachers unions and other liberal organizations that share this agenda are also the key power brokers in the Democratic Party. Thus they are committed to centralization of education funding as one means of centralizing educational decisionmaking. While it is true that teachers unions have relatively more clout in many state capitals than they do in Washington, they nonetheless support centralization because they fundamentally distrust local authorities. Better to fight a single battle than 50, or so they believe.

The immediate challenge to Republicans is to find ways of taking the initiative and winning battles while the research and development of a more comprehensive, long-term agenda is under way. In the near term, much of the leadership must come from the state level, just as ultimately all genuine reforms must be implemented at the state level. State governors are the generals in this theater of political warfare, and conservative policy institutes must work with them and state-based grassroots organizations more closely.

Republican governors have been in the forefront of education reform

What would happen if conservative governors were to embark on a plan to define the "federal partnership" in a way more helpful to their own reform efforts?

in Wisconsin, Michigan, Arizona, and Pennsylvania. They have endorsed school choice and school voucher proposals, backed innovative charter school programs, and pushed for higher achievement standards. What they have not yet talked about much is changing the federal role in education by redirecting or reducing the $34 billion in federal tax dollars now spent by the Department of Education.

What would happen if conservative governors were to embark on a plan to define the "federal partnership" in a way more helpful to their own reform efforts? Why should state education reform and federal education policy proceed on totally different tracks, like two ships passing in the night? To cast the metaphor in military terms, if one ship is carrying a precious cargo called education reform and it is being harassed by another ship attempting to force a change of course, should it not be able to respond in kind?

Why shouldn't governors open a national debate on the efficacy of federal education programs and the wastefulness of much of education spending? They might begin by asking simple questions about specific federal programs that spend billions in the name of improving student achievement. They could, for example

- Ask to see the evidence that the billions of dollars of federal

ESEA Title I funds—now nearly $900 million in California alone—are being well spent. What is the evidence that the funds would not be better spent on parent vouchers to enable disadvantaged students to go to better schools? In concert with the congressional leadership, governors could ask for a GAO audit of the educational results of this 30-year, multimillion-dollar taxpayer investment. They could tell their state education officials to assist in the audit.

- Form an alliance with reform-minded state education officials to actively promote a voucher option for the parents of disadvantaged students to have the choice of a voucher in the same amount as the federal Title I grant.

- Offer cooperation with congressional conservatives in preparing oversight hearings of Department of Education programs in bilingual education. Bring to the committee hearing room the Hispanic parent of a child who is *already* bilingual, who was told by the superintendent in a California town, "What your child needs is not the issue; the district needs the extra money."

- Form an alliance with members of Congress who think states should have more flexibility and fewer federal mandates in educating children with serious handicaps. Why not block grant these funds and give states more flexibility in meeting the needs of students?

- Demand an extensive congressional review of the cumulative impact of federal-court rulings that, in the name of "student rights," impair the ability of classroom teachers and school officials to maintain order in the classroom and to discipline or expel disruptive students. Then seek measures to return control of the classroom to teachers and local school boards.

COURTESY OF NEW HOPE ACADEMY

■ *At school in suburban Maryland:* Having the most up-to-date computers will not help students if political correctness instead of reading and writing is taught.

- Reject the offer of federal funding for student testing by showing that each state can afford to handle this responsibility as part of its constitutional obligations for public education. A governor who thinks his state needs federal funds to pay for student testing has forfeited any claim to leadership in education.
- Reject the $5 billion in federal funding of school construction proposed recently by the Clinton administration. State leaders who think this is "free money" with no strings attached are caught in a time warp; that illusion died in the 1960s.

A few governors have provided leadership in education against formidable odds. Mayors, community leaders, and a few courageous state legislators have moved mountains in starting voucher experiments in several cities. The voucher demonstration programs in school choice now under way in Milwaukee, Cleveland, and elsewhere did not wait on federal leadership.

The veterans of these battles will testify that these confrontations are not purely local in character. The education establishment is a gargantuan national body with local appendages and fiefdoms. When one of the local fortresses is threatened, headquarters mobilizes an army of financial and political resources to repel the attack, with federal judges and bureaucrats assisting. A national debate is needed before these reforms can reach critical mass against entrenched programs and powerful interests that obstruct them.

> Government schools are disgraceful in their mediocrity in white suburbia and in their abject incompetence in most urban areas.

School choice is being advanced today mainly by private organizations, not by legislators or government agencies. Private philanthropists have created CEO America, a program that provides privately funded scholarships to allow inner-city children to escape some of the worst government-run schools in places like San Antonio, Indianapolis, Atlanta, and Los Angeles. The hope and expectation is that these demonstrations of the voucher model in the private sector will pave the way for acceptance of vouchers in the public sector. Yet opposition to vouchers in these cities remains strong.

EDUCATION FUNDING THE REAL PROBLEM

A second major reason that Republican policymakers and conservative policy analysts devote almost no attention to education is that federal education funding (soon to be $35 billion if the president's proposed 1998 budget is adopted) is still only 2 percent of a $1.7 trillion federal budget. It's hard to get people excited about that figure when policymakers have Medicare, the Social Security trust fund, and agricultural subsidies to worry about.

The comparatively small size of the Education Department's outlays actually works to immunize it against conservative criticism. Liberals argue that because the investment is so small, it is silly and even mean-spirited to want to reduce it further. Surely, the argument runs, expanded educational opportunity is worth a mere 2 percent of our taxpayer dollars!

It is hard for conservatives to win a debate on these terms. When argued in the language of budget priorities, education will trump a dozen other federal programs in the voters' minds. When President Clinton says that more education spending is a part of *his* balanced budget, where does that leave the "we can't afford it" line of argument?

Conservatives must understand that this is a losing argument and recast the debate in more realistic terms that make sense to both ordinary taxpayers and local school boards. They should take their cue from the ferocity of the liberal defense of this "small" federal investment: Why is it so important if it is so small? The answer lies not in the dollars but in the sense. The real issue is not the size of the federal budget outlay; it is the disproportionate leverage the funding gives federal bureaucrats and federal courts.

A small school district in Nevada that accepts even one dollar of federal aid for its "disadvantaged" students is subject to the same regulations as the large urban district that takes millions. Even when participation is supposedly voluntary, the pressure for conformity to "federal standards" is enormous. Does anyone doubt that a local school district that uses student tests approved by the federal government will end up adopting texts and standards that help its students show up well on those tests?

TEACHERS UNIONS AND POLITICAL SURVIVAL

The most important reason for Republican inattention to education issues is the survival instinct. The education lobby—what William Bennett has aptly called "the blob"—is large and well funded, and it plays hardball in politics. Teachers unions alone spent an estimated $45 million in PAC dollars in the 1996 election cycle on federal, state, and local races, and 99 percent of those funds went to Democrats.

Is it surprising that the typical Republican congressman, even one with a 90 percent conservative rating, would rather not become a target of this swarm of killer bees? No candidate wants to be tagged an "enemy of education." Nor is the simple pork-barrel factor unimportant: The "clients" who benefit—or think they benefit—from the federal spending in each congressional district are usually well organized.

For similar reasons, conservatives in Congress generally shrink from seeking a seat on the congressional committees that oversee federal education policy and appropriations. The result is that these committees are more liberal than the party as a whole and less willing to take on the education lobby. While this is not the problem it was before the 104th Congress arrived in town, it is still a factor. The interest groups push friends into key committees and then reward them for their friendly voting records.

Conservatives who advocate a serious downsizing of the federal role in education must answer a series of questions that bear on the political feasibility of such initiatives. It is not enough to discuss our goals in academic or theoretical terms. There must be an accompanying political strategy to make them viable. Where is the public-interest counterweight to the education lobby? Who can do battle with this vast army of organized public employees, committed to preserving and expanding the federal role? What is the strategy for

neutralizing or at least diminishing the electoral power of this formidable force?

TAKING EDUCATION SERIOUSLY

The first thing that should be done is to recognize the problem and start taking education seriously as a national disaster zone. Successful policy innovation will require large investments in research and development on a scale proportionate to the $500 billion industry it seeks to impact.

Government schools are disgraceful in their mediocrity in white suburbia and in their abject incompetence in most urban areas. We have had 20 years of commissions and studies and investigative reports by network television and major newspapers, all showing the deplorable condition of standards and a widespread deception over education priorities.

The 1983 *A Nation at Risk* report recommended "increased time on task" as a key to improved student performance, along with a winnowing of elective courses and concentration on core academic subjects. Fourteen years later, these common-sense recommendations have not been implemented in most schools.

Parents involved in education reform are mystified as to why changes aimed at improving academic performance in core subjects are hard to sell to educators. Despite public dissatisfaction with declining standards, the education establishment remains impervious to reform. The answer to any problem is always the same: more money—for smaller classrooms, higher salaries, expanded facilities, and, for the newest panacea, more computers.

But is money the real problem? The evidence suggests not. Education spending has not lagged behind the GNP or growth in personal income. Government spending on K–12 education has more than kept pace with inflation over the past 25

WILLIAM CONNERY

■ *A 1950s class:* School uniforms and strict discipline are just the external manifestations of a fundamental focus on academics instead of political correctness.

years, but educational performance has declined by almost every measure.

In most settings, money is not the real problem. Education standards and expectations are the problem. Our nation is paying a high price for the neglect of basic truths earlier generations understood very well but that many leaders in today's education establishment denigrate. Technology will not replace the need for hard work, teacher competency, parental involvement, and, above all, standards of excellence.

Learning is not a quaint nineteenth-century word for entertainment. Abraham Lincoln did not study *Blackstone's Commentaries* to rap music, and Booker T. Washington did not learn geography by writing letters to the editor about clearcutting.

Our nation's founders understood the importance of education and made provision for it in the organization of local government in one of the three organic acts of the new nation, the Northwest Ordinance of 1787. Education was identified as an important local responsibility of townships in the new federal territories, and land was

explicitly set aside for schools. In this way they provided for public education as a local institution, but they did not make it a continuing federal responsibility. That principle is still valid today.

Recognizing an urgent national interest in education is not the same as advocating the centralization of that important civic responsibility in a federal bureaucracy. Just the opposite is the case: It is precisely because education is so important that we must return control to parents.

Republicans can learn a lesson from the victory in welfare reform. The battle to change federal welfare mandates was successful because conservatives convinced the nation that federal welfare policy was part of the problem, not the solution. The persuasion took many years, but it succeeded. Americans became convinced that pouring more money into job training and "job readiness" would not get results.

Conservatives must begin to frame federal education policy in the same manner—it is part of the problem, not the solution. Adding more federal money to a broken system will only perpetuate problems, not

fix them. The education lobby understands this well, which is why it always wants to shift the debate over education standards from what standards should be to how much should be spent.

Conservatives must work for a new public consensus that educational excellence is the goal of public policy and federal policies stand in the way of that goal. In education jargon, educational outcomes must replace dollar inputs as the measure of sound public policy—at all levels of public education. And those outcomes need to be measured in terms of knowledge acquired in a limited number of academic subjects, not by "self-esteem" or other subjective indicators easily manipulated by administrators.

At the federal level, conservatives must show that education excellence is not advanced by a federal takeover of student testing or additional efforts to "improve access" to higher education. The road to excellence does not run through the Department of Education. That road runs through a region called high standards. It is bounded by high expectations and paved by parental involvement. The most efficient vehicles transporting students along this road in the twenty-first century will be those fueled by competition and choice.

To provide leadership for this development, conservatives must think seriously and creatively about radical changes in education-delivery systems, structures, and financing, including radical models of privatization and decentralization. Tinkering will not work. In education, liberals are the tinkerers: They believe the system is fine and just needs more money.

Conservatives know better, but they haven't devoted the time or resources needed to develop a comprehensive plan for replacing a bankrupt system. Liberals are now encumbered by the unenviable task of defending the bureaucratic fraud that goes by the name of public education. Conservatives are free to think anew and, with courage, can also act anew.

THE ISSUE: CONTROLLING THE CLASSROOM

Do we actually want federal funding of tests in math, science, or other core subjects? Do we want the frontiers of political correctness—gender neutrality, ethnic diversity, and sexual orientation—explored further by the Department of Education? What state will admit to the inability to administer student tests without federal assistance? Can anyone make that argument with a straight face?

When the education experts in a state bureaucracy make a mistake and push statewide implementation of a foolish new curriculum idea, as California did with "whole language" reading instruction, the children pay an awful price. But other states are not affected by the mistake, unless they choose to follow the pied piper. What happens if the national education bureaucracy makes a mistake of this magnitude? Is Congress willing to gamble that the experts in the federal bureaucracy are that much smarter than the experts in Madison, Tallahassee, Austin, and Sacramento?

Conservatives in Congress are mostly neophytes in these matters, and their timidity is understandable given the power and arrogance of the education lobby. The ability of teachers unions to punish their political enemies is often exaggerated, however. When they can gang up on a few dissidents, they are merciless. But they cannot deliver a knockout punch in 200 districts. Dozens of legislators in Indiana and Pennsylvania recently defied the unions and survived the 1996 election; they called the bluff and won. Republicans should take on the teachers union lobby in both direct and indirect ways. The unions may prove to be the paper tiger of American politics once they are put in the spotlight and their vulnerabilities explored.

Clinton has proposed federal funding of a major segment of student testing and federal subsidies for school construction, among other initiatives. To meet that challenge, Republicans must take a cram course in education policy. In the 1980s, Republicans learned how to occupy the high ground on tax policy, public housing, welfare reform, criminal justice, foreign aid, and other issues. There is no reason that they can't learn to do so in education.

The battle over control of student testing is a defensive one, and winning it will not in itself do much to advance education reform. But fighting and winning this battle may give Republicans the self-confidence they need to take on a more ambitious agenda.

Charles L. Heatherly is executive vice president of the Claremont Institute, a nonprofit research organization in California. He was deputy undersecretary of management for the Department of Education and education director of the nation's largest small-business association.

Voucher advocates step up attack

The voucher threat remains alive and well in dozens of states and on Capitol Hill. Voucher bills have been introduced or are anticipated in 24 states, the nonprofit group People for the American Way reported this spring (see map). At the same time, efforts to attach voucher proposals to federal law were in full force. Whether or not 1997 is the year that many states and the federal government jump on the voucher bandwagon depends largely on which side makes itself heard—a well-organized pro-voucher minority or the majority of Americans who still oppose public funding of private schools.

Currently, it's the pro-voucher side that is making the most noise, warns Mary Jean Collins, director of field services for People for the American Way.

After losing high-profile battles at the ballot box in states like California and Washington, voucher advocates have shifted their strategy toward direct lobbying tactics. And they're being persistent—using well-orchestrated bursts of e-mail, faxes, letters and phone calls at critical points in the legislative cycle, capturing call-in lines for radio talk shows about "school choice" and recruiting voucher supporters to testify before committees, Collins says.

These activities create what appears to be a tidal wave of support for vouchers, even though polls show a majority of Americans still oppose them. Even the staunchest defenders of public education eventually "have to look in the mirror and say, 'Am I doing what the people want?' if all the calls and letters are coming from the pro-voucher side," Collins says.

Clearly, that impact is being felt in several states:

■ The Texas Legislature will consider at least three bills this session that would provide vouchers for students attending private and religious schools.

One would offer vouchers to all students attending low-performing schools based on a state testing program, provided those students' requests to transfer to a neighboring school district had been rejected.

■ In Arizona, a proposal to establish "parental choice grants" for students attending private schools recently won approval from the Senate Education Committee and also is being supported by Gov. Fife Symington. It would divert $10 million into vouchers from the general fund.

■ In Florida, the legislature is considering three bills on vouchers, including a push to provide "certificates," or "scholarships," for low-income students throughout the state. A second bill would establish a five-year voucher program in four counties aimed at home-schooled and private school students. The bill also would establish a "choice information center" to give parents help in selecting private and home schooling options.

■ The Colorado Legislature narrowly rejected two voucher bills this session. One would have allowed districts to hold referendums to establish local voucher programs supported by the state. The second would have offered vouchers to home-schooled students and other "homebound" youngsters. New proposals are expected in future sessions.

Meanwhile, Congress has before it a number of bills to fund vouchers.

One proposal would set up a five-year "demonstration program," with a first-year budget of $50 million, that

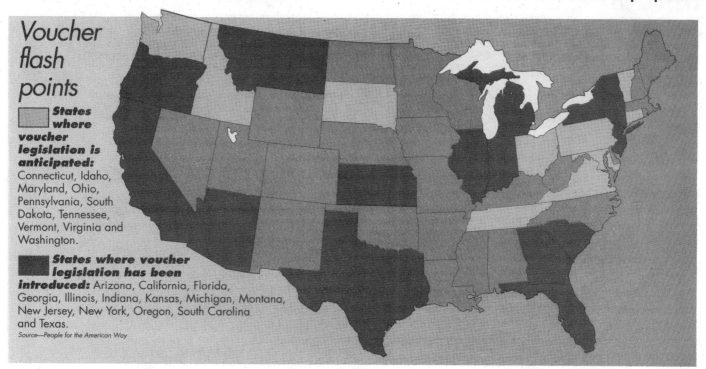

Voucher flash points

States where voucher legislation is anticipated: Connecticut, Idaho, Maryland, Ohio, Pennsylvania, South Dakota, Tennessee, Vermont, Virginia and Washington.

States where voucher legislation has been introduced: Arizona, California, Florida, Georgia, Illinois, Indiana, Kansas, Michigan, Montana, New Jersey, New York, Oregon, South Carolina and Texas.

Source—People for the American Way

would offer vouchers for private and religious schooling to low-income students at 20–30 sites. It would be open to students who currently attend schools with high crime, drug or violence rates and to families with incomes up to 185 percent of the poverty rate.

A second proposal would allow states to use federal block grants to establish voucher programs.

What are the chances that some version of a voucher bill will clear Congress? AFT Legislation director Jerry Morris says, in large part, the outcome will depend on the kinds and amounts of pressure members of Congress receive from back home.

"Privately, we've had representatives approach us and say, 'Where are your members on this ... my mail is running overwhelmingly in favor of vouchers,'" Smith reports. "That creates incredible pressure on even the strongest allies of public education."

AFT members are encouraged to contact state and local affiliates to find out how they might get involved in efforts to fight vouchers, tax credits and other attacks on public schools. Members also are urged to call the AFT's toll-free hotline to Capitol Hill, 800/238-1727, and tell their representatives they oppose these schemes. More information also is available in the AFT forum of America Online (Keyword: AFT) and the union's web page (http://www.aft.org).

Test your voucher savvy

Candidate A says, "I think poor parents should be given the tax dollars allotted for their child's education and allowed to use those dollars in the form of a scholarship to attend a private, public or parochial school of their choosing." Candidate B says, "I favor an education voucher system that transfers taxpayer funds from public schools to private and religious schools."

While the two politicos are basically barking up the same tree—vouchers to pay for private and parochial school tuition—the way they couch their agenda can have an enormous impact on voter attitudes. In fact, recent polls from Peter D. Hart Research show that candidate A's position, sugar-coated with concepts like "scholarships" and "choice," will be supported by 70 percent of voters. Candidate B's no-nonsense voucher platform, on the other hand, will actually make 55 percent of voters *less* likely to support him.

These lessons certainly aren't lost on pro-voucher legislators, who load up voucher bills with the types of mom-and-apple-pie references that will sway the uninitiated. Don't believe us? Take the following short test. Pick the programs and bills that do not include either private school vouchers or tuition tax credits in their original form:

A) The District Educational Choice Act (Florida)
B) The Milwaukee Parental Choice Program (Wisconsin)
C) The Jersey City Children First Education Act (New Jersey)
D) The G.I. Bill for Florida Students
E) Keystone Initiative for a Difference in our Schools or "KIDS" (Pennsylvania)
F) The Ohio Scholarship Plan
G) The Kansas G.I. Bill for Kids
H) Excellence in Teaching Act (federal)
I) Comprehensive Safe Schools Act (New York)
J) Comprehensive Public School Reform Partnership for the District of Columbia (federal)
K) Students First (Minnesota)

Answers: H, I

The 29th Annual Phi Delta Kappa/Gallup Poll Of the Public's Attitudes Toward the Public Schools

By Lowell C. Rose, Alec M. Gallup, and Stanley M. Elam

Illustration by Fred Bell

PLACE A computer in every classroom. Move persistent "troublemakers" into alternative schools. Establish national standards for measuring the academic performance of the public schools. Let parents and students choose which public schools the students will attend. Group students in classes according to ability level. Establish a national curriculum. Use standardized national tests to measure the academic achievement of students. Provide health-care services in schools. These are all measures that the public believes would improve student achievement in the public schools. Probing attitudes about improving achievement was a major focus of the 1997 Phi Delta Kappa/Gallup Poll of the Public's Attitudes Toward the Public Schools, conducted by the George H. Gallup International Institute.

Why do some public schools achieve better academic results than others? The public believes that three factors are important: 1) strong support from parents, 2) the amount of money spent, and, to a lesser extent, 3) the kinds of students in attendance.

This year's poll data make it clear that public schools continue to enjoy strong public support. Most respondents give good grades to the schools in their own communities, and parents of public school students express even stronger satisfaction. While there is an obvious desire for improvement, almost three-fourths (71%) of those surveyed believe that this improvement should come through reforming the existing system rather than through seeking an alternative system.

At the same time, however, the public seems more willing than in earlier years to approve government financial support for students who wish to attend nonpublic schools. This continues a trend tracked by these polls for nearly three decades. As recently as 1993, only 24% of respondents favored "allowing students and parents to choose a private school to attend at public expense." Seventy-four percent were opposed. In 1997, 44% favor this and 52% oppose it. When the words "public expense" are changed to "government expense," the public is exactly divided (48% in favor, 48% opposed).* On the basic "voucher question," asking respondents to indicate whether they would support allowing parents and students to choose a public or nonpublic school to attend with the government paying "all or part of the tuition," this poll shows a virtual deadlock, for the first time, with 49% favoring and 48% opposing. While this is good news to advocates of nonpublic schools, the conditions the public would impose on such support suggest that proposals of this kind are certain to be controversial.

---

*Although on the borderline of statistical significance, this difference reminds us of the need for very careful wording of questions that assess opinion on sensitive issues.

LOWELL C. ROSE is executive director emeritus of Phi Delta Kappa International. ALEC M. GALLUP is co-chairman, with George Gallup, Jr., of the Gallup Organization, Princeton, N.J. STANLEY M. ELAM, who was Kappan editor from 1956 through 1980, is contributing editor of the Phi Delta Kappan.

The public expresses the strong belief that any nonpublic school that accepts public funds should be required to enroll students from a wider range of backgrounds and academic ability than is now the case. This popular conviction would seem to invite the kind of government regulation that has led some proponents of nonpublic schools to oppose the voucher idea.

This year's poll reflects a strong public belief in the important role parents can and should play in the education of their children. Respondents regard the amount of support provided by parents of public school students as a major factor in determining why some schools are better than others; they also believe strongly that parents should be notified if their children have a substance abuse problem or suffer from a sexually transmitted disease.

Other findings in the 1997 Phi Delta Kappa/Gallup poll include the following.

• Majorities in all demographic groups believe that the problems faced by the public schools in urban areas are more serious than those affecting nonurban schools.

• Lack of discipline and inadequate financing are the local school problems most frequently mentioned by respondents. The use of drugs and "fighting, violence, and gangs" are not far behind.

• Forty-six percent of those surveyed give the public schools in their community an A or a B. Fifty-six percent of public school parents give them a grade of A or B, and almost two-thirds (64%) of public school parents give the school their eldest child attends an A or B.

• The public believes that, if given the opportunity, the students most likely to move from public schools to private schools under a voucher system would be the higher-achieving students. Furthermore, the public believes that the academic achievement of these students would *improve* as a result of the move, while the academic achievement of the students remaining in the public schools would stay about the same.

• The public believes the home school movement is a bad thing for the nation; however, fewer respondents hold this belief today than when this question was asked in 1988 and 1985. Moreover, the public feels strongly that home schools should be required to guarantee a minimum level of educational quality.

• The public does not believe that state takeover of failing schools will improve academic achievement. Indeed, a strong majority (69%) believes that achievement would remain the same or get worse.

• Do the public schools overemphasize achievement testing? Approximately half (48%) believe the current emphasis is appropriate; the remaining half are divided between "too much" (20%) and "not enough" (28%).

• There is no consensus regarding the effect on academic achievement of lowering a school's starting age for children. However, a majority (75%) of the public would have students start school at age 5 or under.

• People divide almost equally in assessing the way a part-time job outside of school affects students' academic performance: one-third say it lowers performance, one-third say it improves performance, and one-third say it has no effect.

• The public supports President Clinton's main education initiatives. The President would assess performance of the nation's public schools according to how well students score on achievement tests at two different grade levels; he proposes a five-year, two-billion-dollar program to place a computer with access to the Internet in every classroom; and he seeks a tax credit for each first-year college student in a family with an annual income of $100,000 or less.

• Seven out of 10 respondents (71%) reject the idea that the local public schools are infringing on the right of parents to direct their children's education.

• Children today are getting more parental help with their homework than in earlier years, and Americans in general report an increased willingness to work as unpaid volunteers in their local public schools.

• A majority of public school parents (57%) say they would be more likely to take the school's side than their child's if a teacher or principal reported the child misbehaving or being disruptive in school.

• A majority of the public (60%) indicates that a C is the lowest grade a child of theirs could bring home on a report card without causing them to be upset or concerned.

• Fifty-four percent of Americans believe that the curriculum in their local schools needs to be changed to meet today's needs, while 39% believe it already does so.

• Majorities define curriculum "basics" as including mathematics and English. Pluralities would add history/U.S. government and science to the list.

• A small majority (52%) of the public believes that gifted and talented students should be placed in separate classes. Moreover, 66% believe that grouping students by ability in classrooms improves student achievement overall.

• Almost two-thirds of Americans (63%) believe that extracurricular activities are very important. Another 27% believe they are fairly important. The importance assigned to these activities is substantially greater today than when the question was last asked in 1985.

• A small majority (53%) of the public believes that the emphasis placed on sports such as football and basketball is about right. However, 39% believe there is too much emphasis.

• Ninety-six percent of respondents would require an average grade of C or better for interscholastic athletic eligibility.

• Americans are divided as to whether public schools should be financed through local property taxes, state taxes, or federal taxes. They are also divided as to whether local property taxes or local income taxes should be the main source of school funding.

• A small majority of the public (53%) is at least somewhat satisfied with the steps being taken to deal with the use of drugs in the local schools. Fifty-two percent of respondents believe an educational approach is the best way to deal with the problem; 42% believe severe penalties are best.

• The public gives strong support to "zero tolerance" policies that call for automatic suspension for drug and alcohol possession in school and for carrying weapons of any kind into school.

Improving the Public Schools And Student Achievement

Since some of the proposals being considered for improving student achievement call for alternatives to the public schools, the initial question, in effect, asked whether people would prefer reform or revolution. The answer is clear: 71 % of those responding believe that reform should come through the existing system. This response is uniform across demographic categories.

The question:

In order to improve public education in America, some people think the focus should be on reforming the existing public school system. Others believe the focus should be on finding an alternative to the existing public school system. Which approach do you think is preferable—reforming the existing public school system or finding an alternative to the existing public school system?

	National Totals %	No Children in School %	Public School Parents %	Nonpublic School Parents %
Reforming existing system	71	70	72	67
Finding alternative system	23	23	24	32

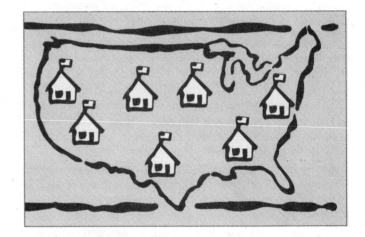

Improving Student Achievement

The question most directly aimed at discovering what the public believes will improve student achievement offered respondents the opportunity to evaluate 10 proposals. A majority of the public assigns either a great deal or quite a lot of importance to eight of them. However, two frequently mentioned reform proposals—lengthening the school year and lengthening the school day—could garner support from only 38% and 25% of respondents respectively.

With relatively few exceptions, there is little difference in the way subgroups in the national population view these measures. However, 75% of blacks (compared to 50% for the national population) feel that placing a computer in every classroom would improve student achievement a great deal. In addition, 59% of blacks and 51% of nonwhites believe that allowing parents and children to attend the public school of their choice would improve student achievement a great deal; the corresponding figure for the nation as a whole is just 39%.

Indeed, blacks favor many of the national reforms proposed in recent years to a much greater extent than does the general population. For example, blacks are more likely to believe that student achievement will be improved a great deal by establishing national standards (58% to 41%), by establishing a national curriculum (58% to 35%), by using standardized tests to measure achievement (52% to 36%), and by providing health-care services in the public schools (65% to 35%).

The question:

Here is a list of measures that have been proposed for improving the academic achievement of public school students. As I read each one, would you tell me whether you believe that measure would improve the achievement of the students in the local public schools a great deal, quite a lot, not very much, or not at all?

	A Great Deal or Quite a Lot %	A Great Deal %	Quite A Lot %	Not Very Much %	Not Much At All %	Don't Know %
Placing a computer in every classroom	81	50	31	13	5	1
Establishing national standards for measuring the academic performance of the public schools	77	41	36	15	6	2
Moving persistent "troublemakers" into alternative schools	75	43	32	14	9	2
Allowing parents and students to attend the public school of their choice	73	39	34	18	7	2
Using standardized national tests to measure the academic achievement of students	67	36	31	23	8	2
Grouping students in classes according to ability level	66	34	32	19	13	2
Establishing a national curriculum	66	35	31	20	10	4
Providing health-care services in schools	61	35	26	25	12	2
Lengthening the school year	38	18	20	33	27	2
Lengthening the school day	25	12	13	38	35	2

State Takeovers

In some states the administration of faltering or failing schools is taken over by the state. People were asked what effect they thought such a move would have on student achievement in the schools in their community. The public is split on this question; 43% believe such a takeover would have no effect, and the rest are evenly divided on whether achievement would improve or get worse.

The question:

Some states have taken over the administration of schools in local school districts where the public schools were considered to be doing a poor job. What effect do you think takeover by the state would have on the academic achievement of students in a public school in your community? Do you think their academic achievement would improve, get worse, or do you think it wouldn't have much effect on their academic achievement?

	National Totals %	No Children in School %	Public School Parents %	Nonpublic School Parents %
Would improve	25	24	25	46
Would get worse	26	25	27	27
Wouldn't have much effect	43	45	42	25

School-Starting Age and Part-Time Work

The current poll probed people's beliefs about the effect on student achievement of starting school a year earlier and of holding a part-time job. There is no consensus on either question. Thirty-seven percent of respondents believe that starting school a year earlier would improve student achievement, 24% disagree, and 37% believe it would make no difference. Blacks are more than twice as likely as whites (75% to 31%) *to* believe that starting school earlier would improve student achievement.

On the question of starting age, three-fourths of Americans would have students start school at age 5 or under. Twenty-six percent would have them start at age 4 or under. Groups in the national population that most strongly support having children start school at age 4 or under include blacks (64%), nonwhites (59%), 18- to 29-year-olds (40%), and urban residents (35%).

Data on public school parents reveal a pattern similar to that for the national population. Sixty-four percent of black parents would prefer a school starting age of 4 or under (compared to 30% for all parents), as would 57% of 18- to 29-year-old parents and 61% of nonwhite parents.

The first question:

In your opinion, what effect would starting a child a year younger than is now generally the case have on the child's academic achievement in elementary and in high school? Do you think starting a year younger would improve the child's achievement, make it worse, or wouldn't it make much difference?

	National Totals %	No Children in School %	Public School Parents %	Nonpublic School Parents %
Improve achievement	37	35	40	37
Make it worse	24	22	25	39
Not much difference	37	40	33	23
Don't know	2	3	2	1

At what age do you think students should start school?

	National Totals '97 %	National Totals '86 %	No Children In School '97 %	No Children In School '86 %	Public School Parents '97 %	Public School Parents '86 %	Nonpublic School Parents '97 %	Nonpublic School Parents '86 %
4 years (or under)	26	29	24	29	30	27	27	29
5 years	49	41	50	40	47	44	44	42
6 years	21	18	22	18	19	20	16	23
7 years (or over)	3	2	3	1	3	2	11	*
Don't know	1	10	1	12	1	7	2	6

*Less than one-half of 1%.

The third question:

What effect do you feel having a part-time job outside of school has on the academic achievement of students in the public schools in this community? Generally speaking, do you feel having a part-time job improves their academic achievement, hurts their academic achievement, or do you feel it does not affect their academic achievement one way or the other?

	National Totals .%	No Children In School .%	Public School Parents .%	Nonpublic School parents .%
Improves achievement	29	31	28	16
Hurts achievement	32	32	30	44
Does not affect achievement	35	34	37	37
Don't know	4	3	5	3

Improving Schools

People frequently ask, "Why are some schools better than others?" This year poll respondents were asked to rate the importance of three factors sometimes offered to explain such differences. The public considers the amount of support from parents of students in the local public schools to be the most important factor in making a school better. However, the amount of money spent on the local public schools is a close second. The kinds of students attending the local public schools is regarded as either quite important or very important by two-thirds of the public but is not considered as important as the other two factors.

The question:

Here are some factors that are sometimes mentioned to explain why the public schools in some places are better than those in others. As I read off each one, would you tell me whether you think that factor is very important, quite important, not very important, or not at all important in determining the quality of the local public schools?

	Very Important %	Quite Important %	Not Very Important %	Not at All Important %	Don't Know %
Amount of support from parents of students in the local public schools	86	11	3	*	*
Amount of money spent on the local public schools	62	29	6	2	1
Kinds of students attending the local public schools	41	26	20	9	4

Percent Responding "Very Important"

	National Totals .%	No Children In School .%	Public School Parents .%	Nonpublic School parents .%
Amount of support from parents of students in the local public schools	86	84	88	92
Amount of money spent on the local public schools	62	59	67	63

President Clinton's Proposals

President Clinton has offered three proposals designed to improve schools, enhance student achievement, or provide incentives for students to succeed in school. These proposals are currently before Congress and may or may not become law.

While all the proposals made by President Clinton attract majority support, the strongest support (82%) is for the proposed tax credit for the parents of first-year college students. This proposal has already been debated in Congress, with the Administration indicating a willingness to compromise on the need for a B average as a condition for second-year aid. Support for the proposal is strong among all groups in the poll.

Two-thirds of the public (66%) favor the proposal for placing a computer with access to the Internet in every public school classroom. Groups strongly in favor of the proposal include blacks (85%), nonwhites (83%), 18- to 29-year-olds (78%), and those in the $50,000 and over income range (78%).

The President's testing proposal has the least support and, based on past experience, is likely to generate the most controversy.

The first question:

President Clinton has proposed a tax credit for families with an annual income of $100,000 or less for each first-year college student. The $1,500 tax credit would also apply to the second year if the student maintained a B average and had no conviction for drugs. in general, do you favor or oppose this proposal?

	National Totals .%	No Children In School .%	Public School Parents .%	Nonpublic School parents .%
Favor	82	79	87	88
Oppose	17	20	12	12
Don't know	1	1	1	*

*Less than one-half of 1%

The second question:

President Clinton has proposed a five-year, two-billion-dollar program that would place a computer with access to the Internet in every public school classroom in the nation. In general, do you favor or oppose this proposal?

	National Totals .%	No Children In School .%	Public School Parents .%	Nonpublic School parents .%
Favor	66	64	70	73
Oppose	32	34	29	26
Don't know	2	2	1	1

	National Totals .%	No Children In School .%	Public School Parents .%	Nonpublic School parents .%
Favor	57	56	59	53
Oppose	37	37	37	42

The third question:

President Clinton has proposed that the performance of the nation's public schools be assessed according to how well students score on achievement tests at two different grade levels. In general, do you favor or oppose this proposal?

Achievement Testing

Testing and its role in school improvement is a frequent subject of debate. Respondents this year were asked their opinion of the level of emphasis on testing in their local public schools. Forty-eight percent responded that the emphasis is about right. The rest were divided between too much and too little. These responses were consistent among all demographic groups.

The question:

In your opinion, is there too much emphasis on achievement testing in the public schools in this community, not enough emphasis on testing, or about the right amount?

	National Totals .%	No Children In School .%	Public School Parents .%	Nonpublic School parents .%
Too much emphasis	20	20	19	24
Not enough emphasis	28	28	26	42
About the right amount	48	46	54	32
Don't know	4	6	1	2

Biggest Problems Facing Local Schools

Efforts at school improvement must, of course, address the problems the public schools face. In all recent polls the public has been asked to indicate the biggest problem facing the local public schools. This year a follow-up question was asked to determine whether the public feels the problems faced by urban schools are more serious than those faced by their nonurban counterparts. Sixty-nine percent said they believe the problems that urban schools face are either much more serious or somewhat more serious.

This year "lack of discipline" and "lack of financial support" were mentioned by 15% of the respondents respectively as the most serious problems facing local public schools. Use

of drugs, designated the number-one problem in last year's poll, was mentioned by 14% of respondents this year, and fighting/violence/gangs was mentioned by 12%. These four problems were the only ones to reach double figures.

One caution needs to be offered relative to the findings reported. The question requires respondents to identify a problem, and they do not have a list from which to choose. That is undoubtedly why so many different problems are mentioned and why the percentage of mentions is so small. (Eleven other problems were mentioned by 2% of respondents.)

The first question:

What do you think are the biggest problems with which the public schools in this community must deal?

	National Totals '97 %	National Totals '96 %	No Children In School '97 %	No Children In School '96 %	Public School Parents '97 %	Public School Parents '96 %	Nonpublic School Parents '97 %	Nonpublic School Parents '96 %
Lack of discipline/more control	15	15	15	16	12	12	22	18
Lack of financial support/funding/money	15	13	15	14	14	13	4	7
Use of drugs/dope	14	16	14	17	14	14	9	12
Fighting/violence/gangs	12	14	12	14	12	15	16	17
Overcrowded schools	8	8	6	6	10	11	17	15
Concern about standards/quality of education	8	4	7	4	8	4	10	9
Pupils' lack of interest/poor attitudes/truancy	6	5	6	5	6	6	3	4
Difficulty getting good teachers/quality teachers	3	3	3	3	4	3	*	3
No problems	2	3	2	2	3	7	*	3
Miscellaneous	9	9	9	8	8	10	13	11
Don't know	10	13	13	15	6	9	4	10

*Less than one-half of 1%.

The second question:

Just your impression, are the problems faced by the public schools in urban areas much more serious, somewhat more serious, somewhat less serious, or much less serious than those faced by the public schools in nonurban areas?

	National Totals %	No Children in School %	Public School Parents %	Nonpublic School Parents %
Much more serious	40	40	40	43
Somewhat more serious	29	29	30	32
Somewhat less serious	16	16	17	16
Much less serious	7	6	7	5
Don't know	8	9	6	4

Grading the Schools

Since 1974 respondents to the Phi Delta Kappa/Gallup education polls have been asked to grade the public schools in their communities on a scale of A to F. In 1981, people were first asked to rate the "nation's public schools" on the same scale. Then, beginning in 1985, parents were asked to grade the public school their oldest child was attending.

One significant generalization derived from responses to these questions over the years is the fact that the closer respondents are to the public schools, the higher the grades they give them. Thus people give the schools in their own community much higher grades than they give the nation's schools. Parents give the schools in the community much higher grades than do those who do not have children in the public schools. By the same token, public school parents, when asked to grade the school their oldest child attends, give that school higher grades than they give to schools in the community as a whole. Current poll findings reinforce the basic generalization: familiarity with the public schools breeds respect for them.

The differences are impressive. Over the last nine years the differences between the percentage of A's and B's given to the nation's public schools and to the local schools have averaged about 23 points. Even more startling is the difference between the percentage of A's and B's parents give to the school their oldest child attends and the percentage of A's and B's given to the nation's schools. Here the difference over the last nine years has averaged 47 percentage points.

Taken together, these items suggest a second generalization: the low grades given the nation's public schools are primarily media-induced. Whereas people learn firsthand about their *children's* schools, they learn about the *nation's* schools primarily from the media.

Local Public Schools

As has been the case for two decades, over four Americans in 10—46% this year—award a grade of A or B to the public schools in their own communities. And almost eight in 10—78% this year—award them at least a grade of C. An even higher percentage of public school parents (56%) assign an A or a B to the schools in their community.

The question:

Students are often given the grades A, B, C, D, and FAIL to denote the quality of their work. Suppose the public schools themselves, in this community, were graded in the same way. What grade would you give the public schools here—A, B, C, D, or FAIL?

	National Totals '97 %	National Totals '96 %	No Children In School '97 %	No Children In School '96 %	Public School Parents '97 %	Public School Parents '96 %	Nonpublic School Parents '97 %	Nonpublic School Parents '96 %
A & B	46	43	42	38	56	57	26	24
A	10	8	8	6	15	15	9	2
B	36	35	34	32	41	42	17	22
C	32	34	33	36	30	29	35	43
D	11	11	11	12	10	9	21	13
FAIL	6	6	7	6	3	4	13	13
Don't know	5	6	7	8	1	1	5	7

Public Schools Nationally

As has been the case since this question was first asked in 1981, about half as many Americans give a grade of A or B to the nation's public schools as give these grades to the local public schools. This year the figures are 22% and 46% respectively. The groups assigning unusually high percentages of A's and B's to the nation's public schools include blacks (44%) and nonwhites (35%).

The question:

How about the public schools in the nation as a whole? What grade would you give the public schools nationally— A, B, C, D, or FAIL?

	National Totals		No Children In School		Public School Parents		Nonpublic School Parents	
	'97 %	'96 %	'97 %	'96 %	'97 %	'96 %	'97 %	'96 %
A & B	22	21	23	20	23	26	24	8
A	2	1	3	1	2	2	2	1
B	20	20	20	19	21	24	22	7
C	48	46	49	47	46	43	38	57
D	15	18	15	19	16	14	15	21
FAIL	6	5	6	5	4	7	6	3
Don't know	9	10	7	9	11	10	17	11

Public School Oldest Child Attends

The parents of public school children are likely to be among the best-informed citizens about the public schools. Since 1985, this poll has asked parents to grade the school their oldest child attends. This year almost two-thirds (64%) of public school parents assign the school their oldest child attends an A or a B. Another 23% assign this school a C, bringing to 87% the proportion of parents giving the school their oldest child attends at least a passing grade of C. The parents who are most likely to give the school their oldest child attends an A or a B include college graduates (75%), parents who live in the East (74%), and those parents whose children are at the top of their class or above-average academically (74%).

The question:

Using the A, B, C, D, FAIL scale again, what grade would you give the school your oldest child attends?

	Public School Parents	
	'97 %	'96 %
A & B	64	66
A	26	23
B	38	43
C	23	22
D	7	6
FAIL	4	5
Don't know	2	1

Public Versus Nonpublic Schools

The current poll featured the usual questions regarding attendance at public, private, or church-related schools with the government paying all or part of the costs. The first question dealt with choosing a private school to attend at public expense. In the past, when this question has been asked, some critics have suggested that the results would be different if the words "government expense" were used in place of "public expense." With this in mind, a split-sample design was used in this year's poll. That is, the sample was divided, and the question was asked both ways. The customary question dealing with the use of vouchers was also asked, along with a question designed to determine whether the public believes any changes in admission policies should be required for nonpublic schools that accept public funds.

Providing for parents and students to attend nonpublic schools at public expense has been strongly opposed in past years. In 1993, for example, the percentage opposing allowing students and parents to choose a private school to attend at public expense was 74%, with only 24% in favor. In 1994 allowing parents to send their school-age children to any public, private, or church-related school of their choice with the government paying "all or part of the tuition" was opposed 54% to 45%. However, with each succeeding year, the opposition has lessened. This year the public can be described as almost equally divided on this issue.

Choosing Private Schools at Public Expense

The current poll is the fourth (starting in 1993) to ask the public its attitude toward allowing parents to choose a private school to attend at public expense. The opposition has been consistent, though it dropped from 74% in 1993 to 65% in 1995 to 61% in 1996. This year the poll shows that 52% oppose such choice while 44% approve it.

The group most likely to oppose this form of choice is the 18- to 29-year-olds (62% opposed, 38% in favor). Groups most likely to support this form of choice include nonwhites (51% in favor, 46% opposed) and urban residents (53% in favor, 45% opposed).

A second form of the question was also asked this year with the words "government expense" substituted for "public expense." When asked in this way, the public is equally divided, with 48% in favor and 48% opposed. Those most likely to support this choice include blacks (72%), nonwhites (68%), 18- to 29-year-olds (70%), professional and business persons (53%), and urban residents (59%).

The first question:

Do you favor or oppose allowing students and parents to choose a private school to attend at public expense?

	National Totals				No Children In School				Public School Parents				Nonpublic School Parents			
	'97 %	'96 %	'95 %	'93 %	'97 %	'96 %	'95 %	'93 %	'97 %	'96 %	'95 %	'93 %	'97 %	'96 %	'95 %	'93 %
Favor	44	36	33	24	44	33	30	21	45	39	38	27	52	60	44	45
Oppose	52	61	65	74	54	63	68	76	50	59	59	72	44	38	51	55
Don't know	4	3	2	2	2	4	2	3	5	2	3	1	4	2	5	*

*Less than one-half of 1%.

The second question:

Do you favor or oppose allowing students and parents to choose a private school to attend at government expense?

	National Totals		No Children in School		Public School Parents		Nonpublic School Parents	
	Gov't Exp. %	Public Exp. %	Gov't Exp. %	Public Exp. %	Gov't Exp. %	Public Exp. %	Gov't Exp. %	Public Exp. %
Favor	48	44	51	44	43	45	50	52
Oppose	48	52	45	54	54	50	44	44
Don't know	4	4	4	2	3	5	6	4

The question most directly associated with vouchers was asked in 1994 and repeated in 1996. When it was first asked in 1994, 45% favored the idea. Support was virtually the same (43%) in 1996; however, this year's poll shows the public equally divided, with 49% in favor and 48% opposed. Both public school parents (55%) and nonpublic school parents (68%) favor allowing parents to send their school-age children to any public, private, or church-related school they choose, with the government paying part or all of the cost.

This issue divides men and women. Women favor permitting the choice by 52% to 45%; men oppose it by 51% to 47%. Other groups in support include blacks (62% to 34%), nonwhites (61% to 36%), 18- to 29-year-olds (55% to 43%), 30- to 49-year-olds (53% to 45%), those who live in the South (56% to 42%), those in the $20,000 to $30,000 income group (55% to 43%), those in the $10,000 to $20,000 income group (53% to 42%), and manual laborers (53% to 44%). Groups in opposition include those 50 years of age and older (56% to 40%), those living in the West (54% to 45%), those in the $50,000 and over income group (57% to 41%), and suburban residents (51% to 45%).

The question:

A proposal has been made that would allow parents to send their school-age children to any public, private, or church-related school they choose. For those parents choosing nonpublic schools, the government would pay all or part of the tuition. Would you favor or oppose this proposal in your state?

	National Totals			No Children In School			Public School Parents			Nonpublic School Parents		
	'97 %	'96 %	'94 %	'97 %	'96 %	'94 %	'97 %	'96 %	'94 %	'97 %	'96 %	'94 %
Favor	49	43	45	46	38	42	55	49	48	68	70	69
Oppose	48	54	54	51	59	57	43	49	51	31	28	29
Don't know	3	3	1	3	3	1	2	2	1	1	2	2

Obligations of Private Schools Accepting Public Funds

One of the issues that comes up in any debate over public funds going to nonpublic schools is the extent to which those schools should be bound by the same obligations that fall on public schools. This year's poll asked whether such schools should be required to accept students from a wider range of backgrounds and levels of academic ability than is now generally the case. The public is strongly in agreement that they should. Seventy-eight percent of the public holds this view. This response is consistent across all demographic groups.

The question:

Do you think nonpublic schools that receive public funding should or should not be required to accept students from a wider range of backgrounds and academic ability than is now generally the case?

	National Totals %	No Children In School %	Public School Parents %	Nonpublic School Parents %
Should be required to accept a wider range	78	78	80	76
Should not	18	17	17	22
Don't know	4	5	3	2

Effects of a Shift to Nonpublic Schools

Another concern raised by those opposing the use of public funds for nonpublic schools is that the students and parents with the financial means to do so might opt for private schools, leaving the public schools to serve the poor and underprivileged. Three of the questions in this year's poll addressed this concern. The responses offer some indication that the concern is warranted.

Almost two-thirds of those surveyed (65%) believe that it would be the higher-achieving students who would take the opportunity to attend private schools. The same percentage believes the result for these students would be improved academic achievement. As for the students remaining in the public schools, 70% of the public believes that their achievement would remain about the same.

Responses to these three questions vary little across the subgroups in the poll.

The first question:

Suppose a large number of students in your local public schools moved to private schools. Just your opinion, who would be most likely to move to the private schools—the higher-achieving students, the lower-achieving students, or the average-achieving students?

	National Totals %	No Children In School %	Public School Parents %	Nonpublic School Parents %
Higher-achieving students	65	67	62	56
Lower-achieving students	8	8	8	10
Average-achieving students	20	19	21	28
No difference	3	3	5	2
Don't know	4	3	4	4

The second question:

Again, just your opinion, how would the academic achievement of those public school students who had moved to the private schools be affected? Do you think their academic achievement would improve, get worse, or remain about the same after moving to private schools?

	National Totals %	No Children In School %	Public School Parents %	Nonpublic School Parents %
Improve	65	68	58	80
Get worse	4	4	4	*
Remain about the same	28	25	35	19
Don't know	3	3	3	1

*Less than one-half of 1%.

The third question:

How about the students who remained in the local public schools? Do you think their academic achievement would improve, get worse, or remain about the same?

	National Totals %	No Children In School %	Public School Parents %	Nonpublic School Parents %
Improve	17	16	19	10
Get worse	11	11	11	10
Remain about the same	70	70	68	80
Don't know	2	3	2	*

*Less than one-half of 1%.

Home Schooling

The Phi Delta Kappa/Gallup poll first addressed the home-school movement in 1985, asking respondents whether the fledgling move toward home schooling was a good thing or a bad thing for the nation. At that time, 73% said they thought it was a bad thing, while 16% said they thought it was a good thing. When the question was repeated in 1988, the proportion who said it was a bad thing had fallen to 59%, and the proportion who said it was a good thing had risen to 28%. Given a continuing increase in the number of students being schooled at home, poll planners deemed it important to revisit the issue this year. While the public still feels that the home-school movement is a bad thing, the margin has now shrunk to just 21 percentage points.

It is interesting to note that nonpublic school parents, who thought the home-school movement was a bad thing in 1985 (by a margin of 71% to 22%), now favor it by 52% to 41%. This is the only group sampled that believes the movement to home schooling is a good thing.

This year's poll also asked respondents whether home schools should or should not be required to guarantee a minimum level of educational quality. Almost nine in 10 respondents (88%) felt that they should. This response is consistent among all groups.

The first question:

Recently, there has been a movement toward home schools—that is, situations in which parents keep their children at home to teach the children themselves. Do you think this movement is a good thing or a bad thing for the nation?

	National Totals			No Children In School			Public School Parents			Nonpublic School Parents		
	'97 %	'88 %	'85 %	'97 %	'88 %	'85 %	'97 %	'88 %	'85 %	'97 %	'88 %	'85 %
Good thing	36	28	16	34	27	16	38	29	14	52	29	22
Bad thing	57	59	73	59	59	72	56	61	75	41	56	71
Don't know	7	13	11	7	14	12	6	10	11	7	15	7

The second question:

Do you think that home schools should or should not be required to guarantee a minimum level of educational quality?

	National Totals %	No Children In School %	Public School Parents %	Nonpublic School Parents %
Should be required	88	88	91	80
Should not be required	10	10		19
Don't know	2	2	1	1

Parents and Their Relationship To the Public Schools

This poll went further than most recent Phi Delta Kappa/Gallup polls in exploring the relationship between the public schools and the parents who send students to those schools. That seems to have been an appropriate decision, given the fact that 86% of the public cites the amount of support from parents of students in the local public schools as the most important factor in determining why schools in some places are better than others.

Infringing on Rights of Parents

One of the charges heard from some critics is that the public schools are infringing on the right of parents to direct their children's education. This seems to be part of a more general feeling among some Americans that the government has too much control over their lives. However, more than seven in 10 respondents (71%) said they do not believe that the public schools are infringing on the rights of parents. Only nonpublic school parents differ.

The question:

People in some communities say the local public schools are infringing on the rights of parents to direct their children's education. In your opinion, are the public schools in your community infringing on the rights of local parents to direct their children's education?

	National Totals %	No Children In School %	Public School Parents %	Nonpublic School Parents %
Yes	infringing	24	20	28
No, not infringing	71	73	70	44
Don't know	5	7	2	6

Help with Homework

The 1986 poll asked parents how much help they gave their oldest child with his or her homework. At that time, 34% said that they provided no help—a figure that fell to 13% when the question was repeated in this year's poll. It also appears that parents who help their children are spending more hours doing so than they did in 1986. Forty-seven percent of this year's respondents say that they help with homework four or more hours a week, compared to 14% who said they spent that much time in the earlier poll. Thirty-nine percent of all public school parents report that they help their children five or more hours per week.

The question:

During the school year, on average, about how many hours a week do you help your oldest child with his or her homework?

	'97 %	'86 %
None	13	34
Up to 1 hour	5	13
1 – 1:59 hours	12	17
2 – 2:59 hours	12	10
3 – 3:59 hours	9	7
4 – 4:59 hours	8	5
5 – 5:59 hours	14	4
6 hours or more	25	5
Undesignated	2	5

Willingness to Volunteer

Much has been made recently of the importance of persons being willing to serve as unpaid volunteers in addressing problems the nation faces. Television recently featured pictures of past U.S. Presidents working at sprucing up inner-city areas. Gen. Colin Powell heads up a Presidential task force to promote volunteerism. Given this backdrop, poll planners thought it important to repeat the 1992 question in which participants were asked about their willingness to serve as unpaid volunteers in the public schools. At that time 59% said that they would be willing to do so. In this year's poll that figure rose to 69%.

The question:

If you were asked, would you be willing to work as an unpaid volunteer in any of the public schools in this community or not?

	Willing to Work as Unpaid Volunteer	
	'97 %	'92 %
NATIONAL TOTALS	69	59
Sex		
Men	64	54
Women	73	64
Race		
White	68	61
Nonwhite	74	49
Age		
19–29 years	72	65
30–49 years	76	65
50–64 years	56	54
65 and over	57	36
Education		
Collee graduage	73	70
High school graduate	63	57
High school incomplete	63	45
Children in School		
No children in schoo	65	51
Public school parents	78	72
Nonpublic school parents	60	49

Parental Support for Teachers and Principals

One of the complaints heard from teachers and principals is that they no longer have the parental support they once enjoyed. Two questions were asked in this poll to explore the support parents give to school personnel.

The first question:

Suppose a teacher or principal reported that your oldest child was misbehaving and being disruptive in school. Whose side do you think you would be more likely to take—the school's or your child's?

	Public School Parents %	Nonpublic School Parents %
The school's side	57	73
Your child's side	25	16
Don't know	18	11

The second question:

What if a teacher or principal reported that your oldest child was not working hard enough at schoolwork? Whose side do you think you would be more likely to take—the school's or your child's?

	Public School Parents %	Nonpublic School Parents %
The school's side	70	70
Your child's side	22	25
Don't know	8	5

Parental Expectations Regarding Achievement

By a 2-1 margin (60% to 28%) respondents in the 1996 Phi Delta Kappa/Gallup poll said that, if forced to choose, they would prefer their sons or daughters to make C grades and be active in extracurricular activities rather than make A grades and not be active. This response led poll planners to ask on this year's poll about the lowest grade a student could bring home without causing the parent to be upset or concerned. A majority (60%) said their child could bring home a

report card with a C without raising concern. This response is consistent among all groups in the poll.

The question:

Regardless of whether you have children in public school, what would be the lowest grade a child of yours could bring home on a report card without upsetting or concerning you?

	National Totals %	No Children In School %	Public School Parents %	Nonpublic School Parents %
A	1	1	*	2
B	21	20	21	22
C	60	58	63	64
D	13	15	11	9
FAIL	3	3	4	1
Don't know	2	3	1	2

*Less than one-half of 1%.

Parental Expectations on Communication

Given today's concern for privacy, one of the important dilemmas for school personnel is how much information regarding student problems should be reported to parents. This is an area, however, where parental expectations are quite clear. Ninety-eight percent of all respondents believe that public schools should be required to notify the parents if their child is found to have a substance abuse problem, and 90% feel that parents should be notified if their child is found to have a sexually transmitted disease. These responses are consistent across all groups surveyed.

The first question:

Do you think that the public schools in your community should or should not be required to notify the parents of a student who is found by school authorities to have a substance abuse problem?

	National Totals %	No Children In School %	Public School Parents %	Nonpublic School Parents %
Should be required	98	98	98	100
Should not be required	1	1	2	*
Don't know	1	1	*	*

*Less than one-half of 1%.

The second question:

How about a sexually transmitted disease? Do you think the public schools in your community should or should not be required to notify the parents of a student who is found by school authorities to have a sexually transmitted disease?

	National Totals %	No Children In School %	Public School Parents %	Nonpublic School Parents %
Should be required	90	89	92	89
Should not be required	9	10	7	10
Don't know	1	1	1	1

*Less than one-half of 1%.

The Curriculum

One question that quickly surfaces in any discussion of school reform is the extent to which the curriculum needs to be changed to meet today's needs. This question was explored in the 1982 poll. At that time a plurality (42%) expressed the view that the curriculum did meet the needs of the day. Fifty percent of public school parents agreed. In this year's poll, however, 54% of respondents say they think the curriculum needs to be changed. Public school parents now call for change by a 53% to 46% margin. Groups most likely to feel the need for change include nonwhites (65%), 18- to 29-year-olds (64%), and clerical and sales personnel (65%).

The question:

Do you think the curriculum in the public schools in your community needs to be changed to meet today's needs, or do you think it already meets today's needs?

	National Totals %	%	No Children In School %	%	Public School Parents %	%	Nonpublic School Parents %	%
Needs to be changed	54	36	54	33	53	42	65	46
Already meets needs	39	42	36	38	46	50	30	44
Don't know	7	22	10	29	1	8	5	10

Curriculum 'Basics'

In every public school forum conducted by Phi Delta Kappa during the 1996–97 academic year, there was agreement that the schools should teach the "basics." The ensuing discussions, however, suggested that there might be a difference of opinion as to what the "basics" included. This year's poll asked respondents to define the term. The responses indicate that mathematics (named by 90%) and English (named by 84%) constitute the heart of the "basics." This seems close to the traditional three R's. Large percentages of respondents would also add science (44%) and history/U.S. government (38%).

A word of caution is required here. The fact that the public wants the basics taught and defines them narrowly should not be interpreted to mean that people do not value other subjects and other parts of the curriculum. In fact, the public assigns great importance even to extracurricular activities (as a later question shows). What seems clear is that, while the public

sees teaching the so-called basics as a central mission, it has many other expectations of its public schools as well.

The question:

People have different ideas as to what constitutes the so-called basic subjects in school. Would you name the school subjects that you consider to be the basics?

	National Totals %	No Children In School %	Public School Parents %	Nonpublic School Parents %
Mathematics	90	89	91	93
English	84	84	84	91
Science	44	41	49	53
History/U.S. government	38	36	40	50
Geography	8	9	8	4
Computer training	8	8	8	12
Physical education	7	7	9	11
Art	5	6	5	8
Social studies	5	4	7	4
Foreign language	5	4	6	13
Music	3	3	3	1
Health education	2	2	4	4
Vocational training	1	2	1	*
Career education	1	1	1	*
Business	1	1	1	2
Other	8	8	7	7
Don't know	1	2	1	2

*Less than one-half of 1%.

Placement of the Gifted and Talented

Whether students who are judged to be gifted and talented should be placed in separate classes is an issue that has implications beyond what is good for gifted and talented students. There are those who argue that removing the gifted and talented from the regular classroom eliminates important role models and results in lower performance on the part of those remaining in the regular classroom. With this in mind, poll planners included a question on the topic in this year's poll. A small majority (52%) of the public supports the placement of gifted and talented students in separate classes. This response takes added significance from the fact that 66% of poll respondents also said they believe that grouping students according to ability will improve student achievement a great deal or quite a lot.

The question:

How do you feel about the placement of gifted and talented students in the local public schools? In your opinion, should gifted and talented students be placed in the same classes as other students, or should they be placed in separate classes?

	National Totals %	No Children In School %	Public School Parents %	Nonpublic School Parents %
Placed in the same classes	44	44	44	44
Placed in separate classes	52	51	52	51
Don't know	4	5	4	5

Importance of Extracurricular Activities

The importance of extracurricular activities has been explored in previous polls. In 1978, 45% of the public judged extracurricular activities to be very important. That figure fell to 31% in 1984, rose to 39% in 1985, and then jumped to 63% in this year's poll. Percentages vary only a little among the groups sampled.

The question:

I'd like your opinion about extracurricular activities such as the school band, dramatics, sports, and the school newspaper. How important are these to a young person's education—very important, fairly important, not too important, or not at all important?

	National Totals %	No Children In School %	Public School Parents %	Nonpublic School Parents %
Vary Important	63	64	62	58
Fairly important	27	26	29	37
Not too important	8	8	7	5
Not at all important	2	2	2	*
Don't know	*	*	*	*

*Less than one-half of 1%.

National Totals	1997 %	1985 %	1984 %	1978 %
Very important	63	39	31	45
Fairly important	27	41	46	40
Not too important	8	14	18	9
Not at all important	2	3	4	4
Don't know	*	3	1	2

*Less than one-half of 1%.

The Role of Interscholastic Sports

Previous polls have not dealt extensively with the role of interscholastic sports in the school program. However, this year's poll included three questions. The first asked about the emphasis placed on such sports as football and basketball. A small majority (53%) of the public believes that the current emphasis is about right. However, 39% feel there is too much emphasis. Public school parents (58%) are a little more inclined than the average to think the present emphasis is appropriate.

In a follow-up question, there was virtual unanimity (96%) on the question of requiring minimum grades and school attendance for participation in sports. When asked how high that minimum should be, 96% would require a grade-point average of C or higher. Men and women tend to take a slightly different view, with only 35% of men suggesting a minimum of an A or a B while 51% of women would require these higher grades.

The first question:

What is your opinion about the way sports, such as football and basketball, are handled in the public schools in your community? Do you feel that there is too much emphasis on sports, not enough emphasis on sports, or about the right amount of emphasis in the local schools?

	National Totals %	No Children In School %	Public School Parents %	Nonpublic School Parents %
Too much emphasis	39	43	33	36
Not enough emphasis	5	4	7	8
About right amount	53	50	58	54
Don't know	3	3	2	2

The second question:

Do you feel that high school students who participate in sports should or should not be required to maintain a minimum grade-point average and school attendance record in order to participate in interscholastic sports?

	National Totals %	No Children In School %	Public School Parents %	Nonpublic School Parents %
Should be required	96	96	96	99
Should not be required	3	3	4	1
Don't know	1	1	*	*

*Less than one-half of 1%.

The third question:

What average grade do you think should be required for participation in interscholastic sports?

	National Totals %	No Children In School %	Public School Parents %	Nonpublic School Parents %
A	3	3	2	4
B	41	42	41	30
C	52	51	55	59
D	2	2	1	5
FAIL	*	*	*	*
Don't know	2	2	1	2

*Less than one-half of 1%.

Dealing with Drugs and Weapons in School

The public continues to believe that drugs and weapons in school are major problems for the public schools. Although school personnel in most situations do not believe these problems are as severe as the public does, schoolpeople must nonetheless deal with the public's concern. The first of three drug-related questions in this poll sought to find out how satisfied people are with steps being taken to deal with the drug problem in their local schools. Perhaps surprisingly, 53% indicate they are either very or somewhat satisfied. The level of satisfaction rises to 65% for public school parents and to 60% for rural residents. However, it falls to 45% for urban residents.

The second question dealt with "zero tolerance" policies calling for automatic suspension of students carrying drugs or alcohol into school. Support for such policies is strong. Eighty-six percent say they support such policies, and this level of support is consistent among all groups.

Respondents were also asked whether they feel an educational approach or severe penalties offer the best means of dealing with the drug problem. A small majority (52%) prefers an educational approach, while 42% favor severe penalties.

These percentages vary little across groups.

Many schools also have "zero tolerance" policies that call for automatic suspension of students who bring weapons to school. Such policies garnered media attention when authorities suspended a student for bring a nail file to school. Regardless of difficulties in application, support for such policies is very strong. Ninety-three percent of poll respondents express support, and that support is consistent among all groups.

The first question:

How satisfied are you yourself with the steps being taken to deal with the use of drugs in the public schools in your community—very satisfied, somewhat satisfied, not very satisfied, or not at all satisfied?

	National Totals %	No Children In School %	Public School Parents %	Nonpublic School Parents %
Very satisfied	17	13	25	11
Somewhat satisfied	36	35	40	35
Not very satisfied	22	24	17	32
Not at all satisfied	20	21	17	17
Don't know	5	7	1	5

The second question:

Some public schools have a so-called zero-tolerance drug and alcohol policy, which means that possession of any illegal drugs or alcohol by students will result in automatic suspension. Would you favor or oppose such a policy in the public schools in your community?

	National Totals %	No Children In School %	Public School Parents %	Nonpublic School Parents %
Favor	86	84	89	93
Oppose	13	15	10	7
Don't know	1	1	1	*

The third question:

In your opinion, which is more effective for dealing with a drug problem in the public schools in your community—an educational approach, pointing out the consequences of drug use, or severe penalties for those violating the school drug policy?

	National Totals %	No Children In School %	Public School Parents %	Nonpublic School Parents %
Educational approach	52	52	53	44
Severe penalties	42	41	43	49
Don't know	6	7	4	7

The fourth question:

Some public schools have a so-called zero-tolerance weapons policy, which means that students found carrying weapons of any kind in school will be automatically suspended. Would you favor or oppose such a policy in the public schools in your community?

	National Totals %	No Children In School %	Public School Parents %	Nonpublic School Parents %
Favor	93	92	95	91
Oppose	5	6	4	9
Don't know	2	2	1	*

*Less than one-half of 1%.

Financing the Public Schools

From time to time, the Phi Delta Kappa/Gallup polls have surveyed public attitudes regarding school finance. The first question on that topic this year repeated one asked in 1986 concerning the source of taxes used to finance the public schools. In findings remarkably similar to those in the 1986 poll, 27% expressed a preference for local property taxes, 34% for state taxes, and 30% for taxes from the federal government. There is certainly no consensus. The two groups that do take a majority position in favor of federal funding are blacks (56%) and nonwhites (54%).

In a second question respondents were reminded that the local property tax is the main source for financing the public schools and were asked whether they would prefer to change to a local income tax system as the principal source of public school funds in their community. Once again, there is no consensus: 43% favor changing to a local income tax system, while 48% oppose it. This lack of consensus characterizes all groups surveyed.

The first question:

There is always a lot of discussion about the best way to finance the public schools. Which do you think is the best way to finance the public schools—by means of local property taxes, by state taxes, or by taxes from the federal government in Washington?

	National Totals		No Children In School		Public School Parents		Nonpublic School Parents	
	'97 %	'86 %	'97 %	'86 %	'97 %	'86 %	'97 %	'86 %
Local property taxes	27	24	30	22	22	28	32	22
State taxes	34	33	35	34	32	32	28	36
Federal taxes	30	24	26	23	37	28	36	22
Don't know	9	19	9	21	9	12	4	20

The second question:

At the present time, local property taxes are the main source for financing the public schools in most states. Thinking about your own community, would you favor or oppose changing the local property tax system to a local income tax system as the principal way to finance the local public schools?

	National Totals %	No Children In School %	Public School Parents %	Nonpublic School Parents %
Favor	43	42	47	39
Oppose	48	49	44	51
Don't know	9	9	9	10

Research Procedure

The Sample. The sample used in this survey embraced a total of 1,517 adults (18 years of age and older), including 1,017 parents of public school children. The sample of public school parents was increased to 1,017 interviews this year from the 500 interviews customarily used. The increased sample size permits analysis and reporting of findings for subgroups within the national public school parent population. A description of the sample and methodology can be found at the end of this report.

Time of Interviewing. The field work for this study was conducted during the period of 3 June to 22 June 1997.

The Report. In the table used in this report, "Nonpublic School Parents" includes parents of students who attend parochial schools and parents of students who attend private or independent schools.

Due allowance must be made for statistical variation, especially in the case of findings for groups consisting of relatively few respondents, e.g., nonpublic school parents.

The findings of this report apply only to the U.S. as a whole and not to individual communities. Local surveys, using the same questions, can be conducted to determine how local areas compare with the national norm.

Design of the sample

For the 1997 survey the Gallup organization used its standard national telephone sample, i.e., an unclustered, directory-assisted, random-digit telephone sample, based on a proportionate stratified sampling design.

Composition of the Sample

Adults	%
No children in school	64
Public school parents	33*
Nonpublic school parents	7*

*Total exceeds 100% because some parents have children attending more than one kind of school.

	National	Public School Parents
Gender	%	%
Men	46	43
Women	54	57
Race		
White	85	83
Nonwhite	13	15
Black	9	11
Undesignated	2	2
Age		
18–29 years	22	12
30–49 years	44	75
50 and over	33	12
Undesignated	1	1
Education		
Total college	56	47
College graduate	23	16
College incomplete	33	31
Total high school	44	53
High school graduate	31	33
High school incomplete	13	20
Undesignated	*	*
Income		
$50,000 and over	30	32
$40,000 and over	42	48
$30,000–$39,999	14	14
$20,000–$29,999	16	13
Under $20,000	20	20
Undesignated	8	5
Region		
East	24	22
Midwest	25	20
South	30	38
West	21	20
Community Size		
Urban	28	26
Suburban	48	49
Rural	24	25
Undesignated	*	*

* Less than one-half of 1%/

The random-digit aspect of the sample was used to avoid "listing" bias. Numerous studies have shown that households with unlisted telephone numbers are different in important ways from listed households. "Unlistedness" is due to household mobility or to customer requests to prevent publication of the telephone number.

To avoid this source of bias, a random-digit procedure designed to provide representation of both listed and unlisted (including not-yet-listed) numbers was used.

Telephone numbers for the continental United States were stratified into four regions of the country and, within each region, further stratified into three size-of-community strata.

Only working banks of telephone numbers were selected. Eliminating nonworking banks from the sample increased the likelihood that any sample telephone number would be associated with a residence.

The sample of telephone numbers produced by the described method is representative of all telephone households within the continental United States.

Within each contacted household, an interview was sought with the youngest man 18 years of age or older who was at home. If no man was home, an interview was sought with the oldest woman at home. This method of respondent selection within households produced an age distribution by sex that closely approximates the age distribution by sex of the total population.

Up to three calls were made to each selected telephone number to complete an interview. The time of day and the day of the week for callbacks were varied so as to maximize the chances of finding a respondent at home. All interviews were conducted on weekends or weekday evenings in order to contact potential respondents among the working population.

The final sample was weighted so that the distribution of the sample matched current estimates derived from the U.S. Census Bureau's Current Population Survey (CPS) for the adult population living in telephone households in the continental U.S.

As has been the case in recent years in the Phi Delta Kappa/Gallup poll series, parents of public school children were oversampled in the 1997 poll. This procedure produced a large enough sample to ensure that findings reported for "public school parents" are statistically significant (see Research Procedure).

Conducting Your Own Poll

The Phi Delta Kappa Center for Professional Development and Services makes available PACE (Polling Attitudes of the Community on Education) materials to enable nonspecialists to conduct scientific polls of attitude and opinion on education. The PACE manual provides detailed information on constructing questionnaires, sampling, interviewing, and analyzing data. It also includes updated census figures and new material on conducting a telephone survey. The price is $55. For information about using PACE materials, write of phone Phillip Harris at Phi Delta Kappa, P.O. Box 789, Bloomington, IN 47402-0789. Ph. 800/766–1156.

Sampling Tolerances

In interpreting survey results, it should be borne in mind that all sample surveys are subject to sampling error, i.e., the extent to which the results may differ from what would be obtained if the whole population surveyed had been interviewed. The size of such sampling error depends largely on the number of interviews.

The following tables may be used in estimating the sampling error of any percentage in this report. The computed allowances have taken into account the effect of the sample design upon sampling error. They may be interpreted as indicating the range (plus or minus the figure shown) within which the results of repeated samplings in the same time period could be expected to vary 95% of the time, assuming the same sampling procedure, the same interviewers, and the same questionnaire.

The first table shows how much allowance should be made for the sampling error of a percentage:

Recommended Allowance for Sampling Error of a Percentage

	In Percentage Points (at 95 in 100 confidence level)* Sample Size						
	1,500	1,000	750	600	400	200	100
Percentages near 20	2	2	3	3	4	5	8
Percentages near 20	3	3	4	4	5	7	10
Percentages near 30	3	4	4	5	6	8	12
Percentages near 40	3	4	5	5	6	9	12
Percentages near 40	3	4	5	5	6	9	13
Percentages near 60	3	4	5	5	6	9	12
Percentages near 70	3	4	4	5	6	8	12
Percentages near 80	3	3	4	4	5	7	10
Percentages near 90	1	1	3	3	4	5	8

*The chances are 95 in 100 that the sampling error is not larger than the figures shown.

The table would be used in the following manner: Let us say that a reported percentage is 33 for a group that includes 1,000 respondents. we go to the row for "percentages near 30" in the table and across to the column headed "1,000."

The number at this point is 4, which means that the 33% obtained in the sample is subject to a sampling error of plus or minus four points. In other words, it is very probable (95 chances out of 100) that the true figure would be somewhere between 29% and 37%, with the most likely figure the 33% obtained.

In comparing survey results in two samples, such as, for example, men and women, the question arises as to how large a difference between them must be before one can be reasonably sure that it reflects a real difference. In the tables below, the number of points that must be allowed for in such comparisons is indicated. Two tables are provided. One is for percentages near 20 or 80; the other, for percentages near 50. For percentages in between, the error to be allowed for lies between those shown in the two tables.

Recommended Allowance for Sampling Error of the Difference

TABLE A	In Percentage Points (at 95 in 100 confidence level)*					
	Percentages near 20 or percentages near 80					
Size of Sample	1,500	1,000	750	600	400	200
1,500	4					
1,000	4	5				
750	5	5	5			
600	5	5	6	6		
400	6	6	6	7	7	
200	8	8	8	8	9	10

TABLE B	Percentages near 50					
Size of Sample	1,500	1,000	750	600	400	200
1,500	5					
1,000	5	6				
750	6	6	7			
600	6	7	7	7		
400	7	8	8	8	9	
200	10	10	10	10	11	13

*The chances are 95 in 100 that the sampling error is not larger than the figures shown.

Here is an example of how the tables would be used: Let us say that 50% of men respond a certain way and 40% of women respond that way also, for a difference of 10 percentage points between them. Can we say with any assurance that the 10-point difference reflects a real difference between men and women on the question? Let us consider a sample that contains approximately 750 men and 750 women.

Since the percentages are near 50, we consult Table B, and, since the two samples are about 750 persons each, we look for the number in the column headed "750," which is also in the row designated "750." We find the number 7 here. This means that the allowance for error should be seven points and that, in concluding that the percentage among men is somewhere between three and 17 points higher than the percentage among women, we should be wrong only about 5% of the time. In other words, we can conclude with considerable confidence that a difference exists in the direction observed and that it amounts to at least three percentage points.

If, in another case, men's responses amount to 22%, say, and women's to 24%, we consult Table A, because these percentages are near 20. We look in the column headed "750" and see that the number is 5. Obviously, then, the two-point difference is inconclusive.

Rethinking and Changing the Educative Effort

The dialogue regarding how to rethink and restructure the priorities of educational services is continuing; this is not surprising. There has been a similar dialogue in every generation of American history. Some of the debate centers on whether change and reform in education today should focus on restructuring how teachers are prepared or on research into the changing conditions of the lives of many American youth today and how to help them better meet the challenges in their lives.

The articles in this unit reflect a wide range of opinion on these concerns. Several new and exciting ideas are being proposed as to how we might reconceive the idea of *school* to encompass much more variety in school learning communities as well as to meet a broader range of the academic and social needs of today's youth.

American educators could have a much better sense of their own past as a profession, and the public could better understand the history of public education. In the United States, a fundamental cycle of similar ideas and practices reappears in school curricula every so many years. The decades of the 1970s and 1980s witnessed the rise of "behavioral objectives" and "management by objectives," and the 1990s have brought us "outcome-based education" and "benchmarking" in educational discourse within the public school system's leadership. These are related behavioral concepts focusing on measurable ways to pinpoint and evaluate the results of educational efforts. Why do we seem to reinvent the "wheel" of educational thought and practice every so many decades? This is an important question worth addressing. Many of our ideas about change and reform in educational practice have been wrongheaded. There is a stronger focus on more qualitative, as opposed to empirical, means of assessing the outcomes of our educative efforts; yet many state departments of education still insist on external, objective assessments and verifications of students' mastery of predetermined academic skills. How does this affect the development of creative, imaginative teaching in schools? We are not sure; but all of us in the education system are concerned, and many of us believe that there really are some new and generative ideas to help students learn basic intellectual skills and content.

The essays in this and later units of this volume explore some of these ideas. There are a variety of myths about what did or did not happen in some "golden age" of our educational past. Our current realities in the field of education reflect differing conceptions of how schooling ought to change. It is difficult to generalize reliably regarding school quality across decades because of several factors; high schools, for instance, were more selective in 1900, when only 7 percent of American youth graduated from them. Today we encourage as many youth as possible to graduate from high school. The social purposes of schooling have been broadened; now we want all youth to complete some form of higher education.

We have to consider the social and ideological differences among those representing opposing school reform agendas for change. The differences over how and in what directions change is to occur in our educational systems rest on which educational values are to prevail. These values form the bases for differing conceptions of the purposes of schooling. Thus the differing agendas for change in American education have to be positioned within the context of the different ideological value systems that underpin each alternative agenda for change.

There are several currently contending (and frequently conceptually conflicting) strategies for restructuring life in schools as well as the options open to parents in choosing the schools that they want their children to attend. On the one hand, we have to find ways to empower students and teachers to improve the quality of academic life in classrooms. On the other hand, there appear to be powerful forces contending over whether control of educational services should be even more centralized or more decentralized (site-based). Those who favor greater parental and teacher control of schools support greater decentralized site management and community control conceptions of school governance. Yet the ratio of teachers to nonteaching personnel (administrators, counselors, school psychologists, and others) continues to decline as public school system bureaucracies become more and more "top heavy."

In this unit, we consider the efforts to reconceive, redefine, and reconstruct existing patterns of curriculum and instruction at the elementary and secondary levels of schooling and compare them with the efforts to reconceive existing conflicting patterns of teacher education. There is a broad spectrum of dialogue developing in North America, the British Commonwealth, Russia, Central Eurasia, and other areas of the world regarding the redirecting of the learning opportunities for all citizens.

Prospective teachers here are being encouraged to question their own individual educational experiences as part of this process. We must acknowledge that our values affect our ideas about curriculum content and the purpose of educating others. This is perceived as vitally important in the developing dialogue over liberating all students' capacities to function as independent inquirers. The dramatic economic and demographic changes in our society necessitate a fundamental reconceptualization of how schools ought to respond to the many social contexts in which they are located. This effort to reassess and reconceive the education of persons is a vital part of broader reform efforts in society as well as a dynamic dialectic in its own right. How can schools, for instance, better reflect the varied communities of interest that they serve? What must they do to become better perceived as just and equitable places in which all young people can seek to achieve learning and self-fulfillment?

This is not the first period in which our citizens have searched their minds and souls to redirect, construct, and, if necessary, deconstruct their understandings regarding formal educational systems. The debate over what ought to be the conceptual and structural underpinnings of national educational opportunity structures has continued since the first mass educational system was formed in the nineteenth century.

When we think of continuity and change, we think of the conceptual balance between cherished traditions and innovations that will facilitate learning without compromising cherished core values and standards. When we think of change in education, we are reminded of such great educational experiments of earlier times as John Dewey's Laboratory School at the University of Chicago, Maria Montessori's Casi di Bambini (children's houses), and A. S. Neill's controversial Summerhill School in England as well as many other innovative experiments in learning theories. Our own time has seen similarly dramatic experimentation.

Each of the essays in this unit relates directly to the conceptual tension involved in reconceiving how educational development should proceed in response to all the dramatic social and economic changes in society.

Looking Ahead: Challenge Questions

What are some issues in the debate regarding educational reform?

What social, political, and economic pressures are placed on our public school systems?

Should the focus of educational reform be on changing the ways educators are prepared, on the changing needs of students, or on both of these concerns?

What are some imaginative new models of schools?

How do we build communities of learners?

Reforming the Wannabe Reformers

Why Education Reforms Almost Always End Up Making Things Worse

Mr. Pogrow uses his own experience and the history of education reform over the past 100 years to argue that the biggest problem in education is with the reformers themselves and with the academicians and researchers who develop the ideas and rationales for the reformers' pet reforms.

STANLEY POGROW

STANLEY POGROW is an associate professor of educational administration at the University of Arizona, Tucson, where he specializes in instructional and administrative uses of computers. He is the developer of the HOTS and SUPER-MATH programs. (E-mail: SPOGROW@mail.ed.arizona.edu)

FOR MORE THAN a decade, we have been buried in proposed reforms. Those responsible for this avalanche of reforms have taken the perspective that there are problems with the education establishment, problems with society, problems with the political structure, problems with current practice—in short, problems with everything except reformers and their proposed reforms.

Reformers typically feel that their solutions would work if only people would get on board. When people do not jump on board, the reformers conclude that the practitioners are at fault or that the society is at fault for socializing individuals in ways that prevent them from appreciating the wisdom of the reforms. When the proposed reforms, lacking popular support, inevitably end up not working, the refrain is that the reforms were implemented in style but not in substance. Once again, the practitioners are at fault.

I will argue that the biggest problem in education is with the reformers themselves and with the academicians and researchers who develop the ideas

and rationales for the reformers' pet reforms. My conclusions stem from my own experience as a reformer, an academician, and the developer of the HOTS (Higher Order Thinking Skills) program[1] and from the history of education reform over the past 100 years.

The State of Education Reform

This appears to be a time when reform is blossoming. The *Kappan* and other major education publications have highlighted dozens of reforms. Examples of current widely advocated

reforms include whole language, vouchers, heterogeneous grouping, teacher empowerment, authentic assessment, and team teaching. Lovers of reform are ecstatic; the traditionalists seem to be on the run.

But this isn't the first instance of hyper-reform in the history of education. Another such period ran from the mid-1960s to the mid-1970s. Almost none of the widely advocated reforms of that period— open space, individualization, community-based education—survived.

Unfortunately, the fate of these earlier reforms is typical. The history of

 From *Phi Delta Kappan*, June 1996, pp. 656-663. © 1996 by Phi Delta Kappa International, Inc. Reprinted by permission.

education reform is one of consistent failure of major reforms to survive and become institutionalized. David Tyack and his colleagues have found that education reforms typically do not last very long. Larry Cuban has noted that the few that do survive are shorn of their ambitious goals and ideals, becoming instead routinized incremental changes to what exists. The only innovations that survive are those that are highly structural in nature, that are easily monitored (e.g., the Carnegie unit), or that create new constituencies. Cuban refers to the historical success of attempted curriculum reform as "pitiful."[2] Indeed, reports of research on the innovations of the late 1980s and early 1990s are starting to appear and are generally disclosing failure.[3]

Does the consistent failure of all but the simplest reforms suggest that educators are stupid, lazy, unimaginative, and uncaring? No! The record of innovation in education is the same as that in other areas. In *Innovation and Entrepreneurship*, Peter Drucker draws on a wide range of human experience to determine the fundamental conditions under which new ideas become successful and enduring innovations in any field. He finds that, historically, the vast majority of innovative ideas and changes throughout human experience have failed to take root. Most remain just interesting ideas. Drucker arrives at the following conclusions regarding the fate of new ideas:

• ideas that become successful innovations represent a solution that is clearly definable, is simple, and includes a complete system for implementation and dissemination;

• successful innovations start small and try to do one specific thing; and

• knowledge-based innovations are least likely to succeed and can succeed only if *all* the needed knowledge is available.[4]

Drucker's conditions for success are a chronicle of human tolerance for uncertainty and ambiguity. Unfortunately, these conditions are violated by virtually every new idea for change that is currently sweeping through the education profession. For example, school restructuring violates all of Drucker's principles. Process learning approaches, in which teachers are left to invent their own methods, violate the first principle. Indeed, students in my educational administration classes decided that only one current reform met all three of Drucker's conditions—integrated social service centers in schools.

Educational practitioners are no less skilled in implementing innova-

tions than practitioners in other professions. The fault lies in the types of reforms they are seduced into pursuing by a reform/academic/research community that is largely out of touch with reality.

Myths of the Reform Process

Education reforms almost always fail because they are usually based on combinations of a number of myths.

Myth 1. You can change instruction via advocacy, inservice, and training. The single biggest tool in promoting reform has been advocacy—followed up by massive doses of conferences, inservice training, and university courses. The scenario goes like this: a sense of urgency is created, and a new terminology is coined; a national fellowship develops among the believers; stories of success appear in a journal such as this; and a massive national network of training is created. The advocacy is driven largely by philosophy, with only a smidgen of technique or research supporting the idea. The word then goes out that the technique is supported by research. In retrospect, the supposed research is never very convincing, and the reforms fade away for lack of a real methodology for implementing them. Some examples of current reforms that are built primarily around advocacy and training are the middle school movement, schoolwide approaches to Title 1, heterogeneous grouping, full inclusion, and a thinking approach to mathematics.

Reality 1. Large-scale reform requires highly specific, systematic, and structural methodologies with supporting materials of tremendously high quality. (Such methodologies are hereafter referred to as "technologies.") All the inservice training, editorials, and articles cannot make up for the absence of a powerful, yet simple, supporting technology. (Technology is a systematic way of doing something consistently and can be either a specific social process or some specific equipment.) Without such technology, almost all training is a waste of time.

For example, consider the case of middle school reform. Thousands of articles and speeches have advocated the development of child-centered curricula. I recently completed a three-year study to identify exemplary middle school curricula. There were few examples of exemplary curricula to be found.[5] The only exemplary math curriculum was 20 years old, and the only exemplary comprehensive science curriculum was Canadian. There were no exemplary comprehensive language

arts or social studies curricula. While everyone has been philosophizing about what middle school curricula should look like, no one has bothered to develop them, despite 40 years of advocacy. The basic tools that are needed aren't there; there is a lot of bull but no beef.

The middle school movement is not a singular example. The reality for teachers and principals is that exemplary programs usually do not exist for the goals schoolpeople are being asked to achieve.

Myth 2. Theory is a useful guide for the design of programs and reforms. This is the most cherished belief of the academic and reform community.

Reality 2. Metaphor is much more important to the design of sophisticated programs than research and theory. The key to developing successful programs is to have the right metaphor. The key metaphor in the HOTS program is the "dinner table conversation in the home." This metaphor was the basis for at least 80% of the design decisions. For example, since dinner table conversation is not linked to formal content, it was decided that HOTS would not link to the regular classroom curriculum—a counterintuitive decision for a Title I program. Once you have the right metaphor, though, theory can fill in some of the gaps and help with perhaps 10% to 15% of the decisions that have to be made.

Myth 3. You can reform education by disseminating knowledge and leaving it up to practitioners to apply that knowledge. The REsearch/Academic/Reform community mentioned above (hereafter referred to as REAR) continually claims that it knows what works, if only others would apply that knowledge. For example, Carl Kaestle found that key researchers blamed "the awful reputation of education research" on how the research is disseminated and on the lack of incentives for practitioners to use research.[6]

The knowledge disseminated by REAR consists primarily of advocacy and general theory. The feeling is widespread in the REAR community that its responsibility is to produce general theory and that it is up to practitioners to figure out how to apply that theory. For example, in describing the success of teachers in designing *libritos* based on knowledge of literacy to develop the reading skills of minority students, Claude Goldenberg and Ronald Gallimore view the local knowledge needed to make implementation decisions as separate from research knowledge.[7] Essentially, they argue that local practitioners must apply theory to develop their own interventions because knowledge of details will invariably be different for each local site.

Reality 3. Reform requires technology, methodology, structure, dosages, and materials. It is far more difficult to figure out how to implement theory than it is to generate it. I am reasonably intelligent, and it took me 14 years of almost full-time effort to figure out how to consistently work just four thinking skills into a detailed and effective curriculum. Thus it makes no sense to expect practitioners to develop their own techniques for implementing a complex reform idea. While there are many talented teachers who can come up with highly innovative techniques, it's too demanding and too much a hit-or-miss proposition. This is not a criticism of educators. No other field expects its practitioners to develop the techniques that they practice. Indeed, in medicine, if individual practitioners invent their own procedures, we call it "malpractice."

The equivalent of expecting teachers to develop the interventions they are going to apply would be asking an actor to perform Shakespeare—but to write the play first. The role of actors is to make the playwright's lines come alive, not to write those lines. The primary role of teachers is to teach, not to develop their own interventions because the REAR community prefers to philosophize and preach. Professional behavior is judged by the quality with which practitioners implement established procedures, not by whether they can invent them.

The simple fact of the matter is that what Goldenberg and Gallimore called local knowledge is as important in education as in medicine. We do need to know how much and what types of services specific students need to improve their performance; we don't need general philosophical statements such as "All students can learn." My own experience is that it is indeed possible for the right type of research to develop techniques and determine implementation details that are applicable to most local conditions—if REAR is so disposed.

But the bottom line is that no amount of advocacy will cause an innovation to succeed if it lacks an underlying technology. The individualized education movement of the 1970s is a classic example of a reform with absolutely no technology that most teachers found simply impossible to carry out. We are repeating this mistake today. Current REAR reforms that have little or no underlying technology include restructuring, site-based man-

agement, full inclusion, constructivism, and portfolio assessment.

Myth 4. The most important change involves radical reformulation of existing practice, i.e., new paradigms. Whenever a new reform idea is presented, it is usually made to sound revolutionary. The most popular phrase used to describe these new ideas is "paradigm shift." The concept of a paradigm shift can be traced to the work of Thomas Kuhn, who has documented how important periodic reformulations are to the evolution of scientific knowledge.[8] In education, most reforms are presented as paradigm shifts. Authentic testing is presented as a paradigm shift away from the evil standardized tests; whole language is a paradigm shift away from the evils of phonics; of course, the biggest paradigm shift of all is restructuring itself (whatever that is).

Reality 4. The most important changes are incremental ones. While paradigm shifts are important in the evolution of knowledge, they are extremely rare. Most fields do not have even one per century. Moreover, they are seldom involved in the creation of breakthrough products. Indeed, most lucrative patents and products are incremental refinements of existing technologies. HOTS did not come from any new paradigm; it came from more than a dozen years of tinkering with combinations of new pieces of technology and 2,000-year-old ideas, as well as lots of observation of teachers and students conversing.

Myth 5. The best way to achieve reform is through schoolwide change/restructuring. The representatives of REAR always start with the assumption that it is critical to change whole schools and systems.

Reality 5. Schoolwide change, while a nice idea, has never worked on a large scale and is probably not necessary. In some cases entire schools may need to change, but there is no evidence that entire schools can be changed on a large scale. In a sense, schoolwide change has become a convenient rallying cry that often provides a smokescreen to cover the failure to deal substantively with the real issues.

Nor is there evidence that whole schools generally need to be changed. My own work suggests that it is possible to produce high levels of learning by providing exemplary activities for just a small part of the day.[9] If we cannot figure out how to provide exemplary learning experiences to every student for an hour a day, we certainly cannot figure out how to consistently

change whole schools in substantive ways.

Myth 6. You can develop learning through reforms designed to enhance correlates of learning, such as self-concept or empowerment. We keep creating reforms that focus on everything but learning. For example, in the 1980s we became absorbed in developing student self-concept, computer literacy, and computer equity. So far in the 1990s we are absorbed with detracking, empowering, eliminating labels, sex equity, changing tests, and increasing democratic participation. While all of these are important and are *related* to learning, they are not learning.

Reality 6. The best way to enhance learning is to develop more powerful programs to enhance learning. Movements built around the correlates of learning never lead to substantial improvements in learning. These correlates should be produced as by-products of increased learning. Unfortunately, we always seem to get sidetracked and end up trying to produce the correlates directly. It is amazing how many different reforms we have distracted ourselves with over the years. (I strongly suspect that teacher empowerment and authentic testing are similar diversions.) REAR is very inventive about developing new ways to engage us in pursuit of sideshow issues. Indeed, REAR often seems to have little interest in developing or defining systematic learning environments.[10]

Myth 7. You can understand large-scale change by understanding what happens on a very small scale. This is the biggest myth of all! Physicists understand that physical processes at the small-scale, individual subatomic particle level are very different from those at the large-scale, aggregate human level. The fundamental problem is that school reform is a large-scale issue, and REAR is virtually ignorant about large-scale processes in education. Researchers study small-scale phenomena for very short periods of time. Their knowledge comes from controlled laboratory research, pilot studies, case studies in a few schools, or a few examples of unusually effective schools. Newer research techniques, such as meta-analysis, have been developed that "pretend" that outcomes were generated on a large scale. REAR then convinces itself and the profession that the knowledge gained from these small-scale investigations is applicable.

Reality 7. It's the scale, stupid! Large-scale change reflects properties that are often diametrically opposed to those in effect in small-scale research. While small-scale success is inspirational, the methods are not necessarily workable on a large scale. The fact that something works in a few class-rooms, in a few schools, with a few teachers, at a few grade levels, for a few weeks, and so on says nothing about whether or how it can be dis-seminated or will actually work on a large scale. Conversely, the fact that a standardized test is inaccurate in the case of a few individuals doesn't mean that it isn't giving an accurate overall picture of large-scale results.

There are almost no cases in which researchers have studied an innova-tive practice on a large scale, as it was happening, over an extended period of time. Indeed, there aren't even appro-priate research methods in education for evaluating large-scale effective-ness.[11] Thus reforms supposedly based on research are, at best, little more than hunches that are usually based on inapplicable studies.[12]

As a profession we do not even ask the right questions about the large-scale efficacy of ideas. For example, in-stead of asking whether full inclusion works, the large-scale point of view would ask whether there exists a suf-ficiently articulated technology to al-low 80% of the sites that exert a reasonable effort actually to make full inclusion work. If full inclusion or any other reform cannot be made to work consistently, we should not attempt to make it national policy. Rather, we should treat such reforms as ideas about which we can learn from those who voluntarily choose to pursue them. Alternative assessment is cur-rently an innovative idea, not a tech-nology or an innovation.

Myth 8. Directive programs cannot be effective on a large scale, and at-tempts to implement such programs rob teachers of their individuality. This myth denies the whole history of the performing arts.

Reality 8. It is possible to develop a new generation of far more powerful programs that can be effective on a large scale. The performing arts have survived and flourished because they have been able to systematize the de-livery of highly creative performances by striking an appropriate balance between directive components—e.g., scripts and choreography—and indi-vidual interpretation. The same thing can be done in education. The success of HOTS and other creative programs, such as Reading Recovery and Junior Great Books, suggests that it is possi-ble to develop programs that combine the best of educational research and pedagogy into specified systems that consistently generate high levels of

learning and also stimulate highly creative forms of interaction between students and teachers on a large scale.

Consequences of the Myths

For the last 100 years REAR has been using the myths described above to develop and promote highly amor-phous and ill-advised reforms. In the absence of substantive methodologies, these reforms are of necessity imple-mented through highly simplistic strategies that are doomed to fail. For example, full inclusion is implemented by eliminating pullouts and treating everyone the same—instead of by de-veloping programs to meet the needs of all students. The nature of the re-forms produced by these myths leads to a number of consequences.

Repeated failure of reform initia-tives. The failure of reforms produces much trauma for practitioners and students. Indeed, reforms based on the above myths fail not only once, but often a number of times. For example, consider the child-centered school. In one incarnation, the advocacy of child-centeredness is associated with the use of middle schools as an alternative to the content orientation of junior high schools. However, at the turn of the century, the goal of child-centeredness was a major rationale for the creation of a new type of school to be called the "junior high school"—as an alternative to the content-oriented high school. Unfortunately, we do not know how to create child-centered schools that in-crease learning and social develop-ment on a reasonably consistent basis. But fear not! REAR will create another type of school that starts a grade lower and will be child-centered for sure.

Massive waste of resources on staff development and dissemination. In the absence of a valid technology and a body of experience for carrying out a proposed reform on a large scale, in-service training and dissemination strategies are largely ritualistic shams that waste time. Staff development gets everyone excited, but little hap-pens. Still, despite its woeful track re-cord, we keep on pushing staff development with religious fervor as *the* key to improving education.

No professional validation stand-ards for considering and implementing reform. We have no tradition of insist-ing on anything approaching reason-able validation of proposed reforms before we rush to implementation. This lack became glaringly evident to me some time ago as I was watching TV. Jonas Salk was announcing that recent work in his lab had convinced

him that AIDS could be cured by a particular type of vaccine. Instead of calling for the production of vaccine, he went on to say that he needed to con-duct large-scale tests over the next five to 10 years to figure out how viable the use and production of the vaccine was. Then the news switched to some education policy maker who was ad-vocating the national adoption of the latest reform proposals for school im-provement. The two news clips cap-tured the difference in professional responsibility between medicine and education, and we looked silly in comparison.

Seymour Sarason expresses the same idea as follows:

> To a significant degree, the major educational problems stem from the fact that educators not only accepted responsibility for schooling but, more fateful, also adopted a stance that es-sentially said: we know how to solve and manage the problems of school-ing in America. Educators did not say: there is much we do not know. . . .
>
> [T]he medical community has made a virtue of its ignorance insofar as its stance with the public is con-cerned. That community did not say that it would be able to cure cancers next year or 20 years from now. On the contrary, it emphasized the com-plexity and scope of the problems, the inadequacies of past and present con-ceptions and practices. . . .[13]

A current example of this lemming-like approach to reform is site-based management. The site-based band-wagon is at least five years old, but there still is no agreement on what it is and no evidence that it is either workable or effective.[14] So why is eve-ryone doing site-based management and so many other current reforms? Indeed, why is the current administra-tive training literature so focused on leadership for change with almost no standards for the conditions under which administrators should resist change? Anyone standing pat is auto-matically seen as reactionary.

Repeated cycling of inadequate pro-gressive and traditional reforms. The absence of adequate validation norms for proposed reforms has meant that the primary reason to adopt reforms is the failure of what exists rather than the demonstrated success of what is being proposed. For example, in a re-cent article, Diane Ravitch noted that "the educational results bear the re-formers out." I read on eagerly, think-ing I was going to find out about improved educational results from some new reform. Unfortunately, her rationale was a litany of the failures of the status quo: "Fewer than half the city's ninth-graders graduate within four years. Of those who do, nearly 40% enter the City University of New York, and only a quarter of those pass all three of its tests of minimal reading, writing, and math skills.[15] Similarly, curriculum theorists point to the repeated failure of nationally generated curricula to argue that curricula should be developed locally—even though there is no evidence offered that locally developed curricula work better.[16]

As legitimate problems with the status quo become apparent, the profession periodically tries progressive ideas. When the progressive reforms fail, the traditionalists come back with their own set of inadequate proposals. Neither side ever seems to get it right. This yo-yo effect has been going on for more than a century and is worse than a broken clock; at least the clock is correct twice a day.

Nowhere is the yo-yo syndrome truer than in Title I. Over the years results have consistently found little effect beyond the third grade. In the next-to-last reauthorization, the traditionalists prevailed, and strict basic skills accountability guidelines were incorporated into the legislation. This had little effect. In the latest reauthorization, progressives moved to the fore, and the legislation emphasized school-wide reform. This probably won't work either. In truth, neither side had large-scale experience in improving learning for educationally disadvantaged students. The sides merely waged political war on the basis of their philosophies and myths. A whole series of fundamental changes that were critical for real improvement were not even considered.[17]

Misleading conclusions and misleading uses of research. When researchers have little experience with the phenomena that they seek to apply their findings to, the result is usually misleading conclusions. That is not to say that researchers deliberately mislead the field. Rather, they mislead one another, which then causes them inadvertently to mislead the field.

Indeed, one of the reasons why HOTS is so effective is that I was ignorant of the research on the development of thinking. In particular, I was ignorant about the fact that nearly everyone agreed that thinking was best developed in content. Thus I didn't think twice when my experience suggested that harnessing the tremendous intellectual potential of educationally disadvantaged students in

grades 4 through 7 required first developing their sense of understanding through immersion in general thinking activities divorced from classroom content.[18] Unfortunately, researchers have no instincts by which to judge whether the conclusions in the literature make sense.[19]

It is impossible to develop a true understanding of the nature of student/teacher interaction from reading research. Indeed, as I was writing this article, the then-latest issue of the prestigious *American Educational Research Journal (AERJ)* arrived. It featured a special section on fostering higher-order thinking skills. I immediately put aside my writing to see whether it had any significant new ideas that could help improve HOTS.

The first of the articles found that teachers were much more likely to ask higher-order thinking questions of higher-performing students than of lower-performing ones.[20] Surprise! In their tortured attempt to explain why this was so, the authors blamed tests, institutional norms, teachers, and so on—but they ignored the obvious possibility that lower-performing students might not in fact know how to respond to such questions.

In the second article, researchers followed one first-grade teacher for four years to learn how she used the research-based knowledge about student learning that they had provided to guide her teaching of addition and subtraction. The researchers concluded that the teacher was teaching differently from the way they would have expected her to. As a result, the authors concluded that "teachers would be better translators of knowledge about children's thinking that we would."[21] Unfortunately, the researchers never did document that the teacher was in fact applying research at all.

The third article studied 12 sixth-graders in two science classrooms. Each student was observed for the equivalent of four lessons to determine why some students understand science concepts while others do not. The researchers solemnly concluded that the differences in engagement and understanding they observed in these students were due to "complex interactions among cognitive qualities of academic tasks, students' knowledge and achievement, and students' motivational and affective orientations in science classrooms." So what else is new?[22] The *AERJ* research was disappointing, silly, misleading, and useless, and it was predicated on the validity of the above myths.

Even more misleading have been the research results from meta-analyses. Meta-analysis is a relatively new technique to make small-scale research seem to be large scale. In meta-analysis, results from a series of individual small-scale studies are aggregated into a single finding. This single finding appears statistically to have been generated from a single large-scale study.

Much of the push for full inclusion and schoolwide models of reform has come from a series of meta-analyses that find small effects from special programs, such as gifted programs.[23] Unfortunately, meta-analyses combine results from a series of studies in which virtually nothing is known about the nature or quality of the interventions that generated the results. Indeed, I have even seen a case in which a researcher generated meta-analysis results for the effects of a program that he was unaware had not been implemented and did not exist. Since the researchers are almost always ignorant about the quality of the programs in the included studies, meta-analysis crunches data generated from primarily weak programs and thereby severely underestimates the impact of effective programs.[24]

Substitution of philosophy of process for philosophy of outcomes, of good intentions for science, and of global good efforts for precise interventions. Faced with the repeated failure of reforms, we have essentially shifted from a focus on outcomes to a focus on processes. We choose up sides based on the process of a proposed approach. People say such things as "I am philosophically opposed to pull-outs" or "I am philosophically opposed to prescriptive programs" or "I am philosophically opposed to phonics." When you cannot produce the outcomes you need, all that's left is to look good philosophically while you fail.

We have also abandoned science and cognition in the design of reforms. Saying "All children *can* learn" says nothing about *what* they can learn, *how fast* different youngsters can learn, *when* different types of children are best able to learn certain things and why, and so on. Or consider the reform breakthrough on how best to use a computer—"Use it as a tool!" That advice says nothing about what to build, how to build it, and what other tools you might need.

In the absence of specific, systematic interventions that work, reformers become obsessed with getting everyone on board, infusing a reform throughout the curriculum, and carrying out the process all the time. Untracking comes to mean that students should *never* be separated according to ability (except for sports, of course). Opposition to the mindless use of standardized tests or rote learning or pull-out programs comes to mean that these technologies should *never* be used.

Yet, despite all these problems, the myths persist. The ultimate reality is that the only way to improve education significantly is by the use of more powerful forms of curricula in the hands of very good teachers who are trained to teach better. All three of these conditions must exist. Any other type of reform is a sham—no matter how compelling its philosophical rationale. Any proposed reform should be tested against whether it is likely to enhance these three conditions consistently and directly.

Why Do Practitioners Tolerate The Ignorance of REAR?

The short answer is that the activities of the REsearch/Academic/Reform community provide hope. Practitioners passionately, even desperately, want to help young people. The hardest thing for a teacher or principal to accept is failure with a student who has potential and needs help. Good practitioners are always seeking answers and searching for something that will help them be more successful. Unfortunately, the answers provided by REAR are more often than not illusory. If you remove yourself from the fray for a moment to sit back and think about it, building movements around such concepts as school restructuring, using the computer as a tool, or creating child-centered schools is silly. But in our desire to help students, we do not sit back.

REAR also provides excuses for failure. It spews out ever more esoteric, jargon-ridden philosophical rationales to explain why apparent failures aren't really failures, why it's impossible to be more systematic, and why a new reform is needed. REAR's intellectual machinations help shield the profession from outside criticism, while also providing rallying cries and rationales for new funding.

Some of the current defense mechanisms being deployed by REAR include blaming society, blaming tests, or claiming that schools are as good as they ever were. Gerald Bracey's 1994 report in this journal promotes the excuse that students who do poorly do so because of demographic factors, such as poverty, that are beyond the control of schools.[25] This is like arguing that we shouldn't expect to be able to fly

because gravity is beyond human control. Given that we have spent billions trying to get schools to perform better for economically disadvantaged students, inadequate progress should not be excused.

Beginning Anew: Reforming the Reformers

Instead of leading, REAR is inhibiting substantive improvement. The members of the REAR community currently act like spoiled siblings who cannot get along. It is time for them to grow up and stop viewing education as a playing field for their ideologies. We need to stop the silly posturing about knowing what works when there is no proof that any of these reforms work on even a small scale. This rhetoric has outlived its usefulness and has become a self-delusional detriment to educational progress. The dissemination of research knowledge and inservice training as the *primary* vehicles for reform has failed and is unworkable.

The sad thing is that many progressive ideas have great potential, if only the technology appropriate for them had been developed. For example, my staff and I recently employed constructivism to develop a unique solution to a classic problem: teaching and learning word problems in math. No, we did not create a national network of courses shot through with hype about the use of constructivism. Rather, we devised a new technology for helping students create their own sense of how language and math go together. We developed a new type of software to enable students to communicate with a lonesome space creature stuck inside their computer—a creature that understands English and speaks math. The result of using this software, along with appropriate teacher interaction, was that students came to view word problems on tests as simple.[26]

Creating better techniques and technologies requires increasing investment in development, slowing the rush to large-scale implementation, and rethinking the role and structure of colleges of education. We no longer need colleges composed largely of individuals and courses that spread the latest incarnations of unworkable myths. Rather, we need organizations that can integrate research and philosophy with the development and large-scale testing of new technologies. Such organizations would have fewer courses and far more joint-development ventures involving university faculty members, students, and practitioners. Teachers and students could

work together to design interventions and collect data on their effectiveness. This would force faculty members to confront the limitations of their ideas and subject them to review by those who must implement them.

One problem might arise in that colleges of education do not have the highly skilled inventors, craftspeople, and tinkerers who can put the pieces together. There are few individuals with expertise in such areas as biology, artificial intelligence, or the integration of social services, which are likely to be critical for generating new technologies. Moreover, very few people in colleges of education have experience in designing technologies. Converting ideas into successful innovations will require new types of knowledge generators, disseminators, and reformers. We need to increase the diversity of skills within education faculties, much as we have increased racial and sexual diversity. What exists in education today is the equivalent of having only theoretical physicists and philosophers on the faculty of an engineering school. I wonder what a bridge built by theoretical physicists and philosophers would look like?

A vibrant research and reform community is critical to the future of education. Unfortunately, for much of this century, these communities have been in a rut. They have been able to generate many innovative ideas but few innovations—that is, effective large-scale reforms.

Education can no longer afford a research and academic community that is detached from the real processes that take place in schools and from the large-scale consequences of the ideas that it proposes. Education can no longer afford a well-intentioned but inept progressive movement and a too-limited traditional movement, each waiting for its 10- to 20-year turn in the limelight. It can no longer afford the piling on of ill-conceived movements to compensate for the inadequacy of current ideas. The result has been inefficiency and waste.

We need to start by being honest and saying that we do *not* know what works for the educationally disadvantaged student, that we do *not* know how to get most students thinking on a higher level, that we do *not* know how to increase their motivation to learn, and that we do *not* know how to systematically blend the best of progressive and traditional ideas. We also need to recognize that caring and empowerment are not enough and that movements are no substitutes for better techniques. Significantly improving the learning of educationally disadvantaged students on a large scale requires fundamental breakthroughs in the development of powerful and highly systematic technologies, and people must be willing to invest a decade of work in the pursuit of that goal. Finally, we need to learn that mass advocacy should follow, not precede, the careful development and large-scale testing of techniques.

It is not easy in any field to develop interventions that avoid prevalent myths, are creative, and meet the criteria set forth by Drucker. However, experience has shown that it is possible to design interventions for education that are practical for large-scale use, that are highly creative, that incorporate many progressive ideals, and that consistently produce higher levels of traditional outcomes. Producing such interventions requires some new skills and some different conceptions of what it means to be a researcher, a reformer, or a practitioner. A few academicians and reformers have taken up the challenge. Far more are needed.

1. For information about the HOTS program, see Stanley Pogrow, "Making Reform Work for the Educationally Disadvantaged," *Educational Leadership,* February 1995, pp. 20–24; idem, *HOTS (Higher Order Thinking Skills): A Validated Thinking Skills Approach to Using Computers with Students Who Are At-Risk* (New York: Scholastic, 1990); idem, "A Socratic Approach to Using Computers with At-Risk Students," *Educational Leadership,* February 1990, pp. 61–67; and idem, "Challenging At-Risk Students: Findings from the HOTS Program," *Phi Delta Kappan,* January 1990, pp. 389–97.

2. For discussions of which types of innovations survive, see David Tyack, Michael Kirst, and Elisabeth Hansot, *Educational Reform: Retrospect and Prospect* (Palo Alto, Calif.: Institute for Research on Educational Finance and Governance, Stanford University, Project Report #79-A5, September 1979); and David Tyack and William Tobin, "The Grammar of Schooling: Why Has It Been So Hard to Change?," *American Educational Research Journal,* Fall 1994, pp. 453–79. For a discussion of what happens to innovations that survive, see Larry Cuban, "What Happens to Reforms That Last? The Case of the Junior High School," *American Educational Research Journal,* Summer 1992, pp. 227–51; and idem, "The Lure of Curriculum Reform and Its Pitiful History," *Phi Delta Kappan,* October 1993, pp. 182–85.

3. For the failure of state-level reform, see Robert A. Frahm, "The Failure of Connecticut's Reform Plan: Lessons for the Nation," *Phi Delta Kappan,* (October 1994, pp. 156–59; and Judith McQuaide and Ann-Maureen Pliska, "The Challenge to Pennsylvania's Education Reform," *Educational Leadership,* December 1993/January 1994, pp. 16–21. For the failure of school restructuring and site-based management, see Jeffrey Mirel, "School Reform Un-plugged: The Bensenville New American School Project, 1991–93," *American Educational Research Journal,* Fall 1994, pp. 481–518; and Di-

anne Taylor and Ira E. Bogotch, "School-Level Effects of Teachers' Participation in Decision Making," *Educational Evaluation and Policy Analysis,* Fall 1994, pp. 302–19.

4. Peter F. Drucker, *Innovation and Entrepreneurship* (New York: Harper & Row, 1985).

5. Stanley Pogrow, "Where's the Beef? Looking for Exemplary Materials," *Educational Leadership,* May 1993, pp. 39–45.

6. Carl F. Kaestle, "The Awful Reputation of Education Research," *Educational Researcher,* January/February 1993, pp. 23–31.

7. Claude Goldenberg and Ronald Gallimore, "Local Knowledge, Research Knowledge, and Educational Change: A Case Study of Early Spanish Reading Improvement," *Educational Researcher,* November 1991, pp. 2–14.

8. Thomas Kuhn, *The Structure of Scientific Revolutions* (Chicago: University of Chicago Press, 1962).

9. My research has shown that you can stimulate the development of thinking skills in educationally disadvantaged students and so spark a wide variety of improvements in learning in just 35 minutes a day of exemplary activities over a two-year period. For a discussion of this 35-minute principle, see Pogrow, "Challenging At-Risk Students"; and idem, "Converting At-Risk Students into Reflective Learners," in Arthur L. Costa, James A. Bellanca, and Robin Fogarty, eds., *If Minds Matter: A Foreword to the Future* (Palatine, Ill.: Skylight Publishing, 1992).

10. In some content fields I could not find expert academicians who were willing to look at curricula and make judgments about the relative quality of the materials; in others, the judges panicked when the moment came to apply the criteria that they had developed. Academicians seemed more interested in making relativistic arguments as to why ratings could not be done.

11. It makes no practical sense to use comparison groups to determine the large-scale effectiveness of an intervention. A more appropriate statistical procedure would be to determine the consistency of effects across 50 to 100 treatment sites and simply to assume that, if consistent effects are occurring, it is a result of the intervention. However, such a study would probably not be published in the top research journals.

12. Here's a personal example of how researchers misapply small-scale findings. Researchers tell me that research has found that engaging students in discussions on the use of computers reduces their enjoyment of the technology and so reduces its potential for learning. Yet Socratic dialogue about computer experiences is the key element in the success of the HOTS program. While the finding cited by researchers is true over the short term, my large-scale experience has consistently found that, after several months of discussing computer use, students exhibit far higher levels of cognitive development and enjoyment than the use of technology alone could generate.

13. Seymour B. Sarason, *The Predictable Failure of Educational Reform* (San Francisco: Jossey-Bass, 1990), pp. 37–38.

14. The fall 1994 issue of *Educational Evaluation and Policy Analysis* featured a special section on site-based management/shared decision making. Two of the four articles were devoted to aspects of conceptualizing what site-based management is.

The third article studied the process of implementing shared decision making in six schools and found heightened conflict with little effect on school reform. The fourth article went beyond process and studied the effects in one district of shared decision making on student achievement and teacher practice. (It was good to find a researcher actually interested in student learning.) The fundamental conclusion was that student achievement had not improved and that teachers had not changed their instructional practices.

15. Diane Ravitch, "First, Save the Schools," *New York Times,* 27 June 1994, p. A-17.

16. For examples of those recommending local curricula, see Larry Cuban, "The Lure of Curricular Reform and Its Pitiful History"; and Decker Walker, *Fundamentals of Curriculum* (New York: Harcourt Brace Jovanovich, 1990), pp. 307–36.

17. For alternative policy recommendations for Chapter 1/Title I, see Stanley Pogrow, "The Forgotten Question in the Chapter 1 Debate: Why Are the Students Having So Much Trouble Learning?," *Education Week,* 26 May 1993, pp. 36, 26; and idem, "What to Do About Chapter 1: An Alternative View from the Street," *Phi Delta Kappan,* April 1992, pp. 624–30.

18. See the theory of cognitive underpinnings in Pogrow, "Challenging At-Risk Students"; and idem, "Converting At-Risk Students."

19. When it became clear that HOTS was producing significant gains, I went back to the research literature to see where the conclusion that thinking should first be developed in content had originated. Almost all the research had been conducted with highly educated adults as subjects; it had nothing to do with educationally disadvantaged students in middle school.

20. Steven Raudenbush, Brian Rowan, and Yuk-Fai Cheong, "Higher Order Instructional Goals in Secondary Schools: Class, Teacher, and School Influences," *American Educational Research Journal,* Fall 1993, pp. 523–54.

21. Elizabeth Fennema et al., "Using Children's Mathematical Knowledge in Instruction," *American Educational Research Journal,* Fall 1993, pp. 555–84.

22. Okhee Lee and Charles W. Anderson, "Task Engagement and Conceptual Change in Middle School Science Classrooms," *American Educational Research Journal,* Fall 1993, pp. 585–610.

23. Edward Baker, Margaret Wang, and Herbert Walberg, "The Effects of Inclusion on Learning," *Educational Leadership,* December 1994/January 1995, pp. 33–35.

24. For a criticism of the tendency of the meta-analyses conducted by Robert Slavin to overlook the effects of high-quality programs and thereby to grossly underestimate the effects of good programs, see Susan Demirsky Allan, "Ability Grouping Research Reviews: What Do They Say About Grouping and the Gifted?," *Educational Leadership,* March 1991, pp. 60–65; and Stanley Pogrow, "Good Statistics About Bad Programs Tell Little," *Educational Leadership,* letter to the editor, October 1991, p. 93.

25. Gerald W. Bracey, "The Fourth Bracey Report on the Condition of Public Education," *Phi Delta Kappan,* October 1994, pp. 114–27.

26. The software is called Word Problem Processors. For more information on this software, contact the author by fax at 520/621-9373.

Sweeping Decentralization of Educational Decision-Making Authority

Lessons from England and New Zealand

BY RICHARD C. WILLIAMS, BARBARA HAROLD,
JAN ROBERTSON, AND GEOFF SOUTHWORTH

The experience with decentralization in New Zealand and England illustrates that the goals of local control and accountability might be more elusive than was initially envisioned by those who designed the system, the authors suggest.

AMONG THE solutions being offered to improve the quality of America's public schools is decentralizing decision-making authority from state educational agencies and school districts to local school sites.[1] The shift is being recommended in the belief that organizations will perform better if those who must implement and are affected by programs and decisions have a greater say in decision making. This development parallels a similar movement in the private sector.[2]

The degree of decentralization varies among states and school districts, ranging from slightly increasing the percentage of district funds allocated to local schools for discretionary spending, to decentralizing decision making to the school principal, to establishing site-based councils that advise the principal—who retains ultimate authority for decisions. These approaches—which Priscilla Wohlstetter and Allan Odden refer to as administrative decentralization and principal control[3]—do not fundamentally change professional and school board control. We refer to them as *limited* models of decentralization.

RICHARD C. WILLIAMS is a professor in the College of Education, University of Washington, Seattle. BARBARA HAROLD is a senior lecturer in the School of Education, University of Waikato, Hamilton, New Zealand, where JAN ROBERTSON is a senior lecturer and director of the Educational Leadership Centre. GEOFF SOUTWORTH is a senior lecturer in the Institute of Education, University of Cambridge, England.

The American education system, when compared to many other national systems, is already quite decentralized. The main responsibility for education rests with the states, which, in turn, have vested extensive decision-making responsibilities in local school boards. However, with the exception of a few places such as Chicago, the American system has only the trappings of true decentralization.[4] In reality, the school board and central administration retain ultimate authority over the most important decisions.

Some advocates argue that we need to decentralize further, to the local school site, if we are to garner the benefits that such an approach can provide. They urge us to adopt a system that would accomplish some or all of the following objectives:

- Devolve the ultimate responsibility for a wide range of decisions from the school board and central administration to the school-site council.
- Change site-council membership so that it consists of a majority of parents and community members and a small minority of teachers and administrators.
- Change the role of the school board and the state to assisting local site councils in implementing their own programs and decisions.
- Allow site councils greater freedom to purchase goods or obtain services for the school from government agencies and private vendors.[5]

From *Phi Delta Kappan*, April 1997, pp. 626-631. © 1997 by Phi Delta Kappa International, Inc. Reprinted by permission.

For our purposes here, we define such changes as a *sweeping* decentralization of decision making. Rather than tinkering with the system by decentralizing a few decisions to professionally controlled councils, sweeping decentralization represents a fundamental shift in the decision-making structure of the school system.

We might well ask some questions. What would happen if a centralized system moved in this direction? Would it result in chaos or more efficiency? Would client interests be better served? What effect would it have on teachers and administrators? Would citizens and parents be capable of providing effective leadership? Two national education systems, England and New Zealand, have implemented just such a sweeping system, and a look at some of their experiences provides some insights into decentralization's likely effect on school sites in the U.S.

We will briefly describe the reforms that have been implemented in these two countries, identify and discuss some common challenges that they have faced when moving in this direction, and discuss lessons that American reformers might learn from these experiences.

New Zealand

During a century of education with a strongly centralized administrative structure, there had been little real change in New Zealand's system. In the 1960s there was growing community concern about the education system. In the late 1980s, discontent on the part of communities and groups that were disadvantaged by the system, such as Maori and women, led the government to decide to restructure its health, education, and other departments to achieve smaller, more effective regional units. A task force commonly referred to as the Picot Committee recommended a system that was more efficient; encouraged greater local decision making, equity, and fairness; and reallocated funds in a way that would most benefit students.

In April 1988 the decentralization of educational administration was recommended in a policy document titled *Tomorrow's Schools*.[6] The Education Act came into effect on 1 October 1989, when schools took over their own administration. The previous regional education boards were disestablished, and schools have since been governed by individual boards of trustees (site councils) consisting of three to five parent representatives, the principal, a staff representative, and, in secondary schools, a student representative.

England

To understand the background of the reforms in England and the context in which they were passed, one needs to recall the mid-1970s. In 1976 the chief inspector of schools gave a speech titled "The Secret Garden." Its message was that "the school curriculum needed to be opened up to the wider interests of all who had a legitimate interest in it; the government, parents, employers; not just teachers and educationists."[7]

The more than 100 Local Education Authorities (LEAs) in England and Wales provided little direct guidance on what was to be taught in schools. Curriculum content was determined mainly by school staffs, along with publishing houses, major national curriculum innovation projects, and local initiatives in specific subject areas. National inspectors' reports on national standards and school curricula and some international comparative studies began to raise concerns about the schools' quality and relevance to the modern world.

In 1988 the government passed the Education Reform Act (ERA). The ERA had two distinct parts. One half of the legislation was concerned with the national curriculum and its related assessment arrangements. It has moved the schools' curricula from being a "secret garden" inhabited only by children and teachers to a public playground in which the central government encourages, even mandates, parents and others to spend time. The second half has "much to do with the Thatcher Government's macro-philosophy that efficiency and quality are best sustained and enhanced in situations where users and customers have choice and the information and the scope to use it as they decide—in other words, where there is a market."[8] There can be other reasons for delegating financial management—such as efficiency, better value, and empowerment of teachers, trustees, and parents—but the prevailing rationale in England is for the purposes of the marketplace.

In this article we will deal mostly with the second half of the 1988 legislation, the delegation of financial management to governing boards that are predominantly composed of parents and citizens (trustees). However, it is important to understand that efforts in England to decentralize the education system by delegating funds to schools have simultaneously been accompanied by a counter flow of centralization of the curriculum, over which the government has taken control.

Under England's decentralization plan, which is called Local Management of Schools (LMS), funds are now routed to individual schools and managed by the school's principal and school trustees, to whom the principal is accountable. Generally speaking, a governing body made up of the principal, elected parents, community members, and some staff members determines how monies will be spent and makes decisions on personnel, faculty, staff development, and equipment.

Lessons to Be Learned

Both New Zealand and England have undergone sweeping decentralization of their education systems. Responsibilities previously resting with centralized educational authorities at the national and regional levels have been delegated to local schools. Further, the governance of schools has been legislated to be shared among teachers, parents, and local citizens, with the lay members outnumbering the professional staff.

In England, by a vote of the parents, a school can "opt out" of the national system. An opted-out school can receive state funds to run the school, but it is essentially freed from many of the rules and policies that govern schools remaining within the system. Both England and New Zealand, however, have a national curriculum for which the local schools are responsible. In England, accountability is to be ensured by school results on national examinations; the New Zealand model, while still mandating accountability, allows the local schools greater discretion in determining how their progress is to be identified and measured. The officers of the Education Review Office carry out effectiveness reviews and assurance audits every three years in each educational institution in New Zealand.

Four cross-national themes have emerged from the experiences of the two countries as they have moved to this more decentralized model: 1) the need for support and training, 2) the problem of lack of time, 3) the puzzle of accountability, and 4) the principal's professional and personal adjustments.

The Need for Support and Training

In many countries, one of the more persistent laments of teachers and local administrators is that the central bureau (district office, local educational authority, or national ministry) seems remote and inefficient. Local teachers and administrators wonder what "those people" do all day. One of the most important things local decision makers realize when a school moves to a decentralized system is that someone has been attending to the myriad concerns that now fall into the laps of the local school staff and governing board.

Typically, head teachers in England and New Zealand have had only minimal training and experience in management and business administration. These head teachers (we will refer to them as "principals") are suddenly responsible for a budget equivalent to millions of dollars, which covers staff salaries, building and grounds maintenance and repair, equipment, and instructional and noninstructional costs. Principals must assume the functions of accountants, maintenance managers, and personnel directors. To complicate the situation, they must make their decisions in cooperation with politically appointed trustees who also have little or no training in these areas. This is proving to be a heavy burden on everyone, especially principals. The obvious need to help local administrators deal with added responsibilities has been handled in three ways: 1) government-sponsored

training and support systems, 2) self-help networks, and 3) contracting out.

Government-sponsored training and support systems. As control has been decentralized to the local schools, support systems have either been formed from previously existing bodies (the LEA in England) or have been newly set up in advance of initiating the reform (the Implementation Unit in New Zealand). In both cases, personnel who are knowledgeable and able to assist local schools provide support, and, as the new system becomes established, their authority and control gradually diminish. In New Zealand in 1989, for the first year of implementation, the School Management Development Project (SMDP) was set up in each of the six teacher colleges. Staff members from each college conducted and coordinated the support and training activities set up for school trustees, staff members, and principals in their respective regions.

Because the needs vary among the governing councils, providers of professional development in both countries have found it difficult to give the right help and support at the right time for those who need it. The principals' assessment of the adequacy of the training and support available to them has been mixed. In New Zealand, after six months, the principals' training was generally viewed as inadequate. A Principals' Implementation Task Force was established, which produced eagerly received training booklets dealing with personnel, property, and school management.

Self-help networks. In England, principals and other school staff members were encouraged to create local self-help networks—groups of principals who informally assist or advise one another on ways to manage their new responsibilities. Clearly, self-help networks are only a partial solution; systematic support is needed as well.

Contracting out. Increasingly, school principals are contracting out various tasks, such as custodial or accounting responsibilities. In some instances several schools contract jointly with a firm or an individual. In both England and New Zealand there is a growing sector of private individuals and firms competing to provide specialized services to schools.

Lack of Time

Decentralization increases the workloads of principals, administrators, and school trustees. Indeed, the complexity of the new tasks has taken up more time than anyone initially envisioned.[9] There are three broad elements that account for this increase in tasks and the time required to discharge them: 1) financial planning and management, 2) the volume of paper, and 3) the amount of consultation required.

Financial planning. Principals, along with their trustees, now need to monitor funds, keeping a check on variables such as expenditures for heating, supplies, and substitute

*The role of the principal in site-based management
obviously becomes more varied and complex.*

■ ■

teachers. In England, although principals may have quickly adjusted to making financial plans, many complain that because their school budgets are set by local politicians on an annual basis, it is almost impossible for them to make long-term forecasts and plans.

Volume of paper. Principals must deal with countless agencies, including private advertisers, retailers, and consultants. The introduction of the national curriculum has also greatly increased the number of reports and policy dicta that must be read. There never seems to be enough time to read all the official documents, which are constantly being altered. In New Zealand this phenomenon is commonly referred to as a "paper war."[10]

Consultation required. Principals must now work closely with their trustees, which requires attending more and longer meetings. The education system is now run by volunteers taking on roles previously played by full-time, paid personnel of the regional education boards and LEAs. Also of importance is the attitude of the trustees toward their responsibilities. Trustees who view themselves as "watchdogs" and trust the principal to run the school unless there is some reason to be concerned take less time than trustees who see themselves as "bosses" elected to run the school on behalf of the parents.

The Problem of Accountability

In both England and New Zealand, the decentralization to local schools has developed within the constraints of national policy frameworks. New Zealand uses a "charter" between the schools and the government that sets out the educational objectives for the schools under the umbrella of the national curriculum framework. An Education Review Office conducts reviews and reports on the extent to which schools are achieving the goals set forth in their charters. The school boards of trustees are required to report regularly to their communities on the charter objectives and how well they are being achieved. In England, similar structures exist. The national curriculum provides a framework of entitlement for each pupil. An Office of Standards in Education ensures that all schools are inspected every four years by teams of registered inspectors who report to the trustees. Trustees formally report once a year to the parents about the school and its achievements.

Undoubtedly, many of the decisions that school councils make will be sound and sensible. There is a downside to this decentralization movement, however. Eric Bolton, a former senior chief inspector of schools, stated succinctly, "It is surely a triumph of hope over experience

to expect that such self-interested, isolated, fragmented decisions, made in thousands of separate institutions, will add up to a sensible, effective, and efficient national school system."[11]

In England, many valuable activities are already suffering. Orchestras and other music groups, drama programs, and visual arts centers, which brought together pupils of similar abilities or needs, were organized at a level over and above the individual school. The list is not confined to the arts; centers for pupils with special needs also fall into this category. A counterbalance of some "higher" authority is needed that will coordinate certain kinds of educational activities that are more cost-effective when more centrally organized.

While New Zealand has not experienced the same problems, there has been concern that personnel and services such as teacher/librarians, museum education officers, and special education—all previously funded centrally—will be affected. Clearly, the devolution of funds to local sites needs to be handled with care; otherwise, some valuable resources and provisions will be lost.

The Changing Role of the Principal

The role of the principal in site-based management obviously becomes more varied and complex. The power to make autonomous decisions on matters closely related to the schools' problems and welfare is valued by the principals in New Zealand and England and has led to innovative programs and practices over the past four years. The freedom to be able to make decisions and to implement change at the local level without a lot of central bureaucratic interference has been appreciated and is an acknowledged benefit of the education reforms in both countries. However, this responsibility also places further demands on principals.

In both New Zealand and England, as in the U.S., principals have traditionally sought to balance educational leadership and organizational management. The reforms have forced educational leaders to pick up many more managerial responsibilities. The time required for these new duties has varied to some degree, depending on the principals' expertise, but the complexity of the management role has usually severely cut into the time available to principals to act as educational leaders in staff and school development.

It is possible to argue that the perception of dual roles is in some ways a false dichotomy and that the two functions can be accommodated and integrated.[12] However, this role integration appears to be essentially an academic resolution of the inherent tensions between the two roles. Principals themselves apparently see the two functions as separate parts of their work, and some appear to have a preference for one over the other.

In England, Geoff Southworth found that some principals appeared to regard their educational leadership not as a role but as an occupation identified with teaching and learning and educational beliefs. Being a principal was not a managerial role for them. For these educational-leadership-oriented principals, school management was a means to an end; now, they fear that the managerial role will become an end in itself, taking them away from what they see as their reason for being a principal. As one principal said, "LMS has turned the role of the principal upside down."[13]

In her study in New Zealand, Jan Robertson found that many of the principals felt that "Nobody knows the things beyond the call of duty that a principal does." One urban primary principal stated a concern that was felt by all in the group: "My problem is that there are so many things that are drawing me out all the time to do other things instead of my being able to stay in the school and concentrate on what I want to do."[14]

Occupying a position at the interface of staff, school-site council, and community has greatly increased principals' stress levels. The situation needs to be closely watched. Research indicates that the principal is a significant factor in the school's effectiveness and development. Therefore, if decentralization reduces the professional leadership of the principal, it may inhibit the effectiveness of the school.

Those who have been directly involved in trying to make decentralization work at the school-site level have commented on the strain they have experienced and the problems they have encountered. Yet it is interesting to note that, when given the choice, many would rather press on with the new system than return to the previous, more centralized system. With all its challenges, they seem to prefer the choices and autonomy that the new system provides over the limitations that are inherent in complex bureaucracies.

Implications for the U.S. Education System

American school districts' plans to decentralize decision making from the central administration to local school sites are, with the exception of the Chicago plan, not as sweeping as those we have described in England and New Zealand. Typically, when American school districts decentralize, they shift some budgetary responsibilities and decision-making authority to the local school site. Some plans require the schools to appoint or elect school-site councils that consist of teachers, parents, citizens, and occasionally students. However, these site councils typically are not composed of a majority of parents and citizens, and their decision-making authority is quite limited, often to an advisory role.

There are *reinvention* advocates in the United States who consider the current decentralization situation to be merely the beginning stages of a system that will ultimately resemble the more sweeping approaches of England and New Zealand. If we do move toward a more complete decentralization to local school sites, what can be learned from these years of experience in New Zealand and England that might inform our policy decisions? We consider three lessons from the New Zealand and England models: the Catch-22 of empowerment, the unbounded need for training, and the cloud of accountability.

The Catch-22 of empowerment. Neighborhoods and attendance areas in school districts—especially in large districts—often differ considerably. Decentralization advocates argue that the students and parents in local schools are best served if their programs are responsive to the unique character and needs of their clients. They consider central school bureaucracies with broad general policies and procedures to be incapable of responding adequately to widely differing local needs. Decentralizing decision making to the local school site empowers the school principal, staff members, parents, and citizens to respond to local needs.

In New Zealand and England, decentralization has resulted in a paradox. When the schools are given more autonomy over a wide range of activities (from curriculum and instruction, to the physical plant and facilities, to budget and personnel—functions previously handled by a central administrative unit), it turns out that school administrators do not have the training, expertise, or, most important, the time to deal with all these matters. The attention of the designated decision makers is divided among a wide range of activities and demands. Further, many parents and teachers do not have the background, time, or inclination to delve into the details of problems that confront the school. Principals are drawn away from their responsibility to provide leadership to the school's instructional program; teachers spend an inordinate amount of time on noninstructional matters for which they have neither training nor interest. As a result, the school—finally given greater discretion over its own destiny—finds it extremely difficult to solve practical problems and get on to more fundamental curricular and instructional matters.

Decentralizing decision making to the local school site will not result in more responsiveness to local needs unless the schools have the capacity to respond. This capacity might be provided in at least three ways:

- a central administrative unit at the district level might provide selected services to the schools,
- schools might be given resources sufficient to allow the school-site councils time to deal adequately with the challenges they face, or

- schools might be given the resources and the freedom to purchase needed services from the private sector.

An unbounded need for training. When school principals, teachers, parents, and citizens are delegated responsibility for decision making, they must understand the matters about which they are to make decisions, appreciate the workings of complex organizations, and have the skills to participate in the decision-making process. Knowledge, understanding, patience, and persistence are required to make decisions about such diverse matters as assessing the instructional program, planning programs, determining disciplinary and other policies, ensuring equity to all students, and dispersing limited resources.

In New Zealand and England, principals typically have had limited formal training in administration, and teachers and parents have had virtually none. In the U.S., principals have considerable training and experience in administering a school within a centralized system. Teachers do have some training in curriculum and instruction, but few have a comprehensive understanding of the workings of a school as a complex organization. Parents and citizens generally have very limited knowledge of these matters.

In England and New Zealand, the delegation of decision-making authority to site councils resulted in a massive and apparently unanticipated demand for inservice training. The need for training varied considerably across the spectrum of councils, depending on the challenges they faced and the makeup of the council. And, considering the turnover of membership on councils, the need for training will be unending.

In the U.S., the same inservice training needs should be anticipated. While American administrators have more initial training in these matters, they generally have limited experience with the kind of collaborative decision making required by this shift in responsibility. Some teachers, through the teacher leadership movement, have acquired such skills and knowledge, but many more need training. Parents and citizens will generally need extensive training.

Who will provide this inservice training? In New Zealand it was provided by a network of regional colleges. In England virtually no provision was made for such training. Both countries have reported that a lack of adequate inservice training is a continuing stumbling block in implementing the school reform program. In the U.S. some school districts have provided orientations for site-council members, and many principals have worked to develop their councils' skills and understandings. However, centralized district offices with diminished resources will not have the capacity to provide this service. Perhaps this need will be filled by local universities, regional educational agencies, principal centers, or private consultants.

Policies that involve any substantial movement toward decentralizing decision making to local sites must include a recognition of this need for inservice training and must provide the resources necessary to develop thoughtful, informed, and competent school-site council members. Without adequate initial and continuing training, the potential benefits of this organizational structure will not be realized.

The cloud of accountability. One of the heralded benefits of decentralizing decision making to the local school site is that accountability for the school's performance can be more clearly affixed. Because the school has been allocated additional resources and the clear authority to determine and operate its school program, it should be much easier to determine the causal relationship between the school's program and functioning and the students' performance on identified outcome measures. However, the experience in New Zealand and England indicates that decentralization to local school sites has in some ways clouded, rather than clarified, the accountability question.

One problem that resulted when dividing up the central budget and dispersing it to local school sites was that the district and the schools lost the benefits of economy of scale—that is, a larger organization generally has the purchasing power to demand a better unit price from the sales source. This applies, for example, to equipment, instructional materials, paper, and cleaning supplies. With parceled-out funds, it also becomes more difficult to provide some kinds of programs and resources in individual schools. As illustrated in New Zealand and England, museums, central libraries with significant collections, large-scale musical or artistic programs, and comprehensive inservice training programs are difficult and expensive to maintain separately in each individual school. These facilities require resources that are beyond the reach of individual schools—resources that have typically been provided by a central administrative agency. Who is to be accountable for providing these valued programs and resources?

A second problem is determining to whom the school is accountable. The movement to local accountability raises afresh the question of whom the school serves. Obviously, schools serve the enrolled students and their parents; however, public schools also serve the local community and the nation. As became apparent in England, a set of individual schools each determining its own program and priorities to fit its own interests is not likely to result in a national education system designed to prepare the students, and thereby the nation, for life in the 21st century.

In some instances, the goals of the local school might be in conflict with national goals, or they might not address broad societal needs.

How can this tension between the interests of the nation and those of the individual schools be resolved? England's answer has been to develop a national curriculum and examination system through which all schools are held accountable. In theory, the nation sets the goals and determines how to measure the outcomes. The schools are given the freedom to determine how to meet those outcomes and are held accountable for the results. This idea has proved difficult to implement. Recently, because of its complexity and expense, the government has attempted to reduce the scale of the national curriculum and the scope of the national testing program. New Zealand has implemented a less centralized system that includes a national curriculum but not a national testing system. However, as the new curriculum framework is implemented, a new monitoring system of national standards will be introduced. Each school has greater autonomy in determining its educational goals and the ways that the school's progress will be measured. In both systems, the accountability issue has been addressed, but the challenge of responding to community and national accountability issues remains largely unresolved.

In the U.S., with responsibility for education resting in each of the 50 states and thousands of school districts, the accountability issue would seem even more vexing. Attempts to develop or coordinate a national standards and assessment program that might anchor an accountability system are under way. However, considering the nation's vastness and diversity, the complexity of the task, and the looming costs, the likelihood of developing a system that would meet the needs of state and national accountability seems slim at best.

Even if a clear accountability system can be developed, the question remains: Who will be responsible if the school is judged unsuccessful? Asked another way, Who will have the authority and responsibility for determining the school's goals and objectives and the responsibility for implementing the school's program? And who will meet the legal and financial obligations that might arise if the governing board acts irresponsibly? The standard answer to questions about the role of lay school boards is that boards have general policy responsibilities and superintendents are responsible for implementing a program to accomplish those policy goals. Anyone acquainted with the workings of school boards knows that the line between the two functions is very fuzzy and often breached. Some school board members become deeply involved in micromanaging school districts. School-site councils with voting memberships that encompass both the professional staff and the lay public would seem to blur even further the question of who is accountable for the schools' performance and obligations.

In summary, sweeping decentralization of educational decision making from the central administration to the local school site is advocated because it provides the school staff, parents, and local citizens an opportunity to develop a school that is responsive to local needs, and it more clearly assigns accountability if the school does not meet agreed-upon standards. The experience in New Zealand and England, however, illustrates that these goals of local control and accountability might be more elusive than was initially envisioned by those who designed the system. Those who advocate a more sweeping or radical approach, similar to the programs that have been introduced in New Zealand and England, must be prepared to address the challenges that others have encountered.

1. Paul T. Hill and Josephine Bonan, *Decentralization and Accountability in Public Education* (Santa Monica, Calif.: RAND Corporation, 1991), p. 9.
2. David Osbourne and Ted Gaebler, *Reinventing Government: How the Entrepreneurial Spirit Is Transforming the Public Sector* (New York: Addison-Wesley, 1992).
3. Priscilla Wohlstetter and Allan Odden, "Rethinking School-Based Management Policy and Research," *Educational Administration Quarterly*, November 1992, pp. 529–49.
4. G. Alfred Hess, Jr., *School Restructuring, Chicago Style* (Newbury Park, Ill.: Corwin, 1991), chap. 9; and Richard F. Elmore, "Models of Restructuring Schools," paper presented at the annual meeting of the American Educational Research Association, New Orleans, 1988.
5. For a source of various perspectives on decentralization, see Paul T. Hill, *Reinventing Public Education* (Seattle: Institute for Education and Training and the Institute for Public Policy and Management, University of Washington, report #DRU-690IET/LE/GGF, April 1994).
6. David Lange, *Tomorrow's Schools* (Wellington, New Zealand: Government Printer, 1988).
7. Eric Bolton, "Imaginary Gardens with Real Toads," in Clyde Chitty and Brian Simons, eds., *Education Answers Back* (London: Lawrence & Wishart, 1993), p. 3.
8. Ibid., p. 5.
9. Robin McConnell and Richard Jefferies, "Report No. 4: Monitoring Today's Schools Research Project," in David Mitchell, ed., *The First Year: Tomorrow's Schools as Perceived by Members of the Boards of Trustees* (Hamilton, New Zealand: University of Waikato, 1991).
10. Cathy Wylie, "Volunteers and Conscripts in the Paper War," *Public Sector*, vol. 13, no. 4, 1990, pp. 14–15.
11. Bolton, p. 8.
12. Meredydd Hughes, "Leadership in Professionally Staffed Organisations," in idem et al., eds., *Managing Education: The System and the Institution* (London: Holt, Rinehart & Winston, 1985), pp. 262–90.
13. Geoff Southworth, "Primary School Headship: An Analysis Derived from an Ethnographic Case Study of One Headteacher's Work" (Doctoral dissertation, University of East Anglia, England, 1993), p. 317.
14. Jan M. Robertson, "Developing Educational Leadership" (Master's thesis, University of Waikato, Hamilton, New Zealand, 1991), p. 142.

Teaching teachers

Graduate schools of education face intense scrutiny

Almost a century after they began popping up on America's burgeoning university campuses, graduate schools of education still labor in a shadowland. Although they award more than a quarter of all the advanced degrees conferred each year in the United States, they remain at the bottom of academia's pecking order. As Prof. John Goodlad, director of the Center for Educational Renewal at the University of Washington, puts it: "The only enterprise with lower status than teaching is the enterprise of teacher education."

Yet the issue of how America teaches its teachers to teach is becoming increasingly crucial. A few years from now, the biggest generation of pupils in history will enter the nation's schools, and they will represent the widest imaginable mix of cultures and socioeconomic backgrounds. To deal with this challenge, the nation will need an estimated 2 million new classroom teachers in the coming decade. Linda Darling-Hammond, professor of education at Teachers College at New York's Columbia University, says the nation has reached "a critical moment for transforming the capacity of the American teaching force."

This past January, 87 leading schools of education—known as the Holmes Group after former Harvard Education Dean Henry W. Holmes—demonstrated that they grasped the importance of the moment. They issued a bluntly worded report in which they warned that unless America's schools of education institute real reforms, they should "surrender their franchise" in teacher training.

Certainly, the challenges facing education schools are extraordinary. Among them: attracting a different breed of prospective teacher; elevating teaching to a true profession; forging stronger intellectual ties to other parts of the academic community; developing new links with the real world of education; turning more research into practice; absorbing the lessons of the cognitive revolution that is rapidly altering what we know about how we learn; and most important, restoring the confidence of citizens despairing over conditions in public schools. In short, can the teaching profession emerge from what Goodlad has called a state of "chronic prestige deprivation" by rejuvenating an educational system that needs a transforming overhaul?

Team teaching. So far, the answer is "Maybe." As the Holmes report indicates, "a few institutions already have stirred the winds of change." Some have forged promising links between the campus and public schools. One of the most important of these experiments is at Teachers College, long an intellectual wellspring for graduate teacher education but infrequently involved directly with the schools. Each week a group of Teachers College students in the first year of their graduate program take the subway to Intermediate School 44, a middle school on Manhattan's gentrifying Upper West Side. The visiting students spend 15 to 30 hours weekly team teaching sixth to eighth graders and being mentored by classroom veterans and TC faculty. Then, in January, the three groups join together full time as a team, breaking up the sense of isolation teachers often feel and apparently enriching the educational experience of IS 44's pupils. Says one enthusiastic student: "I felt I was in a new world for four weeks."

The Teachers College experiment is part of what graduate schools of education call "professional development" programs, the counterpart in education of teaching hospitals in medicine. About 200 institutions have established such programs, which provide real-world settings in which prospective teachers and experienced teachers, too, can hone their professional skills, especially classroom techniques. The extended immersion in professional development is a far cry from the traditional training of most of the nation's 2.8 million teachers and most teachers-to-be. Often, seasoned teachers get their only contact with ongoing professional training from "in-service education," which often consists of little more than quickie workshops.

Extended learning. Another reform designed to improve teaching: five-year academic programs that allow undergraduates to major in a liberal arts discipline and then switch to specialized education courses at the graduate level. Five-year teaching programs are becoming the norm, and about 25 percent of newly hired teachers hold master's degrees.

Surprisingly, some of the nation's most respected schools of education—among them the Harvard Graduate School of Education, top ranked in this year's *U.S. News* survey—believe that training teachers is not their primary function. Although even Harvard is making programmatic changes to increase the prominence of teacher-training, research remains the academic lodestar for the most prestigious institutions. As these institutions see it, their main mission is to build the base of research that educators need to make the wisest decisions in day-to-day practice.

Meanwhile, advances in cognitive-science research are spurring new teaching methods. John Bruer, head of the St.

GRADUATE SCHOOLS OF EDUCATION
WITH THE HIGHEST SCORES IN THE *U.S.* NEWS SURVEY

Rank/School	Overall score	Reputation rank by academics	Rep. rank by school super-intenents	Student selectivity rank	Research activity rank	Facility resources rank	'94 total enrollment	'94 ed. school research	'94 doctoral student/ faculty ratio	'94 acceptance rate
1. Harvard University	100.0	3	1	4	12	1	1,102	$7,100,000	17.3	47.2%
2. Stanford University	99.3	1	2	8	7	9	401	$7,370,982	5.08	39.2%
3. University of California at Berkeley	98.8	6	10	2	2	11	367	$14,000,000	8.35	30.3%
4. Columbia University Teachers College (N.Y.)	98.5	3	10	6	19	2	3,972	$11,498,000	5.36	39.9%
5. University of Wisconsin at Madison	96.2	3	14	9	14	12	1,396	$10,867,641	2.95	37.3%
6. Vanderbilt University (Peabody College) (Tenn.)	95.4	9	8	12	1	29	658	$16,753,048	2.71	53.8%
7. University of Illinois at Urbana-Champaign	92.1	2	19	14	27	24	702	$7,301,000	3.07	37.5%
7. Michigan State University	92.1	6	9	15	5	51	999	$13,295,094	1.29	48.2%
9. Ohio State University	90.8	9	4	70	3	10	2,629	$15,361,911	3.35	59.2%
10. University of California at Los Angeles	89.4	9	13	36	6	44	509	$7,990,520	6.29	44.4%
10. University of Pennsylvania	89.4	25	27	25	15	16	537	$6,999,000	1.71	58.0%
12. NorthwesternUniversity (Ill.)	87.3	25	19	1	59	21	274	$2,386,953	6.11	22.2%
13. Indiana University at Bloomington	86.8	15	15	41	41	17	1,469	$5,284,225	7.17	77.7%
13. University of Virginia	86.8	9	15	18	73	14	906	$2,089,491	2.76	36.7%
15. University of Georgia	86.2	19	46	54	11	4	1,539	$14,522,374	2.92	59.4%
16. Boston College	86.1	52	17	21	30	15	977	$4,429,897	1.88	59.1%
17. University of Kansas	85.2	36	62	16	10	18	1,502	$10,219,861	1.59	60.1%
18. University of Washington	84.9	19	40	19	20	47	511	$5,653,623	2.00	53.4%
19. University of Chicago	84.0	6	11	5	46	84	129	$3,250,000	6.87	66.9%
20. University of Iowa	83.0	24	26	52	18	40	976	$6,197,740	1.96	45.6%
21. University of Maryland at College Park	82.4	19	48	24	20	54	1,155	$7,000,000	1.82	40.9%
22. University of Michigan at Ann Arbor	81.8	9	7	13	81	60	291	$2,250,760	2.38	63.2%
23. University of Southern California	81.6	36	23	45	49	19	786	$3,127,814	3.79	46.8%
24. University of Colorado at Boulder	81.1	33	32	10	52	49	351	$3,300,000	2.31	56.8%
25. University of Minnesota at Twin Cities	80.6	9	29	115	7	20	1,965	$11,037,192	1.56	56.4%
25. Penn State University at University Park	80.6	15	22	65	42	36	1,037	$4,629,763	3.1	45.8%

(continued)

Louis-based James S. McDonnell Foundation, has laid out much of the history of the new research and its implications in *Schools for Thought,* a book much discussed at graduate schools of education. His study discredits teaching practices based on the "mental calisthenics" theory of learning—drill and practice—and lays out three basic requirements before real learning can take place: The learners must have a base of knowledge about the subject upon which to draw; they must be able to monitor their own mental processes and make adjustments as they go about learning, and the material being learned has to be presented to them in a way that has personal meaning. Teachers can control all of

GRADUATE SCHOOLS OF EDUCATION
THE SECOND TIER

Rank/School	Over-all score	Reputation rank by academics	Rep. rank by school super-intendents	'94 ed. school research	'94 doctoral student/ faculty ratio	'94 acceptance rate
27. University of Texas at Austin	80.3	19	21	$1,178,995	5.67	40.6%
28. Syracuse University (N.Y.)	79.7	25	37	$5,607,000	1.70	74.3%
28. University of Oregon	79.7	64	53	$11,795,426	3.12	46.1%
30. Florida State University	77.9	36	38	$6,209,693	2.08	61.0%
31. Boston University	76.6	52	50	$3,585,094	2.19	78.9%
32. University of North Carolina at Chapel Hill	76.3	19	5	$1,388,400	1.16	34.3%
33. Temple University (Pa.)	76.1	52	40	$3,700,000	1.01	45.9%
34. University of Missouri at Columbia	75.6	36	53	$5,317,561	1.31	54.4%
35. University of Arizona	74.8	25	64	$3,979,005	2.32	70.6%
36. University of Florida	74.1	25	53	$2,859,371	1.11	65.0%
37. University of North Carolina at Greensboro	74.0	77	74	$11,816,539	1.80	39.2%
38. University of Connecticut	73.9	52	58	$7,847,241	2.08	62.9%
39. State University of N.Y. at Buffalo	73.6	47	89	$1,926,700	3.40	37.3%
40. New York University	72.9	52	49	$1,400,000	1.05	47.3%
40. Texas A&M University at College Station	72.9	33	40	$6,651,837	1.64	48.1%
42. Cornell University (N.Y.)	72.5	25	25	$928,246	1.94	51.8%
43. College of William and Mary (Va.)	71.3	52	24	$1,375,820	1.53	56.3%
44. Univ. of Pittsburgh-Main Campus	70.8	25	68	$3,776,000	2.58	77.5%
45. George Washington University (D.C.)	70.1	77	36	$4,625,141	1.92	64.5%
46. University of Massachusetts at Amherst	69.6	47	44	$1,375,074	2.35	43.3%
47. Arizona State University at Tempe	67.2	33	40	$3,332,000	1.05	41.8%
48. University of Nebraska at Lincoln	66.8	36	34	$2,361,788	.84	45.2%
49. Rutgers Univ. at New Brunswick (N.J.)	66.1	36	32	$710,693	.55	50.6%
50. University of Tennessee at Knoxville	65.9	36	50	$1,676,301	1.53	51.1%

Note: Schools with the same number rank are tied. Basic data: *U.S. News* and the schools. Reputational surveys conducted by Market Facts Inc. Response rate to reputational surveys: academics, 43 percent; school superintendents, 32 percent.

METHODOLOGY

Here's how U.S. News determined the rankings for the 223 graduate education programs that grant Ph.D.'s or Ed.D.'s:

■ Student selectivity was based on data for doctoral and master's candidates who enrolled in fall 1994: average scores on the verbal, quantitative and analytical parts of the Graduate Record Examination (each counted for 30 percent) and proportion of applicants accepted in the program (10 percent).

■ Faculty resources was based on the current ratio of both full-time doctoral (25 percent) and master's degree (20 percent) candidates to full-time faculty; the proportion of graduate students who were doctoral candidates (10 percent); the number of doctoral (15 percent) and master's (10 percent) degrees granted in 1994, and the percent of faculty given Spencer Foundation-Young Faculty, Fulbright, Guggenheim or Humboldt awards in the past two years (20 percent).

■ Research activity was based on the 1994 dollar total of the publicly and privately funded research administered by the education school (75 percent) and that total divided by the number of faculty members engaged in research (25 percent).

■ Reputation was determined by two U.S. News reputational surveys conducted in early 1995. In the first, education school deans and top faculty were asked to rate by quartiles the reputation of each graduate education program. In the second, a nationwide cross section of 1,000 school superintendents in school districts with more than 5,000 students were asked to select the 25 graduate education programs that offer the highest-quality training.

■ Overall rank was determined by converting into number ranks (from 1 to 223) the scores achieved by each school in the above categories. The highest score in each category—or subcategory—received a rank of 1. The scores for the other schools were then converted into number ranks by sorting them in descending order from the score achieved by the No. 1 school. The rankings for research activity, faculty resources and selectivity were determined by totaling the weighted number ranks of their subvariables. Next, the number ranks in the five indicators were weighted: The two reputational surveys, faculty, selectivity and research each accounted for 20 percent of the final score. The final rankings were then determined by totaling the five weighted number-ranked scores. The weighted score for the top school was given a value of 100 percent. The scores for all the others were then determined by figuring their totals as percentages of the score achieved by the No. 1 school.

these factors, Bruer says. But they cannot teach well when any one of the three is missing.

As they incorporate research advances in their own discipline, schools of education also are adopting proven techniques and modern technologies from their counterparts elsewhere on campus. From business schools, for instance, comes the case-study method; from law schools, the videotape review of student performance. At the University of Virginia's education school, a pioneer in high-tech pedagogy, faculty and students combine the case-study method and computerized technologies to create multimedia and online materials. Virginia offers teachers-to-be computerized simulation of real-life decision making in the classroom.

In the long run, however, the technology, the research and the best of faculty intentions will not satisfy the tough-minded critics who put together the stinging Holmes report. Such critics argue that to avoid a wholesale collapse,

American schools must quickly gain the adherence of a new breed of teacher for whom the classroom is not merely a workplace but the expression of a personal commitment. And there seems to be a new level of commitment among prospective teachers. Indeed, many educators say the atmosphere among young teacher candidates reminds them of that in the 1960s. Herbert Kohl, currently a visiting professor at Carleton College in Northfield, Minn., who wrote the beginning-teacher classic, *36 Children,* observes that "teaching has become exciting again."

Alternate routes. Many of the new teaching enthusiasts are graduates of schools of education. But others are entering the profession through alternate routes, including the Teach for America program, which enlists liberal arts graduates from elite schools. Other programs are attracting military retirees and recently unemployed defense workers to teaching. For example, Capt. William Miller, 48, an operations officer at the

Philadelphia Navy Yard, is preparing for a new career in the classroom by taking night courses at Temple University. He hopes to begin student teaching this summer.

When a group of nontraditional teacher candidates were asked why they had pursued teaching, a striking 80 percent said: "Because of the significance it holds for society." The same spirit seems to inspire the young. Arthur Levine, the new president of Teachers College and a former ranking official at Harvard's graduate education school, delights in retelling the story of the answer given by one young woman when she was asked why she had chosen a career in teaching: because, she replied, "it is my generation's Peace Corps."

BY SANDRA REEVES

For education school rankings in specialty disciplines, see the 1995 *U.S. News* guide to *America's Best Graduate Schools,* now on newsstands.

Failures in school privatization.

LEARNING CURVE

By Elissa Silverman

Late last fall, Baltimore Mayor Kurt Schmoke and the city's school board ostentatiously pulled the plug on a much ballyhooed experiment in school privatization. What went wrong? After all, just three years earlier, Schmoke had been touting Baltimore's contract with a Minnesota company called Education Alternatives Inc. (EAI) as a way to breathe new life into a public school system with a roughly 50 percent dropout rate; and John Golle, the enterprising president of EAI, had promised that "Over the course of the next year, we will convert the existing schools into 'community sanctuaries' that will deliver world-class education." Yet when Schmoke was deciding to cancel the EAI deal he sounded bitter, telling the press, "Even mayors get tired of being kicked around."

Baltimore's experience serves as a cautionary tale for school privatization enthusiasts, of whom there are plenty these days. Senate Majority Leader Bob Dole has pinned America's public education woes on the "dictates, meddling and politically correct dogma of federal bureaucrats." President Clinton has encouraged school districts "to experiment with ideas like chartering their schools to be run by private corporations." And former Assistant Secretary of Education Thomas Payzant told a congressional committee, "If communities want to hire companies to come in and help their schools, they ought to be able to do so."

Unlike vouchers, which guarantee school choice to parents, privatization (or, more accurately, public-private partnerships) guarantees choice to school boards. Under these schemes, local schools can contract out educational services to private vendors. Many schools already contract with private companies to perform administrative functions such as cleaning and food services. Now they can extend the idea to the classroom.

Yet teaching math, grammar or even laissez-faire economics is a far cry from trash pickup or mail delivery, and some consumers question whether its value comes with a hidden price tag. As Baltimore's experience shows, they are probably right to do so.

On the face of it, Golle's offer to Schmoke sounded like a hard one to refuse. EAI, which already managed private "Tesseract" schools in Arizona and Minnesota and one public elementary school in Miami, asked only for the average per-pupil cost, approximately $5,900 this school year, that the Baltimore school system would have spent anyway. In return EAI would save money (by, for example, contracting out administrative services and streamlining bureaucracy), plow some of those savings back into the classroom, improve student performance and even make a respectable profit to boot. "Our mission isn't to act as an employment agency, but to educate children," Golle promises.

Into some of the most impoverished neighborhood schools in Baltimore, EAI brought computers and teddy bears, rocking chairs and VCRs. In classrooms, tables in the shape of trapezoids and rectangles supplanted vertical rows of individual desks. On school walls, banners announcing that "every child has unique gifts and talents" replaced graffiti. Students began their day at a morning meeting, a kind of self-esteem pep rally, where they chanted slogans like: "I'm able to do whatever I put my mind to. I like myself. . . . I'm smart, I'm strong, I'm ready for whatever comes along."

Yet in the end, EAI performed cosmetic surgery—at best—on a school system badly in need of a major transplant. Last August, an independent evaluation by researchers from the Center for Educational Research at the University of Maryland Baltimore County found that despite all the attention focused on physical upgrading and staff development EAI schools were generally on a par with Baltimore public schools in similar neighborhoods. "The evaluation team found Tesseract and comparison schools more alike than different," the August 1995 report concluded.

More importantly, standardized test scores for Tesseract students in Baltimore, already dismal, declined still further in the first two years after EAI took over—while scores both for comparable schools and for the city as a whole showed modest gains. Only last year, the third year of the EAI experiment, did comprehensive test scores rise back to the city average.

Initially EAI claimed just the opposite results, announcing only months after it arrived in the Baltimore schools that it had raised test scores. When the numbers turned out to be based upon a small and unrepresentative group of students, EAI backpedaled, admitting that its report contained an error. Similar "errors" have been discovered in other EAI success stories. A year ago, the company announced a 22.2 percent increase in attendance at one EAI school. But the next day, company officials sheepishly admitted that data had been misread, and the increase was only 2.2 percent. Now John Golle denies ever having promised immediate results. "You don't sprinkle fairy dust around and all of a sudden have [achievement] grow. Perhaps if we had anything to do over again, we would have done a better job of lowering expectations," Golle told *The Baltimore Sun* last summer.

Given its sales pitch, though, EAI's failure to deliver on quality is less startling than its failure to deliver on thrift. The University of Maryland report declared that the "promise that EAI could improve instruction without spending more than Baltimore City was spending on schools has been discredited." "Discredited" is a generous evaluation. Records from the Baltimore City schools show that EAI received almost $18 million *more* over the past three years than comparable city schools. In fact, EAI was slated to receive $8.5 million, or approximately 11.2 percent more, for the 1995–96 school year than the city would ordinarily have spent. But wait a second, wasn't privatization supposed to save money? No, says Baltimore Schools Superintendent and EAI cheerleader Walter Amprey: "EAI just proves that we need to spend more money on our schools."

Despite getting more and performing less, however, audits by the accounting firm Arthur Andersen revealed that EAI did make good on one of its promises: it racked up at least $2.6 million in gross profits in 1992–93 and $4.3 million in 1993–94. The teachers' union accuses EAI of generating a profit by making significant cuts in expensive curricula such as art, music and special education and by pocketing Chapter I money, federal funds specifically granted to provide additional resources for disadvantaged students. The University of Maryland report confirmed that EAI offered fewer classes in art and music than comparable schools. And EAI used Chapter I funding, not, as it had promised, its own capital, to provide funds for its computer labs during its first year.

Indeed, with all its upgrades in equipment and technology, it seems the one thing EAI hasn't improved on is curriculum. In Baltimore, it chose to retain the city curriculum, simply better "aligning" it with the questions asked in comprehensive tests. Yet Baltimore had in its midst a model for a successful public-private partnership in curriculum reform: a grafting of the curriculum from the private Calvert school onto an inner-city elementary school called Barclay. Five years ago, Barclay's principal, Gertrude Williams, had to fight both the teachers' union and the former city schools superintendent to bring the Calvert school approach to her public school, but it has paid off. Calvert focuses on the substance of traditional subjects like phonics, spelling, grammar, reading, writing and math rather than on test preparation, experimental teaching methods or even computers. "We don't need self-esteem exercises; the students build it organically through the curriculum," says Williams. And though the classrooms lack rocking chairs, Barclay parents see the results. Test scores of Barclay students consistently exceed the city average; and the experiment has been deemed such a success that the city will be bringing it to a second elementary school this year.

Meanwhile, EAI has suffered another setback in Hartford, Connecticut, where the Board of Education reversed its original decision to hand over operations of all thirty-two of its schools to the company, restricting it to six instead. In November *Forbes* rated EAI one of its worst-performing stocks. But none of that has stopped Washington, D.C.'s troubled school system, among others, from considering a privatization venture with the company. And none of it has stopped John Golle, though these days he says that EAI's true mission may not be in the inner city, after all: it may be in the suburbs.

IT TAKES A SCHOOL

A new approach to elementary education starts at birth and doesn't stop when the bell rings

By MARGOT HORNBLOWER NORFOLK

THE SIGN ON THE SQUAT BRICK SCHOOL-house in the midst of crime-ridden public-housing projects in Norfolk, Virginia, reads BOWLING PARK ELE-MENTARY: A CARING COMMUNITY. Principal Herman Clark is one of those who does the caring, which is why every year he takes the parents of his pupils on a field trip to local attractions. One year it was to Greensville Correctional Center in Jarratt. "We got the chance to see the electric chair," he says. There have been visits to a prison in Chesapeake and a women's penal institution in Gooch-land. Two months ago, it was a walk through Death Row at Mecklenburg Correctional Center.

"The parents are subjected to a shake-down body search" for weapons or drugs, Clark says. "They hear the door slam. They look at the inmates and see the way the in-mates look back at them. We ask the pris-oners, 'Was there something that led you to this life?' They say, 'Yes, my parents were not there when I was a kid. There was noth-ing to do, so I did this or that [crime].' It is frightening. It makes our parents realize: this is where their child is heading." Every three years, Clark puts his pupils through a similar ordeal. "We target students who have the po-tential to get in trouble," he says. When a group of 26 returned from Deerfield Correc-tional Center, Clark says, "I was glad to see the bullies crying."

The shock treatment of the field trips is just one of many innovative therapies that Clark, a Ph.D. in education, has brought to

his school. Bowling Park is where the rheto-ric of "standing for children" moves beyond talk. If children are to be rescued, the rea-soning goes, who is better equipped to do so than the elementary school, a solid insti-tution already in the business? Yet to rescue children, one must start early—even before birth. And to rescue children, whole families must be rescued along with them—hence the transformation of the neighborhood school into a "caring community." It may sound like a platitude, but it is in fact a revolution, one that is spreading through the country, from inner-city ghettos to prosperous suburbs and rural enclaves, as fast as you can say *ABC.*

> "Schools are being
> called on to be those
> 'surrogate parents'
> that can increase
> 'teachability.'"

One of the most far-reaching programs, which began in Missouri and has spread to 47 states, hires "parent educators" who offer parenting skills and developmental screening

to families with young children, beginning in the third trimester of pregnancy. Bowling Park's Michael Bailey, a soft-spoken Mis-ter Rogers type, hands out flyers in food-stamp lines to encourage new mothers to sign up. Each day he drives out to visit one of the 35 families who have joined the pro-gram. "Hello, teacher!" shrieks Tonesha Sims, 2½, running out of her house to hug him on a recent morning. Bailey spends an hour re-viewing colors and numbers with the pig-tailed toddler. As Bailey leaves, Tonesha begs, "Teacher, can I play with you next week?" Lottie Holloman, 68, her great-grand-mother—and her guardian since Tonesha's mother, a drug addict, abandoned the girl to foster care—credits Bailey with inspiring her to buy books and read to the child. Children in the program get priority for slots in Bowl-ing Park's preschool.

By delving into the critical first three years of life, schools such as Bowling Park are expanding far beyond traditional aca-demics. But to many educators it is a logical evolution. Moving away from a narrow fo-cus on curriculum reform, some schools are assuming responsibility for the foundations of learning—the emotional and social well-being of the child from birth to age 12. Thus anything that affects a child is the school's business—from nutrition to drug-abuse pre-vention to health care and psychological counseling. "Schools are being called on to be those 'surrogate parents' that can increase the 'teachability' of children who arrive on their doorsteps in poor shape," according to

Joy G. Dryfoos, author of the 1994 book *Full-Service Schools*.

Bowling Park was chosen in 1992 as the site of the first CoZi school, a model that combines the education programs of two Yale professors, James P. Comer and Edward Zigler. Over the past three decades, Comer, a psychiatrist, has helped convert 600 mostly inner-city schools to a cooperative management in which parents, teachers and mental-health counselors jointly decide policy and focus on building close-knit relationships with children. Zigler, one of the founders of Head Start, designed "The School of the 21st Century," a program operating on 400 campuses, offering year-round, all-day preschool beginning at three, as well as before- and after-school and vacation programs. Bowling Park combines both approaches in what may be the nation's most comprehensive effort, as Zigler puts it, "[to] make the success of the child in every aspect of development our constant focus." Other CoZi schools are operating in Bridgeport, Connecticut, and in Mehlville, Missouri.

At Bowling Park staff members "adopt" a child; many take on several at a time. Often the child is one whose parent has died or gone to prison, or whose siblings are dealing drugs, or whose single mother neglects him. "We take these kids home with us for the weekend or out to eat or to get a haircut," says principal Clark. "School has to be about more than reading, writing and arithmetic. These kids need so much—and sometimes what they really need is a good hug."

In Clark's office the other day, Rashid Holbrook, 11, fidgeted with his wraparound shades and sought to explain why he had gone after a boy with an ax and spray painted a family's front steps. "I got a bad temper," he says. "When I get home at night, I pile up feelings." Rashid lives with an aunt who, Clark says, takes little interest in him. "My daddy's in prison," the boy says, showing little emotion. "He hit my momma. He went for breaking and entering and a hundred other charges." Interjects Clark: "But you're going in a different direction."

Rashid volunteers that he might be an engineer or a policeman. Why a policeman? "I don't like people doing things to other people," he says. And then after a long pause, "But I do it."

Rashid has been "adopted" by Clayton Singleton, 25, an art teacher. "We've been to art museums and shopping at the mall," says Singleton, pausing during a drawing class that sprawls over the floor of a corridor. "He was getting curious about the man-woman thing, so we had The Talk. Whatever questions he asked, he got the real answer." The talk was timely: only a few weeks before, Rashid had asked the daughter of another teacher if she wanted "to make a baby."

The key to Bowling Park's success, which has shown up in higher test scores and a 97% attendance rate, is getting parents into the school. Many of them had never bothered even to walk their first-graders to class. CoZi offers "parent technicians"—two in Bowling Park's case—to visit parents at home, ask them what they need and spur them to form committees and organize projects. Responding to parent feedback, Bowling Park now offers adult-education courses, adult-exercise classes, a once-a-month Family Breakfast Club at which parents talk about children's books, a singing group and a "room moms" program that puts parents into the classroom to help teachers. Parents also pressed the principal for school uniforms—and now help launder them. Bowling Park's programs are funded through a

> ## "We have fine buildings. Why let them sit vacant 14 hours a day and three months of the year?"

combination of federal funds set aside for inner-city schools, parent fees, private grants and school-district money.

"This is a holistic approach," says CoZi coordinator Lorraine Flood. "If parents are not sitting at the table, we don't find out the underlying reasons for children's academic or behavioral problems." When a mother of children at the school lost her husband to cancer recently, leaving her with six sons, parent technicians set up a workshop on grief. A welfare mother, who had put her child in foster care, found her self-confidence so built up by parenting and adult-education classes and her service in the PTA that she recovered her daughter and got a secretarial job. Recently parent techs held a wedding reception at the school for a mother who finally got married. A grandfather, inspired by a writing workshop, reads his poems at school functions.

But the lessons of Bowling Park, where the student body is overwhelmingly black and low income, are not just for schools that serve the poor. In fact, Zigler's concept of expanding school into a full-day, year-round enterprise is equally crucial to middle-class

parents at Sycamore Hills Elementary School in Independence, Missouri, where students are mostly white.

In Independence all 13 elementary schools work on the 21st Century model. Thirty-five percent of new parents take advantage of the state-funded home-visit program for children younger than age three. "We have fine buildings. Why let them sit vacant 14 hours a day and three months a year?" says superintendent Robert Watkins. "Now we can see a child with a speech impediment at age three and get started on remediation."

Once start-up costs were absorbed for remodeling school basements or buying modular units, the preschool and after-school day care became mostly self-supporting: 85% of the $2 million program comes from parents' fees. "Schools should be a community hub," says fourth-grade teacher Darlene Shaw. In three decades at Sycamore Hills, she has witnessed profound change. "Out of my 23 students today, only one has a stay-at-home mom," she said. "Without consistent, quality day care, kids flounder. And for kids dealing with divorce and single-parent families, school is their stability when things are going crazy at home."

Nicole Argo, one of Shaw's fourth-graders, has tried riding the bus home after school at 3:15 p.m. But she found she would rather stay in Sycamore's after-school program. "It's boring to watch TV at home," she says. "At 21st Century you do projects and go places." So Nicole's parents—an engineer and a human-resources officer—pick her up after work at 4:30—along with her five-year-old sister Amanda—and drop them both off each morning at 6:30, more than an hour before school begins. Nearly a third of Independence's students have a similar 10-hour day on campus. "It's Bobby's second home," says Laurie French, the divorced mother of a nine-year-old with muscular dystrophy. "The staff is like family, and since Bobby was three, we've done a pretty good job raising him together." Although he walks with difficulty, Bobby takes karate lessons in the program. And lately his favorite activity has been crochet, taught at the day-care center by a volunteer grandmother.

Independence and Norfolk have not experienced opposition to their reforms, but that does not mean every school district is ready for change. Overcrowded classrooms, pinched budgets and teachers set in their ways are only a few of the obstacles. Julia Denes, assistant director of Yale's Bush Center of Child Development and Social Policy, warns, however, that not adopting CoZi-like programs will ultimately cost more. "We must invest in children at an early age to prevent special needs and delinquency," she says. That's the message too of principal Clark's field trips.

Striving for Excellence: The Drive for Quality

The debate continues over which academic standards are most appropriate for elementary and secondary school students. Discussion regarding the impact on students and teachers of state proficiency examinations goes on in those states or provinces where such examinations are mandated. We are still dealing with how best to assess student academic performance. Some very interesting proposals on how to do this have emerged in the 1990s.

There are several incisive analyses of why American educators' efforts to achieve excellence in schooling have frequently failed. Today, some interesting proposals are being offered as to how we might improve the academic achievement of students. The current debate regarding excellence in education clearly reflects parents' concerns for more choices in how they school their children.

Many authors of recent essays and reports believe that excellence can be achieved best by creating new models of schooling that give both parents and students more control over the types of school environments available to them. Many believe more money is not a guarantor of quality in schooling. Imaginative academic programming and greater citizen choice can guarantee at least a greater variety of options open to parents who are concerned about their childrenís academic progress in school.

We each wish the best quality of life that we can attain, and we each desire the opportunity for an education that will optimize our chances to achieve our objectives. The rhetoric on excellence and quality in schooling has been heated, and numerous opposing concepts of how schools can reach these goals have been presented for public consideration in recent years. Some progress has been realized on the part of students as well as some major changes in how teacher education programs are structured.

In the decade of the 1980s, those reforms instituted to encourage qualitative growth in the conduct of schooling tended to be what education historian David Tyack referred to in *The One Best System* (Harvard University Press, 1974) as "structural" reforms. Structural reforms consisted of demands for standardized testing of students and teaching, reorganization of teacher education programs, legalized actions to provide alternative routes into the teaching profession, efforts to recruit more people into teaching, and laws to enable greater parental choice as to where their children may attend school. These structural reforms cannot, however, as Tyack noted as early as 1974, in and of themselves produce higher levels of student achievement. We need to explore a broader range of the essential purposes of schooling, which will require our redefining what it means to be a literate person. We need also to reconsider what we mean by the "quality" of education and to reassess the essential purposes of schooling.

When we speak of quality and excellence as aims of education, we must remember that these terms encompass aesthetic and affective as well as cognitive processes. Young people cannot achieve the full range of intellectual capacity to solve problems on their own simply by being obedient and by memorizing data. How students encounter their teachers in classrooms and how teachers interact with their students are concerns that encompass both aesthetic and cognitive dimensions.

There is a real need in the 1990s to enforce intellectual (cognitive) standards and yet also to make schools more creative places in which to learn, places where students will yearn to explore, to imagine, and to hope.

Compared to those in the United States, students in European nations appear to score higher in assessments of skills in mathematics and the sciences, in written essay examinations in the humanities and social sciences, and in the routine oral examinations given by committees of teachers to students as they exit secondary schools.

Policy development for schooling needs to be tempered by even more "bottom-up," grassroots efforts to improve the quality of schools that are now under way in many communities in North America. New and imaginative inquiry and assessment strategies need to be developed by teachers working in their classrooms, and they must nurture the support of professional colleagues and parents.

Excellence is the goal: the means to achieve it is what is in dispute. There is a new dimension to the debate over assessment of academic achievement of elementary and secondary school students. In addition, the struggle continues of conflicting academic (as well as political) interests in the quest to improve the quality of preparation of our future teachers, and we also need to sort these issues out.

No conscientious educator would oppose the idea of excellence in education. The problem in gaining consensus over how to attain it is that the assessment of excellence of both teacher and student performance is always based on some preset standards. Which standards of assessment should prevail? The current debate over excellence in teacher education clearly demonstrates how conflicting academic values can lead to conflicting programmatic recommendations for educational reform.

The 1980s and 1990s have provided educators with many insightful individual and commissioned evaluations of ways to improve the educational system at all levels. Some of the reports addressed higher education concerns (particularly relating to general studies requirements and teacher education), but most of them focused on the academic performance problems of elementary and secondary school students. From literally dozens of such reports, some common themes have developed. Some have been challenged by professional teaching organizations as being too heavily laden with hidden business and political agendas. The rhetoric on school reform extends to the educators in teacher education, who are not in agreement either.

What forms of teacher education and in-service reeducation are needed? Who pays for these programmatic options? Where and how will funds be raised or redirected from other priorities to pay for this? Will the "streaming and tracking" model of secondary school student placement that exists in Europe be adopted? How can we best assess academic performance? Can we commit to a more heterogeneous grouping of students and to full inclusion of handicapped students in our schools? Many individual, private, and governmental reform efforts did *not* address these questions.

Other industrialized nations champion the need for alternative secondary schools to prepare their young people for varied life goals and civic work. The American dream of the common school translated into what has become the comprehensive high school of the twentieth century. But does it provide all the people with alternative diploma options? If not, what is the next step? What must be changed? For one, concepts related to our educational goals must be clarified and political motivation must be separated from the realities of student performance. We must get a clearer picture of "what knowledge is of most worth."

Looking Ahead: Challenge Questions

Identify some of the different points of view on achieving excellence in education. What value conflicts can be defined?

Do teachers see educational reform in the same light as governmental, philanthropic, and corporate-based school reform groups? On what matters would they agree and disagree?

What are the minimum academic standards that all high school graduates should meet?

What are some assumptions about achieving excellence in student achievement that you would challenge? Why?

What can educators do to improve the quality of student learning?

Have there been flaws in American school reform efforts in the past 30 years? If so, what are they?

What choices ought parents and students have in their efforts to optimize the quality of educational services they receive?

What Matters Most

A Competent Teacher for Every Child

BY LINDA DARLING-HAMMOND

The report of the National Commission on Teaching and America's Future offers a blueprint for recruiting, preparing, supporting, and rewarding excellent educators in all of America's schools, according to Ms. Darling-Hammond. For the details, read on.

We propose an audacious goal . . . by the year 2006, America will provide all students with what should be their educational birthright: access to competent, caring, and qualified teachers.[1]

WITH THESE words, the National Commission on Teaching and America's Future summarized its challenge to the American public. After two years of intense study and discussion, the commission—a 26-member bipartisan blue-ribbon panel supported by the Rockefeller Foundation and the Carnegie Corporation of New York—concluded that the reform of elementary and secondary education depends first and foremost on restructuring its foundation, the teaching profession. The restructuring, the commission made clear, must go in two directions: toward increasing teachers' knowledge to meet the demands they face and toward redesigning schools to support high-quality teaching and learning.

The commission found a profession that has suffered from decades of ne-

glect. By the standards of other professions and other countries, U.S. teacher education has historically been thin, uneven, and poorly financed. Teacher recruitment is distressingly ad hoc,

and teacher salaries lag significantly behind those of other professions. This produces chronic shortages of qualified teachers in fields like mathematics and science and the continual hiring

LINDA DARLING-HAMMOND is William F. Russell Professor of Education at Teachers College, Columbia University, New York, N.Y., and executive director of the National Commission on Teaching and America's Future. She is a member of the Kappan *Board of Editorial Consultants.*

 From *Phi Delta Kappan*, November 1996, pp. 193-200. © 1996 by Linda Darling-Hammond. Reprinted by permission.

of large numbers of "teachers" who are unprepared for their jobs.

Furthermore, in contrast to other countries that invest most of their education dollars in well-prepared and well-supported teachers, half of the education dollars in the United States are spent on personnel and activities outside the classroom. A lack of standards for students and teachers, coupled with schools that are organized for 19th-century learning, leaves educators without an adequate foundation for constructing good teaching. Under these conditions, excellence is hard to achieve.

The commission is clear about what needs to change. No more hiring unqualified teachers on the sly. No more nods and winks at teacher education programs that fail to prepare teachers properly. No more tolerance for incompetence in the classroom. Children are compelled to attend school. Every state guarantees them equal protection under the law, and most promise them a sound education. In the face of these obligations, students have a right to competent, caring teachers who work in schools organized for success.

The commission is also clear about what needs to be done. Like the Flexner report that led to the transformation of the medical profession in 1910, this report, *What Matters Most: Teaching for America's Future*, examines successful practices within and outside the United States to describe what works. The commission concludes that children can reap the benefits of current knowledge about teaching and learning only if schools and schools of education are dramatically redesigned.

The report offers a blueprint for recruiting, preparing, supporting, and rewarding excellent educators in all of America's schools. The plan is aimed at ensuring that all schools have teachers with the knowledge and skills they need to enable all children to learn. If a caring, qualified teacher for every child is the most important ingredient in education reform, then it should no longer be the factor most frequently overlooked.

At the same time, such teachers must have available to them schools and school systems that are well designed to achieve their key academic mission: they must be focused on clear, high standards for students; organized to provide a coherent, high-quality curriculum across the grades; and designed to support teachers' collective work and learning.

We note that this challenge is accompanied by an equally great opportunity; over the next decade we will recruit and hire more than two million teachers for America's schools. More than half of the teachers who will be teaching 10 years from now will be hired during the next decade. If we can focus our energies on providing this generation of teachers with the kinds of knowledge and skills they need to help students succeed, we will have made an enormous contribution to America's future.

The Nature of the Problem

The education challenge facing the U.S. is not that its schools are not as good as they once were. It is that schools must help the vast majority of young people reach levels of skill and competence that were once thought to be within the reach of only a few.

After more than a decade of school reform, America is still a very long way from achieving its educational goals. Instead of all children coming to school ready to learn, more are living in poverty and without health care than a decade ago.[2] Graduation rates and student achievement in most subjects have remained flat or have increased only slightly.[3] Fewer than 10% of high school students can read, write, compute, and manage scientific material at the high levels required for today's "knowledge work" jobs.[4]

This distance between our stated goals and current realities is not due to lack of effort. Many initiatives have been launched in local communities with positive effects. Nonetheless, we have reached an impasse in spreading these promising efforts to the system as a whole. It is now clear that most schools and teachers cannot produce the kind of learning demanded by the new reforms—not because they do not want to, but because they do not know how, and the systems they work in do not support their efforts to do so.

The Challenge for Teaching

A more complex, knowledge-based, and multicultural society creates new expectations for teaching. To help diverse learners master more challenging content, teachers must go far beyond dispensing information, giving a test, and giving a grade. They must themselves know their subject areas deeply, and they must understand how students think, if they are to create experiences that actually work to produce learning.

Developing the kind of teaching that is needed will require much greater clarity about what students need to learn in order to succeed in the world that awaits them and what teachers need to know and do in order to help students learn it. Standards that reflect these imperatives for student learning and for teaching are largely absent in our nation today. States are just now beginning to establish standards for student learning.

Standards for teaching are equally haphazard. Although most parents might assume that teachers, like other professionals, are educated in similar ways so that they acquire common knowledge before they are admitted to practice, this is not the case. Unlike doctors, lawyers, accountants, or architects, all teachers do not have the same training. Some teachers have very high levels of skills—particularly in states that require a bachelor's degree in the discipline to be taught—along with coursework in teaching, learning, curriculum, and child development; extensive practice teaching; and a master's degree in education. Others learn little about their subject matter or about teaching, learning, and child development—particularly in states that have low requirements for licensing.

And while states have recently begun to require some form of testing for a teaching license, most licensing exams are little more than multiple-choice tests of basic skills and general knowledge, widely criticized by educators and experts as woefully inadequate to measure teaching skill.[5] Furthermore, in many states the cutoff scores are so low that there is no effective standard for entry.

These difficulties are barely known to the public. The schools' most closely held secret amounts to a great national shame: roughly one-quarter of newly hired American teachers lack the qualifications for their jobs. More than 12% of new hires enter the classroom without any formal training at all, and another 14% arrive without fully meeting state standards.

Although no state will permit a person to write wills, practice medicine, fix plumbing, or style hair without completing training and passing an examination, more than 40 states allow districts to hire teachers who have not met basic requirements. States pay more attention to the qualifications of the veterinarians treating America's pets than to those of the people educating the nation's youngsters. Consider the following facts:

- In recent years, more than 50,000 people who lack the training required for their jobs have entered teaching annually on emergency or substandard licenses.[6]

- Nearly one-fourth (23%) of all secondary teachers do not have even a minor in their main teaching field. This is true for more than 30% of mathematics teachers.[7]
- Among teachers who teach a second subject, 36% are unlicensed in that field, and 50% lack a minor in it.[8]
- Fifty-six percent of high school students taking physical science are taught by out-of-field teachers, as are 27% of those taking mathematics and 21% of those taking English.[9] The proportions are much greater in high-poverty schools and lower-track classes.
- In schools with the highest minority enrollments, students have less than a 50% chance of getting a science or mathematics teacher who holds a license and a degree in the field in which he or she teaches.[10]

In the nation's poorest schools, where hiring is most lax and teacher turnover is constant, the results are disastrous. Thousands of children are taught throughout their school careers by a parade of teachers without preparation in the fields in which they teach, inexperienced beginners with little training and no mentoring, and short-term substitutes trying to cope with constant staff disruptions.[11] It is more surprising that some of these children manage to learn than that so many fail to do so.

Current Barriers

Unequal resources and inadequate investments in teacher recruitment are major problems. Other industrialized countries fund their schools equally and make sure there are qualified teachers for all of them by underwriting teacher preparation and salaries. However, teachers in the U.S. must go into substantial debt to become prepared for a field that in most states pays less than any other occupation requiring a college degree.

This situation is not necessary or inevitable. The hiring of unprepared teachers was almost eliminated during the 1970s with scholarships and loans for college students preparing to teach, Urban Teacher Corps initiatives, and master of arts in teaching (MAT) programs, coupled with wage increases. However, the cancellation of most of these recruitment incentives in the 1980s led to renewed shortages when student enrollments started to climb once again, especially in cities. Be-

tween 1987 and 1991, the proportion of well-qualified new teachers—those entering teaching with a college major or minor and a license in their fields—actually declined from about 74% to 67%.[12]

There is no real system for recruiting, preparing, and developing America's teachers. Major problems include:

Inadequate teacher education. Because accreditation is not required of teacher education programs, their quality varies widely, with excellent programs standing alongside shoddy ones that are allowed to operate even when they do an utterly inadequate job. Too many American universities still treat their schools of education as "cash cows" whose excess revenues are spent on the training of doctors, lawyers, accountants, and almost any students other than prospective teachers themselves.

Slipshod recruitment. Although the share of academically able young people entering teaching has been increasing, there are still too few in some parts of the country and in critical subjects like mathematics and science. Federal incentives that once existed to induce talented people into high-need fields and locations have largely been eliminated.

Haphazard hiring and induction. School districts often lose the best candidates because of inefficient and cumbersome hiring practices, barriers to teacher mobility, and inattention to teacher qualifications. Those who do get hired are typically given the most difficult assignments and left to sink or swim, without the kind of help provided by internships and residencies in other professions. Isolated behind classroom doors with little feedback or help, as many as 30% leave in the first few years, while others learn merely to cope rather than to teach well.

Lack of professional development and rewards for knowledge and skill. In addition to the lack of support for beginning teachers, most school districts invest little in ongoing professional development for experienced teachers and spend much of these limited resources on unproductive "hit-and-run" workshops. Furthermore, most U.S. teachers have only three to five hours each week for planning. This leaves them with almost no regular time to consult together or to learn about new teaching strategies, unlike their peers in many European and Asian countries who spend between 15 and 20 hours per week working jointly on refining lessons and learning about new methods.

The teaching career does not encourage teachers to develop or use growing expertise. Evaluation and tenure decisions often lack a tangible connection to a clear vision of high-quality teaching, important skills are rarely rewarded, and—when budgets must be cut—professional development is often the first item sacrificed. Historically, the only route to advancement in teaching has been to leave the classroom for administration.

In contrast, many European and Asian countries hire a greater number of better-paid teachers, provide them with more extensive preparation, give them time to work together, and structure schools so that teachers can focus on teaching and can come to know their students well. Teachers share decision making and take on a range of professional responsibilities without leaving teaching. This is possible because these other countries invest their resources in many more classroom teachers—typically constituting 60% to 80% of staff, as compared to only 43% in the United States—and many fewer nonteaching employees.[13]

Schools structured for failure. Today's schools are organized in ways that support neither student learning nor teacher learning well. Teachers are isolated from one another so that they cannot share knowledge or take responsibility for overall student learning. Technologies that could enable alternative uses of personnel and time are not yet readily available in schools, and few staff members are prepared to use them. Moreover, too many people and resources are allocated to jobs and activities outside of classrooms, on the sidelines rather than at the front lines of teaching and learning.

High-performance businesses are abandoning the organizational assumptions that led to this way of managing work. They are flattening hierarchies, creating teams, and training employees to take on wide responsibilities using technologies that allow them to perform their work more efficiently. Schools that have restructured their work in these ways have been able to provide more time for teachers to work together and more time for students to work closely with teachers around more clearly defined standards for learning.[14]

Goals for the Nation

To address these problems, the commission challenges the nation to embrace a set of goals that will put us on the path to serious, long-term improvements in teaching and learning for America. The commission has six goals for the year 2006.

- All children will be taught by teachers who have the knowledge, skills, and commitment to teach children well.
- All teacher education programs will meet professional standards, or they will be closed.
- All teachers will have access to high-quality professional development, and they will have regularly scheduled time for collegial work and planning.
- Both teachers and principals will be hired and retained based on their ability to meet professional standards of practice.
- Teachers' salaries will be based on their knowledge and skills.
- High-quality teaching will be the central investment of schools. Most education dollars will be spent on classroom teaching.

The Commission's Recommendations

The commission's proposals provide a vision and a blueprint for the development of a 21st-century teaching profession that can make good on the nation's educational goals. The recommendations are systemic in scope—not a recipe for more short-lived pilot and demonstration projects. They describe a new infrastructure for professional learning and an accountability system that ensures attention to standards for educators as well as for students at every level: national, state, district, school, and classroom.

The commission urges a complete overhaul in the systems of teacher preparation and professional development to ensure that they reflect current knowledge and practice. This redesign should create a continuum of teacher learning based on compatible standards that operate from recruitment and preservice education through licensing, hiring, and induction into the profession, to advanced certification and ongoing professional development.

The commission also proposes a comprehensive set of changes in school organization and management. And finally, it recommends a set of measures for ensuring that only those who are competent to teach or to lead schools are allowed to enter or to continue in the profession—a starting point for creating professional accountability. The specific recommendations are enumerated below.

1. Get serious about standards for both students and teachers. "The Commission recommends that we renew the national promise to bring every American child up to world-class standards in core academic areas and to develop and enforce rigorous standards for teacher preparation, initial licensing, and continuing development."

With respect to student standards, the commission believes that every state should work on incorporating challenging standards for learning—such as those developed by professional bodies like the National Council of Teachers of Mathematics—into curriculum frameworks and new assessments of student performance. Implementation must go beyond the tautology that "all children can learn" to examine what they should learn and how much they need to know.

Standards should be accompanied by benchmarks of performance—from "acceptable" to "highly accomplished"—so that students and teachers know how to direct their efforts toward greater excellence.

Clearly, if students are to achieve high standards, we can expect no less from teachers and other educators. Our highest priority must be to reach agreement on what teachers should know and be able to do in order to help students succeed. Unaddressed for decades, this task has recently been completed by three professional bodies: the National Council for Accreditation of Teacher Education (NCATE), the Interstate New Teacher Assessment and Support Consortium (INTASC), and the National Board for Professional Teaching Standards (the National Board). Their combined efforts to set standards for teacher education, beginning teacher licensing, and advanced certification outline a continuum of teacher development throughout the career and offer the most powerful tools we have for reaching and rejuvenating the soul of the profession.

These standards and the assessments that grow out of them identify what it takes to be an effective teacher: subject-matter expertise coupled with an understanding of how children learn and develop; skill in using a range of teaching strategies and technologies; sensitivity and effectiveness in working with students from diverse backgrounds; the ability to work well with parents and other teachers; and assessment expertise capable of discerning how well children are doing, what they are learning, and what needs to be done next to move them along.

The standards reflect a teaching role in which the teacher is an instructional leader who orchestrates learning experiences in response to curriculum goals and student needs and who coaches students to high levels of independent performance. To advance standards, the commission recommends that states:

- establish their own professional standards boards;
- insist on professional accreditation for all schools of education;
- close inadequate schools of education;
- license teachers based on demonstrated performance, including tests of subject-matter knowledge, teaching knowledge, and teaching skill; and
- use National Board standards as the benchmark for accomplished teaching.

2. Reinvent teacher preparation and professional development. "The Commission recommends that colleges and schools work with states to redesign teacher education so that the two million teachers to be hired in the next decade are adequately prepared and so that all teachers have access to high-quality learning opportunities."

For this to occur, states, school districts, and education schools should:

- organize teacher education and professional development around standards for students and teachers;
- institute extended, graduate-level teacher preparation programs that provide yearlong internships in a professional development school;
- create and fund mentoring programs for beginning teachers, along with evaluation of teaching skills;
- create stable, high-quality sources of professional development—and then allocate 1% of state and local spending to support them, along with additional matching funds to school districts;
- organize new sources of professional development, such as teacher academies, school/university partnerships, and learning networks that transcend school boundaries; and
- make professional development an ongoing part of teachers' daily work.

If teachers are to be ready to help their students meet the new standards that are now being set for them, teacher preparation and professional development programs must consciously examine the expectations embodied in new curriculum frameworks and assessments and understand what they imply for teaching and for learning to teach. Then they must develop effective strategies for preparing teachers to teach in these much more demanding ways.

Over the past decade, many schools of education have changed their programs to incorporate new knowledge. More than 300 have developed extended programs that add a fifth (and occasionally a sixth) year of undergraduate training. These programs allow beginning teachers to complete a degree in their subject area as well as to acquire a firmer grounding in teaching skills. They allow coursework to be connected to extended practice teaching in schools—ideally, in professional development schools that, like teaching hospitals in medicine, have a special mission to support research and training. Recent studies show that graduates of extended programs are rated as better-prepared and more effective teachers and are far more likely to enter and remain in teaching than are their peers from traditional four-year programs.[15]

New teachers should have support from an expert mentor during the first year of teaching. Research shows that such support improves both teacher effectiveness and retention.[16] In the system we propose, teachers will have completed initial tests of subject-matter and basic teaching knowledge before entry and will be ready to undertake the second stage—a performance assessment of teaching skills—during this first year.

Throughout their careers, teachers should have ongoing opportunities to update their skills. In addition to time for joint planning and problem solving with in-school colleagues, teachers should have access to networks, school/university partnerships, and academies where they can connect with other educators to study subject-matter teaching, new pedagogies, and school change. The benefit of these opportunities is that they offer sustained work on problems of practice that are directly connected to teachers' work and student learning.

3. Overhaul teacher recruitment and put qualified teachers in every classroom. "The Commission recommends that states and school districts pursue aggressive policies to put qualified teachers in every classroom by providing financial incentives to correct shortages, streamlining hiring procedures, and reducing barriers to teacher mobility."

Although each year the U.S. produces more new teachers than it needs, shortages of qualified candidates in particular fields (e.g., mathematics and science) and particular locations (primarily inner city and rural) are chronic.

In large districts, logistics can overwhelm everything else. It is sometimes the case that central offices cannot find out about classroom vacancies, principals are left in the dark about applicants, and candidates cannot get any information at all.

Finally, it should be stressed that large pools of potential mid-career teacher entrants—former employees of downsizing corporations, military and government retirees, and teacher aides already in the schools—are for the most part untapped.

To remedy these situations, the commission suggests the following actions:

- increase the ability of financially disadvantaged districts to pay for qualified teachers and insist that school districts hire only qualified teachers;
- redesign and streamline hiring at the district level—principally by creating a central "electronic hiring hall" for all qualified candidates and establishing cooperative relationships with universities to encourage early hiring of teachers;
- eliminate barriers to teacher mobility by promoting reciprocal interstate licensing and by working across states to develop portable pensions;
- provide incentives (including scholarships and premium pay) to recruit teachers for high-need subjects and locations; and
- develop high-quality pathways to teaching for recent graduates, mid-career changers, paraprofessionals already in the classroom, and military and government retirees.

4. Encourage and reward knowledge and skill. "The Commission recommends that school districts, states, and professional associations cooperate to make teaching a true profession, with a career continuum that places teaching at the top and rewards teachers for their knowledge and skills."

Schools have few ways of encouraging outstanding teaching, supporting teachers who take on the most challenging work, or rewarding increases in knowledge and skill. Newcomers who enter teaching without adequate preparation are paid at the same levels as those who enter with highly developed skills. Novices take on exactly

the same kind of work as 30-year veterans, with little differentiation based on expertise. Mediocre teachers receive the same rewards as outstanding ones. And unlicensed "teachers" are placed on the same salary schedule as licensed teachers in high-demand fields such as mathematics and science or as teachers licensed in two or more subjects.

One testament to the inability of the existing system to understand what it is doing is that it rewards experience with easier work instead of encouraging senior teachers to deal with difficult learning problems and tough learning situations. As teachers gain experience, they can look forward to teaching in more affluent schools, working with easier schedules, dealing with "better" classes, or moving out of the classroom into administration. Teachers are rarely rewarded for applying their expertise to the most challenging learning problems or major needs of the system.

To address these issues, the commission recommends that state and local education agencies:

- develop a career continuum linked to assessments and compensation systems that reward knowledge and skill (e.g., the ability to teach expertly in two or more subjects, as demonstrated by additional licenses, or the ability to pass examinations of teaching skill, such as those offered by INTASC and the National Board);
- remove incompetent teachers through peer review programs that provide necessary assistance and due process; and
- set goals and enact incentives for National Board certification in every district, with the aim of certifying 105,000 teachers during the next 10 years.

If teaching is organized as are other professions that have set consistent licensing requirements, standards of practice, and assessment methods, then advancement can be tied to professional growth and development. A career continuum that places teaching at the top and supports growing expertise should 1) recognize accomplishment, 2) anticipate that teachers will continue to teach while taking on other roles that allow them to share their knowledge, and 3) promote continued skill development related to clear standards.

Some districts, such as Cincinnati and Rochester, New York, have already begun to develop career pathways that tie evaluations to salary increments at key stages as teachers move from their *initial license* to *resident teacher* (under the supervision of a mentor) to the designation of *professional teacher*. The major decision to grant *tenure* is made after rigorous evaluation of performance (including both administrator and peer review) in the first several years of teaching. Advanced certification from the National Board for Professional Teaching Standards may qualify teachers for another salary step and/or for the position of lead teacher—a role that is awarded to those who have demonstrated high levels of competence and want to serve as mentors or consulting teachers.

One other feature of a new compensation system is key. The central importance of teaching to the mission of schools should be acknowledged by having the highest-paid professional in a school system be an experienced, National Board-certified teacher. As in other professions, roles should become less distinct. The jobs of teacher, consultant, supervisor, principal, curriculum developer, researcher, mentor, and professor should be hyphenated roles, allowing many ways for individuals to use their talents and expertise without abandoning the core work of the profession.

5. Create schools that are organized for student and teacher success. "The Commission recommends that schools be restructured to become genuine learning organizations for both students and teachers: organizations that respect learning, honor teaching, and teach for understanding."

Many experts have observed that the demands of serious teaching and learning bear little relationship to the organization of the typical American school. Nothing more clearly reveals this problem than how we allocate the principal resources of school—time, money, and people. Far too many sit in offices on the sidelines of the school's core work, managing routines rather than improving learning. Our schools are bureaucratic inheritances from the 19th century, not the kinds of learning organizations required for the 21st century.

Across the United States, the ratio of school staff to students is 1 to 9 (with "staff" including district employees, school administrators, teachers, instructional aides, guidance counselors, librarians, and support staff). However, actual class size averages about 24 and reaches 35 or more in some cities. Teaching loads for high school teachers generally exceed 100 students per day. Yet many schools have proved that it is possible to restructure adults' use of time so that more teachers and administrators actually work in the classroom, face-to-face with students on a daily basis, thus reducing class sizes while creating more time for teacher collaboration. They do this by creating teams of teachers who share students; engaging almost all adults in the school in these teaching teams, where they can share expertise directly with one another; and reducing pullouts and nonteaching jobs.

Schools must be freed from the tyrannies of time and tradition to permit more powerful student and teacher learning. To accomplish this the commission recommends that state and local boards work to:

- flatten hierarchies and reallocate resources to invest more in teachers and technology and less in nonteaching personnel;
- provide venture capital in the form of challenge grants that will promote learning linked to school improvement and will reward effective team efforts; and
- select, prepare, and retain principals who understand teaching and learning and who can lead high-performing schools.

If students have an inalienable right to be taught by a qualified teacher, teachers have a right to be supervised by a highly qualified principal. The job began as that of a "principal teacher," and this conception is ever more relevant as the focus of the school recenters on academic achievement for students. Principals should teach at least part of the time (as do most European, Asian, and private school directors), and they should be well prepared as instructional leaders, with a solid understanding of teaching and learning.

Next Steps

Developing recommendations is easy. Implementing them is hard work. The first step is to recognize that these ideas must be pursued together—as an entire tapestry that is tightly interwoven.

The second step is to build on the substantial work of education reform undertaken in the last decade. All across the country, successful programs for recruiting, educating, and mentoring new teachers have sprung up. Professional networks and teacher academies have been launched, many teacher preparation programs have been redesigned, higher standards for licensing teachers and accrediting education schools have been developed, and, of course, the National Board for Professional Teaching Standards is now fully established and beginning to define and reward accomplished teaching.

While much of what the commission proposes can and should be accomplished by reallocating resources that are currently used unproductively, there will be new costs. The estimated additional annual costs of the commission's key recommendations are as follows: scholarships for teaching recruits, $500 million; teacher education reforms, $875 million; mentoring supports and new licensing assessments, $750 million; and state funds for professional development, $2.75 billion. The total is just under $5 billion annually—less than 1% of the amount spent on the federal savings-and-loan bailout. This is not too much, we believe, to bail out our schools and to secure our future.

A Call to Action

Setting the commission's agenda in motion and carrying it to completion will demand the best of us all. The commission calls on governors and legislators to create state professional boards to govern teacher licensing standards and to issue annual report cards on the status of teaching. It asks state legislators and governors to set aside at least 1% of funds for standards-based teacher training. It urges Congress to put money behind the professional development programs it has already approved but never funded.

Moreover, the commission asks the profession to take seriously its responsibilities to children and the American future. Among other measures, the commission insists that state educators close the loopholes that permit administrators to put unqualified "teachers" in the classroom. It calls on university officials to take up the hard work of improving the preparation and skills of new and practicing teachers. It asks administrators and teachers to take on the difficult task of guaranteeing teaching competence in the classroom. And it asks local school boards and superintendents to play their vital role by streamlining hiring procedures, upgrading quality, and putting more staff and resources into the front lines of teaching.

If all of these things are accomplished, the teaching profession of the 21st century will look much different from the one we have today. Indeed, someone entering the profession might expect to advance along a continuum that unfolds much like this:

For as long as she could remember, Elena had wanted to teach. As a peer tutor in middle school, she loved the feeling she got whenever her partner learned something new. In high school, she served as a teacher's aide for her community service project. She linked up with other students through an Internet group started by Future Educators of America.

When she arrived at college she knew she wanted to prepare to teach, so she began taking courses in developmental and cognitive psychology early in her sophomore year. She chose mathematics as a major and applied in her junior year for the university's five-year course of study leading to a master of arts in teaching. After a round of interviews and a review of her record thus far, Elena was admitted into the highly selective teacher education program.

The theories Elena studied in her courses came to life before her eyes as she conducted a case study of John, a 7-year-old whom she tutored in a nearby school. She was struck by John's amazing ability to build things, in contrast with his struggles to learn to read. She carried these puzzles back to her seminar and on into her other courses as she tried to understand learning.

Over time, she examined other cases, some of them available on a multimedia computer system that allowed her to see videotapes of children, samples of their work, and documentation from their teachers about their learning strategies, problems, and progress. From these data, Elena and her classmates developed a concrete sense of different learning approaches. She began to think about how she could use John's strengths to create productive pathways into other areas of learning.

Elena's teachers modeled the kinds of strategies she herself would be using as a teacher. Instead of lecturing from texts, they enabled students to develop and apply knowledge in the context of real teaching situations. These frequently occurred in the professional development school (PDS) where Elena was engaged in a yearlong internship, guided by a faculty of university- and school-based teacher educators.

In the PDS, Elena was placed with a team of student teachers who worked with a team of expert veteran teachers. Her team included teachers of art, language arts, and science, as well as mathematics. They discussed learning within and across these domains in many of their assignments and constructed interdisciplinary curricula together.

Most of the school- and university-based teacher educators who made up the PDS faculty had been certified as accomplished practitioners by the National Board for Professional Teaching Standards, having completed a portfolio of evidence about their teaching along with a set of rigorous performance assessments. The faculty members created courses, internship experiences, and seminars that allowed them to integrate theory and practice, pose fundamental dilemmas of teaching, and address specific aspects of learning to teach.

Elena's classroom work included observing and documenting the learning and behavior of specific children, evaluating lessons that illustrated important concepts and strategies, tutoring and working with small groups, sitting in on family conferences, engaging in school and team planning meetings, visiting homes and community agencies to learn about their resources, planning field trips and curriculum segments, teaching lessons and short units, and ultimately taking major responsibility for the class for a month at the end of the year. This work was supplemented by readings and discussions grounded in case studies of teaching.

A team of PDS teachers videotaped all their classes over the course of the year to serve as the basis for discussions of teaching decisions and outcomes. These teachers' lesson plans, student work, audiotaped planning journals, and reflections on lessons were also available in a multimedia database. This allowed student teachers to look at practice from many angles, examine how classroom situations arose from things that had happened in the past, see how various strategies turned out, and understand a teacher's thinking about students, subjects, and curriculum goals as he or she made decisions. Because the PDS was also wired for video and computer communication with the school of education, master teachers could hold conversations with student teachers by teleconference or e-mail when on-site visits were impossible.

When Elena finished her rich, exhausting internship year, she was ready to try her hand at what she knew would be a demanding first year of teaching. She submitted her portfolio for review by the state professional standards board and sat for the examination of subject-matter and teaching knowledge that was required for an initial teaching license. She was both exhilarated and anxious when she

received a job offer, but she felt she was ready to try her hand at teaching.

Elena spent that summer eagerly developing curriculum ideas for her new class. She had the benefit of advice from the district mentor teacher already assigned to work with her in her first year of teaching, and she had access to an on-line database of teaching materials developed by teachers across the country and organized around the curriculum standards of the National Council of Teachers of Mathematics, of which she had become a member.

Elena's mentor teacher worked with her and several other new middle school mathematics and science teachers throughout the year, meeting with them individually and in groups to examine their teaching and provide support. The mentors and their first-year colleagues also met in groups once a month at the PDS to discuss specific problems of practice.

Elena met weekly with the other math and science teachers in the school to discuss curriculum plans and share demonstration lessons. This extended lunch meeting occurred while her students were in a Project Adventure/physical education course that taught them teamwork and cooperation skills. She also met with the four other members of her teaching team for three hours each week while their students were at community-service placements. The team used this time to discuss cross-disciplinary teaching plans and the progress of the 80 students they shared.

In addition to these built-in opportunities for daily learning, Elena and her colleagues benefited from the study groups they had developed at their school and the professional development offerings at the local university and the Teachers Academy.

At the Teachers Academy, school- and university-based faculty members taught extended courses in areas ranging from advances in learning theory to all kinds of teaching methods, from elementary science to advanced calculus. These courses usually featured case studies and teaching demonstrations as well as follow-up work in teachers' own classrooms. The academy provided the technologies needed for multimedia conferencing, which allowed teachers to "meet" with one another across their schools and to see one another's classroom work. They could also connect to courses and study groups at the university, including a popular master's degree program that helped teachers prepare for National Board certification.

With the strength of a preparation that had helped her put theory and practice together and with the support of so many colleagues, Elena felt confident that she could succeed at her life's goal: becoming—and, as she now understood, always becoming—a teacher.

1. *What Matters Most: Teaching for America's Future* (New York: National Commission on Teaching and America's Future, 1996.) Copies of this report can be obtained from the National Commission on Teaching and America's Future, P.O. Box 5239, Woodbridge, VA 22194-5239. Prices, including postage and handling, are $18 for the full report, $5 for the summary report, and $20 for both reports. Orders must be prepaid.

2. *Income, Poverty, and Valuation of Non-Cash Benefits: 1993* (Washington, D.C.: U.S. Bureau of the Census, Current Population Reports, Series P-60, No. 188, 1995). Table D-5, p. D-17. See also *Current Population Survey: March 1988/March 1995* (Washington, D.C.: U.S. Bureau of the Census, 1995).

3. *National Education Goals Report: Executive Summary* (Washington, D.C.: National Education Goals Panel, 1995).

4. National Center for Education Statistics, *Report in Brief: National Assessment of Education Progress (NAEP) 1992 Trends in Academic Progress* (Washington, D.C.: U.S. Department of Education, 1994).

5. For reviews of teacher licensing tests, see Linda Darling-Hammond, "Teaching Knowledge: How Do We Test It?," *American Educator,* Fall 1986, pp. 18–21, 46; Lee Shulman, "Knowledge and Teaching: Foundations of the New Reform," *Harvard Educational Review,* January 1987, pp. 1–22; C. J. MacMillan and Shirley Pendlebury, "The Florida Performance Measurement System; A Consideration," *Teachers College Record,* Fall 1985, pp. 67–78; Walter Haney, George Madaus, and Amelia Kreitzer, "Charms Talismanic: Testing Teachers for the Improvement of American Education," in Ernest Z. Rothkopf, ed., *Review of Research in Education, Vol. 14* (Washington, D.C.: American Educational Research Association, 1987), pp. 169–238; and Edward H. Haertel, "New Forms of Teacher Assessment," in Gerald Grant, ed., *Review of Research in Education, Vol. 17* (Washington, D.C.: American Educational Research Association, 1991), pp. 3–29.

6. C. Emily Feistritzer and David T. Chester, *Alternative Teacher Certification: A State-by-State Analysis* (Washington, D.C.: National Center for Education Information, 1996).

7. Marilyn M. McMillen, Sharon A. Bobbitt, and Hilda F. Lynch, "Teacher Training, Certification, and Assignment in Public Schools: 1990–91," paper presented at the annual meeting of the American Educational Research Association, New Orleans, April 1994.

8. National Center for Education Statistics, *The Condition of Education 1995* (Washington, D.C.: U.S. Department of Education, 1995), p. x.

9. Richard M. Ingersoll, *Schools and Staffing Survey: Teacher Supply, Teacher Qualifications, and Teacher Turnover, 1990–1991* (Washington, D.C.: National Center for Education Statistics, 1995), p. 28.

10. Jeannie Oakes, *Multiplying Inequalities: The Effects of Race, Social Class, and Tracking on Opportunities to Learn Mathematics and Science* (Santa Monica, Calif.: RAND Corporation, 1990).

11. *Who Will Teach Our Children?* (Sacramento: California Commission on Teaching, 1985); and Linda Darling-Hammond, "Inequality and Access to Knowledge," in James Banks, ed., *Handbook of Research on Multicultural Education* (New York: Macmillan, 1995), pp. 465–83.

12. Mary Rollefson, *Teacher Supply in the United States: Sources of Newly Hired Teachers in Public and Private Schools* (Washington, D.C.: National Center for Education Statistics, 1993).

13. *Education Indicators at a Glance* (Paris: Organisation for Economic Cooperation and Development, 1995).

14. Linda Darling-Hammond, "Beyond Bureaucracy: Restructuring Schools for High Performance," in Susan Fuhrman and Jennifer O'Day, eds., *Rewards and Reform* (San Francisco: Jossey-Bass, 1996), pp. 144–94; Linda Darling-Hammond, Jacqueline Ancess, and Beverly Falk, *Authentic Assessment in Action: Studies of Schools and Students at Work* (New York: Teachers College Press, 1995); Fred Newman and Gary Wehlage, *Successful School Restructuring: A Report to the Public and Educators by the Center on Organization and Restructuring of Schools* (Madison: Board of Regents of the University of Wisconsin System, 1995); and Ann Lieberman, ed., *The Work of Restructuring Schools: Building from the Ground Up* (New York: Teachers College Press, 1995).

15. For data on effectiveness and retention, see Michael Andrew, "The Differences Between Graduates of Four-Year and Five-Year Teacher Preparation Programs," *Journal of Teacher Education,* vol. 41, 1990, pp. 45–51; Thomas Baker, "A Survey of Four-Year and Five-Year Program Graduates and Their Principals," *Southeastern Regional Association of Teacher Educators (SRATE) Journal,* Summer 1993, pp. 28–33; Michael Andrew and Richard L. Schwab, "Has Reform in Teacher Education Influenced Teacher Performance? An Outcome Assessment of Graduates of Eleven Teacher Education Programs," *Action in Teacher Education,* Fall 1995, pp. 43–53; Jon J. Denton and William H. Peters, "Program Assessment Report: Curriculum Evaluation of a Nontraditional Program for Certifying Teachers," unpublished report, Texas A & M University, College Station, 1988; and Hyun-Seok Shin, "Estimating Future Teacher Supply: An Application of Survival Analysis," paper presented at the annual meeting of the American Educational Research Association, New Orleans, April 1994.

16. Leslie Huling-Austin, ed., *Assisting the Beginning Teacher* (Reston, Va.: Association of Teacher Educators, 1989); Mark A. Smylie, "Redesigning Teachers' Work: Connections to the Classroom," in Linda Darling-Hammond, ed., *Review of Research in Education, Vol. 20* (Washington, D.C.: American Educational Research Association, 1994); and Linda Darling-Hammond, ed., *Professional Development Schools: Schools for Developing a Profession* (New York: Teachers College Press, 1994).

Using Standards to Make a Difference: Four Options

By Thomas P. Thomas

Prodded to completion by the *Goals 2000: Educate America Act,* voluntary national standards have been drafted for approval or for review in an astounding thirteen different disciplines. Heralded by policymakers as well as associations representing teachers, school administrators, school boards, and parents as the proper beginning for the effective transformation of our schools, the debate about what these standards should be is subsiding. Although pockets of dissent and contention remain on the particulars of the National Standards for History and the National Council of Teachers of English/International Reading Association Language Arts Standards, the overall work can now go ahead to consider how the standards are to be realized by all of America's students. The American Federation of Teachers declared, "Until you know where you're going, you won't know you've arrived. Goals 2000 gives us a destination—high standards for all students. . . ."

So now that we know where we are going, how are we going to get students there? What vehicle or vehicles will schools use to get all students to where we want them to be? The decision rests in part on how the standards are em-

A plan for standards implementation is presented with an intent to better students' educational experiences, not just increase test scores

Thomas P. Thomas, formerly a consultant for the Illinois State Board of Education in School and Student Assessment, is currently an assistant professor in the College of Education at Roosevelt University in Chicago.

 From *Educational Horizons*, Spring 1997, pp. 121-125. © 1997 by Thomas P. Thomas. Reprinted by permission.

ployed. Using the experience of Illinois as a case study, we will discuss four options for the use of standards: standards for advisement, for accountability, for curriculum design, and for the construction of artifacts. Which of these options are most likely to impact the lives of students? More important, will this impact lead to higher levels of learning and skill development?

Standards for Advising Curriculum and Instruction

In Illinois, a two-year initiative to develop the Illinois Academic Standards is coming to completion. A revision of the State Goals for Learning adopted by the state legislature in 1985 during the reform-minded days of *A Nation at Risk*, the new content standards were drafted by committees with attention given to the national voluntary standards. Why the need for revision? In part, it remedied limitations of the original state goals. Some goals (e.g., mathematics) were hastily developed and merited further refinement. Then there were political motivations. The original goals were drafted by fewer than 150 people, giving them limited buy-in from various stakeholders. The new content standards expanded involvement in authorship, if nothing else. The state board had recently appointed a new superintendent and new leadership demands high profile initiatives, such as revisiting what all Illinois students should know and be able to do. Further, Illinois wishes to continue to receive financial benefit from the federal Goals 2000 legislation. But perhaps the single most significant reason for revision: over the past decade, the 1985 State Goals for Learning—thirty-four general statements of what students should be able to know and do upon completion of schooling in six fundamental learning areas (biological and physical sciences, fine arts; language arts, mathematics, physical development and health; and social sciences)—had limited visible effect on what or how well students learned.

When the state goals were promulgated, the state board of education stipulated that all school districts attend to these goals by developing learning objectives derived from the broadly stated goals, and submitting learning assessment plans (bureaucratically labeled "LAPs") that indicated how students were performing in regularly (a four-year cycle or more frequently) meeting the objectives for the state goals. District superintendents asked for and received time to implement this assessment plan over a five-year timetable. LAPs were to be annually submitted. However, the state board quickly recognized it did not have the resources to review this documentation. The requirement for submission was replaced with a district superintendents's assurance that LAPs were maintained. Three years into implementation, the state agency realized that the LAP was a formality for many school districts. Re-

porting was often done through the agency of a commercial test publisher, and the state goals remained in the background of concerns for many school boards, administrators, and faculty.

One of the criticisms leveled against the goals was that their focus was too general. As such, they were not true guideposts to indicate the particulars of what schools were to teach. The NCTE/IRA Language Arts Standards have also been criticized as being more exhortation than specification. But specificity of itself does not ensure acceptance. Responding to the call for detail, the Illinois board of education produced a series of knowledge and skills statements and learning objectives specific to particular grades. This enhancement did not significantly advance the transformation of the schools. Whether general or specific, this "Field of Dreams" approach ("If you build it, they will come") has become suspect as a means to effect educational reform. How then can the states get school people to attend to standards?

Standards for Accountability

Enter state testing. Diane Ravitch speaks for a significant number of policymakers and school professionals when she states: "Standards alone are not likely to change anyone's behavior or expectations. Whether developed at the national or state level, standards must precede and be linked to student tests; for the standards to matter to teachers and students, the tests must be based on the standards. . . . If the standards form the basis for the state's testing program, they will not be ignored." Following the direction taken by numerous states, Illinois instituted state testing, the Illinois Goal Assessment Program (IGAP), in the late 1980s at various grade levels. IGAP expanded a program intended originally to sample student performance statewide in reading, writing, and mathematics to a school-accountability instrument. From 1990–92, panels of Illinois teachers were called in to set "cut scores" for tests in reading, writing, mathematics, science, and social science, indicators of whether students exceed, meet, or do not meet performance levels deemed appropriate for a student in the designated grade.

This statewide testing program established the use of the state goals for accountability. Schools were to be judged effective or ineffective in providing service to students in achieving the goals. Some states moved accountability beyond school accountability to individual student responsibility (e.g., Ohio). In legislation as well as the rules and regulations established by the Illinois Board of Education, a formula was determined: if more than 50 percent of students performed at the "does not meet" state standards level on the aggregate of tests, the school was to

be monitored by the state agency for improvement. If the school's improvement plan did not meet criteria for monitoring student achievement and indicate progress toward meeting state goals, the school was to be placed on an academic watch list. The intent of this further monitoring was to ensure that state testing was not the only measure used to determine the efforts of school personnel in providing service. Within three years of this legislation, the monitoring or "quality review" aspect of accountability was dropped and the state test became, as it is in many states, the centerpiece of accountability.

One lesson learned with the approach of testing to the standards and holding schools accountable for their students' academic performance was that the process often did not begin positively. Connecticut, California, and Kentucky all had to report bad news about the performance of their students in the first year that criterion-referenced testing tied to standards was administered. Fortunately for Kentucky, things improved

> *"Whether developed at the national or state level, standards must precede and be linked to student tests; for the standards to matter to teachers and students, the tests must be based on the standards. . . ."*

sufficiently in three years, with student performance shifting from the bottom two levels as the top levels increased.

In Illinois, testing for accountability appears to have had little effect. The move to the IGAP does not appear to have created a dramatic focusing by school people on state goals or widespread reforms. Although scores did improve in mathematics at all grade levels (a possible explanation is provided below), reading scores remained stable or actually decreased from 1993 to 1996. Student performance in reading in 1995 was so startlingly low that State Superintendent Joseph Spagnolo ordered a study to determine if the reading test was reliable. The review, although not flattering, revealed no technical problems with the instrument. The 1996 reading assessment offered no turnaround in student performance, with tenth-grade reading sliding to a new low.

> *Schools were to be judged effective or ineffective in providing service to students in achieving the goals.*

Does testing bring about a greater awareness of standards and does it induce restructuring of curriculum and instruction in line with the standards? It certainly serves notice to schools that are not performing well on state testing to do something. Unfortunately, this "something" is not always a critical reading of the performance standards that determine the test's construction and performance levels. The next step is reasonable if often unwelcome: if schools cannot determine what kind of curriculum and instruction they need for students to do well on the state test, the state can prescribe a curriculum and suggest instructional activities. Standards can facilitate this process as well.

Standards for Prescribing Curriculum and Instruction

Standards are used as a basis for drafting a state curriculum framework. California's framework for the disciplines, published in the early 1990s, has been perhaps the most visible and influential of the state curriculum guides. Kentucky also developed a curriculum framework to coordinate with its standards and assessment program. In Illinois, the state goals for learning were placed under review, and after two years of deliberation the Illinois Academic Standards were produced for public review and comment. Illinois' new academic standards, although not

as specific as California or Kentucky regarding instructional recommendations, do move distinctly toward prescription. The authors redefined the 1985 state goals, developed academic standards from these proposed state goals, and established learning benchmarks "as bridges between the stated standards and the measurements that will be used to determine achievement." This level of detail lets school administrators and teachers know at each grade level of testing what the state specifically expects students to know and be able to do. If students are to perform well on state assessments, school personnel will do well to heed the benchmarks.

Providing schools with a curriculum framework that aligns with state assessment inevitably affects the lives of students. The voice of the state is likely to be heard clearly in the curriculum choices and instructional activities demanded of teachers. But when one voice dominates, whose voices are stilled? It is improbable that teachers will complacently allow their voices to be quieted. In her study of four classroom teachers and their curriculum construction, Rebecca Killen Hawthorne effectively argues, "Faced with multiple, competing, and at times conflicting influences upon their instructional programs, classroom teachers pick and choose, depending on circumstances. . . . In such a manner, teachers translate curriculum potential into operational curriculum. . . ." If the stakes become high enough, however, a teacher might reluctantly concede some control of the curriculum to state prescription. This decision inevitably transforms the teacher's work with young people.

Can we be sure that this perceived "micro-managing" of the classroom is reform? Every teacher has particular topics or activities that is his or her passion for teaching or for sharing a given discipline. These showcase elements in the curriculum are selected by the teacher to provide not only knowledge and skills but to share their enthusiasm for what the community is learning together. The very best teachers have a full repertoire of these topics and activities. What is a teacher to do if the directives of a state framework in curriculum choices and instructional designs do not coordinate with the best pieces of a teacher's craft? And do students gain or lose from the decision to adhere to the framework?

The voices of students in curriculum construction (and in many classrooms) are already timid or quiet unless they rise up and speak in a rebellious if immature shout. How will the voice of the state impact on their contribution to the work of determining what is most important for them to know, to do, to share? Curriculum frameworks, then, are likely to make a difference—but is it a difference that we want to make in the classrooms of conscientious, creative, and dynamic teachers?

Standards for the Construction of Artifacts

Standards have also been used to design and re-design instructional artifacts: the tools, props, equipment, and agencies a teacher uses in conducting his or her craft. An artifact can range from something as mundane as a blackboard or overhead projector to a textbook, a lesson plan, a worksheet, or an Internet Web page. The production of recent textbooks demonstrates how standards can be used as specifications for the construction of an educational artifact. The National Council of Teachers of Mathematics Standards, used in the construction of California's curriculum framework, have clearly become the conceptual base for most of the elementary and high school mathematics texts published in the past half decade. California demands that all textbooks go through an adoption screen for eligibility to be sold to the public schools. Texas, another major adoption state, also has state standards that coordinate with the NCTM voluntary standards. School districts in every other state are now given the opportunity to purchase textbooks that are blueprinted around the demands of these two large-population text adoption states. Whether in science, social science, language arts, health, or the fine arts, teachers who rely on textbooks to determine their classroom activities are adopting a curriculum designed to address the standards of Texas and California.

> *Providing schools with a curriculum framework that aligns with state assessment inevitably affects the lives of students.*

The results? In Illinois, student performance on state testing in mathematics reveals a success story. The Illinois State Goals for Learning, both old and revised, also reflect the NCTM standards. Teachers in Illinois are using textbooks, a primary artifact, that coordinate with state standards, and more and more students are achieving these standards. Combined with a heightened public focus on mathematics, it could be argued that it is the textbooks that are helping to make the difference.

For some, this suggested correlation is disturbing. Recognizing the marketplace supremacy of adoption states over textbook production could lead a curriculum planner to despair. We can lament that many teachers depend on textbooks to drive their curriculum and instruction and that smaller markets cannot dramatically influence how textbooks are being written. Suggesting another direction, however, may provide hope. If artifacts can so dramatically direct teaching and learning, why not have teachers and students decide on the artifacts they want to use? In a democratic school, attention can be given to what artifacts, besides or even instead of the "sacred text," can be selected, modified, or invented that both allow the voice of the teacher and the voice of the students to be heard *and* address state standards. What projects can be devised, what performance-based assessments can be borrowed, adapted, or constructed, that authentically reflect the learning experiences students, teachers, and the state (expressed in standards) find significant? How can pre-service and professional-development workshops assist teachers in developing a full range of artifacts and facilitate their skills in using them?

Coming back one last time to the Illinois experience, a scoring rubric was developed precedent to state assessment on the dynamics of effective writing. *Write on, Illinois* was promulgated as an approach for teaching and evaluating student writing in workshops throughout the state. When state testing came on-line, the rubric was adopted for the assessment, and student performance has been responsive to the initiative. The success of this effort to improve student writing worked because it met a need. Many teachers found in the rubric and workshops a more effective tool for teaching and evaluating student writing. It also was a cost-effective tool. There was no need to dramatically restructure teaching or the classroom, nor did the effort demand a substantial resource commitment.

Bring tools into the classroom that will be authentic to the gathered community as well as to the state standards.

The proposal is for teachers to look at the standards not with a reactive perspective ("How will the state try to change the way I teach?") but with a proactive perspective ("What artifacts can I create or adopt with my students that will address these standards while allowing us the opportunity to learn together as a personal community?") Teachers and students should look around for artifacts that might be helpful—whether they be short stories, sets of discussion questions, cooperative group projects, pieces of video, simulations, procedures for journal writing, or science experiments. Bring tools into the classroom that will be authentic to the gathered community as well as to the state standards. If there is a conflict between the aspirations of the classroom community and state standards, consider together ways that this conflict might be creatively resolved. This is part of the craft of teaching: knowing how to find the tools, how to create some of the hard-to-find tools, how to make use of these artifacts in a way that responds to the group of learners that the teacher sees every day, and how to share these artifacts with others in the profession. It demands of the teacher (and those who provide resources to teachers in pre-service, administration, and professional growth) the commitment to be ever alert and receptive to new tools and to make critical and imaginative use of mandated artifacts.

Having found a voice in the classroom by using standards for accountability and prescription, states are not likely to let their influence wane. It is time to engage in imaginative and constructive dialogue, discovering artifacts that will allow for the passion of the teacher, at his or her best moments, to shine through while moving all students in the classroom community closer to the standards established by the wider educational, political, and social community.

1. "School Reform: Getting It Right," *American Educator* 18, no. 3 (Fall 1994): 13.

2. Diane Ravitch, *National Standards in American Education* (Washington, D.C.: The Brookings Institution, 1995), 24.

3. The IGAP does not assess in all state goals and it was expected that school districts would be responsible for evidencing in their school improvement plans how they were assessing fine arts, physical development and health and listening, speaking and student knowledge of literature and literary criticism. Like the earlier LAP system, many schools made no changes in the way they educate students in these areas and did not respond to the state charge.

4. Kentucky Department of Education, *Transformations: Kentucky's Curriculum Framework* (Frankfort, Ky.: Kentucky Department of Education, 1993).

5. *Preliminary Draft: Illinois Academic Standards* (Springfield, Ill.: Illinois State Board of Education, 1996).

6. Rebecca Killen Hawthorne, *Curriculum in the Making: Teacher Choice and the Classroom Experience* (New York: Teachers College Press, 1992), 5.

7. Illinois State Board of Education, *Write on, Illinois!* (Springfield, Ill: Illinois State Board of Education, 1994).

The Challenges of National Standards in a Multicultural Society

by Cherry A. McGee Banks

Ms. Banks argues that numerous considerations have not been addressed in the course of developing national standards.

Cherry A. McGee Banks is Associate Professor of Education, University of Washington, Bothell.

Since the late 1980s, national standards have been part of the discourse on school reform. An examination of that discourse reveals the extent to which the development and implementation of national standards have been shaped by forces that minimize the importance of diversity in U.S. society. Diversity is a salient characteristic of U.S. society. It is manifested in the racial and ethnic diversity of its citizens, their multiple identities, and the social-class positions they occupy. Developing and implementing national standards in a multicultural society should incorporate and give voice to diversity. When diversity is recognized as an important component of national standards questions such as "Whose Standards?" "Who benefits from the standards?" and "Whom will the standards harm?" will be raised by people outside the standards movement, but rarely by those within it.

When questions related to equity are raised by people inside the standards movement, they are addressed with a promise of high standards for all students. However, this promise will go unfulfilled if it is not accompanied by essential resources. In this article, I discuss the development of national standards and examine three types of standards: content, performance, and opportunity to learn. I then discuss multicultural literacy, a standard that is missing from the discourse on national standards.

From *Educational Horizons*, Spring 1997, pp. 126–132. © 1997 by Cherry A. McGee Banks. Reprinted by permission.

The Development of National Standards

The development of national standards can be viewed as a case study in the way to develop educational policy without recognition of the complex characteristics of U.S. schools and students. The developers of national standards, who used a "top down" approach, did not realize the extent to which state governments and local school districts would oppose attempts to direct school reform from the federal level. Nor were they prepared to provide funding to address the tremendous inequalities in the facilities, resources, curricula, and teachers in schools.[1] Most important, the purpose of schooling has not been a significant topic in the discourse on national standards. The assumption that schooling was essentially preparation for the world of work was such a fundamental part of the thinking of those framing national standards that it was rarely questioned. The idea that schooling should also be a means for developing democratic values and commitments to social justice and equity was rarely considered or discussed.[2]

The standards movement was officially launched in 1989 when President George Bush held an education summit for the nation's governors in Charlottesville, Virginia. The summit took place at a time when the manufactured reality that our schools were in a dire condition and that drastic action was required was widely accepted without question.[3] The lack of discourse about the multiple interpretations of student performance and the realities of U.S. schools resulted in a national obsession about fixing the nation's schools. There was increasing concern about the ability of U.S. students to compete in a global economy. Business leaders pointed out that the U.S. economy had undergone significant changes, but the nation's schools had remained essentially the same as they had been for most of the twentieth century. The perceived mismatch between schools and the needs of the economy was the focus of media attention. Books describing how bad U.S. schools had become and listing what every educated person needed to know became best-sellers.[4] Proposed solutions for fixing the schools included returning to the basics, developing a national curriculum, and using standardized tests to assess student knowledge.

Within this atmosphere, President Bush and the state governors proposed six goals to guide educational reform and to raise the achievement levels of all students by the year 2000. The goals, known as America 2000, moved national standards to the center of school reform discourse. To support America 2000, Congress created the National Council on Education Standards and Testing (NCEST) in 1991 to advise it on matters related to standards and testing. "Raising Standards for American Education," a report issued by NCEST in 1992, defined and affirmed the importance of content standards, performance standards, assessment, and opportunity to learn.

President Clinton, who attended Bush's education summit, began work on his own education program after he became president in 1993. His education program, which proposed voluntary goals for the states, was signed into law in 1994 as the Goals 2000: Educate America Act. Communities throughout the United States began using Goals 2000 to facilitate their own standards-based education improvements. In 1996, state governors joined with business leaders to issue a policy statement endorsing academic and performance standards. The policy statement, along with an appropriation bill that amended the Goals 2000: Educate America Act, was designed to strengthen the role of the states in the standards movement and to make standards more palatable to the conservatives who saw national standards as an expansion of the federal government's role in education. Language related to opportunity-to-learn and the National Education Standards and Improvement Council were eliminated from Goals 2000. Little, however, was done to assuage the concerns of educators who believe that standards can increase race and class stratification in U.S. society.

The Meaning and Possible Consequences of National Standards

National standards is a multifaceted idea. Three types of standards comprise national standards: content, performance, and opportunity to learn. Each type of standard provides different insights into the meaning and possible consequences of national standards. Some aspects of national standards focus on course content and teaching methods. Others focus on student performance; still others focus on factors that influence student achievement.

Content Standards

Content standards provide a structure to guide curriculum and instruction by framing core academic content areas in terms of what and how teachers should teach and what students should know and be able to do. Emphasis is put on students' developing an understanding of the key concepts and issues in the content area and being able to reason and communicate in ways that are characteristic of the discipline. Content standards have been developed in a number of disciplines, including history, science, and mathematics.

The National History Standards (NHS) are an example of content standards. The NHS, frequently misrepresented in the media as a school text, was a series of guide-

Little, however, was done to assuage the concerns of educators who believe that standards can increase race and class stratification in U.S. society.

lines for teaching U.S. and world history. The first version of the history standards was published in November 1994. Those standards were revised in the spring of 1996 and reduced from three volumes to one. Both versions were directed by Charlotte Crabtree and Gary B. Nash at the National Center for History in the Schools at the University of California, Los Angeles, and funded by the National Endowment for the Humanities and the U.S. Department of Education. The development of the history standards purported to be an objective approach for reforming schools. However, the response they received

tion of the standards by the U.S. Congress. Sen. Slade Gordon of Washington state led the attack on the history standards on the floor of the U.S. Senate. He argued that the standards were not balanced or objective because they emphasized what was negative in America's past and celebrated "politically correct" culture and causes.

The attack on the original version of the history standards and their forced revision raises the specter of political power coupled with intimidation, public attack, and humiliation as a means to create "official" history.[7] The original history standards were neither

the margins. Students need to understand how these struggles are reflected in quests for equality today. The discourse on the national history standards was shaped by forces that muted the importance of diversity in U.S. society. In arguing against the history standards, conservatives failed to recognize that U.S. history is the story of all its peoples, not just the powerful few who want school history to tell only their stories.

Opportunity to Learn Standards

Opportunity-to-learn (OTL) is a concept that was introduced in the 1960s by researchers who were trying to validate cross-national comparisons of mathematics achievement. These researchers recognized that achievement is complex and influenced by many factors. They identified three different levels of curricula that influence achievement: the intended curriculum, the implemented curriculum, and the attained curriculum. The intended curriculum is articulated by officials at the national level. The implemented curriculum is enacted by teachers in their classrooms. Student achievement on standardized tests provides evidence of the attained curriculum. Disaggregating the curriculum into three components reveals the extent to which education is a highly contextualized system and highlights the relationship between educational experiences and student achievement.

Are you saying, Senator, that after the thirty-seventh rewrite of this textbook, we should cut out some of the minor characters of American history to explain the importance of horses, pigs, and chickens?

upon their publication, which included political intervention and the privileging of conservative ideological perspectives, suggested otherwise.

The response to the NHS was immediate, bitter, and widespread. The NHS were perceived by conservatives as not focusing on what was most worth knowing in history.[5] Conservatives believed the NHS devoted too much space to women and people of color. Critics of the standards—many of whom are not historians—counted the number of times historical figures they admired were included in the standards. They concluded that major historical figures had been omitted or slighted in the NHS.[6] Conservatives called for the repeal of the NHS and the development of what they termed "true reliable national standards."

Even though the NHS were strongly supported by the two leading history professional associations, the American Historical Association and the Organization of American Historians, the attacks continued and eventually culminated in an official repudia-

as radical nor as irresponsible as they were described by their critics. They did, however, provide a framework for teachers and students to uncover unlearned lessons from the past and to study U.S. history from the perspective of the vanquished as well as the victors. The attacks on the history standards helped to maintain the established history curriculum and to halt efforts to legitimize the histories, voices, and experiences of groups who traditionally have been excluded from school history.[8]

Democracy requires citizens who understand that the development of the United States has not been a straight path to freedom, liberty, and justice.[9] Many groups of Americans have been victimized in the past and are still being victimized today. If we are to build a just society, we must give students opportunities to learn from our mistakes as well as to celebrate our victories. An authentic history of the U.S. must not only include the stories of people who are at the center of U.S. society; also it must include the historic struggles of people on

Opportunity to learn (OTL) is used by advocates of disenfranchised students to acknowledge the political and economic link between schools and society and to identify and demonstrate how factors such as income and access to knowledge, influence academic achievement. OTL is also used to identify how variables such as quality of school facilities, availability of teaching materials, and teacher expertise influence achievement. Language related to opportunity to learn was included in both America 2000 and Goals 2000. However, it was deleted from the 1996 budget bill for Goals 2000 and from the 1996 National Education Summit policy statement. Conservatives were able to argue successfully that OTL standards would take attention away from achievement and put the focus on resources or input variables. They took the position that OTL issues should be addressed at the state level, not directed by the federal government. As a result, addressing OTL factors will likely have a low priority as states and local school districts respond to the national standards. The money saved by deleting OTL standards from the national standards agenda will be paid for by sacrificing the futures of disenfranchised students.

OTL factors highlight the inequalities that exist in the educational experiences of many low-income students and students of color. For example, students who are placed in general or vocational tracks have limited access to college preparatory courses.[10] Students of color and low-income students are disproportionately represented in general and vocational tracks. In 1985, 51.5 percent of white students and only 28.1 percent of black and Hispanic students were enrolled in academic math classes.[11] Students who are tracked into college-preparatory courses have greater access to more challenging and rewarding curricula than students in lower tracks. Students in college-preparation tracks are disproportionately from advantaged socioeconomic groups. Moreover, important gate-keeping courses such as calculus are not available in many schools with large numbers of low-income students and students of color.

> *The discourse on the national history standards was shaped by forces that muted the importance of diversity in U.S. society.*

OTL factors also call attention to the differences in the quality and credentials of teachers of students who teach in central city schools and those who teach in middle-class suburban schools. Students in the central city are more likely to be taught by teachers who have less experience and who are less qualified than suburban teachers. In 1983, more than 14 percent of the new teachers in central cities were uncertified in their primary fields of instruction. This was almost double the percentage of such teachers in suburban districts.[12]

Schools in central-city schools have fewer resources and less funding than suburban schools. In *Savage Inequalities,* Jonathan Kozol describes a school that offered a computer course but did not have computers for students.[13] Disparity in funding among districts is especially evident when school districts that are primarily populated by upper-middle-class students are compared to school districts in which most of the students are from low-income families. For example, in the 1990–91 school year New York City, which has a large percentage of low-income students and students of color, spent $7,300 per student, while Great Neck, a nearby suburban school district, spent $15,000 per student.[14]

Given the tremendous disparity in educational resources and opportunities of U.S. students, it is understandable why OTL factors are embraced by advocates of disenfranchised students. OTL standards are very meaningful for low-income students, students of color, students who do not speak English as their first language, and other disenfranchised students. Disparity in the educational resources affects the course offerings, facilities, books, computers, labs, the quality of teachers, and the quality of teaching in the schools they attend. School reform efforts that do not acknowledge these disparities will fail.

Performance Standards

Performance standards provide concrete examples and explicit definitions of what students need to know and be able to do in order to demonstrate proficiency in the skills and knowledge specified by content standards. Most advocates of national standards believe that performance standards are a logical consequence of content standards and that content standards would be meaningless without performance standards. Therefore, as new curriculum frameworks are being developed, new assessments are also being developed. The New Standards Project developed and piloted performance tasks that are designed to provide information on what students know and can do. These tasks, sometimes referred to as authentic assessment, are also intended to improve teaching and curriculum. They include videotapes of performances, debates, exhibitions, teacher observations and inventories of student work, as well as other examples of student behavior

> *Therefore, as new curriculum frameworks are being developed, new assessments are also being developed.*

in real-world situations. Although these new approaches to assessment will be more closely aligned to the curriculum than in the past, they do not provide a means for educators and policymakers to differentiate levels of achievement in terms of OTL factors.

Proponents of performance standards claim that differentiating levels of achievement in terms of OTL factors is not necessary. They argue that performance standards are the best hope for low-income students and students of color because performance standards promote "high standards for all students." Without resources, that slogan will be an empty promise. Low-income students and students of color will be left to suffer the consequences of low performance on their own. Consequences such as grade retention, placement in remedial programs, and denial of diplomas can have a devastating impact on students. Moreover, these kinds of consequences are not only ineffective, they may serve as justifications for further exclusion.

Parents who are concerned about consequences that will likely be viewed as a confirmation of their students' low ability will have very few options available to them. They can talk to their children's teachers; have their children transferred to new schools; put their children in private or parochial schools; complain to the principal, superintendent, or school board; implement a tutorial program at home; or engage in some other form of action. All of these options assume that all students have informed active, and academically capable parents. Students whose parents face language, financial, or other barriers to active school involvement will not likely benefit from performance standards.

The lack of recognition and response to the connection between assessment and performance, perhaps more than any other aspect of the standards movement, raises historic and troubling concerns related to fairness, justice, and educational equality. Even though we know that unequal resources can affect quality of teachers, availability of advanced courses, the safety of the school environment, and other factors that can contribute to what students know and can do, performance assessments do not account for these factors. Without information on the factors that contribute to high and low performance, students from low-income families as well as many students of color may fall victim to historic beliefs about their genetic inferiority that are accepted by many educators. The success of *The Bell Curve* attests to the continuing saliency of beliefs about inherited ability and academic achievement.[15]

Highly motivated students who have high potential should not be penalized for factors in the school or community environment that are beyond their control. To be effective, assessments must consider the adequacy of re-

> *To be effective, assessments must consider the adequacy of resources when identifying what a student knows and can do.*

sources when identifying what a student knows and can do. In that way assessment will not simply be a way to identify what students know and can do. They will identify what students know and can do as a result of their educational experiences.

National standards will not substitute for needed resources and programs such as bilingual education. The number of students who do not speak English is increasing as the funding for bilingual programs is decreasing. In 1990, 14 percent of school-age youths lived in homes in which English was not their first language.[16] Parents whose children speak English poorly will be more interested in what the school is doing to teach their children English than their children's scores on tests that they had trouble reading.

The Missing Standard: Multicultural Literacy

In a society that continues to be deeply divided along race, gender, and social-class lines, students need to recognize and understand the historic and contemporary role of diversity in U.S. society. Multicultural literacy will provide a framework for teachers to develop course content that will challenge students to recognize the multifaceted and complex ways in which structural inequality continues to exist in U.S. society.[17] For example, even though many African-Americans have historically viewed education as a means to upward mobility, many inner-city African-American students know that an education will not necessarily result in a bet-

ter life.[18] They see many people in their communities who have a very difficult time securing gainful employment even when they have a high school diploma. In 1992, more than half of African-American high school graduates, compared to almost three-fourths of high school dropouts were unemployed. While less than twenty percent of white high school graduates, compared to mroe than one third of high school dropouts were unemployed.[19] White males and females are more likely to hire a white female over either an African-American male or female.[20] These data suggest that blacks have fewer economic incentives to stay in school than whites.

Racial incidents and gender discrimination are increasing in U.S. society and in the nation's schools. Prejudice and discrimination not only indicate the level of injustice in our society, they are also barriers to learning.[21] Multicultural literacy helps schools to resolve intergroup tensions in the schools and society and students to develop the knowledge, skills, and commitment needed to participate in personal, social, and civic action to make our society more democratic and just.[22] Teachers need support and further education to work effectively with students to reduce sexism, racism, and class inequality.

> *Many of the advocates of national standards seem prepared to abandon these students if they are not able to succeed against great odds.*

Multicultural literacy would provide a vehicle for schools to recognize the importance of educating the hearts as well as the minds of students. It would also provide a basis for students to think deeply about citizenship in a pluralistic democratic society and encourage students to engage in citizen action to extend the principles of freedom, equality, and justice. Multicultural literacy is needed to develop creative and reflective citizens who are prepared to compete in a global workforce, but who also have the skills, knowledge, and confidence to question the status quo and to work for social justice.[23]

Conclusion

The standards movement is our latest magic bullet in a long line of school-reform strategies. Standards provide a false sense of security by suggesting that we have found a way to cure our educational ills. However, the cure may prove to be more deleterious than the problems. The active involvement of politicians, commentators, and political appointees in what should have been a professional and academic endeavor raises questions about who constructs school knowledge and for what purposes. The almost exclusive focus on the relationship between schooling and the world of work potentially marginalizes subjects such as art, music, and foreign languages and raises the question of what knowledge will be privileged in the school curriculum. Most important, even though diversity is increasing in U.S. society, content that can help students become effective citizens in a pluralistic democratic society has been jeopardized by the standards movement. Many of the responses to the history standards questioned whether the roles of women and people of color should be integral parts of U.S. history.

National standards obscure more than they reveal. They divert attention from the realities of schools in low-income, rural, and urban communities. Those realities include schools with leaky roofs, limited access to advanced curricula offerings, and teachers who are overworked and underpaid. In the next few decades, the nation's schools will enroll increasing numbers of low-income students, students of color, and students who do not speak English as their first language. These students will need more than content and performance standards to increase their academic achievement and social success in school. Many of the advocates of national standards seem prepared to abandon these students if they are not able to succeed against great odds. If educators ignore how opportunities to learn influence student performance, these students are likely to be blamed for their academic failure and doomed to second-class citizenship.

1. Michael W. Apple, "The Dangers of a National Curriculum," *In These Times* 17 (November 15, 1993): 26–27.

2. James A. Banks, *Educating Citizens in a Multicultural Society* (New York: Teachers College Press, 1997).

3. David C. Berliner, Bruce J. Biddle, and James Bell, *The Manufactured Crisis: Myths, Fraud, and the Attack on America's Public Schools* (Reading, Mass.: Addison Wesley, Longman, 1996).

4. Diane Ravitch and Chester E. Finn, Jr., *What Do Our 17-Year-Olds Know?* (New York: Harper & Row, 1987) and E. D. Hirsch, Jr., *Cultural Literacy: What Every American Needs to Know* (Boston: Houghton Mifflin, 1987).

5. Lynne V. Cheney, "The End of History," *Wall Street Journal,* 20 October 1994, 26, and David W. Sax, "The National History Standards: Time for Common Sense," *Social Education* 60 (January 1995): 44–48.

6. Robert Cohen, "Moving Beyond Name Games: The Conservative Attack on the U.S. History," *Social Education* 60 (January 1995): 49–54.

7. Gary B. Nash and Ross E. Dunn, "National History Standards: Controversy and Commentary," *Social Studies Review* 34 (Winter 1995): 4–12.

8. Joyce Appleby, "Controversy Over the National History Standards," *OAH Magazine of History* 9 (Spring 1995), 4.

9. Arthur M. Schlesinger, Jr., *The Cycles of American History* (Boston: Houghton Mifflin, 1986).

10. Gretchen Guiton and Jeannie Oakes, "Opportunity to Learn and Conceptions of Educational Equality," *Educational Evaluation and Policy Analysis* 17 (Fall 1995): 323–336.

11. National Center for Education Statistics, *The Condition of Education* (Washington, D.C.: U.S. Department of Education, 1985).

12. Linda Darling-Hammond, "Inequality and Access to Knowledge," in *Handbook of Research on Multicultural Education,* ed. James A. Banks and Cherry A. McGee Banks (New York: Macmillan, 1995).

13. Jonathan Kozol, *Savage Inequalities* (New York: Crown Publishing, 1991).

14. Ibid.

15. Richard Hernstein and Charles Murray, *The Bell Curve* (New York: Free Press, 1994).

16. Committee on Developing a Research Agenda on the Education of Limited-English-Proficient and Bilingual Students Board on Children, Youth, and Families, *Improving Schooling for Language-Minority Children* (New York: National Academy Press, 1997).

17. James A. Banks and Cherry A. McGee Banks, *Handbook of Research on Multicultural Education* (New York: Macmillan, 1995).

18. William Julius Wilson, *When Work Disappears: The World of the Urban Poor* (New York: Knopf, 1996).

19. Antoine M. Garibaldi, "African-American Students as Dropouts," in *Encyclopedia of African-American Culture and History,* ed. Jack Salzman, David Lionel Smith, and Cornel West (New York: Macmillan, 1996), 181–184.

20. Luethel Tate Green, "Gender Differences and African-American Education" in *Encyclopedia of African-American Culture and History,* ed. Jack Salzman, David Lionel Smith, and Cornel West (New York: Macmillan, 1996), 181–184.

21. Claude M. Steele and Joshua Aronson, "Stereotype Threat and the Intellectual Test Performance of African Americans," *Journal of Personality and Social Psychology* 69, No. 5: 797–811.

22. Cherry A. McGee Banks and James A. Banks, "Teaching for Multicultural Literacy," *Louisiana Social Studies Journal* 16 (Fall 1989): 5–9.

23. Ibid.

The Case for National Standards and Assessments

DIANE RAVITCH

Education means to lead forth, but it is impossible to lead anyone anywhere without knowing where you want to go. If you do not know what you are trying to accomplish, you will not accomplish much. Content standards—what children are expected to learn—are necessary for educational improvement because they are the starting point for education. When educators fail to agree on what children should learn, it means that they have failed to identify their most fundamental goals. In the absence of such agreement by educators, decisions about what should be learned are left to the marketplace—textbook publishers, testmakers, and interest groups.

In 1994 Congress passed a law intended to begin the process of creating national content and performance standards (but not national assessments: states will continue to be responsible for assessment). Supporters of national standards in education make the following claims.

Standards can improve achievement by clearly defining what is to be taught and what kind of performance is expected. They define what teachers and schools should be trying to accomplish. They can raise the quality of

---

Diane Ravitch is senior research scholar in the School of Education, New York University, New York City. This article is excerpted from her book National Standards in American Education: A Citizen's Guide. *Copyright 1995, The Brookings Institution. Reprinted with permission. Copies of the book (list price $22.95) may be ordered by contacting The Brookings Institution at (202) 797-6258 or (800) 275-1447.*

education by establishing clear expectations about what students must learn if they are to succeed. If the goals of teaching and learning are spelled out, students understand that their teachers are trying to help them meet externally defined standards, and parents know what is expected of their children in school.

Standards (national, state, and local) are necessary for equality of opportunity. Standards establish the principle that all students should encounter the same educational opportunities and the same performance expectations, regardless of who their parents are or what neighborhood they live in. One essential purpose of standards is to ensure that students in all schools have access to equally challenging programs and courses of study, that expectations for learning are equally high for almost all children, and that all teachers are well prepared to teach.

National standards provide a valuable coordinating function. In the absence of explicit standards, the pieces of the educational system operate without coherence and often at odds with each other. Teacher education proceeds without sure knowledge of what is to be taught, giving rise to the frequent complaint that schools of education stress pedagogy and ignore content. In-service courses for current teachers focus on process and group dynamics, rather than building teachers' understanding of what they are to teach. The content of textbooks determines what is taught, and their content is based on the checklists of textbook adoption committees in big states such as California and Texas. Tests drive the curriculum, based on what testmakers think is being taught; teachers teach what they think is likely to be on the standardized tests that their students take. With teachers teaching to the test and using the textbook as their course guide, the textbook and test publishers—*faute de mieux*—define the curriculum and set the actual standards low enough so that every state can claim to be "above the national norm."[1]

Content standards make it possible to coordinate the various parts of the educational system to promote student learning. Teachers can use content standards to prepare their lessons. Textbook writers can use them to write materials for the schools. Colleges and universities can use them to prepare teachers so that they will know what they are expected to teach. Software designers can use them to create new technology that will teach what children are supposed to learn. Testing experts can use them as the basis for tests that children will take to determine whether or how well they have met the standards. Seen this way, explicit content standards clearly can become an organizing force for education, in which all the different pieces of the system are focused on the same goal: helping children learn at high levels of achievement.

There is no reason to have different standards in different states, especially in mathematics and science, when well-developed international standards have already been developed for these fields. International assessments of mathematics and science have identified clear parameters for what is expected of students at various ages. Why should state and local standards depart radically from international standards? In addition, because so many Americans move from state to state and from region to region, there is no justification for extreme variation among state educational standards.

Standards and assessments provide consumer protection by supplying accurate information to students and parents. Who would willingly send their child to a school where a full curriculum was not available, where few students enrolled in advanced classes, where teachers did not know their subject area, where expectations for achievement were low, and where student performance was consistently poor? Students and their parents have the right to know whether their school offers a full curriculum, appropriate facilities (such as a library and science laboratories), and a well-educated staff; how student achievement compares to other schools in the district and the state; and how their individual performance measures up to the school's expectations.

Standards and assessments serve as an important signaling device to students, parents, teachers, employers, and colleges. Standards tell everyone in the educational system what is expected of them; assessments provide information about how well expectations have been met. Standards tell students what they need to do to succeed in school; assessments tell them whether they are making progress. Assessments also tell employers and colleges whether high school graduates truly possess the necessary knowledge and skills for work or further study.

NOTE

1. John Jacob Cannell, *Nationally Normed Elementary Achievement Testing in America's Public Schools: How All Fifty States Are Above the National Average* (Daniels, West Va.: Friends for Education, 1987).

Teachers Favor Standards, Consequences ... And A Helping Hand

Last October, Peter D. Hart Research Associates, one of the country's leading opinion research firms, conducted a survey among a nationally representative sample of AFT teachers. The survey assessed teachers' experiences with and attitudes toward a range of educational issues, exploring two critically important areas in particular depth: classroom discipline and academic standards. The commentary that follows reviews the survey's main findings regarding academic standards.

CONSIDERABLE TIME was devoted in the survey to the area of academic performance and standards, with a particular emphasis on the issue of "automatic promotion," that is, promoting children who have not truly mastered the academic skills and knowledge of the previous grade level. The results show significant teacher discontent in this area.

- Teachers receive students each fall with widely varying levels of preparation, which is a significant barrier to effective teaching.
- Automatic promotion is the single biggest cause of the tremendous disparities in student preparation, and teachers feel that practice should end.
- Teachers acknowledge that they play a role in automatic promotion, but describe conditions that often make it the lesser of two evils—teachers need better alternatives than choosing between retention and automatic promotion.

Variations in student preparation.

Nearly three in five (59%) teacher members say that students arrive at the beginning of the year with such dif-

ferent levels of preparation that teachers must spend time reviewing old material so that less-prepared students are not left behind. This problem is particularly serious in urban areas, where more than 70% of teachers say that they must devote considerable teaching time to determining what students know and then trying to get the entire class to the same starting point. Even in nonurban schools, though, nearly one in every two (47%) teachers say that differentials in student preparation cause them to waste valuable teaching time.

Teacher members pinpoint three reasons why preparation levels are mixed. The first problem is teachers at earlier grades within the district teaching different materials and preparing students differently. This does not appear to be much of a problem for primary teachers (just 14% say this happens very or fairly often), but does pose a problem at the secondary level (36%). While only about one in ten suburban teachers cite this problem, twice as many rural teachers (22%) and nearly three times as many urban teachers (31%) do. The lack of curriculum standardization is further confirmed in a survey question regarding latitude in teaching, as more than three in five respondents report that teachers in their districts have "a lot of latitude" in deciding what to teach, within general guidelines set by the school or district.

The second cause of varying student preparation levels is students' transferring into new schools from outside districts. Secondary level teachers generally say that students changing districts (32% happens very or fairly often) is about as common a problem as intradistrict lack of standardization. In contrast, primary teachers cite district changes as the single most common cause of different preparation levels, with nearly half (46%) saying this happens very or fairly often in their school. Primary school teachers in urban areas, where families tend to be

From *American Educator,* Spring 1996, pp. 18-21. © 1996 by the American Federation of Teachers. Reprinted by permission.

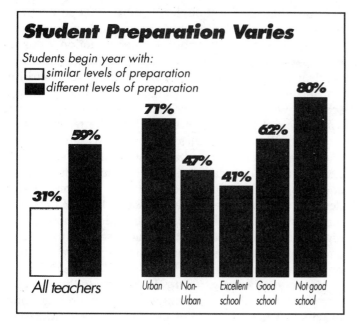

Student Preparation Varies

Students begin year with:
- ☐ similar levels of preparation
- ■ different levels of preparation

31% — All teachers (similar)
59% — All teachers (different)
71% — Urban
47% — Non-Urban
41% — Excellent school
62% — Good school
80% — Not good school

more transitory, face an especially tough challenge in this regard (54%).

The third and most important reason for inconsistent student preparation is that some students are promoted without truly mastering the previous grade's academic material, i.e., automatic promotion. This is a widespread problem, with two in five teacher members overall saying this happens very or fairly often. Especially alarming is the number of students in urban districts being inappropriately promoted. More than seven in ten (72%) teachers say they think over 5% of their current students (approximately one per class) were promoted without having mastered last year's academic material and skills, with 36% saying that more than one-fifth of their students are not adequately prepared (see the following table). In urban districts, the corresponding figures are 80% and 49%, meaning that for urban teachers today, it is commonplace to face a classroom filled with many academically unprepared students.

Teachers clearly do not view the problem of automatic promotion lightly. They universally believe that automatic promotion is harmful to education, as 94% agree (77% strongly) with the following statement:

> Promoting students who are not truly prepared creates a burden for the receiving teachers and classmates. Automatic promotion inevitably brings down standards and impedes education.

Causes of automatic promotion. Teachers recognize that they play a significant role in promoting students who are not truly ready for the next grade level. More than half (54%) of teacher members say that they have promoted unprepared students during the past year. Indeed, the top two reasons cited as causes of automatic promotion center on decisions being made by

teachers themselves that retention can be worse than promoting unprepared students.

Six in ten (61% major/minor cause of automatic promotion) teacher members fear that students repeating the same grade might create social and disciplinary problems for a class because they are then older than the other students. As mentioned previously, middle school teachers face more disciplinary problems than do teachers at other levels, so it comes as no surprise that a considerable majority of them (73%) cite this as a cause for automatic promotion. As we might expect, this reservation about retention is less of a concern at the high school level (48%). Male secondary school teachers also are disproportionately more likely to view concerns about po-

Students Promoted Without Mastering Materials or Skills

	All Teachers	Urban Schools	Nonurban Schools
	%	%	%
More than 20%	36	49	22
6% to 20%	36	31	41
5% or less	28	20	37

tential discipline problems as a reason for automatic promotion, with nearly seven in ten citing this as a cause, as opposed to only half of the female secondary school teachers surveyed.

Teachers are equally concerned (61% major/minor cause) that students are commonly promoted because many teachers believe that repeating a grade is not academically helpful for a student. Teachers in high school are again less likely to subscribe to this belief, with only half of them citing this as a major or minor cause of automatic promotion; presumably this is because teachers at this level can fail a student in a class without this necessarily leading to retention.

The core problem lying behind these decisions to reluctantly promote unprepared students is that teachers operate within a system that lacks sufficient alternatives to retention. Too often, they face a dilemma with no satisfactory solution: automatically promote, and burden a colleague with an unqualified student, or retain the student in a setting that does neither the student nor next year's class any real good. Teachers justify sending unprepared students on to the next grade level as, in essence, choosing the lesser of two genuine evils.

Fully half (52% major/minor cause) of those surveyed cite the lack of alternative settings, such as special classes or tutoring programs, as a factor in automatic promotion. While grade level does not seem to differentiate between availability of alternatives to retention, district area does. This is a major problem for urban teachers—they rank

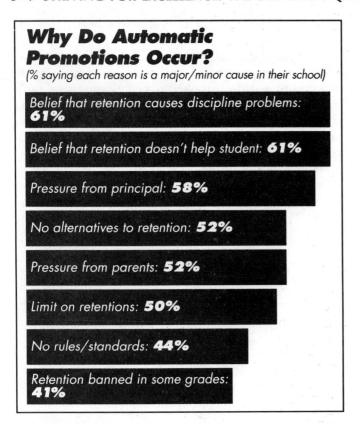

Why Do Automatic Promotions Occur?

(% saying each reason is a major/minor cause in their school)

Belief that retention causes discipline problems: **61%**

Belief that retention doesn't help student: **61%**

Pressure from principal: **58%**

No alternatives to retention: **52%**

Pressure from parents: **52%**

Limit on retentions: **50%**

No rules/standards: **44%**

Retention banned in some grades: **41%**

it nearly as highly (64%) as the two factors discussed previously—but is not as much of one for suburban teachers (36%). Teachers in rural areas and small towns fall somewhere in between these two groups in citing this as a problem (46%). In addition, male secondary school teachers (57%) are more likely than are female secondary school teachers (44%) to cite lack of alternatives as a cause, as are teachers under age 35 (62%) compared to those age 50 and over (48%).

Another cause of students being sent to the next grade without mastering the previous year's academic material is external pressure to promote. Unlike on the issue of discipline, however, school administrators are at least as culpable as are parents in this area. Six in ten (58% major/minor cause) respondents say that teachers in their school are pressured by principals and other administrators not to retain students, while 52% say parental pressure is a problem. Administration pressure is especially prevalent at the primary level, with two-thirds of elementary teachers citing this as a cause for automatic promotion. Male secondary school teachers (60%) also tend to believe pressure from principals and other administrators is a likely cause for automatic promotion more often than do their female counterparts (42%). Interestingly, while teachers also experience some external pressure from parents and administrators when it comes to giving out grades, this happens far less often than does pressure to promote. It is mainly when a student faces possible retention, apparently, that serious external pressure to relent on academic standards is brought to bear on teachers.

Somewhat smaller though still substantial proportions of teacher members cite school promotion and retention guidelines as a source of automatic promotion. Four in nine (44% major/minor cause) say that their school has no clear rules or standards for retention, so it is hard for teachers to justify not promoting a student (53% in urban schools). Other teachers say that there are rules, but the rules themselves are a problem: Half the teachers surveyed say that school rules do not allow them to retain more than a certain number of students, so some students who are not ready must be sent to the next grade, and 41% say that their school actually requires all students in certain grades to be promoted. Both of these are mainly problems in elementary and middle schools, with high school teachers citing them as lesser factors. Urban teachers also see these as more significant factors than do nonurban teachers.

Homework and grading. Responses to the survey's questions regarding academic workload and grading provide further evidence of insufficient standardization and slipping standards. About two in five respondents say that teachers in their school reduce the difficulty and amount of work they assign because students cannot or will not do it. Grade level affects whether or not teachers reduce homework assignments, with half of senior high school and 43% of middle school teachers saying this happens very or fairly often. Slightly smaller proportions of teachers at these grade levels say that colleagues in their own schools generally assign less homework than they believe is academically necessary and appropriate because they don't believe students today will do that amount of work (44% high school and 35% middle school teachers). Most teachers at all levels assign between two and five hours of homework per week, with an average of about three hours.

The survey also finds considerable variation in grading. A majority (63%) of teachers say that they have a lot of latitude in grading, with high school teachers especially reporting this to be true (74%). As a result, most teachers think that students in different classes who do the same quality of work often receive different grades. Most AFT teachers also agree that this use of different standards and grading systems in evaluating students results in confusion over what a grade really means. An overwhelming 85% majority agree that a grade should reflect real performance, and that students, teachers, and parents should all know what it means.

When asked how much weight they give to academic achievement, just 12% of teachers say that they award grades at the end of a marking period based solely upon achievement as opposed to effort, improvement, or other factors. Another three in ten say that 80% to 99% of a grade they assign reflects academic achievement, 41% cite a lower percentage, and 17% could not answer the question. Individual teachers also differ in their systems of grading, with more than half (58%) using an absolute standard and 25% grading on a curve.

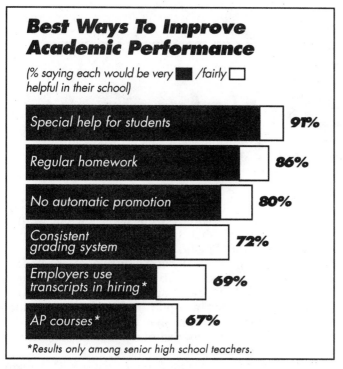

Best Ways To Improve Academic Performance

(% saying each would be very ■ /fairly ☐ helpful in their school)

Special help for students	91%
Regular homework	86%
No automatic promotion	80%
Consistent grading system	72%
Employers use transcripts in hiring*	69%
AP courses*	67%

*Results only among senior high school teachers.

THIS SURVEY was designed primarily to be a "census" of AFT teacher members, measuring their personal experiences with and underlying attitudes toward crucial educational problem areas. As such, it did not explore in any great depth support for policy options for dealing with these problems. Nevertheless, the research suggests two broad directions that schools must take to improve educational standards and achievement.

Bring more standardization and continuity to education. Teachers occupy an educational environment full of uncertainty and inconsistency. They cannot be certain what a new student has been taught or whether misbehavior will be punished. For schools to work the way they should, teachers believe this situation must change. The following are some of the key indications of teachers' desire for increased stability and predictability in their work environment.

- 53% of teacher members favor more standardization of what is taught at each grade level, so students would arrive at the start of the year with similar levels of preparation, even at the cost of teacher flexibility.
- 52% say that having a consistent grading system, based on achievement rather than a curve, would be very helpful in their school.
- 85% agree that a grade should reflect real achievement, and students, teachers, and parents should all know what a given grade means.
- 84% agree that consistent academic standards would reduce disruption in schools caused by educational fads.

- 96% feel that clear and consistently enforced discipline standards are a very or extremely important goal for schools today.

Raising student achievement requires both carrots and sticks. AFT teachers are broadly supportive of the union's focus on raising standards and increasing student accountability in the educational process. Teachers advocate a number of "tough love" measures to enhance achievement today.

- 86% believe that assigning regular homework and holding students accountable for its completion would be helpful in improving academic standards and performance in their schools.
- 80% of teachers feel that making promotion dependent on meeting real standards and ending the practice of automatic promotion would enhance achievement.
- More than half of teachers believe that having more employers use school transcripts in hiring would be very helpful in improving academic standards and performance.

More broadly, seven in ten teachers believe that student motivation and achievement would improve a great deal (48%) or a fair amount (23%) if there were *clearer consequences*—in terms of promotion, admission to college or trade school, and employment opportunities—for success or failure in meeting educational standards. The breadth of support for increasing the consequences for students is particularly striking, as large majorities of teachers at all grade levels, and in both urban and nonurban areas, support a move in this direction.

While getting tough is certainly a necessary step, teachers also clearly tell us that it is by no means a sufficient answer to today's educational challenges. Children will need a helping hand as well.

Fully 90% of AFT teacher members agree (72% strongly so) that the practice of automatic promotion means that students are not getting the help that they need in school. And the single reform that teachers say would be most important for improving standards and performance in their school (82% very helpful) is "providing special help for students who are not meeting academic standards in order to minimize the number of retentions." Support for this direction is widespread, as it ranks first among teachers at every grade level and in all district types. This serves as an important reminder that, while teachers want to uphold standards and demand accountability, their ultimate goal is not reprimanding failure but helping students to succeed.

Morality and Values in Education

Morality has always been a concern of educators. There has possibly not been a more appropriate time to focus attention on ethics, on standards of principled conduct, in our schools. The many changes in American family structures in the past 30 years make this an important public concern, especially in the United States. We are told that all nations share concern for their cherished values. We need to reexamine how best to teach students to be ethical decision makers. There are also substantive values controversies regarding curriculum content, such as the dialogue over how to infuse multicultural values into school curricula. On the one hand, educators need to help students learn how to reason and how to determine what principles should guide them in making decisions in situations where their own well-being and/or the well-being of another is at stake. On the other hand, educators need to develop reasoned and fair standards for resolving the substantive values issues to be faced in dealing with questions about what should or should not be taught.

There is frustration and anger among some American youth, and we must address how educators can teach moral standards and ethical decision-making skills. This is no longer simply something desirable that we might do; it has become something that we *must* do. How it is to be done is the subject of a national dialogue that is now occurring.

Students need to develop a sense of genuine caring both for themselves and others. They need to learn alternatives to violence and human exploitation. Teachers need to be examples of morally responsible and caring persons who use reason and compassion in solving problems in school. Further, there is no compromise necessary in maintaining classroom order and control. Cruel teachers will produce in their students the idea that it is "OK" to be mean and brutish when they are in authority. Our children need teachers who can be moral examples whom students can truly admire and respect. Such teachers will exemplify self-respect and self-discipline and will encourage these values in their students.

Some teachers voice their concerns that students need to develop a stronger sense of character that is rooted in a more defensible system of values. Other teachers express concerns that they cannot do everything and are hesitant to instruct on morality and values. Most believe that they must do something to help students become reasoning and ethical decision makers.

What teachers perceive to be worthwhile and defensible behavior informs our reflections on what we as educators should teach. We are conscious immediately of some of the values that affect our behavior, but we may not be as aware of what informs our preferences. Values that we hold without being conscious of them are referred to as tacit values—values derived indirectly after reasoned reflection on our thoughts about teaching and learning. Much of our knowledge about teaching is tacit knowledge, which we need to bring into conscious cognition by analyzing the concepts that drive our practice. We need to acknowledge how all our values inform, and influence, our thoughts about teaching.

Teachers need to help students develop within themselves a sense of critical social consciousness and a genuine concern for social justice. The debate on this issue continues in professional literature. Insight into the nature of moral decision making should be taught in the context of real current and past social problems and should lead students to develop their own skills in social analysis relating to the ethical dilemmas of human beings.

There is a need for teachers to develop principles of professional practice that will enable them to respond reasonably to the many ethical dilemmas that they now face. A knowledge base on how teachers derive their knowledge of professional ethics is developing; further study of how teachers' values shape their professional practice is very important. Educational systems at all levels are based on the desirability to teach certain fundamental beliefs as well as the disciplines of knowledge (however they may be organized in different cultures). School curricula are based on certain moral assumptions (secular or religious) as to the worth of knowledge—and the belief that certain forms of knowledge are more worthy than others. Schooling should not only transmit national and cultural heritages, including our intellectual heritage; it should also be a fundamentally moral enterprise in which students learn how to develop tenable moral standards in the contexts of their own visions of the world.

The controversy over teaching morality deals with more than the tensions between secular and religious interests in society—although acknowledging such tensions is valuable. Moral education is also more than a debate over the merits of methods used to teach students to make morally sound, ethical choices in their lives—although this also is critically important and ought to be done. We argue that the construction of educational processes and the decisions about the substantive content of school curricula involve moral issues as well.

One of the most compelling responsibilities of schools is that of preparing young persons for their moral duties

Teaching students to respect all people, to revere the sanctity of life, to uphold the right of every citizen to dissent, to believe in the equality of all people before the law, to cherish freedom to learn, and to respect the right of all people to their own convictions—these are principles of democracy and ideals worthy of being cherished. An understanding of the processes of ethical decision making is needed by the citizens of any free nation; thus, this process should be taught in a free nation's schools.

What part ought the schooling experience play in the formation of such things as character, informed compassion, conscience, honor, and respect for self and others? From Socrates onward (and, no doubt, before him), we have wrestled with these concerns. Aristotle noted in his *Politics* that there was no consensus as to what the purposes of education should be in Athens, that people disputed what Athenian youth ought to be taught by their teachers, and that youth did not always address their elders with respect. Our present situation is far more serious than the one Aristotle confronted in fifth century B.C. Athens. The issue of public morality and the question of how best to educate to achieve responsible social behavior, individually and collectively, are matters of great significance today.

The articles in this unit constitute an overview of moral education with considerable historical and textual interpretation. This unit can be used in courses dealing with the historical or philosophical foundations of education.

Looking Ahead: Challenge Questions

What is moral education? Why do so many people wish to see a form of moral education in schools?

Are there certain values about which most of us can agree? Should they be taught in schools? Why, or why not?

Should local communities have total control of the content of moral instruction in their schools, as they did in the nineteenth century? Explain your reasoning.

What is the difference between indoctrination and instruction?

Is there a national consensus concerning the form that moral education should take in schools? Is such a consensus likely if it does not now exist?

What attitudes and skills are most important for a responsible approach to moral decision making?

What can teachers do to help students become caring, morally responsible persons?

Finally, can virtue be taught (Plato's question)? If so, how?

as free citizens of free nations. Governments have always wanted schools to teach the principles of civic morality based on their respective constitutional traditions. Indeed, when the public school movement began in the 1830s and 1840s, the concept of universal public schooling as a mechanism for instilling a sense of national identity and civic morality was supported. Indeed, in every nation, school curricula have certain value preferences imbedded in them.

For whom do the schools exist? Is a teacher's primary responsibility to his or her client, the student, or to the student's parents? Do secondary school students have the right to study and to inquire into subjects not in officially sanctioned curricula? What are the moral issues surrounding censorship of student reading material? What ethical questions are raised by arbitrarily withholding information regarding alternative viewpoints on controversial topics?

Teachers cannot hide all of their moral preferences. They can, however, learn to conduct just and open discussions of moral topics without succumbing to the temptation to indoctrinate students with their own views.

Professional Ethics and the Education of Professionals

by Kenneth A. Strike

Plato opens the Meno[1] dialogue by asking whether virtue can be taught. He leads Meno through a discussion about the relationship between virtue, wisdom, and knowledge, and concludes with a discussion of whether it is possible to identify genuine teachers of virtue. Despite some pretenders—the sophists and the heads of some notable families—the dialogue concludes pessimistically that no genuine teachers of virtue have been found and that becoming virtuous seems more divine dispensation than instruction.

Professional schools in the United States have begun teaching professional ethics without having given much thought to Plato's concerns. Courses in professional ethics are widespread in medicine, law, and business, and instruction in professional ethics is increasingly common in education. My purpose here is to reflect on the aspirations of such endeavors with a special emphasis on educational professionals. I am partly motivated by Plato's concern. I wonder whether virtue can be taught. At least I doubt that it can be taught in courses in professional ethics. Perhaps we should aspire to something more modest than virtue.

A shared ethical language is key in focusing on ethical discussion rather than shared moral beliefs.

Kenneth A. Strike is a professor in the department of education at Cornell University.

From *Educational Horizons,* Fall 1995, pp. 29-36. © 1995 by Kenneth A. Strike. Reprinted by permission.

What professional ethics is supposed to be about for professional educators is puzzling.

I shall begin by telling three tales. The first is a thought experiment I have occasionally used to raise issues about professional ethics. I ask people to imagine that they are responsible for teaching a course in business ethics. They are also to imagine that, by some quirk of time, they have the young Ivan Bosky in their class. Their problem is to think of an argument with the power to persuade him not to engage in insider trading.

I place two restrictions on the task. I point out that the problem is not to persuade Bosky that insider trading is wrong. I stipulate that Bosky already knows this. The problem is to persuade him not to do what he knows to be wrong when he believes that he will substantially benefit from doing it. I also forbid threats. Bosky is to be persuaded to want to do what is right because it is right.

My most important reason for assigning this task is to persuade people to reflect on the connection between instruction in professional ethics and moral behavior. Another is to encourage them to reflect on their own goals for teaching ethics. A final concern is that the appropriate focus of professional ethics might differ depending on the professional area.

Consider a contrast between the role of ethics in medicine versus the role of ethics in business. The principal engine driving the concern for ethics in medicine is medical technology. Developments in medical technology generate new possibilities that demand an ethical understanding. Not only are these often life-and-death issues, but they are also intimately associated with money and lawyers. There is thus great incentive for moral reflection.

In contrast, fiscal misbehavior more than technological development generates concern for business ethics. The task is to dissuade business people from engaging in activities they know to be wrong, but which may be highly profitable. Thus, the emphasis shifts from moral complexity to moral motivation. For those of philosophical inclination who teach about ethics, this is not a trivial change. Philosophers often have much of interest to say about moral complexity. Their usefulness in motivating good behavior is less clear.

What professional ethics is supposed to be about for professional educators is puzzling. It seems doubtful that many new ethical puzzles are being generated by emerging educational technologies. Nor are teachers responsible for large amounts of other peoples' money. Although new moral agendas do occasionally wash up on educators' shores, they do not arrive amid swarms of dollars and lawyers. Moreover, they are frequently treated as policy issues to be decided by democratic discussion and not as matters for the professional determination of educators. Hot topics such as multiculturalism, AIDS, or gay rights are more likely to be viewed as matters for public debate than as matters of the ethics of a professional community.

Should we instruct educators in ethics to curb their moral abuse? Should we persuade them not to beat children, not to sell them drugs, or not to steal from their school districts? If so, we must face the problem of moral motivation. Motivating to goodness is not reasonably conceived of as persuading people that child abuse, drug pushing, or theft is wrong. Most educators know this, and those who do not are beyond the aid of philosophy. Are we to exhort to good behavior? If so, we will need to discover exhortations that actually motivate and that can be effectively made in a brief time in a classroom setting. I am not overly optimistic about such projects. Evil people are rarely made virtuous by good arguments or sermonettes.

Is there anything else we might do? To suggest what this something else is, I come to my second and third stories. I once coauthored a paper entitled "Who Broke the Fish Tank?"[2] This article discussed a teacher who, in order to discover the perpetrator of the destruction of the classroom fish tank and the untimely demise of its occupants, punished an entire class. The paper's purpose was to focus attention on the unfairness of group punishment. The journal in which the article appeared is targeted to teachers, who were asked to write in with responses. About twenty teachers responded. Their responses were noteworthy. For the most part, respondents viewed the problem as one of classroom management. They assumed that the sole end to be achieved was the establishment of order in the classroom and that this required the identification of the destroyer of the fish tank. Various proposals were generated for doing this. They ranged from fairly coercive to an emphasis on explaining the seriousness of the matter to the children.

Arguably, most of these teachers failed to identify any moral issues in this case. None of the teachers discussed the fairness of group punishment. Nor did they see a problem of nurturance emphasizing the moral growth of the children involved. Instead, they saw a "strategic" problem. They conceptualized the case as concerned with discovering effective means to the desired outcome of classroom order. They did not assess the desirability of the ends sought. They did not judge their preferred means by any standard of fairness. Nor did they question the means other than its effectiveness.

The third story: In one of my fall classes I gave an assignment that asked students to analyze a case in moral terms. A student came to my office to discuss a plagiarism case. Her concern was that I would not allow her to discuss the case from a religious perspective. After assuring her that I was not in the business of persecuting people for their religious convictions, I constructed the following interpretation of the problem. Imagine, I suggested, that you are a principal in a public school. Your task is not just deciding for yourself what is right in this case, it is also persuading the community that your decision is reasonable. Your community contains people with varied religious convictions and people with none at all. How will you persuade them?

My point was to persuade the student that in public contexts moral arguments need to be made in a "public language." I would suggest that a public language suitable for discussing the ethical issues of education should have at least three characteristics. First, it should have sufficient richness and sophistication to allow us to discuss educational issues cogently. Second, it must be a language the vast majority of competent moral speakers in a society can speak conscientiously, despite disagreements about fundamental convictions. Finally, it must be widely shared. Public speech is the common speech of a morally pluralistic society.[3]

I think that a public language adequate to the needs of public education should be composed of three kinds of sublanguages.

As educators we are in charge of children who need to be treated with kindness and compassion, who have needs and projects that must be respected, who need to grow and mature.

Seeking a shared language instead of shared convictions reduces the temptation to think of professional ethics as the transmission of ethical rules instead of a shared way of thinking through ethical issues.

First, we need a rights language. Educators need to be able to talk competently about due process, equal opportunity, privacy, and democracy. We need to understand how to apply the moral concepts that have been developed to regulate civic affairs to education. Education, after all, is a civic affair.

Second, we need a language of caring or nurturance.[4] As educators we are in charge of children who need to be treated with kindness and compassion, who have needs and projects that must be respected, who need to grow and mature. A language of nurturance and caring is required to discuss these matters.

Finally, we need a language of integrity about subject matter. Education deals not just with people—it deals with ideas. Teachers need to respect evidence and argument, they need to respect the values internal to their subject matters, they need an ethic appropriate to the life of the mind and the pursuit of truth.

Requiring educators' competence in this tri-part public moral language also implies a need for certain virtues, especially those of wisdom and judgment. These three sublanguages serve different purposes and can conflict. For example, is our primary goal in grading fairness? Then we need to talk about due process. We will need a language of rights. Is our purpose to encourage? Then we need to talk about nurturance. Is our purpose to promote intellectual growth? Then we must discuss the characteristics of evidence, argument, and criticism. Each orientation may be appropriate to grading. But fair grades may discourage. Encouraging grades may not provide intellectually stimu-

lating feedback. Educators need to know how to balance such concerns in particular cases. There are no firm rules, but judgments can be more or less sensitive to context and individual need.

The young lady whom I urged to consider persuading persons outside her faith seemed amenable to pursuing her project my way, but she was much puzzled about *how* to proceed. It turned out that she had wished to focus on forgiveness, which she thought was irredeemably religious in its character. I asked her whether she thought that a judge in a court of law could find sincere penance relevant in sentencing. She thought so. What followed was a long and complex discussion about the connections between penance, forgiveness, and punishment and how these concepts might be connected to the plagiarism case.

The paper that resulted was satisfactory, but more to the point, it was expressed in a set of widely shared moral concepts. Moreover, it included the elements of rights, nurturance, and intellectual integrity as relevant considerations. She was able to address the questions of fairness involved in making the judgment that plagiarism had occurred. Her concern for forgiveness allowed her to discuss the needs of the guilty student for a suitable form of nurturance—that engendered by repentance and forgiveness. Finally, she was able to discuss the importance of intellectual honesty in education. Thus concepts concerning rights, nurturance, and intellectual integrity were all involved. Moreover, because she was required to balance these concerns, she was called upon to exhibit the qualities of wisdom and judgment—to balance competing claims apart from definitive guidelines.

By suggesting that such concepts are widely shared, I do not mean that everyone would have agreed with either her argument or its conclusion. I mean that the concepts employed in constructing the argument would have been acceptable and intelligible to a range of people despite differences of religion or fundamental conviction. Few people would have been excluded from the discussion, because its very terms presupposed convictions that they could not share.

I believe that a language for educators consisting of concepts of rights, nurturance, and intellectual integrity meets my three criteria for a public ethical language. For this reason it is suitable for instruction in professional ethics. There is also considerable anecdotal evidence that educational professionals are not skilled in its concepts, which my second story should illustrate. The teachers who responded were unable to discuss the case by asking whether it is proper to punish without proof of wrongdoing or whether the punishment fits the offense.[5] Finally, teaching a public ethical language is a task that can plausibly be addressed in the classroom. It can be done effectively by us-

ing cases and suitable structured discussions thereof. It does not require us to believe that we can redeem character in the typical classroom setting. We are not trying to persuade people to be better or to be good. We are merely doing the kind of thing routinely done in the classroom. We are teaching a set of concepts and how they apply to their characteristic phenomena. I do not want to claim that this is all that professional ethics might be about, but it is at least a task that is both worthy and attainable.

Perhaps the reader has found my talking about moral languages an odd way to talk about the kinds of moral concepts that are important to teaching. One reason for this emphasis is its focus on ethical discussion rather than on shared moral beliefs. A moral language might be thought of as a set of concepts and argument strategies. Seeking a shared language instead of shared convictions reduces the temptation to think of professional ethics as the transmission of ethical rules instead of a shared way of thinking through ethical issues.

Thinking of teaching ethics as teaching a language also allows us to connect instruction in ethics to important points about how people learn to see and interpret their world. Consider an example from sport. Suppose that we wish to teach tennis. Teaching a sport requires more than a set of motor skills. To be able to play the game one needs to be able to describe it. To do so students will need such concepts as "serve," "volley," "backhand," "service line," and "ace." They will need to be able to construct such sentences as "The depth of her approach shots is the reason her net game is so successful." People who learn to say such things are also learning how to *see* the game. Concepts are perceptual categories. Those who lack the concept of serve and volley can observe ball swatting and net rushing, but cannot see a tactic in a game. Users of a common language, moreover, are also learning the standards of appraisal that pertain to the game. They are learning how to think about strategy and how to judge the aesthetics of the sport. Without the vocabulary, one cannot

Ethical concerns, when they are considered at all, are viewed as placing boundaries on acceptable means.

play the game. Without the vocabulary, there is no game. One may hit rubber orbs with stringed paddles, but one cannot serve aces or hit backspin lobs. The vocabulary constitutes the game. Learning to play requires learning to talk in a certain way. So it is also with ethics.

A final reason for this way of thinking about teaching ethics is that learning to speak a certain language is community constituting. When we learn a language—when we learn to think about and to see issues in certain ways—we begin to become part of a community. We begin to feel bonds with others like-minded people. We begin to understand them and they us. We begin to form habits of mind and ways of seeing the world that unite us in a common endeavor. And we may begin to acquire the wisdom and judgment required to apply the language deftly and to deal with children in morally enlightened ways.

Unhappily the opposite is also true. Where there is not ethical community, no community of shared speech, ethical language will atrophy. We must recognize that students are unlikely to acquire, maintain, and become sophisticated in the use of a suitable moral language unless that language is widely employed in their professional communities. People do not become proficient in languages that they do not use.

My second story provides some reason for concern here. Those teachers who responded to my queries seemed unable to address the issues employing the kinds of concepts that seemed to me to be appropriate. As I noted, their language might best be described as instrumental and strategic—as concerned solely with efficient means to unreflective ends. Concern for justice, nurturance, and intellectual integrity was not evident. Why not?[6]

Some possibilities are the kinds of research traditions that have tended to inform educational thought, the kinds of moral languages that have been popular in schools of education, and the authority structure of schools. In many contexts educators are taught to think of their practice as regulated by empirical research findings that inform them about successful means to achieve publicly identified goals. They are often discouraged from being reflective about the legitimacy or desirability of the ends, which are viewed either as private and subjective or as objects of public decision. Ethical concerns, when they are considered at all, are viewed as placing boundaries on acceptable means. In short the language is strategic and instrumental. Other educators have been taught to speak a moral language that speaks excessively about values, implicitly seeing all value issues as private and as matters of personal feelings. They may view any attempt to achieve a public understanding of what is right or best as a form of illicit imposition.[7] The importance and coexistence of

these two incommensurable and dysfunctional languages—neither of which manages to integrate the concepts of rights, nurturance, and intellectual integrity into the dialogue of educators in more than a superficial way—may explain much about the inability of educators to speak a more robust moral language in their practice.

Another obstacle may be the anti-dialogical authority structure of schools.[8] Teachers are rarely asked to engage in moral dialogue with other educational professionals about the ethical issues of their practice. Their practice is often solitary. When ethical issues burst beyond the classroom they may take the form of dealing with an angry parent and be adjudicated by an administrator, who in turn may be quite concerned for the opinion of the school district's lawyer. The hierarchical authority structure of schools means that they are not always places where educators have good and frequent opportunities to discuss ethical issues.

Although the ethical discourse of educators can be community constituting, we should also note that the idea of a public moral language is connected to the idea of democratic pluralistic societies as morally bilingual. There are, in our society, various moral languages associated with religious convictions, philosophical traditions, chosen life styles, ethnic group membership, culture, and personal history. I do not see the public moral language as either a competitor with or replacement for these various forms of moral speech. Indeed, I think that it is appropriate and necessary in liberal democracies that the moral speech of most individuals consist of one or more "particularistic" moral languages spoken to members of particular communities and a kind of common moral language spoken with those who may be strangers in public spaces.

One author has described public moral language as a moral pidgin,[9] a language for those who have "left home" and who need to discourse with others outside their primary community. It is not the moral language of church, family, ethnic group, or cultural tradition. In this sense it is a second language. John Rawls' characterization of his theory of liberal justice as an overlapping consensus[10] also assumes that many people already have a primary viewpoint to which they are attached, and that is the language of a particular community.

As Rawls, and many others, have argued,[11] any language that can function as an overlapping consensus must strive for a degree of impartiality between the various moral contenders and perspectives in society, and it must as a consequence be a "thin" language. It cannot express a viewpoint on every issue of human concern or ground itself in some vision of the ultimate purpose of human life. It must emphasize civic matters. God and the good are sidestepped. This necessary thinness of public ethical language

limits the extent to which it can be community constituting. No public community can be constituted by a moral conception as thick and robust as those that constitute many religious communities. Public communities must be thin, they must be consistent with much diversity, and they are unlikely to be the primary objects of allegiance of many of their members.

In a society whose moral life is characterized by this moral bilingualism, individuals are likely to find themselves engaging in an internal dialectic between their moral languages. They may have a need for moral integration. They are likely to seek assurance that in speaking the public moral language, they are not also subtly rejecting their most fundamental convictions. For example, I suspect that the young lady who wished to write on forgiveness routinely explains to herself that claims about human dignity are grounded in notions that we are all created in God's image. She will attempt to construct a religious interpretation of the point and meaning of the public ethic, and if she cannot, her attachment to it will be greatly weakened.

What this example suggests is that often the motivation to follow the precepts of the public ethic comes from attachments and values formed in primary moral communities and then transferred to the public domain. Constructing a public ethic eliminates many concepts that help people understand why they should be moral. Those concepts that link morality to religion or to any fundamental conception of the human good are privatized by constructing a suitably thin public ethic. The public ethic thus may simply lack cognitive resources to articulate why people should be moral. Much of what we might wish to say to the Ivan Boskys in our classes cannot be uttered in the public language.

These considerations mean that a liberal culture such as ours must seek to strike a precarious balance between its subsidiary moral communities and its public life, including that of its public schools. If the bonds with private moral communities are too strong or are articulated in certain ways, civic life may be torn apart by "sectarian strife." On the other hand, a society that seeks to live too much of its moral life inside a public morality may find that it has had to thicken this public morality so much that it has become intolerant of diversity.[12] The state becomes the servant of a nation, a people (Volk), and other peoples within its bounds become second-class citizens. Another possibility, however, is that a society might continue to have a thin public morality, but also behave in such a way that its private moral communities are weakened. In such a society the public ethic may lose its grip on peoples' allegiance because there are no moral communities into which people are initiated whose practices and commitments sustain such allegiances. I suspect that a society where the public morality is thin and non-public moral communities are weak should expect to find numerous Ivan Boskys in its professions. It is naive to believe that courses in professional ethics will do much to change this.

Thus there are numerous limits on what we can expect of instruction in professional ethics. Instruction in professional ethics can help people to begin to learn sophistication in public moral discourse. But this function is limited by the diversity and infelicity of speech forms in schools of education. It can be community constituting, but this is limited by the need to respect diversity. Although competent instruction in professional ethics may help to form those virtues of wisdom and judgment on which balanced moral reflections depend, such instruction is limited in its power. It is unlikely to form character deeply or to reform those who are morally damaged. Academic instruction in professional ethics has little redemptive potential. If the society wishes to protect itself from corrupt professional practice, it would do well to redirect its attention and its resources to the moral socialization of its children and to strengthening institutions that initiate the young into the practices and understandings of a sustainable moral life.

While I do conclude from this discussion that instruction in professional ethics is unlikely to do what the public thinks it is primarily intended to do, to cure serious wrongdoing, I do not think that it is a pointless activity. To get a picture of its genuine possibilities, we need to talk more broadly about the character of professional and moral socialization. Ultimately, we must come to think of professional ethics against the background of what Charles Taylor calls the dialogical character of human life. In Taylor's words, "We become full human agents, capable of understanding ourselves, and hence of defining our identity, through our acquisition of rich human languages of expression."[13]

Something like Taylor's view is presupposed in the little I have said about initiation into professional communities. Professionals achieve a sense of professional identity and a professional value system by engaging in dialogue with a professional community, during which time they acquire a language distinctive to the profession that contains, among other things, criteria, explicit and implicit, for making ethical professional decisions. Instruction in professional ethics needs to be thought about as part of the process of community formation in education.

1. Plato, *Meno* (New York: Bobbs-Merril, 1949).
2. K. A. Strike and J. F. Soltis, "Who Broke the Fish Tank? And Other Ethical Dilemmas," *Instructor* 95 (1986): 5, 36–39.
3. For a work that emphasizes teaching the language of rights see K. Strike and J. Soltis, *The Ethics of Teaching* (New York: Teachers College Press, 1992).
4. See N. Noddings, *Caring: A Feminine Approach to Ethics and Moral Education* (Berkeley: University of California Press, 1984).
5. Another illustration: A few years ago I attended a parents' night at a local school. The school was, at that time, engaged in a program called assertive discipline. This program involved writing names of student offenders on the board. I was struck that in classroom after classroom the teachers had not thought to erase the names from the board prior to the appearance of the parents. Moreover, several teachers took time to explain the point of the names. I was unable to detect any concern for the privacy or the confidentiality of this information. Moreover, when I mentioned the matter (politely—my child wasn't on the board that day), my concern attracted expressions of bewilderment from several teachers and from the principal.
6. Of course my survey was hardly scientific. Yet many observers have noted the lack of an adequate moral language among educators. See J. Goodlad, *Teachers for Our Nation's Schools* (San Francisco: Jossey-Bass, 1990).
7. See L. E. Raths, M. Harmin, and S. B. Simon, *Values and Teaching* (Columbus, Ohio: Charles E. Merrill, 1966).
8. See N. Burbules, *Dialogue in Teaching* (New York: Teachers College Press, 1993).
9. Jeffrey Stout, *Ethics After Babel* (Boston: Beacon Press, 1988).
10. J. Rawls, "Justice as Fairness; Political, Not Metaphysical," *Philosophy and Public Affairs* 17 (1987): 251–276.
11. See, for example, Bruce Akermann, "Why Dialogue," *Journal of Philosophy* 86 (1989): 1, 5–22.
12. Two examples of this may be the kind of "Civic Republicanism" that links a civic culture to a kind of "big tented" Protestantism (see R. N. Bellah et al., *Habits of the Heart* (New York: Harper & Row, 1985); and R. Pratte, *The Civic Imperative: Examining the Need for Civic Education* (New York: Teachers College Press, 1988) and the view that Americans are or should be a distinctive kind of people (see A. Schlesinger, *The Disuniting of America* (New York: W. W. Norton & Company, 1992).
13. Charles Taylor, *Multiculturalism and the Politics of Recognition: An Essay* (Princeton, N. J.: Princeton University Press, 1992), 32.

The Last Freedom:

Religion, the Constitution, and the Schools

Joseph P. Viteritti

JOSEPH P. VITERITTI, *a new contributor to* COMMENTARY, *is a research professor at New York University and the author, most recently, of "Choosing Equality: Religious Freedom and Educational Opportunity Under Constitutional Federalism," Yale Law & Policy Review, Fall 1996.*

THE DEBATE over the proper relationship between church and state, a debate as old as the Republic, has in our time taken on fresh intensity. The flashpoints range from abortion to the role of the so-called religious Right in American politics, but among the most delicate issues involved are those concerning education, in particular public support for private and parochial schools.

As is usual when it comes to education, much of the battle lately has been taking place on the local level. Thus, in 1990, at the urging of black parents frustrated with the wretched quality of the schools, a law was passed in Wisconsin making taxpayer-funded scholarships available so that poor families in Milwaukee could send their children to schools of their choosing, be they public or private; but when in 1995 the law was amended to include parochial schools, the Wisconsin supreme court held that this violated federal and state constitutional standards for the separation of church and state, and put a temporary stop to the program just before the school year was to begin. In Cleveland, Ohio, the constitutionality of a similar program was upheld by a state trial court, but is now under appeal. Meanwhile, in New York City, a brouhaha has erupted over the offer of the Catholic Archdiocese to take 1,000 of the worst-performing students in the public-school system and educate them in Catholic schools. The chancellor of New York's Board of Education, Rudy Crew, declared that he would accept the offer only if the Archdiocese found private funds to pay for the program, *and* if the schools involved removed any signs, indications, or lessons marking them as religious.

As in Milwaukee and Cleveland, the subject under discussion in New York quickly changed from the ills of public education to the establishment clause of the First Amendment ("Congress shall make no law respecting an establishment of religion") and what it signifies. And that requires us to take a quick look back at history.

The idea of a religious establishment had a quite specific meaning in 18th-century Europe, where it referred to a single official church supported by public funds. This was a condition common in many countries in which ecclesiastic and state authority were still closely intermingled, and where membership in the established church was required to hold public office or to be eligible for other social privileges. But in colonial America, owing to the distinct origin of each settlement, religious establishment took on a more ambiguous, and a more diffuse, significance. In most of New England, each town selected its own minister—usually a Congregationalist—and supported him with local taxes; New York, although favoring Anglicanism, was slightly more pluralistic; Rhode Island, Pennsylvania, Delaware, and New Jersey had no establishments at all; in the South, the Anglican establishment was replaced by a system of nonpreferential aid that taxed citizens to support the churches of their choice.

This pattern of diversity was carried over into the early decades of the Republic. By the time the First Congress adopted the Bill of

Rights in 1789, every state except Connecticut had a constitutional provision protecting religious freedom, but only in a limited sense. Six states granted the right to theists only; all but two required religious tests for public office; in some, the franchise was conditioned upon membership in a Christian church, and a person could be criminally prosecuted for not observing the Sabbath. But more important for our purposes is the fact that in almost all states, education was deemed inseparable from religious instruction, and responsibility for providing both resided with the clergy.

As it happens, the establishment clause of the First Amendment applied to none of these arrangements, being designed merely to prevent the establishment of a *national* church. And in the meantime, the same Congress that drafted the Bill of Rights also voted to support chaplains in the military and in both of its own houses, and used these words in reenacting the Northwest Ordinance and providing for a system of schools: "Religion, morality, and knowledge being necessary to good government . . . schools and the means of education shall forever be encouraged."

IT IS a measure of the distance we have traversed from such elastic early understandings that today's conventional wisdom should be the one reflected in many of the arguments put forward in the court cases in Wisconsin and Ohio and in the position adopted so reflexively by the New York City schools chancellor—namely, that an impenetrable "wall of separation" (in Thomas Jefferson's metaphor) is needed to protect government and religion from each other, and that the First Amendment enshrines that principle in constitutional law. To be sure, there are some legal historians who argue that the First Amendment was never intended to prohibit government support to religion so long as it was not limited to a single established church. But theirs is decidedly a minority view. Most contemporary scholars favor an interpretation of the First Amendment that proscribes any direct aid to sectarian institutions,* and over the last 50 years this interpretation has found its way into the reasoning of the Supreme Court.

The landmark opinion was written in 1947 by Justice Hugo Black, who in *Everson* v. *Board of Education* invoked the Jeffersonian metaphor

*See Leonard W. Levy, *The Establishment Clause: Religion and the First Amendment* (1994).

of a wall of separation to extend the strictures of the establishment clause from the federal government to the states. That decision, in turn, gave rise to a number of subsequent judicial actions regulating the relationship between religion and education. But not until 1971, in *Lemon* v. *Kurzman,* did the Court take a giant step by promulgating a three-part test, the so-called *Lemon* test, forbidding any government action in this sphere that (1) had no secular purpose; (2) had a "primary effect" of advancing religion; or (3) fostered "excessive entanglement" between church and state.

Two years later, in *Committee for Public Education* v. *Nyquist,* the Court invalidated a New York law that had offered tuition allotments for the poor and tax relief to parents sending their children to private and parochial schools. Focusing on the second prong of the *Lemon* test, the Court noted that "insofar as such benefits render assistance to parents who send their children to sectarian schools, their purpose and inevitable effect are to aid and advance those religious institutions."

Here, and in a whole string of other cases in the 1970's, a pattern was set whereby the wholly secular purpose of improving educational opportunities for disadvantaged children became entangled in the Court's preoccupation with preventing any benefit, however incidental, to church-connected schools. Not surprisingly, the resulting decisions were tortured in their reasoning and confusing in their effect. Thus, loans of textbooks by public-school systems to nonpublic schools were approved on the grounds that they could be considered a financial benefit "to parents and children, not to the nonpublic schools"— though even so, the Court worried lest the textbooks become "instrumental in the teaching of religion." But while lending textbooks was approved, lending instructional materials and equipment was deemed to have "the unconstitutional effect of advancing religion because of the predominantly religious character of the schools benefiting from the act." Again, although it was permissible to provide bus transportation to parochial schools, the Court found that states were under no obligation to provide the same level of service to public- and parochial-school students; in addition, a bus ride to a park or a museum *from* a parochial school was declared to be in violation of the Constitution. And so forth.

The ultimate message conveyed by all this convoluted decision-making, routinely justified on grounds of protecting religious liberty, was that public money allocated for education belonged not to taxpayers and their children but to the public-school "system." By definition, families wanting to provide their children with an education reflecting their religious values stood outside that system and its aims, and were entitled to none of its benefits.

T HE ECONOMIC disadvantage at which this put religious families was one thing, and perhaps could be regarded by them as a price that had to be paid. But something else has been going on in recent decades which, in the name of religious freedom, has amounted to a positive infringement on *their* freedom: namely, the transformation of the public schools into vehicles of a secularist orthodoxy which is not merely neutral on questions of religious faith and values but positively hostile.

Consider, for example, the predicament of religious parents in New York City who cannot afford a private religious education and whose children therefore end up in the public schools. Several years ago, such parents were confronted with a new sex-education program that involved the distribution of condoms. When the program was implemented, a number of Catholic and Jewish groups pleaded for "opt-out" alternatives, so that their children would not have to be subjected to teachings which actively violated the precepts of their respective religions. To this, the Board of Education turned a deaf ear: for parents offended by the program, the only "opt-out" provision was to leave the public-school system altogether and exercise their religious freedom at their own expense—or, to put it more accurately, to accept a significant financial penalty, imposed by the state, for holding their religious beliefs in the first place.

Although the program in question has since been revised, the militantly secularist ethos embodied in it remains an animating factor in public education throughout the country, protected by a whole line of Supreme Court decisions. Nor is this all: in a period in which, under the banner of multiculturalism, educators have gone to the ends of the earth to show "sensitivity" to minorities defined by race, ethnicity, and sexual orientation, the line of tolerance has been peremptorily drawn at individuals whose identity is defined by faith.

Fortunately, however, that is not quite the whole story. Not only are local initiatives like the ones in Wisconsin, Ohio, and New York City becoming more common, whatever tem-

porary setbacks they may encounter, but the Supreme Court itself has entered upon a reconsideration of its jurisprudence. I would trace the beginning of the change to 1983, when, in *Meuller* v. *Allen*, the Court upheld a Minnesota statute granting a tax deduction to families for expenses incurred for tuition, textbooks, and transportation. The relief was made available to *all* parents, regardless of whether their children attended public, private, or parochial schools.

This decision was notable not only because it validated benefits for parochial-school parents, but for two other reasons as well: it drew a distinction between direct and indirect aid to religious institutions (the former being prohibited, the latter permitted), *and* it endorsed the concept of parental choice. Writing for the majority, Justice William Rehnquist asserted that

> aid to parochial schools [was being made] available only as a result of decisions of individual parents . . . [and] no "imprimatur of state approval" . . . . can be deemed to have been conferred on any particular religion, or on religion generally.

While recognizing that most of the parents who had taken advantage of the program sent their children to Catholic schools, Rehnquist, who was about to become Chief Justice, deemed that it was time to relax the "primary-effect" prong of the *Lemon* test.

Continuing the line of *Meuller*, a unanimous Court ruled in 1986 that the First Amendment was not violated when a (blind) student used a public scholarship to attend a Bible college. In 1990, the Court held that public schools must allow student religious clubs to meet on campus under the same terms as other clubs; to do otherwise, the Court reasoned, would violate First Amendment freedom-of-association and free-exercise-of-religion rights (as well as the Fourteenth Amendment), and would demonstrate "not neutrality but hostility toward religion." In 1993, the Court upheld the right of a Catholic high-school student to receive the services of a sign-language interpreter at public expense. And in 1995 the Court rejected an attempt by the University of Virginia to exclude a student newspaper with a religious message from the services and benefits that were awarded to other student organizations on campus.

All in all, the First Amendment jurisprudence that has been evolving over the last fifteen years suggests a shift in balance, with the

Court relaxing the strict approach to the Amendment's establishment clause that prevailed in the prior decade and relying more heavily on the clause immediately following it, the one which guarantees "free exercise." In the University of Virginia case, Justice Anthony Kennedy distinguished neatly between "government speech endorsing religion, which the establishment clause forbids, and private speech endorsing religion, which the free-exercise clause protects." In so doing, the Court has also begun to set standards that would permit the government to support school choice if three criteria are met:

1. Public aid is given to an individual parent or student rather than to an institution.

2. Any benefit accrued by an institution is the result of individual choices made by the parent or student.

3. Aid is appropriated on a religiously neutral basis to those who attend private and parochial schools as well as to those who attend public schools.

OPPONENTS OF this trend say that it represents an aberration from the Court's by-now longstanding tradition of maintaining a wall of separation between church and state. In fact, however, the opposite is true: what is going on is more akin to a restoration. *Everson* notwithstanding, up until the early 1970's the Supreme Court was clearly accommodationist on this issue, and was especially sympathetic to the rights of parents wishing to determine the kind of schooling their children would have. As early as 1925, the Court supported parental prerogatives in the face of a compulsory-education law (itself motivated by anti-Catholic sentiment) that would have required all children in Oregon to attend public school. As the Court explained in *Pierre* v. *Society of Sisters:*

> The child is not the mere creature of the state; those who nurture him and direct his destiny have the right, coupled with the high duty, to recognize and prepare him for additional obligations.

Five years later, in *Cochran* v. *Board of Education,* upholding a Louisiana law that set aside tax funds to supply textbooks for children in public, private, and parochial schools, the Court enunciated a "child-benefit theory": although some of the participating students attended sectarian institutions, nevertheless "the schoolchildren and the state alone are the beneficiaries."

Even *Everson* is less clear-cut than strict separationists make it out to be. In addition to containing Justice Black's edict on the wall of separation, the decision supported the right of parochial-school children to receive transportation services at public expense. To be consistent with the establishment clause of the First Amendment, wrote the majority, the state of New Jersey could not "contribute tax funds to the support of an institution which teaches the tenets of faith of any church." But, on the other hand, the Court went on:

> [O]ther language of the Amendment commands that New Jersey cannot hamper its citizens in the free exercise of their own religion. Consequently, it cannot exclude Catholics, Lutherans, Mohammedans, Baptists, Jews, Methodists, Nonbelievers, Presbyterians, or the members of any faith, because of their faith or lack of it, from receiving the benefits of public-welfare legislation.

Finally, in 1970, just one year prior to issuing the *Lemon* standard, the Court upheld tax exemptions for religious institutions and endorsed the principle of "benevolent neutrality" as opposed to total separation (*Walz* v. *Tax Commission*). Even the *Lemon* opinion itself contains language that should be discomfiting to any strict separationist:

> Our prior holdings do not call for a total separation between church and state; total separation is not possible in an absolute sense. Some relationship between government and religious organizations is inevitable.

True, just as the prior history of Court jurisprudence is nowhere near so seamless as strict separationists like to argue, the Court's recent record is not totally consistent, either. The most notable exception to the new pattern of accommodation occurred in 1990, when the Court ruled, in *Oregon Department of Human Resources* v. *Smith,* that religious believers are not entitled to exemptions from generally applicable governmental requirements. But this decision, which seemed to fly in the face of a long line of cases dealing with religious minorities—from conscientious objectors in the military to Amish seeking exemptions from compulsory-education laws—elicited a response from other branches of government that was itself noteworthy. The Religious Freedom Restoration Act, signed into law by President Clinton in 1993, prohibits the government from burdening a person's exercise of religion unless it can be demonstrated that the burden "is in furtherance of a compelling governmental interest" and "is the least restrictive means of furthering" that interest. The federal courts are still trying to determine whether the Act amounts to an unconstitutional attempt by Congress to usurp judicial power and overturn *Smith;* however that question gets resolved, the Act itself affirms a growing sentiment in the nation that is already, as we have seen, exerting an influence on public policy.

STILL, THE direction of events is by no means certain. Last year, President Clinton signed a "Memorandum on Religion in Schools." Proclaiming that the First Amendment "does not convert schools into religion-free zones," he instructed the Secretary of Education and the Attorney General to develop guidelines on the appropriate role of religion in public-school districts. The memorandum was itself a response to a document drafted by an unusual coalition of Jewish, Christian, Muslim, and civil-rights groups, and both the initial document and the executive memorandum may be seen as signs of accommodation to the new public mood. But both are inadequate at best.

For example, the consensus document declares the right of students in public schools to read their Bibles and pray in informal settings; at the same time, out of concern for students who choose not to pray, or who might be offended by prayer, it *prohibits* any form of official religious prayer. Elsewhere, it urges that school administrators be given substantial discretion to *excuse* students from lessons which, for religious reasons, are objectionable to them or their parents.

Note the difference between the two sets of injunctions. In the first instance, whether or not prayer is considered a normal part of the school day by a majority of the community, individual students are to be saved the embarrassment of nonparticipation in it by virtue of a general prohibition. By contrast, no such effort to avoid stigmatization is on display in the case of students who may not want to hear, for example, what the Board of Education thinks they should know about sex; at

most, they are to be excused from a prescribed school activity and allowed to leave the room where it is taking place. Once again, the secularist "system" decides what is or is not legitimate, and once again religion is put on the defensive.

Of course, even under the best of circumstances, and with all the good will in the world, it would be extremely difficult to force the square peg of religion into the round hole of secularism—even a secularism more neutral than the current brand of government-enforced anti-religion. Christian groups, for example, have advocated the right to conduct prayer of some sort in public classrooms. But in addition to all the other valid objections that can be raised against this idea, it is highly improbable that any real prayer could be composed under such auspices that would not succeed in offending other religious minorities. What would result from the process of negotiation would inevitably be so devoid of spiritual meaning as hardly to merit being called a prayer.

To say this, however, is not to give up on the search for accommodation but to expose the need for a genuine accommodation. Our Bill of Rights, written to protect individuals from excessive governmental power, has from time to time been used in ways that tend unduly to impose that power on the truly religious among us, and to burden them in the exercise of their rights. For anyone who still adheres to the liberal tradition of tolerance, here is perhaps the last frontier of freedom.

If government-run schools are to remain secular, as no doubt they should, there is no good reason why the devoutly religious should not have alternatives—just as they do in other free nations, from Canada to Europe to Australia—that would permit them to educate their children in a setting that supports their values and convictions, under state-imposed educational standards but without taint, without encumbrance, and without financial penalty. This goal, which can be achieved without giving direct support to religious institutions, strikes a balance between the disestablishment of religion and its free exercise—the inextricably twinned aims of the First Amendment. It is sound public policy, it is fair, and it has even been upheld as constitutional by the United States Supreme Court.

Diane Berreth and Sheldon Berman

The Moral Dimensions of Schools

Small schools, caring adults, community service, and parent involvement can foster the virtues of empathy and self-discipline in our students— from preschool through high school.

© Lloyd Wolf

Trustworthiness, respect, responsibility, justice, fairness, integrity, caring—these concepts are at the heart of good character. Yet these are lofty words that are difficult for young people to appreciate or for teachers to set as instructional goals.

Amitai Etzioni, a George Washington University sociologist and leader in character education, has formulated a conceptual framework that helps turn character development into accessible skills for both teachers and students. Rather than focusing on

particular character traits, he identifies two underlying skills, empathy and self-discipline, that are prerequisites for character development. *Empathy* allows the child to appreciate the perspectives and feelings of another, to sense violations of justice and care, and to better distinguish right from wrong. *Self-discipline* provides the ability to take action and delay or even forego gratification in order to remain committed to a set of values or goals. Together, these skills provide the foundation for moral behavior.

Concerns for safety and order in schools have led to a raft of violence-prevention programs, from conflict resolution training to metal detectors and security guards. We believe that such programs, though well-intentioned, are incomplete. The missing piece in prevention programs is character development through the skills of empathy and self-discipline. Without these skills, we run the risk that schools will become locked-down, oppressive institutions built around fear rather than responsiveness. Nurturing empathy and self-discipline is our best hope for establishing an ethic rooted in shared rights and responsibilities.

To nurture empathy and self-discipline in our young people, we need to help them

- Learn basic decision-making and perspective-taking skills.
- Delay gratification and persist through obstacles.
- Develop a consistent set of positive values they can translate into action.
- Learn how to act responsibly.
- Have opportunities to successfully test skills.

Further, we need to structure all learning activities within a developmental context. What empathy and self-discipline mean to children

 From *Educational Leadership,* May 1997, pp. 24-27. © 1997 by the Association for Supervision and Curriculum Development. All rights reserved.
Reprinted by permission.

changes with age, life stage, and experience.

Confronting Challenges

Children today face an extremely challenging social environment. They experience growing economic disparity, the increasing acceptance of violence and abuse, a sense of disenchantment with government, and society's emphasis on self-interest and material goods. Too many young people feel hopeless, helpless, and powerless.

Such feelings and experiences undermine children's ability to help others, to trust, and to see meaningful possibilities for their own future. Young people are easily seduced by a material culture that promotes instant gratification. And the violence they see around them desensitizes them to their own pain and that of others.

Although adults have created this environment, our children most vividly live out the contradictions between our words and our deeds. If we wish to address the crisis in character we observe in our young people, we must confront those circumstances in

---

We can help children develop social skills and moral values through modeling, direct instruction, experience, and continual practice.

---

our environment. Children are the mirrors in which we can see our own reflection. We must hold ourselves and our social, educational, and political leaders accountable for living the values of trustworthiness, respect, responsibility, justice, fairness, integrity, and caring. Adults need to demonstrate to young people that it is possible to live one's values and advocate for a more just and responsible society.

But adults also need to help schools become moral communities where students experience the values

we hold dear. Our vision of a school as a moral community that nurtures empathy and self-discipline is the exception today. Making such schools commonplace will take concerted effort by the local school community and the citizenry at large.

Principles for a Moral School Community

How can schools best support the work of families in building these qualities? What would a moral school community look like?

- *The school community collaboratively develops, clearly states, and celebrates core moral values.* Members of the school community can develop mission statements, codes of responsibility, and shared moral values. Students thus get a sense of contributing to the common good. To encourage students to live these values, we can provide time for peer leadership, cross-grade tutoring, caring for plants and animals, and beautifying the school. We can display posters and essays focusing on empathy and self-discipline. We can engage in regular rituals that emphasize caring, such as matching first-year students with older students for orientation and holding recognition assemblies that celebrate caring in both adults and students.

- *Adults exemplify positive moral values in their work with one another and with students.* Children—especially adolescents—often see the contradictions in values that adults live by. We cannot erase all contradictions, but we can help model moral behavior by developing codes of conduct for our own work—as teachers, administrators, school board members, parents, and even cafeteria workers.

- *The school functions as the hub of the neighborhood community.* The alliances we build with parents, business leaders, and community members strengthen the moral support structure children need to develop character. We can

keep the school building open on evenings and weekends and plan activities, classes, and programs that serve all ages. We can encourage parents and community members to share their expertise.

- *Students develop skills in goal setting, problem solving, cooperation, conflict resolution, and decision making.* We can help children develop social skills and moral values through modeling, direct instruction, experience, and continual practice. Norma Haan and her colleagues[1] found that though children could think in profoundly empathic and moral terms, they lacked the skills to handle moral conflicts. To learn these skills in a history class, for example, students could collaboratively study strategies that real diplomats use to diffuse international conflict.

- *Students are involved in decision making within their classroom and school.* We must provide students with age-appropriate opportunities to participate in the decisions that affect their lives. The *practice* of democracy is vital. Even very young children can participate in class meetings to discuss rules and moral values. High school students can serve on screening committees for new faculty members, be representatives to the school improvement committee, and meet with department committees to review new courses.

- *Educators use a problem-solving approach for discipline.* To develop self-discipline, children need structures and limits with clear consequences to guide their behavior. We enhance students' ownership and sense of responsibility when we include children in the development of rules and consequences. Beginning at the preschool level, we can teach and use conflict management and mediation skills and use discipline problems and conflicts as opportunities to enhance students' social skills.

- *School communities provide opportunities for service—within and outside of the school.* K-12 service learning provides ways to develop empathy and practice self-discipline. Young children can take responsibility for a nature area near the school. Older children can volunteer in nursing homes and community agencies, become active in social and political organizations, provide peer leadership, or tutor younger students.

We must also engage young people in asking the hard questions about how we, collectively, live up to high moral standards—questions about the roots of violence, economic disparities, and environmental crises. We must allow students to make their own informed decisions and take re-

---

Empathy and self-discipline provide the foundation on which people build moral behavior.

---

sponsible action. Students need to experience being part of the solution rather than remaining passive observers.

- *Students and staff members appreciate diversity in cultures and beliefs through both study and direct experience.* We can help the entire school community develop empathy by consistently expanding the boundaries of family, religious, class, cultural, national, or racial groups. We can encourage discussions of literature and offer direct contact with people who differ in age or culture, thus providing the common ground for resolving differences and developing caring relationships. Through telecommunications, students and adults can collaborate with people in other communities, states, and countries.
- *At least one caring adult is personally connected with each child.* Such relationships are fostered through smaller schools or "houses" within schools. Mentors, tutors, and adult advisors should pair with students on a long-term basis.

Young people need structure and guidance, yet they also need developmentally appropriate opportunities to take risks and overcome failure. Empathy and self-discipline evolve through practice in real-life situations.

Character and Meaning
At heart, character education is helping young people develop a sense of social responsibility—a personal investment in the well-being of others and in the future of the planet. We can teach the virtues we hold dear only when we step out of our own perspective, empathize with others, and see the future consequences of our actions.

Character education means helping students understand, through experience, that what they value matters and that living these virtues lends meaning and richness to their own lives. Young people begin to see that their actions and choices create the world as it is and as it will be. When students grasp the positive difference they can make in the world, they grow in responsibility, respect, self-discipline, integrity, empathy—all the virtues we wish to see.

[1]See N. Haan, E. Aerts, and B. Cooper, *On Moral Grounds: The Search for Practical Morality* (New York: New York University Press, 1985).

Diane Berreth is Deputy Executive Director at ASCD; **Sheldon Berman,** the author of *Children's Social Consciousness* (Albany: State University of New York, 1997), is Superintendent of Schools, Hudson Public Schools, Hudson, MA 01749 (e-mail: shelley@concord.org). A version of this article appears in *Character Building for a Democratic, Civil Society,* by The Communitarian Network (Washington, D.C.: Author, 1997).

RELIGION

PUBLIC SCHOOLS, RELIGION, AND PUBLIC RESPONSIBILITY

". . . Children whose families practice any of the world religions other than Christianity either see them given passing, less significant regard or ignored entirely [in the classroom]."

by Barbara McEwan

THERE IS an old joke that can be heard in faculty lounges around the nation: "There will be prayer in the schools as long as we're giving tests." The irony of the comment also encapsulates the basic constitutional protections of free religious exercise as balanced against government prohibitions against the establishment of religion. Put simply, students do have the right to their free exercise of religious beliefs, and the government—in this case public school educators—must refrain from advancing one religious perspective. A student who is praying silently before a meal or a test is exercising his or her First Amendment right to religious expression. A teacher who devotes class time to making Christmas decorations that will be hung in the classroom is violating First Amendment protections from the establishment of religion.

Dr. McEwan is associate professor of education, Oregon State University, Corvallis.

In 1963, the Supreme Court stated in *School District of Abington Township v. Schempp* and *Murray v. Curlett:* "The place of religion in our society is an exalted one, achieved through a long tradition of reliance on the home, the church and the inviolable citadel of the individual heart and mind. We have come to recognize through bitter experience that it is not within the power of government to invade that citadel, whether its purpose or effect be to aid or oppose, to advance or retard. In the relationship between man and religion, the State is firmly committed to a position of neutrality."

While the separation of church and state may seem a straightforward, self-explanatory concept, the issues can become clouded in daily public school practice. Teacher and administrator education programs as well as school districts frequently fail to inform educators adequately as to their professional responsibilities in this area. As a result, there is more misinformation to be had than there is evidence of a commitment to maintaining legal and equitable standards.

Educators who plan a series of activities around the theme of religious holidays express reticence about mentioning religion in the legitimate secular context of teaching history, music, literature, or art. In the case cited above, the Supreme Court advocated the direct opposite of these practices. " . . . It might well be said that one's education is not complete without a study of comparative religion or the history of religion and its relationship to the advancement of civilization." Religion can and should play a significant role in the lives of young people. Actively practiced or not, it is an integral part of the diverse cultures represented in today's society.

A holiday party that occurs primarily because it is in keeping with a teacher's cultural heritage well might be considered an example of how the government establishes religion. While educators must refrain from advancing one particular religious perspective, the influence of religious thought should be included in a global curriculum if it accurately is to reflect the U.S.'s multicultural society. To remove religion from the educational conversation is to pull a

From *USA Today Magazine*, May 1997, pp. 70-72. © 1997 by the Society for the Advancement of Education. Reprinted by permission.

critical thread from the weave of culture and provide students with a limited understanding of their world.

Misunderstandings or misinterpretations of the law have led to classroom practices that often are the reverse of what the Court intended in its rulings. For instance, there have been cases in which children who chose to spend their free reading time engrossed in Bible stories have had their books pulled from their hands as they are told, "You can't do that in school." At the same time, Christmas decorations are displayed prominently on the bulletin boards and walls of their classrooms. School administrators develop policies that respond more to the predominant values held in their communities than to the rulings of the Supreme Court. As a result, they will allow the celebrations of religious holidays, stating, "We'll have Halloween until somebody complains."

The impetus for creating a classroom environment of equity is that public school educators are responsible for ensuring that all students experience an equal educational opportunity in their classrooms. Psychological and physiological information on human development and brain research indicate that young people need to feel that they are an accepted part of their learning communities in order to be able to achieve to the level of their maximum potential. While at one time the neighborhoods of middle America may have been indeed homogeneous in nature, that assumption no longer is valid.

Too often, educators adhere to a false expectation that their students will act, think, and look like them. This may be true in a monocultural society. In the U.S., though, demographics clearly reflect the fact that this is a multicultural society and its system of compulsory education ensures that any public school classroom is likely to include students who represent a broad sampling of diverse religious, political, and cultural values.

My work in the area of educational law has led me to interactions with teachers and school administrators from all over the country. They have convinced me that, despite legal considerations, the policies relating to religion in the schools can be characterized as confusing, misinformed, and misguided. Classroom teachers are faced

with trying to find their way through a particularly sensitive balance that encourages them to teach about all aspects of cultural diversity, respect family values, and, at the same time, not intrude on the privately held beliefs of students. In short, educators find themselves trying to make sense of a situation that can appear very much like a classic Catch-22.

While classroom festivities may hold pleasant associations for the educators who plan them, what frequently is absent from their considerations is the sense of isolation experienced by youngsters whose families do not celebrate the holiday being observed. These children are left to decide if they will participate in activities they personally do not value or remove themselves from the classroom and their peers, an act that emphasizes their differences. While there certainly are exceptions to these scenarios, it is remarkably rare to find school administrators and teachers who act as if they are even aware of the law's expectations or simply choose to ignore them.

Educators have a responsibility to protect all students from discrimination based on their race, national origin, disability, age, marital status, sex, and religion. Classroom activities celebrating one religion's holiday while ignoring others can result in some students who will feel excluded in spirit, if not in fact, from their classmates and teachers. Educators must determine if an activity is being carried out for the knowledge it imparts or is being done to advance a single religious perspective.

In many cases, the answer to that question will depend on how the activity is staged. For instance, calling a December vocal concert "Our Winter Music Festival" is appropriate. However, if the concert is comprised of 12 Christmas songs, two about snow, and one about Chanukah, the activity may fail to meet the standard of neutrality. On the other hand, if that same concert presented an overview of songs of the season as well as religious music in even balance, the standard would be well-met. Teachers who deny students the right to exercise various religious practices while establishing one dominant religion through holiday celebrations don't just convey the message that the only religion with true merit is the one they are choosing to favor, but attenuate the potential positive impact of the moral values embedded in all theologies.

While to some the act of maintaining this balance seems an impossibly difficult task, the Supreme Court has developed succinct language to guide educators in their practices, advocating a standard of "wholesome neutrality." This posture of neutrality is not one of disinterest or disaffection, but, rather, a professional stance in which all perspectives are appreciated equally and no one perspective is presented as being more acceptable than another. Certainly, the common values we all share as a society are reflected in the belief systems of the world's religions, and a classroom built on wholesome neutrality would be an environment in which children can explore the similarities as well as the differences, finding value in both.

In *Lee v. Weisman* (1992), the Court dealt with prayers at graduation ceremonies. In its ruling, the majority stated clearly that maintaining an environment of wholesome neutrality is of importance not just to students in the public schools, but to the well-being of society. The findings of the Court state in part, "The lessons of the First Amendment are as urgent in the modern world as in the 18th Century when it was written. One timeless lesson is that if citizens are subjected to state-sponsored religious exercises, the State disavows its own duty to guard and respect that sphere of inviolable conscience and belief which is the mark of a free people."

Educators concerned with equity recognize that these ill-informed practices may have the effect of alienating some students. Young people whose religious holiday is the one that dominates the celebratory activities in October, December, or April are given the impression that their religion is somehow more important than all the others. In addition, the practice of favoring one religion over others has the effect of encouraging students to view minority religious practices as curiosities, particularly when they are grouped under the generic designation of "non-Christian."

The fact that Chanukah falls around the same time as Christmas is one of the most notable examples. Many teachers are unfamiliar with Judaism and Jewish holidays. As a result, it is not uncommon for students to hear Chanukah described as the "Jewish Christmas," a statement that ill serves both Christianity and Judaism.

In an effort to skirt constitutional authority, schools will focus on the more secular aspects of Christmas in the mistaken belief that Santa Claus and a Christmas tree are not religious symbols. To the children whose families do not celebrate Christmas, though, Santa Claus is very much the emblem of practices that do not occur in their homes. If the songs being sung and the messages being given to children in the month of December include statements about Santa visiting the homes of "good little boys and girls," what are non-Christian children to think when they know Santa never will visit their homes? Furthermore, when Santa Claus is the dominant image of classroom holiday cele-

> **"Classroom activities celebrating one religion's holiday while ignoring others can result in some students who will feel excluded in spirit, if not in fact, from their classmates and teachers."**

brations, those Christian children whose families adhere to a more fundamentalist viewpoint are given to understand that what is really important about Christmas are the means by which they get presents.

Some teachers erroneously believe that a classroom containing one menorah and otherwise festooned with red and green holiday decorations has met the standard for equity. Such classrooms are more likely to be considered unfortunate examples of tokenism.

Conversely, children whose families practice any of the world religions other than Christianity either see them given passing, less significant regard or ignored entirely. Other religious holidays—those that do not fall during December—tend to be utterly ignored. Kwanzaa, a holiday that falls in the latter part of December and con-

tinues for seven days, occasionally is mentioned, but it often is misrepresented as an African holiday, when in fact it is an African-American creation.

A curriculum that represents many cultures and moral perspectives could provide teachers with significant opportunities to explore the shared insights of social justice, respect, and responsibility provided by the world religions. Such a curriculum would be a positive step toward creating a community tolerant of differences and enhanced by similarities, as opposed to one that emphasizes holiday parties and favors just one viewpoint.

A curriculum built on balance and equity is not difficult to achieve, but does take a little forethought. One seventh-grade teacher developed a curriculum for the month of October that would present an in-depth study of Mexico. On Oct. 31, the integrated program culminated in a fiesta the students had planned and staged. They wore costumes, had special food, danced, and played games. Other classrooms in the same school were engaged in Halloween parties, but this one avoided the exclusionary effect that such a party might have had on some students who do not celebrate that holiday and instead had all the students actively involved in a curriculum-based party that was entirely appropriate to the school's mission. Certainly, a study of Mexico would include the religious influences present in that country, and in that context, a discussion of religion is fitting.

Religion already is a part of the curriculum. It is interwoven into motivations for exploration and wars as well as peace; it is a theme that runs through much of our literary and musical heritage; and it is a predominant topic in philosophy. Rather than fearing religion's presence, we should reach out and embrace its power.

I recently had an opportunity to visit a school with a room set aside where volunteers could interact with and counsel students who had been assigned an in-school suspension for some behavioral infraction. The volunteers had decorated the room with sayings from Gandhi, Jesus, Mohammed, Buddha, Martin Luther King, Jr., Moses, and others who have contributed to the moral conversation of our world societies. The presence of so many diverse voices all speaking about the value of truth, honesty, respect, and responsibility created a powerful montage and at the same time represented the essence of what religion in the schools can and should be.

Managing Life in Classrooms

All teachers have concerns regarding the "quality of life" in classroom settings. All teachers and students want to feel safe and accepted when they are in school. There exists today a reliable, effective knowledge base on classroom management and the prevention of disorder in schools. This knowledge base has been developed from hundreds of studies of teacher/student interaction and student/student interaction that have been conducted in schools in North America and Europe. We speak of managing life in classrooms because we now know that there are many factors that go into building effective teacher/student and student/student relationships. The traditional term *discipline* is too narrow and refers primarily to teachers' reactions to undesired student behavior. We can better understand methods of managing student behavior when we look at the totality of what goes on in classrooms, with teacher responses to student behavior as a part of that totality. Teachers have tremendous responsibility for the emotional climate that is set in a classroom. Whether students feel secure and safe and whether they want to learn depend to an enormous extent on the psychological frame of mind of the teacher. Teachers must be able to manage their own selves first in order to effectively manage the development of a humane and caring classroom environment.

Teachers bear moral and ethical responsibilities for being witnesses to and examples of responsible social behavior in the classroom. There are many models of observing life in classrooms. Arranging the total physical environment of the room is a very important part of the teacher's planning for learning activities. Teachers need to expect from students the best work and behavior that they are capable of achieving. Respect and caring are attitudes that a teacher must communicate to receive them in return. Open lines of communication between teachers and students enhance the possibility for congenial, fair dialogical resolution of problems as they occur.

Developing a high level of task orientation among students and encouraging cooperative learning and shared task achievement will foster camaraderie and self-confidence among students. Shared decision making will build an *esprit de corps*, a sense of pride and confidence, which will feed on itself and blossom into high-quality performance. Good class morale, well-managed, never hurts academic achievement. The importance of emphasizing quality, helping students to achieve levels of performance that they can feel proud of having attained, and encouraging positive dialogue among them leads them to take ownership in their individual educative efforts. When that happens, they literally empower themselves to do their best.

When teachers (and prospective teachers) discuss what concerns them about their roles (and prospective roles) in the classroom, the issue of discipline—how to manage student behavior—will usually rank near or at the top of their lists. A teacher needs a clear understanding of what kinds of learning environments are most appropriate for the subject matter and ages of the students. Any person who wants to teach must also want his or her students to learn well, to acquire basic values of respect for others, and to become more effective citizens.

There is considerable debate among educators regarding certain approaches used in schools to achieve a form of order in classrooms that also develops respect for self and others. The dialogue about this point is spirited and informative. The bottom line for any effective and humane approach to discipline in the classroom, the necessary starting point, is the teacher's emotional balance and capacity for self-control. This precondition creates a further one—that the teacher wants to be in the classroom with his or her students in the first place. Unmotivated teachers cannot motivate students.

Helping young people learn the skills of self-control and motivation to become productive, contributing, and knowledgeable adult participants in society is one of the most important tasks that good teachers undertake. These are teachable and learnable skills; they do not relate to heredity or social conditions. They can be learned by any human being who wants to learn them and who is cognitively able to learn them. We know also that these skills are learnable by virtually all but the most severely cognitively disabled persons. There is a large knowledge base on how teachers can help students learn self-control. All that is required is the willingness of teachers to learn these skills themselves and to teach them to their students. No topic is more fundamentally related to any thorough examination of the social and cultural foundations of edu-

tive techniques combined with humane but clear principles of procedure seem to be most effective. Teachers need to realize that before they can control behavior, they must identify what student behaviors are desired in their classrooms. They need to reflect, as well, on the emotional tone and ethical principles implied by their own behaviors. To optimize their chances of achieving the classroom atmosphere that they wish, teachers must strive for emotional balance within themselves; they must learn to be accurate observers; and they must develop just, fair strategies of intervention to aid students in learning self-control and good behavior. A teacher should be a good model of courtesy, respect, tact, and discretion. Children learn by observing how other persons behave and not just by being told how they are to behave. There is no substitute for positive, assertive teacher interaction with students in class.

This unit addresses many of the topics covered in basic foundations courses. The selections shed light on classroom management issues, teacher leadership skills, and the rights and responsibilities of teachers and students. In addition, the articles can be discussed in foundations courses involving curricula and instruction. This unit falls between the units on moral education and equal opportunity because it can be directly related to either or both of them.

Looking Ahead: Challenge Questions

What are some things that can be done to help students and teachers to feel safe in school?

What is a good technique for learning self-control?

What should be the behavioral standards in schools? On what factors should they be based?

Does a peer approach seem like a workable solution to undesirable behavior? Why, or why not?

What ethical issues may be raised in the management of student behavior in school settings?

Do any coercive approaches to behavioral management in schools work better than noncoercive ones?

Why is teacher self-control a major factor in just and effective classroom management strategies?

cation. There are many sound techniques that new teachers can use to achieve success in managing students' classroom behavior, and they should not be afraid to ask colleagues questions and to develop peer support groups with whom they can work with confidence and trust.

Teachers' core ethical principles come into play when deciding what constitutes defensible and desirable standards of student conduct. As in medicine, realistic preven-

Creating School and Classroom Cultures that Value Learning:
The Role of National Standards

by Geneva D. Haertel

Implementing national standards can help create positive learning environments for students from diverse backgrounds.

Increased diversity in our nation's school population and in children's education experiences has placed greater and greater demands on the public school system. This diversity makes it imperative to use commonly held educational content and performance standards. Such standards can ensure that all students will be expected to learn essential and rigorous content at levels needed to achieve academic success. The use of such standards can also help develop classroom and school cultures that are task-oriented rather than competitive. The focus of a task-oriented school culture is each child's own progress in learning, rather than comparisons among classmates' performances. Creating task-oriented classroom and school cultures that value learning for its own sake reaps academic and motivational benefits for students.

Increased Diversity

Diversity among public school students is increasing nationwide. Demographers have documented a drop in the percentage of white, non-Hispanic students enrolled in public schools since 1976. Simultaneously, the U.S. pre-K to grade 12 student population has decreased from 43 to 41 million, while minority enrollment, as a proportion of

Geneva D. Haertel, Ph.D., is a Senior Research Associate at the Center for Research in Human Development and Learning at Temple University.

 From *Educational Horizons*, Spring 1997, pp. 143-148. © 1997 by Geneva D. Haertel. Reprinted by permission.

> *Too often the schools that serve such impoverished children also reflect the neglect, scarce resources, and despair that characterize poor neighborhoods.*

total enrollment, has risen from 24 percent to 30 percent. In Florida, California, New Jersey, New York, and Texas, where large numbers of immigrants locate, minority enrollment in schools is exceeding majority enrollment. In California, for example, most students (52 percent) are minority group members. Demographers estimate that in less than twenty years, 70 percent of California's students will be minorities and 50 percent of them will use a first language other than English on their first day of school.[1] Not only is racial, ethnic, and linguistic diversity increasing among public school enrollees, but economic heterogeneity as well. Increasing numbers of students' families are plagued by poverty, unemployment, frequent relocation, limited access to high-quality medical and social services, and crime-ridden neighborhoods.[2] Too often the schools that serve such impoverished children also reflect the neglect, scarce resources, and despair that characterize poor neighborhoods.

Variations in children's educational experiences have also increased due to the range in the tangible and intangible resources available to schools within the same districts and states. Deteriorating school buildings, increased school violence, and high staff turnover now characterize many schools, especially those in our nations' inner cities and isolated rural areas. These conditions contrast sharply with those of wealthy, suburban schools, where computer and science laboratories contain the latest equipment and teachers have abundant professional and community resources that enrich their students' learning experiences. Increased divergence in school resources exposes children to greater variation in the quality of education.

Over the past decade, several educational movements have further contributed to variations in student populations and in instruction, content, and learning environments. The following section will briefly describe some of the most pervasive movements.

Multiculturalism has both broadened and deepened the traditional K-12 curricula. The goal of multicultural education, as stated by experts in the field, is to reform schools and other educational institutions so that students from diverse racial, ethnic, and linguistic groups will receive equal educations.[3] Multicultural education involves institutional changes in curricula, instructional materials, teaching styles, students' and educators' attitudes, perceptions, beliefs, and behaviors, and the goals, norms, and culture of schools. The movement has sensitized many educators to differences in the prior knowledge and experiences of children from diverse backgrounds and familiarized students with the histories of diverse cultures and their contributions.

The **inclusion** of students with disabilities in regular classrooms has also increased diversity in schools nationwide. Because inclusion stresses bringing instructional services to the handicapped child, rather than the student to the services, it has encouraged curriculum adaptations, environmental adaptations of the classroom, behavior support plans, cooperative learning, peer tutoring, and team teaching. These support systems increase the diversity of students' curricula, instruction, and culture.

Technologies, as conduits to new knowledge, resources, and higher-order thinking skills, have entered classrooms and schools nationwide. Personal computers, CD-ROMS, on-line services, the World Wide Web, and other innovative technologies have enriched curricular resources and altered the types of instruction available. The new Office of Technology Assessment (OTA) report, "Teachers and Technology: Making the Connection," provides evidence that schools' access to technologies is rising steadily. OTA reports 5.8 million computers are available in schools for instruction—about one computer for every nine students. Approximately 35 percent of schools can access on-line services, 30 percent have CD-ROMS, and nearly all have TVs and VCRs. Most of these technologies are used for traditional instruction, such as presenting information, basic skills practice, word processing, and developing computer literacy. Teachers are, however, beginning to use more innovative applications—using desktop publishing, developing mathematical and scientific reasoning with computer simulations, gathering information using on-line services and CD-ROM databases, and communicating via E- mail.[4] Thus, the use of technologies is altering the curriculum content and instructional experiences available to students—a trend that will likely accelerate with the passage of time.

The **school-choice movement** has promoted the development of unique school learning environments. From the creation of magnet schools centered around particular themes, such as the visual and performing arts, science and technology, and other spe-

cialty areas, to the design of charter schools that reflect the values, philosophy, and preferences of particular community groups, school choice has changed the menu of public school experiences. School choice has encouraged greater variation in the goals, curricula, instructional approaches, and culture of schools.

The **service-learning movement** involves students applying academic knowl-

> *This curricular and instructional incoherence can contribute to many children and youths' failure to meet their academic potential.*

edge to meet their communities' needs. Service learning exerts an influence on the school culture via its emphasis on student self-direction, workplace relationships, parent and community involvement, and school-community partnerships. Service learning usually involves varied groups, including parents, school personnel, and community members. The community becomes an extension of the classroom, and in many cases, students participate in project environments that differ physically, culturally, and economically from the environments of their own families and neighborhoods. Service learning addresses concerns of the larger community, including homelessness, hunger, poverty, illiteracy, and environmental problems. Schools that engage in service-learning projects provide students with a vastly different type of instruction than traditional classroom learning, and the content that students are exposed to in the service-learning projects is not restricted by traditional subject areas. Thus, service learning greatly increases the types of content, instruction, and values that students experience.

The final trend to be mentioned is **reduced dependence on textbooks,** such as the basal reader series, and increased reliance on trade books, curriculum frameworks, and teacher-developed materials. Alternatives to textbooks have made student materials more challenging, accommodated student ethnic, racial, and cultural diversity, and expanded the instructional experiences of children and youth.

In summary, diverse student populations and varied content, instruction, and learning environments have increased the likelihood that children who have completed the same grade or academic level will nonetheless not have mastered key knowledge and skills to

When students hold ability goals, they view school as a competitive enterprise in which only a few children can be top performers.

the same degree. This curricular and instructional incoherence can contribute to many children and youths' failure to meet their academic potential. National standards can provide common targets toward which students, parents, teachers, and local schools direct their efforts to ensure that all children and youth have opportunities to learn crucial knowledge and skills.

The Impact of Standards and Goals on Students

National standards not only provide a response to increased diversity, but can also confer educational and psychological advantages on students. In educational environments, practices such as goal-setting, high expectations, and standards are associated with increased academic performance and motivational benefits. Psychological and behavioral research establishes that these practices are essential to attain desired outcomes. Without a conscious effort to make decisions and take actions that can result in such outcomes, individuals are unlikely to achieve desired ends.[5]

Behavioral research has identified several necessary conditions for individuals to attain challenging goals and standards. They must be aware of the type and level of knowledge and skill required; be nurtured in their commitment to act in ways that will lead to attainment; be provided with effective strategies and resources; and believe that attaining the stand-

ard is beneficial to them. The ways in which standards affect children's learning, motivation, and behavior are similar in every academic subject. We will now examine how and in what ways standards and goals can help create task-oriented classroom and school cultures where learning is valued.

Task-Oriented versus Ability-Oriented Goals

Recent research on student learning and motivation has identified purposes and goals as crucial to students' efforts to learn. The purposes of schooling vary among students, although two perspectives dominate. Students who hold a task-, or mastery-oriented, perspective regard schooling as an opportunity to acquire knowledge and skills and to solve problems. Other students regard schooling as a competitive game in which some students win and others lose. Students who take this perspective are regarded as having an ability, ego, or performance orientation toward schooling. These two types of goals create different levels of engagement in learning tasks, learning approaches, and attitudes toward learning and school.[6]

Students who view schooling as task-oriented and hold task-related goals are more interested in learning; plan their time; employ more rigorous and conceptually demanding learning strategies; and are undeterred by occasional mistakes. Task-oriented students report positive feelings about learning new content and skills. They seek opportunities to succeed that allow them to pursue their own interests using available resources.

When students hold ability goals, they view school as a competitive enterprise in which only a few children can be top performers. These students judge every academic task by its potential to make them look capable or incompetent. Engagement in school tasks, thus, depends on the task's potential impact on their self-worth. A task perceived as too difficult is avoided because it can make a student look "unable." In addition, these students seldom persevere at challenging tasks: to exert a great effort in completing a task suggests that the individual has little ability. "Self-handicapping" strategies are used by many children, but especially those who hold ability goals. These strategies buffer children's self-worth. They include procrastination, exerting little effort, or selecting learning activities that are very easy or very hard. In any case, there are plausible excuses, other than low ability, for a poor performance.

Students with task-oriented goals are more positive about learning and school than their peers who hold ability goals. Having ability-oriented goals is associated with disruptive behavior, low self-esteem, and alienation. Ultimately, the academic performance and school citizenship of ability-

oriented students become threatened by the disengagement, anxiety, fear of failure, low self-worth, and negative attitudes toward learning that often accompany such goals.

The emphases that teachers and schools place on task versus ability goals vary. Recent research studies demonstrate that students are sensitive to the orientation stressed in their learning environments. Particular classroom and schoolwide practices and policies affect which goal orientation stu-

Holding high standards for children who are low achievers or those in need of greater-than-usual instructional assistance is crucial to improving their learning.

dents embrace. Among these influences are: teacher behaviors and beliefs; instructional strategies; the nature of schoolwork and learning tasks; classroom and schoolwide organization and grouping practices; the way authority is shared and decision-making occurs; and evaluation and recognition systems.[7] Using standards can stress a task-oriented perspective toward schooling and thereby positively influence students' motivation and learning.

National Standards and Task-Oriented Classrooms and Schools

Schools change in response to both recognized needs and stated standards and goals. National standards, if they fulfill their promise, alter teachers' expectations and actions and the culture of schools and classrooms. These changes would lead to enhanced student achievement. Although national standards define domains of subject matter to be mastered to varying degrees of competence, their reform potential may require further strengthening by specifying standards and goals at the state, district, school, or even classroom level. An illustration of how standards can influence classroom and school culture through evaluation and recognition systems is presented below.

National, state, and local standards apply to all students, not just the academically talented and economically advantaged. Educational research has clearly demonstrated the relationships among teachers' expectations, attributions, and behaviors. A teacher's expectation that students will master the curriculum content presented is related to maximizing student achievement.[8] Holding high standards for children who are low achievers or those in need of greater-than-usual instructional assistance is crucial to improving their learning. Many of these children, who often are at risk of school failure, are placed in categorical programs with watered-down curricula and little academic rigor.[9] If all students are expected to master challenging content and skills, a classroom and school climate must emphasize the academic growth and motivation of each student—a task-oriented culture. Such a culture would emerge from teachers' high expectations for student learning, the design of meaningful learning tasks and assessments aligned with content and performance standards, and a cooperative community of learners and teachers.

The way student performance is assessed has a powerful effect on school and classroom culture. Norm-referenced assessment compares the academic performances of students to other students, whereas criterion-referenced assessments compare student performances to standards. Many norm-referenced assessments ignore students' levels of competence and prior experiences when they enter the educational system. Criterion-referenced measurement, on the other hand, necessarily takes into consideration students' levels of achievement when they begin and their growth along a continuum of knowledge and skills. Norm-referenced assessments may reinforce the tendency of many students to strive to get the highest score on the test—which contributes to the misguided, but seductive, belief that the primary objective of academic endeavors is to attain the highest test score. Norm-referenced assessments can lead children to avoid errors—rather than learning from their mistakes. Getting the correct answer to a test question becomes the critical concern of these students, rather than gaining new knowledge and succeeding at the learning task. Thus, the use of norm-referenced assessment contributes to an ability-oriented, competitive culture. By comparison, the use of criterion-referenced assessment stresses the importance of each student's performance against a standard. The focus is on student progress and growth on the task at hand, not on comparisons among students.

Student performance on national, state, and local standards can be assessed using a norm- or criterion-referenced approach. A norm-referenced approach is more likely to use content and performance standards to encourage competitiveness. The presence of standards alone does not guarantee the creation of task-oriented classrooms. However, if educators are aware of the impact of goals and standards on student learning, motivation, and citizenship, they can use standards to create task-oriented learning environments that nurture each student's achievement, support the development of powerful learning strategies, and foster positive attitudes toward learning and school.

Conclusions

National standards can leverage reform in the nation's schools and classrooms. The standards will impact students by identifying a core of common educational outcomes that students, regardless of their characteristics, backgrounds, or prior educational experiences, will be expected to achieve. The implementation of the standards will provide all children with opportunities to learn academically rigorous curriculum and higher-order thinking skills. Such standards will influence not only the content to which students are exposed, but also the selection, design, and alignment of learning tasks and assessments.

Given these changes and the subsequent challenge for students to attain high levels of academic performance, educators can seize the opportunity and design task-oriented learning environments that confer academic and motivational benefits on students. Within such learning environments, students are more likely to achieve challenging levels of academic performance and become motivated learners who are well-prepared for the twenty-first century.

1. Eugene E. Garcia, "Language, Culture, and Education," in *The Review of Research in Education*, Vol. 19, ed. Linda Darling-Hammond (Washington, D.C.: American Educational Research Association, 1993), 51–98, and National Center for Education Statistics, *Secondary Education*, Vol. 1 of *The Condition of Education*, (Washington, D.C.: Author: 1991).
2. Margaret C. Wang and Edmund W. Gordon, eds., *Educational Resilience in Inner-City America: Challenges and Prospects* (Hillsdale, N.J.: Lawrence Erlbaum Associates, 1994); Andrea A. Lash and Sandra L. Kirkpatrick, "Interrupted Lessons: Teacher Views of Transfer Student Education," *American Educational Research Journal* 31 (1994): 813–843; and Leonard C. Rigsby, Maynard C. Reynolds, and Margaret C. Wang, eds., *School-Community Connections: Exploring Issues for Research and Practice* (San Francisco: Jossey-Bass Publishers, 1995).
3. James A. Banks, "Multicultural Education: Historical Development, Dimensions, and Practice" in *The Review of Research in Education*, Vol. 19, ed. Linda Darling-Hammond (Washington, D.C.: American Educational Research Association, 1993), 3–49.
4. Office of Technology Assessment, *Teachers and Technology: Making the Connection* (Washington, D.C.: U.S. Government Printing Office, 1995).
5. Catherine D. Ennis, "Health Education," in *Handbook of Research on Improving Student Achievement*, ed. G. Cawelti (Arlington, Va.: Educational Research Service, 1995).
6. Bernard Weiner, "Attributional Theory of Achievement Motivation and Emotion," *Psychological Bulletin* 71 (1985): 3–25; John G. Nicholls, "Conceptions of Ability and Achievement Motivation," in *Student Motivation*, Vol. 1 of *Research on Motivation in Education*, ed. R. Ames and C. Ames (New York: Academic Press, 1984), 39–68; John G. Nicholls, *The Competitive Ethos and Democratic Education* (Cambridge, Mass.: Harvard University Press, 1989); and E. S. Elliot and C. S. Dweck, "Goals: An Approach to Motivation and Achievement," in *Journal of Personality and Social Psychology* 54 (1988): 5–12.
7. Carole Ames, "Achievement Goals, Motivational Climate, and Motivational Processes," in *Motivation in Sport and Exercise*, ed. G. C. Roberts (Champaign, Ill.: Human Kinetics, 1992), 161–176; Carole Ames, "Classrooms: Goals, Structures, and Student Motivation," in *Journal of Educational Psychology* 84 (1992): 261–271; Joyce Epstein, "Family Structures and Student Motivation: A Developmental Perspective," in Vol. 3 of *Research on Motivation in Education*, ed. C. Ames and R. Ames (New York: Academic Press, 1989), 259–295; and Phyllis C. Blumenfeld, "Classroom Learning and Motivation: Clarifying and Expanding Goal Theory," in *Journal of Educational Psychology* 84 (1992): 272–281.
8. Jere Brophy and Carolyn Evertson, *Student Characteristics and Teaching* (New York: Longman, 1981); Jere Brophy and Thomas Good, "Teacher Behavior and Student Achievement," in *Handbook of Research on Teaching*, 3rd ed., ed. Merlin C. Wittrock (New York: Macmillan Publishing Company, 1986), 328–375; and Thomas Good, "Teacher Expectations," in *Talks to Teachers*, ed. David Berliner and Barok Rosenshine (New York: Random House, 1987), 159–200.
9. Barbara Means and Michael Knapp, eds., "Teaching Advanced Skills to Educationally Disadvantaged Students: Final Report" (Washington, D.C.: U.S. Department of Education, Office of Planning, Budget and Evaluation, 1991).

Converting Peer Pressure

Audrey Gartner

Audrey Gartner is co-director of the Peer Research Laboratory, Graduate School and University Center, City University of New York.

A new hopelessness has arisen about our society's ability to educate young people today. Race and class discrimination is no longer considered the purported cause of poor school performance. The problem, we're told, is the students themselves. Peer pressure is blamed for everything from poor grades to drug abuse.

Supporting this argument is new research by Steinberg, et al. (*Beyond the Classroom*). In a survey of 20,000 teenagers, the authors found that, while parents have little influence on youngsters' attitudes toward school, peers are very influential in producing negative attitudes.

But there are, in fact, a large number of programs in school that utilize peers to provide a very different and positive message. Student-to-student programs such as peer drug education, peer tutoring, peer mediation, peer mentoring, youth helplines, and peer counseling are found in thousands of schools around the country. Research indicates that they are effective and, equally important, cost-effective. For example, a meta-analysis of 143 adolescent drug-prevention programs showed that peer approaches are more persuasive than any other program in reducing drug use among young people. Another study determined that cross-age tutoring among students was most cost-effective in comparison with three other well-known reform strategies—reduced class size, computer-assisted instruction, and a longer school day.

In peer programs, students become role models, and imbue the programs with their own idiom and style. To varying degrees, students feel good about themselves for being able to help someone else, a key element in all peer programs. These programs appeal to a wide variety of young people. In fact, those students who are not the "best" students often make exemplary tutors. And, in assuming this role, they have the most room for personal change. For example, if a tutor is a below average student a much greater growth potential exists.

In all of these programs and others like them, students receive training and supervision by adults to carry out their peer activities. In a junior high school anti-drug program implemented by the Peer Research Laboratory, peer helpers met as a group twice a week with a teacher for training in listening and communication skills and how to handle one-to-one interactions, and they learned about substance abuse prevention. The training focused on the problems facing today's youth and how to cope with everyday school and family situations. These peer helpers staffed a rap room in their school, where students dropped in to talk about their concerns with other students, receive information and get support from others who shared the same experiences.

Converting Students to Helpers

Students who use a rap room or receive tutoring assistance often are put in the unique position not only of receiving help, but offering help to their peers as well. The

In peer programs, students become role models, and imbue the programs with their own idiom and style.

helping process works both ways. These students understand, in a very personal way, how it feels to need help and to receive it, preparing them, in turn, to give help to someone else.

We tested the premise of whether the opportunity of being converted from helpee to helper would improve student learning. As part of a drop-out prevention effort, a tutoring program was started in three New York City high schools, and tutees were involved with tutors in training activities and in refining elements of the program. They were also given the opportunity to become tutors the following semester if they successfully passed the course in which they were being tutored. Compared with similar students who were being tutored as part of a traditional tutoring program at three other high schools, the first group of tutees had higher rates of completion in tutored courses

and received significantly higher grades in tutored subjects.

In all school-based peer activities, there is a tacit alliance between the students and the adults in the schools. It is an association that builds on the students' strengths, style and similarity—they understand each other's language—combined with the teaching and training skills of the school staff. Each of the partners is allied in sending critical messages: "It's good to achieve." "Drugs ruin people's lives." "There is a lot to look forward to."

The scope and positive impact of peer programs could be widely expanded by giving all students the opportunity of playing the helping role. It is through the act of helping others that really powerful learning takes place for the helper. We need educational visionaries to lead schools in this process of unlocking this learning and helping power. Students, indeed, are the most overlooked resource in most schools.

The crucial importance of youth participation in meaningful roles such as youth-helping-youth programs can go a long way in spreading pro-learning messages, as well as preventing substance abuse, teen pregnancy, AIDS, and delinquency. The challenge is to have as many students as possible—a critical mass—involved in these activities, so that positive peer pressure becomes "the thing to do." The ultimate goal is the creation of student-centered, peer-focused schools.

Photo by Audrey Gartner

Changing the Way Kids Settle Conflicts

By using the Students Against Violence program, teachers can help children deal with their own—and others'—disagreements in positive ways.

Gerri Holden

Someone takes your parking space—what do you do? Someone cuts ahead of you in line at the football game—what do you say? A man bumps into your cart in the grocery store and keeps going. How does that make you feel?

These adult conflicts are similar to the issues that children face every day. Missing pencils, line cutting, and being pushed or shoved are real concerns to elementary school children. Whether they are prepared and confident enough to handle them depends on whether they possess certain skills—the ability to negotiate, to compromise, and to resolve conflicts peacefully.

As a 2nd grade teacher in Pittsburgh, I have a growing concern for students who are exposed to violence or who are displaying more violent behavior. Increasingly, children who learn good conflict management skills find themselves trying to negotiate with kids who would rather fight—even over minor matters like cutting into line, taking a pencil, and touching a classmate's desk.

Many kids are unable to share or to negotiate for what they want; they are unable to consider the other person's point of view. They assume hostile intent; they believe the other person is intentionally causing them shame, embarrassment, or ridicule.

Many of these children have witnessed adults handling problems by shouting or hitting.

I was in the hallway when some 3rd graders were walking downstairs from a second-floor class. All the way down, one child was loudly protesting. "He cut in, he cut in!" The alarm in his voice prompted me to investigate. I found that both youngsters were vying for second place in line. The one who wasn't succeeding was red-faced, flushed, and crying profusely. His face reflected pure rage. I touched his shoulder, and he was shaking. Only by talking quietly to him and getting him to take deep breaths was I able to calm him down. He was ready to fight. This was a power play and he was losing.

Although the problem of violence exists in elementary school, we usually don't attempt to fix it until middle school or high school. Tragically, "without intervention, 40 percent of childhood bullies become adult felons," according to a recent study (Brendtro and Long 1995).

We clearly need a curriculum to help these kids. But as Johnson and Johnson (1995) point out,

> Teaching students the procedures and skills they need to resolve conflicts constructively has been relatively ignored . . . despite considerable research evidence indicating that the constructive management of conflict increases classroom productivity.

When I first decided to teach my 2nd graders about conflict manage-

> **These kids assume hostile intent; they believe the other person is intentionally causing them shame, embarrassment, or ridicule.**

ment, antiviolence strategies, drug avoidance, and safety, I could find no materials suitable for elementary school children. So I created my own. I wrote a program called "Students Against Violence" (Holden 1990) that is geared for grades 1–5.

Creating a Refuge

Children also have a sense of helplessness and fear about the violence and terror that surrounds them. "What may appear to be a nonchalant guntoting mentality—even habit—among school youth is as often the result of terror, the need for safety, and a perceived lack of options." say Haberman and Dill (1995).

Students in my classroom have expressed their fear of gunshots in the night. One child talked about the bloodstains on her street from a gang fight the day before. She had to look at them as she walked to her school bus. I've seen these children's faces mirroring the horror of what is becoming an everyday occurrence.

In addition, more and more children are the victims of violent crimes committed by adults. Teachers and parents cannot watch their children 24 hours a day, so we must teach them how to get help and how to help themselves.

As an antidote to the environment these children face, I attempt to create a classroom that looks and feels physically and emotionally safe. I place peace posters around the room. I use stuffed animals. I display signs and banners about love, respect, and kindness. The atmosphere says "We do not fight here. We are calm here. We are secure and protected here."

Each morning, the children begin class by reciting their class motto: "We are smart. We are important. We can learn. We care and share. Our teacher loves us." Students then read the brief "newsroom message" that I write on the chalkboard each day. I call them "Star Students" and provide a short, positive message. Next, the children recite their class rules. They know them by heart and they may recite them in any order they like. The rules are short and direct: "Show respect," "No pushing or fighting," "Smile," and "Always do your best," for example.

Finally, the children recite their rap song, "Hugs Not Slugs":

Hugs not slugs is what we say,
We are kind in every way.
We do our best.
We are good.
We solve our problems like we should.
We never fight.
We never bite.
We always share.
We do what's right.

So if you want to join our club,
Just remember,
Hugs Not Slugs!

Integrating the Message

Children need to feel a part of something; they need to belong. Therefore, we have a Students Against Violence club. The children receive membership cards and stickers or stars just for being members in good standing. They must sign a contract promising to avoid violence.

I infuse all of the program's lessons into my curriculum. (My 2nd grade class is self-contained; the children remain together for every subject but gymnasium, music, and art.) For one reading session, I read *The Berenstain Bears Get into a Fight*. Right after I teach vocabulary and comprehension, we apply what we've learned in discussing questions such as "What do the cubs do when they get angry?" "How do the cubs finally solve their problems?" "Is it normal for people to argue?"

I particularly enjoy a lesson called "Year of the Child," included in a social studies or health class. It addresses young people's concerns under four major themes: "I'm Home Alone But Acting Grown," "I Know How to Handle Stranger Danger," "I can Cope, I Don't Need Dope!" and "Get A Grip! Gangs Aren't Hip." Under "Stranger Danger," for example, I have students complete sentences such as "If someone I do not know offers me candy, I will . . ." Under "Gangs Aren't Hip," students answer questions like "What does it mean to be violent?" "Is it a good idea to join a gang?" and "Is it okay to hit someone because you are angry?"

Another lesson, "Make a Better World," follows a map skills lesson. We create an imaginary country called SAV—the acronym for my program. We name cities and streets (Peaceful Avenue in Love Land, for example.) We draw a map of our cities that includes the names of buildings and stores (Friendship Builders is a business that helps people make friends). We write a history of the

You will not rid your classrooms of all disagreements, nor should you try.

country. We even design a flag and postage stamps.

You Can't Do It All

Once we understand some basics about conflict, we are in a better position to control it. Here are some of the things I've learned since starting my program.

- *Teachers can't do it all.* You may have one or two children you just can't reach. They may have severe behavior problems that go beyond the scope of your classroom.
- *It takes time for behavior to change; learning takes place only through repetition.* Don't get frustrated—or lose hope—if you do not see immediate changes in your students. I always say that perhaps my difficult student will be the 3rd grade teacher's success story.
- *The ability to see the other person's point of view is difficult for adults as well as children.* In fact, this is really a grown-up skill that many of us adults are not so good at.
- *Violent behavior may have any of a number of causes, and in a specific incident, we may not know what the student is thinking.* Children do not walk into our classrooms and announce that they are angry and so plan to hit their classmates. They do not necessarily tell us that they are sad or worried or afraid. Having a good student-centered program helps alleviate the stress this ambivalence causes teachers.
- *Conflict is unavoidable.* You will not rid your classrooms of all disagreements, nor should you try. Conflict is a normal part of life. I have finally come to accept that

some days are just bad days for kids. They can be just as cranky and irritable as any adult and therefore more prone to conflicts and arguments.

- *Remember that every conflict is not serious, so don't overreact.* You want to eliminate the violent conflict and teach your kids how to manage the rest.
- *Adults must model ways of handling conflicts peacefully and compliment children who are doing so as well.* I never pass up opportunities to point out when children are settling their problems appropriately.

Watching New Habits Unfold

Once I've taught my students what to do, I can step out of the way and allow them to help one another. And they do. For example, one day when I was demonstrating my program to a visiting teacher, I noticed that a young boy was angry at a classmate. Apparently, he had been sent to the principal's office after the two of them got into a fight in another classroom. Before I began my lesson, I acknowledged the problem and said I hoped they would work it out.

After the lesson, I told the children to work in their groups. As my guest and I watched, two other students immediately went to the child who was upset and attempted to help him work out his problem with his classmate. They cared about him and they now had the skills to help him resolve his problem peacefully. Although he resisted at first, he eventually expressed his anger, got over it, and made up with his pal.

This was the program in action. Without adult supervision, these 7-year-olds were able to help one another solve their problems. And they also got their classwork done—very well, in fact. They did what Johnson and Johnson (1995) said successful anti-violence programs must do: help students change their habits, attitudes, and values, and replace violent behavior with nonviolent or positive behavior.

I hope this happens on a larger scale. Too long have I lived among those who hate peace. I've grown weary of it, and I am offended by it. We must all join forces to combat the epidemic that is destroying our young. We have to start—the kids will do the rest.

References

Brendtro, L., and N. Long. (February 1995). "Breaking the Cycle of Conflict." *Educational Leadership* 52, 5: 52–56.

Haberman, M., and V. S. Dill. (Summer 1995). "Commitment to Violence Among Teenagers in Poverty." *Kappa Delta Pi Record,* p. 148.

Holden, G. (1990). *Students Against Violence.* Westminster, Calif.: Teacher Created Materials.

Johnson, D. W., and R. T. Johnson. (1995). *Reducing School Violence Through Conflict Resolution.* Alexandria, Va.: ASCD.

Gerri Holden teaches 2nd grade at Colfax Elementary School in Pittsburgh. She can be reached at 601 Marshall Ave., Pittsburgh, PA 15214.

Discipline Alternatives

Six Surefire Strategies to Improve Classroom Discipline

With these timely tips, you can start your year off right!
By Martin Henley

Teachers spend as much as 30 percent of their instructional time on discipline, with the majority of student behavior problems being minor distractions such as goofing off or talking out of turn. Keeping more than two dozen young people engaged in learning while handling problems usually generated by two or three students can not only test your patience but also ruin a perfect lesson. Instead of playing the role of air traffic controller, begin the school year with these six strategies for keeping kids focused on your lessons.

1 Move around the room

The front of the classroom is a natural place to be when conducting large-group instruction. However, "frontal teaching" opens up the possibility for many minor discipline problems related to restlessness, daydreaming, or lack of interest.

Rather than rooting yourself to the front of the classroom, move around the room. You can teach just as effectively from the back, side, or middle of the classroom, so let the entire room be your stage. If you need to write something on the board or flip a transparency, ask a student for help. Students enjoy helping you, and doing so keeps them involved in the lesson. As a result, disruptions during your lesson will be kept to a minimum.

2 Teach social skills

This may seem like an additional burden piled on you while you're hard-pressed to meet the demands of the curriculum, but that's not the case. You're already teaching social skills; they're hidden in day-to-day conversation. For example, every time you talk with a student about a procedure for doing a task or give explanations about a misbehavior, you're giving a minilesson on social skills.

If you're concerned about how to fit teaching social skills into your busy schedule, you can relax. Lessons about conflict resolution can be drawn from children's literature and chapter books. Math and science teach about numbers and facts, but these subjects also provide lessons about anticipating consequences and learning from experience. In addition, teaching methods such as cooperative learning, brainstorming, and peer tutoring promote social skills while enriching students' understanding of the curriculum. The amount of time you spend correcting student behavior can be reduced if you bring social skills out into the open and make them a part of your curriculum.

3 Have a sense of humor

You are probably already aware of the positive effects that laughter has on the body. A good chuckle helps to remove irritations and releases tension. Humor can also be the bridge to friendship—it supports relationships and builds group cohesiveness.

If you find ways to enjoy yourself in the classroom by integrating your

Reprinted with permission from *Learning,* August 1997, pp. 43-45. © 1997 by The Education Center, Inc.

interests and hobbies into your curriculum, your sense of humor will surface. Keep in mind that your temperament sets the mood for the entire class. The more of yourself you share with your students, the more fun you will all have.

4 Don't take unruly behavior personally

When I was teaching, my pet peeve was tattling. Maybe that's because I'm a lawyer's son and early on in life I learned the difference between direct observation and hearsay. Whenever a student tattled, I knew that I had to be careful not to respond negatively. Unacknowledged pet peeves can cause a minor discipline issue to snowball into a major confrontation between you and a student.

Be aware of student behavior that throws your emotional gyroscope into a tailspin. Consider that therapists, lawyers, and judges can't make sound professional judgments if they react personally to the people who come to them for help. The same holds true for you. Emotional detachment presents the opportunity for clear thinking, while an impulsive reaction to misbehavior will model precisely the type of behavior that you want your students to eliminate.

5 Look for causes of discipline problems

Ethan was a well-mannered kindergartner who came to class one morning all out of sorts. He was so irritable and argumentative that his teacher sent him to the principal's office. In tears, Ethan confided to the principal that his feet hurt because in a rush, his mother had mistakenly dressed him in a pair of shoes that belonged to his brother and were two sizes too small. Ethan didn't tell his teacher about his feet hurting because he didn't want the other kids to know he was wearing his brother's shoes.

There's always a reason for misbehavior. In exemplary schools, good discipline concentrates on the causes of discipline problems rather than the symptoms. When misbehavior occurs, look for the source of the trouble and see whether there's something within the classroom or school environment that you can change. When confronted with the problem of teasing and bullying, consider the impact of student cliques. When students fail to finish assignments, analyze the interest level of the materials and your presentation.

6 Promote student responsibility

Ms. Levy ran a tight ship. Her students understood that breaking rules would lead to swift consequences. Her class was referred to as the model class, and her students complied with the rules—until the day she was absent. When the substitute arrived, so did the misbehavior.

Don't mistake compliance for responsible behavior. When all control resides with the teacher, students will toe the line because they fear the consequences. Responsible behavior cannot be dictated; the classroom belongs to everyone, not just the teacher.

Classroom events offer many ways to teach and learn responsibility:

- Develop classroom rules together so that the rules are initiated by students rather than forced upon them.
- Use cooperative learning and peer tutoring so that students can help others and feel useful.
- Hold discussions to troubleshoot problems. Honest dialogue about feelings communicates a sense of community and shared priorities.
- Sharing the responsibility of classroom housekeeping teaches students the importance of contributing and giving something back to the class.

Give it a try

As you start off a new school year, think back and recall the number of times in a day that you've had to speak to students about their behavior. You'll have a pretty good idea about how much time you're devoting to discipline. Give these ideas a try. You'll see results. I guarantee it!

***

Martin Henley is a professor at Westfield State College in Westfield, Massachusetts, and has been an educator for 25 years. He's the author of Teaching Self-Control: A Curriculum for Responsible Behavior *(National Educational Service, 1997).*

Classroom Climate and First-Year Teachers

Sally J. Zepeda
University of Oklahoma
Norman, Oklahoma

Judith A. Ponticell
Texas Tech University
Lubbock, Texas

For first-year teachers, classroom climate is a perplexing arena. In their teacher preparation programs, teachers observe classrooms, students, and other teachers. Instruction unfolds, rules and procedures are enforced, and student and teachers subtly negotiate classroom space and interactions. What beginning teachers see is an end-product. Missing are important insights into the nature of the classroom processes and interactions that build the finished classroom climates they observe.

Experienced teachers view classroom climate holistically (Cushing, Sabers, and Berliner 1992). When they plan for teaching, they ask questions about the organization, interaction, and management implications of instructional strategies and classroom activities. Beginning teachers, however, tend to view instruction and management as separate functions. When they plan for teaching, they tend to think in terms of content to be covered and activities to keep students busy. Often, the organization, interactions, and management implications of a lesson are an afterthought, generally confronted after classroom problems occur.

Despite all the literature over the last 45 years reporting the problems of first-year teachers (Smith 1950; Dropkin and Taylor 1963; Veenman 1984; Rust 1994), schools still treat beginning teachers like their experienced colleagues. They are assigned the same number of classes, duty periods, extracurricular responsibilities, and, most often, the least-favored students. Although some schools and school districts are attempting to improve the entry of beginning teachers into their first teaching positions through induction programs and mentoring (Gehrke 1991; Eckmier and Bunyan 1995), many schools and school districts continue to provide unspecialized, infrequent supervision and staff development that ignores the needs of beginning teachers.

For this study, we looked at seven first-year high school teachers in the Chicago area who volunteered to participate. Three teach in suburban public schools, two in urban public schools, and two in urban parochial schools. Despite their different settings, we found important commonalities in their first-year experiences. In this article, we share what we learned from 127 observations and 159 tape-recorded interviews regarding the complex, interrelated nature of their problems with interactions with students, the development of classroom routines and procedures, and the selection of content and instruction. We explore tensions they felt between their ideals about teaching and the realities of the classroom. Finally, we share some thoughts about teacher preparation and school-based support for beginning teachers.

Interrelated Problems

These first-year teachers faced a variety of problems simultaneously. One problem would give rise to another, creating a complex network of challenges. A scaffolding effect occurred in which one problem compounded the seriousness of another. For example, unfamiliarity with the school's curriculum led to unfocused teaching, students responding with off-task behaviors, more time spent on discipline than on teaching, disappointment, and disillusion.

These first-year teachers entered teaching, first and foremost, with the desire to make a difference in students' lives. They found that this intent eroded with their inability to (1) establish positive relationships with their students; (2) set clear expectations and classroom routines and procedures; and (3) select and deliver content in ways that were meaningful to high school students.

Relationships with Students

Teachers interact with students on a daily basis, and the patterns of interaction that contribute to the climate of a classroom are built over time. In their observations of classrooms and in their student teaching experiences, beginning teachers see a more mature climate of education. First-year teachers must establish and maintain interactions with students on a long-term basis, yet their point of reference is based upon short-term observations. Thus, first-year teachers do not know exactly how to speak to or develop relationships with students as learners or as people (Tye and Tye 1984).

Our first-year teachers were confused about their relationships with students. They learned that being a student's friend and trying to establish one's professional self are often at odds with each other. A personal desire to touch deeply the lives of students takes a shocking back seat to establishing order, rules and procedures, and dealing with school or district content specifications. While beginning teachers must consider the individual instructional needs of their students (Borko 1986), our first-year teachers struggled with the conflict between idealistic images of relationships with students and the need to establish authority. They tended to focus on order and efficiency without looking at how instructional content and strategies and students' interests and needs related to the degree of order and efficiency needed.

Routines and Procedures

The development of classroom routines and procedures causes a great deal of distress for beginners (Veenman 1984). Their most immediate experience with classrooms—student teaching—took place in classrooms with already-established routines. Consequently, they had to learn how to communicate expectations for classroom behavior. As a result, discipline problems were common in their classes.

> Our first-year teachers struggled with the conflict between idealistic images of relationships with students and the need to establish authority.

Experienced teachers' stories about students and advice about establishing order greatly influenced our first-year teachers, sending a clear message to "be in charge." But these messages were hard to accept. Our first-year teachers struggled with balancing stories they heard about "keeping the lid" on student behavior with idealistic notions of student-teacher relationships. First, their understanding of rules and procedures developed "context free" during the summer prior to the beginning of their first teaching assignments. Second, they based their rules and procedures upon those existing in the classrooms in which they did their student teaching, then used them for different groups of students. Furthermore, these first-year teachers relied heavily on their last experience and memory of how "students-in-general" behave, and this last experience was the college classroom.

Our first-year teachers had the impression that students simply knew how to go to school. As Ihle (1987, 95) observed, "The worst classroom disciplinarian . . . is likely to be the teacher who keeps reminding the students they must behave." However, these reminders are not linked to clearly understood rules and expectations. These first-year teachers based their rules and procedures on a weak foundational understanding of teaching and learning, enforcing rules inconsistently and often damaging relationships with their students. Teachers find it difficult to develop a positive classroom climate when they act like the students' friend one day and the next day act upon perceived or real advice that students must be controlled.

Content and Instruction

First-year high school teachers are usually subject matter specialists who are degreed and certified in specific content areas. As our first-year teachers struggled to discover and/or develop their own teaching personalities and styles, they often relied on content and their identification with content as a vehicle for making sense of themselves and learning. Using college content, these first-year teachers believed they had the knowledge needed to keep students busy for a prescribed amount of time.

Our first-year teachers faced difficulties with students' reactions to both content selected and instructional strategy. One first-year teacher observed, "I can't seem to get things right, to get students to see how one piece of information fits in with what has just been taught."

These first-year teachers did not know how curriculum unfolds into units and lessons that are manageable and understandable for students. Moreover, they expressed difficulties aligning their instructional techniques to the content and learning styles of their students. One first-year teacher reported that he "tried to teach at the same level that I learned at in college. I felt like most of the time I wasn't making myself clear. Everything was just going over their heads." Another noted, "I never taught American Literature before. I was never responsible for organizing a plan of content. I would plan for long hours, but the organization just never came together for me or my students."

Their college coursework did not help them to interpret high school curriculum. They missed the critical link between organizing content, teaching, and engaging students in learning. As a result, our first-year teachers had little credibility with students, and students reacted with troublesome behavior.

Preparing Teachers

While we cannot generalize from a study of seven first-year teachers that every first-year teacher goes through the same experiences, we believe that the problems our first-year teachers encountered will sound familiar to many first-year teachers. With impending teacher shortages, the "greying" of the profession, an increase in alternatively certified teachers, and a high attrition rate among first-year teachers, we must begin to think of preservice teacher preparation, student teaching or internship, and the first-year of teaching as a continuous learning experience. Both teacher preparation and school-based supports for beginning teachers must:

- focus on real classrooms. Lecture-based coursework and school-based staff development will not enhance classroom-specific problem solving.
- address teaching in a holistic fashion. In the case of classroom climate, coursework and staff development must focus on the interrelatedness of organization, interaction, and management implications of content, instructional strategies, and classroom activities.
- follow a reality-based continuum of content and experience that enables the development of skills and resolution of problems over time. Important

questions to ask in coursework and schools are: What does the beginning teacher know at this time? What teaching tasks should the beginning teacher be realistically expected to use at this time? What content or skill does the beginning teacher need to complete these tasks at this time?

- reframe preservice clinical experiences, student teaching, and the first-year teaching experience as a single induction continuum, to university supervisors, mentors, peer coaches, other teaching colleagues, and school administrators must be reexamined to determine who is responsible for giving what kind of information, assistance, and support at what time to foster growth and improvement in beginning teachers.

Authors

Sally J. Zepeda is Assistant Professor of Educational Leadership and Policy Studies at the University of Oklahoma, in Norman. Her research interests include supervision of instruction and teacher evaluation, mentoring, and induction. Dr. Zepeda is a member of the Golden Apple Chapter of Kappa Delta Pi.

Judith A. Ponticell is Assistant Professor of Curriculum, Instruction, and Educational Leadership at Texas Tech University, in Lubbock. Her research interests include teachers as learners, individual and organizational change processes, and teacher and administrator induction. She is the 1994 recipient of the Distinguished Research Award from the Association of Teacher Educators.

References

Borko, H. 1986. Clinical teacher education: The induction years. In *Reality and reform in clinical teacher education*, ed. J. V. Hoffman and S. A. Edwards, 45–64. New York: Random House.

Cushing, K. S., D. S. Sabers, and D. C. Berliner. 1992. Olympic gold: Investigations of expertise in teaching. *Educational Horizons* 70(3): 108–14.

Dropkin, S., and M. Taylor. 1963. Perceived problems of beginning teachers and related factors. *Journal of Teacher Education* 14(4): 384–89.

Eckmier, J., and R. Bunyan. 1995. Mentor teachers: Key to educational renewal. *Educational Horizons* 73(3): 124–29.

Gehrke, N. J. 1991. Seeing our way to better helping of beginning teachers. *The Educational Forum* 55(3): 233–42.

Ihle, R. 1987. Defining the big principal—What schools and teachers want in their leaders. *National Association of Secondary School Principals Bulletin* 71(500): 94–98.

Rust, F. O. 1994. The first year of teaching: It's not what they expected. *Teacher & Teacher Education* 10(2): 205–17.

Smith, H. P. 1950. A study of the problems of beginning teachers. *Educational Administration and Supervision* 36(5): 257–64.

Tye, K. A., and B. B. Tye. 1984. Teacher isolation and school reform. *Phi Delta Kappan* 65(5): 319–22.

Veenman, S. 1984. Perceived problems of beginning teachers. *Review of Educational Research* 54(2): 143–78.

Equal Opportunity in Education

As we move toward the end of this century we find that there is an immense amount of unfinished business before us in the area of intercultural relations in the schools and in educating all Americans regarding how multicultural our national population demographics really are. We are becoming more and more multicultural with every passing decade. This further requires us to take steps to ensure that all of our educational opportunity structures remain open to all persons regardless of their cultural backgrounds or gender. There is much unfinished business as well with regard to improving educational opportunities for girls and young women; the remaining gender issues in American education are very real and directly related to the issue of equality of educational opportunity.

Issues of racial prejudice and bigotry still plague us in American education, despite massive efforts in many school systems to improve racial and intercultural relations in the schools. Many American adolescents are in crisis as their basic health and social needs are not adequately met and their educational development is affected by crises in their personal lives. The articles in this unit reflect all of the above concerns plus others related to efforts to provide equality of educational opportunity to all American youth and attempts to clarify what multicultural education is and what it is not.

The "equity agenda," or social justice agenda, in the field of education is a complex matrix of gender- and culture-related issues aggravated by incredibly wide gaps in the social and economic opportunity structures available to citizens. We are each situated by cultural, gender-based, and socioeconomic factors in society; this is true of all persons, everywhere. We have witnessed a great and glorious struggle for human rights in our time and in our nation. The struggle continues to deal more effectively with educational opportunity issues related to cultural diversity and gender.

The effort to improve equality of opportunity in the field of education relates to a wide range of both cultural and gender issues still confronting our society. Although there has been a great, truly historic, effort to achieve social justice in American society, that effort must continue. We need to see our social reality in the context of our "wholeness" as a culturally pluralistic society in which there remain unresolved issues in the field of education for both cultural minorities and women. Women's issues and concerns have historically been part of the struggle for civil liberties.

The "Western canon" is being challenged by advocates of multicultural perspectives in school curriculum development. Multicultural educational programming, which will reflect the rapidly changing cultural demographics of North American schooling, is being advocated by some and strongly opposed by others. This controversy centers around several different issues regarding what it means to provide equality of opportunities for culturally diverse students. The traditional Western cultural content of general and social studies and language arts curricula is being challenged as Eurocentric.

Helping teachers to broaden their cultural perspectives and to take a more global view of curriculum content is something the advocates of culturally pluralistic approaches to curriculum development would like to see integrated into the entire elementary and secondary school curriculum structure. North America is as multicultural a region of the world as exists anywhere. Our enormous cultural diversity encompasses populations from many indigenous "First Americans" as well as peoples from every European culture, plus many peoples of Asian, African, and Latin American nations and the Central and South Pacific Island groups. There is spirited controversy over how to help all Americans to better understand our collective multicultural heritage. There are spirited defenders and opponents of the traditional Eurocentric curriculum.

The problem of inequality of educational opportunity is of great concern to American educators. One in four American children does not have all of basic needs met and lives under poverty conditions. Almost one in three lives in a single-parent home, which in itself is no disadvantage—but under conditions of poverty, it often is. More and more concern is expressed over how to help children of poverty. The equity agenda of our time has to do with many issues related to gender, race, and ethnicity. All forms of social deprivation and discrimination are aggravated by great disparities in income and accumulated wealth. How can students be helped to have an equal opportunity to succeed in school? We have wrestled with this dilemma in educational policy development for decades. How can we advance the just cause of the educational interests of our young people more effectively?

Some of us are still proud to say that we are a nation of immigrants. As we became a new nation, powerful demographic and economic forces impacted upon the makeup of our population. In addition to the traditional minority/majority group relationships that evolved in the United States, new waves of immigrants today are again enhancing the importance of concerns for achieving equality of opportunity in education. In light of these vast sociological and demographic changes, we must ensure that we will remain a multicultural democracy.

The social psychology of prejudice is something that psychiatrists, social psychologists, anthropologists, and sociologists have studied in great depth since the 1930s. Tolerance, acceptance, and a valuing of the unique worth of every person are teachable and learnable attitudes. A just society must be constantly challenged to find meaningful ways to raise human aspirations, to heal human hurt, and to help in the task of optimizing every citizen's potential. Education is a vital component to that end.

Teachers can incorporate into their lessons an emphasis on acceptance of difference, toleration of and respect for the beliefs of others, and the skills of reasoned debate and dialogue.

We must remain alert to keep our constitutional promises. Although it is not easy to maintain fair opportunity structures in a culturally pluralistic society, we must continually try.

The struggle for optimal representation of minority perspectives in the schools will be a matter of serious concern to educators for the foreseeable future. From the many court decisions upholding the rights of women and cultural minorities in the schools over the past 40 years has emerged a national consensus that we must strive for the greatest degree of equality in education as may be possible. The triumph of constitutional law over prejudice and bigotry must continue.

As we look with hope to our future, we seek compassion in the classroom for our respective visions of the world.

Looking Ahead: Challenge Questions

How do you respond to calls for the integration of more multicultural content into school studies?

What do you know about how it feels to be poor? How do you think it would feel in school? How would you respond?

What is multicultural education? To what does the national debate over multiculturalism in the schools relate? What are the issues regarding it?

If you are a female, have you ever felt that you were discriminated against or, at the least, ignored? Describe your experiences.

If you are a male, have you ever felt that you were being favored? Relate your experiences.

How can schools more effectively address the issues of gender bias?

How do children learn to be prejudiced? How can they learn tolerance and acceptance of diversity?

How would you define the remaining equity issues in the field of education? How would you rank order them?

Are there social class issues that affect students' lives in schools? Explain them.

The Challenge of Affirmative Action

By Valerie Ooka Pang,
David Strom,
& Russell L. Young

Affirmative action has been and continues to be a complex social issue that demands courageous and difficult decisions. Many questions arise in the discussion: Is it best to be color-conscious or color-blind? How can a nation ensure equity for all people? Though Supreme Court Justices like Sandra Day O'Connor, Antonin Scalia, and Clarence Thomas have ruled that the Constitution protects individuals and not groups, the United States is clearly not a color-blind society, and many individuals have been and continue to be discriminated against due to their membership in groups based on race, ethnicity, religion, gender, class, and sexual orientation.

The purpose of this paper is to look at the challenge of using affirmative action programs when there are competing groups of underrepresented people struggling for limited school resources. We view affirmative action as actions that address past and current patterns of discrimination and promote the goal of diversity in society. Many people believe these programs represent preferential treatment primarily based on race and gender, while others see affirmative action programs as crucial means to be inclusive of the diversity in society.

In this paper we present the case study of a San Francisco high school where sev-

Valerie Ooka Pang, David Strom, and Russell L. Young are faculty members in the School of Education at San Diego State University, San Diego, California.

eral Asian-American students did not feel they were treated fairly because of their ethnicity. The students are an example of a group within the underrepresented community who feel they are being discriminated against because they have done well. The case of Lowell High School brings to the surface conflicting values. The challenge is how to balance competing goals. Several tensions have emerged. In this situation, the goals of affirming diversity and addressing historical patterns of discrimination are in conflict with the goal of equal treatment of each person.

The Case of Lowell High School in San Francisco

In San Francisco at Lowell High School, Chinese-American students are finding themselves in the middle of a fierce discussion on affirmative action. Last year, 94 Chinese Americans were denied admissions to the school.[1] These students had scores that were comparable or higher than other students admitted from other ethnic groups. The year before, 90 Chinese-American students were turned away under the same conditions. The debate has fueled dialogue over the importance of academic opportunities and quotas.

In 1994, three Chinese-American students, Brian Ho, Patrick Wong, and Hilary Chen, and their parents filed a federal

class-action lawsuit against this school and its desegregation plan, which does not allow more than 40 percent of students to come from one ethnic group. This suit challenges a 1983 court desegregation decision limiting the number of Chinese Americans who can enroll in the school. Every year, 1,800 students apply for about 700 new freshman positions in the ninth grade class.[2] For the fall of 1995, Chinese Americans had to score a minimum of 63 on the school's admission index of 69, while Whites and other Asians had to score at least 60, and Latinos and Blacks had to have scores of at least 55. There is also an affirmative action category that admits Blacks and Latinos who score in the range of 50 to 54.

Lowell High School is one of the most coveted public schools in the Bay Area and many students would like the opportunity to attend. The case study provides students the opportunity to discuss how affirmative action goals clash in real life. Discussions may help students understand that group and individual goals can be sources of tension, especially when trying to be equitable.

In a democracy, it is crucial for students, teachers, and parents in our communities to work together to solve problems. The challenge is not only to define equity, but also to get people to work together toward a common goal that may not seem to benefit the individual directly or immediately.

From *Multicultural Education*, Summer 1997, pp. 4-8. © 1997 by the National Association for Multicultural Education. Reprinted by permission.

Strategies for Promoting the Goal of Diversity in Society

What Should Be Done at Lowell High?

As the debate over the admissions policy continues, the following simulated conversation among the Chinese-American parents and the children who filed the lawsuit, the school personnel, and other Lowell High School parents about the admissions policy presents some of the perspectives in the controversy:

School Personnel: We're sorry, but your children will not be allowed to go to Lowell. You will have to send your children to another school because our school is already 40 percent Chinese American and we need more diversity at Lowell.

Chinese American Parent 1: That's not fair. Our children have done what you told them to do. They have earned mostly A's and they have also been leaders in the community volunteering many hours in hospitals, nursing homes, and recreation centers. They have also gotten high scores on their standardized tests, and their scores are higher than other students you are admitting. We don't understand why our children can't get in. If we send them to another school, our kids will not get as good of an education.

Other Parents: We know you want your children to go to the best schools. We do too, but there are already many Chinese Americans going to the school. For us to ever achieve equity in society, we need spaces for other students.

Chinese-American Students Filing Suit: Quotas are unfair. Quotas always discriminate against someone. We know what it is to be called "Chink" or "Chinaman." We do not oppose affirmative action, but we have worked hard and it is not fair to exclude us while other less qualified students are allowed into Lowell High School.

Chinese-American Parent 2: We don't want to stick out in this lawsuit. Our kids didn't get in either and they were qualified. We know your kids didn't get in and were also qualified. So why don't we work together.

Chinese-American Parent 1: What can we do?

Non-Chinese-American Parent: Let's get together and ask the district why there aren't more opportunities for all these qualified students.

Another Parent: Why can't other schools be as outstanding as Lowell? Why isn't the district doing something to help other schools become excellent?

Before discussing the alternative of creating other excellent schools, the next section presents the new admissions policies at Lowell High School.

Lowell High School: New Admissions Policies

San Francisco Unified School District has revised their admissions policies for Lowell High School.[3] The new policies are similar to the earlier ones. Under the new proposal

. . . approximately 80 percent of the 9th grade Lowell class for the 1996–7 school year will be admitted using the same point criteria for all students. The process for point determination remains unchanged. The remaining approximately 20 percent will be admitted on a "value added" diversity basis open to all ethnic groups who meet socio-economic disadvantage criteria and high academic achievement performance. Students who qualify for this "value added" pool to Lowell will be required to attend a special six-week summer session prior to their freshman year. This summer session will also be open to all incoming Lowell students.[4]

The new 20 percent "value diversity" category differs little from past affirmative action practices. The suit that was filed by the Chinese American students and their parents has not been settled.[5]

Since the class action suit involves a high school, students may be able to relate to this issue and it may be a meaningful case study of equity for them to address through an issues-centered approach.

Using an Issues-Centered Approach with Students: Raising the Issue of Affirmative Action in the Classroom

An issues-centered approach is consistent with our national ideals as an exercise in democratic values. It fosters examination, discussion, and resolution of public issues in a multicultural society. The approach encourages students to consider other perspectives, develop their own "voice" without the filters of others, respect and listen to others, and foster a sense of community through dialogue and collaborative solutions. It is an effective way to teach controversial topics like affirmative action.

When engaged in the process, students develop critical-thinking skills by sorting through their competing and conflicting values and arriving at a thoughtful decision after considering alternatives and their consequences. Students must develop the ability to engage in discussion of controversial issues which are sources of tension so they can become informed participants in society.[6] Since this approach is open-ended, teachers usually take a neutral role during the discussion, though they also must make sure that the discussion does not stop. Teachers may ask students questions to keep the momentum of the dialogue moving.

Following are several components of an issues-centered unit.[7]

- Teachers introduce students to the issue. The teacher can begin by presenting the case of Lowell High School. Additional resources can be provided for students to read, such as newspaper articles from the *San Francisco Examiner* or other articles on affirmative action.
- Students review information and define the major issue. The teacher may ask the following questions and write the responses on the board. In addition, it may help students to focus by having them write their answers quickly on a sheet of paper before they

are asked to share their perspectives with the class orally.
- What is the main issue at Lowell High School?
- Who are the main participants in the problem?
- Students clarify terms and share information. Students may be asked:
- How would you define affirmative action?
- What is a level playing field?
- What are the important points being made?
- What tensions do you see?
- Students examine their values. These questions can help students to identify what their own conflicting values are in this situation:
- What values are conflicting in this issue?
- Which values do you think are most important?
- In the final segment of the approach, students come to a decision and give an analysis of how they came to their final position. The teacher may ask:
- What are possible solutions at Lowell?
- What are the consequences to each alternative suggested?
- What do you think should be done at Lowell? What policies should be adopted? Why?

To extend the approach, after students discuss what they think should be done, they can form teams where the group role-plays the solutions by choosing various roles like the Chinese-American students who filed the suit, other Asian-American students, African-American, Anglo-American, and Latino students, parents, teachers, and the school board.

A teacher can also have students get involved in a mock trial where the state supreme court is hearing the case brought to them by the Chinese-American students. Students would take on the roles of lawyers, plaintiffs, parents, school boards, teachers, and judges. This would actively involve students in the process and stimulate further discussion.

Background Information for Teachers

Affirmative action is a complex issue. Before teachers have students grapple with the issue in class, teachers are advised to examine the issue themselves. Students may need teachers to provide some direction, because the issue is like an onion with many layers. There are many issues at the core of this situation as indicated by the following questions:

- What is equity?

- What is the purpose of affirmative action?
- What protections does the fourteenth amendment provide individuals? groups?
- What is the responsibility of society towards its members: equality of opportunity or equality of results?
- How can minority interests be protected from the majority?
- Should affirmative action be implemented? Is so, how? If not, why?
- What policies should be implemented at Lowell?
- Why aren't there more Lowells?
- There is only one Lowell High School. How can school districts be encouraged to create more excellent schools?

In preparation for class discussions, the teacher should examine the issue of why there aren't more schools like Lowell.

Why Aren't There More Lowells?

One of the questions that arose in the simulated discussion was why aren't there more Lowell High Schools. Many skeptics would say, "Because it can't be done."

Skeptics often think of a pie as an analogy for resources. There is one pie and a set number of pieces to go around. With this perception, it becomes necessary to fight for a slice of the pie, rather than work together to build more bakeries that could produce more pies. Often people's viewpoints are based upon the economic assumption that there just isn't enough money. However, a long-term goal can have a longer impact, but often it is more difficult to implement.

Using another example, when two people love each other, they may have or adopt a child. They do not love their partner any less because they now share their love with a child. Instead, their capacity to love grows. In terms of the pie analogy, the pie becomes twice as large, it does not shrink.

Excellent schools can be a model for others. If one school is successful, the others can be successful too. In fact, Deborah Meier has shown that affirming schools can be built for all children.[8] Meier is the director of schools that have been extremely successful in school reform. With the help of teachers, parents, and students, she reinvented schools by creating a group of four Central Park East schools (CPESS) in East Harlem. The secondary school graduates 95 percent of its students and 90 percent of those students go on to college. Most of the students are Latinos and African Americans who come from low-income families.

The number of students in the Central Park East schools ranges from 250 to 400.

The small size of the schools allows faculty to respond to the needs of the students more quickly: for example, a class schedule for the entire school can be changed in a week. In addition, one of the most important philosophical aspects of the school is respect:

A good school for anyone is a little like kindergarten and a little like a good post-graduate program—the two ends of the educational spectrum, at which we understand that we cannot treat any two human beings identically, but must take into account their special interests and styles even as we hold all to high and rigorous standards. . . . The main difference between the advantaged and the disadvantaged is that the latter need such flexible schools even more. When people think "those kids' need something special, the reply we offer at CPESS is, Just give them what you have always offered those who have the money to buy the best, which is mostly a matter of respect. (p. 49)[9]

The Manhattan Center for Math and Science was also created using the Central Park East model. It houses an elementary school, a junior high, and high school. Franklin High had previously served the area, but was closed when the Manhattan school opened. It had only a seven percent graduate rate and 44 percent of the students attended class on any given day.[10] Principal Cole Genn and his assistant principal, Gene Brown, wanted to change the community's feeling of hopelessness about the school to one of success.

The administrators involved community people from institutions and businesses such as Columbia Teachers College and General Electric at the Manhattan Center. Parents also became involved. Within four years, all but four of 154 students graduated from High School and went on to college.[11] Parents beamed with pride because their young people were being admitted to prestigious universities like M.I.T., Harvard, Amherst, Cornell, Trinity, and Wesleyan. The Manhattan class of 1986 was featured on the cover of *The New York Times.* Although many had said that these schools could not be created, parents, students, community people, and school personnel believed in the potential of each student. Together they worked to provide students with skills, confidence, and opportunities. Meier and Genn are revolutionary educators. Their vision was not limited. They made the pie larger and this gave many more students the opportunity to go to excellent schools.

Affirmative Action Addresses Past Patterns of Discrimination

In the case of Lowell High School, the goal of the district is to address past patterns of discrimination by encouraging broad representation of diverse students in the school. It is difficult to respond to Chinese-American students who believe they have not been treated equally. They are members of a group which has been and continues to be subjected to discrimination and social oppression. However, in this particular context, they are not victims of a pattern of exclusion. Since 40 percent of the school is Chinese American, there is little to suggest a conspiracy to keep the Chinese Americans as a group out of the school. The issue of providing access to students from all groups is the most pressing issue at the school. Students from all groups should have the opportunity to attend the Lowell.

> In order to fight racial oppression, it may be necessary for individuals, at particular times, to place the collective good before their own personal needs.

While it may appear that the rights of individual Chinese-American students are being denied, the rights of Chinese Americans as a group are not being denied. In this particular case, the primary goals of Lowell should be to have an integrated population and to address the past pattern of exclusion. Race does matter and has since the beginning of our nation. To argue that we live in a color-blind society, and thus the Chinese-American students should be allowed into Lowell, denies that race matters. People are not the same, nor are they treated the same. In order to fight racial oppression, it may be necessary for individuals, at particular times, to place the collective good before their own personal needs.

In addition to competing values, there are many myths in society. These myths serve to keep the status quo and do not encourage an inclusionary society. The following are myths that act as obstacles to addressing and finding ways to solve our equity issues, and the comments that follow are responses to those myths.

- **Preferences need to be done away with.** William H. Gray III, President of the United Negro College Fund, remarked: "Our society has been loaded with preferences. Preferences for veterans, preferences for senior citizens, preferences for farmers. Government contracting has had preference for small business—small white business—that far exceeds the preferences for [businesses owned by] minorities. I don't see anyone saying let's stop that preference. . . . The only one they want to get rid of is race."[12]

- **Merit can be objectively measured.** Merit is a subjective measure and is judged by the person who is doing the measuring. That person will determine what is valuable.

- **The resource pie is limited and each person must fight to get their share.** Our nation does not have limited resources, rather the problem is limited visions. Communities can create more excellent schools like what Deborah Meier and Cole Genn have accomplished in New York City.

- **Admission quotas are a major tool in affirmative action programs.** Quotas can be used to allow people to get in, but they also can be used to exclude others. When quotas are used to encourage more diversity in our institutions, they are only a short-term answer to social discrimination.

- **The Supreme Court ruled against racial preference in the *Bakke* case.** Though the Supreme Court ruled that the use of quotas was unlawful in this case, there have been numerous cases where courts have upheld the use of quotas in cases where there is evidence of discrimination. In addition, the Supreme Court ruled in the *Bakke* case that race could be considered in admissions programs created to increase the participation of underrepresented groups.[13]

Today there is a great deal of racism, sexism, homophobia, and classism in society. Children must be taught to include people rather than exclude them. Society will not change without the participation of a diversity of citizens. In order to have equal opportunity and equal results, we must have programs like affirmative action that create an equitable playing field and affirm our diversity as a nation.

Conclusion

Harvard Professor Randall Kennedy's following remarks point to the core issue: "What is required is to create political institutions that address the needs and aspirations of all Americans, not simply whites, who have long enjoyed racial privilege, but people of color who have long suffered racial exclusion from policy making forums."[14] Students need to understand that though the affirmative action debate is often seen from a winners and losers perspective, this is a limiting perception. Rather, affirmative action is really about encouraging all people to participate in society.

Lani Guinier suggests an alternative to the winner-take-all majoritarianism; she recommends through dialogue, compromise, and consensus "the principle of taking turns."[15] Guinier believes that when all citizens are empowered to participate in society, the majority does not lose, rather they "simply learn to take turns" which is a "positive-sum solution that allows all . . .to feel that they participate" in a meaningful way.[16]

Sherman Schwartz reiterates Guinier's viewpoint and explains how the majority may not understand that its actions are limiting the abilities of others to participate in society. He states:

> Affirmative-action hiring plans . . .are not intended to deny jobs to whites but to make jobs available to blacks. Any harm to whites [or Asians] is entirely unintentional. . . . Centuries of discrimination are so embedded in institutions and attitudes that whites are often unaware of their impact. . . . Affirmative-action plans that allocate a relative handful of business or other opportunities for qualified minorities are thus nothing like the racist laws that subjected human beings to brutality, poverty, and powerlessness. Only the most willful blindness fails to see this.[17]

What are the goals of schools? Are they intended only to provide children with reading, writing, mathematics, and computer skills? Or are they also intended to transmit American values like equality, freedom, democracy, and diversity. Today, few would argue against racial equality; however, racial equality is an ideal. When confronted with affirmative action in one's personal life, individuals may feel they are being threatened and treated unfairly. For example, when a qualified person from an underrepresented group is hired, many individuals may resent her because they do not understand that this person is bringing with her not only skills and knowledge needed for the position, but also a different set of experiences and information that enrich the organization. Students need to struggle with the complexities and dilemmas that are aspects of affirmative action programs. What happened at Lowell is a good example.

People from all groups feel that they have struggled and been victims of discrimination; the historical record of discrimination towards groups like African-Americans is shameful. Many European-American groups like the Irish, Italians, and Polish also faced severe discrimination. However European Americans have been able to assimilate more easily into the macroculture, while people of color continue to face the barrier of discrimination. We must look at the historical context of discrimination and its impact on society when everyone does not have the opportunity to develop her/his talents and interests. Stanley Crouch wrote, "Unless Americans begin to assert the commonality of their fates, . . .and are convinced that a superb work force can include people from many backgrounds through fair practices, the squabble will continue and the bitterness will deepen in all directions."[18]

As Cornel West has stated, race does matter.[19] Gender, class, and social orientation also matter in our society. One of the questions we have asked Non-African-American teachers in our classes is "Would you rather be Black?" Most say no, because they realize that African Americans face myriad social stigmas. People discriminate against African Americans because of color. Would you rather be rich or poor? Would you rather be male or female? By posing these questions, teachers can attempt to confront social oppression by bringing the issues to students on a personal level. Dialogue in a supportive and trusting atmosphere is crucial to moving forward.

As John Dewey explained, democracy is a social process where we dialogue and live together, rather than a form of government.[20] Democracy should provide us with the tools to change our institutions so that they are more fair and just. Even though the need for community is inherent in the human condition, it does not occur automatically, nor does it come about when people live in the same neighborhoods; communities are formed because of shared interests and a willingness to work for common issues.[21] This process is often challenging and difficult. Tensions will arise just as they did at Lowell High School; however, in a place where community is important, members will work to find solutions that strengthen the community rather than tear it apart.

Affirmative action refers to programs that are affirming, affirming our interconnections and diversity with each other.[22] Taking turns and encouraging a broad participation of the community are two critical aspects of our democratic values. More Lowell High Schools must be created because every child must have an opportunity to attend a school which is dedicated to and effective with all its students.

> Injustice anywhere is a threat to justice everywhere. We are caught in an inescapable network of morality, tied in a single garment of destiny. What affects one directly, affects all indirectly.
>
> —*Martin Luther King, Jr.*

Notes

1. Elaine Woo, "Caught on the Wrong Side of the Line? The Los Angeles Times, Thursday, 13 July 1995, pp. A1, A15; and "Suit Allowed Over Race Quotas in S. F. Schools," San Diego Union- Tribune, Saturday, 30 September, 1995, p. A3.
2. Woo., A15.
3. Waldemar Rojas, "Letter to Parents, Lowell High School Admissions Process," January 20, 1996, pp. 1–2.
4. Ibid., p. 1.
5. Venise Wagner, "Elite S. F. School Faces new Policy," San Francisco Examiner, December 21, 1995, Newsbank 1995 EDU 101:A5.
6. James Shaver, "Rationales for Issues-Centered Social Studies Education," The Social Studies, 83, 3, 95–99.
7. Shirley Engle & Anna Ochoa. Education for Democratic Citizenship: Decision-making 'in the Social Studies. New York: Teachers College Press, 1988.
8. Deborah Meier. 1995. The Power of Their Ideas. Boston, MA: Beacon Press, p. 49.
9. Ibid., p. 49.
10. Seymour Fliegel & James MacGuire, 1993. Miracle in East Harlem. New York: Random House.
11. Ibid., p. 151
12. Voices, Los Angeles Times, Sunday, April 30, 1995, p. A24.
13. Peter Irons & Stephanie Guitton (Eds.) May It Please The Court. New York: New Press, 1993, p. 318.
14. Lani Guinier. The Tyranny of the Majority. New York: Free Press, 1994, p. 6.
15. Ibid.
16. Guinier, p. 6–7.
17. Sherman Schwartz, "The Blind Spot in Strict Scrutiny." The Los Angeles Times, Sunday, 18 June 1995, p. M1.
18. Stanley Crouch, "Someone Ate My Bowl of Privilege," The Los Angeles Times, Sunday, 18 June 1995, pp. M1, M6.
19. Cornel West. Race Matters. Boston, MA: Beacon Press, 1993.
20. John Dewey, *Democracy and Education: An Introduction to the Philosophy of Education*. New York: Macmillan, 1916.
21. Valerie Ooka Pang, Geneva Gay & William B. Stanley, 1995. "Expanding Conceptions of Community and Civic Competence for a Multicultural society," *Theory and Research in Social Studies Education* 23(5), pp. 302–331.
22. Geneva Gay. Private Interview. April, 1995, San Francisco, Ca.

SOCIAL CLASS ISSUES IN FAMILY LIFE EDUCATION*

Robert Hughes, Jr. and Maureen Perry-Jenkins**

Beginning with an examination of cultural and structural frameworks for considering social class, we examine the research evidence regarding social class differences in parenting and marriage. Additionally, family life education literature is reviewed regarding how families in different social classes respond to various forms of intervention. Finally, we offer recommendations about how to include social class issues in the content and delivery of family life education.

From an ecological perspective, family life educators have been increasingly oriented towards the development of prevention and intervention models that consider families in context. Within this framework, there has been an increased emphasis on understanding the diversity of family experiences that has challenged researchers and family life educators to pay closer attention to issues of race, class, and gender as they affect families. These three deeply interrelated social categories place families within a hierarchical social system that offers differential rewards and resources to those members at different levels of the hierarchy. Although there has been some attention to these matters in our research on families, there has been less attention to these issues in family life education. In a recent handbook devoted to family life education, Arcus and Thomas (1993) state, "gender, class and ethnicity have received little attention as factors that might affect family life education programs" (p. 23). In those cases in which there has been attention to these issues, ethnicity and gender have received most of the attention. Indeed, in the same handbook (Arcus, Schvaneveldt, & Moss, 1993), there are chapters on gender and ethnicity in regards to family life education, but there is no chapter on social class.

The purpose of this article is to begin to examine the meaning of social class in the lives of families. Specifically, our first aim is to discuss how social class can lead family members to assign different meanings and values to their behaviors and life circumstances. As Kohn (1977) and others have shown, social class fosters values which, in turn, affect our daily interactions with spouses, children, and friends. Our second aim is to address the importance of social class as a critical issue to be considered by family life educators as they seek to support families.

CONCEPTUAL AND MEASUREMENT ISSUES

Theoretical Perspectives on Social Class

Despite the fact that most of us have an intuitive sense about social class and can even describe our position in this social hierarchy, it has proven to be a slippery idea for researchers to conceptualize. Two distinct theoretical approaches to understanding social class have been proposed in the literature. The *cultural approach* views class differences as indicative of subcultural variation among those of different socioeconomic levels who hold different cultural values (Baca Zinn & Eitzen, 1990). Historically, this approach has often led to comparisons across social categories, with the middle class representing better or more adaptive values, such as self-direction and independence, as compared to working- or lower-classes. A criticism of the cultural approach is its susceptibility to being used evaluatively; that is, there is a tendency to blame individuals in certain social conditions for their situation. The rationale for this view is that if these individuals had good or the right values they could succeed in this society.

In opposition to the cultural view, a *structural approach* places emphasis on external social forces that situate families at certain positions within the hierarchy. Baca Zinn and Eitzen (1990) argue that, although many family patterns may be differentiated by social class, we cannot assume that these cultural norms are stable traits specific to a class level or that they are passed from generation to generation. Rather, Baca Zinn and Eitzen propose that structural conditions in American society shape the ways in which families function. Rapp's (1982) work on class and family illustrates how households are shaped differently based on economic resources. Specifically, families with more secure economic resources can more easily aspire to a cultural ideal in the U. S. of self-support and autonomy than those individuals who are marginalized in our economic structures.

*The authors wish to thank Laurie Kramer and Robert Moreno for their thoughtful comments on this manuscript.

**Robert Hughes, Jr. is an Associate Professor and Extension Specialist in Family Relations and Human Development, The Ohio State University, 1787 Neil Avenue, Columbus, OH 43210. Maureen Perry-Jenkins is an Assistant Professor in Consumer and Family Studies, University of Massachusetts, Amherst, MA 01003.

Key Words: culture, family life education, marriage, parenting, social class.

The distinction between the cultural and structural approaches to social class is critical. A cultural approach focuses on values and goals situated within a specific class where "those in the higher socioeconomic levels are said to have cultural values that mold successful individuals while those at lower socioeconomic levels are said to have different cultural values" (Baca Zinn & Eitzen, 1990, p. 94). A structural analysis examines how people within certain classes come to embrace particular values as a way to cope with the opportunity structure in our society.

Each of these theoretical approaches presents family researchers and practitioners with difficulties. Recognizing that in our current class structure families tend to hold different values across levels suggests that interventions and family life education programs must be sensitive to those differing values and must work within different belief systems. This is not to suggest that we accept a cultural approach that compares all other groups to the optimal middle class, but rather our aim should be to value the differing goals and ideals that individuals hold at different levels of the hierarchy and recognize how beliefs and behaviors are adaptive within different contexts. At the same time, in acknowledging that our society is based on an inequitable social structure that distributes rights, power, and privileges differentially to families, we should also be charged with reforming a social system that allows for such inequality. Keeping these goals in mind, the following discussion not only focuses on the importance of valuing various belief systems across class levels but also challenges the system that may enforce what the ruling class views as the correct belief system.

Defining and Measuring Social Class

Gecas (1979), in his review of the research on social class, suggests that a major problem in interpreting the findings in this field stems from differences in the measurement and categorization of class. Researchers differ on issues of whether class is a discrete or continuous variable, whether it is a unidimensional or multidimensional concept, whether it is constructed within one's community or in society at large, and whether it is a subjective or objective phenomenon.

According to Kohn (1979), who is perhaps the most well known social scientist to examine the implications of social class for family life, the two most important aspects of social class are education and occupational position. Income is of secondary importance in Kohn's conceptualization of class. He proposes that the stratification system in the United States is best thought of as a continuum of social class positions with no sharp demarcations. He argues, however,

that most research on class and families resorts to a rather simplistic model that includes four class levels: lower class (unskilled manual workers), working class (semi-skilled and skilled workers), middle class (white collar workers and professionals), and the elite (differentiated in terms of wealth and lineage, rather than occupation). Despite the challenges researchers face in operationalizing the concept of class, most recognize its importance and utility in family research. As Kohn (1979) concludes,

> [social class] is useful because it captures the reality that the intricate interplay of all these variables creates different basic conditions of life at different levels of the social order. Members of different social classes, by virtue of enjoying (or suffering) different conditions of life, come to see the world differently—to develop different conceptions of social reality, different aspirations and hopes and fears, different conceptions of the desirable. (p. 48)

In contrast to Kohn's conceptualization, the two most pervasive indices of socioeconomic status in the literature, which were developed by Warner (1960) and Hollingshead and Redlich (1958), combine indicators of education and income into a single index. It should be noted, however, that disagreement exists about which indicators should be used to assess class. Erickson and Gecas (1991) describe in detail the complex and often opposing ways that factors such as income and education can influence parental roles. For example, research indicates that as fathers' educational levels increase, so does involvement with their children (Lamb, 1986). In contrast, Model (1981) has found that as men's incomes rise, father involvement tends to *decrease*. In short, the combined effects of education and income, at least in the case of father involvement, appear to dilute the main effects of each indicator examined separately. To complicate the story even more, as wives' incomes and educational levels become more comparable to their husbands, men assume more household and child-care chores. Thus, the impact of both husbands' and wives' education and income is intricately intertwined. As Erickson and Gecas (1991) conclude, these findings suggest that family scholars need to pay greater attention to how specific indicators of class, such as income, education, or occupational prestige, can influence family life in different ways and under different conditions.

Yet another thorny issue related to the measurement of social class is identifying the member of the household whose characteristics have the most influence on the economic well-being of the family (Entwisle & Astone, 1994; Hauser, 1994). In addressing the measurement of social class, Hauser (1994) writes:

> [It is] better to focus on the characteristics of one adult in the household, a head of household, householder, or principal earner, who may be male or female and to ascertain educational attainment, labor force status, and occupational position of that person regardless of gender. . . . (p. 1542)

He suggests in a footnote that, when time and resources permit or when one is interested in maternal employment, then it would be useful to collect data on both parents in a dual-earner household.

Taking a stronger stance than Hauser, Perry-Jenkins and Folk (1994) propose that it is critical in dual-earner households to assess the combined effects of both parents' class levels. Their findings on perceptions of marital equity and conflict suggest that the *combination* of spouses' class levels (e.g., both spouses are middle class, a middle-class husband is married to a working class wife) can hold different implications for spouses' assessments of their marital relationship. They argue that examining the class level of only one adult in the family overlooks the ways in which the husband's and wife's individual socio-economic standings interact to affect aspects of their marital relationship and parenting.

This review of some of the key problems plaguing the conceptualization of social class, as well as its measurement, suggests that researchers' and practitioners' choice of indicators of class should be dictated in large part by their research question and the family outcomes of interest. Ideally, the more indices of social class that can be assessed the better, because it is then possible to examine the direct and interactive effects of factors such as education, income, and occupational prestige.

SOCIAL CLASS AND FAMILY LIFE EXPERIENCE

In this section we briefly review the current patterns of social class in American society and the research evidence regarding variations in parenting and marital experience.

The Class System in America

Despite difficulties in defining social class, demographers have provided a portrait of America's class structure. Gilbert and Kahl (1993) present a taxonomy of social class that includes six defined classes (see Table 1). These authors define class in terms of income and type of occupation, with higher classes having more resources and jobs that require more education and self-direction. Based on these categories, Gilbert and Kahl estimated that in 1990, the majority of the population was middle class, working class, or working poor. It should be noted that Gilbert and Kahl would be the first to acknowledge the imprecision in these estimates and to suggest that the conceptualization of social class categories is an inexact science at best. Thus, the question of whether certain class groups are growing or shrinking is subject to the idiosyncrasies in how groups are defined.

If one examines median family income, however, which in 1988 was $32,000, the proportion of families that fell near this median amount declined, whereas the proportion that fell either further below or above this level increased. Thus, these authors suggest that the American class structure, and its inherent differences in access to opportunity, is moving in the direction of greater inequality. It is these class inequalities that are played out daily in the lives of family members. As research in the area of social class and families illustrates, occupational experiences can shape social values, and these values are then brought home to affect relationships with spouses and children (Kohn, 1977). It must also be recognized that individuals and families are not passive recipients of the opportunities or hardships that social class contexts offer, but are active agents in choosing contexts, changing contexts (upward mobility), and fighting against the inequities in the social system (labor uprisings, unions). The following discussion will examine linkages between social class and family life with attention to how ecological contexts can affect families and, conversely, how family members can affect their environments (Bronfenbrenner, 1979).

Social Class and Parenting

In his now classic book, *Class and Conformity: A Study in Values,* Kohn (1977) proposed a very straightforward thesis: There are substantial differences in the ways parents of differing social classes raise their children. Much of the early research in this area examined class differences in discipline styles, with early findings suggesting that working-class families were more likely to use physical punishment as a parenting technique, whereas middle-class parents used reasoning, guilt, and threats more often (Bronfenbrenner, 1958). Gecas (1979) concluded that middle-class parents place greater emphasis on independence and achievement than their working-class counterparts, whereas the latter group relies more on commands and directives in parenting. Despite these consistent differences, Gecas points out that, at best, the category of social class explains only 10% of the variance in parenting practices. In his words, the number is "hardly an empirical bedrock upon which to build a theory" (Gecas, 1979, p. 377).

Table 1
Demographics of Social Class in the United States

Class	Occupations	Income($)	Population(%)
Capitalist	Investors, heirs, top executives	750,000+	1
Upper middle	University-trained professionals, managers	70,000-749,999	14
Middle	White-collar, lower level professionals, managers, skilled blue collar workers	40,000-69,999	30
Working	Semiskilled blue collar and low level white collar	20,000-39,999	30
Working poor	Laborers, service workers	13,000-19,999	20
Underclass	Unemployed or erratically employed	0-12,999	5

Note. From *The American Class Structure* (p. 311), by D. Gilbert and J. A. Kahl, 1993, Belmont, CA: Wadsworth. Copyright 1993 by Wadsworth. Adapted with permission.

The process, however, of how social class as a macro concept gets translated to influence the more micro aspects of family life is worth examining. A process approach reshapes the nature of the questions asked about social class. Specifically, Kohn makes the case that it is not social class that predicts parenting style, but rather the fact that middle- and working-class parents differ in their values regarding appropriate child behavior. For example, if conformity to authority is a parental value, then disobeying authority figures will be judged more harshly than if parents value self-direction and independence in their children. Kohn proposes that the difference in values across class groups are a function of occupational conditions. Specifically, middle- and working-class occupations differ on three key characteristics: (a) the degree to which one manipulates ideas and symbols versus physical objects; (b) the degree to which a job requires flexibility, thought, and judgment versus a standardization of rules; and (c) the closeness of supervision. These work experiences then get translated into values surrounding one's beliefs regarding self-direction and conformity or internal versus external standards that determine behavior. It is these values that emerge from one's work conditions that Kohn has related to the degree to which parents value self-direction or conformity in their children's behavior. As values of self-direction increase, parents become more concerned with children's internal states and rely more on reasoning, explaining, and psychological techniques of discipline. In contrast, as values of conformity increase, parents express greater concern with external aspects of their child's behavior and tend to rely more on commands and physical punishment (see a review by Gecas, 1979 for a more detailed explanation of these processes).

Ribbens (1994) argues that Kohn takes a deterministic view of family interaction patterns whereby parenting and marital relationships are viewed solely as outcomes of social class. She suggests that this mechanistic approach disregards the opposite flow of influence in which individuals' personal characteristics, family demands, and relationships may lead them to chose certain types of occupations or approach economic mobility in different ways. From a more interactionist perspective, Ribbens has shown ways in which women attempt to rise above their work situations or class limitations and also offer different meanings to their child-rearing behaviors that are not determined by their work. Ribben's work forces us to address the interaction between social class and family life and to consider the dynamic interplay between these worlds.

There is additional evidence of differences in parental values based on social class. Strom, Griswold, and Slaughter (1981) examined maternal attitudes in a multiethnic sample that was stratified by social class. Regardless of the ethnic group (African American, Latino, and White), there were social class differences. Lower-class parents encouraged less creativity and playfulness, were more easily frustrated by their children, and were more controlling than middle-class parents. Although there was a main effect for class, it was primarily between the lower- and upper-class parents that the differences occurred. Similarly, Schafer and Edgerton (1985) found that authoritarian and conforming values were negatively correlated with mothers' education and family income; self-directing values were positively correlated with indices of social class.

Social class differences in the degree of paternal involvement have been documented in a number of studies (Erickson & Gecas, 1991). Mothers' employment in the work force has different implications for dual-earner (primarily working-class couples) than for dual-career (primarily middle-class) couples. Whereas middle-class couples have the resources to buy relief such as hired household help (Holmstrom, 1972), working-class families deal with juggling work and family demands by requiring greater paternal involvement in child care (Nock & Kingston, 1984).

These results provide evidence that there are significant differences in the values and practices of different classes of parents. Much of the work discussed thus far has examined the linkages between social class and parenting styles because this area has received the most attention in the research. More recently, however, some family scholars have begun to examine how social class is related to the marital relationship and the division of both paid and unpaid labor in families.

Social Class and Marriage

In the few classic studies on blue-collar marriage, Komarovsky (1962), Rubin (1976), and LeMasters (1975) poignantly illustrate the linkages between social class and marital relations. Each of these researchers depicted working-class marriages as unions in which men and women had segregated activities: Wives were responsible for home and family, and husbands took on the role of good providers. It was quite clear, however, that this arrangement was far from satisfactory for many of the wives in these marriages. Rubin and LeMasters suggested that the middle- class ideals for marriage that include companionship, communication, and equality were drifting into the working class and establishing new notions of marriage that led wives to question their relationships. Although husbands were happy to maintain the status quo, wives were pushing husbands to communicate, share, and become intimate partners—a development that made many men nervous and women frustrated (LeMasters, 1975; Rubin, 1976).

More recent research by Rubin (1994) and Stacey (1991) on working-class families suggests that, although women in these households enjoy their paid employment, many still "suffer plenty of guilt and anxiety about not fulfilling their maternal role in traditional ways" (Rubin, p. 79). These women, more so than their middle-class counterparts, place little or no responsibility on fathers for the care and nurturance of their children. Thus, there is often less marital conflict in situations in which wives demand very little from their spouses, as in blue-collar families, whereas in middle-class families, wives often expect and may, in fact, demand more father involvement, which can result in greater marital strife (Perry-Jenkins & Folk, 1994).

Women's employment has had an impact on how work and family issues are negotiated. In the case of working-class women, a common assumption is that, if they are working, it is solely out of financial necessity. As Ferree (1987) points out, they are often viewed as a homogeneous group presumed to be "traditional—that is, willing to accept patriarchal authority, reluctant to work outside the home, and prepared to sacrifice themselves endlessly to family demands" (p. 289). Research suggests, however, that not all working-class women work only for financial reasons and that motives such as expanding one's competence and interacting with other adults are valued aspects of employment. This is not to say that these same women do not struggle with negotiating the demands of a job and a family, or that the struggle cannot lead to increased marital discord or greater overload for women.

In a related study by Perry-Jenkins and Folk (1994), social class was defined by the interaction of both husbands' and wives' class position in dual-earner families. Results from this research indicated that the interaction between spouses' class levels held different consequences for the ways in which the division of labor, perceptions of its equity, and evaluations of marriage related to one another. For example, for couples in which both spouses had middle-class occupations, wives' perceptions of equity in the marriage were strongly related to marital quality. In contrast, for working-class wives married to middle-class husbands, perceptions of equity were unrelated to assessments of the marriage. These findings suggest that working-class women may not hold as high as expectations for equity as middle-class women and, consequently, equity is unrelated to assessments of marriage. These studies on marriage offer further support for the notion that social class influences values, which, in turn, can affect one's expectations for marriage.

SOCIAL CLASS AND FAMILY LIFE EDUCATION PROGRAMS

In addition to growing knowledge about the influences of social class on family life, there have been some efforts to examine how the social class of family members interacts with the process and outcome of family life education. In this section, we will examine some of this work and consider ways that it can be strengthened.

Parent Education

In the late 1970s and early 1980s, there were a number of studies that were designed to consider the effectiveness of behavior modification programs on parents with difficult children. The impetus for this research was the observation by Patterson (1974) that behavioral parent training may be less effective with lower socioeconomic status families than with middle-class families. Additionally, Wahler (1980) sought to identify those aspects of lower-class mothers' lives that might account for the ineffectiveness of the parenting programs. In particular, he noted that parents with conflictual relationships with kin and friends had more negative interactions with their children. He hypothesized that this lack of social support may have a negative influence on lower-class mothers.

Since these initial observations, several researchers have examined the effectiveness of parent training programs with different social classes. Several studies found that the parent training programs were less effective with lower socioeconomic parents than with middle-class parents (Dumas & Albin, 1986; Webster-Stratton & Hammond, 1990; Zegiob & Forehand, 1975, 1978). However, there have also been studies that have found no social class differences in the effectiveness of parent training programs (Rogers, Forehand, Griest, Wells, & McMahon, 1981; Strain, Young, & Horowitz, 1981).

The conflicting results may be due to numerous factors including differences in the measurement of social class, the actual class comparisons that were made, and treatment methods. Several researchers used the Hollingshead Index as an indicator of class (e.g., Webster-Stratton & Hammond, 1990), whereas others used only mother's education and family income (e.g., Strain et al., 1981). These differences make it difficult to compare the results from these various studies. Additionally, those studies that have used class measures such as the Hollingshead have ended up with somewhat different comparisons. For example, Zegiob and Forehand (1975, 1978) compared the lowest social class and the highest social class, whereas other researchers have used samples that included the full range of social classes (e.g., Rogers et al., 1981). It may be that there are differences when the extremes of social class are compared that are not apparent when the full range of social classes is present.

In addition to these measurement issues, there are important issues with regard to treatment that need to be considered. Knapp and Deluty (1989) assert that the differences in outcomes in various behavioral parent training programs may be due to differences in the treatment program itself. They suggest that the programs that are more successful with lower socioeconomic status families are less dependent on reading and discussion formats and utilize more role playing, modeling, and coaching in the training methods. To test this hypothesis, they compared lower- and middle-class mothers on a program based either on reading and discussion or on demonstration and practice. Social class was determined using the Hollingshead Index. Lower- and middle-class parents were randomly assigned to either the discussion or demonstration formats. The results indicated that, for lower-class mothers, only those participating in the demonstration method showed improvements over time, whereas middle-class mothers showed improvements with both treatment methods. These findings indicate that some teaching methods may reflect social class differences in program effectiveness whereas others may not. Interestingly, regardless of treatment method, lower-class mothers reported no improvements in their children's behavior, whereas both groups of middle-class mothers reported significant improvements in their children's behavior. These differences may indicate reporting differences, the failure to address appropriate concerns of lower-class parents, or parents' inability to implement the suggested solutions. Additional findings by McGaw and Sturmey (1989) regarding the reading level of parenting programs indicate that, when the reading level of materials was lowered, parents gained more knowledge about parenting. Also, they found that there was a strong positive correlation between social class level and knowledge gained from the readings. Overall, these results do not suggest that behavioral parenting programs are less effective with lower-class parents, but that some treatment strategies are more effective than others with lower-class parents.

Marriage and Family Enrichment and Therapy

Unlike the work with parents, there is little information about how families of different social classes respond to marriage and family educational or therapy programs. One of the problems may be that many types of marriage or family enrichment primarily reach middle-class families. In a review of 85 marriage enrichment studies, Giblin, Sprenkle, and Sheehan (1985) found that the educational range of the samples was from 11 to 17 years, with a mean of 15 years, which suggests that most of these programs primarily serve a very well educated population. The fact that these researchers found no differences in the effectiveness of marriage enrichment due to education or income may have resulted from the limited range of these variables within these samples. At the very least, we know that studies of marriage enrichment have rarely included less educated couples.

The general inadequacy of family therapy to consider class issues has been voiced in a recent review of the intervention process in family therapy. Friedlander, Wildman, Heatherington, and Skowron (1994) conclude:

> family therapists lack basic information about the demographics (race, ethnicity, SES, or family structure) of family therapy—who is referred for and who completes therapy (i.e., dropout rates), who is most likely to benefit from or be harmed by family therapy, and what family-therapist matchings on demographics or cultural variables, if any, facilitate progress in family therapy. (p. 411)

Ironically, in a recent guide for therapists, Vogel (1989) writes, "It is apparent to any practitioner of family therapy that there are major differences in the problems which families present and the manner in which they present them that are a function of *social class* [emphasis added] and ethnic background. (p. 662)

There is at least one study that documents social class variations in response to marital therapy. Cline, Mejia, Coles, Klein, and Cline (1984) found that lower- and middle-class husbands responded to therapists in differing ways. Middle-class men's marital relationships improved when therapists were reflective and encouraged the discussion of emotions. However, this same technique had just the opposite effect on lower-class husbands. The most successful techniques for lower-class men were those that helped the man understand the workings of his marriage without altering his style of marriage. There were also some differences between middle- and lower-class wives' responses to therapy. The authors conclude that "no one marital therapy technique will be appropriate for the different sexes and with those of different SES backgrounds" (Cline et al., 1984, p. 691).

Also, Boyd-Franklin (1989) offers important information regarding different approaches to middle- and lower-class African American families. She recommends very different methods for working with middle-class versus poor African American families. With poor families, she describes the need to deal with basic issues of food and shelter, as well as to function as a facilitator with other agencies that contribute to the well-being of the family. With middle-class families, she suggests that issues such as anger, keeping up appearances, and racism are important to consider, but otherwise offers a traditional therapeutic approach to treatment. Boyd-Franklin's work demonstrates that both ethnic and class variations need to be considered in family therapy.

IMPLICATIONS AND RECOMMENDATIONS FOR FAMILY LIFE EDUCATORS

This review indicates that there are important differences in family relations due to social class and that families of different social classes respond differently to family life education and family therapy. The evidence reported in this article regarding social class variation indicates the necessity for family life educators to consider social class issues along with ethnicity, gender, and other factors that influence families. Just as it has become commonplace to consider variations due to ethnicity and gender, we should add considerations of class. Below are some ideas for how to incorporate social class issues into family life education.

Measuring and Reporting Social Class

Without data on social class, it will be difficult to begin to document and assess the ways in which it influences family life education: As a first step, it is important for family life educators to begin collecting and reporting information about social class as a part of program evaluation, along with the other usual demographic information. Complicating the measurement of social class is the fact that the term is used loosely. Our suggestion is that family life educators and program evaluators should be more precise in their use of social class indices. To more accurately understand class variations, it would be useful to collect data on income, education, and occupational position at the very least. These indices can then be examined separately as influences on family outcomes or can be combined into a socioeconomic index. Entwisle and Astone (1994) include sample questions that can be used to assess education, income, and occupational prestige from both child and adult informants. The appendix to their article also includes the 1992 job status codes for various occupations (Nakao & Treas, 1992).

A critical issue to keep in mind when assessing social class is the nature of the evaluation question being addressed. As discussed earlier, Erickson and Gecas (1991) point out that it may be that different indicators of class, such as educational level and income, work in different ways to affect family process; teasing apart these differing effects is important. At a more macro level, however, broader indices of socioeconomic status allow us to categorize families in a global way that is a marker for the resources and privileges accorded to them in our current societal structure.

Another approach to dealing with issues of social class is to measure values directly. Kohn (1977) has made the case that social class is a marker variable for different values, particularly in regard to issues of self-direction and power. The advantage of this approach is that it avoids making any stereotypical assumptions about families in a particular class having certain values and gets directly at the particular values of the families involved in a specific program. This kind of data would also provide a means to assess variations in the effectiveness of programs across groups with different values.

There are several measures that could be used to assess values. Schaefer and Edgerton's (1985) measure of parental modernity may be one useful way to assess values in regards to parenting. This measure could be adapted to reflect these same values in regards to marriage. Another viable measure of workplace conditions and values is Moos' (1986) Work Environment Scale that assesses 10 dimensions of one's work experience and includes subscales on autonomy, control, support, and aspects of work that have been linked to parental values.

Responding to Social Class Variation

In addition to measuring and reporting social class as a routine part of family life education reports, family life educators will also need to examine their own values and the values reflected in their curricula. Through self-awareness, educators will more easily understand their own implicit class values. Aponte (1985) provides some helpful ideas regarding how to become more aware of one's own values. Additionally, through research, the arts, and personal experience, educators can learn more about the values and experiences of families that are not similar to their own. For example, there are many novels, autobiographies, and films that can provide insight into the lives of families in various social classes. It can also be valuable to gather ideas from others who have more experience working with various social classes. Ultimately, greater experience teaching and learning from families at various economic levels will be the best method for improving the skills of educators.

Attention will also have to be given to the issues addressed in parenting and family life education curricula. Often these curricula reflect only middle-class values and concerns. Parenting is often reduced to guidance techniques, overlooking the important role parents play in ensuring basic needs (e.g., providing food, clothing, and shelter) and maintaining children's safety. Likewise, in regards to marital issues such as balancing work and family, the program focus is frequently related to time management solutions and other techniques that address the issues of professional working couples rather than the strains and stresses of working- or lower-class husbands and wives. For example, the question of how to identify and afford quality child care for a low-income family is rarely addressed in mainstream work-family seminars. In short, to address families from various social classes, family life educators will also need to identify issues that are relevant to these families.

The findings that parenting and marital experiences vary by social class do not mean that family life educators should immediately create rigid programs that are designed exclusively for lower or upper classes. Just as there are variations across class, there are also variations within class. A more flexible program development strategy is needed that incorporates knowledge of general patterns with an appreciation of differences. Family scholars and practitioners are faced with the challenges of developing research strategies and programs that are sensitive to potential class differences while respecting individual differences; this is the same challenge that emerges when considering race, ethnicity,

and gender. Although some might conclude that individual differences are so great that it is unproductive to focus on generalities, it is our contention that being aware of potential differences across groups acknowledges diversity and will lead us to develop more appropriate and culturally sensitive research and intervention programs.

Assimilation, Multicultural, and Social Reconstruction Orientations

In this final section, we deal with the most troublesome issue in regards to social class and the implications for practitioners. As noted in the beginning, the theoretical position one takes regarding social class leads to quite different ideas about how to approach intervention. The specific perspective taken by family life educators will raise different questions. We outline three perspectives—assimilation, multicultural, and social reconstruction. Each position has its own advantages, risks, and limitations.

Assimilation view. The assimilation view documents the way things are in our current social hierarchy while also, inherently, supporting notions of the way things should be; in other words, the ultimate goal is the "middle-class ideal" (Baca Zinn & Eitzen, 1990). Proponents of this approach assert that we have important scientific knowledge about what works in this society and that it is unfair and unethical not to convey this information. Likewise, there is research knowledge about types of behavior that are helpful and harmful. To respect values that run counter to this knowledge is to do great harm.

There are two problems with this approach. First, the assimilation orientation has a "blame the victim" mentality toward differences; that is, the reason why lower-class families are lower class is their failure to adopt appropriate values and practices that could lift them out of poverty (Ryan, 1971). Second, this approach has historically led family scholars to assume that all families should aspire to a certain type of parenting or a correct form of marriage that most often fits a White, middle-class model. Nevertheless, this perspective reminds us that there should be some limits on respecting all cultural values (e.g., condoning family violence).

Multicultural view. A multicultural approach to these issues acknowledges class differences, as well as ethnic and race differences, without labeling one group as deficient or another as better. From this perspective, values held by family members are not viewed as fixed and unchanging. We see some value in shaping and developing family life education programs that pay attention to class difference, because class is related to values regarding parenting and marriage. We propose that it is critical to obtain information about education and occupation because it may give us some insights

into parental belief systems. Perhaps even more valuable would be assessments of parental values regarding self-direction versus conformity, reasoning versus commands, physical punishment versus guilt and natural consequences. This approach suggests that working with the family's belief system is the approach most likely to yield results.

From this multicultural perspective, it is also possible to assist families in examining and learning various cultural values. Aponte (1985) suggests that therapists make values explicit and negotiate them with their clients. Just as we can talk about biculturism across ethnic and racial domains, we can conceptualize biculturalism regarding social class. In this instance, the family life educator's role may be to assist families in learning to be bicultural across social class. The risk with this approach is that family life educators may fail to provide families with the skills and knowledge to improve their lives or to adapt to the larger society. Or in an effort to be respectful of differences, family life educators will overlook harmful or questionable practices based on values that are not thoroughly examined.

Social reconstruction view. In contrast to either an assimilation or multicultural orientation, the social reconstruction approach sees differences as based on the individual's and family's adaptation to their social circumstances (Baca Zinn & Eitzen, 1990). A social reconstruction approach suggests that family life educators focus on changing the structural conditions that lead to lower class families having little power and control over their lives. It should be realized, however, that changing the structural features of an inequitable society, features that lead some families to have less access to power and resources, is no small task. According to Schmid (1995), this approach prepares citizens to work actively toward social equality. From this perspective, family life educators may also help family members become more aware of their values and the values of professionals and institutions they encounter so that they can more successfully negotiate with them.

The following examples illustrate how family life educators might use a social reconstruction approach to address inequities and power differences. It is often the case that working-class jobs are highly structured, allowing little flexibility or creative thinking. The solution that work-family scholars have offered to the problem is a top down approach whereby management creates ways to give a voice to all employees in the form of work groups or rewards for innovative thinking. A bottom up approach, however, would encourage employees to express their ideas without waiting to be asked. In this case, employees could be taught to develop their own solutions and present them to supervisors and employers.

In another context, working-class parents could be taught advocacy skills for dealing with school teachers and principals. That is, parents could acquire the abilities for confronting the structural inequities in society that restrict opportunities for their children. A similar advocacy training could be made available to women in lower-class families to help them deal more effectively with their husbands.

The risk of the social reconstruction approach is that it could lead to encouraging people to adopt a combative class warfare approach to resolving problems. This approach is especially dangerous when these recommendations are given to individuals who may already be marginalized and who lack significant power. Additionally, this perspective may fail to encourage people to develop other adaptive approaches to dealing with family life, rather than expecting institutions and the culture at large to change.

CONCLUSION

In summary, this article documents that there are important class differences in family processes and interventions that have been overlooked in the design of family life education programs. Progress in creating effective family life education will only be possible with increased attention to social class variations. This article challenges family scholars and practitioners to re- examine the complexity of social class as it is conceptualized in our research and enacted in daily life.

REFERENCES

Aponte, H. (1985). The negotiation of values in therapy. *Family Process, 24*, 323–338.

Arcus, M. E. Schvaneveldt, J. D., & Moss, J. J. (1993). *Handbook of family life education* (Vols. 1 & 2). Newbury Park, CA: Sage.

Arcus, M. E. & Thomas J. (1993). The nature and practice of family life education. In M. E. Arcus, J. D. Schvaneveldt, & J. J. Moss (Eds.) *Handbook of family life education: The practice of family life education* (Vol. 2, pp. 1–32). Newbury Park; CA: Sage.

Baca Zinn, M. & Eitzen, D. S. (1990). *Diversity in families*. New York: Harper & Row.

Boyd-Franklin, N. (1989). *Black families in therapy*. New York: Guilford.

Bronfenbrenner, U. (1958). Socialization and social class through time and space. In E. E. Maccoby, T. M. Newcomb, & E. L. Harley (Eds.), *Readings in social psychology* (pp. 400–425). New York: Holt, Rinehart, & Winston.

Cline, V. B., Mejia, J., Coles, J., Klein, N., & Cline, R. A. (1984). The relationship between therapist behaviors and outcome for middle- and lower-class couples in marital therapy. *Journal of Clinical Psychology, 40*, 691–704.

Dumas, J. E., & Albin, J. B. (1986). Parent training outcome: Does active parental involvement matter? *Behavior Research Therapy, 24*, 227–230.

Entwisle, D. R. & Astone, N. M (1994). Some practical guidelines for measuring youths' race/ethnicity and socioeconomic status. *Child Development, 65*, 1521–1540.

Erickson, R. J. & Gecas, V. (1991). Social class and fatherhood. In F. W. Bozett & S. M. Hanson (Eds.) *Fatherhood and families in cultural context* (pp. 114–137). New York: Springer Verlag.

Ferree, M. M. (1987). Family and job for working-class women: Gender and class systems seen from below. In N. Gerstel & H. Gross (Eds.), *Families and work* (pp. 289–301). Philadelphia: Temple University Press.

Friedlander, M. L., Wildman, J., Heatherington, L., & Skowron, E. A. (1994). What we do and don't know about the process of family therapy. *Journal of Family Psychology, 8*, 390–416.

Gecas, V. (1979). The influence of social class in socialization. In W. R. Burr, R. Hill, F. I. Nye, and I. Reiss (Eds.), *Contemporary theories about the family. Vol. 1: Research-based theories* (pp. 365–404). New York: Free Press.

Giblin, P., Sprenkle, D. H., & Sheehan, R. (1985). Enrichment outcome research: A meta-analysis of premarital, marital and family interventions. *Journal of Marital and Family Therapy, 3*, 257–271.

Gilbert, D., & Kahl, J. A. (1993). *The American class structure: A new synthesis*. Belmont, CA: Wadsworth.

Hauser, R. M. (1994). Measuring socioeconomic status in studies of child development. *Child Development, 65*, 1541–1545.

Hollingshead, A. B., & Redlich, F. C. (1958). *Social class and mental illness*. New York: Wiley.

Holmstrom, L. L. (1972). *The two-career family*. Cambridge, MA: Schenkman.

Knapp, P. A., & Deluty, R. H. (1989). Relative effectiveness of two behavioral parent training programs. *Journal of Clinical Child Psychology, 18*, 314–322.

Kohn, M. L. (1977). *Class and conformity: A study in values*. Homewood, IL: Dorsey Press.

Kohn, M. L. (1979). The effects of social class on parental values and practices. In D. Reiss & H. A. Hoffman (Eds.), *The American family* (pp. 45–68). New York: Plenum.

Komarovsky, M. (1962). *Blue-collar marriage*. New York: Vintage Books.

Lamb, M. E. (1986). *The father's role: Applied perspectives*. New York: Wiley.

LeMasters, E. E. (1975). *Blue-collar aristocrats: Life-styles at a working class tavern*. Madison, WI: University of Wisconsin Press.

McGaw, S., & Sturmey, P. (1989). The effects of text readability and summary exercises on parental knowledge of behavior therapy: The Portage parent readings. *Educational Psychology, 9*, 127–132.

Model, S. (1981). Housework by husbands: Determinants and implications. *Journal of Family Issues, 2*, 225–237.

Moos, R. (1986). *Work environment scale manual* (2nd ed.) Palo Alto, CA: Consulting Psychologists Press.

Nakao, K. & Treas, J. (1992). *The 1989 socioeconomic index of occupations: Construction from the 1989 occupational prestige scores* (General Social Survey Methodological Report No. 74).

Chicago: University of Chicago, National Opinion Research Center.

Nock, S. L., & Kingston, P. W. (1984). The family work day. *Journal of Marriage and the Family, 46*, 333–343.

Patterson, G. R. (1974). Interventions for boys with conduct problems: Multiple settings, treatments and criteria. *Journal of Consulting and Clinical Psychology, 42*, 471–481.

Perry-Jenkins, M., & Folk, K. (1994). Class, couples, and conflict: Effects of the division of labor on assessments of marriage in dual-earner families. *Journal of Marriage and the Family, 56*, 165–180.

Rapp, R. (1982). Family and class in contemporary America: Notes toward and understanding of ideology. In B. Thorne & M. Yalom (Eds.), *Rethinking the family: Some feminist questions* (pp. 168–187). New York: Longman.

Ribbens, J. (1994). *Mothers and their children: A feminist sociology of childrearing*. Newbury Park, CA: Sage.

Rogers, T. R., Forehand, R., Griest, D. L., Wells, K. C., & McMahon, R. J. (1981). Socioeconomic status: Effects on parent child behaviors and treatment outcome of parent training. *Journal of Clinical Child Psychology, 10*, 98–101.

Rubin, L. B. (1976). *Worlds of pain: Life in the working-class family*. New York: Basic.

Rubin, L. B. (1994). *Families on the fault line: America's working class speaks about the family, the economy, race, and ethnicity*. New York: HarperCollins.

Ryan, W. (1971). *Blaming the victim*. New York: Pantheon.

Schaefer, E. S., & Edgerton, M. (1985). Parent and child correlates of parental modernity. In I. E. Sigel (Ed.), *Parental belief systems* (pp. 287-318). Hillsdale, NJ: Erlbaum.

Schmid, K. (1995). Multicultural family science. In R. Day, K. R. Gilbert, B. H. Settles, & W. R. Burr (Eds.), *Research and theory in family science* (pp. 54–70). New York: Brooks/Cole.

Stacey, J. (1991). *Brave new families: Stories of domestic upheaval in late twentieth century America*. New York: Basic Books.

Strain, P. S., Young, C. C., & Horowitz, J. (1981). Generalized behavior change during oppositional child training. *Behavior Modification, 5*, 15–26.

Strom, R., Griswold, D., & Slaughter, H. (1981). Parental background: Does parent education matter? *Child Study Journal, 10*, 243–260.

Vogel, W. (1989). Family and couple therapy. In A. Lazare (Ed.), *Outpatient psychiatry*. (2nd ed., pp. 655–664). Baltimore: Williens & Wilkens.

Wahler, R. G. (1980). The insular mother: Her problems in parent-child treatment. *Journal of Applied Behavior Analysis, 13*, 207–219.

Warner, W. L. (1960). *Social class in America*. New York: Harper & Row.

Webster-Stratton, C., & Hammond, M. (1990). Predictors of treatment outcome in parent training for families with conduct problem children. *Behavior Therapy, 21*, 319–337.

Zegiob, L. E., & Forehand, R. (1975). Maternal interactive behavior as a function of socioeconomic status, race and sex of child. *Child Development, 46*, 564–568.

Zegiob, L. E., & Forehand, R. (1978). Parent-child interactions: Observer effects and social class differences. *Behavior Therapy, 9*, 118–123.

Accommodating Cultural Differences and Commonalities in Educational Practice

By Ronald Gallimore & Claude Goldenberg

Taking account of diversity in schools is a major challenge in a multicultural society. On one level the issue is simple: Everyone's heritage is due respect, and differences should be regarded as strengths on which to build rather than deficits to be stigmatized or overcome. But on another level there is an often unrecognized paradox: too exclusive a focus on group differences can "all too easily become the basis for creating stereotypes . . ." that blind educators to qualities that students have in common (Fillmore, 1982, p. 24).

How can educators be responsive to cultural differences and avoid stereotypes that mask commonalties shared by different cultural groups? One way is to distinguish between different functions of culture. In this essay we distinguish between the group-defining function and other adaptive functions to show why educators need to accommodate cultural commonalities as well as differences.

Some Functions of Culture

Culture evolves over time in response to adaptive challenges. One result of this evolutionary process is beliefs and practices that help us adapt to persistent as well as changing circumstances. These beliefs and practices are organized as models or

---

Ronald Gallimore is a faculty member at the University of California, Los Angeles, and Claude Goldenberg is a faculty member at California State University, Long Beach.

schema about how things work, what is ideal, and which practices are proper and help individuals or groups survive and

> **Cultural features . . . are neither static nor rigid. As circumstances and environments change, our understanding of how things work and how to respond are modified and changed to meet new challenges. We change just enough to make things work . . .**

prosper (LeVine, 1977). Cultural models are so familiar and mundane that their functions and effects are often unseen, invisible, unnoticed. The evidence of their workings [is] often most apparent in everyday routines in

communities, homes, workplaces, play yards, and schools. What activities are carried out, why they are valued, who should participate, and the rules of interaction are coded into our cultural models.

Cultural features—models of belief and practice and their associated activities—are neither static nor rigid. As circumstances and environments change, our understanding of how things work and how to respond are modified and changed to meet new challenges. We change just enough to make things work—we are satisfiers rather than maximizers, happy with just good enough. The more our environments change, the more we try to keep things the same. The more we try to keep them the same, the more we have to change (Edgerton, 1992). Beliefs and practices are borrowed from others with whom we come in contact or share an ecological niche; alternative ways of organizing daily activities are tried, adapted, and adopted.

In the modern world this process is accelerated by technologies that amplify direct contact, distanced communication, and social and commercial exchange. Changes are made slowly, gradually, and are built on existing beliefs and practices. For example, natives of Spain, Turkey, and Morocco gradually adopted beliefs and practices encountered in Northern Europe after migrating to obtain employment (Roosens, 1994). Culture is not a straitjacket or a cake of custom, it is a storehouse of adaptive solutions to the challenges of existence (Weisner, Gallimore, & Jordan, 1988).

Some cultural features—beliefs, practices, and everyday activities—mark boundaries among groups—clans, tribes, ethnic, and reference groups. Which features mark boundaries are a product of many different historical circumstances. Sometimes two groups occupied the same ecological niche, or monopolized different territories or resources. In some cases ethnic boundaries arose from the interdependence of two groups, with each providing services or goods to the other, sometimes voluntarily, sometimes coerced by the more powerful group. A critical function of boundary markers is to distinguish between "us" and "others."

For example, some scholars have concluded that the function of kosher dietary laws was to differentiate the Jews from their "gentile" neighbors (Harris, 1985, p. 337). Ethnic boundaries help an individual identify who is a fellow member of the "in" group, who is and is not a person with shared perceptions and understandings. (Barth, 1969, p. 15). The borders between ethnic groups define both self and group identity, feelings of belonging, and continuity through time; shared meanings and traditions; self-ascribed genealogical and social filiation, including related forms of family and group bonds (Roosens, 1994).

In contemporary human history, an important function of boundaries is the political and economic advantage that ethnic unity can achieve. In the United States, for example, ethnically defined groups succeeded in building coalitions to pass legislation requiring equity in school funding, hiring, mortgage granting, etc. The unified political action which ethnic groups can muster means, paradoxically, using ethnic categories to rid society of inequities arising from ethnic distinctions (Wright, 1994). Ron Edmonds, advocate of effective schools for minority students, wrote that poor and ethnic groups "are far more likely to be served by politics than by any equity interests to be found in the educational research establishment" (Edmonds, 1978, p. 34). To unify a group for effective political action, ethnic identity must remain relatively impervious to changing circumstances. Otherwise, membership would wax and wane, and the advantages of collective action would be threatened.

One reason ethnic boundaries persist is that they are marked by only a limited set of cultural features the particularities of which are often a product of historical and ecological circumstances (Barth, 1969). What features mark boundaries do not depend on their persistence, or their resistance to change in many domains of belief and practice. This allows for very substantial differences among individuals within an ethnic group—differences that do not affect those features that define the boundary between "us" and "others."

This flexibility regarding most beliefs and practices permits a group to remain unified around core features while allowing great variation within the group on thoughts, feelings, and behavior (LeVine, 1984, p. 68). Individuals within a group can maintain their group identity and still enjoy the adaptive advantages of many beliefs and practices, even those borrowed from the "others." The borrowing and loaning of cultural features are often a two-way process between groups.

This brings us to a key idea. Two well-differentiated ethnic groups living in the same ecological niche are likely to share many cultural beliefs and practices in common (Barth, 1969; Edgerton, 1971; LeVine, 1977). For example, many individuals emigrated from Spain, Sicily, Morocco, and Turkey to work in the factories and mines of Northern Europe (Roosens, 1994). Many in these groups sharply differentiate themselves, and are treated as different by co-resident Northern Europeans, as distinct ethnic groups. Yet the boundaries between groups, that is, what differentiates them, are limited cultural features such as tastes in clothing and food, home furnishing styles, male and female role norms, and religious beliefs (Roosens, 1994). These immigrants come to share, however, many other cultural features with their new Northern European neighbors.

Even those who intend to return to their native land adopt cultural beliefs and practices which give them an adaptive advantage in their new, even if possibly temporary, Northern European homes: They use modern medicines and technologies, take new kinds of jobs, learn new skills, aspire to higher education for their children, seek and attain material abundance, and subscribe to public social security systems, some of which entail adoption of beliefs and practices not present in their native lands.

Adapting Instruction to Culture

The behavior of immigrants to Northern Europe reflects a fundamental principle: Individuals living in the same ecologies will adopt cultural models of adaptation if they offer advantage. What has this principle to do with adapting instruction to cultural variability within groups? It suggests that educators may expect to find many commonalities as well as differences among the ethnic groups that attend America's schools.

Our two-pronged argument is this:

(1) Schools must deal with students from many different groups and should therefore be aware of potential discontinuities between home and school—e.g., attitudes toward discipline, beliefs about how children learn, the nature and quality of learning experiences in the pre-school years and beyond—and design programs that will foster common understandings and complementary efforts.

(2) But at the same time, schools should not assume that ethnic diversity always implies broad-based cultural differences among groups, or conversely homogeneity within groups. Different groups living in the same ecological niche can be expected to have many cultural features—beliefs and practices—in common. Schools therefore should also build on commonalties between schools and families—e.g., beliefs about the value of formal schooling, school achievement, good behavior, and parent support and involvement. Building on commonalties is no less important than being sensitive to differences in forging productive relationships with families.

Discontinuities and Complementarities

Families who emigrate from Mexico to the United States are ethnically different and distinct from other families in this country. Racially, historically, psychologically, they identify with others whose families hail from central and northern Mexico who also speak Spanish and share Indian and Spanish ancestors. These are the people Carey McWilliams (1948, 1968) wrote about a half-century ago. Our longitudinal studies in a California community suggest that on some dimensions of belief and practice immigrant Mexican parents are different from their fellow residents (Goldenberg & Gallimore, 1995; Reese, Balzano, Gallimore, & Goldenberg, 1995).

For example, they subscribe to a cultural model of preschool child development that places a higher emphasis on moral development than on school readiness skills, a pattern exhibited by groups with origins in small-scale agrarian communities where earning a living depends on face-to-face interactions and the cooperative work of family members (LeVine & White, 1986). For the immigrant Mexican parents, it is vital that a child learn the difference between right and wrong, obedience and respect for elders, and to be a full participant in family life. They place less emphasis in the preschool years on the uses of language and print than families in which literacy is both a means of earning a living and an important child development goal (Goldenberg & Gallimore, 1995). This difference matters because the amount of preschool literacy experience is a significant precursor of early reading development in early elementary school. Children with lots of preschool literacy experience have an advantage in early elementary school (Adams, 1990).

On the other hand, some of the cultural models of child development held by the immigrant Mexican families differ little from other Americans: The Mexican immigrant parents value schooling, are available to the children, and are interested in and capable of providing literacy-enhancing experiences, particularly when children are younger. Activities involving literacy are more frequent than suggested by many stereotypes of low income Spanish-speaking families.

Indeed, we found in our studies that the within group variability was substantial. While some families, by their own report and researchers' observations, do not always provide certain experiences, they are motivated to help their children, and eagerly adopt new models of and opportunities for child development and learning. With few exceptions, parents eagerly respond to materials, activities, and suggestions from their school. In one study, over 40 percent of all observed learning activities involved use of materials from school. Once their children entered school the range and frequency of literacy was greatly increased by parents' taking advantage of new materials and ideas the children brought home. In short, many have already adopted beliefs and practices available in the ecological/cultural niche of urban United States and exhibited adaptive flexibility (Goldenberg & Gallimore, 1995).

Yet for all their variability and willingness to adopt new beliefs and practices that benefit their children, the families are not abandoning their ethnic identity. Almost without exception we found a strong endorsement of what the families consider traditional Mexican values of *educación*, that include family solidarity, knowing right from wrong, and obedience, and respect for elders. These parents are strongly identified with their heritage.

One father said: "We Mexicans come from an old tradition, a tradition of the *ranchos* where the father and mother are respected. Regarding siblings, the younger ones respect the older ones" (Reese, *et. al.*, 1995). One mother complained that in the United States children are given too much freedom which results in gangs, drugs, and other urban woes. She said "One cannot tell [young people] anything because [they say] they are going to call the cops on you.... We Mexicans are not like that. This is one of the customs that I don't want them to learn." She described immigrant Mexican families who have educated their children in the same way that they had been educated in Mexico. The result were hard-working young adults who stayed out of trouble, which she said was not always true when parents gave their children too much freedom and autonomy. For many of the families in our study, their adherence to traditional values is a boundary they believe distinguishes them and their group from other groups in their communities.

Yet, even as ethnic identity remains strong, changes in cultural belief and practice were evident in the more than ten years we

have been interviewing and observing in homes of immigrant Latino families:

> ... *educación* for these immigrant parents has a much stronger component of "formal schooling." The immigrant parents in our sample clearly wish to maintain many of the traditional family values of responsibility and respect taught to them by their own parents, our target children's grandparents. But with its greater emphasis on formal schooling—for both boys and girls—these immigrant parents' cultural model of *educación* is itself undergoing change. It is adapting to the exigencies of life in a society where education—in the English sense of the word—[both matters and is more available]. (Goldenberg & Gallimore, 1995)

As they adapt to a new society they may be reaching out and adopting cultural models and practices that provide advantages to themselves and their children. But they are not abandoning all they brought with them.

Commonalties and Collaboration

Ethnic differences, therefore, should not obscure cultural compatibilities. In a study of Latino immigrants and their kindergartners, we found that teachers' attempts to involve parents in children's literacy development led both to greater parent satisfaction and to enhanced student achievement (Goldenberg & Arzubiaga, 1994 April; Goldenberg and Gallimore, 1995), suggesting again that parents and teachers shared many values and beliefs about educating children. The more teachers attempted to involve parents in children's academic learning—by sending home activities or through messages or phone calls home—the more satisfied parents were with both the academic content of their child's classroom and with the extent to which they felt involved in their children's learning.

In addition, teacher attempts to involve parents also predicted children's literacy development at the end of kindergarten. The more teachers attempted to involve parents in children's learning, the higher were children's end-of-year literacy scores. There was no relationship between teacher parent-involvement efforts and beginning of year achievement, so we ruled out the explanation that teachers involved were more likely to reach out to parents of higher achieving students. Furthermore, there was a striking relationship between teachers' parent involvement attempts and changes in child achievement in relation to other kindergartners across the year ($r = .58$; $p<.01$).

In other words, the more the teacher attempted to involve a child's parents in his or her academic learning in kindergarten,

the more a child gained in relative achievement standing from the beginning of the year to the end. Students whose teachers took the initiative to involve parents in children's learning gained ground in comparison to peers; students whose teachers did not take the initiative to involve parents, slipped back in their relative achievement standing.

These results illustrate an important continuity between Latino parents and children's teachers: An interest in children's academic achievement and a belief in the importance of parents' playing a productive role in promoting it. When teachers take advantage of this continuity by facilitating parent involvement, the results are greater parent satisfaction and improved learning by children. When children move on to first and second grade, we have found the relationships hold between teachers' parent involvement efforts and parents' satisfaction. For these older children, parents are more satisfied when their child receives homework they feel is of high quality and that promotes learning and motivation.

Parents are also more satisfied when they feel informed of their child's progress and when the academic content of the classroom is high. This is clearly in keeping with the values and beliefs we have heard parents express for the past ten years. They want their child's school experience to be academically challenging. Indeed, as we have reported before, on occasion parents will comment that United States schools are less demanding than those in their native countries (Goldenberg & Gallimore, 1991; Reese, *et. al.*, 1995).

Surface and Reality in Cultural Commonalties and Differences

In the introduction to this essay we developed the idea that only a few cultural beliefs and practices mark the boundary between groups. Yet in many contexts these limited differences are so compelling at first analysis that they may obscure substantial commonalties. Indeed, the perspective we presented in the first part of this essay would predict this—that all of us are inclined to notice those differences that mark boundaries between groups, because of the social and political functions they serve. But as Fillmore (1982) and Ogbu and Matute-Bianchi (1986) warned, this very predictable human response can, when allowed to operate freely in educational settings, produce a surface response that is insensitive to underlying realities.

In the study on the effects of kindergarten teachers' parent involvement efforts on parent satisfaction and children's achievement (Goldenberg & Arzubiaga, 1994 April), half the teachers were Latinas who spoke Spanish fluently, and the other half were Anglos with varying degrees of skill in Spanish. When we compared the achievement change of children taught by Latinas and Anglos, there was a significant difference. Those taught by the Latina teachers improved from fall to spring, whereas the Anglo teachers' children declined. At first glance this suggests the bridging of discontinuities between child and school cultures (in the form of Latina, fluent-Spanish teachers) improved children's achievement—a result that is inconsistent with previous findings that teacher ethnicity is **unrelated** to Latino children's achievement (Vierra, 1984).

However, further analyses of our data suggested a more complex interpretation was required. Because they were rated much higher at promoting parent-involvement, Latina teachers were benefiting from this powerful effect on children's achievement. When we statistically removed the contribution of parent-involvement, the effect of teacher ethnicity disappeared. The critical variable affecting student progress was teachers' parent-involvement efforts, not teacher ethnicity and language per se. No doubt teacher ethnicity and language contributed to communication and rapport between teachers and parents, but it was not the fact of these shared qualities. It was how teachers behaved that mattered, not their ethnic status.

The importance of teacher action over teacher status was also the argument of one of the Latina teachers, Ms. Delgado—an argument she presented to us **prior** to the study. While she recognized that many children have less access to academic learning opportunities than others, Ms. Delgado also maintained a strong belief (supported by educational research) that children of immigrant Latinos, like other children, can be taught what they need to know in order to be successful in school:

[Some] teachers think these kids are deprived so [they think] all we need to let them do is play all day here. That really makes me mad because I came from [an immigrant Latino] background like this. . . . These kids can learn but they have to be taught. If more teachers realized this and did what they were supposed to do, more of these kids would go on to college (Goldenberg, 1994, p. 185).

Conclusion

Our examples and analyses raise an intriguing possibility: Is accommodating to culturally different children a matter of making changes in teaching, staffing, or curriculum that are sensitive to differences? Or can we also accommodate to culturally different children by recognizing similarities and consistencies, as well as differences and discontinuities, across groups? Cultural accommodation cuts both ways—making changes if needed but recognizing similarities when they exist and not allowing ourselves to see only the cultural features that distinguish a group from others. Ignoring one kind of accommodation over the other is not in the best interest of children or families.

As we confront the challenges posed by this most recent wave of immigrants to the United States, educators must be aware of discontinuities that must be skillfully and sensitively handled. At the same time, they must be equally sensitive to what the families, children, teachers, and administrators share.

References

Adams, M. (1990). *Beginning To Read: Thinking and Learning about Print*. Cambridge, MA: MIT Press.

Barth, F. (1969). Introduction. In F. Barth, (ed.) *Ethnic Groups and Boundaries: The Social Organization of Culture Difference* (pps. 9–38). London, United Kingdom: George Allen & Unwin.

Edgerton, R. B. (1971). *The Individual in Cultural Adaptation: A Study of Four East African Peoples*. Berkeley, CA: University of California Press.

Edgerton, R. B. (1992). *Sick Societies: Challenging The Myth of Primitive Harmony*. New York: Free Press.

Edmonds, R. (July, 1978). A discussion of the literature and issues related to effective schooling. Paper prepared for the National Conference on Urban Education, St. Louis, MO.

Fillmore, L. W. (1982). Cultural Perspectives on Second Language Learning. *TESL Reporter* 14(2): 23–31.

Goldenberg, C. & Gallimore, R. (1991). Local knowledge, research knowledge, and educational change: A case study of first-grade Spanish reading improvement. *Educational Researcher, 20* (8), 2–14.

Goldenberg, C. (1994). Promoting early literacy achievement among Spanish-speaking children: Lessons from two studies. E. Hiebert (Ed.) *Getting Reading Right From the Start: Effective Early Literacy Interventions* (pp. 171–199). Boston, MA: Allyn & Bacon.

Goldenberg, C. & Arzubiaga, A. (1994, April). The effects of teachers' attempts to involve Latino parents in children's early reading development. Paper presented at the annual meeting of the American Educational Research Association, New Orleans, LA.

Goldenberg, C. & Gallimore, R. (1995). Immigrant Latino parents' values and beliefs about their children's education: Continuities and discontinuities across cultures and generations. In Pintrich, P. R. & Maehr, M. (Eds.). *Advances in Motivation and Achievement: Culture, Ethnicity, and Motivation, Vol. 9* (pp. 183–228). Greenwich, CT: JAI Press.

Harris, M. (1985). *Good to Eat: Riddles of Food and Culture*. New York: Simon & Schuster.

LeVine, R. A. (1984). Properties of culture: an ethnographic view. In R. A. Shweder & R. A. LeVine, (Eds.) *Culture theory: Essays on Mind, Self, and Emotion* (pps. 67–87). Cambridge, United Kingdom: Cambridge University Press.

LeVine, R. (1977). Child rearing as cultural adaptation. In P. Leiderman, S. Tulkin, & A. Rosenfeld (Eds.), *Culture and Infancy* (pp. 15–27). New York: Academic Press.

Levine, R. & White, M. (1986). *Human Conditions: The Cultural Basis of Educational Development*. New York: Routledge & Kegan Paul.

McWilliams, C. (1948, 1968). *North from Mexico: The Spanish- speaking People of the United States*. New York: Greenwood Press.

Ogbu, J. U. & Matute-Bianchi, M. E. (1986). Understanding Sociocultural Factors; Knowledge, Identity, and School Adjustment. In *Beyond Language: Social and Cultural Factors in Schooling Language Minority Students*. Bilingual Education Office, California State Department of Education (eds) (pps. 73–142). Los Angeles, CA: Evaluation, Dissemination and Assessment Center, California State University, Los Angeles

Reese, L., Balzano, S., Gallimore, R., & Goldenberg, C. (1995). The Concept of Educación: Latino family values and American schooling. *International Journal of Educational Research, 23,* 1, 57–81.

Roosens, E. (1994, November). Education for living in pluriethnic societies. Paper presented at Carnegie/Jacobs Foundation Conference "Frontiers in the Education of Young Adolescents," November 3–5, Marbach Castle, Germany.

Vierra, A. (1984). The relationship between Chicano children's achievement and their teachers' ethnicity. *Hispanic Journal of Behavioral Science, 6,* 285–290.

Weisner, T. S., Gallimore, R., & Jordan, C. (1988). Unpackaging cultural effects on classroom learning: Hawaiian peer assistance and child-generated activity. *Anthropology and Education Quarterly, 19,* 327–353.

Wright, L. (1994) One drop of blood. *The New Yorker,* July 25, pp. 46–55.

Children's Views of Poverty: A Review of Research and Implications for Teaching

by Judith A. Chafel

This article is the author's revision of a copyedited version that inadvertantly appeared in Volume 61, Number 1, of The Educational Forum. *That version was entitled, "Children's Views of Social Inequality: A Review of Research and Implications for Teaching."*

Despite its social as well as developmental significance, not much attention has been directed to children's conceptions of poverty. The oversight is surprising because a sizable proportion of children in our society are poor—one out of every five younger than 18 years, or 16.9 percent of whites, 39.9 percent of Hispanics, and 46.6 percent of blacks (U. S. Bureau of the Census 1993). What do children think about a dilemma that profoundly affects so many of them?

That children think about poverty is evidenced by a number of sources: news reports, children's literature, and empirical research. Consider this striking example. The Minneapolis *Star Tribune* depicted the case of Roy, an 18-year-old, recalling a tough childhood marred by economic hardship. Roy vividly revealed that in elementary school, "They'd tease me because I had to wear second

Judith A. Chafel is Associate Professor of Curriculum and Instruction at Indiana University in Bloomington. Her research interests include young children's social cognition, child and family policy, and child poverty.

hand clothes and eat free hot lunches." As he explained, "It was bad because there were separate hot lunch lines, one for people who paid for lunch and one for people who didn't" (Hopfensperger 1992, 1A).

Myriad images of poverty appear in children's literature. For example, a picture book for young children entitled *My Daddy Don't Go to Work* focuses on the theme of joblessness and how it affects family relationships. On the first page of text, a child of color explains: "My daddy don't go to work. He would, if he could. He goes out looking for a job every day. But he can't find a place that needs him. He says, 'Things are tough' (Nolan 1978, no page number).

A small body of empirical work has analyzed children's reflections about poverty. Utilizing a Piagetian clinical interview method, Leahy (1983b, 81) captured this response offered by a 6-year-old boy about why people are impoverished: "The poor people don't have no jobs. They couldn't pay for no jobs because they don't have no money to get a job." The child further explained that the poor suffered privation "because they live in Africa and nobody gives them no food and they have to eat out of the garbage."

Regardless of how directly or indirectly children experience poverty, knowing what they think about it is worthwhile. Children use data that their knowledge of the economic system provides in forming constructions of social reality. Their ideas about poverty may be linked with other aspects of their developments—e.g., self-concepts, social relationships with others, and school achievement. While these linkages have yet to be studied and verified empirically, an awareness of their possibility enhances our understanding of children's development. Furthermore, children's conceptions of poverty may suggest possible teaching interventions. Such interventions may be necessary to assist those whose development is thwarted by the damaging effects of economic privation or those whose conception of others is obscured by stereotypical thinking, to cite but two examples (Chafel 1995).

This article surveys research spanning a period of nearly 50 years (Estvan 1952; Furby 1979; Leahy 1981; 1983a; 1983b; 1990; Ramsey 1991; Simmons and Rosenberg 1971; Stendler 1949; Tudor 1971) to highlight what is known about children's conceptions of poverty. Because research focusing directly on children's ideas about poverty is sparse, it was necessary to broaden the search to include these related concepts: social class, occupational stratification, and economic inequality. Organized thematically, the review discusses the problems that researchers identified for study, the procedures they employed to investigate children's conceptions, and age-related findings they obtained for U. S. children mostly of elementary school age or younger. Fol-

lowing the review, specific implications for teaching are drawn.

Regrettably, existing studies on the topic are, on the whole, dated. During the past 50 years, the nation has undergone a number of social changes that have profoundly affected popular thinking about the economically disadvantaged—e.g., the Civil Rights Movement, the War on Poverty, and television (Chafel 1995). Influences such as these have broadened and sharpened popular conceptions. We must take these changes into account when considering the applicability of the findings of these studies to the children of today. Clearly, more research is needed.

RESEARCH PROBLEMS INVESTIGATED

Although only a small body of literature exists on topics related to children's conceptions of poverty, the problems investigated by researchers have been numerous and diverse. Stendler (1949) studied children's conceptions of social class; the symbols they associated with it; whether status influenced their friendships and activities; and, finally, their class-related attitudes. Differentiating three conceptually distinct dimensions of social- class awareness, Tudor (1971) examined the cognitive, behavioral, and evaluative components involved in children's understandings of status. She appraised when children are able to perceive class distinctions; when they are able to recognize class-related behavior; and, finally, when they assign positive or negative judgments to cognitive cues. Simmons and Rosenberg (1971) studied children's awareness of occupational stratification, equality of opportunity for themselves and others, their occupational aspirations, and their knowledge of the social class to which they and their peers belonged.

While the above studies focused on social class and occupational stratification, others have concentrated more specifically on poverty. Estvan (1952, 7) scrutinized the "complex interplay of perceptual, cognitive, and attitudinal elements" involved in children's awareness. He studied children's perception of poverty as a social problem; their knowledge of its consequences and extensiveness; and their judgments about it and sense of concern. Concentrating on a somewhat different problem, Furby (1979) analyzed the explanations that children offered about why unequal distribution of personal belongings exists, and their evaluations of it. Leahy (1981) inquired into whether children's conceptions of rich and poor people shift with age, from emphasizing observable characteristics (possessions, behavior, appearance) to non-observable ones (traits, thoughts); and whether their comprehension of the sociocultural aspects of class (i.e., members' perceptions of their life chances, class consciousness) progresses. In a follow-up study, Leahy (1983a) appraised the explanations

and justifications that children offered for economic inequality, and their ideas about social mobility and change. Finally, Ramsey (1991) investigated young children's ability to categorize people as rich or poor and their understandings of the nature and causes of class differences.

These researchers have drawn primarily upon interviews and pictures to investigate a variety of problems relating to children's conceptions of poverty. Viewed as a whole, they define what we know about children's ideas. Although these problems are many, we can synthesize them into a small number of common themes: awareness of social and economic status, class-related attitudes, explanations for and judgments about inequality, and ideas concerning social mobility and change. The findings discussed in the article address these four areas of social knowledge.

Awareness of Social and Economic Status

In her study of poor and middle-class children in a small New England town, Ramsey (1991) found that 3-, 4-, and 5-year-old children rarely commented spontaneously about social class. They were able accurately to distinguish "rich" from "poor" when sorting photographs of the two groups. Most of the children considered the two as being more different than alike. In their open-ended descriptions of the pictures that they were shown, job and attire were the only class-related attributes upon which the children spontaneously commented. These attributes were mentioned by 25 percent and 27 percent of the sample, respectively.

From her findings in a highly industrialized, heterogeneous community of 15,000 people, Stendler (1949) identified a developmental progression in children's understandings of status, a series of stages which she referred to as pre-awareness, beginnings of awareness, acceptance of adult stereotypes, and recognition of individual differences regardless of class. The stages can be illustrated with a sampling of typical responses, but it should be pointed out that Stendler (1949) found more than one stage at a given grade. When asked to provide reasons for their ratings of pictures, first graders cited something observable or judged conduct or degree of cleanliness—e.g., a gas station worker was wealthy because he named some symbols of class for homes and recreation—e.g., whether homes were crowded or up-to-date—but the more immature types of reasoning found among the younger children were still apparent. Finally, sixth and eighth graders relied almost exclusively on monetary reasons for their ratings of clothing, homes, and recreation—e.g., the presence of a silver coffee service—or qualifications for jobs—e.g., "You need a lot of education to be a doctor" (Stendler 1949, 60). Thus, the oldest children demonstrated a much better understanding of social class symbols than the younger children.

The children also rated themselves and their classmates, providing reasons for their ratings on the latter. The first graders were unable accurately to identify their own class membership (with most saying rich), while the sixth and eighth graders rated themselves "in-between" wealthy and poor. When ascertaining class membership of their classmates, the youngest children had difficulty providing reasons for their choice, but older ones cited more universally recognized symbols of class, such as occupation or the section of town where one lived. First graders accurately rated about 33 percent of the time, fourth graders more than 50 percent, and sixth and eighth graders 68 percent and 78 percent, respectively. Responses on the "Guess Who Test," in which children associated social class symbols with their classmates, revealed a similar pattern of findings, showing increasing agreement with adult ratings, as children progressed through the grades. The largest increment measured by the test occurred between fourth and sixth grades.

On Tudor's (1971) measures, first, fourth, and sixth graders from a metropolitan center in the U. S. South classified figures representing various socioeconomic status groups on the basis of families and belongings and then responded to class-related questions about the pictures. The children's ability to perceive class-related cues grew substantially between the first two grades and, to a lesser extent, from grades 4 to 6. Because the sixth graders achieved a nearly perfect score, Tudor (1971) concluded that the developmental process of perceiving class-related cues is complete by that age. She found awareness of the behavioral correlates of class by first graders, but the children's scores were low. Between grades 1 and 4, awareness grew substantially, with smaller growth occurring between grades 4 and 6.

In their study of children in Baltimore, Simmons and Rosenberg (1971) assessed the ratings that third- to twelfth-grade children made of various occupations, and found them similar at every age to those of adults. The children were aware of the existence of an occupational stratification system but did not believe that its rewards were available to all. When asked whether they believed in the concept of equal opportunity, not every child could reply to the query, but 70 percent of elementary-age children able to do so said that they did not subscribe to the concept. Some subjects in Simmons and Rosenberg's sample indicated which children do not have an equal chance in life. Of these subjects, 68 percent viewed the problem as stemming from ethnic, racial, or socioeconomic disadvantage. When questioned about themselves, at all age levels the children were sanguine about their own chances and, with age, they became even more so. These latter findings conflict with those of Stendler (1949), whose subjects became increasingly realistic about their life chances as they grew older. By eighth grade, these children demonstrated a strong relationship between their choice of occupation and their social class.

Also, Simmons and Rosenberg (1971) found that 15 percent of elementary-age children were acquainted with the term "social class." When asked to identify their own class membership, at all ages they tended to overrate it, but they became increasingly more realistic with age. Similarly, less than 35 percent of elementary-age children were able to rate their peers when asked to name someone richer or poorer than themselves but, with age, they became increasingly able to do so. In sum, the elementary- age children in Simmons and Rosenberg's (1971) study were aware of the existence of status differences and barriers to opportunity but were unable to apply that knowledge to themselves and, in the case of the former, to their peers.

Utilizing a Piagetian clinical interview, Leahy (1981) appraised qualitative differences in the responses that children from 5 to 18 years of age in Washington, D. C., New York, and Boston offered when asked to describe rich or poor people. From the data, he identified a tentative developmental sequence, consisting of three categories of person perception: peripheral, psychological, and socioecentric. Progressive changes in decentration distinguish these categories, from focusing on external observable qualities—appearances, behaviors, possessions—to noting inferred, internal states—thoughts, traits—to recognizing that class membership affects class consciousness and life chances. Generally, the first category became less frequent with age, the other two more so, with a shift from peripheral to psychological conceptions occurring at age 10, though children of varying levels may have similar conceptions (Leahy 1983b).

While 5- and 6-year-olds cited peripheral aspects—e.g., "the poor 'don't have no food to eat'"—children between 10 and 14 cited psychological aspects—e.g., "poor people are 'lazy. They are poor because they don't want to work.'" Older adolescents turned to sociocentric views—e.g., "poor people 'are not being recognized as part of the system. They are neglected, ignored, treated wrong'" (Leahy 1983b, 96; Chafel in press). Leahy (1981) observed an increasing ability with age on the part of the children in his study to use a multiple-classificatory framework in thinking about rich and poor to recognize their similarities and differences; for example, rich and poor are alike because "they're both human beings" (Leahy 1983b, 96).

To sum up, children as young as preschool age are aware of social and economic status differences, although young children make only gross distinctions between "rich" and "poor" (Ramsey 1991). With age, they become increasingly adept at discerning universally accepted symbols of class, noting finer distinctions, and associating them with money (Leahy 1981; Stendler 1949; Tudor 1971). That Ramsey (1991) observed no age-related increment among her preschoolers on the last point may possibly be explained, as she speculated, by the segregated nature of children's lives. When thinking about rich and poor, young children emphasize differences between the two, whereas older ones also perceive similarities (Leahy 1981; Ramsey 1991). With age, too, children grow increasingly cognizant of their own social status and that of their peers (Simmons and Rosenberg 1971; Stendler 1949). There is, however, some disagreement about children's perceptions of their own life chances. In Stendler's (1949) study, they became increasingly more realistic with age while, in Simmons and Rosenberg's (1971) work, they were optimistic at every age. Ego- inflation, perception of a more upwardly mobile social system, or the desire for more favorable self-presentation might account for the latter findings (Chafel 1995). According to Simmons and Rosenberg (1971), elementary-age children are aware that life chances differ for different groups in society.

At what age do children first become aware of status differences? Stendler (1949) reported the beginnings of awareness from before grade 4 to beyond grade 6; adult stereotypes were solidly established before grade 6 and through grade 8. Tudor (1971) described onset at grade 1; substantial growth occurred between grades 1 and 4. By contrast, Ramsey (1991) observed awareness of social class differences on the part of preschoolers, and Leahy (1981) saw it in 5- to 7-year-olds. The different measures used and the time lapse between studies may account for these discrepancies.

Class-Related Attitudes

In Stendler's (1949) study, grade 1 children associated wealth with "good," and poverty with "bad"—e.g., "He's rich because he's smarter" (Stendler 1949, 82). Grade 4 children were not as likely to see the two social classes as so dichotomous, with some increment in the number of children saying that the person shown might be "anyone" (Stendler 1949, 83). Grade 6 children demonstrated little change from the previous level, but there was some increase in criticism of the rich and praise of the poor. Grade 8 children displayed responses that completely reversed those of the grade 1 children, revealing a "halo effect" for the poor; they were "likely to think that the poor are more likely than the rich to do the acceptable thing, but that they are also a bit more likely to do the unacceptable" (Stendler 1949, 85). Grade 8 children were more apt to believe that a bad—as opposed to a good—deed could be done by "anyone." As they advanced through the grades, then, the children in this study relied more on individual as opposed to class differences to assess behavior.

Does social class influence the friendships that children make? Stendler (1949) found that children generally made friends with others of similar background. Grade 1, 6, and 8 children in their out-of-school activities very definitely made friends with those of their own group. Grade 4, 6, and 8 children in their in-school activities either slightly overselected from or tended to make friends with those of like status. Stendler (1949) reasoned that children might be more free to decide upon their friendships with in-school activities, whereas, with out-of-school ones, they might be influenced more by parental persuasion or other considerations, but overall the children were quite homogeneous in their choices. Stendler (1949) speculated that such homogeneity might have resulted from the town's stratified social structure. In addition, children designated someone they would not like to have as a friend.

Of those children rejected, 66 percent belonged to the working class, 21 percent came from white-collar homes, and 13 percent were upper-middle class. The children's rejections did not vary noticeably by grade; but, more than the other age groups, first graders tended to reject upper-middle-class children. Thus, lower status children were the most likely to be rejected, upper status the least.

Ramsey (1991, 78) asked the preschool children in her study about "whether rich and poor people would be friends." A response was elicited from 87 percent of the children, with 52 percent responding positively and 48 percent negatively. There were no age differences in the way the children responded. Estvan (1952) appraised the attitudes that 10- and 11- year-old children from a Midwestern city displayed about poverty—their judgments about it and sense of concern. These children demonstrated considerable awareness of poverty and were in agreement concerning their "extreme rejection," "disapproval," and "condemnation" of it (Estvan 1952, 37, 44, 50). On her evaluative measure, Tudor (1971) investigated whether grade 1, 4, and 6 children assigned positive or negative judgments to cognitive cues about social class, but no significant effects emerged, perhaps because of measurement problems (Chafel 1995).

Clearly, children do have class-related attitudes. At a young age, they tend to see wealth and poverty dichotomously but, as they grow older, they assess behavior more on individual rather than class terms (Stendler 1949). Children select friends from among those of their own social background, rejecting those of lower status more frequently than those of higher status (Stendler 1949). Finally, there is limited evidence to suggest that older elementary children denounce poverty (Estvan 1952).

Explanations

Ramsey (1991, 78) queried the preschoolers in her study about "why some people had more money than others," but most were unable to provide an answer. Children alluded to concrete monetary transactions, saying, for example, that poor people "forgot to go to the store to get their money," indicating the children's only limited comprehension of poverty's causes (Ramsey 1991, 79).

Leahy (1983a; 1983b; 1990) saw an age-trend in children's explanations for wealth and poverty: from 6 to 11 years (peripheral conceptions), they lacked causal reasoning to explain it and viewed inequality in terms of definitional criteria like ownership of possessions. From 11 to 14 years (psychological conceptions), they explained inequality by referring to equity (e.g., effort, intelligence). Finally, from 14 to 17 years (sociocentric conceptions), they continued to ascribe to a belief that the economy rewards differences in merit, although some acknowledged class competition. To illustrate, the youngest children said that poor people "can't buy a job," "have no money," "got no food," or "spend their money on dumb things," while older children suggested that rich people "have better education," are "smarter," "have better jobs," or "work harder" (Leahy 1990, 115). Similarly, Harrah and Friedman (1990) observed that children 8, 11, and 14 years of age cited equity factors as reasons for wealth, poverty, and unemployment.

Furby (1979) questioned children about the unequal distribution of wealth in society. In reply to the statement, "why some people have more than others," kindergarten, second-, and fifth-grade children offered highly similar reasons, most frequently citing differences in the amount of money available, the passive acquisition of possessions, and preferences and needs (Furby 1979, 185). By eleventh grade, equity conceptions appeared as a new dimension in the children's responses—"some people *work hard and achieve*"—and an increasing perception of inequality as being beyond individual control (Furby 1979, 187).

Judgments

Leahy (1983a, 113) asked children, "Should some people be rich, while others are poor?" and "Should some people be poor, while others are rich?" Analyses of replies revealed a developmental shift with age in how children justify and challenge economic inequality. From 6 to 11 years of age, the children demonstrated a concern for consequences—e.g., "Poor should not suffer"—but also used definitional criteria—e.g., "They should be rich because they have a lot of money"—to rationalize status (Leahy 1983a, 114; Leahy 1983b, 99). From 11 to 14 years, they justified inequality by means of equity or challenged it by equality principles—e.g., "I think that they should all be the same"

(Leahy 1983b, 99). The notion of the rich helping the poor increased (at 11 years), and then subsequently declined (Leahy 1990). Finally, from 14 to 17 years, they continued to employ equity as a justification, with fatalistic ideas—e.g., "There will always be poorer people"—and notions of class conflict evident (Leahy 1983b, 99). Equality challenges to poverty also increased at age 14, but then diminished in frequency at age 17 (Leahy 1990). With age, the children in Leahy's (1983a) study increasingly saw economic inequality as being legitimate (Leahy 1990).

When the children in Furby's (1979, 192) study were asked to evaluate the unequal distribution of possessions ("How do you feel about some people having a lot more things than other people?"), kindergartners and second graders found it difficult to render a judgment, but did communicate various non-evaluative sentiments (e.g., a norm of sharing). The fifth graders more readily evaluated, offering more negative than positive judgments—e.g., a norm of equality—but most of their replies were also nonevaluative. Eleventh graders evaluated more than the younger children, also giving more negative than positive assessments. A salient positive evaluation at this age referred to the idea that "some people work harder than others" (Furby 1979, 194). Furby (1979) found more evenly distributed positive and negative judgments in responses from adults in the study. A small percentage of Ramsey's (1991, 78) subjects displayed a norm that supported the giving of money by the rich to the poor in reply to a question about "what rich and poor people might do together." The belief was communicated by significantly more older than younger children.

Social Mobility and Change

Only Leahy (1983a, 113) queried children about their conceptions of social mobility and change, asking "What would have to happen so that there would be no poor people?" Egocentrically bound and lacking causal reasoning, the youngest children in his study viewed the economy as operating on behalf of their interests or those of the poor. For example, they explained, "You can go to the bank and ask them for money" (Leahy 1990, 117). Between 6 and 11 years of age, the concept of the wealthy providing assistance to the poor increased, but then declined substantially (Leahy 1990). Older children relied on equity (e.g., work, effort) to account for social mobility and change. The idea that social change could be brought about by sharing wealth was evident at this level, too. The oldest children increasingly made references to changing the system, class conflict, or the futility of it. Equity still distinguished the children's responses, and sociocentric challenges to poverty were rare (Leahy 1983b).

Children think about whether economic privation should exist, why it does, and what can be done to alleviate it. Developmentally, they progress in their justifications of poverty from a concern for its consequences to challenging it with equality conceptions to legitimizing it with equity ones and a belief in fatalism (Leahy 1983a; 1983b; 1990). Leahy (1983b) observed that children increasingly ascribe to individual, psychological, and equity explanations for poverty rather than social and structural ones like racism or the economy. Furby (1979) noted a somewhat different developmental trend toward a belief in equity and the perception of inequality as beyond individual control—due to environmental characteristics or chance. The discrepancy may possibly be explained by the different questions the two studies asked of children. With age, children and adults increasingly legitimize economic inequality (Furby 1979; Leahy 1983a; 1983b; 1990). Challenges to poverty appear in the thinking of younger children, but later decline in importance (Leahy 1983a; 1983b; 1990). Viewed as a whole, research suggests that equity is an increasingly important factor with development in children's explanations of and justifications for poverty, and their ideas about social mobility and change.

IMPLICATIONS FOR TEACHING

This research indicates that children of elementary school age or younger are cognizant of social and economic inequality. With age, their conceptions increasingly become similar to adult views (Chafel 1995). What children think about poverty has profound social meaning. Today, a sizable proportion of children and families in this country are economically deprived. Furthermore, the gap between rich and poor, as measured by rising income inequality, has widened and a "conservative populism" has surfaced against the impoverished (Committee on Ways and Means 1994; Judis 1994; U. S. Bureau of the Census 1993). If these socially divisive trends continue unabated, they may threaten our survival as a democratic society.

Education should strive to develop in young people a caring and sensitive outlook towards every group that comprises society. While multicultural education has fostered this ideal for some time, it has done so mainly from the perspective of racial and ethnic diversity. Economic diversity has received far less emphasis, with educators avoiding poverty because it represents a conflictual topic, though such avoidance may prove harmful to the democratic process (Moore, Lare, and Wagner 1985; Passe 1995). Accordingly, this final section considers pedagogical implications of the research just reviewed from two perspectives: curriculum development and teacher education.

Curriculum Development

At a very early age, children become aware of status differences in society, so the goal of any curriculum effort should be directed to helping them develop a positive orientation towards every social class. The research just reviewed pointed out the components of social-problem awareness—perception, cognition, and attitudes—and the content of that awareness—e.g., occupations, attire, homes, and recreation. This information can be used to ascertain what the scope of the curriculum should be and provide guidance in designing learning experiences (Estvan 1952).

Educators should gear learning experiences to children's developing capabilities, as Aboud (1988) suggested. From 3 to 7 years of age, children are focused on self and influenced by their emotions. They note gross distinctions between rich and poor, concentrating on differences rather than similarities (Aboud 1988; Leahy 1981; Ramsey 1991). From 7 to 12 years, they grow less egocentric. Cognition overtakes emotion in saliency, the peer group assumes importance, and the child shifts from focusing on external, observable social class differences to noting nonobservable, internal characteristics and traits, and recognizes similarities as well as differences among groups (Aboud 1988; Leahy 1981). In addition, the child is able to think about poverty in causal terms at about 11 years of age and imagine possible solutions (Leahy 1983a; 1983b; 1990).

Activities for the younger age group should provide them an opportunity to become acquainted with social class differences, recognize and express a variety of emotions about these differences, and identify positively with children from these groups (Aboud 1988). Experiences for older ages should enable them to assess others on the basis of internal as opposed to external qualities; focus on similarities between and differences within groups; understand that others may have different points of view from theirs that may all be legitimate; and comprehend that causes of poverty are numerous and complex, but that inequities can be remedied (Aboud 1988; Bianchi 1993; Blank 1989; Chafel 1993; Corcoran, Duncan, Gurin, and Gurin 1985).

Leahy (1983a; 1983b; 1990) noted a developmental progression in children's explanations for and justifications of poverty and ideas about social mobility and change. The period from 11 to 14 years of age and beyond, when equality and sharing notions of wealth were evident in their replies, appears to be a good time to broaden their perspectives about specific ways to alleviate economic privation. With age, the children in Leahy's (1983a; 1983b; 1990) study increasingly saw poverty as inevitable.

Drawing upon the developmental characteristics just described and the suggested activities that correspond to them, teachers can design units of study appropriate for their particular age and socioeconomic group. Units of study for younger children—3 to 7 years of age—should focus on observable manifestations, while older children—7 to 12 years of age—should focus on more advanced topics—How are rich and poor alike or different? Why are people poor? What obligations does society have towards the economically dispossessed? The following suggestions are intended as initial points of departure. By observing children's responses to the activities provided, teachers can devise additional ones.

To illustrate briefly, teachers of younger, middle-class children might design a unit of study around the question, "What is poverty?" The children may have some awareness of its physical manifestations—e.g., attire, occupations. Themes to be pursued might include how you can tell someone is poor; what it might be like to be poor; and how the children feel when they see someone who is poor. A variety of picture books are available on the topic of poverty; they can be used to stimulate discussions and role plays with children about these issues. These experiences can help children to identify with those of different groups vicariously, experience a range of emotions about them, and consider concepts and problems from different perspectives. While research has not addressed children's emotional reactions to topics such as these, they may find poverty distressing, so they should be reassured about their own security (Feder-Feitel 1994).

Teachers of older middle-class children might design a unit of study around issues like how rich and poor are alike or different, why some people are poor, how they can be assisted, and societal obligations to the economically dispossessed. Again, children may have some previously held conceptions, so teachers might explore with them their belief systems and facts that confirm or disprove them (Feder-Feitel 1994). Beliefs pertaining to the above questions might provide starting points, which then could serve as topics for study. For example, some children might say that people are poor because they are lazy or do not want to work. As a group, the class then might go about researching the complex reasons why some people live in poverty.

Depending on whether inner-city or rural children of poverty are being taught, such questions must be very differently shaped. These children will need different kinds of assurance, and such discussions may add greatly to their understanding of themselves and people of other socioeconomic backgrounds.

Various forms of role play could be used by teachers to understand and explore with children their perceptions, beliefs, attitudes, and feelings. For example, children could be provided with a variety of props—pictures, toys, dress-up clothes—and asked to role play a family living under very different socioeconomic conditions.

Through such experiences, children can be helped to think critically about social and economic inequality. While the research just reviewed says nothing about the types of experiences that inspire children to empathize with the poor, it is reasonable to assume that they acquire images from a variety of sources: books, television, movies, newspapers, parents, teachers, and peers. Subtle messages can be communicated via the media, and children may interpret these messages in a variety of ways. Through skillful discussion, teachers can help children to recognize and become critical of negative connotations (Banks 1993). While exploring why some people are poor, for example, teachers might talk with children about the sources of their beliefs and how they might ascertain their validity.

School systems can support teachers in these efforts, most readily through in-service activities. Relevant books, films, guest speakers, and discussion groups on the causes of economic privation and society's obligations towards the poor can enhance teachers' knowledge and broaden their perspectives. Curriculum coordinators and supervisors can also assist teachers in researching resources for developing units of study about poverty.

Teacher Education

Teachers play a critical role in determining the success of these curriculum efforts by demonstrating a willingness to introduce and explore social class themes; by establishing an atmosphere of acceptance and respect for diversity of every kind; by valuing divergent perspectives about controversial issues like poverty; and by creating a social climate of sensitivity, respect, and cooperation in the classroom. Teacher educators can offer courses on poverty that provide useful strategies for classroom discussions with children and design field experiences in which preservice teachers work with economically disadvantaged youngsters or do volunteer work with impoverished populations like the homeless. Through readings, discussions, field experiences, and other means, students can become sensitive to the problem of poverty and learn to develop effective ways of exploring the issue with children.

Schools may perpetuate the status quo or they can transform it by nurturing paradigms of social thinking that encourage critical thinking and democratic values (Minuchin and Shapiro 1983). Children of elementary school age and younger are aware of poverty, a problem of substantial proportions in U. S. society. The pedagogical implications of the research reviewed here suggest that much can be done to encourage a humane outlook towards the impoverished and increase understanding of all socioeconomic classes.

REFERENCES

Aboud, F. E. 1988. *Children and prejudice.* New York: Basil Blackwell.

Banks, J. 1993. Multicultural education for young children: Racial and ethnic attitudes and their modification. In *Handbook of research on the education of young children,* ed. B. Spodek, 236–50. New York: Macmillan.

Bianchi, S. 1993. Children of poverty: Why are they poor? In *Child poverty and public policy,* ed. J. A. Chafel, 91–125. Washington, D. C.: Urban Institute Press.

Blank, R. 1989. Poverty and policy: The many faces of the poor. In *Prophetic visions and economic realities; Protestants, Jews, and Catholics confront the bishops' letter on the economy,* ed. C. R. Strain, 156–68. Grand Rapids, Mich.: W. B. Eerdmans.

Chafel, J. A. 1993. Conclusion: Integrating themes about child poverty in search of a solution. In *Child poverty and public policy,* ed. J. A. Chafel, 327–45. Washington, D. C.: Urban Institute Press.

Chafel, J. A. 1995. Children's conceptions of poverty. In *Advances in early education and day care,* ed. S. Reifel, 7: 27–57. Greenwich, Conn.: JAI Press.

Chafel, J. A. in press. Societal images of poverty: Child and adult beliefs. *Youth and Society.*

Committee on Ways and Means, U. S. Congress House of Representatives. 1994. Overview of entitlement programs: 1994 Green Book. Washington, D. C.: U. S. Government Printing Office.

Corcoran, M., G. Duncan, G. Gurin, and P. Gurin. 1985. Myth and reality: The causes and persistence of poverty. *Journal of Policy Analysis and Management* 4(4): 516–36.

Estvan, F. 1952. The relationship of social status, intelligence, and sex of ten-and eleven-year-old children to an awareness of poverty. *Genetic Psychology Monograph* 46: 3–60.

Feder-Feitel, L. 1994. Homelessness and poverty. *Creative Classroom* (October): 54–61.

Furby, L. 1979. Inequalities in personal possessions: Explanations for and judgments about unequal distribution. *Human Development* 22(3): 180–202.

Harrah, J., and M. Friedman. 1990. Economic socialization in children in a midwestern American community. *Journal of Economic Psychology* 11(4): 495–513.

Hopfensperger, J. 1992. Children in need: In inner cities and outstate, economic hardships come early and achingly for many in Minnesota. *Minneapolis Star Tribune,* 25 October, 1A.

Judis, J. 1994. The new era of instability. *New York Times,* 10 November, A35.

Leahy, R. L. 1981. The development of the conception of economic inequality: I. Descriptions and comparisons of rich and poor people. *Child Development* 52(2): 523–32.

Leahy, R. L. 1983a. The development of the conception of economic inequality: II. Explanations, justifications, and concepts of social mobility and change. *Developmental Psychology* 19(1): 111–25.

Leahy, R. L. 1983b. The development of the conception of social class. In *The child's construction of social inequality,* ed. R. L. Leahy, 79–107. New York: Academic Press.

Leahy, R. L. 1990. The development of concepts of economic and social inequality. In *Economic stress: Effects on family life and child development,* vol. 46 of *New directions for child development,* ed. V. McLoyd and C. Flanagan, 107–20. San Francisco: Jossey-Bass.

Minuchin, P., and E. Shapiro. 1983. The school as a context for social development. In *Socialization, personality, and social development,* vol. 4 of *Handbook of child psychology,* ed. E. M. Hetherington, 197–274. New York: Wiley.

Moore, S. W., J. Lare, and K. A. Wagner. 1985. *The child's political world: A longitudinal perspective.* New York: Praeger.

Nolan, M. S. 1978. *My daddy don't go to work.* Minneapolis: Carolrhoda Books.

Passe, J. 1995. *Elementary school curriculum.* Madison, Wisc.: Brown & Benchmark.

Ramsey, P. G. 1991. Young children's awareness and understanding of social class differences. *The Journal of Genetic Psychology* 152(1): 71–82.

Simmons, R., and M. Rosenberg. 1971. Functions of children's perceptions of the stratification system. *American Sociological Review* 36(2): 235–49.

Stendler, C. 1949. *Children of Brasstown.* Urbana: University of Illinois, Bureau of Research and Service.

Tudor, J. F. 1971. The development of class awareness in children. *Social Forces* 49(3): 470–76.

U. S. Bureau of the Census. 1993. Current Population Reports, Series P60–185, Poverty in the United States: 1992. Washington, D. C.: U. S. Government Printing Office.

EARLY CHILDHOOD EDUCATION: ISSUES OF ETHNICITY AND EQUITY

EDITH W. KING
University of Denver

ABSTRACT

In this article attention is placed on what is considered personal and cultural knowledge versus school knowledge; so that educators can begin to question classic concepts of early learning. Included are the accounts of thoughtful, perceptive adults which help us to recognise that the foundation for traditional education of young children was almost totally based in Western tradition.

Defining Ethnicity

What is ethnicity? In recent years ethnicity has come to play an important role in everyday living. It influences almost everyone. It affects our behaviour in the social spheres of our lives. Consider that ethnicity can affect how we spend our money, how we vote, even where we live or where we go out to dine. We use ethnicity as a filter for forming our identities, opinions and attitudes toward others. Sociologists acknowledge that ethnicity is central to many peoples' images and concepts of self-identity. Furthermore, sociologists recognise that individuals function on a continuum of ethnic affiliations ranging from non-recognition of one's ethnicity in daily life to an almost complete identification with an ethnic group in all activities, choices, and designations in daily actions.

Since the rise to prominence of this concept in the 1960s, ethnicity has been defined by numerous social scientists as: *a sense of peoplehood and commonality derived from kinship patterns, a shared historical past, common experiences, religious affiliations, language or linguistic commonalities, shared values, attitudes, perceptions, modes of expression and identity.*

Some Important Issues That Sociologists Have Addressed About Ethnicity

Why has ethnicity arisen as an important issue in our daily lives? The persistence of ethnicity and one's ethnic identification in contemporary, highly diverse societies is due to both negative and positive factors. When the primary reason for group affiliation is hostility from the majority group, it is inevitable that ethnicity seems more to confine and constrict the individual than to provide opportunities and enhance the quality of life. But people are usually drawn to ethnic identification because of the advantages it offers. The ethnic group can be a buffer between the individual and the broader society; individuals use ethnicity as a filter for forming their opinions, tastes, values and habit patterns. Ethnic affiliations also help organise social, economic, political, and religious interaction, both among individuals and among groups.

The Social Construction of Ethnicity

In exploring the concept of ethnicity or one's ethnic identity, we inevitably encounter questions about the "reality" of the social

From *Education and Society*, Vol. 14, No. 1, 1996, pp. 25-32. © 1996 by James Nicholas Publishers. Reprinted by permission.

world in which the individual exists. It seems appropriate, here to cite the theory of the social construction of reality and to apply it to the meaning of ethnicity and ethnic identity. The leading theorists on the topic of the social construction of reality are Peter Berger and Thomas Luckmann, whose ideas and insights help clarify the significance of the social construction of ethnicity and ethnic identity.

Berger and Luckmann contend that the reality of everyday life presents itself to us as a world we share with others. We share a common sense about what is reality and, therefore, our everyday life is characterised by a taken-for-granted reality. But human beings are unique among living creatures, for they can experience and exist in several provinces of meaning or taken-for-granted realities. These can be enclaves within the paramount reality. The theatre provides an excellent metaphor for coexisting realities. To this point Berger and Luckmann tell us:

> The transition between realities is marked by the rising and falling of the curtain. As the curtain rises, the spectator is "transported into another world" with its own meanings and an order that may or may not have much [to do] with the order of everyday life. As the curtain falls, the spectator "returns to reality." (Berger and Luckmann, 1966; 25).

So it is with ethnicity and an individual's ethnic identity. Within the ethnic group, the taken-for-granted world calls for conduct, use of language, referents, mutual affinities and antipathies that are implicit and unspoken. These ways are shared with others of the same ethnic and racial affiliations. The same individual functions within the majority society in the taken-for granted reality of the supermarket, the street traffic or the daily newspaper. Common habit patterns take over to guide conduct. A person pays the price posted and does not bargain with the cashier at the supermarket; goes on the green light and halts on the red light, not chancing the traffic just because no cars are apparent; and comprehends the news story on the front page about rising food prices. We accept and function within cultural continuities even from childhood. Our view of reality and of the world helps us to make sense of our experiences. We interpret social events in the light of meanings we attach to them. Here our ethnicity or our ethnic identification and ethnic affiliation come forth to interpret the meaning of everyday occurrences.

Often, growing up in the ethnic enclave, ghetto or barrio socialises children into the belief that all the world is Mexican American or Jewish or Italian or Puerto Rican. It is useful to realise that children hold these conceptions quite naturally and logically. Biographies and personal histories reveal how the chance factors of everyday life can affect people's conceptions of the ethnic and social world that surrounds them. Examples of the type of socialisation that lulls a child into believing that most of the existing society that she or he will ever encounter is made of people of the same ethnicity or race as the child, are revealed in these statements compiled from experienced teachers' accounts of their childhood socialisation. Following are some excerpts from adults recalling childhood impressions and remembrances of experiences that influenced their attitudes toward various ethnic groups:

. . . As a young child I had limited contact with people of colour. I knew that they existed because I would see them on the buses, or at the shopping malls, or at the movies when I would go. I never really thought too much about them though, because I never met a person of colour, nor did I ever have an opportunity to speak with one.

. . . An ethnic experience that I remember was when we went out to eat once at a Chinese restaurant. I was totally amazed to see a room full of Chinese people. The food was totally weird to me, and watching the people using chop-sticks, kept me mesmerised during the entire meal.

. . . I am a product of the South. In the 1950s my town was a racially segregated city. It was two cities in one. The blacks lived in an area referred to as "coloured" town and rarely mingled with the white population except when catching the bus. In "coloured" town were churches, schools, small stores—all the essentials to keep the blacks from mingling with the whites. On Saturdays on Main Street there were no blacks doing their weekly shopping[,] only crowds of white people. Blacks did not buy their shoes at Thompson's or ice cream at the Dairy Queen. Although my neighbourhood was only three blocks from "coloured" town, I never visited that area of town nor did any of my friends. It was off limits to us. Sometimes our parents would drive blacks home from their jobs cleaning our houses or yards, but we were never invited to ride along. (King, Chipman and Cruz-Janzen, 1994; 106–107).

These comments demonstrate the power of the social construction of ethnicity on an individual's attitudes, opinions and actions.

Remembering and Recounting Early Experiences for the Social Construction of Ethnic Identity: In the United Kingdom and in the USA

Earlier in this chapter a theory of the social construction of ethnicity was elaborated and some brief anecdotes or recollections were cited. Here now are two more detailed and in depth accounts of mature women recalling the social construction of ethnic, social class, and gender identity in the early childhood years of their lives. The intricate intertwining of the social forces of ethnicity, social class, and gender are evident in the stories of these two women, one of them, currently living in the United States, is of Mexican American ethnic affiliation; the other woman is a citizen of Britain of Panjabi and British affiliation.

My Socialization: The Account of a Mexican American Woman. The wind howled in the distance. Thunder rattled the windows, raindrops pelted the roof. My mother screamed in agony, writhing in pain. The rickety old bed trembled beneath her weight. The house was small, two bedrooms. There was nothing out of the ordinary about it, it was just a house. A small house in a small village in the state of Zacatecas in Mexico. My brother and two sisters were sleeping on one bed, oblivious to my mother's pain and my imminent entrance into their lives. It was 2:00 AM on a hot summer's night and I entered the world screaming and kicking at the medicine woman. I entered a country that I would never call my home, because at one month of age I was taken to the United States of America. My green card temporary passport to enter the USA did not even have a picture on it because I was so small. During my childhood in the United States, I was socialised into my Mexican culture, and acculturated into my American culture (see pp.—for definitions of terms used here). Each culture had different roles and expectations for my ethnic affiliation, my social class level and my gender. For the longest time, there was a battle going on inside me, one culture expected the opposite of the other. In time, I learned to synthesise both into the person I am today.

My Social Class Background: My father had nineteen brothers and sisters. Of those nineteen children, twelve survived. My grandfather was a farmer. He had been orphaned when he was six years old, both his parents having died of diseases. My grandfather was very handsome, his complex-

ion was white, like a Spaniard. He had blond hair and blue eyes. My grandmother was beautiful, she was dark-skinned with distinct Aztec Indian features. Neither of my grandparents had any formal schooling. They brought their children up in a three room cabin. One room was for storing feed for the animals; another room served as the kitchen; the third room was a bedroom where everyone slept. When many of my father's brothers and sisters married, their spouses and children would live with my grandparents, too. Their lives were filled with hardships.

By third grade my father, one of the many children, had to drop [out] of school to help his father on the ranch. At times, the family did not have enough food; neither could they afford shoes or warm clothes for their many children. My father wore his brothers' hand-me-down clothes all of his childhood and adolescence. My mother's family was in similar circumstances. Her father was a farmer. They had ten children with my mother being the oldest. My mother dropped out of school in the sixth grade because her mother needed her help caring for the rest of the children. At the age of eleven, my mother found herself caring for her siblings doing the cooking and cleaning for a family of twelve. So at the age of sixteen my mother married my father who was just eighteen and they went to live in my paternal grandfather's log cabin along with too many other people.

After a number of years of marriage my parents came to the United States looking for work and a better life for their children. They worked hard all of their lives to provide for us their six children, all those things that they never had. My father worked as a cook for quite sometime; then he got a job working in a steel mill. He has worked there for twenty years. My mother got a maintenance job cleaning offices. Now she is a supervisor with an office maintenance company. They both provided us with everything that we needed. We had a house, a yard, clothes, toys, food, and love. We were never without the necessities of life. But, one day I realised that our family now living in America, was considered poor! This came about because at my elementary school I made friends with a little Anglo girl named Sandra. Sandra was the daughter of a city council man. I would visit her big, beautiful house. I can still see it in my mind today. I could not believe that she and each one of her sisters had their own bedroom. I had to share my bedroom with my three sisters. She had a bicycle of her own. I had to share mine with my sisters. She had many beautiful dresses. I had to wear the dresses that belonged to my sisters. I felt inferior to Sandra because she seemed to have so many more things than I did. Also, it was at this young age, seven years old, that I began to feel ashamed of my parents. They were not "important" like other children's parents seemed to be in our neighbourhood and community. My parents spoke with an accent and my father wore "guaraches", Mexican sandals. I was mortified when one day, my father showed up at school wearing his "guaraches." As I was writing about this incident I remembered two other incidents that made me realise that my family was considered poor. I remember having to take home applications for free lunch. My mother would fill them out and have us return the forms to school. I was embarrassed when the teacher gave me an application in front of the class. I was also embarrassed when I had to return it. I felt ashamed because I thought that my classmates would think that we were really poor, when we weren't. Also, I recall that one Christmas, a food basket arrived at our house from my school. My school had collected food items to give to poor families during the holiday season. I was so angry that this basket of food arrived at MY house because I thought that then other people would label us as "poor." I took in the images around me, on television, at school; and I thought less of myself and my family because of this.

The Social Construction of Ethnic Identity:
As every other person in the world, I have also been socialised, a lifelong process of internalising the values of one group of people. I have been socialised to be a part of two different cultures; the Mexican and the American cultures. It has been a difficult road, a clash between the values and attitudes of one culture, and those of another.

My socialisation into the Mexican culture occurred first. We lived in "little Mexico", as we have fondly nicknamed our part of town. It was filled with brown people, speaking Spanish. Spanish was my first language. From the time that I was born until I entered kindergarten, everything and everyone around me was Mexican. Except for "Sesame Street" on the television, I did not know that any other world existed. It was not until I entered the public school that I began to encounter the dominant American society in which I actually lived. In my Mexican world of those pre-school years the family was most important. We did everything together. The reason that my two brothers and three sisters and I most often got punished was for fighting with each other. We have a very large extended family now living here in our city in the United States. I grew up with many cousins. I remember the family parties. We would laugh, eat, watch our parents make fools of themselves, play, fight, and stay up until we couldn't stand it any more. A cohesiveness exists within the Mexican family that cannot be easily broken;

but this cohesiveness has both negative and positive consequences. A negative consequence is that such close family ties tend to cause a dependence on one's family and, in my opinion, many Mexican parents bring up their children to be dependent on them. In my family, my parents did everything for us. My mother cooked and cleaned for all of us, never expecting any help from her children.

The dominant American cultural values disapprove of dependence. Many people in the United States believe that the Mexican family is dysfunctional because it encourages dependence on others. I think that it makes life a little harder because you learn to expect people to do things for you. It is harder for you to get out on your own if that is what you really want to do. What happens many times in the Mexican culture is that young ladies and young men do not leave their homes until they are married and are ready to start their own family. However, they are still dependent on the family to help them with child care or other needs. From what I have seen in the American culture, many American parents expect their children to be fully independent by the time that they are eighteen years old.

It has been a struggle. My Mexican culture is constantly clashing with my American culture. If I had to choose today, I would be American. I grew up here, it is what I know. When I am around Mexicans, which is almost always, I realise how different I am. But then, when I am around Americans, I realise that I am very different from them, too. I just can't be one or the other. I am both. I have been socialized with the values and attitudes of both cultures. It is lonely sometimes because you feel different from everyone else. It is like you are standing on the border of both countries. One foot is in the United States and the other foot is in Mexico, but neither country claims you. Yet, it is also nice to be different sometimes because it makes you feel unique. There is no one else like me. I have accepted it!

(Maria del Carmen Salazar; excerpts from unpublished project for the seminar, "Diversity in Education", Univ. of Denver, 1995)

Biculturalism in Britain: One Mother's View

Writing in an article in the British journal, *Multicultural Teaching to Combat Racism in School and Community* (Vol. 13, No. 1, Autumn, 1994), Vinod Hallan, an administrator of an Equal Opportunity Program in the Midlands of England, clarifies her own social construction of ethnic identity, through the experiences of returning to India with her young son to visit the members of their family that remained there.

As a British person I have lived 33 of my 40 years in England, so I should not have been surprised when, on a recent educational visit to the USA, I was constantly referred to as "our English guest" or "our English visitor." I was amazed at how much they admired my English and confused when, on a formal occasion, I received the compliment: "you English always dress so well."

I was puzzled because in all my 33 years in England nobody had ever referred to me in those terms. In England I am always referred to as Indian. Why was my "Englishness" so prominent in the USA and so unrecognised here? . . .

The real surprise came last Christmas when, having left at the age of seven, I returned to India for a holiday. Indian people are able to recognise what they call "Non-Residential Indians" (NRIs) especially the English NRIs, from a distance. My eight year old son, who is not fluent in Panjabi, suddenly found himself in an environment which he did not fully comprehend, where customs and traditions were not always familiar. There was a different emphasis on food, particularly towards vegetarianism, and fast food was a rarity. He was constantly looking for the "safe" and familiar. The street games played by the children of his age were new to him, and, as he spoke little Panjabi and no Hindi, and they spoke only Hindi and no English, it was clear from day one that to stay within the bounds of the safe, he would be spending most if not all of his stay, with me and my parents or with other English speakers. He spent his spare time watching English language broadcasts on cable TV, MTV and BBC Asia, and after the first few days he was missing his Big Mac, chips, and bacon sandwiches, and he was bored.

In my son I was witnessing an amplification of my "Englishness" and a reduction of my "Indianess." As he was only fluent when communicating in English, it was no surprise when some of my relatives began to call him "Angrez"—the Englishman. But here lies the dilemma experienced by English people whose parents originate from outside Europe, particularly those who do not have a white skin and therefore do not "blend in" with most of the British population. In England he is seen as an outsider, an Indian, but in India he is seen as an outsider, the "Angrez", so where does his ethnic identity lie, and what epithet correctly describes his ethnicity?

Many Asian and African-Caribbean people do not like the tag "ethnic minority group" as it places them at a disadvantage. They feel that ethnic minority groups are subordinated segments of society whose characteristics are held in low esteem by the dominant group, conjuring up notions of culturally deficient people whose history, customs and values are of little consequence. Their perceptions are reinforced by fascist political parties, insensitive media and ethnocentric institutions, to an extent where some young black children deny their own colour and firmly believe themselves to be white. The conclusion that I am beginning to draw from this is that black people need to explore new terms which more accurately describe their ethnicity, terms which establish them as part of the "mainstream" where their "Britishness" is recognised first and only then their additional cultural heritage, in a similar way to American citizens who describe themselves as American-Irish, American-Italian, or African-American and where the extended experience of more than one culture is recognised, valued and accepted. For, contrary to popular belief, few black children are torn between two cultures; the majority are bilingually advantaged and bi-culturally proficient. Is this really surprising? Children who are raised in a pluralised society, particularly those whose parents were immigrants, not only acquire the behavioural and social patterns of their parents' ethnic group but also those of the host society. This is most likely to occur with children from a minority ethnic group, is also common among children of mixed marriages, and majority group children who live with minority group children. They have the advantage of being able to function in two different cultures by switching from one set of values to another. It is not surprising therefore that individuals who are biculturally or even multiculturally competent find the existing ethnic identity tags limiting and in many case inaccurate. Ethnicity has been described as a set of beliefs, attitudes and behaviour which distinguishes one cultural group from another. For many of our youngsters their beliefs, attitudes and behaviour spans more than one culture, and so do not readily fit into an accepted ethnic group. Educationalists are no different to the rest of society. Generally they are only proficient in one culture and language, and have direct experience of only one ethnic group. Children who are bi-culturally proficient quickly learn that these people can only function in one particular part of their repertoire, similar to the way the bilingual children learn that some people can only understand and function using a limited part of their own total language ability. In school, I have seen five year olds switch from speaking Panjabi to speaking English, simply by turning their heads from their parents to the teacher.

For my own son I would like to think that there will be a time, in the not too distant future, when he will be able to describe his ethnicity in his own terms, and that people will accept him for what he thinks he is, rather than what they think he should be.

(Excerpted from Vinod K. Hallan. "Whose Ethnicity Is It Anyway", *Multicultural Teaching,* Vol. 13, No. 1, Autumn, 1994, pp. 14–16).

Some Conclusions

Educational sociologists and curriculum theorists have analysed the construction of knowledge, categorising this knowledge so that it brings to our attention new ramifications for what is learned in schools. In this article attention has been raised to consider what is personal and cultural knowledge; school knowledge; and popular knowledge so that educators can begin to question classic concepts of learning. Through the accounts of thoughtful, perceptive adults, educators can recognise that the grounding and philosophy for traditional education of young children was almost totally based in Western European culture and tradition, with little regard for those children and their families whose traditions, heritage, language and customs stemmed from other cultures. The outmoded conception of readiness in the early childhood curriculum, where the teacher plays a passive role merely waiting for the student to develop physically and intellectually, takes no regard or concern for what may have happened to the individual in the family setting or the broader society. Given the crises and traumas in our modern world, this is naive and inappropriate. We no longer exist in an unchanging and safe society. Further, the conventional wisdom that proffers a curriculum model assuming children grow and develop in the same way, at the same time and they all should be able to function in the mainstream or majority society is errant. Additionally, at the beginning of this century the conventional image of the teacher of young children was a loving, gentle WOMAN, but at the close of this century is this conception still appropriate? Those of us who are committed to the vision of equality of educational opportunity in our society and for a worldwide society are asking now at the close of the 20th Century—just what has diversity brought? What will the future hold? Can this vicious rise of racism, sexism, classism, homophobia be contained? Is equity for all our children an attainable goal in the 21st century?

REFERENCES

Allport, Gordon. *The Nature of Prejudice.* Garden City, N.J.: Doubleday Anchor Books, 1954.

Banks, James A. *Multiethnic Education: Theory and Practice.* Needham Hts., Mass: Allyn and Bacon. (1994, 1988, 1981).

Barth, Frederick. (editor) *Ethnic Groups and Boundaries.* Boston: Little, Brown, 1969.

Berger, Peter and Thomas Luckmann. *The Social Construction of Reality.* New York: Anchor Books, 1966.

Fishman, Joshua. *Bilingual Education: An International Sociological Perspective.* Rowley, Mass: Newbury House, 1976.

Hallan, Vinod. "Whose Ethnicity Is It Anyway?" *Multicultural Teaching.* Volume 13, No. 1, (Autumn, 1994) pp. 14–16.

King, Edith. *Teaching Ethnic and Gender Awareness.* 2nd edition. Dubuque, Iowa: Kendall/Hunt. 1990.

King, Edith W., Marilyn Chipman, Marta Cruz-Janzen. *Educating Young Children in a Diverse Society.* Needham Hts. Mass.: Allyn and Bacon, 1994.

Salazar, Maria del Carmen. Unpublished project for seminar, "Diversity in Education", Denver, CO. University of Denver, 1995.

Address for Correspondence: *Professor Edith W. King, College of Education, University of Denver, 2450 S. Vine Street, Denver, Colorado, 80208 USA.*

RACE AND CLASS CONSCIOUSNESS AMONG LOWER- AND MIDDLE-CLASS BLACKS

THOMAS J. DURANT, JR.
Louisiana State University

KATHLEEN H. SPARROW
University of Southwestern Louisiana

Past studies have revealed that to a great extent, America is a racially stratified society. Early studies revealed that race was a significant factor influencing the life chances and social status of Blacks in America (Cox, 1948; Davis, Gardner, & Gardner, 1941; Drake & Cayton, 1945; DuBois, 1899; Frazier, 1957; Johnson, 1943; Myrdal, 1964). During the 1960s, the U.S. Riot Commission report (1967) concluded that "Our nation is moving toward two societies, one Black, one White—separate and unequal; discrimination and segregation have long permeated much of American life; they now threaten the future of every American." More recent studies have also found that race continues to be a primary factor influencing Black life chances in America (Clark, 1978, 1980; Pettigrew, 1980; West, 1993; Willie, 1989). Past studies have concluded that racial stratification gives rise to race consciousness, which emerges from members of both the dominant and subordinate racial groups (Allen, 1970; Brown, 1931; Ferguson, 1936; Park, 1913, 1923; Pitts, 1974; Rose, 1964).

On the other hand, America is also stratified by social class, which gives rise to class consciousness among members of both the dominant and subordinate classes. As such, both race consciousness and class consciousness are two forms of group consciousness that result from social structured inequality, based on race and class. The theoretical value in studying these concepts lies in their capacity to enhance our understanding of the nature, patterns, and variations in race and class consciousness among subgroups of the Black population. For example, many believe that increased social mobility among Blacks and the reduction of racial prejudice and discrimination have led to an increase in class consciousness and a decrease in race consciousness (Handy, 1984).

Whereas some attention has been given to structural determinants of race and class consciousness among Blacks, little attention has been given to the attributes of race and class consciousness based on the perceptions of lower-class Blacks, compared to middle-class Blacks. Although an earlier study (Handy, 1984) compared the level of race and class consciousness among Blacks and their social correlates, a content analysis of the qualities, patterns, and variations in race and class consciousness respectively, was not conducted. In other words, what are the elements that comprise race and class consciousness? And what are the attitudinal patterns of race and class consciousness, as perceived by lower-class

From *Journal of Black Studies*, January 1997, pp. 334-351. © 1997 by Sage Publications, Inc. Reprinted by permission.

Blacks, compared to middle-class Blacks? This study will explore these questions.

The specific objectives of this study are (1) to lay the background for the current study by briefly reviewing the broader issue on the significance of race versus class in determining the life chances of Blacks, (2) to discuss the sociological meaning and derivation of the concepts of race consciousness and class consciousness, and (3) to discuss and summarize the results of a study on differences in attitudinal patterns of race consciousness and class consciousness among lower-class Blacks, compared with middle-class Blacks of a large southern city.

THE CLASS PERSPECTIVE

Wilson (1978), the chief proponent of the class perspective, contends that the life chances of Blacks have more to do with their economic class position than with their race. In other words, race can no longer be considered as important as class in determining the life chances of Blacks. Wilson states that access to higher paying jobs is increasingly based on education and that relations between racial groups are shaped largely by the character of the economic system of production. According to Wilson, American society has undergone three stages in Black-White relations—preindustrial, industrial, and modern; each period has brought a distinct pattern of race relations.

In the preindustrial period, largely characterized as a slave-based plantation economy of the South, the social order was such that the slaveholding elite relegated Blacks to indefinite servitude and promoted its own class interests. In stage two, the industrial period, a new pattern of race relations evolved. This period was characterized by a growing industrial system that put Whites and Blacks into competition for jobs in the North, which produced racial tension and even riots, and a system of Jim Crow segregation laws was imposed by Whites in the South. In stage three, the modern period, class replaces race as the most important factor influencing Black life chances. This development contributed to internal class differentiation within the Black communities.

In summary, Wilson (1978) argues that race is less determinative of fortunes and destinies than it once was, and that Blacks with the requisite skills can now advance economically whereas the Black underclass without the skills cannot advance. Proponents of the class perspective would probably argue that increased social mobility among Blacks has increased their class consciousness and decreased their race consciousness.

THE RACE PERSPECTIVE

Willie (1989), a chief critic of Wilson's (1978) class perspective, argues that race, not class, is the primary factor underlying the plight of Blacks in America. Willie states that there is a "unified Black experience" within the United States that transcends class. He makes the point that race is the most pervasive factor in the Black experience. Willie cites the large gaps that still exist between Blacks and Whites in employment, education, housing, and other similar socioeconomic characteristics that are not treated equal in the marketplace. In identifying race as an explanation, Willie stresses the role that institutional racism plays in American life. He contends that White elites have structured institutional life so that valued items such as wealth, status, and power flow to the advantaged White group.

Willie's (1989) perspective has been supported by Pettigrew (1980), who argues that race remains as important as ever in determining the life chances of Blacks. According to Pettigrew, the Black poor are far worse off than the White poor and the Black middle class still has a long way to go before it catches up with the White middle class in economic security, status, and wealth. Clark (1978, 1980), also notes that Whites continue to control corporate, educational, and governmental life and hence Blacks always remain vulnerable to White racism. Proponents of the race perspective would probably argue that the persistence of racial discrimination and subordination of Blacks has made Blacks more race conscious than class conscious.

EVOLUTION OF THE CONCEPTS OF RACE CONSCIOUSNESS AND CLASS CONSCIOUSNESS

Our perspective is that race consciousness and class consciousness involve interaction between two components: (1) status, based on race and class; and (2) attitudinal perceptions of race and class. The basic assumption of this perspective is that both race (ascribed status) and class (achieved status) are determinants of social inequality, which in turn lead to attitudinal formations that are conceptualized here as race consciousness and class consciousness. In other words, race consciousness and class consciousness are manifestations of one's racial and class status, as determined by the system of social stratification (Frazier, 1957; Hewitt, 1970; Noel, 1968). Noel (1968) uses the term ethnic stratification to refer to a system wherein some relatively fixed group membership, such as race, religion, or nationality, is used as a major criterion for assigning social positions and their attendant rewards. Achieved status factors, such as education, income, and occupation, may act in concert with ethnic or ascribed factors, such as race, in determining one's position in the stratification system (Noel, 1968). Both Frazier (1957) and Noel (1968) assumed that racial and class inequality may give rise to different types of social and psychological attitudes, such as racial or class identity and class consciousness.

To gain an understanding of the theoretical meaning and usage of the concepts of race consciousness and class consciousness, it is essential to provide some background on the sociological evolution of these concepts. For Karl Marx (1969), class consciousness involved an awareness of common interests and common membership in a distinct community of economic interests that lead to social action on the part of group members. For Marx, social action was viewed as the prerequisite for the transformation of society into a new social order. Marx implied that class consciousness will inevitably arise in response to conflict and oppression that are inherent in the class system (Abrahamson, Mizruchi, & Hornung, 1976). When the proletariat develops consciousness of its distinct interests, it becomes a "class in itself" rather than a class "for itself" (Heller, 1969, p. 9). Marx postulated the relationship between social structure and class consciousness was that social existence determines one's class consciousness.

A critical issue concerning Marx's definition of class consciousness that has been raised by contemporary scholars, who have sought to define the concept, is whether both attitudinal and behavioral (class actions) elements must be included in the definition of class consciousness. Morris and Murphy (1966) address this issue by asserting that it is theoretically useful to view class consciousness with or without class action on the part of individual members. However, others argue that it is essential to the very idea of class consciousness that some sort of commitment to class interest or ideology be present together with participation in a program of action in the name of the class (Glantz, 1958; Leggett, 1968; Manis & Meltzer, 1963). However, Lewis (1965) states that class consciousness involves a common predisposition to class action held by people of a particular class and an awareness of common class interests. Moreover, Landecker (1963) distinguished three types of class consciousness, namely class status consciousness, class structure consciousness, and class interest consciousness. This suggests that class consciousness is a multifaceted concept that can take a number of interrelated attitudinal forms that derive from different dimensions of group structure.

Our view is that it is theoretically useful to study class consciousness as an attitudinal predisposition toward class status, position in the class structure, and class interests, which are predisposed indicators of social action. In other words, we believe there is value in treating attitudes about class consciousness as predisposed social actions, while recognizing that attitudes and behavior may not always coincide. In other words, subjective attitudes toward class do not necessarily coincide with objective class status. Also, it is important to note that class consciousness among Blacks is not static but changes with the dynamic transformations of racial and class status in society. And all of the above factors influence variation in class consciousness among Blacks.

Early attempts to define the concept of race consciousness have been made by a number of scholars (Brown, 1931; Ferguson, 1936; Park, 1913, 1923). These scholars assumed that race consciousness, as a major form of group consciousness, emerges among both domin[ant] and subordin[ant] racial groups. They viewed race consciousness as a tendency toward sentimental and ideological identification with a racial group (Woldemikael, 1989). Accordingly, the individual who is race conscious considers race as an object of loyalty, devotion, and pride, exalting its virtues, taking pride in achievements, and possessing a feeling of solidarity among group members (Brown, 1931; Ferguson, 1936; Hraba, 1979). Awareness of Black subordination and inequality relative to Whites has also been viewed as an element of race consciousness (DuBois, 1953).

A more recent definition of race consciousness emphasizes affective commitment to Blacks in their relations to Whites (Pitts, 1974). Two components have been viewed as essential to the definition of race consciousness, namely (1) accepting the racial identity and groupings of others on the basis of race; and (2) acting to redefine the inequality in status, privilege, and power between the two racial groups (Woldemikael, 1989). In addition to these definitions, recent studies have focused on a wide range of concepts that imply the existence of race consciousness, such as racial group identity, black nationalism, and racial subordination (Broman, Neighbors, & Jackson, 1988; Gurin & Epps, 1975; Woldemikael, 1989).

The common assumption of most of the above conceptualizations of race consciousness is that race consciousness emerges when members of a particular racial group become aware of their position and status vis-à-vis other racial groups and develop a sense of collective identity that may be expressed in different social and psychological forms, such as loyalty, devotion, pride, commitment, and identity. For example, the common thread of historical experience, referred to by Thompson (1974) as the "Black experience," created a strong Black group identity and an awareness of the bond of unity and strength that lies in the group (Erikson, 1966).

THEORETICAL PERSPECTIVE

For the purpose of this study, class consciousness is defined as one's perception of the meaning of social class in terms of awareness of factors that influence social class position. This awareness could be expressed in terms of one's perception of appropriate behavior, lifestyle, social action, and status inequality.

For the purpose of this study, race consciousness is defined as one's awareness of his racial identity and group membership, as reflected by attitudinal expressions of identity, devotion, unity, pride, culture, status, behavior, and iniquities. As such, race consciousness may be expressed in different forms, and is not static, due to social changes, differentiation, transformations, and stratification occurring within the group as well as within the larger society. Thus the type and degree of race consciousness of members of a particular racial group may vary over time.

Two dimensions of race consciousness are included in this study—individual and collective. Individual race consciousness is an orientation that one's racial identity, status, and actions are a function of individual efforts and attitudes about race. Collective race consciousness is defined as an awareness of common racial group identity, and the need for collective group actions to further the collective group interests (Gurin & Epps, 1975; Lopreato & Hazelrigg, 1972).

It should also be noted that racial and class groups overlap, which may sometimes lead to competing and conflicting behavior and attitudes of group members. For example, a Black physician may view himself as a member of the middle class, but due to racial prejudice and discrimination against him, may hold the perception that his racial status takes preceden[ce] over his class status in terms of prestige and attendant rewards. On the other hand, many middle-class Blacks may identify more with other Blacks in their own class rather than with Blacks of the lower class (Rose, 1964). However, many lower-class Blacks may expect middle-class Blacks to identify with their race because of the prevalence of the common foe of racial discrimination and the commonality of the Black experience. Thus this discrepancy may place many Blacks in a race and class dilemma and may influence their level of consciousness about membership in their race and in their class. This suggests that both race and class consciousness evolve from social structured inequality based on membership in different groups—race and class—that can lead to both conflict and consensus.

One of the assumptions of this study is that Black attitudes toward race and class are shaped by their experiences and their status within the race and class hierarchy. As mentioned earlier, attitudes and perceptions toward race and class do not necessarily coincide with the objective reality. For example, it is possible that middle-class Blacks may perceive their race as being relatively more important than their class because they have experienced rejection and discrimination by Whites regardless of their class. For example, a nationwide poll revealed that 61% of all Blacks sampled believed that Whites either do not care whether Blacks get a break or were actively trying to keep Blacks down (Herbers, 1978).

Based on the above theoretical assumptions, in this study we expect race consciousness and class consciousness to differ between lower-class and middle-class Blacks. Also, due to the past Black experience that has been a part of the current and historical experiences of Blacks in America, both lower-class and middle-class Black[s] are expected to have higher race consciousness than class consciousness. The significance of race and class by Blacks will be determined on the basis of perceptions pertaining to subjective attitudes that reflect the meaning attached to race and class.

METHODOLOGY

The location of the study was a southern city with a total population of approximately 200,000 in which Blacks comprised 30% of the total population. A representative sample of 205 subjects was selected by an area-stratified random-block-sampling method. First, the entire study area was divided into blocks based on the stratifying criteria of race and socioeconomic status. Using the U.S. Bureau of the Census *Block Statistics* (1970) publication, which lists the percentage Black population by block, any block with 25% or more Blacks was considered. New additions of blocks with 25% or more Blacks that developed since the 1970 census were determined by knowledgeable informants, mainly real estate agents.

A group frequency distribution of the mean house value for each eligible block was obtained from the U.S. Bureau of the Census *Block Statistics* (1970). From this distribution, house values were divided into four quartiles. Each quartile was representative of the percentage of Blacks in the total population of the city. Each block quartile was fully enumerated on a listing, and the number of dwellings per block was obtained from U.S. *Block Statistics*. Each intersection and midblock was numbered, and a random number was chosen as the starting point. Individuals aged 18 and older were randomly selected in each household and interviewed, using the personal interview technique.

Social class was defined on the basis of education and income. Those individuals with at least some college education and with an income of $16,000 or more were defined as

middle class. Those with no college education and earning less than $16,000 were defined as lower class. Class consciousness was operationalized by a 6-item Likert-type scale derived by a factor-analysis procedure that was used to measure the extent of attitudes, awareness, and commitment to one's class as a group. Both individual race consciousness and collective race consciousness were respectively operationalized by Likert-type scales that were used to measure the extent of attitudes, awareness, and commitment to one's race. Each scale was also constructed with the use of factor analysis. In all of the scales, each item had five response levels: (1) *strongly disagree*, (2) *disagree*, (3) *undecided*, (4) *agree*, and (5) *strongly agree*.

DISCUSSION OF FINDINGS

Table 1 shows the mean scores for each of the three types of class and race consciousness for lower-class and middle-class Blacks. The data clearly show that lower-class Blacks express more class consciousness than middle-class Blacks. The data also show that there is more compatibility of race consciousness than class consciousness between lower- and middle-class Blacks. These results are also supported by the data in Table 2, which show the mean response level for each item for each of the three types of consciousness for lower-class Blacks compared to middle-class Blacks. In other words, our data reveal that there is more consensus among Blacks of the study about the meaning of their race than the meaning of their class. This finding suggests that increased social mobility and social differentiation occurring within the Black population have resulted in differential perceptions of the meaning of social class. This finding also reflects an increasing awareness of class differences between middle-class and lower-class Blacks, whereas at the same time, both groups express a similar degree of race con-

TABLE 1

Class Consciousness and Race Consciousness By Social Class: Mean Scores

	Lower Class			Middle Class		
	M	**SD**	**Range**	**M**	**SD**	**Range**
Class consciousness	10.0	2.4	4.7 to 16.9	7.9	1.7	4.3 to 11.7
Race consciousness individual	4.5	1.9	1.9 to 8.5	3.3	2.2	1.6 to 7.8

TABLE 2

Class Consciousness and Race Consciousness By Social Class: Mean Response Level[a]

	Item	Lower Class	Middle Class
CC1	It is more important to have a career with prestige than a skilled job making lots more money.	2.74	2.08
CC2	Immediate success is more important than long range planning.	2.68	2.30
CC3	If people would just work hard, they would get ahead in life.	3.47	2.20
CC4	Community decisions should be made by those individuals who are financially well off.	1.87	1.50
CC5	The wealth of our country should be divided up equally so that people would have an equal chance to get ahead.	3.61	2.75
CC6	One should choose friends and associates from his own social class.	2.64	2.10
RC1	Schools with mostly Black children should have mostly Black teachers and principals.	3.18	3.25
RC2	Only if Blacks pull together in civil rights groups and activities can anything be done about discrimination.	4.01	4.07
RC3	The only way Blacks will gain their civil rights is by constant protest and pressure.	3.40	2.83
RC4	The attempt to "fit in" and do what's proper has not paid off for Blacks. It does not matter how "proper" you are, you will still meet serious discrimination.	3.97	4.03
RC5	Educated Blacks who have good jobs should try to use their talents and leadership abilities to help other Blacks.	4.56	4.50
RC6	The best way to overcome discrimination is through pressure and social action.	3.30	3.02
RI1	The Black Panther Party and other similar militant organizations have not done a lot for Blacks.	2.81	3.45
RI2	Blacks should not identify with Africa by wearing African-styled clothing, jewelry, and hairstyles.	3.16	3.55
RI3	The best way to overcome discrimination is for each individual Black to be even better trained and more qualified than the most qualified White person.	4.11	3.65
RI4	Many Blacks have only themselves to blame for not doing better in life; if they tried harder, they would do better.	4.56	4.50
RI5	Blacks may not have the same opportunities as Whites, but many Blacks have not prepared themselves enough to make use of the opportunities that come their way.	4.16	3.92

NOTE: CC = Class Consciousness; RC = Race Consciousness: Collective Orientation; RI = Race Consciousness: Individual Orientation.
a. 1 = Low, 5 = High.

sciousness. Thus we can conclude that both lower-class Blacks and middle-class Blacks believe that they are victimized by their race. Consequently, Blacks tend to have a more similar awareness of the meaning of their race than the meaning of their class.

The fact that there are differences and similarities in race consciousness and class consciousness between lower-class and middle-class Blacks does not identify differences in specific attitudinal dispositions toward race and class. To assess the substantive differences in specific attitudes, a content analysis of the responses to the items that comprise race consciousness and class consciousness was conducted. Table 3 shows the responses to the

TABLE 3

Class Consciousness Among Lower- and Middle-Class Blacks: Percentage of Agreement and Difference

Class Consciousness Item	LC	MC	D
The wealth of our country should be divided up equally so that people would have an equal chance to get ahead.	73	36	37
If people would just work hard, they would get ahead in life.	68	35	33
Immediate success is more important than long range planning.	39	12	33
One should choose friends and associates from his own social class.	35	10	25
It is more important to have a career with prestige than a skilled job making lots more money.	35	13	22
Community decisions should be made by those individuals who are financially well off.	11	00	11

NOTE: LC = Lower Class, MC = Middle Class, D = Difference.

class consciousness items for lower-class and middle-class Blacks. The data reveal that much larger proportions of lower-class Blacks, compared to middle-class Blacks, agreed with the class consciousness items. In essence, lower-class Blacks were much more likely to feel that the inequality gap in wealth in America should be reduced or eliminated. Almost three fourths of lower-class Blacks, compared to only 36% of middle-class Blacks, reported that the wealth of our country should be divided up equally so that people would have an equal chance to get ahead. A larger proportion of lower-class Blacks than middle-class Blacks felt that people could get ahead in life if they worked hard.

Although less than half of the lower-class Blacks agreed with the remainder of the four class consciousness items, in all cases these proportions were much higher than those for middle-class Blacks. One observation of particular interest is that 35% of lower-class Blacks and only 10% of middle-class Blacks agreed that "one should choose his friends and associates from his own social class." Surprisingly, this suggests a greater orientation toward interclass integration among middle-class Blacks than lower-class Blacks.

Table 4 shows the responses to items pertaining to individual race consciousness for lower-class and middle-class Blacks. A much larger percentage of middle-class Blacks (67%) than lower-class Blacks (31%) believed that

militant organizations, such as the Black Panther Party, have not done a lot for Blacks. This indicates that middle-class Blacks were more strongly opposed to militant strategies as the best means for the advancement of Blacks. However, both lower-class and middle-class Blacks overwhelmingly disagreed that many Blacks have not prepared themselves enough to take advantage of the opportunities that come their way. Thus regardless of social class, Blacks of the study felt that their status and opportunities were limited because of their race.

There was a high degree of consensus among both groups that the best way to overcome racial discrimination is for each Black person to be better trained and more qualified than the most qualified White person when competing for the same job. Neither lower-class Blacks nor middle-class Blacks tended to blame themselves for not doing better in life or for lack of hard work, although the percentage of middle-class Blacks who expressed this attitude was almost twice as large as that for lower-class Blacks. This finding suggests that Blacks who blame themselves for racial discrimination would be tantamount to blaming the victim. Slightly more than one third of lower-class Blacks compared to one fourth of middle-class Blacks agreed with the statement that Blacks should not attempt to express their identity by wearing African attire. This suggests that middle-class Blacks tend to approve of such "Afrocentric" expressions of

TABLE 4

Individual Race Consciousness Among Lower- and Middle-Class Blacks:
Percentage of Agreement and Difference

Individual Race Consciousness Item	LC	MC	D
The Black Panther Party and other similar militant organizations have not done a lot for Blacks.	31	67	36
Blacks may not have the same opportunities as Whites, but many Blacks have not prepared themselves enough to make use of the opportunities that come their way.	06	15	09
The best way to overcome discrimination is for each individual Black to be even better trained and more qualified than the most qualified White person.	76	68	08
Many Blacks have only themselves to blame for not doing better in life; if they tried harder, they would do better.	12	23	11
Blacks should not identify with Africa by wearing African-styled clothing, jewelry and hairstyles.	37	25	12

NOTE: LC = Lower Class, MC = Middle Class, D = Difference.

culture slightly more than Blacks from the lower class.

Table 5 shows the responses to the items pertaining to collective race consciousness. The data reveal several patterns of race consciousness that are highly prevalent among both lower-class and middle-class Blacks, namely: (1) the need for unity among Blacks, (2) the consensus that race/color is a basis for discrimination, and (3) the expectation that Blacks with educational and economic means and resources should help elevate less fortunate Blacks (items 4, 5, and 6). These responses suggest that both lower-class and middle-class Blacks feel that Blacks must pool their resources, unite, and take action on behalf of their own interests to combat racial discrimination if they are to make substantial progress. These responses reveal that regardless of social class, Blacks feel that race is still a dominant factor that influences life chances and opportunities. These responses also reveal that racial discrimination is expected by most Blacks, over which they have little control.

Strong but somewhat less prevalent among both lower-class and middle-class Blacks was the attitude that Blacks must engage in constructive actions to overcome racial discrimination and gain full socioeconomic equality. However, lower-class Blacks tended to be more oriented toward protests and social pressure than did middle-class Blacks. As shown in Table 5, at least 60% of lower-class Blacks agreed with items 1 and 2 that "the only way to gain civil rights and overcome discrimination is through constant protest, pressure, or social action," compared to less than half of the middle-class Blacks. However, middle-class Blacks, being in a better position to take advantage of available opportunities, were more likely to agree that "schools with mostly Black children should have Black teachers and principals." This is not only an expression of racial unity but also an awareness of the importance of power and control over their own social institutions.

SUMMARY

It was found in this study that both race and class are perceived as important factors influencing social stratification—that is, who gets what, how much, and why. As an alternative to exploring this question with the use of socioeconomic status or structural variables, our study focuses on attitudinal perceptions of Blacks about the meaning of their race and class. In this way, our study captures the perceptions of the reality of race and class of both lower-class and middle-class Blacks based on their beliefs, observations, experiences, and socialization.

Increasing social status differentiation and socioeconomic opportunities have apparently

TABLE 5

Collective Race Consciousness Among Lower-Class and Middle-Class Blacks: Percentage of Agreement and Difference

Collective Race Consciousness Item	*LC*	*MC*	*D*
The only way Blacks will gain their civil rights is by constant protest and pressure.	65	43	21
The best way to overcome discrimination is through pressure and social action.	60	43	17
Schools with mostly Black children should have mostly Black teachers and principals.	47	52	05
Only if Blacks pull together in civil rights groups and activities can anything be done about discrimination.	85	80	05
The attempt to "fit in" and do what's proper has not paid off for Blacks. It does not matter how "proper" you are, you will still meet serious discrimination.	87	83	04
Educated Blacks who have good jobs should try to use their talents and leadership abilities to help other Blacks.	98	100	02

NOTE: LC = Lower Class, MC = Middle Class, D = Difference.

led to differential perceptions about social class among Blacks. Our study reveals that lower-class Blacks have much more class consciousness than middle-class Blacks. Specifically, lower-class Blacks express much more consciousness about the inequality gap between them and the middle class, especially in terms of the distribution of wealth, power, and prestige.

Our study reveals that both lower-class and middle-class Blacks are more race conscious than class conscious, but middle-class Blacks are slightly more race conscious than class conscious. The implication here is that regardless of social class, most Blacks feel that race is still a very significant factor in determining their life chances and opportunities. Black middle-class individuals, in spite of their socioeconomic achievements, are often confronted with racial discrimination, racial barriers, and blocked opportunities due to their race. Our study found that lower-class Blacks tend to place greater emphasis on protests, social pressures, and social actions to eliminate racial discrimination. However, three attitudinal patterns were found among both lower-class and middle-class Blacks: (1) the belief that racial discrimination imposes real and serious obstacles to socioeconomic progress for Blacks, (2) the need for Blacks to unite to combat racial discrimination, and (3)

the expectation that Blacks with the most education and economic means should help elevate less fortunate Blacks.

On the basis of the findings of our study, we can conclude that, indeed, race is still seen by Blacks as a very important factor that can inhibit their progress. Yet the interaction between race and class, accompanied by increasing social diversity and differentiation within the Black population and in the larger society, makes the assessment of the influences of race and class a much more complex matter than heretofore. However, race is likely to continue to be a real issue in the future, whereas increasing status differentiation will likely lead to greater differences in perceptions about class.

REFERENCES

Abrahamson, M., Mizruchi, E., & Hornung, C. (1976). *Stratification and mobility.* New York: Macmillan.

Allen, R. L. (1970). *Black awakening in capitalist America.* New York: Anchor Doubleday.

Broman, C. L., Neighbors, H. W., & Jackson, J. S. (1988). Racial group identification among Black adults. *Social Forces, 67,* 146–158.

Brown, W. (1931). The nature of race consciousness. *Social Forces, 10,* 90–97.

Clark, K. B. (1978, October 5). The role of race. *New York Times Magazine,* p. 24.

Clark, K. B. (1980, March 22). Race, not class is still at the wheel. *New York Times,* p. 22.

Cox, O. (1948). *Caste, class and race.* New York: Doubleday.

Davis, A., Gardner, B., & Gardner, M. (1941). *Deep south: A social anthropological study of caste and class.* Chicago: University of Chicago Press.

Drake, S. C., & Cayton, H. R. (1945). *Black metropolis: A study of negro life in a northern city* (Vol. 2). New York: Harcourt, Brace & World.

DuBois, W.E.B. (1899). *The Philadelphia negro.* New York: Schocken.

DuBois, W.E.B. (1953). *The souls of Black folk.* New York: Fawcett. (Originally published in 1903).

Erikson, E. (1966). The concept of identity in race relations: Notes and queries. In T. Parsons & K. Clark (Eds.), *The negro American* (pp. 227–253). Boston: Beacon.

Ferguson, E. (1936). Race consciousness among American negroes. *Journal of Negro Education, 7,* 32–40.

Frazier, E. F. (1957). *Black bourgeoisie.* New York: Macmillan.

Glantz, O. (1958). Class consciousness and political solidarity. *American Sociological Review, 23,* 375–382.

Gurin, P., & Epps, E. (1975). *Black consciousness, identity and achievement.* New York: John Wiley.

Handy, K. (1984). Race and class consciousness among southern Blacks. *Sociological Spectrum, 4,* 383–403.

Heller, C. (1969). *Structured social inequality: A reader in comparative social stratification.* New York: Macmillan.

Herbers, J. (1978, February 26). Decade after Kerner report: Division of races persists. *New York Times,* p. A1.

Hewitt, J. (1970). *Social stratification and deviant behavior.* New York: Random House.

Hraba, J. (1979). *American ethnicity.* Itasca, IL: Peacock.

Johnson, C. (1943). *Patterns of negro segregation.* New York: Harper.

Landecker, W. (1963). Class crystallization and class consciousness. *American Sociological Review, 28,* 219–229.

Leggett, J. (1968). *Class, race and labor: Working class consciousness in Detroit.* New York: Oxford University Press.

Lewis, L. (1965). Class consciousness and inter-class sentiments. *The Sociological Quarterly, 6,* 325–338.

Lopreato, J., & Hazelrigg, L. (1972). *Class conflict and mobility: Theories and studies of class structure.* San Francisco: Chandler.

Manis, J., & Meltzer, B. (1963). Some correlates of class consciousness among textile workers. *American Sociological Review, 69,* 177–184.

Marx, K. (1969). *The communist manifesto.* Chicago: Regnery.

Morris, R., & Murphy, R. (1966). A paradigm for the study of class consciousness. *Sociology and Social Research, 50,* 314–324.

Myrdal, G. (1964). *An American dilemma.* New York: McGraw-Hill.

Noel, D. (1968). A theory of the origin of ethnic stratification. In N. Yetman & H. Steele (Eds.), *Majority and minority* (pp. 32–44). Boston: Allyn & Bacon.

Park, R. E. (1913). Racial assimilation in secondary groups with particular reference to the negro. *American Sociological Society, 8,* 66–83.

Park, R. E. (1923). Negro race consciousness as reflected in race literature. *American Sociological Review, 1,* 505–516.

Pettigrew, T. (1980). The changing—not declining—significance of race. *Contemporary Sociology, 9,* 19–21.

Pitts, J. (1974). The study of race consciousness: Comments on new directions. *American Journal of Sociology, 80,* 665–687.

Rose, P. I. (1964). *They and we: Racial and ethnic relations in the United States.* New York: Random House.

Thompson, D. (1974). *Sociology of the Black experience.* Westport, CT: Greenwood.

U.S. Bureau of the Census. (1970). *Block statistics.* Washington, DC: Author.

U.S. Riot Commission. (1968). *Report of the National Advisory Commission on Civil Disorders.* New York: Bantam.

West, C. (1993). *Race matters.* Boston: Beacon Press.

Willie, C. (1989). *Caste and class controversy on race and poverty.* Dix Hills, NY: General Hall.

Wilson, W. J. (1978). *The declining significance of race.* Chicago: University of Chicago Press.

Woldemikael, T. (1989). A case study of race consciousness among Haitian immigrants. *Journal of Black Studies, 20,* 224–239.

Thomas J. Durant, Jr. is a full professor of sociology at Louisiana State University—Baton Rouge. He received his Ph.D. degree in sociology from the University of Wisconsin—Madison. His research interests include ethnic minorities, social stratification, and global development.

Kathleen H. Sparrow is director of minority affairs and professor of sociology at the University of Southwestern Louisiana. She received her Ph.D. in sociology from Louisiana State University—Baton Rouge. Her interests are ethnic minorities, race relations, and social stratification.

ONE DROP OF BLOOD

Do ethnic categories protect us or divide us? The way that Washington chooses to define the population in the 2000 census could trigger the biggest debate over race in America since the nineteen-sixties.

LAWRENCE WRIGHT

WASHINGTON in the millennial years is a city of warring racial and ethnic groups fighting for recognition, protection, and entitlements. This war has been fought throughout the second half of the twentieth century largely by black Americans. How much this contest has widened, how bitter it has turned, how complex and baffling it is, and how far-reaching its consequences are became evident in a series of congressional hearings that began last year in the obscure House Subcommittee on Census, Statistics, and Postal Personnel, which is chaired by Representative Thomas C. Sawyer, Democrat of Ohio, and concluded in November, 1993.

Although the Sawyer hearings were scarcely reported in the news and were sparsely attended even by other members of the subcommittee, with the exception of Representative Thomas E. Petri, Republican of Wisconsin, they opened what may become the most searching examination of racial questions in this country since the sixties. Related federal agency hearings, and meetings that will be held in Washington and other cities around the country to prepare for the 2000 census, are considering not only modifications of existing racial categories but also the larger question of whether it is pro-

per for the government to classify people according to arbitrary distinctions of skin color and ancestry. This discussion arises at a time when profound debates are occurring in minority communities about the rightfulness of group entitlements, some government officials are questioning the usefulness of race data, and scientists are debating whether race exists at all.

Tom Sawyer, forty-eight, a former English teacher and a former mayor of Akron, is now in his fourth term representing the Fourteenth District of Ohio. It would be fair to say that neither the House Committee on Post Office and Civil Service nor the subcommittee that Sawyer chairs is the kind of assignment that members of Congress would willingly shed blood for. Indeed, the attitude of most elected officials in Washington toward the census is polite loathing, because it is the census, as much as any other force in the country, that determines their political futures. Congressional districts rise and fall with the shifting demography of the country, yet census matters rarely seize the front pages of home-town newspapers, except briefly, once every ten years. Much of the subcommittee's business has to do with addressing the safety concerns of postal workers and overseeing federal statistical measurements.

The subcommittee has an additional responsibility: it reviews the executive branch's policy about which racial and ethnic groups should be officially recognized by the United States government.

"We are unique in this country in the way we describe and define race and ascribe to it characteristics that other cultures view very differently," Sawyer, who is a friendly man with an open, boyish face and graying black hair, says. He points out that the country is in the midst of its most profound demographic shift since the eighteen-nineties—a time that opened "a period of the greatest immigration we have ever seen, whose numbers have not been matched until right now." A deluge of new Americans from every part of the world is overwhelming our traditional racial distinctions, Sawyer believes. "The categories themselves inevitably reflect the temporal bias of every age," he says. "That becomes a problem when the nation itself is undergoing deep and historic diversification."

Looming over the shoulder of Sawyer's subcommittee is the Office of Management and Budget, the federal agency that happens to be responsible for determining standard classifications of racial and ethnic data. Since 1977, those categories have been set by O.M.B. Statistical

From *The New Yorker,* July 25, 1994, pp. 46–50, 52–55. © 1994 by Lawrence Wright. Reprinted by permission of The Wendy Weil Agency, Inc.

Directive 15, which controls the racial and ethnic standards on all federal forms and statistics. Directive 15 acknowledges four general racial groups in the United States: American Indian or Alaskan Native; Asian or Pacific Islander; Black; and White. Directive 15 also breaks down ethnicity into Hispanic Origin and Not of Hispanic Origin. These categories, or versions of them, are present on enrollment forms for schoolchildren; on application forms for jobs, scholarships, loans, and mortgages; and, of course, on United States census forms. The categories ask that every American fit himself or herself into one racial and one ethnic box. From this comes the information that is used to monitor and enforce civil-rights legislation, most notably the Voting Rights Act of 1965, but also a smorgasbord of set-asides and entitlements and affirmative-action programs. "The numbers drive the dollars," Sawyer observes, repeating a well-worn Washington adage.

The truth of that statement was abundantly evident in the hearings, in which a variety of racial and ethnic groups were bidding to increase their portions of the federal pot. The National Coalition for an Accurate Count of Asian Pacific Americans lobbied to add Cambodians and Lao to the nine different nationalities already listed on the census forms under the heading of Asian or Pacific Islander. The National Council of La Raza proposed that Hispanics be considered a race, not just an ethnic group. The Arab American Institute asked that persons from the Middle East, now counted as white, be given a separate, protected category of their own. Senator Daniel K. Akaka, a Native Hawaiian, urged that his people be moved from the Asian or Pacific Island box to the American Indian or Alaskan Native box. "There is the misperception that Native Hawaiians, who number well over two hundred thousand, somehow "immigrated" to the United States like other Asian or Pacific Island groups," the Senator testified. "This leads to the erroneous impres-

sion that Native Hawaiians, the original inhabitants of the Hawaiian Islands, no longer exist." In the Senator's opinion, being placed in the same category as other Native Americans would help rectify that situation. (He did not mention that certain American Indian tribes enjoy privileges concerning gambling concessions that Native Hawaiians currently don't enjoy.) The National Congress of American Indians would like the Hawaiians to stay where they are. In every case, issues of money, but also of identity, are at stake.

I N this battle over racial turf, a disturbing new contender has appeared. "When I received my 1990 census form, I realized that there was no race category for my children," Susan Graham, who is a white woman married to a black man in Roswell, Georgia, testified. "I called the Census Bureau. After checking with supervisors, the bureau finally gave me their answer: the children should take the race of their mother. When I objected and asked why my children should be classified as their mother's race only, the Census Bureau representative said to me, in a very hushed voice, 'Because, in cases like these, we always know who the mother is and not always the father.' "

Graham went on to say, "I could not make a race choice from the basic categories when I enrolled my son in kindergarten in Georgia. The only choice I had, like most other parents of multiracial children, was to leave race blank. I later found that my child's teacher was instructed to choose for him based on her knowledge and observation of my child. Ironically, my child has been white on the United Sates census, black at school, and multiracial at home—all at the same time."

Graham and others were asking that a "Multiracial" box be added to the racial categories specified by Directive 15—a proposal that alarmed representatives of the other racial

groups for a number of reasons, not the least of which was that multiracialism threatened to undermine the concept of racial classification altogether.

According to various estimates, at least seventy-five to more than ninety per cent of the people who now check the Black box could check Multiracial, because of their mixed genetic heritage. If a certain proportion of those people—say, ten per cent—should elect to identify themselves as Multiracial, legislative districts in many parts of the country might need to be redrawn. The entire civil-rights regulatory program concerning housing, employment, and education would have to be reassessed. School-desegregation plans would be thrown into the air. Of course, it is possible that only a small number of Americans will elect to choose the Multiracial option, if it is offered, with little social effect. Merely placing such an option on the census invites people to consider choosing it, however. When the census listed "Cajun" as one of several examples under the ancestry question, the number of Cajuns jumped nearly two thousand per cent. To remind people of the possibility is to encourage enormous change.

Those who are charged with enforcing civil-rights laws see the Multiracial box as a wrecking ball aimed at affirmative action, and they hold those in the mixed-race movement responsible. "There's no concern on any of these people's part about the effect on policy—it's just a subjective feeling that their identity needs to be stroked," one government analyst said. "What they don't understand is that it's going to cost their own groups"—by losing the advantages that accrue to minorities by way of affirmative-action programs, for instance. Graham contends that the object of her movement is not to create another protected category. In any case, she said, multiracial people know, "to check the right box to get the goodies."

Of course, races have been mixing in America since Columbus arrived. Visitors to Colonial America found plantation slaves who were as light-skinned as their masters. Patrick Henry actually proposed, in 1784, that the State of Virginia encourage intermarriage between whites and Indians, through the use of tax incentives and cash stipends. The legacy of this intermingling is that Americans who are descendants of early settlers, of slaves, or of Indians often have ancestors of different races in their family tree.

Thomas Jefferson supervised the original census, in 1790. The population then was broken down into free white males, free white females, other persons (these included free blacks and "taxable Indians," which meant those living in or around white settlements), and slaves. How unsettled this country has always been about its racial categories is evident in the fact that nearly every census since has measured race differently. For most of the nineteenth century, the census reflected an American obsession with miscegenation. The color of slaves was to be specified as "B," for black, and "M," for mulatto. In the 1890 census, gradations of mulattoes were further broken down into quadroons and octoroons. After 1920, however, the Census Bureau gave up on such distinctions, estimating that three-quarters of all blacks in the United States were racially mixed already, and that pure blacks would soon disappear. Henceforth anyone with any black ancestry at all would be counted simply as black.

Actual interracial marriages, however, were historically rare. Multiracial children were often marginalized as illegitimate half-breeds who didn't fit comfortably into any racial community. This was particularly true of the offspring of black-white unions. "In my family, like many families with African-American ancestry, there is a history of multiracial offspring associated with rape and concubinage," G. Reginald Daniel, who teaches a course in mul-tiracial identity at the University of California at Los Angeles, says. "I was reared in the segregationist South. Both sides of my family have been mixed for at least three generations. I struggled as a child over the question of why I had to exclude my East Indian and Irish and Native American and French ancestry, and could include only African."

Until recently, people like Daniel were identified simply as black because of a peculiarly American institution known informally as "the one-drop rule," which defines as black a person with as little as a single drop of "black blood." This notion derives from a long-discredited belief that each race had its own blood type, which was correlated with physical appearance and social behavior. The antebellum South promoted the rule as a way of enlarging the slave population with the children of slaveholders. By the nineteen-twenties, in Jim Crow America the one-drop rule was well established as the law of the land. It still is, according to a United States Supreme Court decision as late as 1986, which refused to review a lower court's ruling that a Louisiana woman whose great-great-great-great-grandmother had been the mistress of a French planter was black—even though that proportion of her ancestry amounted to no more than three thirty-seconds of her genetic heritage. "We are the only country in the world that applies the one-drop rule, and the only group that the one-drop rule applies to is people of African descent," Daniel observes.

People of mixed black-and-white ancestry were rejected by whites and found acceptance by blacks. Many of the most notable "black" leaders over the last century and a half were "white" to some extent, from Booker T. Washington and Frederick Douglass (both of whom had white fathers) to W. E. B. Du Bois, Malcolm X, and Martin Luther King, Jr. (who had an Irish grandmother and some American Indian ancestry as well). The fact that Lani Guinier, Louis Farrakhan, and Virginia's former governor Douglas Wilder are defined as black, and define themselves that way, though they have light skin or "European" features, demonstrates how enduring the one-drop rule has proved to be in America, not only among whites but among blacks as well. Daniel sees this as "a double-edged sword." While the one-drop rule encouraged racism, it also galvanized the black community.

"But the one-drop rule is racist," Daniel says. "There's no way you can get away from the fact that it was historically implemented to create as many slaves as possible. No one leaped over to the white community—that was simply the mentality of the nation, and people of African descent internalized it. What this current discourse is about is lifting the lid of racial oppression in our institutions and letting people identify with the totality of their heritage. We have created a nightmare for human dignity. Multiracialism has the potential for undermining the very basis of racism, which is its categories."

But multiracialism introduces nightmares of its own. If people are to be counted as something other than completely black, for instance, how will affirmative-action programs be implemented? Suppose a court orders a city to hire additional black police officers to make up for past discrimination. Will mixed-race officers count? Will they count wholly or partly? Far from solving the problem of fragmented identities, multiracialism could open the door to fractional races, such as we already have in the case of the American Indians. In order to be eligible for certain federal benefits, such as housing-improvement programs, a person must prove that he or she either is a member of a federally recognized Indian tribe or has fifty per cent "Indian blood." One can envision a situation in which nonwhiteness itself becomes the only valued quality, to be compensated in various ways depending on a person's pedigree.

Kwame Anthony Appiah, of Harvard's Philosophy and Afro-American Studies Departments, says, "What the Multiracial category aims for is not people of mixed ancestry, because a majority of Americans are actually products of mixed ancestry. This category goes after people who have parents who are socially recognized as belonging to different races. That's O.K.—that's an interesting social category. But then you have to ask what happens to their children. Do we want to have more boxes, depending upon whether they marry back into one group or the other? What are the children of these people supposed to say? I think about these things because—look, my mother is English; my father is Ghanaian. My sisters are married to a Nigerian and a Norwegian. I have nephews who range from blond-haired kids to very black kids. They are all first cousins. Now according to the American scheme of things, they're all black—even the guy with blond hair who skis in Oslo. That's what the one-drop rule says. The Multiracial scheme, which is meant to solve anomalies, simply creates more anomalies of its own, and that's because the fundamental concept—that you should be able to assign every American to one of three or four races reliably—is crazy."

These are sentiments that Representative Sawyer agrees with profoundly. He says of the one-drop rule, "It is so embedded in our perception and policy, but it doesn't allow for the blurring that is the reality of our population. Just look at—What are the numbers?" he said in his congressional office as he leafed through a briefing book. "Thirty-eight per cent of American Japanese females and eighteen per cent of American Japanese males marry outside their traditional ethnic and nationality group. Seventy per cent of American Indians marry outside. I grant you that the enormous growth potential of multiracial marriages starts from a relatively small base, but the truth is it starts from a fiction to begin with;

that is, what we think of as black-and-white marriages are not marriages between people who come from anything like a clearly defined ethnic, racial, or genetic base."

The United States Supreme Court struck down the last vestige of anti-miscegenation laws in 1967, in Loving v. Virginia. At that time, interracial marriages were rare; only sixty-five thousand marriages between blacks and whites were recorded in the 1970 census. Marriages between Asians and non-Asian Americans tended to be between soldiers and war brides. Since then, mixed marriages occurring between many racial and ethnic groups have risen to the point where they have eroded the distinctions between such peoples. Among American Indians, people are more likely to marry outside their group than within it, as Representative Sawyer noted. The number of children living in families where one parent is white and the other is black, Asian, or American Indian, to use one measure, has tripled—from fewer than four hundred thousand in 1970 to one and a half million in 1990—and this doesn't count the children of single parents or children whose parents are divorced.

Blacks are conspicuously less likely to marry outside their group, and yet marriages between blacks and whites have tripled in the last thirty years. Matthijs Kalmijn, a Dutch sociologist, analyzed marriage certificates filed in this country's non-Southern states since the Loving decision and found that in the nineteen-eighties the rate at which black men were marrying white women had reached approximately ten percent. (The rate for black women marrying white men is about half that figure.) In the 1990 census, six per cent of black householders nationwide had nonblack spouses—still a small percentage, but a significant one.

Multiracial people, because they are now both unable and unwilling to be ignored, and because many of them refuse to be confined to tradi-

tional racial categories, inevitably undermine the entire concept of race as an irreducible difference between peoples. The continual modulation of racial differences in America is increasing the jumble created by centuries of ethnic intermarriage. The resulting dilemma is a profound one. If we choose to measure the mixing by counting people as Multiracial, we pull the teeth of the civil-rights laws. Are we ready for that? Is it even possible to make changes in the way we count Americans, given the legislative mandates already built into law? "I don't know," Sawyer concedes. "At this point, my purpose is not so much to alter the laws that underlie these kinds of questions as to raise the question of whether or not the way in which we currently define who we are reflects the reality of the nation we are and who we are becoming. If it does not, then the policies underlying the terms of measurement are doomed to be flawed. What you measure is what you get."

SCIENCE has put forward many different racial models, the most enduring being the division of humanity into three broad groupings: the Mongoloid, the Negroid, and the Caucasoid. An influential paper by Masatoshi Nei and Arun K. Roychoudhury, entitled "Gene Differences between Caucasian, Negro, and Japanese Populations," which appeared in Science, in 1972, found that the genetic variation among individuals from these racial groups was only slightly greater than the variation within the groups.

In 1965, the anthropologist Stanley Garn proposed hundreds, even thousands, of racial groups, which he saw as gene clusters separated by geography or culture, some with only minor variations between them. The paleontologist Stephen Jay Gould, for one, has proposed doing away with all racial classifications and identifying people by clines—regional divisions that are used to account for the diversity of snails and of song-birds, among many other species. In this Gould follows the anthropologist Ashley Montagu, who waged a lifelong campaign to rid science of the term "race" altogether and never used it except in quotation marks. Montagu would have substituted the term "ethnic group," which he believed carried less odious baggage.

Race, in the common understanding, draws upon differences not only of skin color and physical attributes but also of language, nationality, and religion. At times, we have counted as "races" different national groups, such as Mexicans and Filipinos. Some Asian Indians were counted as members of a "Hindu" race in the censuses from 1920 to 1940; then they became white for three decades. Racial categories are often used as ethnic intensifiers, with the aim of justifying the exploitation of one group by another. One can trace the ominous example of Jews in prewar Germany, who were counted as "Israelites," a religious group, until the Nazis came to power and turned them into a race. Mixtures of first- and second-degree Jewishness were distinguished, much as quadroons and octoroons had been in the United States. In fact, the Nazi experience ultimately caused a widespread reëxamination of the idea of race. Canada dropped the race question from its census in 1951 and has so far resisted all attempts to reinstitute it. People who were working in the United States Bureau of the Census in the fifties and early sixties remember that there was speculation that the race question would soon be phased out in America as well. The American Civil Liberties Union tried to get the race question dropped from the census in 1960, and the State of New Jersey stopped entering race information on birth and death certificates in 1962 and 1963. In 1964, however, the architecture of civil-rights laws began to be erected, and many of the new laws—particularly the Voting Rights Act of 1965—required highly detailed information

about minority participation which could be gathered only by the decennial census, the nation's supreme instrument for gathering demographic statistics. The expectation that the race question would wither away surrendered to the realization that race data were fundamental to monitoring and enforcing desegregation. The census soon acquired a political importance that it had never had in the past.

Unfortunately, the sloppiness and multiplicity of certain racial and ethnic categories rendered them practically meaningless for statistical purposes. In 1973, Caspar Weinberger, who was then Secretary of Health, Education and Welfare, asked the Federal Interagency Committee on Education (FICE) to develop some standards for classifying race and ethnicity. An ad-hoc committee sprang into being and proposed to create an intellectual grid that would sort all Americans into five racial and ethnic categories. The first category was American Indian or Alaskan Native. Some members of the committee wanted the category to be called Original Peoples of the Western Hemisphere, in order to include Indians of South American origin, but the distinction that this category was seeking was so-called "Federal Indians," who were eligible for government benefits; to include Indians of any other origin, even though they might be genetically quite similar, would confuse the collecting of data. To accommodate the various, highly diverse peoples who originated in the Far East, Southeast Asia, and the Pacific Islands, the committee proposed a category called Asian or Pacific Islander, thus sweeping into one massive basket Chinese, Samoans, Cambodians, Filipinos, and others—peoples who had little or nothing in common, and many of whom were, indeed, traditional enemies. The fact that American Indians and Alaskan Natives originated from the same Mongoloid stock as many of these peoples did not stop the committee from putting them in a separate racial category.

Black was defined as "a person having origins in any of the black racial groups of Africa," and White, initially, as "a person having origins in any of the original peoples of Europe, North Africa, the Middle East, or the Indian subcontinent"—everybody else, in other words. Because the Black category contained anyone with any African heritage at all, the range of actual skin colors covered the entire spectrum, as did the White category, which included Arabs and Asian Indians and various other darker-skinned peoples.

The final classification, Hispanic, was the most problematic of all. In the 1960 census, people whose ancestry was Latin-American were counted as white. Then people of Spanish origin became a protected group, requiring the census to gather data in order to monitor their civil rights. But how to define them? People who spoke Spanish? Defining the population that way would have included millions of Americans who spoke the language but had no actual roots in Hispanic culture, and it excluded Brazilians and children of immigrants who were not taught Spanish in their homes. One approach was to count persons with Spanish surnames, but that created a number of difficulties: marriage made some non-Hispanic women into instant minorities, while stripping other women of their Hispanic status. The 1970 census inquired about people from "Central or South America," and more than a million people checked the box who were not Hispanic; they were from Kansas, Alabama, Mississippi—the central and southern United States, in other words.

The greatest dilemma was that there was no conceivable justification for calling Hispanics a race. There were black Hispanics from the Dominican Republic, Argentines who were almost entirely European whites, Mexicans who would have been counted as American Indians if they had been born north of the Rio Grande. The great preponderance of Hispanics are mestizos—a continuum of many different genetic backgrounds. Moreover, the fluid Latin-American concept of race differs from the rigid United States idea of biologically determined and highly distinct human divisions. In most Latin cultures, skin color is an individual variable—not a group marker—so that within the same family one sibling might be considered white and another black. By 1960, the United States census, which counts the population of Puerto Rico, gave up asking the race question on the island, because race did not carry the same distinction there that it did on the mainland. The ad-hoc committee decided to dodge riddles like these by calling Hispanics an ethnic group, not a race.

In 1977, O.M.B. Statistical Directive 15 adopted the FICE suggestions practically verbatim, with one principal exception: Asian Indians were moved to the Asian or Pacific Islander category. Thus, with little political discussion, the identities of Americans were fixed in five broad groupings. Those racial and ethnic categories that were dreamed up almost twenty years ago were not neutral in their effect. By attempting to provide a way for Americans to describe themselves, the categories actually began to shape those identities. The categories became political entities, with their own constituencies, lobbies, and vested interests. What was even more significant, they caused people to think of themselves in new ways—as members of "races" that were little more than statistical devices. In 1974, the year the ad-hoc committee set to work, few people referred to themselves as Hispanic; rather, people who fell into that grouping tended to identify themselves by nationality—Mexican or Dominican, for instance. Such small categories, however, are inconvenient for statistics and politics, and the creation of the meta-concept "Hispanic" has resulted in the formation of a peculiarly American group. "It is a mixture of ethnicity, culture, history, birth, and a presumption of lan-

guage," Sawyer contends. Largely because of immigration, the Asian or Pacific Islander group is considered the fastest-growing racial group in the United States, but it is a "racial" category that in all likelihood exists nowhere else in the world. The third-fastest-growing category is Other—made up of the nearly ten million people, most of them Hispanics, who refused to check any of the prescribed racial boxes. American Indian groups are also growing at a rate that far exceeds the growth of the population as a whole: from about half a million people in 1960 to nearly two million in 1990—a two-hundred-and-fifty-nine-per-cent increase, which was demographically impossible. It seemed to be accounted for by improvements in the census-taking procedure and also by the fact that Native Americans had become fashionable, and people now wished to identify with them. To make matters even more confounding, only seventy-four per cent of those who identified themselves as American Indian by race reported having Indian ancestry.

Whatever the word "race" may mean elsewhere in the world, or to the world of science, it is clear that in America the categories are arbitrary, confused, and hopelessly intermingled. In many cases, Americans don't know who they are, racially speaking. A National Center for Health Statistics study found that 5.8 per cent of the people who called themselves Black were seen as White by a census interviewer. Nearly a third of the people identifying themselves as Asian were classified as White or Black by independent observers. That was also true of seventy per cent of people who identified themselves as American Indians. Robert A. Hahn, an epidemiologist at the Centers for Disease Control and Prevention, analyzed deaths of infants born from 1983 to 1985. In an astounding number of cases, the infant had a different race on its death certificate from the one on its birth certificate, and this finding led to staggering increases in the

infant-mortality rate for minority populations—46.9 per cent greater for American Indians, 48.8 per cent greater for Japanese-Americans, 78.7 per cent greater for Filipinos—over what had been previously recorded. Such disparities cast doubt on the dependability of race as a criterion for any statistical survey. "It seems to me that we have to go back and reëvaluate the whole system," Hahn says. "We have to ask, 'What do these categories mean?' We are not talking about race in the way that geneticists might use the term, because we're not making any kind of biological assessment. It's closer to self-perceived membership in a population—which is essentially what ethnicity is." There are genetic variations in disease patterns, Hahn points out, and he goes on to say, "But these variations don't always correspond to so-called races. What's really important is, essentially, two things. One, people from different ancestral backgrounds have different behaviors—diets, ideas about what to do when you're sick—that lead them to different health statuses. Two, people are discriminated against because of other people's perception of who they are and how they should be treated. There's still a lot of discrimination in the health-care system."

Racial statistics do serve an important purpose in the monitoring and enforcement of civil-rights laws; indeed, that has become the main justification for such data. A routine example is the Home Mortgage Disclosure Act. Because of race questions on loan applications, the federal government has been able to document the continued practice of redlining by financial institutions. The Federal Reserve found that, for conventional mortgages, in 1992 the denial rate for blacks and Hispanics was roughly double the rate for whites. Hiring practices, jury selection, discriminatory housing patterns, apportionment of political power—in all these areas, and more, the government patrols society, armed with little more than statistical information to insure equal and fair treatment. "We need these categories essentially to get rid of them," Hahn says.

The unwanted corollary of slotting people by race is that such officially sanctioned classifications may actually worsen racial strife. By creating social-welfare programs based on race rather than on need, the government sets citizens against one another precisely because of perceived racial differences. "It is not 'race' but a *practice* of racial classification that bedevils the society," writes Yehudi Webster, a sociologist at California State University, Los Angeles, and the author of "The Racialization of America." The use of racial statistics, he and others have argued, creates a reality of racial divisions, which then require solutions, such as busing, affirmative action, and multicultural education, all of which are bound to fail, because they heighten the racial awareness that leads to contention. Webster believes that adding a Multiracial box would be "another leap into absurdity," because it reinforces the concept of race in the first place. "In a way, it's a continuation of the one-drop principle. Anybody can say, 'I've got one drop of *something*—I must be multiracial.' It may be a good thing. It may finally convince Americans of the absurdity of racial classification."

In 1990, Itabari Njeri, who writes about interethnic relations for the Los Angeles *Times*, organized a symposium for the National Association of Black Journalists. She recounts a presentation given by Charles Stewart, a Democratic Party activist: "If you consider yourself black for political reasons, raise your hand." The vast majority raised their hands. When Stewart then asked how many people present believed they were of pure African descent, without any mixture, no one raised his hand. Stewart commented later, "If you advocate a category that includes people who are multiracial to the detriment of their black identification, you will replicate what you saw—an empty room. We cannot afford to have an empty room."

Njeri maintains that the social and economic gap between light-skinned blacks and dark-skinned blacks is as great as the gap between all blacks and all whites in America. If people of more obviously mixed backgrounds were to migrate to a Multiracial box, she says, they would be politically abandoning their former allies and the people who needed their help the most. Instead of draining the established categories of their influence, Njeri and others believe, it would be better to eliminate racial categories altogether.

That possibility is actually being discussed in the corridors of government. "It's quite strange—the original idea of O.M.B. Directive 15 has nothing to do with current efforts to 'define' race," says Sally Katzen, the director of the Office of Information and Regulatory Affairs at O.M.B., who has the onerous responsibility of making the final recommendation on revising the racial categories. "When O.M.B. got into the business of establishing categories, it was purely statistical, not programmatic—purely for the purpose of data gathering, not for defining or protecting different categories. It was certainly never meant to *define* a race." And yet for more than twenty years Directive 15 did exactly that, with relatively little outcry. "Recently, a question has been raised about the increasing number of multiracial children. I personally have received pictures of beautiful children who are part Asian and part black, or part American Indian and part Asian, with these letters saying, 'I don't want to check just one box. I don't want to deny part of my heritage.' It's very compelling."

This year, Katzen convened a new interagency committee to consider how races should be categorized, and even whether racial information should be sought at all. "To me it's *offensive*—because I think of the Holocaust—for someone to say what a Jew is," says Katzen. "I don't think a government agency should be defining racial and ethnic categories—that certainly was not what was ever intended by these standards."

I s it any accident that racial and ethnic categories should come under attack now, when being a member of a minority group brings certain advantages? The white colonizers of North America conquered the indigenous people, imported African slaves, brought in Asians as laborers and then excluded them with prejudicial immigration laws, and appropriated Mexican land and the people who were living on it. In short, the nonwhite population of America has historically been subjugated and treated as second-class citizens by the white majority. It is to redress the social and economic inequalities of our history that we have civil-rights laws and affirmative-action plans in the first place. Advocates of various racial and ethnic groups point out that many of the people now calling for a race-blind society are political conservatives, who may have an interest in undermining the advancement of nonwhites in our society. Suddenly, the conservatives have adopted the language of integration, it seems, and the left-leaning racial-identity advocates have adopted the language of separatism. It amounts to a polar reversal of political rhetoric.

Jon Michael Spencer, a professor in the African and Afro-American Studies Curriculum at the University of North Carolina at Chapel Hill, recently wrote an article in *The Black Scholar* lamenting what he calls "the postmodern conspiracy to explode racial identity." The article ignited a passionate debate in the magazine over the nature and the future of race. Spencer believes that race is a useful metaphor for cultural and historic difference, because it permits a level of social cohesion among oppressed classes. "To relinquish the notion of race—even though it's a cruel hoax—at this particular time is to relinquish our fortress against the powers and principalities that still try to undermine us," he says. He sees the Multiracial box as politically damaging to "those who need to galvanize peoples around the racial idea of black."

There are some black cultural nationalists who might welcome the Multiracial category. "In terms of the African-American population, it could be very, very useful, because there is a need to clarify who is in and who is not," Molefi Kete Asante, who is the chairperson of the Department of African-American Studies at Temple University, says. "In fact, I would think they should go further than that—identify those people who are in interracial marriages."

Spencer, however, thinks that it might be better to eliminate racial categories altogether than to create an additional category that empties the others of meaning. "If you had who knows how many thousands or tens of thousand or millions of people claiming to be multiracial, you would lessen the number who are black," Spencer says. "There's no end in sight. There's no limit to which one can go in claiming to be multiracial. For instance, I happen to be very brown in complexion, but when I go to the continent of Africa, blacks and whites there claim that I would be 'colored' rather than black, which means that somewhere in my distant past—probably during the era of slavery—I could have one or more white ancestors. So does that mean that I, too, could check Multiracial? Certainly light-skinned black people might perhaps see this as a way out of being included among a despised racial group. The result could be the creation of another class of people, who are betwixt and between black and white."

Whatever comes out of this discussion, the nation is likely to engage in the most profound debate of racial questions in decades. "We recognize the importance of racial categories in correcting clear injustices under the law," Representative Sawyer says. "The dilemma we face is trying to assure the fundamental guarantees of equality of opportunity while at the same time recognizing that the populations themselves are changing as we seek to categorize them. It reaches the point where it becomes an absurd counting game. Part of the difficulty is that we are dealing with the illusion of precision. We wind up with precise counts of everybody in the country, and they are precisely wrong. They don't reflect who we are as a people. To be effective, the concepts of individual and group identity need to reflect not only who we have been but who we are becoming. The more these categories distort our perception of reality, the less useful they are. We act as if we knew what we're talking about when we talk about race, and we don't."

Serving Special Needs and Concerns

People learn under many different sets of circumstances, which involve a variety of educational concerns both within schools and in alternative learning contexts. Each year we include in this section of this volume articles on a variety of special topics that we believe our readers will find interesting and relevant.

The journal literature thematically varies from year to year. Issues on which several good articles may have been published in one year may not be covered well in other years in the professional and trade publications. Likewise, some issues are covered in depth every year, such as articles on social class or education and school choice.

The first article in this unit this year is from the popular press and deals with why some students growing up in very socially disadvantaged personal situations are able to transcend the difficulties of their circumstances. What are the reasons some young people develop the personal resilience to overcome the obstacles confronting their development as persons? We can learn much from these young people as to how they succeed in life despite the hardships they encounter.

Several other topics of significant interest are included in this unit this year. The influence of family and cultural context on the schooling of students is examined with a focus on intercultural relations between families and their students and the teachers who serve them. Some impor-

tant considerations related to multicultural education are raised. Another article deals with how Christopher Columbus should be dealt with in school curricula, and this article reviews how this is done from a multicultural curricular point of view. On another interesting topic, a look is taken at how we celebrate the major times of achievement in the rites of passage to adulthood, the phenomenon of high school graduation ceremonies having been selected as an example. Going against the prevailing rhetoric on the role and usefulness of computers and education, Todd Oppenheimer is critical of how computer technology is used in schools and discusses the negative curricular impacts that can occur when school systems sacrifice other important services to pay the costs of obtaining computer technology.

Work-study programs at the high school level are probed to learn what makes a work-study experience an educational experience as well. When is work related to a school program educational? What are the criteria for determining this? Finally, we consider some of the remaining gender issues related to how girls are treated in American schools.

Since first issued in 1973, this ongoing anthology has sought to provide discussion of special social or curriculum issues affecting the teaching/learning conditions in schools. Fundamental forces at work in our culture during

the past several years have greatly affected millions of students. The social, cultural, and economic pressures on families have produced several special problems of great concern to teachers. Serving special needs and concerns requires greater degrees of individualization of instruction and greater attention paid to the development and maintenance of healthier self-concepts by students.

Looking Ahead: Challenge Questions

What factors enable some young people (children and teenagers) to overcome adverse personal circumstances to become very successful persons?

What makes a family's cultural heritage an important force in its interaction with teachers and school systems in general?

Why do we celebrate the important rites of passage into adulthood? Give some examples of how we celebrate.

How would you evaluate Todd Oppenheimer's argument regarding computers in schools?

What multicultural curriculum issues are raised by the articles in this unit?

What unfinished gender issues remain to be resolved in American schools?

CULTURE & IDEAS

INVINCIBLE KIDS

*Why do some children survive
traumatic childhoods unscathed?
The answers can help every child*

Child psychologist Emmy Werner went looking for trouble in paradise. In Hawaii nearly 40 years ago, the researchers began studying the offspring of chronically poor, alcoholic, abusive and even psychotic parents to understand how failure was passed from one generation to the next. But to her surprise, one third of the kids she studied looked nothing like children headed for disaster. Werner switched her focus to these "resilient kids," who somehow beat the odds, growing into emotionally healthy, competent adults. They even appeared to defy the laws of nature: When Hurricane Iniki flattened Kauai in 1992, leaving nearly 1 in 6 residents homeless, the storm's 160-mpg gusts seemed to spare the houses of Werner's success stories.

Werner's "resilient kids," in their late 30s when Iniki hit, helped create their own luck. They heeded storm warnings and boarded up their properties. And even if the squall blew away their roofs or tore down their walls, they were more likely to have the financial savings and insurance to avoid foreclosure—the fate of many of Iniki's victims. "There's not a thing you can do personally about being in the middle of a hurricane," says the University of California–Davis's Werner, "but [resilient kids] are planners and problem solvers and picker-uppers."

For many of America's children, these are difficult times. One in five lives in poverty. More than half will spend some of their childhood living apart from one parent—the result of divorce, death or out-of-wedlock birth.

Child abuse, teen drug use and teen crime are surging. Living in an affluent suburb is no protection: Suburban kids are almost as likely as those in violent neighborhoods to report what sociologists call "parental absence"—the lack of a mother and father who are approachable and attentive, and who set rules and enforce consequences.

In the face of these trends, many social scientists now are suggesting a new way of looking at kids and their problems: Focus on survivors, not casualties. Don't abandon kids who fail, but learn from those who succeed.

Such children, researchers find, are not simply born that way. Though genes play a role, the presence of a variety of positive influences in a child's environment is even more crucial; indeed, it can make the difference between a child who founders and one who thrives.

The implications of such research are profound. The findings mean that parents, schools, volunteers, government and others can create a pathway to resiliency, rather than leaving success to fate or to hard-wired character traits. Perhaps most important, the research indicates that the lessons learned from these nearly invincible kids can teach us how to help *all* kids—regardless of their circumstances—handle the inevitable risks and turning points of life. The Search Institute, a Minneapolis-based children's research group, identified 30 resiliency-building factors. The more of these "assets" present in a child's environment, the more likely the child was to avoid school problems, alco-

hol use, early sexual experimentation, depression and violent behavior.

Like the factors that contribute to lifelong physical health, those that create resilience may seem common-sensical, but they have tremendous impact. Locate a resilient kid and you will also find a caring adult—or several—who has guided him. Watchful parents, welcoming schools, good peers and extracurricular activities matter, too, as does teaching kids to care for others and to help out in their communities.

From thug to Scout. The psychologists who pioneered resiliency theory focused on inborn character traits that fostered success. An average or higher IQ was a good predictor. So was innate temperament—a sunny disposition may attract advocates who can lift a child from risk. But the idea that resiliency can be molded is relatively re-

ROBERT DOLE. He came of age during the tough years of the Great Depression. Later, he overcame a nearly fatal war injury.

"Why me, I demanded? ... Maybe it was all part of a plan, a test of endurance and strength and, above all, of faith."

cent. It means that an attentive adult can turn a mean and sullen teenage thug—a kid who would smash in someone's face on a whim—into an upstanding Boy Scout.

That's the story of Eagle Scout Rudy Gonzalez. Growing up in Houston's East End barrio, Gonzalez seemed on a fast track to prison. By the time he was 13, he'd already had encounters with the city's juvenile justice system—once for banging a classmate's head on the pavement until blood flowed, once for slugging a teacher. He slept through classes and fought more often than he studied. With his drug-using crew, he broke into warehouses and looted a grocery store. His brushes with the law only hardened his bad-boy swagger. "I thought I was macho," says Gonzalez. "With people I didn't like, [it was], 'Don't look at me or I'll beat you up.' "

Many of Gonzalez's friends later joined real gangs. Several met grisly deaths; others landed in prison for drug dealing and murder. More than a few became fathers and dropped out of school. Gonzalez joined urban scouting, a new, small program established by Boy Scouts of America to provide role models for "at risk" youth. At first glance, Gonzalez's path could hardly seem more different than that of his peers. But both gangs and Boy Scouts offer similar attractions: community and a sense of purpose, a hierarchical system of discipline and a chance to prove loyalty to a group. Gonzalez chose merit badges and service over gang colors and drive-by shootings.

Now 20, Gonzalez wears crisply pressed khakis and button-down shirts and, in his sophomore year at Texas A&M, seems well on his way to his goal of working for a major accounting firm. Why did he succeed when his friends stuck to crime? Gonzalez's own answer is that his new life is "a miracle." "Probably, God chose me to do this," he says.

There were identifiable turning points. Scoutmaster John Trevino, a city policeman, filled Gonzalez's need for a caring adult who believed in him and could show him a different way to be a man. Gonzalez's own father was shot and killed in a barroom fight when Rudy was just 6. Fate played a role, too. At 14, using survival skills he'd learned in scouting, Gonzalez saved the life of a younger boy stuck up to his chin in mud in a nearby bayou. The neighborhood hero was lauded in the newspaper and got to meet President Bush at the White House. Slowly, he began to feel the importance of serving his community—another building block of resiliency. For a Scout project he cleaned up a barrio cemetery.

Something special. Once his life started to turn around, Gonzalez felt comfortable enough to reveal his winning personality and transcendent smile—qualities that contributed further to his success. "When I met him, I wanted to adopt him," says his high school counselor, Betty Porter. "There's something about him." She remembers Gonzalez as a likable and prodigious networker who made daily visits to her office to tell her about college scholarships—some she didn't even know about.

BILL CLINTON. He lost his father in an auto wreck before he was born. Later, he coped with an alcoholic, occasionally violent stepfather.

"My mother taught me about sacrifice. She held steady through tragedy after tragedy and, always, she taught me to fight."

A little bit of help—whether an urban scouting program or some other chance to excel—can go a long way in creating resiliency. And it goes furthest in the most stressed neighborhoods, says the University of Colorado's Richard Jessor, who directs a multimillion-dollar resiliency project for the John D. and Catherine T. MacArthur Foundation. Looking back, Gonzalez agrees. "We were just guys in the barrio without anything better to do," he says. "We didn't have the YMCA or Little League, so we hung out, played sports, broke into warehouses and the school." Adds Harvard University's Katherine Newman: "The good news is that kids are motivated. They want to make it. The bad news is that there are too few opportunities."

Resiliency theory brightens the outlook for kids. Mental health experts traditionally have put the spotlight on children who emerge from bad childhoods damaged and scarred. But statistics show that many—if not most—children born into unpromising circumstances thrive, or at least hold their own. Most children of teen mothers, for example, avoid becoming teen parents themselves. And though the majority of child abusers were themselves abused as children, most abused children do not become abusers. Similarly, children of schizophrenics and children who grew up in refugee camps also tend to defy the odds. And many Iowa youths whose families lost their farms during the 1980s farm crisis became high achievers in school.

Living well. A person who has faced childhood adversity and bounced back may even fare *better* later in life than someone whose childhood was relatively easy—or so Werner's recently completed follow-up of the Kauai kids at age 40 suggests. Resilient children in her study reported stronger marriages and better health than those who enjoyed less stressful origins. Further, none had been on welfare, and none had been in trouble with the law. Many children of traumatic, abusive or neglectful childhoods suffer severe consequences, including shifts in behavior, thinking and physiology that dog them into adulthood. But though Werner's resilient kids turned adults tended to marry later, there was little sign of emotional turmoil. At midlife, these resilient subjects were more likely to say they were happy and only one third as likely to report mental health problems.

Can any child become resilient? That remains a matter of debate. Some kids, researchers say, simply may face too many risks. And the research can be twisted to suggest that there are easy answers. "Resiliency theory assumes that it's all or nothing, that you have it or you don't," complains Geoffrey Canada, who runs neighborhood centers for New York's poorest youth. "But for some people it takes 10,000 gallons of water, and for some kids it's just a couple of little drops."

In fact, as Canada notes, most resilient kids do not follow a straight line to success. An example is Raymond Marte, whom Canada mentored, teaching the youth karate at one of his Rheedlen Centers for Children and Families. Today, Marte, 21, is a freshman at New York's Bard College. But only a few years ago, he was just another high school dropout and teenage father, hanging out with gang friends and roaming the streets with a handgun in his pocket. "This is choice time," Canada told

"The values my family [instilled] left me with the sense I must make something out of my life to justify my survival."

Marte after five of the boy's friends were killed in three months. Marte re-enrolled in school, became an Ameri-Corps volunteer and won a college scholarship. Today, when he walks the streets of his family's gritty Manhattan neighborhood, he is greeted as a hero, accepting high-fives from friends congratulating the guy who made it out.

Good parenting can trump bad neighborhoods. That parents are the first line in creating resilient children is no surprise. But University of Pennsylvania sociologist Frank Furstenberg *was* surprised to find that adolescents in the city's most violence prone, drug-ridden housing projects showed the same resilience as middle-class adolescents. The expectation was that the worst neighborhoods would overwhelm families. Inner-city housing projects do present more risk and fewer opportunities. But good parenting existed in roughly equal proportions in every neighborhood.

Sherenia Gibbs is the type of dynamo parent who almost single-handedly can instill resiliency in her children. The single mother moved her three children from a small town in Illinois to Minneapolis in search of better education and recreation. Still, the new neighborhood was dangerous, so Gibbs volunteered at the park where her youngest son, T. J. Williams, played. Today, six years later, Gibbs runs a city park, where she has started several innovative mentoring programs. At home, Gibbs sets aside time to spend with T. J., now 14, requires him to call her at work when he gets home from school or goes out with friends and follows his schoolwork closely. Indeed, how often teens have dinner with their family and whether they have a curfew are two of the best predictors of teen drug use, according to

the National Center on Addiction and Substance Abuse at Columbia University. How often a family attends church—where kids are exposed to both values and adult mentors—also makes a difference. Says Gibbs: "The streets will grab your kids and eat them up."

Some resiliency programs study the success of moms like Gibbs and try to teach such "authoritative parenting" skills to others. When a kid has an early brush with the law, the Oregon Social Learning Center brings the youth's whole family together to teach parenting skills. Not only is the training effective with the offending youth, but younger brothers and sisters are less likely to get in trouble as well.

Despite the crucial role of parents, few—rich or poor—are as involved in their children's lives as Gibbs. And a shocking number of parents—25 percent—ignore or pay little attention to how their children fare in school, according to Temple University psychology professor Laurence Steinberg. Nearly one third of students across economic classes say their parents have no idea how they are doing in school. Further, half the parents Steinberg surveyed did not know their children's friends, what their kids did after school or where they went at night. Some schools are testing strategies for what educator Margaret Wang, also at Temple, calls "educational resilience."

One solution: teaching teams, which follow a student for a few years so the child always has a teacher who knows him well. In Philadelphia, some inner-city schools have set up "parents' lounges," with free coffee, to encourage moms and dads to be regular school visitors.

Given the importance of good parenting, kids are at heightened risk when parents themselves are troubled. But it is a trait of resilient kids that in such circumstances, they seek out substitute adults. And sometimes they become substitute adults themselves, playing a parental role for younger siblings. That was true of Tyrone Weeks. He spent about half his life without his mother as she went in and out of drug rehabilitation. Sober now for three years, Delores Weeks maintains a close relationship with her son. But Tyrone was often on his own, living with his grandmother and, when she died, with his basketball coach, Tennis Young. Young and Dave Hagan, a neighborhood priest in north

Philadelphia, kept Weeks fed and clothed. But Weeks also became a substitute parent for his younger brother, Robert, while encouraging his mother in her struggle with cocaine. Says Weeks, "There were times when I was lost and didn't want to live anymore."

Like many resilient kids, Weeks possessed another protective factor: a talent. Basketball, he says, gave him a self-confidence that carried him through the lost days. Today, Weeks rebounds and blocks shots for the University of Massachusetts. Obviously, not all kids have Weeks's exceptional ability. But what seems key is not the level of talent but finding an activity from which they derive pride and sense of purpose.

Mon Ye credits an outdoor leadership program with "keeping me out of gang life." Born in a Cambodian refugee camp, Ye has lived with an older brother in a crime-ridden Tacoma, Wash., housing project since his mother's death a few years ago. Outdoor adventure never interested him. But then parks worker LeAnna Waite invited him to join a program at a nearby recreation center (whose heavy doors are dented with bullet marks from gang fights). Last year, Ye led a youth climb up Mount Rainier and now plans to go to college to become a recreation and park supervisor.

It helps to help. Giving kids significant personal responsibility is another way to build resiliency, whether it's Weeks pulling his family together or Ye supervising preteens. Some of the best youth programs value both service to others and the ability to plan and make choices, according to Stanford University's Shirley Brice Heath. The Food Project—in which kids raise 40,000 pounds of vegetables for Boston food kitchens—is directed by the young par-

"We're all inbred with a certain amount of resiliency. It's not until it's tested . . . that we recognize inner strength."

ticipants, giving them the chance to both learn and then pass on their knowledge. Older teens often find such responsibility through military service.

Any program that multiplies contacts between kids and adults who can offer advice and support is valuable. A recent study of Big Brothers and Big Sisters found that the nationwide youth-mentoring program cuts drug use and school absenteeism by half. Most youth interventions are set up to target a specific problem like violence or teen sex—and often have little impact. Big Brothers and Big Sisters instead succeeds with classic resiliency promotion: It first creates supportive adult attention for kids, then expects risky behavior to drop as a consequence.

The 42,490 residents of St. Louis Park, Minn., know all about such holistic approaches to creating resiliency. They've made it a citywide cause in the ethnically diverse suburb of Minneapolis. Children First is the city's call for residents to think about the ways, big and small, they can help all kids succeed, from those living in the city's Meadowbrook housing project to residents of parkside ranch houses. The suburb's largest employer, HealthSystem Minnesota, runs a free kids' health clinic. (Doctors and staff donate their time.) And one of the smallest businesses, Steve McCulloch's flower shop,

DIANNE FEINSTEIN. The California senator was raised in privilege, but her mother was mentally ill and at times violent.

"I've never believed adversity is a harbinger of failure. On the contrary, [it] can provide a wellspring of strength."

gives away carnations to kids in the nearby housing project on Mother's Day. Kids even help each other. Two high school girls started a Tuesday night baby-sitting service at the Reformation Lutheran Church. Parents can drop off their kids for three hours. The cost: $1.

The goal is to make sure kids know that they are valued and that several adults outside their own family know and care about them. Those adults might include a police officer-volunteering to serve lunch in the school cafeteria line. Or Jill Terry, one of scores of volunteers who stand at school bus stops on frigid mornings. Terry breaks up fights, provides forgotten lunch money or reassures a sad-faced boy about his parents' fighting. The adopt-a-bus-stop program

was started by members of a senior citizens' group concerned about an attempted abduction of a child on her way to school.

Another volunteer, Kyla Dreier, works in a downtown law firm and mentors Angie Larson. The 14-year-old has long, open talks with her mother but sometimes feels more comfortable discussing things with another adult, like Dreier.

Spreading out. St. Louis Park is the biggest success story of over 100 communities nationwide where the Search Institute is trying to develop support for childhood resiliency. In a small surburb, it was relatively easy to rally community leaders. Now Search is trying to take such asset building to larger cities like Minneapolis and Albuquerque, N.M.

In St. Louis Park, resiliency is built on a shoestring budget. About $60,000 a year—all raised from donations—covers the part-time staff director and office expenses. But that's the point, says Children First Coordinator Karen Atkinson. Fostering resiliency is neither complicated nor costly. It's basic common sense—even if practiced too rarely in America. And it pays dividends for all kids.

BY JOSEPH P. SHAPIRO WITH DORIAN FRIEDMAN IN NEW YORK, MICHELE MEYER IN HOUSTON AND MARGARET LOFTUS

ARE YOU WORKING WITH PARENTS?

Family and Cultural Context: A Writing Breakthrough?

Susan Evans Akaran and Marjorie Vannoy Fields

It was the second semester in my kindergarten class in Kotlik, Alaska. I had been trying to get the children to write stories instead of merely labeling pictures, but I was getting nowhere. "Tell us about your drawing," I said to Sasha after he had done a beautiful drawing. We had been practicing this activity for about a week and a half. At this point Sasha was supposed to tell us about his story, and the class was going to help him write it. But it wasn't working.

"What is happening in your picture?" I tried again after getting no answer.

"Mouse, girl, bed, stairs . . ." was the child's response.

"What is the girl doing?" I asked.

After many attempts on different days and with different children, I finally got sentences like "The girl is eating an apple in bed" and "He is harpooning the seal." But these were still labels for pictures, not stories. Even the children who could write easily were not writing down their stories. Why was this? These children tell stories all the time. Their

Susan Evans Akaran, B.A., is a primary teacher in Kotlik, Alaska, for the Lower Yukon School District. She recently received her Early Childhood Endorsement through a distance-delivery program.

Marjorie Vannoy Fields, Ed.D., is a professor of early childhood education at the University of Alaska Southeast in Juneau. Marjorie is the author of several books and articles in the field and is a former member of the NAEYC Governing Board.

The first person "I" in this article is Susan Akaran. Marjorie Fields was her mentor in the process described and her editor in writing about it. Photographs courtesy Susan E. Akaran.

Yup'ik (Eskimo) culture has a rich oral history through storytelling.

I decided that I needed to expose the children to more story writing so they would understand what a story is. However, since school began I had modeled writing for the children and taken dictation of their stories, descrip-

In winter, daylight in Kotlik looks like this.

 From *Young Children*, May 1997, pp. 37-40. © 1997 by the National Association for the Education of Young Children. Reprinted by permission.

tions of events, and ideas. Why wasn't it working? I began to think about what was relevant and meaningful to these children in this community (Bredekamp & Rosegrant 1992). I decided that my students did not see story writing as either relevant or meaningful; they saw no link between their own oral language and the written language activities at school.

The Yup'ik culture is enriched and passed on through oral stories of the old days and of new happenings. Elders from the community visit our school each year to share some of the old stories. However, the Yup'ik language is an oral language; only recently have outsiders come and put it into writing. This new form of the language is not usually written or read by the remaining fluent Yup'ik speakers. Reading and writing in Yup'ik are done mostly in school programs trying to reestablish a language that is nearly extinguished.

But instruction in Yup'ik is not the answer (NAEYC 1996); my students' first language is English, not Yup'ik. As in other places, these children have lost their own language as a result of educational practices common when their parents and grandparents were in school: punishing

Child's story—Sasha and Evan. Susie let us go on her sled. We use a sled so we can carry heavy stuff and light stuff. We carry mail, boxes, tanks, and people. Skidoos break down. We can go hunting, go Emmonak and drive to school with them.

Background: Kotlik is a very small and isolated Alaska Native American village. There are no roads in or out, therefore the river boat for summer travel and the sled pulled by snow machine for winter travel are essential. The use of both sled and skidoo illustrates how people combine the traditional and the new cultures.

Native American children for speaking their own language, and sending them away from their homes to boarding schools. Along with learning English, my students' families also developed bad feelings and mistrust toward schools.

Bridging the gap between school and home is a big job, but I thought it might be the missing piece to my puzzle. My thinking turned to ways of enlisting parents as partners and putting an emphasis on the oral language used at home (Bredekamp & Rosegrant 1995). I wanted to relate the school writing activities to children's home environment. A plan took shape: How about making a class book of stories told to my students by their family members?

Because we were studying animals, and animals are so significant to this culture, it dawned on me that this might be just the thing to make the connection. I sent a letter home to parents asking that they tell their children a story about a personal adventure involving animals (see Figure 1). The plan was for the children to retell the story at school for me to record. When all of the stories were recorded and children had illustrated them, we would compile them into a book.

Figure 1. The Project

- Parents tell their child a story.
- Children retell stories at school.
- Children illustrate stories.
- Children share stories with the group.
- Stories are made into books.
- Children write letters to parents.
- Stories are shared with parents, and books are taken home.

Because we were studying animals, and animals are such a big piece of what makes this culture thrive, it dawned on me that this might be just the thing to make a connection. How about involving family members in sharing some of their own stories? I sent home a letter to the parents asking that they tell a story to their child. The child would then bring the story back to me and retell it. We would compile all of the stories and make a book of them.

𝔖𝔭𝔢𝔠𝔦𝔞𝔩 𝔥𝔬𝔪𝔢𝔴𝔬𝔯𝔨 𝔞𝔰𝔰𝔦𝔤𝔫𝔪𝔢𝔫𝔱

We are collecting stories. Please tell your child a true story about animals. It could be a hunting story, a traditional story, or a personal experience. Tomorrow I will ask your child to tell me your story. We will put the story in a special class book, and your child will illustrate his or her page. We hope to get everyone a special copy of our book at the end of the year. Thanks for your help with this project.

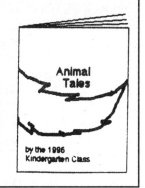

Animal Tales

by the 1996 Kindergarten Class

Figure 2. Some of the Stories We Recorded and Ilustrated

Seal Hunting

Once we were going to our camp. We were playing on the sand. We heard somebody shoot and we hear boats. We go chase the seal and my mama almost hit it. I get my spear and I hit it on it's brain. It float in salty water.

Eagle

My grandma saw a big eagle and she run and she hide and that big eagle circle her and she hide and she circle her. She go in her tent. The eagle go.

About the Whale

That bear was trying to bite me. I take BB gun and next I shoot it on the leg. I bring it down to our camp. Next we cut it up. We make it to parka. We put zipper. We throw the body away. We let the whale eat it.

The Bear

We saw a bear track. My dad saw a fox and he shoot it. We go get it. We bring it to our house.When we bring it to our house, we cut it.We save the skin.

Hunting

Me and my dad catch three ptarmigans and we cook them. We go take a ride. We catch and we eat those ptarmigans. We go home.

That Moose

When my dad see moose trail, he go run after them. Those moose run away.

Although I encourage my students to write independently, I decided to take dictation from them for this activity so that I could use it as a modeling tool.

I sent the letter home to six families a day rather than to everyone simultaneously. This method had two purposes: to allow for alternative stories if a family did not respond right away and to keep me from being overwhelmed with too many stories all at once. As the children came in with their stories, I went to them, one by one, and wrote the stories in big print, using a laptop computer (see Figure 2). I thought that this process demonstrated respect for the child involved. The computer also facilitated the editing process: we read and reread each story until the child decided that it sounded right. The children were fascinated to see their stories in big print.

I copied and bound 30 books over the weekend. On Monday I read the book to the class, and they were thrilled! Each child took a copy of the book, and they all practiced reading their stories to one another and to the group. Their interest continued all week, in contrast to their interest in other writing projects, which the children had ignored after completion. I suggested that they share the books with parents during our quarterly open house. The class was excited. Each child wrote a letter inviting his or her parents and grandparents to come. Six children volunteered to read to the whole group, while others read individually with their parents.

The highlight for me was the reading by a child who had been identified as having special needs. He surprised me by saying that he wanted to read his story aloud to the whole group. He hid under the easel until I asked him if he was ready to share. He immediately stood up, got a copy of the book, and began to read his story in a loud, clear voice. Although he was not actually able to track the words, he knew what a reader does (Fields & Spangler 1995). He stared at the page with his undivided attention, eyes moving from left to right, and spoke the words as if he were reading them. He told the story as he remembered it, which amazed the audience, who all know him well.

During the remainder of the school year, my students—at all levels of reading ability—continued to read and study the books. Many of the children told me they read

Child's story—William and Matthew. This is a boat. It has a steering wheel. It has a tank and tools and spears. In summer we go riding to catch mukluk (seal). Now it's winter. There's no water. The water is frozen.

Child's story—Leeandy and Joseph. This is a mukay house. The stove is made of iron. Fire is in the stove and heat go out of the chimney. People sit down and splash water on the stove. They cool off by the door. When they are done, they wash up with clean water and scrubber.

Background: The mukay (steam bath house) is an important part of the traditional culture and continues to be since the village does not have running water.

Child's Story—Sharon O. and Wilma. They got woods. The Kindergarten people is behind the logs. People get logs 'cause they need for the stove, when they get cold. They get 'em from the water. Us get big woods at far away.

Background: This photo shows the heating system but as the story indicates, there are no trees in the vast tundra of Alaska.

their own copies at home, and I did see the books sitting out as if recently read when I visited their homes informally. In addition, children continued their enthusiasm for bookmaking. They began to make their own books, with less guidance from me. During literacy center time I would hear them ask one another, "How do you spell that?" "What letter is that?" "What are you writing?" "Where is the picture to go with it?" "Is that true or pretend?" A whole new world of writing, creating, and sharing ideas emerged. The children's journal writing also became more focused on ideas and stories.

As I read to my class, the words *author* and *illustrator* took on new meaning. The children wanted to know more about these people: Who wrote these books? What do they look like? Where did they get that idea? How did they know that? They related to authors as people like themselves—clear evidence that they had come to see themselves as writers.

References

Bredekamp, S., & T. Rosegrant. 1992. *Reaching potentials: Appropriate curriculum and assessment for young children.* Vol 1. Washington, DC: NAEYC.

Bredekamp, S., & T. Rosegrant. 1995. *Reaching potentials: Transforming early childhood curriculum and assessment.* Vol 2. Washington, DC: NAEYC.

Fields, M., & K. Spangler. 1995 *Let's begin reading right: Developmentally appropriate beginning literacy.* Columbus, OH: Merrill.

NAEYC. 1996. Position statement: Responding to linguistic and cultural diversity—Recommendations for effective childhood education. *Young Children* 51 (2): 4–12.

For further reading

Brock, D. R., & E. L. Dodd. 1994. A family lending library: Promoting early literacy development. *Young Children* 49 (3): 16–21.

Cohen, L. E. 1997. How I developed my kindergarten backpack program. *Young Children* 52 (2): 69–71.

Garcia, E. E. 1997. Research in review. The education of Hispanics in early childhood: Of roots and wings. *Young Children* 52 (3): 5–14.

Greenberg, P. [1969] 1990. Reading: A key to their future: A freedom. In *The devil has slippery shoes: A biased biography of the Child Development Group of Mississippi—A story of maximum feasible poor parent participation,* 154–170. Reprint, Washington, DC: Youth Policy Institute.

Gutwirth, V. 1997. A multicultural project for primary. *Young Children* 52 (2): 72–78.

Helm, J. 1994. Family theme bags: An innovative approach to family involvement in the school. *Young Children* 49 (4): 48–52.

Johnston, L., & J. Mermin. 1994. Easing children's entry to school: Home visits help. *Young Children* 49 (5): 62–68.

Manning, M., G. Manning, & G. Morrison. 1995. Letter-writing connections: A teacher, first-graders, and their parents. *Young Children* 50 (6): 34–38.

Soto, L. D., 1991. Research in review. Understanding bilingual/bicultural young children. *Young Children* 46 (2): 30–36.

The teacher made this doll so that the children could have a doll that looked like them.

EDUCATION

Pomp and Promises

On Graduation Day in America, not every story about schools has to be a grim one

By John McCormick
and Aric Press

NO YOUNGSTER GETS INTO HOLY Trinity High School each day without getting past Brother Philip Smith. He's there every morning at 5, pushing the papers around his desk before heading for the front door. There he shakes each student's hand (there are roughly 400 kids in the school), welcoming them by name to another day of shared adventure, and incidentally preparing them for that inevitable moment when they will have

to greet a prospective client, or boss, or in-law. So it was entirely appropriate on graduation Saturday for Brother Philip, the school's president, to be standing on the stage of a grand old church on Division Street in Chicago, where 94 seniors of Holy Trinity High School marched toward him, a diploma in one hand, one final handshake in the other.

It was, as these ceremonies should be, a pageant. Prayers were recited in four languages (English, Spanish, Tagalog and Tenagit). Families whooped in several more. The principal, Charlene Szumilas, was brief: be generous, work hard, do us honor. The valedictorian, Abraham Cruz, expressed gratitude to his family and his school; next fall, he's headed for Notre Dame. A recent grad sang the mandatory "Wind Beneath My Wings." As each member of the class of '97 marched toward Brother Philip, it was difficult to maintain eye contact. The beaming and the welling up kept getting in the way.

It is graduation season, one of those rare occasions of pride and accomplishment that can still be enjoyed across all demographic lines. It's easy to forget in post-GI Bill America that only about a quarter of the nation's adults hold a college degree; as a public rite of passage that spans the generations, nothing compares to

high-school-commencement exercises. And for families, however bruised, unconventional or simply traditional, it's both takeoff and landing—children in robes, on the cusp of adulthood, boys with Jordanesque ear studs, girls balancing on towering platform shoes, clutching the arms of parents who are about to set them loose on the world, whether they like it or not. By the best estimates there are 2.6 million members of the class of '97. The most famous, Chelsea Clinton, received her diploma at Sidwell Friends School in Washington, D.C., last Friday, an event at once so uplifting and so egalitarian that the First Parents were allowed to enjoy the occasion without benefit of a press conference or a process server.

These ceremonies take place at a time when high-school diplomas have never been so necessary or so insufficient. The economy has changed radically. The era when high-school students could drop out and still find decent work in factories or farms is long dead. So the prospects are poor for the 800,000 or so kids who entered high school in 1993 but aren't graduating this year. Not that this year's diplomas, however hard-earned, can be comfortably viewed as anything more than a baton pass in the educational relay race. Workers with a high-school education have long made less than those with a college degree; according to federal statistics the gap has widened in recent years. About 60 percent of the class of '97 expect to start college next fall.

However vivid this springtime optimism, it's only a brief respite from the ongoing problems in American education. The critical

SHARON FARMER—THE WHITE HOUSE
The First Graduate: *Chelsea with Mom and Dad*

From *Newsweek*, June 16, 1997, pp. 44-46. © 1997 by Newsweek, Inc. All rights reserved. Reprinted by permission.

litany is all too familiar; standards are too low, and grades are too high. Legislatures debate whether publicly funded colleges should spend their days doing remedial work for kids with high-school degrees. Collectively the nation's school buildings are in dreadful repair. They are both overcrowded and underused. New brain research teaches the importance of early education; lip service is paid but little else. That's all true and will be again when schools open in the fall.

But it's spring and, for just a moment, time to enjoy a breather from the justified criticism, time to tell different stories. Consider the demographic changes felt so acutely in some schools. Compared with graduating classes two decades ago, the number of whites is down, while Hispanic and Asian populations continue to grow. What do these numbers mean for the class of '97? Look at the yearbook pictures of Stuyvesant High School, one of four fiercely competitive New York City public high schools that admit only on the basis of an admissions test. In 1964, well before he put a foot in his mouth, spinmeister Dick Morris was caption of Stuyvesant's debate team; its members were all white and all male. This year the coed team (national champions for the seventh consecutive season) is led by the children of immigrants from Bangladesh, Korea and Israel. "My age group has reached a genuine post-racial consciousness," says team president Reihan Salam, 17. His ambition: to be a "rabble-rouser" in the cause of economic justice.

Stuyvesant, like Walnut Hills in Cincinnati or Thomas Jefferson in Alexandria, Va., are exceptional places. More typical is Venice High School, just a few miles inland from the famous Muscle Beach along the Pacific Ocean. "We in public schools feel very isolated," says principal Bud Jacobs. Schools like his have most of the kids—nationwide a steady 87 percent go to public school—but take most of the trouble and blame, too. Carrying a walkie-talkie, Jacobs patrols his 29-acre campus during class breaks, set on keeping his kids safe. (The emergency buttons on his handset read FIRE, FIGHT, WEAPON, TRESPASSER, DRUGS.). Venice High loses almost 40 percent of its freshman class before graduation; one in four has "limited English proficiency," and one in three is poor enough to get government-funded meals.

Determined to survive, Venice developed a foreign-language magnet program that attracts kids from across Los Angeles and each year sends a few dozen to the most prominent colleges in the country. More impressive, relying mostly on students drawn from the neighborhood polyglot population, the school has won the past two National Science Bowl competitions. A kid like Gregorio Mendez, the son of a day laborer who left Mexico four years ago, sees Venice for exactly what it is: a chance. He graduates this month with a certificate of merit in English lit and plans to attend a community college in the fall. "I was happy here," he says. "I have a good opportunity to be something." That's the button Bud Jacobs want to push.

Despite the changing hue of the class of '97, fully integrated schools are still rare. Whites have continued to push outward into exurbia and the pioneering reaches of the sun belt; multiculturalism is a matter for the curriculum committee, not the welcoming committee. For Southfield, one of the inner-ring suburbs of Detroit, this pattern has meant that Southfield High went from 88 percent white 20 years ago to 86 percent black this year. But the proms are still outrageous, and most kids still go to college (if anything, the number has gone up). Senior Wyatt Schrock heads for the University of Michigan in August. He spent last summer in a business-education camp at Northwestern University. "I was with kids from all over the nation, and I was more prepared than most," he says. "I have no complaints about Southfield High."

For all the educational fads the class of '97 has had to endure, and for all the diversity it embodies, there seems to be one constant in its success: someone or some institution told its kids they could make it. In Chicago, Holy Trinity's kids, as they have for 87 years, come from the working class. The only important difference is that instead of selling kielbasa at the fair to make tuition, mothers now sell tortillas. Brother Philip braces them with a grip and a grin every morning. The English Department pushes them into speech and essay contests. Every scholarship won is posted and announced to the underclassmen. The kids—more than 90 percent of whom go on to college—get the message. The basketball season ended abruptly two months ago with a difficult loss. After the mourning ended in the locker room, senior Richard Brown turned to the others and said, "Let's get out of here and go make something of ourselves." He will, and with any luck, so will the rest of the class of '97.

With DONNA FOOTE *in Los Angeles,*
LESLIE KAUFMAN *in New York,*
DANIEL McGINN *in Detroit and*
PAT WINGERT *in Washington*

Are Diplomas Destiny?

Your guidance counselor was right: the more you learn, the more you earn. A look at graduates and their incomes:

High-school grads	1979	1997*
Total	3.1 mil.	2.6 mil.
Going to college	49.3%	62%
White	82%	72%
Black	12	13
Hispanic	4	10
Asian	1	5
Native American	1	1

Earnings†	1979	1995
WITHOUT A HIGH-SCHOOL EDUCATION		
Males	$29,723	$23,338
Females	17,093	16,319
HIGH-SCHOOL GRADUATES		
Males	37,508	32,708
Females	21,473	21,961
COLLEGE GRADUATES		
Males	55,751	61,717
Females	30,915	37,924

*ESTIMATES. 1979 DEMOGRAPHIC DATA ARE PROJECTIONS FOR 1978. NUMBERS MAY NOT ADD TO 100 DUE TO ROUNDING. †AVERAGE ANNUAL EARNINGS IN 1995 DOLLARS. SOURCES: NATIONAL CENTER FOR EDUCATION STATISTICS; BLS; CURRENT POPULATION SURVEY, CENSUS BUREAU

The Computer

D E L U S I O N

There is no good evidence that most uses of computers significantly improve teaching and learning, yet school districts are cutting programs–music, art, physical education–that enrich children's lives to make room for this dubious nostrum, and the Clinton Administration has embraced the goal of "computers in every classroom" with credulous and costly enthusiasm

TODD OPPENHEIMER

Todd Oppenheimer is the associate editor of Newsweek Interactive. He has won numerous awards for his writing and investigative reporting.

In 1992 Thomas Edison predicted that "the motion picture is destined to revolutionize our educational system and . . . in a few years it will supplant largely, if not entirely, the use of textbooks." Twenty-three years later, in 1945, William Levenson, the director of the Cleveland public schools' radio station, claimed that "the time may come when a portable radio receiver will be as common in the classroom as is the blackboard." Forty years after that the noted psychologist B. F. Skinner, referring to the first days of his "teaching machines," in the late 1950s and early 1960s, wrote, "I was soon saying that, with the help of teaching machines and programmed instruction, students could learn twice as much in the same time and with the same effort as in a standard classroom." Ten years after Skinner's recollections were published, President Bill Clinton campaigned for "a bridge to the twenty-first century . . . where computers are as much a part of the classroom as blackboards." Clinton was not alone in his enthusiasm for a program estimated to cost somewhere between $40 billion and $100 billion over the next five years. Speaker of the House Newt Gingrich, talking about computers to

the Republican National Committee early this year, said, "We could do so much to make education available twenty-four hours a day, seven days a week, that people could literally have a whole different attitude toward learning."

If history really is repeating itself, the schools are in serious trouble. In *Teachers and Machines: The Classroom Use of Technology Since 1920* (1986), Larry Cuban, a professor of education at Stanford University and a former school superintendent, observed that as successive rounds of new technology failed their promoters' expectations, a pattern emerged. The cycle began with big promises backed by the technology developers' research. In the classroom, however, teachers never really embraced the new tools, and no significant academic improvement occurred. This provoked consistent responses: the problem was money, spokespeople argued, or teacher resistance, or the paralyzing school bureaucracy. Meanwhile, few people questioned the technology advocates' claims. As results continued to lag, the blame was finally laid on the machines. Soon schools were sold on the next generation of technology, and the lucrative cycle started all over again.

Today's technology evangels argue that we've learned our lesson from past mistakes. As in each previous round, they say that when our new hot technology—the computer—is compared with yesterday's, today's is bet-

From *The Atlantic Monthly*, July 1997, pp. 45-48, 50-56, 61-62. © 1997 by Todd Oppenheimer. Reprinted by permission.

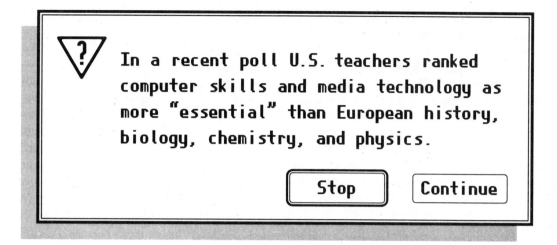

In a recent poll U.S. teachers ranked computer skills and media technology as more "essential" than European history, biology, chemistry, and physics.

Stop   Continue

ter. "It can do the same things, plus," Richard Riley, the U.S. Secretary of Education, told me this spring.

How much better is it, really?

The promoters of computers in schools again offer prodigious research showing improved academic achievement after using their technology. The research has again come under occasional attack, but this time quite a number of teachers seem to be backing classroom technology. In a poll taken early last year U.S. teachers ranked computer skills and media technology as more "essential" than the study of European history, biology, chemistry, and physics; than dealing with social problems such as drugs and family breakdown; than learning practical job skills; and than reading modern American writers such as Steinbeck and Hemingway or classic ones such as Plato and Shakespeare.

In keeping with these views New Jersey cut state aid to a number of school districts this past year and then spent $10 million on classroom computers. In Union City, California, a single school district is spending $27 million to buy new gear for a mere eleven schools. The Kittridge Street Elementary School, in Los Angeles, killed its music program last year to hire a technology coordinator,; in Mansfield, Massachusetts, administrators dropped proposed teaching positions in art, music, and physical education, and then spent $333,000 on computers; in one Virginia school the art room was turned into a computer laboratory. (Ironically, a half dozen preliminary studies recently suggested that music and art classes may build the physical size of a child's brain, and its powers for subjects such as language, math, science, and engineering—in one case far more than computer work did.) Meanwhile, months after a New Technology High School opened in Napa, California, where computers sit on every student's desk and all academic classes use computers, some students were complaining of headaches, sore eyes, and wrist pain.

Throughout the country, as spending on technology increases, school book purchases are stagnant. Shop classes, with their tradition of teaching children building skills with wood and metal, have been almost entirely replaced by new "technology education programs." In San Francisco only one public school still offers a full shop program—the lone vocational high school. "We get kids who don't know the difference between a screwdriver and a ball peen hammer," James Dahlman, the school's vocational-department chair, told me recently. "How are they going to make a career choice? Administrators are stuck in this mindset that all kids will go to a four-year college and become a doctor or a lawyer, and that's not true. I know some who went to college, graduated, and then had to go back to technical school to get a job." Last year the school superintendent in Great Neck, Long Island, proposed replacing elementary school shop classes with computer classes and training the shop teachers as computer coaches. Rather than being greeted with enthusiasm, the proposal provoked a backlash.

Interestingly, shop classes and field trips are two programs that the National Information Infrastructure Advisory Council, the Clinton Administration's technology task force, suggests reducing in order to shift resources into computers. But are these results what technology promoters really intend? "You need to apply common sense," Esther Dyson, the president of EDventure Holdings and one of the task force's leading school advocates, told me recently. "Shop with a good teacher probably is worth more than computers with a lousy teacher. But if it's a poor program, this may provide a good excuse for cutting it. There will be a lot of trials and errors with this. And I don't know how to prevent those errors."

The issue, perhaps, is the magnitude of the errors. Alan Lesgold, a professor of psychology and the associate director of the Learning Research and Development Center at the University of Pittsburgh, calls the computer an "amplifier," because it encourages both enlightened study practices and thoughtless ones. There's a real risk, though, that the thoughtless practices will dominate, slowly dumbing down huge numbers of tomorrow's adults. As Sherry Turkle, a professor of the sociology of science at the Massachusetts Institute of Technology and a longtime observer of children's use of computers, told me, "The possibilities of using this thing poorly so outweigh the chance of using it well, it makes people like us, who are fundamentally optimistic about computers, very reticent."

Perhaps the best way to separate fact from fantasy is to take supporters' claims about computerized learning one by one and compare them with the evidence in the academic literature and in the everyday experiences I have observed or heard about in a variety of classrooms.

Five main arguments underlie the campaign to computerize our nation's schools.

- Computers improve both teaching practices and student achievement.
- Computer literacy should be taught as early as possible; otherwise students will be left behind.
- To make tomorrow's work force competitive in an increasingly high-tech world, learning computer skills must be a priority.
- Technology programs leverage support from the business community—badly needed today because schools are increasingly starved for funds.
- Work with computers—particularly using the Internet—brings students valuable connections with teachers, other schools and students, and a wide network of professionals around the globe. These connections spice the school day with a sense of real-world relevance, and broaden the educational community.

"The Filmstrips of the 1990s"

CLINTON'S vision of computerized classrooms arose partly out of the findings of the presidential task force—thirty-six leaders from industry, education, and several interest groups who have guided the Administration's push to get computers into the schools. The report of the task force, "Connecting K–12 Schools to the Information Superhighway" (produced by the consulting firm McKinsey & Co.), begins by citing numerous studies that have apparently proved that computers enhance student achievement significantly. One "meta-analysis" (a study that reviews other studies—in this case 130 of them) reported that computers had improved performance in "a wide range of subjects, including language arts, math, social studies and science." Another found improved organization and focus in students' writing. A third cited twice the normal gains in math skills. Several schools boasted of greatly improved attendance.

Unfortunately, many of these studies are more anecdotal than conclusive. Some, including a giant, oft-cited meta-analysis of 254 studies, lack the necessary scientific controls to make solid conclusions possible. The circumstances are artificial and not easily repeated, results aren't statistically reliable, or, most frequently, the studies did not control for other influences, such as differences between teaching methods. This last factor is critical, because computerized learning inevitably forces teachers to adjust their style—only sometimes for the better. Some studies were industry-funded, and thus tended to publicize mostly positive findings. "The research is set up in a way to find benefits that aren't really there," Edward Miller, a former editor of the *Harvard Education Letter*, says. "Most knowledgeable people agree that most of the research isn't valid. It's so flawed it shouldn't even be called research. Essentially, it's just worthless." Once the faulty studies are weeded out, Miller says, the ones that remain "are inconclusive"—that is, they show no significant change in either direction. Even Esther Dyson admits the studies are undependable. "I don't think those studies amount to much either way," she says. "In this area there is little proof."

Why are solid conclusions so elusive? Look at Apple Computer's "Classrooms of Tomorrow," perhaps the most widely studied effort to teach using computer technology. In the early 1980s Apple shrewdly realized that donating computers to schools might help not only students but also company sales, as Apple's ubiquity in classrooms turned legions of families into Apple loyalists. Last year, after the *San Jose Mercury News* (published in Apple's Silicon Valley home) ran a series questioning the effectiveness of computers in schools, the paper printed an opinion-page response from Terry Crane, an Apple vice-president. "Instead of isolating students," Crane wrote, "technology actually encouraged them to collaborate more than in traditional classrooms. Students also learned to explore and represent information dynamically and creatively, communicate effectively about complex processes, become independent learners and self-starters and become more socially aware and confident."

Crane didn't mention that after a decade of effort and the donation of equipment worth more than $25 million to thirteen schools, there is scant evidence of greater student achievement. To be fair, educators on both sides of the computer debate acknowledge that today's tests of student achievement are shockingly crude. They're especially weak in measuring intangibles such as enthusiasm and self-motivation, which do seem evident in Apple's classrooms and other computer-rich schools. In any event, what is fun and what is educational may frequently be at odds. "Computers in classrooms are the filmstrips of the 1990s," Clifford Stoll, the author of *Silicon Snake Oil: Second Thoughts on the Information Highway* (1995), told *The New York Times* last year, recalling his own school days in the 1960s. "We loved them because we didn't have to think for an hour, teachers loved them because they didn't have to teach, and parents loved

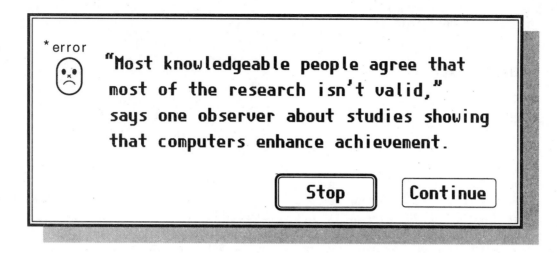

*error

"Most knowledgeable people agree that most of the research isn't valid," says one observer about studies showing that computers enhance achievement.

Stop   Continue

them because it showed their schools were high-tech. But no learning happened."

Stoll somewhat overstates the case—obviously, benefits can come from strengthening a student's motivation. Still, Apple's computers may bear less responsibility for that change than Crane suggests. In the beginning, when Apple did little more than dump computers in classrooms and homes, this produced no real results, according to Jane David, a consultant Apple hired to study its classroom initiative. Apple quickly learned that teachers needed to change their classroom approach to what is commonly called "project-oriented learning." This is an increasingly popular teaching method, in which students learn through doing and teachers act as facilitators or partners rather than as didacts. (Teachers sometimes refer to this approach, which arrived in classrooms before computers did, as being "the guide on the side instead of the sage on the stage.") But what the students learned "had less to do with the computer and more to do with the teaching," David concluded. "If you took the computers out, there would still be good teaching there." This story is heard in school after school, including two impoverished schools—Clear View Elementary School, in southern California, and the Christopher Columbus middle school, in New Jersey—that the Clinton Administration has loudly celebrated for turning themselves around with computers. At Christopher Columbus, in fact, students' test scores rose before computers arrived, not afterward, because of relatively basic changes: longer class periods, new books, after-school programs, and greater emphasis on student projects and collaboration.

During recent visits to some San Francisco-area schools I could see what it takes for students to use computers properly, and why most don't.

On a bluff south of downtown San Francisco, in the middle of one of the city's lower-income neighborhoods, Claudia Schaffner, a tenth-grader, tapped away at a multimedia machine in a computer lab at Thurgood Marshall Academic High School, one of half a dozen special technology schools in the city. Schaffner was using a physics program to simulate the trajectory of a marble on a small roller coaster. "It helps to visualize it first, like 'A if for Apple' with kindergartners," Schaffner told me, while mousing up and down the virtual roller coaster. "I can see how the numbers go into action." This was lunch hour, and the students' excitement about what they can do in this lab was palpable. Schaffner could barely tear herself away. "I need to go eat some food," she finally said, returning within minutes to eat a rice dish at the keyboard.

Schaffner's teacher is Dennis Frezzo, an electrical-engineering graduate from the University of California at Berkeley. Despite his considerable knowledge of computer programming, Frezzo tries to keep classwork focused on physical projects. For a mere $8,000, for example, several teachers put together a multifaceted robotics lab, consisting of an advanced Lego engineering kit and twenty-four old 386-generation computers. Frezzo's students used these materials to build a tiny electric car, whose motion was to be triggered by a light sensor. When the light sensor didn't work, the students figured out why. "That's a real problem—what you'd encounter in the real world," Frezzo told me. "I prefer they get stuck on small real-world problems instead of big fake problems"—like the simulated natural disasters that fill one popular educational game. "It's sort of the Zen approach to education," Frezzo said. "It's not the big problems. Isaac Newton already solved those. What come up in life are the little ones."

It's one thing to confront technology's complexity at a high school—especially one that's blessed with four different computer labs and some highly skilled teachers like Frezzo, who know enough, as he put it, "to keep computers in their place." It's quite another to grapple with a high-tech future in the lower grades, especially at everyday schools that lack special funding or technical support. As evidence, when *U.S. News & World Report* published a cover story last fall on schools that make computers work, five of the six were high schools— among them Thurgood Marshall. Although the sixth was an elementary school, the featured program involved children with disabilities—the one group that does show consistent benefits from computerized instruction.

Artificial Experience

CONSIDER the scene at one elementary school, Sanchez, which sits on the edge of San Francisco's Latino community. For several years Sanchez, like many other schools, has made do with a roomful of basic Apple IIes. Last year, curious about what computers could do for youngsters, a local entrepreneur donated twenty costly Power Macintoshes—three for each of five classrooms, and one for each of the five lucky teachers to take home. The teachers who got the new machines were delighted. "It's the best thing we've ever done," Adela Najarro, a third-grade bilingual teacher, told me. She mentioned one boy, perhaps with a learning disability, who had started to hate school. Once he had a computer to play with, she said, "his whole attitude changed." Najarro is now a true believer, even when it comes to children without disabilities. "Every single child," she said, "will do more work for you and do better work with a computer. Just because it's on a monitor, kids pay more attention. There's this magic to the screen."

Down the hall from Najarro's classroom her colleague Rose Marie Ortiz had a more troubled relationship with computers. On the morning I visited, Ortiz took her bilingual special-education class of second-, third-, and fourth-graders into the lab filled with the old Apple IIes. The students look forward to this weekly expedition so much that Ortiz gets exceptional behavior from them all morning. Out of date though these machines are, they do offer a range of exercises, in subjects such as science, math, reading, social studies, and problem solving. But owing to this group's learning problems and limited English skills, math drills were all that Ortiz could give them. Nonetheless, within minutes the kids were excitedly navigating their way around screens depicting floating airplanes and trucks carrying varying numbers of eggs. As the children struggled, many resorted to counting in whatever way they knew how. Some squinted at the screen, painstakingly moving their fingers from one tiny egg symbol to the next. "*Tres, cuatro, cinco, seis . . . ,*" one little girl said loudly, trying to hear herself above her counting neighbors. Another girl kept a piece of paper handy, on which she marked a line for each egg. Several others resorted to the slow but tried and true—their fingers. Some just guessed. Once the children arrived at answers, they frantically typed them onto the screen, hoping it would advance to something fun, the way Nintendos, Game Boys, and video-arcade games do. Sometimes their answers were right, and the screen did advance; sometimes they weren't; but the children were rarely discouraged. As schoolwork goes, this was a blast.

"It's highly motivating for them," Ortiz said as she rushed from machine to machine, attending not to math questions but to computer glitches. Those she couldn't fix she simply abandoned. "I don't know how practical it is. You see," she said, pointing to a girl counting on her fingers, "these kids still need the hands-on"—meaning the opportunity to manipulate physical objects such as beans or colored blocks. The value of hands-on learning, child-development experts believe, is that it deeply imprints knowledge into a young child's brain, by transmitting the lessons of experience through a variety of sensory pathways. "Curiously enough," the educational psychologist Jane Healy wrote in *Endangered Minds: Why Children Don't Think and What We Can Do About It* (1990), "visual stimulation is probably not the main access route to nonverbal reasoning. Body movements, the ability to touch, feel, manipulate, and build sensory awareness of relationships in the physical world, are its main foundations." The problem, Healy wrote, is that "in schools, traditionally, the senses have had little status after kindergarten."

Ortiz believes that the computer-lab time, brief as it is, dilutes her students' attention to language. "These kids are all language-delayed," she said. Though only modest sums had so far been spent at her school, Ortiz and other local teachers felt that the push was on for technology over other scholastic priorities. The year before, Sanchez had let its librarian go, to be replaced by a part-timer.

When Ortiz finally got the students rounded up and out the door, the kids were still worked up. "They're never this wired after reading group," she said. "They're usually just exhausted, because I've been reading with them, making them write and talk." Back in homeroom Ortiz showed off the students' monthly handwritten writing samples. "Now, could you do that on the computer?" she asked. "No, because we'd be hung up on finding the keys." So why does Ortiz bother taking her students to the computer lab at all? "I guess I come in here for the computer literary. If everyone else is getting it, I feel these kids should get it too."

Some computerized elementary school programs have avoided these pitfalls, but the record subject by subject is mixed at best. Take writing, where by all accounts and by my own observations the computer does encourage practice—changes are easier to make on a keyboard than with an eraser, and the lettering looks better. Diligent students use these conveniences to improve their writing, but the less committed frequently get seduced by electronic opportunities to make a school paper look snazzy. (The easy "cut and paste" function in today's word-processing programs, for example, is apparently encouraging many students to cobble together research materials without thinking them through.) Reading programs get particularly bad reviews. One small but carefully controlled study went so far as to claim that Reader Rabbit, a reading program now used in more than

100,000 schools, caused students to suffer a 50 percent drop in creativity. (Apparently, after forty-nine students used the program for seven months, they were no longer able to answer open-ended questions and showed a markedly diminished ability to brainstorm with fluency and originality.) What about hard sciences, which seem so well suited to computer study? Logo, the high-profile programming language refined by Seymour Papert and widely used in middle and high schools, fostered huge hopes of expanding children's cognitive skills. As students directed the computer to build things, such as geometric shapes, Papert believed, they would learn "procedural thinking," similar to the way a computer processes information. According to a number of studies, however, Logo has generally failed to deliver on its promises. Judah Schwartz, a professor of education at Harvard and a co-director of the school's Educational Technology Center, told me that a few new applications, when used properly, can dramatically expand children's math and science thinking by giving them new tools to "make and explore conjectures." Still, Schwartz acknowledges that perhaps "ninety-nine percent" of the educational programs are "terrible, really terrible."

Even in success stories important caveats continually pop up. The best educational software is usually complex—most suited to older students and sophisticated teachers. In other cases the schools have been blessed with abundance—fancy equipment, generous financial support, or extra teachers—that is difficult if not impossible to duplicate in the average school. Even if it could be duplicated, the literature suggests, many teachers would still struggle with technology. Computers suffer frequent breakdowns; when they do work, their seductive images often distract students from the lessons at hand—which many teachers say makes it difficult to build meaningful rapport with their students.

With such a discouraging record of student and teacher performance with computers, why has the Clinton Administration focused so narrowly on the hopeful side of the story? Part of the answer may lie in the makeup of the Administration's technology task force. Judging from accounts of the task force's deliberations, all thirty-six members are unequivocal technology advocates. Two thirds of them work in the high-tech and entertainment industries. The effect of the group's tilt can be seen in its report. Its introduction adopts the authoritative posture of impartial fact-finder, stating that "this report does not attempt to lay out a national blueprint, nor does it recommend specific public policy goals." But it comes pretty close. Each chapter describes various strategies for getting computers into classrooms, and the introduction acknowledges that "this report does not evaluate the relative merits of competing demands on educational funding (e.g., more computers versus smaller class sizes)."

When I spoke with Esther Dyson and other task-force members about what discussion the group had had about the potential downside of computerized education, they said there hadn't been any. And when I asked Linda Roberts, Clinton's lead technology adviser in the Department of Education, whether the task force was influenced by any self-interest, she said no, quite the opposite: the group's charter actually gave its members license to help the technology industry directly, but they concentrated on schools because that's where they saw the greatest need.

That sense of need seems to have been spreading outside Washington. Last summer a California task force urged the state to spend $11 billion on computers in California schools, which have struggled for years under funding cuts that have driven academic achievement down to among the lowest levels in the nation. This task force, composed of forty-six teachers, parents, technology experts, and business executives, concluded, "More than any other single measure, computers and network technologies, properly implemented, offer the greatest potential to right what's wrong with our public schools." Other options mentioned in the group's report—reducing class size, improving teachers' salaries and facilities, expanding hours of instruction—were considered less important than putting kids in front of computers.

"Hypertext Minds"

TODAY'S parents, knowing firsthand how families were burned by television's false promises, may want some objective advice about the age at which their children should become computer literate. Although there are no real guidelines, computer boosters send continual messages that if children don't begin early, they'll be left behind. Linda Roberts thinks that there's no particular minimum age—and no maximum number of hours that children should spend at a terminal. Are there examples of excess? "I haven't seen it yet," Roberts told me with a laugh. In schools throughout the country administrators and teachers demonstrate the same excitement, boasting about the wondrous things that children of five or six can do on computers: drawing, typing, playing with elementary science simulations and other programs called "educational games."

The schools' enthusiasm for these activities is not universally shared by specialists in childhood development. The doubters' greatest concern is for the very young—preschool through third grade, when a child is most impressionable. Their apprehension involves two main issues.

First, they consider it important to give children a broad base—emotionally, intellectually, and in the five senses—before introducing something as technical and one-dimensional as a computer. Second, they believe that the human and physical world holds greater learning potential.

The importance of a broad base for a child may be most apparent when it's missing. In *Endangered Minds*, Jane Healy wrote of an English teacher who could readily tell which of her students' essays were conceived on a computer. "They don't link ideas," the teacher says. "They just write one thing, and then they write another one, and they don't seem to see or develop the relationships between them." The problem, Healy argued, is that the pizzazz of computerized schoolwork may hide these analytical gaps, which "won't become apparent until [the student] can't organize herself around a homework assignment or a job that requires initiative. More commonplace activities, such as figuring out how to nail two boards together, organizing a game . . . may actually form a better basis for real-world intelligence."

Others believe they have seen computer games expand children's imaginations. High-tech children "think differently from the rest of us," William D. Winn, the director of the Learning Center at the University of Washington's Human Interface Technology Laboratory, told *Business Week* in a recent cover story on the benefits of computer games. "They develop hypertext minds. They leap around. It's as though their cognitive strategies were parallel, not sequential." Healy argues the opposite. She and other psychologists think that the computer screen flattens information into narrow, sequential data. This kind of material, they believe, exercises mostly one half of the brain—the left hemisphere, where primarily sequential thinking occurs. The "right brain" meanwhile gets short shrift—yet this is the hemisphere that works on different kinds of information simultaneously. It shapes our multi-faceted impressions, and serves as the engine of creative analysis.

Opinions diverge in part because research on the brain is still so sketchy, and computers are so new, that the effect of computers on the brain remains a great mystery. "I don't think we know anything about it," Harry Chugani, a pediatric neurobiologist at Wayne State University, told me. This very ignorance makes skeptics wary. "Nobody knows how kids' internal wiring works," Clifford Stoll wrote in *Silicon Snake Oil*, "but anyone who's directed away from social interactions has a head start on turning out weird. . . . No computer can teach what a walk through a pine forest feels like. Sensation has no substitute."

This points to the conservative developmentalists' second concern: the danger that even if hours in front of the screen are limited, unabashed enthusiasm for the computer sends the wrong message: that the mediated world is more significant than the real one. "It's like TV commercials," Barbara Scales, the head teacher at the Child Study Center at the University of California at Berkeley, told me. "Kids get so hyped up, it can change their expectations about stimulation, versus what they generate themselves." In *Silicon Snake Oil*, Michael Fellows, a computer scientist at the University of Victoria, in British Columbia, was even blunter. "Most school would probably be better off if they threw their computers into the Dumpster."

Faced with such sharply contrasting viewpoints, which are based on such uncertain ground, how is a responsible policymaker to proceed? "A prudent society controls its own infatuation with 'progress' when planning for its young," Healy argued in *Endangered Minds*.

> Unproven technologies . . . may offer lively visions, but they can also be detrimental to the development of the young plastic brain. The cerebral cortex is a wondrously well-buffered mechanism that can withstand a good bit of well-intentioned bungling. Yet there is a point at which fundamental neural substrates for reasoning may be jeopardized for children who lack proper physical, intellectual, or emotional nurturance. Childhood—and the brain—have their own imperatives. In development, missed opportunities may be difficult to recapture.

The problem is that technology leaders rarely include these or other warnings in their recommendations. When I asked Dyson why the Clinton task force proceeded with such fervor, despite the classroom computer's shortcomings, she said, "It's so clear the world is changing."

Real Job Training

IN the past decade, according to the presidential task force's report, the number of jobs requiring computer skills has increased from 25 percent of all jobs in 1983 to 47 percent in 1993. By 2000, the report estimates, 60 percent of the nation's jobs will demand these skills—and pay an average of 10 to 15 percent more than jobs involving no computer work. Although projections of this sort are far from reliable, it's a safe bet that computer skills will be needed for a growing proportion of tomorrow's work force. But what priority should these skills be given among other studies?

Listen to Tom Henning, a physics teacher at Thurgood Marshall, the San Francisco technology high school. Henning has a graduate degree in engineering, and helped to found a Silicon Valley company that manufactures electronic navigation equipment. "My bias is the physical reality," Henning told me, as we sat outside a shop where he was helping students to rebuild an old motorcycle. "I'm no technophobe. I can program computers." What worries Henning is that computers at best engage only two senses, hearing and sight—and only two-dimensional sight at that. "Even if they're doing three-dimensional computer modeling, that's still a two-D replica of a three-D world. If you took a kid who grew up on Nintendo, he's not going to have the necessary skills. He needs to have done it first with Tinkertoys or clay, or carved it out of balsa wood." As David Elkind, a professor of child development at Tufts University, puts it, "A dean of the University of Iowa's school of engineering

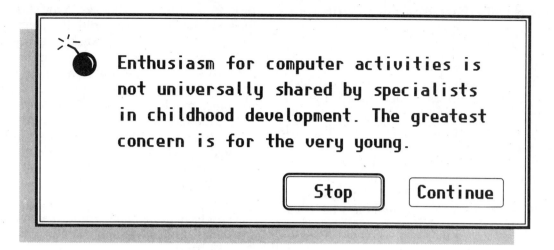

Enthusiasm for computer activities is not universally shared by specialists in childhood development. The greatest concern is for the very young.

Stop   Continue

used to say the best engineers were the farm boys," because they knew how machinery really worked.

Surely many employers will disagree, and welcome the commercially applicable computer skills that today's high-tech training can bring them. What's striking is how easy it is to find other employers who share Henning's and Elkind's concerns.

Kris Meisling, a senior geological-research adviser for Mobil Oil, told me that "people who use computers a lot slowly grow rusty in their ability to think." Meisling's group creates charts and maps—some computerized, some not—to plot where to drill for oil. In large one-dimensional analyses, such as sorting volumes of seismic data, the computer saves vast amounts of time, sometimes making previously impossible tasks easy. This lures people in his field, Meisling believes, into using computers as much as possible. But when geologists turn to computers for "interpretive" projects, he finds, they often miss information, and their oversights are further obscured by the computer's captivating automatic design functions. This is why Meisling still works regularly with a pencil and paper—tools that, ironically, he considers more interactive than the computer, because they force him to think implications through.

"You can't simultaneously get an overview and detail with a computer," he says. "It's linear. It gives you tunnel vision. What computers can do well is what can be calculated over and over. What they can't do is innovation. If you think of some new way to do or look at things and the software can't do it, you're stuck. So a lot of people think, 'Well, I guess it's a dumb idea, or it's unnecessary.'"

I have heard similar warnings from people in other businesses, including high-tech enterprises. A spokeswoman for Hewlett-Packard, the giant California computer-products company, told me the company rarely hires people who are predominantly computer experts, favoring instead those who have a talent for teamwork and are flexible and innovative. Hewlett-Packard is such a believer in hands-on experience that since 1992

it has spent $2.6 million helping forty-five school districts build math and science skills the old-fashioned way—using real materials, such as dirt, seeds, water, glass vials, and magnets. Much the same perspective came from several recruiters in film and computer-game animation. In work by artists who have spent a lot of time on computers "you'll see a stiffness or a flatness, a lack of richness and depth," Karen Chelini, the director of human resources for LucasArts Entertainment, George Lucas's interactive-games maker, told me recently. "With traditional art training, you train the eye to pay attention to body movement. You learn attitude, feeling, expression. The ones who are good are those who as kids couldn't be without their sketchbook."

Many jobs obviously will demand basic computer skills if not sophisticated knowledge. But that doesn't mean that the parents or the teachers of young students need to panic. Joseph Weizenbaum, a professor emeritus of computer science at MIT, told the *San Jose Mercury News* that even at his technology-heavy institution new students can learn all the computer skills they need "in a summer." This seems to hold in the business world, too. Patrick MacLeamy, an executive vice-president of Hellmuth Obata & Kassabaum, the country's largest architecture firm, recently gave me numerous examples to illustrate that computers pose no threat to his company's creative work. Although architecture professors are divided on the value of computerized design tools, in MacLeamy's opinion they generally enhance the process. But he still considers "knowledge of the hands" to be valuable—today's architects just have to develop it in other ways. (His firm's answer is through building models.) Nonetheless, as positive as MacLeamy is about computers, he has found the company's two week computer training to be sufficient. In fact, when he's hiring, computer skills don't enter into his list of priorities. He looks for a strong character; an ability to speak, write, and comprehend; and a rich education in the history of architecture.

The Schools That Business Built

NEWSPAPER financial sections carry almost daily pronouncements from the computer industry and other businesses about their high-tech hopes for America's schoolchildren. Many of these are joined to philanthropic commitments to helping schools make curriculum changes. This sometimes gets businesspeople involved in schools, where they've begun to understand and work with the many daunting problems that are unrelated to technology. But if business gains too much influence over the curriculum, the schools can become a kind of corporate training center—largely at taxpayer expense.

For more than a decade scholars and government commissions have criticized the increasing professionalization of the college years—frowning at the way traditional liberal arts are being edged out by hot topics of the moment or strictly business-oriented studies. The schools' real job, the technology critic Neil Postman argued in his book *The End of Education* (1995), is to focus on "how to make a life, which is quite different from how to make a living." Some see the arrival of boxes of computer hardware and software in the schools as taking the commercial trend one step further, down into high school and elementary grades. "Should you be choosing a career in kindergarten?" asks Helen Sloss Luey, a social worker and a former president of San Francisco's Parent Teacher Association. "People need to be trained to learn and change, while education seems to be getting more specific."

Indeed it does. The New Technology High School in Napa (the school where a computer sits on every student's desk) was started by the school district and a consortium of more than forty businesses. "We want to be the school that business built," Robert Nolan, a founder of the school, told me last fall. "We wanted to create an environment that mimicked what exists in the high-tech business world." Increasingly, Nolan explained, business leaders want to hire people specifically trained in the skill they need. One of Nolan's partners, Ted Fujimoto, of the Landmark Consulting Group, told me that instead of just asking the business community for financial support, the school will now undertake a trade: in return for donating funds, businesses can specify what kinds of employees they want—"a two-way street." Sometimes the traffic is a bit heavy in one direction. In January, *The New York Times* published a lengthy education supplement describing numerous examples of how business is increasingly dominating school software and other curriculum materials, and not always toward purely educational goals.

People who like the idea that their taxes go to computer training might be surprised at what a poor investment it can be. Larry Cuban, the Stanford education professor, writes that changes in the classroom for which business lobbies rarely hold long-term value. Rather, they're often guided by labor-market needs that turn out to be transitory; when the economy shifts, workers are left unprepared for new jobs. In the economy as a whole, according to a recent story in *The New York Times*, performance trends in our schools have shown virtually no link to the rises and falls in the nation's measures of productivity and growth. This is one reason that school traditionalists push for broad liberal-arts curricula, which they feel develop students' values and intellect, instead of focusing on today's idea about what tomorrow's jobs will be.

High-tech proponents argue that the best education software does develop flexible business intellects. In the *Business Week* story on computer games, for example, academics and professionals expressed amazement at the speed, savvy, and facility that young computer jocks sometimes demonstrate. Several pointed in particular to computer simulations, which some business leaders believe are becoming increasingly important in fields ranging from engineering, manufacturing, and troubleshooting to the tracking of economic activity and geopolitical risk. The best of these simulations may be valuable, albeit for strengthening one form of thinking. But the average simulation program may be of questionable relevance.

Sherry Turkle, the sociology professor at MIT, has studied youngsters using computers for more than twenty years. In her book *Life on the Screen: Identity in the Age of the Internet* (1995) she described a disturbing experience with a simulation game called SimLife. After she sat down with a thirteen-year-old named Tim, she was stunned at the way

> Tim can keep playing even when he has no idea what is driving events. For example, when his sea urchins become extinct, I ask him why.
> Tim: "I don't know, it's just something that happens."
> ST: "Do you know how to find out why it happened?"
> Tim: "No."
> ST: "Do you mind that you can't tell why?"
> Tim: "No, I don't let things like that bother me. It's not what's important."

Anecdotes like this lead some educators to worry that as children concentrate on how to manipulate software instead of on the subject at hand, learning can diminish rather than grow. Simulations, for example, are built on hidden assumptions, many of which are oversimplified if not highly questionable. All too often, Turkle wrote recently in *The American Prospect*, "experiences with simulations do not open up questions but close them down." Turkle's concern is that software of this sort fosters passivity, ultimately dulling people's sense of what they can change in the world. There's a tendency, Turkle told me, "to take things at 'interface' value." Indeed, after mastering SimCity, a popular game about urban plan-

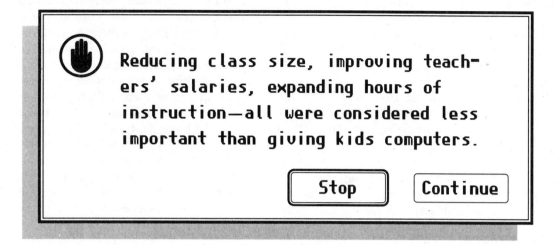

Reducing class size, improving teachers' salaries, expanding hours of instruction—all were considered less important than giving kids computers.

[Stop]   [Continue]

ning, a tenth-grade girl boasted to Turkle that she'd learned the following rule: "Raising taxes always leads to riots."

The business community also offers tangible financial support, usually by donating equipment. Welcome as this is, it can foster a high-tech habit. Once a school's computer system is set up, the companies often drop their support. This saddles the school with heavy long-term responsibilities: maintenance of the computer network and the need for constant software upgrades and constant teacher training—the full burden of which can cost far more than the initial hardware and software combined. Schools must then look for handouts from other companies, enter the grant-seeking game, or delicately go begging in their own communities. "We can go to the well only so often," Toni-Sue Passantino, the principal of the Bayside Middle School, in San Mateo, California, told me recently. Last year Bayside let a group of seventh- and eight-graders spend eighteen months and countless hours creating a rudimentary virtual-reality program, with the support of several high-tech firms. The companies' support ended after that period, however—creating a financial speed bump of a kind that the Rand Corporation noted in a report to the Clinton Administration as a common obstacle.

School administrators may be outwardly excited about computerized instruction, but they're also shrewdly aware of these financial challenges. In March of last year, for instance, when California launched its highly promoted "Net-Day '96" (a campaign to wire 12,000 California schools to the Internet in one day), school participation was far below expectations, even in technology-conscious San Francisco. In the city papers school officials wondered how they were supposed to support an Internet program when they didn't even have the money to repair crumbling buildings, install electrical outlets, and hire the dozens of new teachers recently required so as to reduce class size.

One way around the donation maze is to simplify: use inexpensive, basic software and hardware, much of which is available through recycling programs. Such frugality can offer real value in the elementary grades, especially since basic word-processing tools are most helpful to children just learning to write. Yet schools, like the rest of us, can't resist the latest toys. "A lot of people will spend all their money on fancy new equipment that can do great things, and sometimes it just gets used for typing classes," Ray Porter, a computer resource teacher for the San Francisco schools, told me recently. "Parents, school boards, and the reporters want to see only razzle-dazzle state-of-the-art."

Internet Isolation

IT is hard to visit a high-tech school without being led by a teacher into a room where students are communicating with people hundreds or thousands of miles away—over the Internet or sometimes through video-conferencing system (two-way TV sets that broadcast live from each room). Video conferences, although fun, are an expensive way to create classroom thrills. But the Internet, when used carefully, offers exciting academic prospects—most dependably, once again, for older students. In one case schools in different states have tracked bird migrations and then posted their findings on the World Wide Web, using it as their own national notebook. In San Francisco eighth-grade economics students have E-mailed Chinese and Japanese businessmen to fulfill an assignment on what it would take to build an industrial plant overseas. Schools frequently use the Web to publish student writing. While thousands of self-published materials like these have turned the Web into a worldwide vanity press, the network sometimes gives young writers their first real audience.

The free nature of Internet information also means that students are confronted with chaos, and real dangers. "The Net's beauty is that it's uncontrolled," Stephen Kerr, a professor at the College of Education at the University of Washington and the editor of *Technology in the Future of Schooling* (1996), told me. "It's information by anyone, for anyone. There's racist stuff, bigoted, hate-group stuff, filled with paranoia; bomb recipes; how to engage in various kinds of crimes, electronic and otherwise; scams and swindles. It's all there. It's all available." Older students may be sophisticated enough to separate the Net's good food from its poisons, but even the savvy can be misled. On almost any subject the Net offers a plethora of seemingly sound "research." But under close inspection much of it proves to be ill informed, or just superficial. "That's the antithesis of what classroom kids should be exposed to," Kerr said.

This makes traditionalists emphasize the enduring value of printed books, vetted as most are by editing. In many schools, however, libraries are fairly limited. I now volunteer at a San Francisco high school where the library shelves are so bare that I can see how the Internet's ever-growing number of research documents, with all their shortcomings, can sometimes be a blessing.

Even computer enthusiasts give the Net tepid reviews. "Most of the content on the Net is total garbage," Esther Dyson acknowledges. "But if you find one good thing you can use it a million times." Kerr believes that Dyson is being unrealistic. "If you find a useful site one day, it may not be there the next day, or the information is different. Teachers are being asked to jump in and figure out if what they find on the Net is worthwhile. They don't have the skill or time to do that." Especially when students rely on the Internet's much-vaunted search software. Although these tools deliver hundreds or thousands of sources within seconds, students may not realize that search engines, and the Net itself, miss important information all the time.

"We need *less* surfing in the schools, not more," David Gelernter, a professor of computer science at Yale, wrote last year in *The Weekly Standard*. "Couldn't we teach them to use what they've got before favoring them with three orders of magnitude *more*?" In my conversations with Larry Cuban, of Stanford, he argued, "Schooling is not about information. It's getting kids to think about information. It's about understanding and knowledge and wisdom."

It may be that youngsters' growing fascination with the Internet and other ways to use computers will distract from yet another of Clinton's education priorities: to build up the reading skills of American children. Sherry Dingman, an assistant professor of psychology at Marist College, in Poughkeepsie, New York, who is optimistic about many computer applications, believes that if children start using computers before they have a broad foundation in reading from books, they will be cheated out of opportunities to develop imagination. "If we think we're going to take kids who haven't been read

to, and fix it by sitting them in front of a computer, we're fooling ourselves," Dingman told me not long ago. This doesn't mean that teachers or parents should resort to books on CD-ROM, which Dingman considers "a great waste of time," stuffing children's minds with "canned" images instead of stimulating youngsters to create their own. "Computers are lollipops that rot your teeth" is how Marilyn Darch, an English teacher at Poly High School, in Long Beach, California, put it in *Silicon Snake Oil*. "The kids love them. But once they get hooked. . . . It makes reading a book seem tedious. Books don't have sound effects, and their brains have to do all the work."

Computer advocates like to point out that the Internet allows for all kinds of intellectual challenges—especially when students use E-mail, or post notes in "newsgroup" discussions, to correspond with accomplished experts. Such experts, however, aren't consistently available. When they are, online "conversations" generally take place when correspondents are sitting alone, and the dialogue lacks the unpredictability and richness that occur in face-to-face discussions. In fact, when youngsters are put into groups for the "collaborative" learning that compute defenders celebrate, realistically only one child sits at the keyboard at a time. (During my school visits children tended to get quite possessive about the mouse and the keyboard, resulting in frustration and noisy disputes more often than collaboration.) In combination these constraints lead to yet another of the childhood developmentalists' concerns—that computers encourage social isolation.

Just a Glamorous Tool

IT would be easy to characterize the battle over computers as merely another chapter in the world's oldest story: humanity's natural resistance to change. But that does an injustice to the forces at work in this transformation. This is not just the future versus the past, uncertainty versus nostalgia; it is about encouraging a fundamental shift in personal priorities—a minimizing of the real, physical world in favor of an unreal "virtual" world. It is about teaching youngsters that exploring what's on a two-dimensional screen is more important than playing with real objects, or sitting down to an attentive conversation with a friend, a parent, or a teacher. By extension, it means downplaying the importance of conversation, of careful listening, and of expressing oneself in person with acuity and individuality. In the process, it may also limit the development of children's imaginations.

Perhaps this is why Steven Jobs, one of the founders of Apple Computer and a man who claims to have "spearheaded giving away more computer equipment to schools than anybody else on the planet," has come to a grim conclusion: "What's wrong with education cannot be fixed with technology," he told *Wired* magazine last year. "No amount of technology will make a dent. . . .

You're not going to solve the problems by putting all knowledge onto CD-ROMs. We can put a Web site in every school—none of this is bad. It's bad only if it lulls us into thinking we're doing something to solve the problem with education." Jane David the consultant to Apple, concurs, with a commonly heard caveat: "There are real dangers," she told me, "in looking to technology to be the savior of education. But it won't survive without the technology."

Arguments like David's remind Clifford Stoll of yesteryear's promises about television. He wrote in *Silicon Snake Oil,*

"Sesame Street" ... has been around for twenty years. Indeed, its idea of making learning relevant to all was as widely promoted in the seventies as the Internet is today.
So where's that demographic wave of creative and brilliant students now entering college? Did kids really need to learn how to watch television? Did we inflate their expectations that learning would always be colorful and fun?

Computer enthusiasts insist that the computer's "interactivity" and multimedia features make this machine far superior to television. Nonetheless, Stoll wrote,

I see a parallel between the goals of "Sesame Street" and those of children's computing. Both are persuasive, expensive and encourage children to sit still. Both display animated cartoons, gaudy numbers and weird, random noises. . . . Both give the sensation that by merely watching a screen, you can acquire information without work and without discipline.

As the technology critic Neil Postman put it to a Harvard electronic-media conference, "I thought that television would be the last great technology that people would go into with their eyes closed. Now you have the computer."

The solution is not to ban computers from classrooms altogether. But it may be to ban federal spending on what is fast becoming an overheated campaign. After all, the private sector, with its constant supply of used computers and the computer industry's vigorous competition for new customers, seems well equipped to handle the situation. In fact, if schools can impose some limits—on technology donors and on themselves—rather than indulging in a consumer frenzy, most will probably find themselves with more electronic gear than they need. That could free the billions that Clinton wants to devote to technology and make it available for impoverished fundamentals: teaching solid skills in reading, thinking, listening, and talking; organizing inventive field trips and other rich hands-on experiences; and, of course, building up the nation's core of knowledgeable, inspiring teachers. These notions are considerably less glamorous than computers are, but their worth is firmly proved through a long history.

Last fall, after the school administrators in Mansfield, Massachusetts, had eliminated proposed art, music, and physical-education positions in favor of buying computers, Michael Bellino, an electrical engineer at Boston University's Center for Space Physics, appeared before the Massachusetts Board of Education to protest. "The purpose of the schools [is] to, as one teacher argues, 'Teach carpentry, not hammer,'" he testified. "We need to teach the whys and ways of the world. Tools come and tools go. Teaching our children tools limits their knowledge to these tools and hence limits their futures."

Columbus in the Curriculum: Shoring Up a Hero

SHARON L. KNOPP

When I teach Human Relations, a course or workshop on multiculturalism, to current and future teachers, I include a section on Christopher Columbus. Howard Zinn's (1980, pp. 1–11) portrayal of the Columbian encounter is always a traumatic experience for my students, an experience not unlike (though perhaps not as important as) losing Santa Clause! This was especially true before the media coverage of the debate surrounding the celebration of the quincentenary of Columbus's first arrival in the Western Hemisphere; it was rare to find a student who had heard anything other than glory assigned to this very "American" hero. It is possible that they had simply forgotten the complexity of this man and his "accomplishments," but more likely that they had never heard anything but praise.

We should not be dependent on a sensationalist media for the training of our teachers, and I was curious to see what kind of education today's school children are receiving on this topic before arriving in my classroom. Having been inadequately trained myself, I was hopeful that current editions of textbooks reflect the current debate about Columbus's laudatory status, and that students trained with these new books might enter my future classrooms better informed.

I began where our education about Christopher Columbus usually begins: in elementary school, often in our first year of class. According to the American Textbook Council, the United States elementary social studies curriculum is dominated by three publishers: Macmillan, Houghton Mifflin, and Silver Burdett. Although it is impossible to know exactly how dominant, because of the secrecy of a competitive industry, in some states, these three publishers enjoy an estimated 80% of the market (Sewall, 1992). An analysis of their curriculum then will tell us much about the collective training of United States students in their most formative years, perhaps the years when we are most eager to believe in heroes and to be influenced by them.

SAMPLE AND METHOD

The entire elementary social studies series (grades 1–6) of Macmillan (1987), Houghton Mifflin (1991), and Silver Burdett (1991) were analyzed. This included 15 books in which Columbus appeared, in the edition closest to the quincentenary of 1992. Many school districts, of course, are still using older editions, and my teachers-in-training must have used older editions still, so this analysis represents the *best* likely education they might have received. The teachers' editions were used to include curriculum that students might be told, as well as what they read. I looked at Columbus's treatment as a hero, by noting his frequency of appearance, adjectives used to describe him and his enterprise, his presentation pictorially, and critical thinking questions asked about him. I also evaluated the treatment of native perspective, associated questions that reveal what is "important" about Columbus, and skills associated with the pedagogy of Columbus curriculum.

I also considered the factual accuracy of the story. Numerous contemporary scholars call into question the interpretation of Columbus's contribution. Part of their question is based on values and ideology, but another part is based on the discovery and examination of primary materials previously unavailable. In "The Columbian Quincentenary," the National Council for the Social Studies (1991, p. 1) urges educators to "examine seriously the available scholarship to enhance our knowledge about 1492" and to "provide students with basic, accurate knowledge about Columbus's voyages, their historical setting, and unfolding effects."

Ascertaining accuracy is no small task given that leading Columbian scholars continually debate what *is* fact and how to interpret primary data. Perhaps the most popular source material for social studies authors on Columbus is Samuel Eliot Morison's *Admiral of the Ocean Sea* (1942), an unabashed celebrant of Columbus heroism. For an alternative perspective, I have relied on Kirkpatrick Sale's *The Conquest of Paradise,* one of the most scholarly critiques of Columbus, which includes examination of source materials not available to Morison. Both studies are pointedly ideological, and neither author is less controversial. The question for this analysis is, how is the controversy represented in our textbooks?

The purpose for this article is not a comparative evaluation of the relative superiority of one series over another. My students were, for the most part, equally

From *Equity & Excellence in Education,* Vol. 28, No. 3, 1995, pp. 57-64. © 1995 by Greenwood Publishing Group, Inc., Westport, CT. Reprinted by permission.

ignorant of the debate. And teachers need to know how to evaluate their own texts, including future adoptions and texts issued by smaller publishers. I therefore did my evaluation, and now report my findings, holistically, as the composite picture of Columbus presented together by the dominant textbook publishers. Specific citations are given only for examples that stand out as exceptional in some way.

In 1991, Sewall (p. 14) wrote, "we may expect some strenuous efforts during the next two years among some curriculum planners to obtain compensatory revision in texts" in response to the quincentenary debate. To test this hypothesis, I reviewed the all new 1993 Macmillan/McGraw Hill series, *The World Around Us*, written by a completely different list of authors. Has significant compensatory revision occurred? Once again, this evaluation is not meant to compare Macmillan with the other publishers, especially since it includes a comparison with an earlier Macmillan series. Rather the purpose is to consider the difference that time and public debate may have made in our texts, with the expectation that similar changes may be forthcoming with other publishers.

FINDINGS

Columbus's status as a hero is certainly reflected in his frequency of appearance in the curriculum of our elementary students. They will learn something about him in each of five different grades. (Like Santa Claus, he does indeed arrive yearly!) Among the three series together, then, he appears in 15 books. This is particularly curious given that he is made to be relevant during years in which children are learning about "Living in Families" (Columbus did very little of this himself [Sale, 1990, pp. 53–4]), "Communities" (Columbus was shipped home in chains and forever banished from Espanola for his failure to create and maintain community [Sale, 1990, p. 182]), and "People and Neighborhoods" (Columbus failed miserably at getting along with his neighbors, both natives and colonials; even Columbus celebrants do not dispute this).

"Discovery"

Traditionally, Columbus's greatest act of heroism is considered to be his "discovery" of a New World. Native American critique of this concept has perhaps been the simplest and easiest perceptual bias for non-Indians, including publishers, to grasp. How can you discover a world that is populated with millions of people? Obviously, someone else had already discovered it. In defense of those who have used the word, all of us make discoveries in our lifetimes that are indeed new to us, but have been known for a very long time by others. From our perspective, it is a discovery. The problem then is not that Columbus did not discover anything. It is that

using this word places the education of our children narrowly in the perspective of Europeans, ignoring the perspective of the indigenous people he "discovered."

Authors and publishers have clearly understood this bias and taken pains to make amends linguistically. In the series studied, the word "discovered" is still used, but often it is put in quotes, acknowledging the natives' prior occupation, sometimes Lief Ericson's previous landing, and always presenting discovery as a European perspective. Holiday units most often "celebrate" Columbus, sometimes simply "remember" him, because he was "one of the first people to make this trip [across the Atlantic]" or because he was the "first European of modern times to reach America." Rather than say "discovered," the books are more likely to use careful phrases like "found new land," "went ashore," "landed," "visited," "reached" or even "stumbles on" the "New World."

Certainly these changes do reflect a growing sensitivity to Columbus detractors, but the use of the term "New World" still ignores the fact that it was an old world to those who had been living there, and it asserts the persistence of the European perspective. Furthermore, much opinion has been written about the appropriateness of "celebrating" this encounter (Harjo, 1991).

Adjectives

If the writers are more careful about the bias in labeling Columbus's accomplishment, they are much less concerned about bias in describing the man. He is called "special," "brave," "famous," "adventurous," "thoughtful," "determined," "great," "important," and "bold." There are, of course, many people, including Morison, who would agree with all of these descriptors. But there are also those who would add some much less flattering ones to the list. Sale, and some of his sources who might even agree with the words above, would also include such words as "lying," "self-serving," "greedy," "cruel," or "irresponsible." The controversy about the personality, motives, and merits of the man does not appear in these books. Nor the possibility that one can be great and famous and still have some serious flaws that are just as important for children to ponder as are virtues.

Negative descriptors appear in only two cases. The voyage across the Atlantic is called "frightening," thus confirming Columbus's bravery. And he is called "bitter" and "disappointed" because he died never knowing he had found a "New World" and would therefore be "surprised" that we would celebrate a holiday in his honor. Readers are thus taught to feel sympathy and admiration for such a humble and unfortunate man.

Pictures

At the elementary level, texts are dominated by pictures that not only capture children's attention, but teach them many of their lessons as well. In the 15 books there are 24 pictures related to Columbus. Not surprisingly, by far the greatest number (11) are of ships, portraying action and a vehicle of transportation, both of which are assumed to capture the imagination of children (possibly more so for boys than for girls). Interestingly, these pictures also reflect the text's preoccupation with Columbus's time at sea, not his time on land, where he is subject to the greatest criticism. There are also five maps, reinforcing the importance of the voyage itself. Each series has one map of the first voyage only; two series later add a map of all four voyages (see also Knopp, 1995b).

Next, there are five pictures of Columbus with Isabella and Ferdinand, including three pictures of leave-taking at the departure of the first voyage. There is, in fact, no evidence that Columbus saw the sovereigns at all on that day, much less in view of the harbor. The source for such a portrayal is the imagination of artists and fictional historians, long after Columbus's death (Sale, 1990, p. 20). This suggests that our social studies texts are books of the arts rather than the kind of serious scholarship that the National Council for the Social Studies urges us to share with our students. Both portrayals, fiction and scholarly research, have merits of their own, but education supposedly attempts to teach us to distinguish between the two. That distinction is not made in our elementary textbooks, and students are not taught that there is a difference. Similarly, there are four portraits of Columbus. Only one caption states that it was painted 20 years after his death. Sale (1990, p. 214) says that the earliest was done 50 years after his death, none are authenticated, all look different, and therefore, all are products of the artists' imagination.

Two pictures represent Columbus staking claim to the new land, and neither shows any natives, either nearby or in the distance. One shows a holiday parade, again reinforcing his status as a hero. And one is of school children taking the Pledge of Allegiance. The teacher's edition tells that it was written in commemoration of the 400th anniversary of Columbus's landing, thus associating love of Columbus with American patriotism.

Questionable Facts and Omissions

The distinction between fact and fiction is an important lesson for students and a continual quest for scholars. The indiscriminate mingling of the two is evident in the telling of the Columbus story where there appear numerous "facts" of questionable veracity and omissions of some considerable significance. It would hardly be fair to blame elementary textbook writers for this problem, since "there is probably no other area of modern history with more elaborate fantasies pretending to be sober fact than in Columbian studies, even in works by the most celebrated and reputable" (Sale, 1990, p. 20). Indeed, Sale himself has been accused of passing on at least one such

fantasy, albeit probably unwittingly (Lynch, 1993, pp. 254–69).

Columbus's life before 1492: Perhaps to encourage readers to identify with their subject matter, elementary writers cannot resist painting an embellished picture of Columbus's early years. Not until high school (Knopp, 1995a) does one text admit that we know very little about this topic (less than the earlier texts provide). He is said to have first gone to sea at various ages between 14 and 19, with contradictory ages even given in the same series! Three books call him a "captain," one even saying that he was "one of the most skilled sea captains in Portugal." There is, in fact, *no* evidence of Columbus having captained *any* vessel at all before 1492 (Sale, 1990, p. 16).

The source for many embellishments, repeated by Morison, is the biography of Columbus written by his son Fernando. Fernando was only four years old at the time of the first voyage and 14 when he accompanied his father on the fourth voyage. His source material included stories spun over the years by the crew and Columbus, who was known for his exaggerations and lies. Fernando's book is full of inaccuracies (Sale, 1990, pp. 20–21).

Flat earth theory: Many of my students believed that Columbus proved the earth was round, and that sailors had been afraid to go on his expedition because they thought they would fall off the edge of the earth. One book in this study reinforces that falsehood by saying that Columbus was right about the most important thing—the world *is* round. Actually, Columbus did nothing to make that point, since he did not go all the way around the earth; it was Magellan's expedition which later did. Furthermore, no serious sailors of Columbus's time believed that ships disappeared off the edge of the earth. They commonly disappeared over the horizon, and then returned (Sale, 1990, p. 14).

Mutiny at sea: Two of the series tell of Columbus's crew being close to mutiny. Such a story, of course, gives the great captain a further opportunity to demonstrate his greatness. After studying Columbus's journal directly, Sale (p. 60–61) finds no mention by the captain himself of any mutiny at all. The crew's complaints have apparently been turned into stories of mutiny by subsequent "historiofabulists" in order to further construct a hero.

Who first sighted land?: This story is also embellished beyond the known facts. One text says that Columbus saw fire, thought it must be on land and when it was acknowledged by the crew, he ordered that anchors be dropped. According to his journal, however, when Columbus saw a flickering light, he was so uncertain that he did not declare the citing of land. His royal steward thought he saw it too, but the royal inspector could see nothing, and no one on the other ships mentioned it. So he simply told his crew to keep a sharp lookout. There were no dropping of anchors. It was not until four hours later that Juan Rodriguez Bermejo sighted land. According to Sale (1990, pp. 62–3), Columbus's earlier sighting had been too far away from land to be true.

One book actually names the first person to site land as Rodrigo de Triana, not Bermejo. Morison names him de Triana and Sale does not explain the difference. More importantly, what no text mentions is the fact that Ferdinand and Isabella had promised a significant monetary reward to the first person to sight land, and Columbus claimed and received that reward for himself. In any exercise on values clarification, this would be an important piece of information about a person's character, and might cause our student to add some words of their own to the list of descriptors about our hero.

Landfall—where?: The location of landfall, when given, is always named San Salvador, for that is what Columbus named it. But which island is San Salvador? He did not record the information necessary to determine that. In fact, scholars have made persuasive arguments for 12 different places, and this question is probably irresolvable (Sale, 1990, p. 66). But once again, controversy (even enticing mystery!) is omitted from the texts.

Success or failure?: Whether Columbus was a success or a failure depends in part on what he set out to accomplish, what he thought he accomplished, and what he actually did accomplish. All series say that his goal was to find a water route to the "Indies." Some books leave us with the impression that Indies meant India, but others correct that error by saying that he was looking for Asia, including China and Japan (which was then referred to as the Indies). We all know that he did not find Asia, and one book says that failure was the cause for his bitterness at the time of his death. In fact, Columbus's extensive writings about his own bitterness all focus on his lack of recognition and compensation for his accomplishments, not on lack of accomplishment itself (Sale, 1990, pp. 187–88). Although most historians still believe that he thought he had found Asia, there is now compelling evidence that he did indeed know that he had found a new continent on the third voyage, and new lands had been his intention all along (Sale, 1990, p. 358).

One book says that his goal was "to become rich," that is, to find gold. His journal is certainly filled with this obsession. The series leave us to think that he did not find gold or any riches, and so do most historians. But according to Sale (1990, pp. 180–81), whose sources include Columbus's writings and the royal court's revenue records, extensive gold was found on Espanola during the third voyage, making him and the Crown very wealthy. He died with seven servants at his deathbed, lamenting that he should have had more compensation!

So, although one book says that Columbus's disrepute among his contemporaries was due to the failure of all four voyages, thus leaving readers today to think, "if they only knew . . . ," there is significant evidence that both Columbus and his contemporaries did know, in fact knew more than our students do today. If *they* only knew, he might not be so reputable today.

La Navidad: As mentioned earlier, these elementary texts spend most of their time on Columbus at sea, rather than on land. The omission of the story of La Navidad is symbolic of this important bias. La Navidad was the first European settlement established by our hero, and although he returned to Europe after giving instructions to the men left behind to treat the Indians well, on return to La Navidad, during the Second Voyage, he found their fortress completely destroyed and all the Spaniards dead, their bodies "miserably deformed and corrupted." One eyewitness explained the violent change of disposition of the friendly natives toward the colonists as retaliation for the "licentious conduct of our men towards the Indian women" (Sale, 1990, p. 139). For the first time, the meeting of two worlds takes on an undeniably dark aspect.

We have no reason to blame Columbus himself for his colonists' behavior during his first absence, but we do have reason to begin to question the glory of his enterprise. Furthermore, their behavior seems to have been even worse, not better, when he was present to govern. One text says that Columbus left some sailors behind to start a new settlement (unnamed), and their fate is never discussed. La Navidad is not otherwise mentioned in any of the series, and one book begins with the second settlement, Isabella, as if it were the first, thereby avoiding an explanation of the significance of the real beginning. No text tells that Columbus was expelled and permanently barred from Espanola in 1500 for his failure to govern adequately, and thus we learn neither of the beginning nor the end of his rule.

Thus, our children who grow up with the relatively uncensored violence of their television sets, are schooled in the censorship of real life violence, and thereby lose an opportunity to study the causes, consequences, and prevention of future violence. Not knowing their own history, they are condemned to repeat it. Similarly, these series completely omit the slavery that was instituted under Columbus's colonial rule and the tribute system by which the natives were forced to bring him gold. Although these events are mentioned relative to subsequent colonial rule, Columbus's reputation is not challenged by any association with such currently condemned practices.

Native Perspectives

Far less is said about the natives of the West Indies than about Columbus, and most often nothing is said at all. We are told that Columbus named them Indians. Two books refer to them as Arawak. Current thought, however, is that the Arawak were distant relations on the South American mainland, and that the people Columbus first met were Taino (Sale, 1990, p. 97). None of the books refer to them as Taino. One mentions the Carib further south as "fierce warriors and conquerors." Such a description might help to justify the Europeans' conquering behaviors, but it was apparently fabricated by

Columbus who never set foot on a Carib island, and it was quite the opposite of reports from people who did meet them (Sale, 1990, pp. 130–32). At the least we can say that the nature of the Caribs is historically debatable. Two books mention that Columbus took six natives back to Spain with him. They fail to mention that these were captives, and that he started out with perhaps two dozen (Sale, 1990, p. 122). The rest died on the trip while all of the Europeans returned safely.

An important writer about the Columbian encounter was Bartolome de Las Casas, who himself held slaves in the encomienda system instituted by Columbus, before taking religious vows as a friar. He arrived in Espanola in 1502, just two years after Columbus was deemed incompetent to rule the island. His writings express great admiration for the Admiral's courage and bravery, but absolute condemnation of his horribly cruel treatment of the natives, who came to hate the colonists. His perspective, and the native perspective he reports, is nowhere mentioned in the curriculum on Columbus. What is reported instead are quotes from Columbus's journal of the first voyage, before the Taino learned that they had to defend themselves against the Europeans. Those impressions are quite positive, and the subsequent change in Columbus's reports is never mentioned.

So relations between Columbus and the Taino, when mentioned at all, are depicted as favorable. What happened to them then? Nothing is said about the fate of these reportedly good people, except "most disappeared" and "many died from diseases." One wonders how and why people "disappear," especially from a child's perspective!

Skills and Concepts

Skills that are taught in conjunction with the curriculum are reading and writing time lines, graphic organizers, map reading, outlining, listening, writing, persuasion, oral reporting, and doing research. None of these, obviously need be specific to the actual story of Columbus and could be accomplished with many other subjects. A problem that occurs with the research assignments is that they invariably lead to biographies of Columbus, which are filled with far more falsehoods, omissions, and embellishments than the social studies texts (Bigelow, 1991).

Noncontroversial concepts that are Columbus-related include the preColumbian era, exploration, navigation, cartography, and signs of land at sea. More questionable concepts that are taught are holidays (the question is not asked whether Columbus deserves one), leadership (Columbus is used as a role model of good leadership), and studying hard, believing in what you're doing, daring to be wrong, and never giving up (other ways to not only admire, but also *be* like Columbus, uncritically).

These are standard concepts in the Columbus lessons, but Houghton Mifflin stands out by adding concepts that are more controversial and much less flattering. These include contagious disease, decisionmaking (whether to fund Columbus; another series says uncritically that this was the most important decision of Isabella's reign), colonialism, expansion (occupying or controlling another country through war, purchase, or trade), force and violence, and comparison of European exploration to the Crusades, concluding that the arrival of Europeans was a tragedy for the Indians. Concepts such as these certainly represent a departure from the traditional presentation of Columbus as hero.

Critical thinking

Questions included in the text tell us what the authors think is important about Columbus. For the most part, they are questions about the voyages themselves, about the goal of the expeditions, and why Columbus is remembered today. There are no questions about the native inhabitants of his discoveries, and this omission reflects the lack of information provided.

Critical thinking questions provide students with an opportunity to apply and expand what the book has taught them. These are typical topics suggested by the authors (with my critique added in parentheses):

- Speculate on Columbus's feelings, personality traits (What the historiofabulists too often present as fact, though this is not pointed out in this assignment. Students are encouraged to do the same, uncritically.)
- Would you rather sail in a caravel or a Viking ship? (Is this supposed to be the lesser of two evils?)
- Why is 1992 important to all Americans? (Does this question lead students to think that it *is* important to all Americans, and for the same reasons?)
- What can we learn from making mistakes? (Reference is to Columbus's geographical miscalculations, not human relations mistakes.)
- How would you persuade Queen Isabella if you were Columbus?
- What are Columbus's leadership qualities? (Assumes strengths and provides no information to assess weaknesses; some of his contemporaries would say that Columbus did not possess all the strengths they suggest.)
- Tell about a place you'd like to explore. What might be the dangers? What would you expect to find? (Not *whom* might you expect to find, or what might be your responsibilities.)

All of these questions are interesting, though certainly less interesting and challenging than they could have been, and not at all without ideological implications. Furthermore, none of them are about the native people encountered. Only these questions addressed the Indian perspective:

- Who in your opinion really discovered America? Why?
- Which group do you think was more astonished by the other, Indians or Europeans? Why?
- Today, many Native Americans object to reading or hearing that Columbus "discovered" America. Native Americans do not agree with the European explorers who called America a "new world." Why? Do you agree or disagree? Explain.

These questions from the texts represent a beginning at viewing events from another perspective. But none of them lead to any criticism of Columbus or address his treatment of Indians. Students are not given enough information to consider more critical questions.

Further in their texts, Houghton Mifflin does offer more challenging questions. For example:

- What effect did Spanish explorers' attitudes and actions towards Indians have on Indian cultures? Did they act properly? How should they have treated the Indians?
- Imagine you are an Iroquois. Write a reaction to the explorers.
- Europeans' treatment of the Indians ranged from enslavement to acceptance of them as equals. What factors contributed to the Europeans' harsh treatment of the Indians? Why didn't more Europeans follow the examples of William Penn or Roger Williams? (Teachers' notes ask the teacher to point out that many Europeans were fleeing harsh treatment themselves. The expected conclusion therefore must be that they are products of their times, and therefore somehow excused. Were not Penn and Williams and Las Casas also products of their times?)

These questions are more complex and potentially more critical, but they come *after* the sections on Columbus, who therefore escapes this kind of analysis, and too little information is provided to address his responsibility anyway.

The critical thinking questions in these series then begin to address perspectives that have not been addressed in traditional textbooks, but they are a cautious beginning that easily excuse Columbus himself. Furthermore, if critical thinking is left to end-of-chapter questions (or worse yet, only teachers' editions), and omitted from the actual text, students may be asked to answer questions that the authors seem to have resolved themselves, in Columbus's favor.

A 1993 PERSPECTIVE

The last edition of the Macmillan Social Studies series was 1987, the one in widest use at the time of the quincentenary. It is being replaced by the Macmillan/McGraw-Hill series, *The World Around Us.* This new series began in 1990, and that edition contains problems typical of the three sets already analyzed. Columbus is "special," "great," and "talented" because he discovered a new world. The inhabitants were Indians. In 1990 he is actually called an American, though that misnomer is omitted in 1991. In both years the two books assert that people in Columbus's time thought that the earth was flat and ships would fall off the edge if they sailed too far.

The 1993 edition included three new authors with credentialed multicultural perspectives, and it is indeed different from the earlier series in significant ways. First, some of the errors discussed earlier have been corrected. Teachers are told that we are not sure where Columbus first landed. Many people say it was San Salvador. Some say it was Samana Cay Island. In this series, Columbus did discover gold and become rich. The reason that he died disappointed and angry was not because he failed in any of his goals, but rather because he thought the Spanish government held back on his rewards.

There is still confusion about Columbus's perception of his accomplishment. One book asks students to write a paragraph to *convince Columbus* of the value of his voyages even though he did not reach the riches of Asia. One wonders why Columbus would need to be convinced, especially given that he spent the last years of his life writing voluminously to convince others of the values of his voyages. It might be interesting to compare his writings with those of the students. Another asks, "if Columbus had landed in South America, do you think he would have known he had reached a land unknown to him?" The answer is, "Probably not, because he was sure he was exploring the Indies and coast of Asia." Although most of the books refer to the Indies as Asia and its islands, one still says that he thought he had reached India. Actually, Columbus did land in South America, so a new error is introduced. And a subsequent book quotes Columbus as writing in 1502, "I have come to believe that this is a mighty continent which was before unknown." So although some important new information is added about Columbus's own perception, the inconsistencies within the series will leave students confused.

The Smithsonian Institution attempted to balance the perception of the significance of Columbus's arrival with their quincentenary exhibit and associated curricula, *Seeds of Change.* The general theme purports that each hemisphere contributed new things to the other. This series reflects that theme in one sadly humorous assertion that the east got maize, yams, sweet potatoes and tobacco in exchange for Roman Catholic place names given to the west! This is simply a lesson in place names, and no thought is given to whether this was a worthy exchange.

Nevertheless, the perspective of the native peoples has been expanded. They are not called Taino, but the name Arawak is used consistently. The first book in the series even begins from the native perspective: "Long ago, Arawak Indians in another part of America saw something that they had never seen before." Columbus comes second. A new artist's version of the landfall includes Arawak observers, and the captain is simply disembarking, not staking claim. Students are asked to speculate on the feelings of each side. This series includes boxes on "multicultural perspectives" that question the perspectives implied in words like "discovery," "encounter," "New World," and "celebration."

The controversy of 1992 is further discussed with questions about how people's view of history changes over time, and how people can have different points of view about the same historical event. A contemporary Native American (unnamed) is quoted regarding the "invasion" of 1492. The different perspectives of Spaniards and Arawak will be relatively easy for students to surmise, but this lesson could be deepened by adding the perspective of Las Casas and the concept of dissent within one group. La Navidad is introduced (though not by name) as "the beginning of tense relations between Europe and the Americas—the clash of two cultures." Unfortunately, readers are told that the cause is unknown, thus depriving them of an exploration of the roots of violence, and leaving them to think that the Arawak were responsible for the ensuing tension.

The most notable change in this series is that Columbus's status as a hero is greatly diminished, and it is done so by authors that can most fairly be called *careful*. There are *no* heroic adjectives. We simply "think" about him and how he came to America, and remember him for reaching them. Many holidays are for "people in our country's history"—not great or famous people, just people. In the second book he is one of four famous people: Columbus, Benjamin Franklin, Harriet Tubman and Susan B. Anthony. What strange bedfellows! A slave trader and an abolitionist. All are known for working hard to help America grow (does this imply the United States?). Columbus sailed to America; because of him other people came to live here. Franklin helped to free America from England. Tubman helped free African Americans. Anthony helped women to get the vote. Does Columbus belong in a group of liberators? The selection of two women, including one Black, suggests just how careful the authors are to please everyone, but the incongruity is heightened by the fact that Columbus is the only one for whom there is a national holiday.

There is no information given to make students question his worth as a national hero. The decimation of the Arawak is attributed to the conquistadors, *not* to Columbus. The conquistadors are those who conquered Indian *empires* (Aztec and Incan), and Columbus never encountered these peoples. As in all other social studies books I have seen, Columbus is not counted among the conquistadors, who have debatable merit. He is not given credit, as he should be, for instituting the encomienda system, which included the first European institution of slavery in the western hemisphere. Nor are students ever told that he was removed and forever banned from Espanola for his failure to properly govern the island's colonists who hated him. As usual, his "accomplishments" on land are ignored.

Critical thinking questions in this series introduce some new perspectives. First, students are asked in what ways Queen Isabella had more wisdom than King John of Portugal. The answer is that she realized she had more to gain than to lose from Columbus's voyage. Since she and John were both making their best educated guesses, it seems fairer to say that such "wisdom" comes from hindsight, and that she was, more realistically, a greater risk-taker. How could she "realize" what there was to gain from a voyage that ultimately brought only surprises?

Readers are also asked if Columbus might have been "exaggerating" when he said that a fish jumped into his boat. Teachers are to explain that he was probably trying to convince people that he had found a land rich in resources, and so he might have exaggerated. Dishonesty then is treated like a somewhat typical fisherman's tale. His credibility is further questioned, and exonerated, in a passage about the fact that he kept two logs at sea and deceived his crew into thinking they had gone less distance than they really had. What does this tell you about him, readers are asked. Possible answer: "that he was clever and knew when to tell people what they wanted to hear." Every child knows how to do this, but adults are much more likely to call them dishonest than clever. What lesson are we teaching students here? If teachers choose to ask the "building citizenship" questions, students will ponder the questions, was Columbus right or wrong, and does the end justify the means? Given the weight of a national holiday attributed to this man's accomplishment, the answer is fairly clear. The authors have not done enough to encourage readers to consider an alternative view, one that is critical of Columbus's character. How differently might they answer these questions if they knew that Columbus later made his sailors sign an oath swearing to say always that Cuba was not an island, but the Asian continent, and that the penalty for stating a differing opinion was financial, as well as having their tongue cut out (Sale, 1990, pp. 147–48).

In summary, the authors of this 1993 series have been careful not to praise Columbus, careful not to criticize him, and careful not to ask provocative questions with enough information provided to encourage critical answers. Although astute students may wonder why we bother to have a national holiday in his honor, few will see any reason to suggest that others might be more deserving.

SUGGESTIONS TO TEACHERS

The current debate about the accomplishments and character of Christopher Columbus clearly began in the public media, not the schools. An earlier quiet debate continues in Columbian scholarship but has barely begun to reach our classrooms. Many elementary teachers will say that it is not appropriate to present lessons on the dark side of human nature to such young children. The dark side of Columbus should be left in the dark until they are old enough to handle it. This argument ignores the fact that our children are fed a constant diet of violence, exploitation, and moral dilemma in the fiction and "news" of their television sets, if not within their own neighborhoods and families. What preparation are they being given to confront and conquer these issues?

My son took a copy of Howard Zinn's chapter on Columbus to his fifth grade teacher and asked why they were not learning this information. The teacher said that he did not think the students would be interested. My son came home and asked for multiple copies. It seemed that Howard Zinn had become a hot underground item on the playground. Not surprisingly, the students who were most interested were members of racial and cultural minorities.

My own students (mostly White majority) tell me that they are angry (and they seem *very* angry) to learn the whole story of Columbus. It is not Columbus they care about. They care about truth and deception. If they cannot trust what they were taught about Columbus, how can they trust anything they have been taught? By learning alternative viewpoints in college, rather than throughout their education, they are learning cynicism. I would much rather that students learn and continually cultivate an educated skepticism. The only way to learn a healthy skepticism is to learn to examine the "facts" from all sides. Thus, it is not valuable to simply praise or condemn Columbus. It is valuable to assess *all* the lessons he taught us through the process of critical thinking. And rather than scapegoating Columbus himself, we need to apply those lessons to the parallels in our own current behaviors.

Teachers who would like to commit themselves to an education in critical thinking would do well to try these things: (1) read Samuel Eliot Morison's *Admiral of the Ocean Sea;* (2) read Kirkpatrick Sale's *The Conquest of Paradise;* (3) assume that neither author knows and tells all of the truth; (4) use *Rethinking Columbus* to develop your own exercises in critical thinking (remembering that *Rethinking Columbus* is not itself above critique [Lynch, 1993, pp. 271–73]); and (5) apply what you have learned from this exercise to all areas of the curriculum.

REFERENCES

Bigelow, B. (1991). Once upon a genocide: Christopher Columbus in children's literature. *Rethinking Columbus.* Milwaukee, WI: Rethinking Schools, 23–30.

Harjo, S. S. (1991). We have no reason to celebrate an invasion. *Rethinking Columbus.* Milwaukee, WI: Rethinking Schools, 4–5.

Knopp, S. L. (1995a). *Critical thinking and Columbus: Secondary social studies.* Unpublished manuscript.

Knopp, S. L. (1995b). *Opportunities lost: Columbus in the geography curriculum.* Unpublished manuscript.

Lynch, L. D. (1993). Columbus in myth and history. In L. J. McCrank, (ed.), *Discovery in the archives of Spain and Portugal: Quincentenary essays, 1492–1992* (pp. 227–87). Binghampton, NY: Haworth Press.

Morison, S. E. (1942). *Admiral of the ocean sea.* Boston: Little, Brown.

National Council for the Social Studies. (1991, October). *The Columbian quincentenary.* Washington, DC.

Sale, K. (1990). *The conquest of paradise: Christopher Columbus and the Columbian legacy.* New York; Penguin Books.

Sewall, G. (Ed.). (1991, Spring). *Social Studies Review, 8.* "Columbus and the Quincentenary" p. 12–14. New York, NY: American Textbook Council.

Sewall, G. (Dir.). (1992, June). Telephone consultations with American Textbook Council. New York.

Zinn, H. (1980). *A People's History of the United States.* New York: Harper & Row.

Sharon L. Knopp is a Multicultural and Gender Equity Consultant.

When Is Work a Learning Experience?

Simply placing young people in workplaces does not guarantee that they will learn. The authors discuss seven principles, derived from a youth apprenticeship demonstration project, that make work-based learning effective.

BY MARY AGNES HAMILTON
AND STEPHEN F. HAMILTON

WORK-BASED learning is a promising complement to conventional school-based learning and a key component of school-to-work opportunities systems. But its promise can be fulfilled only if the experience is of high quality. Workplaces are no more magical than schools; simply placing young people in them does not guarantee that they will learn.

We directed a youth apprenticeship demonstration project for four years. Beginning in grade 11, a total of 100 young people were apprentices in three occupational areas: manufacturing and engineering technology, health care, and administration and office technology. Seven high schools in the Binghamton, New York, area were involved, along with 11 firms, including hospitals, factories, and insurance

MARY AGNES HAMILTON and STEPHEN F. HAMILTON direct the Cornell Youth and Work Program, which is located in the Department of Human Development and Family Studies, College of Human Ecology, Cornell University, Ithaca, N.Y. (http://www.human. cornell.edu/youthwork/). This article is based on material in Mary Agnes Hamilton and Stephen F. Hamilton, Learning Well at Work: Choices for Quality *(National School-to-Work Opportunities Office, 1997).*

companies. The project's chief lessons can be summarized in seven principles for high-quality work-based learning. Note that, although we emphasize work-based learning, the principles also address school-based learning, and connecting activities constitute the key elements of a school-to-work opportunities system, according to the School-to-Work Opportunities Act of 1994.

The seven principles and associated recommendations identify areas in which adults teaching young people in schools and workplaces must make choices that determine the quality of work-based learning. Although we derived the principles from youth apprenticeship programs, we believe that they may be adapted to other types of work-based learning, particularly as the latter become more intensive.

Technical Competence

Principle 1. Youths gain basic and high-level technical competence through challenging work. Work-based learning beyond the exploratory level (e.g., field trips) teaches young people how to perform work tasks. Technical competence includes not only mastering procedures but also understanding the fundamental principles and concepts underlying the procedures, gaining capacity for analytical judgment, and becoming computer literate.

To foster the acquisition of technical competence, designers of work-based learning programs use the same approach used by the designers of classroom instruction: they develop a curriculum. A work-based learning curriculum identifies and sequences learning objectives and specifies the tasks, projects, and activities that enable young people to achieve them.

In addition to learning how to perform work tasks, youths learn how to learn. They acquire a firm foundation of knowledge and skills, appreciation for expertise, confidence in their own ability, and understanding that learning continues for a lifetime. They must learn specific work skills, but those skills should be understood as a foundation for continuous learning, not as ultimate or sufficient in themselves. Through work-based learning, youths prepare to function in learning organizations.

Teaching young people how to perform work tasks is the essence of employment programs—and to a lesser degree of worklike experience programs. In some ways it is also the easiest objective to achieve. Young people in our demonstration project quickly learned to perform a wide range of tasks that are usually considered beyond the capacity of teenagers. They successfully ran tests in pathology labs, published corporate newsletters in human resources departments, tested photographic film quality, and performed a range of other tasks that are usually done by adults with at least two years of postsecondary education. Some filled in when their supervisors were on vacation, demonstrating their capacity to meet employers' expectations for adults.

The most challenging aspect of designing employment programs involves the identification of appropriate learning objectives and then the planning and sequencing of tasks, projects, and other activities that enable youths to achieve those objectives. Because education is fundamental to acquiring high-level technical skills, employers must collaborate with high schools and community colleges, which can provide the disciplinary base for skills and further skill learning, but only if they know what they should be teaching and set high academic standards.

Recommendations. 1) Identify work tasks that teach technical competence; 2) organize learning objectives as modules in core and elective units; and 3) design a multi-year learning plan that is increasingly challenging.

Breadth

Principle 2. Youths gain broad technical competence and understand all aspects of the industry through rotation and projects. Breadth is certainly a quality of technical learning, but it is so critical that it deserves separate treatment. Teaching young people technical competence in a single, specialized area is relatively easy compared to achieving broad technical competence. Broad training teaches young people how to continue learning and reduces the chance that their skills will become obsolete. Multiple skills enable a worker to move readily from one assignment to another, to participate in flexible work teams, and to respond to rapid changes in production that result from changing markets and technology and from short production runs and customized products.

The phrase "all aspects of the industry," which is prominent in the School-to-Work Opportunities Act and in the Perkins Act supporting vocational education, denotes the goal of introducing youths to the larger context in which they do their work—the economic and organizational structures surrounding them. An old story about two stonemasons illustrates the point. When asked, "What are you doing?" one replied, "I'm squaring this stone." The second said, "I'm building a cathedral." Workers who know how their actions contribute to the whole are more motivated than those

whose vision is narrow. They can answer questions and solve problems that go beyond their immediate setting. And they can aspire to a range of career possibilities. A stone finisher can do only one job. A cathedral builder might become a foreman, a contractor, or an architect.

Rotation is the most important way to ensure breadth of experience. Youths should move systematically through several different placements to acquire a variety of skills but also to learn what different units contribute and how they function. Frequent rotations are especially important in the first year or two; they may become less frequent as youths specialize in later years. Program coordinators in some of the firms in our demonstration project were very creative in finding ways to help participants become acquainted with their organizations. For example, moving patients from one part of a hospital to another via wheelchair, gurney, or walking is an excellent way for youths to learn how to deal with patients while also learning about the locations and functions of many different parts of the hospital. A brief placement in the mail room can serve the same purpose for youths in administration and office technology. The tool room can help orient youths in manufacturing and engineering technology.

Project-based learning also ensures breadth and introduces youths to all aspects of an industry. By their nature, projects cut across boundaries and engage young people in aspects of work beyond their daily assignments. Seniors in the demonstration project framed an issue related to their occupational area, planned a complex long-term project that would benefit others, researched their chosen issue using a range of resources, applied academic knowledge, and exhibited their findings.

Recommendations. 1) Inform youths about all aspects of the industry; 2) rotate youths through several departments or placements; and 3) support projects and activities that teach multiple skills and broad knowledge.

Personal and Social Competence

Principle 3. Youths gain personal and social competence in the workplace. Bringing young people into a workplace is quite different from hiring new adult employees. Normal hiring processes are designed to ensure that new employees already have most of the knowledge, skills, and attitudes required to fill a particular position.

Work-based learning programs bring young people who are unqualified for regular employment into a workplace and, over an extended time, qualify them.

Employers frequently say that the qualifications they value most in entry-level employees are not technical skills but such traits as punctuality, reliability, and diligence. They claim that people who have demonstrated personal and social competence can be trained in technical skills. In other words, it is easier to teach people how to work than how to be workers.

Before employers can teach personal and social competence, they must explicitly determine their standards, formulate appropriate learning objectives, and teach young people to achieve them. This is different from using standards to select or dismiss people or, at the opposite extreme, from misdirecting youths by excusing them from meeting standards. Employers teach youths what their standards are and how to meet them.

Meeting during the spring of our demonstration project's second year, workplace teachers concluded that personal and social competence is generic across all industries and collaborated to produce a "Guide to Evaluating Social and Personal Competence," which was used in all three of the occupational areas in which we placed apprentices: manufacturing and engineering technology, health care, and administration and office technology.

The idea of systematically teaching personal and social competence is new and challenging to many people in business. When we interviewed adults who worked with youths in the demonstration project, they said that teaching personal and social competence was more challenging than teaching technical competence. Working with youth apprentices raised new issues for managers, but we learned that many middle managers were uncertain about how to handle issues related to personal and social competence with adult employees as well. Some said they became better managers of adults after learning to deal with youths.

Personal competence encompasses self-confidence, initiative, motivation, commitment to continuous improvement, and career planning. Learning to act like an adult was a common theme in our interviews with youth apprentices, who spoke of growing self-confidence and often noted a contrast between their behavior at work and their behavior in school.

Social competence includes learning about organizational systems—the pur-

Rotation

Over four years apprentice Brian LaPorte rotated through several departments at the Raymond Corporation, a manufacturer of electrically powered fork lift trucks, gaining skills in machining, electronics, and engineering design. During his first year he learned to calibrate the guidance system for two truck models, to check the microprocessors, and to use variable power supplies, chart recorders, and multimeters. The procedures he performed required inductive as well as deductive thinking. Through his work he discovered an aptitude for and curiosity about electronics. At the end of the first year, Brian's manager noted on his evaluation that the next step for him was to master "more hands-on troubleshooting." In an interview at the end of his second year, Brian described a complex task he learned to perform:

> At first I worked with electrical boards. "Wire guidance," they called it, for the trucks. I had to put the circuit board into the fork lift. Then I had to tune it in to where they go by themselves. They'll steer themselves on this grid on the floor, and you have to tune it to stay on the grid. And, you know, it took me quite a while to get it to where I could do it by myself.

poses of an organization, its structure, how one department connects to another, the roles of people in the organization, obligations to clients and customers, and how to gain access to information. Work tasks and projects can provide insights into how the firm operates. When young people understand how their work contributes to the firm as a whole, they are more enthusiastic and more productive.

Some youths have difficulty meeting workplace expectations. For example, poor health care may result in frequent absences. Others may simply fail to understand what is expected and why they should comply. In such instances, convening a small case-management meeting can illuminate the problem and generate strategies to solve it. Participants in the demonstration project's case-management meetings typically included the youth, parents, a school counselor and teacher, the firm's apprenticeship coordinator, and one or more coaches or mentors.

Project-Based Learning

For his senior project at Anitec and Binghamton High School, Blair Dury's coach, Robert Kage, gave him an architectural layout for a new silver analysis laboratory and challenged him to produce a functional design package for its electrical services.

Blair gathered information about power requirements for the test equipment, for the chemical exhaust fans, and for general room power and lighting by reading equipment specifications and nameplate data and interviewing lab technicians and engineers. Design steps included applying the information to size electrical circuits according to the National Electrical Code; specifying the required conduit, wire, circuit breakers, disconnect switches, and so on; and calculating lighting levels. He reviewed all work with the facilities project engineer at each stage.

The design package Blair presented at his exhibition included architectural auto-cad plan-view drawings with associated elevation views, schematics, and single-line diagrams, a bill of materials, and standard construction notes and a scope of work. Panel members who evaluated the exhibition commended the depth of his knowledge about electrical power requirements, the numerous skills acquired in executing the project, the connections to academic knowledge and skills, and the range of resources used.

Recommendations. 1) Recognize personal and social competencies as key learning objectives; 2) systematically teach personal and social competence in context; and 3) through case management, provide extra assistance to youths who lack personal and social competence.

Expectations and Feedback

Principle 4. Workplace teachers convey clear expectations to youths and assess progress toward achieving them. A description of the apprentice's position explains the nature and conditions of employment and outlines associated career possibilities and educational requirements. In addition, working with representatives of workplaces and schools, we developed a Mutual Expectations Agreement, which describes in detail the roles of the key players in a work-based program: employers, schools, apprentices, and parents. Ideally, all four parties sign the agreement at the beginning of the work experience, following a discussion of its contents and of other initial expectations. Work-based learning makes demands on employers that they do not ordinarily face. The agreement helps to spell out expectations without being legalistic.

Evaluation notebooks detail employers' expectations for what youths will learn and serve as a record of their progress and a means for workplace teachers to communicate with them, with schoolteachers and parents, and with one another as the youths rotate through a variety of assignments. Another reason for documenting learning is to substantiate credentials, which are a critical component of work-based learning. Yet no institution can unilaterally issue truly portable credentials. Educational and occupational credentials open career paths for their bearers only when the institutions granting them are accepted as legitimate and the criteria used in granting them are well established and widely recognized. Accreditation agencies review schools and colleges for this purpose. State and professional certification boards govern the granting of credentials in medicine, law, and other professions. Journeyworkers' papers granted to registered apprentices testify that they have met criteria established by unions or state or federal departments of labor. State licenses attest that barbers, hairdressers, plumbers, and electricians have proved their mastery of health and safety issues in those occupations.

Several industry groups are currently developing occupational skills standards, and a National Skills Standards Board has been established. These efforts are steps in the right direction, but years may pass before widely accepted standards and credentials are available for more than a few occupational areas. In the meantime, local and regional standards can communicate to young people what it takes to get a job and to educators what employers expect of schools.

In the absence of standards and associated credentials, individual young people are best advised to build portfolios substantiating their work-related competencies. The use of portfolios as evidence of learning is gaining momentum in secondary education as a reaction against the limitations of conventional grades and test scores. Many colleges are willing to examine students' portfolios instead of or in addition to their transcripts and SAT scores. Work-based learning should be recorded in a portfolio that will be manageable and convincing both to prospective employers and to postsecondary educational institutions. Young people could include completed evaluation notebooks, project reports, letters of recommendation, selected work samples, and a school transcript in their portfolios. A "certified résumé," listing experiences and competencies and signed by a manager, would be useful by itself or as part of a portfolio.

Recommendations. 1) State expectations for behavior and learning at the outset of the work experience; 2) regularly monitor and document the acquisition of competence; 3) provide feedback on progress to youths, school, parents, and firm; 4) encourage youths to assemble a portfolio; and 5) eventually use industrywide standards to provide portable credentials.

Teaching Roles

Principle 5. Youths learn from adults with formally assigned teaching roles. The greatest investment that employers make in work-based learning is the time that is devoted to teaching young people. This would be a substantial investment if adults and youths were paired off one-to-one, as apprentices historically were with independent master craftsmen. Work-based learning as conducted in our demonstration project, in which youths rotate through several departments of a sizable firm, requires that many adults work with each young person. We have records of 251 different adults

in 11 firms who worked extensively with the 100 youths in the project; many of them taught more than one youth. This is a low estimate of the ratio of adults to young people because we know that many other adults were also involved. All adults engaged in any type of work-based learning program need some basic information about the program and the participants, which requires communication, orientation, and continuing support.

We labeled four critical teaching roles at the workplace: coordinator, manager, coach, and mentor. Most adults we interviewed (65 of 70) described interacting with youths in more than one role, such as coaching and mentoring or managing and mentoring. More than one adult might play the same role for a single youth. The point of distinguishing the four roles is to ensure that all are attended to and to promote appropriate orientation, training, and communication. The key responsibilities associated with each role follow.

Coordinator. A coordinator designs a multi-year plan that delineates a career path with various branches, goals, and objectives for learning; core and elective competency units; a rotation plan; and desired academic degrees. The coordinator also links work-based learning to a workplace's strategic plan.[1] For example, a strategic plan might call for cross-training workers, upgrading workers' skill sets, establishing self-managed work teams, and creating a learning organization.

The coordinator is responsible for recruiting, orienting, and supporting adult participants who work with apprentices. The coordinator oversees

rotation, schedules youths in participating departments, and meets with managers to review apprentices' learning progress at each stage.

Coordinators also facilitate communication between the workplace, youths, schools, and families. They collect and distribute young people's evaluation reports, call and facilitate case management meetings, and participate in planning, training, and program development.

Manager. The learning in a department or unit is supervised by a manager. Together with coaches, managers decide what youths will learn within a department (or comparable unit), which work tasks will enhance their learning, and in what order the tasks should be

Gaining Competence

As a junior, Donald Tolerson initiated conversations with his apprenticeship coordinator and managers at the IBM Corporation at Endicott about his desire to learn more and be more productive at work. Consequently, they increased the level of his work on the manufacturing line and in engineering during his senior year, and he began to see how his personal and social skills would enable him to do a good job in a high-performance workplace.

Being on a manufacturing line definitely taught me a lot of discipline, about being to work on time, about how important it is, and getting my job done. Being where I am now is teaching me to have a good outlook for quality. It's showing me how well-rounded you have to be to do a certain job sometimes and how to interact with people. I'm always calling up engineers, asking them questions about blueprints, their quality plans, and it's made my communication better. A lot of it is knowing how well I have to know my job in order to do a good job.

presented. They review youths' learning progress and determine whether the assigned tasks enable them to achieve learning objectives, to contribute to the team's productivity, and to experience continuous learning and challenge.

Managers also assign coaches. Coaches must be sensitive to and interested in young people. They must grasp the principles underlying the program, and they must be competent workers.

Finally, managers organize assessment. Coaches assess young people's learning, but the system of assessment and documentation is designed and maintained centrally by the managers to ensure consistency.

Coach. A coach demonstrates how to do a task while a youth watches.[2] While performing the task, the coach points out important features and checks the youth's understanding by asking questions and encouraging the youth to ask questions. (Reciprocal questioning is also part of the other functions.)

A coach explains how to perform a task correctly. Coaches may explain either while demonstrating or at another time. The explanation sets out performance criteria, points out what problems are likely to occur, and indicates possible problem- solving strategies. Coaches also explain why a task is performed in a certain way. They communicate specifications, provide information about the business management or scientific principles underlying the procedure, and explain how the task relates to other tasks.

Coaches model problem solving. They are responsible for teaching youths to perform routine tasks and for fostering their understanding of what they are doing and why, as well as their capacity to cope with nonroutine events. "Thinking out loud" is the best example of modeling problem solving.

Coaches monitor and critique youths' performance. They give clear and immediate feedback. As the youth gains competence, the coach extends the interval between checks, encouraging the youth to monitor his or her own performance and to seek help when difficulties arise.

Mentor. The task of a mentor is to initiate youths into the workplace culture. When they engage in work-based learning, young people enter a new culture with its own rules, conventions, and norms. A mentor's explanations about the culture of the workplace facilitate the young person's adjustment to the work setting. Mentors advise youths on career directions and opportunities and might describe the hierarchy in an occupational area and explain the educational requirements associated with each step.

Mentors also help to resolve problems. A mentor might help a young person resolve a problem with a manager, with school, with family members, or with peers.

Coaches often become mentors, but not all adults who are effective as coaches are accepted by youths as mentors. We allowed apprentices to choose their own mentors. Other programs assign adults as mentors and train them to perform these functions. We do not insist on our terminology, but we think it is important to distinguish coaching, which entails teaching technical competence, from mentoring, which is teaching personal and social competence. The two responsibilities are quite different and need not be assumed by the same people.

Recommendations. 1) Assign clear teaching roles and responsibilities to coordinators, managers, coaches, and mentors; 2) authorize teaching roles in job descriptions and performance assessments; and 3) orient, train, and support adults who teach young people.

Academic Achievement

Principle 6. Youths achieve high academic standards. If the distinction between head and hand, between academic and vocational education, was ever valid, it is no longer. Jobs that pay well increasingly require a combination of knowledge, communication, problem solving, and technical skill that sounds like a classic definition of the well-educated person.

High school students hoping to have rewarding careers without graduating from four-year colleges must enroll in courses previously considered appropriate only for those bound for selective colleges. Work-based learning presents a major challenge and a tremendous opportunity for schools to connect academic learning more closely with the real world, a connection that will benefit not only the students in what have been general and vocational tracks but also college-bound students, many of whom are adept at learning abstract information for tests but unable to use what they have learned by applying it to solve real problems.

Young people should know while they are in high school what they will have to do to achieve their career goals. If their goal is first to graduate from a four-year college, then it is clear what they must do to gain admission. When employers publicly advocate higher academic standards and then use those standards to make hiring decisions, they send a very powerful message. When schools reorganize to teach all students, they will help to release human resources that are currently wasted when we define more than half of our high school students as unable to learn.

Our demonstration project showed that specific institutional practices are needed to communicate high standards and help young people meet them. Courses designed to teach high-level content in engaging ways are one

> *Coaches must be sensitive to and interested in young people.*

Questioning

Earl Lee, a manager at IBM Endicott, explained how he managed apprentice Donald Tolerson's work and learning. As a *manager* he designated areas in a large department where Tolerson would work. As a *coach,* he insisted on high standards in work products. The intensity of the relationship that resulted led to Tolerson's accepting Lee as a *mentor* who could teach him workplace rules, advise him about his career path, and counsel him about his social life.

On Monday mornings we had a one-on-one meeting. I told him what we should try to do with the project, and then I would give Don, say, a week or so to do some things with it, and he would walk back in with his outline—this was what he thought he wanted to do. And I basically had Don justify that outline. I could have pretty easily told Don, "This is what I want you to do." But I thought it was important that Don be able to rationalize and justify why he made the decision he made. What I was really trying to get out of him was problem solving, critical thinking. Whenever he came to me and he was at a roadblock and didn't know where to go, I would ask him, "What do you think you would do?" And what I wanted from him were two or three different alternatives because if he understood the problem and he understood the options he had, then we could go down and jointly evaluate and analyze each option. And that's the way we went through things.

such practice. Schedules must become more flexible to enable work-based learning. Another needed reform is the creation of comprehensive advising systems involving not only school counselors but also teachers, parents, and mentors at the work site. Teachers and counselors will be most effective if they are able to learn firsthand about the academic content of contemporary workplaces through visits, meetings, and internships.

Finally, curricula and instructional practices should integrate academic education with vocational education and school-based learning with work-based learning.

Recommendations. Workplaces, schools, and postsecondary institutions should work closely together to 1) set high academic standards; 2) specify courses and degrees related to the career areas; and 3) open multiple options for postsecondary education.

Career Paths

Principle 7. Youths identify and follow career paths. A career path traces a lifelong occupational journey involving both education and employment—not a single job or even a single occupation. By this definition, some career paths are smooth and direct, while others are rough and full of dead ends; some lead to well-paid and prestigious employment, but others do not.

A path is not a track. It allows for changes in direction and can lead toward several destinations. A good career path provides a sense of direction and a purpose for academic achievement so that a young person is well prepared even if he or she later chooses a different path. No one has ever been able to predict precisely where his or her own or someone else's career will lead, and certainty about the future is now inconceivable. But if we can give more young people a better sense of what they can do in the future and what they have to do to prepare, they will be better able to make good choices and to adapt to uncertainty.

A high school senior without a vision of a career path may see no reason to take an additional math or science course in the senior year and may therefore opt to take no more than the required courses. A student who takes an extra science course because she wants to becomes a physical therapy assistant not only prepares for that career goal but also preserves the option of continuing her studies to become a physical therapist or a physician, options foreclosed or at least

made less attainable if she takes only the minimum requirements to graduate from high school.

Employers who invest in work-based learning to improve the quality of their future work force should take a long view of what is needed. They cannot expect that every youth will continue in a related career path, much less that all will become their employees. Employers can increase the return on their investment by selecting young people who have already had exploratory work-based learning experience and who have learned enough about the occupational area to make a reasonable commitment to a related career path. If employers in a community join together to provide a range of work-based and school-based learning opportunities, all students will be better able to decide whether they wish to participate in work-based learning and, if so, in what occupational area.

Recommendations. 1) Provide opportunities for career exploration and information on related careers; 2) advise youths about career paths, coordinating planning with high school and college advisors and parents; and 3) pay particular attention to the postsecondary school transition.

Next Steps

The experience of operating a youth apprenticeship demonstration project has left us optimistic about the prospects for creating a more effective system to foster the transition from adolescence into adulthood in the United States, a system that uses workplaces as learning environments for youth. The experience has also revealed the magnitude of the task. Following are the steps we see as most critical to success.

1. *Restructure schools and workplaces.* Commitment is more than willingness to participate. An employer, for example, might join a school-to-work partnership primarily as a gesture of support to the community but without accepting its aims and its guiding principles. If an employer is motivated by no more than civic duty, then a downturn in earnings will quickly terminate participation. Similarly, if schools are primarily concerned about dealing with students who are not served well by current programs, they are unlikely to engage in the kind of restructuring that school-to-work requires, especially enabling all students to meet high academic standards.

The opposite of commitment is rejection, but in many ways straightforward rejection is less insidious than participation without commitment. The greatest threat to the integrity of school-to-work is its nominal adoption, perhaps simply by using the term to describe current activities without attempting the restructuring that true commitment entails.

We see a striking parallel between the kinds of commitments school-to-work requires of schools and of work-

<hr />

Academic Learning And the Real World

Joyce Golden's account of a marginal math student explaining the concept and use of standard deviation helps illustrate the rationale for work-based learning. Her opportunity to visit workplaces and meet the people from business brought a new dimension to her classroom.

When material can be made meaningful to their everyday life as it is in the workplace, it has some relevance. I had a couple of good examples this year where apprenticeships were a factor in my classroom instruction, and that would not have happened if I had not been familiar with the work environment. One was teaching standard deviation with a student who was doing very poorly in math. I was able to day, "Gee, I think we use standard deviation in the workplace. I wonder if someone could tell us what that means?" And sure enough [finger snap], it came to life, and he explained exactly what a standard deviation was, why it was important to the statistical research of the company, and how he was using it on a regular basis. No problem whatsoever because it was in a meaningful context for him. So that was application for the whole class, but he would not have volunteered if I hadn't known enough to go for it. It was my familiarity with what they were doing and what he was doing that made me able to use that kind of knowledge. Unfortunately, few teachers have had those opportunities.

> *Nominal adoption is the greatest threat to school-to-work.*

places. Both schools and workplaces must be willing to:

- increase the breadth and depth of learning,
- ensure equal access to learning,
- assign staff to organize and monitor work-based learning, and
- maintain a learning organization.

2. *Form partnerships.* The demonstration project confirmed that partnership is essential among employers, employees, and their organizations; educators and school systems; legislators and government agencies; parents; youths; and community organizations. Once they have committed themselves to the goals of school-to-work, the partners must define their roles and responsibilities and establish a working relationship that enables each one to contribute. They succeed when the partners are able to establish a joint strategy, respect one another's needs and strengths, and negotiate to resolve their differences. The partner organizations and groups have purposes, cultures, and structures that keep them separate from one another. Changing a single institution is daunting enough; creating functional partnerships is a challenge of the first magnitude because it requires coordinating changes in several institutions. Institutional inertia and self-protective tendencies are serious barriers. But there is no alternative. None of the partners can succeed alone.

3. *Build a school-to-work system.* No single type of work-based learning is adequate by itself. Field trips, service learning, youth-run enterprises, and other approaches all increase young people's awareness of their own talents and inclinations and of the opportunities available to them. Youths who enter apprenticeship programs need to have explored careers beforehand via work-based opportunities. Employers who wish to use youth apprenticeship as a means of improving the quality of their work force will find that their investment pays off at a higher rate if they first provide young people with job shadowing and other exploratory opportunities. If the investment required by youth apprenticeship is too great, then cooperative education, internships, and other types of work-based learning may suffice. Nearly three-quarters of high school seniors work during at least part of the school year. Augmenting standard youth jobs to make them into opportunities for work-based learning has greater potential for involving all youths than any other step. The goal should be to provide in every community a complement of work-based learning opportunities to meet a range of needs among both young people and employers.

Moreover, in addition to work-based learning, a school-to-work opportunities system includes appropriate and effective school-based learning and multiple connections between the two. Although we have not addressed those components separately, the demonstration project confirmed that work-based learning must be supported by changes in schools and by an array of connecting activities, as the principles and choices described above make clear.

A *system* differs from a *program*. A system is:

- inclusive—it has a place for everyone who needs one;
- comprehensive—it addresses the full range of relevant issues;
- integrated internally—its components are closely linked (e.g., school-based learning and work-based learning);
- connected externally—it builds on what comes before and leads on to something else (e.g., school-to-work connects with higher education and with the labor market); and
- comprehensible—participants understand it and can navigate through it with help of parents and other advisors.

4. *Continue research and development.* We do not yet know how to accomplish the goals of school-to-work. Research and development cannot answer all the questions that remain, but it would be unwise to proceed without continued monitoring and testing. Ideally this investigation will be done in a manner and on a schedule that informs practitioners who are designing and operating systems. We hope that the principles and choices proposed here will serve as a framework for some of the needed research and development.

Conclusion

The growing disparity between the well-educated affluent and the inadequately educated who struggle to maintain a decent standard of living must be reduced if the United States is to remain a prosperous and secure democracy. Education cannot reduce that disparity without complementary changes in the economy, particularly the labor market. But education—in the form of the school-to-work initiative, and especially work-based learning—is a powerful means of improving the knowledge and skills of the American work force, which is, after all, most of our citizens. Work-based learning that adheres to the principles we have stated will contribute to but also depend on never-ending progress toward the promise of freedom and opportunity that is the American dream.

---

1. Heidi Bowne, former vice president for human resources at the Raymond Corporation, alerted us to the importance of linking youth apprenticeship with a firm's strategic plan and demonstrated how that can be done. Bowne made sure that the program with the young people contributed to a human resource strategy that was, in turn, a part of the firm's strategic plan. The Raymond Corporation was committed to increasing the skill level and flexibility of its employees and designed its apprenticeships to produce highly skilled workers with many competencies.

2. Some programs use the German term *Meister* (master) for the person who performs this role. We have not done so for several reasons. A German *Meister* is literally a master of a craft, and only a *Meister* is formally permitted to train apprentices. In practice, however, most German apprentices spend most of their time working alongside a journeyworker; the *Meister* functions more as what we call a manager. In the United States, a coach is more like what the Swiss call a *Lehrmeister*, who is formally trained and certified as an apprentice trainer, but without the courses and examinations that would qualify him or her as master of a trade.

SEVENTY-FIVE YEARS LATER . . .

Gender-Based Harassment in Schools

KATHRYN SCOTT

On the seventy-fifth anniversary of women's suffrage, we can celebrate significant advances in the legal status, opportunities, and achievements of women in the United States. Whereas in the early twentieth century, sex-segregated education was the norm in secondary schools and higher education, today's public policy upholds integrated institutions. The 1972 Civil Rights Act Title IX prohibited sexual or racial discrimination against students and staff in public education. Since then, legal challenges by students and women activists have resulted in greater gender equity in student access, curriculum, academic achievement, and extra-curricular activities, including sports.

Although women have gained greater access and visibility in the public arena, glaring disparities among the experiences of females, males, and people of color are evident today in both public and private spheres. What has gone largely unnoticed in schools is widespread gender-based harassment—unwanted and unwelcome sexual words or actions that can begin as early as the elementary years (Best 1983; Bogart, et al. 1992).

Sexual harassment and domestic violence became front page news in the 1990s with events such as the Anita Hill—Clarence Thomas Senate hearings, the Navy Tailhook scandal, and the O.J. Simpson trial. Although the 1964 Civil Rights Act made it illegal to engage in sexual or racial discrimination in the workplace, it was not until 1986 that the courts recognized sexual harassment on the job as a form of illegal discrimination and determined that allowing an environment of sexual harassment is unlawful (Meritor State Bank v. Vinson). Since then, plaintiffs have brought successful court suits using a definition of sexual harassment that includes individual cases of harassment as well as a sexually hostile work environment. However, the majority of instances of sexual harassment in the workplace and in schools are never reported.

Identifying Sexual Harassment

What constitutes gender-based harassment? Considerable misunderstanding surrounds the distinction between flirting, which is generally welcomed by the recipient, and sexual harassment, which is demeaning and unwanted. Under the law, the distinction is determined not by the intent of the behavior, but by its impact. Sexual harassment is any type of unwelcome conduct, verbal or nonverbal, directed toward an individual because of his or her gender. It is often more an expression of power than sexual interest and is considered a form of sex discrimination under the law (Seigel, Hallgarth, and Capek 1992). If the initiator believes that she or he is just being "cool" or "joking around" but the respondent feels demeaned or degraded, then harassment has occurred (see Chart 1). Targets of unwanted sexual talk or actions, usually females, often feel intimidated, embarrassed, and afraid, often blaming themselves.

Social norms, however, perpetuate and may actually encourage gender-based harassment through the barrage of sexual images in television, music, movies, and other media. Social norms also support gender stereotypes that treat females as sex objects and males as predators. Teachers and administrators frequently overlook or excuse gender-based harassment among peers as "boys will be boys," normal childhood teasing, or teenage flirting. When complaints are made by students, they are often downplayed or ignored by adults (Bogart et

Chart 1

A Comparison of the Impact of Flirting and Sexual Harassment

Flirting	Harassment
Feels good	Feels bad
Reciprocal (two-way)	Power-based (one-way)
Feel attractive	Feel degraded
Feel in control	Feel powerless
Open-ended	Invasive
Flattered	Demeaned
Confident	Confused
Self-assured	Afraid

Adapted from It's Not Fun/It's Illegal: The Identification and Prevention of Sexual Harassment to Teenagers. *St. Paul: Minnesota Department of Education, 1988, p. 70.*

From *Social Education,* September 1995, pp. 293–297. © 1995 by the National Council for the Social Studies. Reprinted by permission.

Chart 2

Myths and Realities about Gender-Based Harassment

1. MYTH: Sexual harassment is just having fun.
REALITY: Sexual harassment is in the eye of the beholder. Joking or teasing can be one-sided, at the expense of another who experiences harassment.

2. MYTH: Saying "no" is usually enough to stop harassment.
REALITY: Sexual harassment is often motivated by power and a "no" may be ignored or even trigger escalation. It is often difficult for a student to say "no" to a school authority, such as a teacher or coach, or even a popular peer.

3. MYTH: A girl who dresses in a sexually attractive way is asking to be harassed.
REALITY: This statement blames the victim. A response of sexual harassment differs from sexual attraction, which can be expressed in a complimentary way. Unfortunately social norms encourage males to be sexually aggressive or "macho," often at the expense of females.

4. MYTH: If a student has flirted in the past with a harasser, then there's nothing s/he can do.
REALITY: Flirting is a mutual encounter that makes both individuals feel good. What is wanted one day may be unwelcome another and is not an excuse for unwelcome sexual aggression.

5. MYTH: Most males enjoy getting sexual attention at school.
REALITY: As reported in a 1993 study for the American Association of University Women, the majority of boys have experienced sexual harassment, unwanted talk or behaviors, though they may be generally less upset by it than females, unwilling to acknowledge it as unwanted.

6. MYTH: Given the many responsibilities teachers have to educate students, schools can not be expected to intervene when verbal or nonphysical sexual harassment occurs among students.
REALITY: Under the law, schools have the responsibility to ensure students a learning environment free of sexual harassment, which is a form of sex discrimination that can be verbal or nonverbal as well as physical.

7. MYTH: Calling a boy "sissy" or "wimp" would not be considered gender-based harassment.
REALITY: The English language has many gender-based terms of derision. "Sissy" and "wimp" are terms that incorporate negative stereotypical images of females to insult males (and females at times).

8. MYTH: Elementary-aged students are too young to sexually harass other students or experience effects of sexual harassment from peers.
REALITY: Starting at very young ages, children tease each other using sexual stereotypes of females and males. Sexual touching and verbal abuse with sexually explicit language among elementary school students are increasing.

9. MYTH: Sexual harassment cannot occur between same-sexed peers.
REALITY: More than 20 percent of harassment of males is by other males. Homophobic terms such as "fag," "queer," or "homo" are common insults of boys. Although less common, girls harass other girls by initiating sexual rumors or writing bathroom graffiti.

10. MYTH: Students usually report incidents of sexual harassment.
REALITY: Most incidents of sexual harassment go unreported. Victims may think that reporting will not make any difference, that they will not be taken seriously, or that they will be blamed for the behavior.

For more information, see: Minnesota Department of Education (MDE). Girls and Boys Getting Along: Teaching Sexual Harassment Prevention in the Elementary Classroom. St. Paul: Minnesota Department of Education, 1993; Nan Stein and Lisa Sjostrom. Flirting or Hurting? A Teacher's Guide on Student-to-Student Sexual Harassment in Schools (grades 6–12). Washington, D.C.: National Education Association, 1994; Susan Strauss. Sexual Harassment and Teens: A Program for Positive Change. Minneapolis, Minnesota: Free Spirit Publishing Inc., 1992.

al. 1992; Stein 1993). Chart 2 discusses some of the common myths about sexual harassment held by young people and adults alike.

Harassment Is Widespread

Two recent nationwide surveys of students provide substantial documentation of sexual harassment in schools and its effects on students (AAUW 1993; Stein, Marshall, and Tropp 1993). In a survey of more than 1,600 girls and boys that was conducted by Louis Harris and Associates for the educational foundation of the American Association of University Women (AAUW 1993), 81 percent of all students reported at least one incident of school-related sexual harassment, defined as "unwanted and unwelcome sexual behavior which interferes with your life" (see Chart 3). The AAUW study presents further evidence in support of an earlier survey of readers of the magazine *Seventeen* in which 39 percent of the female respondents indicated that they experienced some form of sexual harassment daily in school-related activities (Stein, Marshall, and Tropp 1993).

Researchers in the AAUW study took a representative sample of African American, Hispanic, and white students in grades 8–11 from seventy-nine schools nationwide. Boys (76 percent) as well as girls (85 percent) reported being targets of sexual harassment, with girls (66 percent) likely to experience harassment more frequently than were boys (49 percent). Peer-to-peer harassment typified the majority of incidents (79 percent), most of which occurred in the classrooms or hallways where other students or adults were likely to be bystanders.

Sexual comments, jokes, gestures, or looks were the most frequent (66 percent) forms of harassment. Girls were more likely to experience almost every form of harassment than were boys (see Chart 3), with the most notable exception that boys were more likely to be harassed by being called gay (23 percent) than were girls (10 percent). Boys were also much more likely to be harassed by other boys alone or in a group (38 percent) than were girls by other girls (13 percent). More than half of all respondents knew of complaints of harassment that had been ignored by school officials.

One-third of harassed students first experienced unwanted sexual talk or actions as early as elementary school, with the majority first aware of unwelcome sexual behavior in the middle school or junior high grades. However, twice as many boys (36 percent) as girls (17 percent) could not remember the grade in which they first encountered sexual harassment. Adults in the school setting (e.g., teachers, coaches, bus drivers) were responsible for almost 20 percent of incidents. Girls (25 percent) in general were more likely than were boys (10 percent) to be targets of adult sexual harassment, with African American girls (33 percent) the most frequent targets.

The greatest gaps between girls' and boys' experiences of harassment reported in the AAUW study appeared in the greater discomfort and educational harm experienced by girls (Chart 4). Boys tended to take sexual overtures in stride with less emotional, educational, or behavioral impact on their lives. Whereas only 24 percent of the boys became "very upset" or "somewhat upset" by their experiences, 70 percent of the girls felt this way. Harassment influenced females to such an extent that a far greater proportion of them stayed home from school, participated less frequently in classroom discussions, had difficulty concentrating in class and studying, and made lower test grades and report card grades as a result of being harassed (see Chart 5). Girls also took greater pains than did boys to avoid the person(s) who harassed them (69 percent) and restricted their activities at school (34 percent).

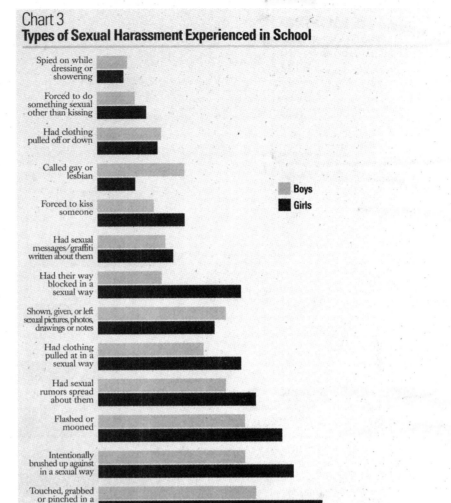

Chart 3
Types of Sexual Harassment Experienced in School

(Boys, Girls) Categories from top to bottom: Spied on while dressing or showering; Forced to do something sexual other than kissing; Had clothing pulled off or down; Called gay or lesbian; Forced to kiss someone; Had sexual messages/graffiti written about them; Had their way blocked in a sexual way; Shown, given, or left sexual pictures, photos, drawings or notes; Had clothing pulled at in a sexual way; Had sexual rumors spread about them; Flashed or mooned; Intentionally brushed up against in a sexual way; Touched, grabbed or pinched in a sexual way; Sexual comments, jokes, gestures or looks.

Adapted from AAUW. Hostile Hallways. *Washington, DC: The Educational Foundation of the American Association of University Women, 1993.*

Understanding Gender-Based Harassment

The differential impact of sexual harassment on females and males should not be surprising, given the greater cultural and structural power generally bestowed on males in U.S. culture. Males learn from a very early age that they can use informal power to intimidate others verbally and physically, often in quite socially acceptable ways. In contrast, females are socialized to eschew power through nurturing roles and put other people's feelings first (Stein 1993). They may at times stifle their own feelings so as not to hurt another and, in the process, internalize others' condescension, disapproval, or even hostility, resulting in their lowered self-esteem. As a consequence, females may not recognize situations of harassment or abuse.

Beginning in the elementary school years and throughout adulthood, females who do object to harassment are often silenced through ridicule, blame, or exclusion (Bogart et al. 1992). For example, females who respond negatively to being harassed may be accused of being "too sensitive" or "not being able to take a joke." Or they may be accused by males of having "asked for it" by wearing attractive clothes. The fear of disapproval or rejection by males may also be sufficient to create a wall of silence supported by other women who do not want to take the risk of "rocking the boat." Especially during middle school years, both boys and girls are more likely to adopt peer norms at whatever price to achieve acceptance.

Legal Sanctions Against Harassment

Until the 1990s, there were no significant legal decisions defining a school's responsibility should gender-based harassment occur. In 1992, the U.S. Supreme Court unanimously ruled in the case of Franklin v. Gwinnett County

Public Schools that under Title IX of 1972 a student could seek monetary damages from the schools and school officials. The student bringing charges had been subjected to unwanted sexual attention from a high school social studies teacher in suburban Atlanta, Georgia, and was discouraged from filing charges by the district.

Another ground-breaking case was the first ruling on student-to-student harassment by the U.S. Department of Education that determined in 1993 that the Minnesota Eden Prairie Schools had violated federal law in "failing to take timely and effective responsive action to address . . . multiple or severe acts of a sexual harassment" (cited in Eaton 1994). This decision stemmed from complaints filed on behalf of eight elementary-grade girls who, while riding the school bus, had been repeated targets of a group of boys calling them "bitches" with "stinky vaginas."

In recognizing peer harassment, the Office for Civil Rights (OCR) declared that a school district violated Title IX "when it knew or should have known that a sexually hostile environment exists due to student-to-student harassment." A hostile environment was defined as one where "acts of a sexual nature are sufficiently severe or pervasive to impair educational benefits," including school-related activities such as school busing (cited in Eaton 1994). Although the Eden Prairie Schools had policies in effect prohibiting student-to-student harassment, they had considered the bus incidents as instances of "bad language," while the OCR considered the instances from the point of view of the victims, declaring "there is no question that even the youngest girls understood that the language and conduct being used were expressions of hostility toward them on the basis of their sex."

Policy and Prevention

With the growing public awareness of gender-based harassment and willingness of courts to permit monetary restitution, educators have an increased impetus to ensure that their schools are free from sexually hostile environments and that students are aware of their right to a gender-safe education. Districts have the obligation to develop and implement a school policy to handle the problem (see Chart 6). Although many

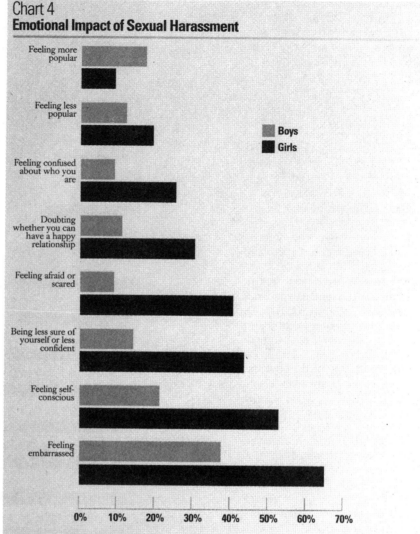

Chart 4
Emotional Impact of Sexual Harassment

- Feeling more popular
- Feeling less popular
- Feeling confused about who you are
- Doubting whether you can have a happy relationship
- Feeling afraid or scared
- Being less sure of yourself or less confident
- Feeling self-conscious
- Feeling embarrassed

■ Boys
■ Girls

0% 10% 20% 30% 40% 50% 60% 70%

Adapted from AAUW. Hostile Hallways. *Washington, DC: The Educational Foundation of the American Association of University Women, 1993.*

school districts have written policies barring harassment, only rarely are they fully understood or enforced (Eaton 1994).

By involving teachers, administrators, and students in creating a policy, schools can begin to address the issue at the grassroots level. With a clear statement of what constitutes gender-based harassment and a complaint procedure that ensures confidentiality, educators can send a message that complaints will be taken seriously and that students will be protected from retaliation. Parents and school staff also need to be educated about the problem and informed of the policy.

Although most acts of gender-based harassment occur in school corridors and classrooms in full view of others,

most teachers and administrators are unclear about what constitutes illegal harassment or are unaware of the widespread prevalence of gender-based harassment and its impact on students. No longer is it advisable for teachers or administrators to ignore student harassment or dismiss student complaints. Educators and parents have a responsibility to teach today's youth respect for others, educate them to respond to abuse, and intervene where a hostile climate exists.

Sources

American Association of University Women. *Hostile Hallways: The AAUW Survey on Sexual Harassment in America's Schools.* Washington, D.C.: American Association of University Women Educational Foundation, 1993.

Chart 5
Educational Impact of Sexual Harassment

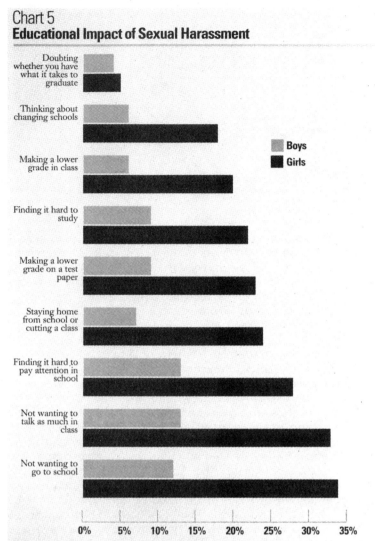

Boys
Girls

Doubting whether you have what it takes to graduate

Thinking about changing schools

Making a lower grade in class

Finding it hard to study

Making a lower grade on a test paper

Staying home from school or cutting a class

Finding it hard to pay attention in school

Not wanting to talk as much in class

Not wanting to go to school

0% 5% 10% 15% 20% 25% 30% 35%

Adapted from AAUW. Hostile Hallways. Washington, DC: The Educational Foundation of the American Association of University Women, 1993.

Chart 6

What Are the Key Elements of a Good Sexual Harassment Policy?

The Process of Adopting a Policy
In writing a sexual harassment policy, include representatives from all the constituencies in each school such as teachers, staff members, and students if possible.

Prohibition of Sexual Harassment
The policy should contain a clear and forceful statement by the school superintendent and/or top administrators that harassment is prohibited and will not be tolerated.

Definition of Sexual Harassment
The policy should concisely describe what behavior is prohibited and should include specific examples.

Complaint Procedures
The policy should clearly explain how to file a complaint.

Sanctions
The policy should detail what sanctions will apply for engaging in prohibited activity.

Confidentiality
Confidential investigations are critical to protect everyone involved.

Protection Against Retaliation
Students will not be comfortable coming forward unless they are confident that they will be treated fairly and not further harmed.

Investigations
The policy should provide for a neutral and well-trained investigator to follow up on complaints.

Policy Distribution
The policy must reach every member of the community.

Education and Training
All students, teachers, and staff should participate in education and training on sexual harassment.

Support Services
The policy should include information about individuals such as nurses, counselors, psychologists, and social workers who are available to help students determine if they have been harassed and cope with the effects of harassment.

Mechanisms for Feedback
Procedures are needed for an annual review of the policy, procedures, and programs at each school as well as an annual evaluation of the sensitivity of those handling and investigating complaints.

Adapted from NOW Legal Defense and Education Fund Legal Resource Kit in Issues Quarterly: An Intelligent Resource for Research, Policy, and Action Affecting the Lives of Women and Girls. Published by the National Council for Research on Women, 1994, vol. 1(1), p. 8.

Best, Raphaella. *We've All Got Scars: What Boys and Girls Learn in Elementary School.* Bloomington: Indiana University Press, 1983.

Bogart, K., S. Simmons, N. Stein, and E. P. Tomaszewski. "Breaking the Silence: Sexual and Gender-Based Harassment in Elementary, Secondary, and Post-Secondary Education." In *Sex Equity and Sexuality in Education,* edited by S. S. Klein. Albany: State University of New York Press, 1992.

Eaton, Susan. "Sexual Harassment at an Early Age: New Cases Are Changing the Rules for Schools." In *The Best of the Harvard Education Letter.* Cambridge, Massachusetts: Harvard Graduate School of Education, 1994.

Seigel, D. L., S. A. Hallgarth, and M. E. Capek. *Sexual Harassment: Research and Resources.* New York: The National Council for Research on Women, 1992.

Stein, Nan, N. L. Marshall, and L. R. Tropp. *Secrets in Public: Sexual Harassment in Our Schools.* Wellesley, Massachusetts: Wellesley College Center for Research on Women, 1993.

Stein, Nan D. "It Happens Here, Too: Sexual Harassment and Child Sexual Abuse in Elementary and Secondary Schools." In *Gender and Education,* edited by S. K. Biklen and D. Pollard. Ninety-Second Yearbook of the National Society for the Study of Education. Chicago: University of Chicago Press, 1993.

Kathryn Scott, professor of educational theory and practice at Florida State University, has published more than twenty articles and book chapters on gender in education. She teaches social studies education for elementary teachers.

The Profession of Teaching Today

The task of helping teachers to grow in their levels of expertise in the classroom falls heavily on those educators who provide professional staff development training in the schools. Meaningful staff development training is extremely important. Several professional concerns are very real in the early career development of teachers. Level of job security or tenure is still an issue, as are the concerns of first-year teachers and teacher educators. How teachers interact with students is a concern to all conscientious, thoughtful teachers.

We continue the dialogue over what makes a teacher "good." There are numerous external pressures on the teaching profession today from a variety of public interest groups. The profession continues to develop its knowledge base on effective teaching through ethnographic and empirical inquiry on classroom practice and teacher behavior in elementary and secondary classrooms across the nation. Concern continues as to how best to teach to enhance insightful, reflective student interaction with the content of instruction. We continue to consider alternative visions of literacy and the roles of teachers in fostering a desire for learning within their students.

All of us who live the life of a teacher are aware of those features that we associate with the concept of a good teacher. In addition, we do well to remember that the teacher/student relationship is both a tacit and an explicit one—one in which teacher attitude and emotional outreach are as important as student response to our instructional effort. The teacher/student bond in the teaching/learning process cannot be overemphasized; teaching is a two-way street. We must maintain an emotional link in the teacher/student relationship that will compel students to want to accept instruction and attain optimal learning. What, then, constitutes those most defensible standards for assessing good teaching?

The past decade has yielded much in-depth research on the various levels of expertise in the practice of teaching. We know much more now than in the 1970s about specific teaching competencies and how they are acquired. Expert teachers do differ from novices and experienced teachers in terms of their capacity to exhibit accurate, integrated, and holistic perceptions and analyses of what goes on when students try to learn in classroom settings. We can now pinpoint some of these qualitative differences.

As the knowledge base of our professional practice continues to expand, we will be able to certify with greater precision what constitutes acceptable ranges of teacher performance based on more clearly defined procedures of practice, as we have, for example, in medicine and dentistry. Medicine is, after all, a practical art as well as a science—and so is teaching. The analogy in terms of setting standards of professional practice is a strong one. Yet the emotional pressure on teachers that theirs is also a performing art, and that clear standards of practice can be applied to that art, is a bitter pill to swallow for many. Hence, the intense reaction of many teachers against external competency testing and any rigorous classroom observation standards. The writing, however, is on the wall: the profession cannot hide behind the tradition that teaching is a special art, unlike all others, which cannot be subjected to objective observational standards, aesthetic critique, or to a standard knowledge base. Those years are behind us. The public demands the same levels of demonstrable professional standards of practice as are demanded of those in the medical arts.

Likewise, we have identified certain approaches to working with students in the classroom that have been effective. Classroom practices such as cooperative learning strategies have won widespread support for inclusion in the knowledge base on teaching. The knowledge base of the social psychology of life in classrooms has been significantly expanded by collaborative research between classroom teachers and various specialists in psychology and teacher education. This has been accomplished by using anthropological field research techniques to ground theory of classroom practice into demonstrable phenomenological perspectives. Many issues have been raised—and answers found—by basic ethnographic field observations, interviews, and anecdotal record-keeping techniques to understand more precisely how teachers and students interact in the classroom. A rich dialectic is developing among teachers regarding the description of ideal classroom environments. The methodological insight from this research into the day-to-day realities of life in schools is transforming what we know about teaching as a professional activity and how to best advance our knowledge of effective teaching strategies.

Creative, insightful persons who become teachers will usually find ways to network their interests and concerns with other teachers and will make their own opportunities for creative teaching in spite of external assessment procedures. They acknowledge that the science of teaching involves the observation and measurement of teaching be-

processes and formulate questions according to their perceptions of how students are responding to the material.

To build their aspirations, as well as their self-confidence, teachers must be motivated to an even greater effort for professional growth in the midst of these fundamental revisions. Teachers need support, appreciation, and respect. Simply criticizing them while refusing to alter social and economic conditions that affect the quality of their work will not solve their problems, nor will it lead to excellence in education. Not only must teachers work to improve their public image and the public's confidence in them, but the public must confront its own misunderstandings of the level of commitment required to achieve teacher excellence—and their share of responsibility in that task. Teachers need to know that the public cares about and respects them enough to fund their professional improvement in a primary recognition that they are an all-important force in the life of this nation. The articles in this unit consider the quality of education and the status of the teaching profession today.

Looking Ahead: Challenge Questions

What is "expertise" in teaching? Be specific; use examples.

What are some ways in which teacher/student classroom interaction can be studied?

What do you think of efforts to "reinvent" schools? What are your own visions of what is possible in schooling?

Why has the knowledge base of teaching expanded so dramatically in recent years?

List by order of importance what you think are the five most vital issues confronting the teaching profession today. What criteria did you use in ranking these issues? What is your position on each of them?

What does gaining a student's assent to a teacher's instructional effort mean to you?

What are the most defensible standards to assess the quality of a teaching performance?

What is the role of creativity in the classroom?

What political pressures do teachers in the United States face today?

Can teachers be sufficiently imaginative in their teaching and still get students to meet standardized objective test requirements? What are the issues to be considered regarding assessment of student learning?

haviors but that the art of teaching involves the humanistic dimensions of instructional activities, an alertness to the details of what is taught, and equal alertness to how students receive it. Creative, insightful teachers guide class

THE QUIET REVOLUTION

Rethinking Teacher Development

Reforms that invest time in teacher learning and give teachers greater autonomy are our best hope for improving America's schools.

Linda Darling-Hammond

Over the last decade, a quiet revolution in teaching has been under way. The profession has begun to engage in serious standard-setting that reflects a growing knowledge base and a growing consensus about what teachers should know and be able to do to help all students learn according to challenging new standards. Most states have launched efforts to restructure schools and to invest in greater teacher knowledge.

Changes are also taking place in teacher preparation programs across the country; performance-based approaches to licensing and accreditation are being reconsidered; and a new National Board for Professional Teaching Standards has created assessments for certifying accomplished teachers. School districts and grass roots networks are creating partnerships to support teacher development and to rethink schools.

These initiatives are partly a response to major changes affecting our society and our schools. Because rapid social and economic transformations require greater learning from all students, society is reshaping the mission of education. Schools are now expected not only to offer education, but to ensure learning. Teachers are expected not only to "cover the curriculum" but to create a bridge between the needs of each learner and the attainment of challenging learning goals.

These objectives—a radical departure from education's mission during the past century—demand that teachers understand learners and their learning as deeply as they comprehend their subjects, and that schools structure themselves to support deeper forms of student and teacher learning than they currently permit. The invention of 21st century schools that can educate all children well rests, first and foremost, upon the development of a highly qualified and committed teaching force.

As recently as 10 years ago, the idea that teacher knowledge was critical for educational improvement had little currency. Continuing a tradition begun at the turn of the 20th century, policymakers searched for the right set of test prescriptions, textbook adoptions, and curriculum directives to be packaged and mandated to guide practice. Educational reform was "teacher proofed" with hundreds of pieces of legislation and thousands of discrete regulations prescribing what educators should do.

More recent efforts differ from past strategies that did not consider how ideas would make it from the statehouse to the schoolhouse. New initiatives are investing in the front lines of education. Policymakers increasingly realize that regulations cannot transform schools; only teachers, in collaboration with parents and administrators, can do that.

Indeed, solutions to all of the problems that educational critics cite are constrained by the availability of knowledgeable, skillful teachers and school conditions that define how that knowledge can be used. Raising graduation requirements in mathematics, science, and foreign language, for example, is of little use if there are not enough teachers prepared to teach those subjects well. Concerns about at-risk children cannot be addressed without teachers prepared to meet the diverse needs of students with varying learning styles, family situations, and beliefs about what school means for them.

In policy terms, betting on teaching as a key strategy for reform

From *Educational Leadership,* March 1996, pp. 4–10. © 1996 by the Association for Supervision and Curriculum Development. All rights reserved. Reprinted by permission.

means investing in stronger preparation and professional development while granting teachers greater autonomy. It also means spending more on teacher development and less on bureaucracies and special programs created to address the problems created by poor teaching. Finally, we must put greater knowledge directly in the hands of teachers and seek accountability that will focus attention on "doing the right things" rather than on "doing things right." Such reforms demand changes in much existing educational policy, in current school regu- lations, and in management structures.

Possibilities for Transforming Teaching

Several current efforts hold great promise to transform teaching: redesigning initial teacher preparation, rethinking professional development; and involving teachers in research, collaborative inquiry, and standard-setting in the profession. Given the fact that fully half of the teachers who will be teaching in the year 2005 will be hired over the next decade (and large-scale hiring will continue into the decade thereafter), this is a critical time to transform the quality of teacher preparation.

New ideas about teacher preparation. Over the past decade, many schools of education have made great strides in incorporating new understandings of teaching and learning into their programs for prospective teachers. More attention to learning and cognition has accompanied a deepening appreciation for content pedagogy and constructivist teaching. In addition, teacher preparation and induction programs are increasingly helping prospective teachers and interns develop a reflective, problem-solving orientation by engaging them in teacher research, school-based inquiry, and inquiry into student's experiences. These approaches help teachers build an empirical understanding of learners and a capacity to analyze what occurs in their classrooms and in the lives of their students.

Efforts to develop teachers as managers of their own inquiry stand in contrast to earlier assumptions [about] teacher induction and about teaching generally: beginning teachers need to focus only on the most rudimentary tasks of teaching with basic precepts and cookbook rules to guide them, and more seasoned teachers should be the recipients, not the generators, of knowledge. Teacher preparation is now seeking to empower teachers to use and develop knowledge about teaching and learning as sophisticated and powerful as the demands of their work require.

Professional development schools. A growing number of education schools are working with school systems to create professional development schools that will prepare teachers for what schools must *become,* not only schools as they *are.* Too often there is a disparity between the conceptions of good practice that beginning teachers are taught and those they encounter when they begin teaching.

Professional development schools, which now number several hundred across the country, prepare beginning teachers in settings that support state-of-the-art practice and provide needed coaching and collaboration. Where districts and schools of education are creating professional development school partnerships, they are finding ways to marry state-of-the-art practice for students and state-of-the-art preparation and induction for teachers (Darling-Hammond 1994).

Regulations cannot transform schools; only teachers, in collaboration with parents and administrators, can do that.

Teacher education reformers are beginning to recognize that prospective teachers, like their students, learn by doing. As teacher educators, beginning teachers, and experienced teachers work together on real problems of practice in learner-centered settings, they can begin to develop a collective knowledge base and a common set of understandings about practice.

Collaborative inquiry and standard-setting. In addition to these reforms, important initiatives are under way to develop more meaningful standards for teaching, including performance-based standards for teacher licensing; more sophisticated and authentic assessments for teachers; and national standards for teacher education, licensing, and certification. These national efforts are being led by the National Board for Professional Teaching Standards (NBPTS), Interstate New Teacher Assessment and Support Consortium (INTASC), and National Council for Accreditation of Teacher Education (NCATE).

The new standards and assessments take into explicit account the multicultural, multilingual nature of a student body that possesses multiple intelligences and approaches to learning. The standards reflect the view of teaching as collegial work and as an intellectual activity. In many restructuring schools and schools of education, prospective, new, and veteran teachers are conducting school-based inquiry, evaluating programs, and studying their own practices—with one another and with university-based colleagues.

In many restructured schools, teachers are developing local standards, curriculum, and authentic student assessments. Those who develop assessments of their own teaching—for example, through the certification process of the National Board for Professional Teaching Standards—also discover that careful reflection about standards of practice stimulates an ongoing learning process.

Issues in Teacher Preparation

If we are to sustain these promising new initiatives, however, we must confront deeply entrenched barriers. As an occupation, teaching has historically been underpaid and micromanaged, with few investments in teachers' learning and few supports for teachers' work. By contrast, European and Asian countries hire a greater number of teachers who are better prepared, better paid, better supported, and vested with more decision-making responsibility. The conditions that enable these countries to provide much greater time and learning opportunity for teachers suggest that rethinking school staffing and scheduling must go hand in hand with redesigning teacher development.

By the standards of other professions and of teacher preparation in other countries, U.S. teacher education has been thin, uneven in quality, and under-resourced. While a growing number of teachers participate in rigorous courses of study, including intensive internships (increasingly, five- or six-year programs), many still attend underfunded undergraduate programs that their universities treat as "cash cows." These programs, typically less well-funded than any other department or professional school on campus, produce greater revenues for educating future businessmen, lawyers, and accountants than they spend on educating the future teachers they serve (Ebmeier et al. 2990, Sykes 1985).

In addition to the tradition of emergency certification that continues in more than 40 states, some newly launched alternative certification programs provide only a few weeks of training for entering teachers, skipping such fundamentals as learning theory, child development, and subject matter pedagogy and placing recruits in classrooms without previous supervised experience. Each year about 20,000 individuals enter teaching without a license, while another 30,000 enter with substandard credentials.

In addition to lack of support for beginning teacher preparation, districts spend less than one half of 1 percent of their resources on staff development. Most corporations and schools in other countries spend many times that amount. Staff development in the United States is still characterized by one-shot workshops rather than more effective, problem-based approaches that are built into

teachers' ongoing work with colleagues. As a result, most teachers have few opportunities to enhance their knowledge and skills over the course of their careers. The lack of investment in teacher knowledge is a function of the factory model approach to schooling adopted nearly a century ago, which invested in an administrative bureaucracy to design, monitor, and inspect teaching, rather than in the knowledge of the people doing the work. As a consequence, preservice and inservice investments in teacher knowledge have been quite small compared to those in many other countries.

In contrast to the traditions of U.S. education, teachers in these countries make virtually all decisions about curriculum, teaching, and assessment because of the greater preparation and inservice support they receive. They are almost never hired without full preparation, a practice enabled by subsidies that underwrite teacher preparation and by salaries that are comparable to those in other professions.

In the former West Germany, for example, prospective teachers earn the equivalent of two academic majors in separate disciplines prior to undertaking two additional years of rigorous teacher preparation at the graduate level. This training combines pedagogical seminars with classroom-based observation and intensively supervised practice teaching (Burns et al. 1991, OECD 1990, Kolstad et al. 1989).

Preparation in Luxembourg, a seven-year process, extends beyond the baccalaureate degree to professional training that blends pedagogical learning with extensive supervised practice teaching (OECD 1990).

In France, new models of teacher education send candidates through two years of graduate teacher education, including an intensively supervised yearlong internship in schools.

Most European and Asian countries are extending both their preservice education requirements and inservice learning opportunities for teachers (OECD 1990). Five-year programs of teacher preparation and in-

tensive internships are becoming the norm around the world (Darling-Hammond and Cobb 1995).

Beginning teachers in Japan receive at least 20 days of inservice training during their first year on the job, plus 60 days of professional development. Master teachers are released from their own classrooms to advise and counsel them (Stigler and Stevenson 1991, OECD 1990).

In Taiwan, candidates pursue a four-year undergraduate degree, which includes extensive courses on child learning, development, and pedagogy, prior to a full-year teaching practicum in a carefully selected and supervised setting.

After their preparation as apprentices, beginning teachers in the People's Republic of China work with a reduced teaching load, observing other teachers and preparing under the supervision of master teachers. They work in teaching teams to plan lessons and do peer observations (Paine 1990). Schools in China provide ongoing supports for collegial learning.

In most of these European, and many Asian, countries, teachers spend between 15 and 20 hours per week in their classrooms and the remaining time with colleagues developing lessons, visiting parents, counseling students, pursuing research, attending study groups and seminars, and visiting other schools.

By contrast, most U.S. elementary teachers have three or fewer hours for preparation per week (only 8 minutes for every hour in the classroom), while secondary teachers generally have five preparation periods per week (13 minutes for every hour of classroom instruction) (NEA 1992). In most U.S. schools, teachers are not expected to meet with other teachers, develop curriculum or assessments, or observe one another's classes—nor is time generally provided for these kinds of activities.

Investing in Time for Teacher Learning

Other countries are able to afford these greater investments in teachers' knowledge and time for collaborative work because they hire fewer non-teaching staff and more teachers who assume a broader range of decision-making responsibilities.

In the United States, the number of teachers has declined to only 53 percent of public school staff, while the number of nonteaching specialists and other staff has increased (NCES 1993). And only about 75 percent of teachers take primary responsibility for classrooms of children. The remainder work in pullout settings or perform nonteaching duties. A system in which lots of staff work outside the classroom to direct and augment the work of teachers unintentionally increases the need for greater coordination, raises class sizes, and reduces time for classroom teachers to collaborate.

While fewer than half of all public education employees in the United States work primarily as classroom teachers, classroom teaching staff comprise more than three-fourths of all public education employees in Australia and Japan, and more than 80 percent in Belgium, Germany, the Netherlands, and Spain (OECD 1992). These hiring patterns give a greater number of teachers per student more time each week for professional development activities, studies with colleagues, and meetings with parents and individual students. In their study of mathematics teaching and learning in Japan, Taiwan, and the United States, Stigler and Stevenson note that one reason

> Asian class lessons are so well crafted is that there is a very systematic effort to pass on the accumulated wisdom of teaching practice to each new generation of teachers and to keep perfecting that practice by providing teachers the opportunities to continually learn from one another (1991).

In addition, teaching in most other countries is not as bureaucratically organized as it is in the United States. It is not uncommon, for example, in Germany, Japan, Switzerland, and Sweden, for teachers to teach multiple subjects, counsel students, and teach

the same students for multiple years (Shimahara 1985, OECD 1990). Where similar arrangements for personalizing teacher-student relationships have been tried in the United States, student achievement is significantly higher because teachers know their students better both academically and personally (NIE 1977, Gottfredson and Daiger 1979).

Professionalizing teaching may call for rethinking school structures and roles and reallocating educational dollars. If teachers assume many instructional tasks currently performed by others (for example, curriculum development and supervision), the layers of bureaucratic hierarchy will be reduced. If teachers have opportunities for collaborative inquiry and learning, the vast wisdom of practice developed by excellent teachers will be shared across the profession. If teachers are more carefully selected and better trained and supported, expenditures for management systems to control incompetence will decrease. And if we make investments at the beginning of teachers' careers for induction support and pre-tenure evaluation, we should see a decline in the money needed to recruit and hire new entrants to replace the 30 percent who leave in the first few years.

These early investments will also reduce the costs of band-aid approaches to staff development for those who have not learned to teach effectively and the costs of remediating, or trying to dismiss, poor teachers—not to mention the costs of compensating for the effects of their poor teaching on children. In the long run, strategic investment in teacher competence should free up resources for innovation and learning.

Rethinking Schooling and Teaching Together

Ultimately, the quality of teaching depends not only on the qualities of those who enter and stay, but also on workplace factors. Teachers who feel enabled to succeed with students are more committed and effective than those who feel unsupported in their

learning and in their practice (Haggstrom et al. 1988, McLaughlin and Talbert 1993, Rosenholtz 1989). Those who have access to teacher networks, enriched professional roles, and collegial work feel more efficacious in gaining the knowledge they need to meet the needs of their students and more positive about staying in the profession.

Teachers in schools with shared decision making, according to a recent survey, were most likely to see curriculum reforms accompanying transformations in teaching roles (LH Research 1993). For example, 72 percent of teachers in site-based managed schools believed that cooperative learning had had a major impact on their schools, compared to only 35 percent of teachers in schools that had not restructured. Also more prevalent in restructuring schools were more rigorous graduation standards, performance-based assessment practices, emphasis on in-depth understanding rather than superficial content coverage, accelerated learning approaches, connections between classroom practices and home experiences of students, and teacher involvement in decisions about school spending (LH Research 1993).

Teachers in such schools were more likely to report that their schools were providing structured time for teachers to work together on professional matters—for example, planning instruction, observing one another's classrooms, and providing feedback about their teaching. More opportunities to counsel students in home visits and to adapt instruction to students' needs were also cited. In addition to feeling less constrained by district routines or standardized curriculums, teachers were more optimistic about their relationships with principals, their working conditions, and the educational performance of students. In brief, teachers in restructured schools were more confident about the professional status of teachers and more likely to view themselves as agents, rather than targets, of reform (LH Research 1993).

The attempts across the country are still embryonic and scattered rather than systemic, but the possibilities for rethinking teacher preparation and revamping how schools structure teacher time and responsibilities are probably greater now than they have ever been. Although current efforts are impressive, it is important to realize that American education has been down this path before. The criticisms of current educational reformers—that our schools provide most children with an education that is too passive and too rote-oriented to produce learners who can think critically, synthesize and transform, experiment and create—are virtually identical to those of progressive educators at the turn of the century, in the 1930s, and again in the 1960s.

An underinvestment in teacher knowledge and school capacity killed all of these efforts to create more universal, high- quality education. "Progressive education," Cremin argued, "demanded infinitely skilled teachers, and it failed because such teachers could not be recruited in sufficient numbers" (1965). Because of this failure, during each wave of reform, learner-centered education gave way to standardizing influences that "dumbed down" the curriculum: in the efficiency movement of the 1920s, the teacher-proof curriculum reforms of the 1950s, and the back-to-the-basics movement of the 1970s and '80s. Disappointment with the outcomes of these attempts to simplify and prescribe school procedures, however, led in turn in each instance to renewed criticisms of schools and attempts to restructure them.

Current efforts at school reform are likely to succeed to the extent that they are built on a strong foundation of teaching knowledge and are sustained by a commitment to structural rather than merely symbolic change. Major changes in the productivity of American schools rest on our ability to create and sustain a highly prepared teaching force for all, not just some, of our children.

References

Burns, B. P. Hinkle, R. Marshall, C. S. Manegold, F. Chideya, T. Waldrop, D. Foote, and D. Pedersen. (December 2, 1991). "The Best Schools in the World." *Newsweek:* 50–64.

Cremin, L. A. (1965). *The Genius of American Education.* New York: Vintage Books.

Darling-Hammond, L. (1994). *Professional Development Schools: Schools for Developing a Profession.* New York: Teachers College Press.

Darling-Hammond, L., and V. L. Cobb. (1995). *A Comparative Study of Teacher Training and Professional Development in APEC Members.* Washington, DC: U.S. Department of Education.

Ebmeier, H., S. Twombly, and D. Teeter. (1990). "The Comparability and Adequacy of Financial Support for Schools of Education." *Journal of Teacher Education* 42: 226–235.

Gottfredson, G. D., and D. C. Daiger. (1979). *Disruption in Six Hundred Schools.* Baltimore, Md.: The Johns Hopkins University, Center for Social Organization of Schools.

Haggstrom, G. W., L. Darling-Hammond, and D. W. Grissmer. (1988). *Assessing Teacher Supply and Demand.* Santa Monica, Calif.: RAND Corporation.

Kolstad, R. K., D. R. Coker, and C. Edelhoff, (January 1989). "Teacher Education in Germany: An Alternative Model for the United States." *The Clearing House* 62, 5: 233–234.

LH Research. (1993). *A Survey of the Perspective of Elementary and Secondary School Teachers on Reform.* Prepared for the Ford Foundation. New York: LH Research.

McLaughlin, M. W., and J. E. Talbert. (1993). "New Visions of Teaching." In *Teaching for Understanding: Challenges for Policy and Practice,* edited by D. K. Cohen, M. W. McLaughlin, and J. E. Talbert. San Francisco: Jossey-Bass.

NCES. (1993). *The Condition of Education, 1993.* Washington, D.C.: National Center for Education Statistics, U.S. Department of Education.

NEA (1992). *The Status of the American School Teacher.* Washington, D.C.: National Education Association.

NIE. (1977). *Violent Schools—Safe Schools: The Safe School Study Report to Congress.* Washington, D.C.: National Institute of Education.

OECD. (1990). *The Training of Teachers.* Paris: Organization for Economic Cooperation and Development.

OECD. (1992). *Education at a Glance, OECD Indicators.* Paris: Organization for Economic Cooperation and Development.

Paine, L. W. (1990). "The Teacher as Virtuoso: A Chinese Model for Teaching." *Teachers College Record* 92: 49–81.

Rosenholtz, S. (1989). *Teacher's Workplace: The Social Organization of Schools.* New York: Longman.

Shimahara, N. K. (1985). "Japanese Education and Its Implications for U.S. Education." *Phi Delta Kappan* 66: 418–421.

Stigler, J. W., and H. W. Stevenson. (Spring 1991). "How Asian Teachers Polish Each Lesson to Perfection." *American Educator.* 12–47.

Sykes, G. (1985). "Teacher Education in the United States." In *The School and the University,* edited by B. R. Clark, pp. 264–289. Los Angeles: University of California.

Linda Darling-Hammond is Co-Director, National Center for Restructuring Education, Schools, and Teaching, Box 110, Teachers College, Columbia University, New York, NY 10027.

A New Look at School Failure and School Success

BY WILLIAM GLASSER, M.D.

The cause of both school failure and marriage failure is that almost all people believe in and practice stimulus/response psychology, Dr. Glasser contends. He suggests a better alternative—CHOICE THEORY^{SM}—to nurture the warm, supportive human relationships that students need to succeed in school and that couples need to succeed in marriage.

JOHN IS 14 years old. He is capable of doing good work in school. Yet he reads and writes poorly, has not learned to do more than simple calculations, hates any work having to do with school, and shows up more to be with his friends than anything else. He failed the seventh grade last year and is well on his way to failing it again. Essentially, John chooses to do nothing in school that anyone would call educational. If any standards must be met, his chances of graduation are nonexistent.

We know from our experience at the Schwab Middle School, which I will describe shortly, that John also knows that giving up on school is a serious mistake. The problem is he doesn't believe that the school he attends will give him a chance to correct this mistake. And he is far from alone. There may be five million students between the ages of 6 and 16 who come regularly to school but are much the same as John. If they won't make the effort to become competent readers, writers, and problem solvers, their chances of leading even

minimally satisfying lives are over before they reach age 17.

Janet is 43 years old. She has been teaching math for 20 years and is one of the teachers who is struggling unsuccessfully with John. She considers herself a good teacher but admits that she does not know how to reach John. She blames him, his home, his past teachers, and herself for this failure. All who know her consider her a warm, competent person. But for all her warmth, five years ago, after 15 years of marriage, Janet divorced. She is doing an excellent job of caring for her three children, but, with only sporadic help from their father, her life is no picnic. If she and her husband had been able to stay together happily, it is almost certain that they and their children would be much better off than they are now.

Like many who divorce, Janet was aware that the marriage was in trouble long before the separation. But in the context of marriage as she knew it, she didn't know what to do. "I tried, but nothing I did seemed to help," she says. She is lonely and would like another marriage but, so far, hasn't been able to find anyone she would consider marrying. There may be more than a million men and women teaching school who, like Janet, seem capable of relationships but are either divorced or unhappily married. No one doubts that marriage failure is a huge problem. It leads to even more human misery than school failure.

William Glasser, M.D., is the founder and president of the William Glasser Institute in Chatsworth, Calif. In 1996 he changed the name of the theory he has been teaching since 1979 from "control theory" to CHOICE THEORY^{SM}. He is currently writing a new book on the subject. All his books are published by HarperCollins.

I bring up divorce in an article on reducing school failure because there is a much closer connection between these two problems than almost anyone realizes. So close, in fact, that I believe the cause of both these problems may be the same. As soon as I wrote those words, I began to fear that my readers would jump to the conclusion that I am blaming Janet for the failure of her marriage or for her inability to reach John. Nothing could be further from the truth. The fact that she doesn't know something that is almost universally unknown cannot be her fault.

If you doubt that the problems of John and Janet are similar, listen to what each of them has to say. John says, "I do so little in school because no one cares for me, no one listens to me, it's no fun, they try to make me do things I don't want to do, and they never try to find out what I want to do." Janet says, "My marriage failed because he didn't care enough for me, he never listened to me, each year it was less fun, he never wanted to do what I wanted, and he was always trying to make me do what he wanted." These almost identical complaints have led John to "divorce" school, and Janet, her husband.

Are these Greek tragedies? Are all these students and all these marriages doomed to failure no matter what we do? I contend they are not. *The cause of both school failure and marriage failure is that almost no one, including Janet, knows how he or she functions psychologically.* Almost all people believe in and practice an ancient, commonsense psychology called stimulus/response (SR) psychology. I am one of the leaders of a small group of people who believe that SR is completely wrongheaded and, when put into practice, is totally destructive to the warm, supportive human relationships that students need to succeed in school and that couples need to succeed in marriage. The solution is to give up SR theory and replace it with a new psychology: *choice theory.*

To persuade a teacher like Janet to give up what she implicitly believes to be correct is a monumental task. For this reason I have hit upon the idea of approaching her through her marriage failure as much as through her fail-

> **To persuade a teacher like Janet to give up what she implicitly believes to be correct is a monumental task.**

ure to reach students like John. I think she will be more open to learning something that is so difficult to learn if she can use it in both her personal and her professional lives. From 20 years of experience teaching choice theory, I can also assure her that learning this theory can do absolutely no harm.

If John could go to a school where choice theory was practiced, he would start to work. That was conclusively proved at the Schwab Middle School. To explain such a change in behavior, John would say, "The teachers care about me, listen to what I have to say, don't try to make me do things I don't want to do, and ask me what I'd like to do once in a while. Besides, they make learning fun." If Janet and her husband had practiced choice theory while they still cared for each other, it is likely that they would still be married. They would have said, "We get along well because every day we make it a point to show each other we care. We listen to each other, and when we have differences we talk them out without blaming the other. We never let a week go by without having fun together, and we never try to make the other do what he or she doesn't want to do."

Where school improvement is concerned, I can cite hard data to back up this contention. I also have written two books that explain in detail all that my staff and I try to do to implement choice theory in schools. The books are *The Quality School* and *The Quality School Teacher.*[1] Where marriage failure is concerned, I have no hard data yet. But I have many positive responses from readers of my most recent book, *Staying Together,*[2] in which I apply choice theory to marriage.

The most difficult problems are human relationship problems. Technical problems, such as landing a man on the moon, are child's play compared to persuading all students like John to start working hard in school or helping all unhappily married couples to improve their marriages. Difficult as they may be to solve, however, relationship problems are surprisingly easy to understand. They are all some variation of "I don't like the way you treat me, and even though it may destroy my life, your life, or both our lives, this is what I am going to do about it."

READERS familiar with my work will have figured out by now that choice theory used to be called control theory because it teaches that the only person whose behavior we can control is our own. I find choice theory to be a better and more positive-sounding name. Accepting that you can control only your own behavior is the most difficult lesson that choice theory has to teach. It is so difficult that almost all people, even when they are given the opportunity, refuse to learn it. This is because the whole thrust of SR theory is that we do not control our own behavior, rather, our behavior is a response to a stimulus from outside ourselves. Thus we answer a phone in response to a ring.

Choice theory states that we never answer a phone because it rings, and we never will. We answer a phone—and do anything else—because it is the most satisfying choice for us at the time. If we have something better to do, we let it ring. Choice theory states that the ring of the phone is not a stimulus to do anything; it is merely *information*. In fact, all we can ever get from the outside world, which means all we can give one another, is information. But information, by itself, does not make us do anything. Janet can't make her husband do anything. Nor can she make John do anything. All she can give them is information, but she, like all SR believers, doesn't know this.

What she "knows" is that, if she is dissatisfied with someone, she should try to "stimulate" that person to change. And she wastes a great deal of time and energy trying to do this. When she discovers, as she almost always does, how hard it is to change another person, she begins to blame the person, herself, or someone else for the failure. And from blaming, it is a very short step to punishing. No one takes this short step more frequently and more thoroughly than husbands, wives, and teachers. As they attempt to change their mates, couples develop a whole repertoire of coercive behaviors aimed at punishing the other for being so obstinate. When teachers attempt to deal with students such as John, punishment—masquerading as "logical consequences"—rules the day in school.

Coercion in either of its two forms, reward or punishment, is the core of SR theory. Punishments are by far the more common, but both are destructive to relationships. The difference is that rewards are more subtly destructive and generally less offensive. Coercion ranges from the passive behaviors of sulking and withdrawing to the active behaviors of abuse and violence. The most common and, because it is so common, the most destructive of coercive behaviors is criticizing—and nagging and complaining are not far behind.

Choice theory teaches that we are all driven by four psychological needs that are embedded in our genes: the need to belong, the need for power, the need for freedom, and the need for fun. We can no more ignore these psychological needs than we can ignore the food and shelter we must have if we are to satisfy the most obvious genetic need, the need for survival.

Whenever we are able to satisfy one or more of these needs, it feels very good. In fact, the biological purpose of pleasure is to tell us that a need is being satisfied. Pain, on the other hand, tells us that what we are doing is not satisfying a need that we very much want to satisfy. John suffers in school, and Janet suffers in marriage because neither is able to figure out how to satisfy these needs. If the pain of this failure continues, it is almost certain that in two years John will leave school, and of course Janet has already left her marriage.

If we are to help Janet help John, she needs to learn and to use the most important of all the concepts from choice theory, the idea of the *quality world*. This small, very specific, personal world is the core of our lives because in it are the people, things, and beliefs that we have discovered are most satisfying to our needs. Beginning at birth, as we find out what best satisfies our needs, we build this knowledge into the part of our memory that is our quality world and continue to build and adjust it throughout our lives. This world is best thought of as a group of pictures, stored in our brain, depicting with extreme precision the way we would like things to be—especially the way we want to be treated. The most important pictures are of people, including ourselves, because it is almost impossible to satisfy our needs without getting involved with other people.

Good examples of people who are almost always in our quality worlds are our parents and our children—and, if our marriages are happy, our husbands or wives. These pictures are very specific. Wives and husbands want to hear certain words, to be touched in certain ways, to go to certain places, and to do specific activities together. We also have special things in our quality world. For example, the new computer I am typing this article on is very much the computer I wanted. I also have a strong picture of myself teaching choice theory, something I believe in so strongly that I spend most of my life doing it.

When we put people into our quality worlds, it is because we care for them, and they care for us. We see them as people with whom we can satisfy our needs. John has long since taken pictures of Janet and of most other teachers—as well as a picture of himself doing competent schoolwork—out of his quality world. As soon as he did this, neither Janet nor any other SR teacher could reach him. As much as they coerce, they cannot make him learn. This way of teaching is called "bossing." Bosses use coercion freely to try to make the people they boss do what they want.

To be effective with John, Janet must give up bossing and turn to "leading." Leaders never coerce. We follow them because we believe that they have our best interests at heart. In school, if he senses that Janet is now caring, listening, encouraging, and laughing, John will begin to consider putting her into his quality world. Of course, John knows nothing about choice theory or about the notion of a quality world. But he can be taught and, in a Quality School, this is what we do. We have evidence to show that the more students know about why they are behaving as they do, the more effectively they will behave.

Sometime before her divorce, Janet, her ex, or both of them took the other out of their quality worlds. When this happened, the marriage was over. If they had known choice theory and known how important it is to try to preserve the picture of a spouse in one's quality world, they could have made a greater effort than they did to care, listen, encourage, and laugh with each other. They certainly would have been aware of how destructive bossing is and would have tried their best to avoid this destructive behavior.

As I stated at the outset, I am not assigning blame for the failure of Janet's marriage. I am saying that, as soon as one or the other or both partners became dissatisfied, the only hope was to care, listen, encourage, and laugh and to completely stop criticizing, nagging, and complaining. Obviously, Janet and her ex-

husband would have been much more likely to have done this if they had known that the only behavior you can control is your own.

When Janet, as an SR teacher, teaches successfully, she succeeds with students because her students have put her or the math she teaches (or both) into their quality worlds. If both she and the math are in their quality worlds, the students will be a joy to teach. She may also succeed with a student who does not particularly want to learn math, but who, like many students, is open to learning math if she gives him a little attention.

John, however, is hard core. He is more than uninterested; he is disdainful, even disruptive at times. To get him interested will require a real show of interest on her part. But Janet resents any suggestion that she should give John what he needs. Why should she? He's 14 years old. It's his job to show interest. She has a whole classroom full of students, and she hasn't got the time to give him special attention. Because of this resentment, all she can think of is punishment.

> **When Janet punishes John, she gives him more reasons to keep her and math out of his quality world.**

When Janet punishes John, she gives him more reasons to keep her and math out of his quality world. Now he can blame her; from his standpoint, his failure is no longer his fault. Thus the low grades and threats of failure have exactly the opposite effect from the one she intends. That is why she has been so puzzled by students like John for so many years. She did the "right thing," and, even though she can see John getting more and more turned off, she doesn't know what else to do. She no more knows why she can't reach John than she knows why she and her husband found it harder and harder to reach each other when their marriage started to fail.

FROM THE beginning to the end of the 1994–95 school year, my wife Carleen and I worked to introduce Quality School concepts into the Schwab Middle School, a seventh- and eighth-grade school that is part of the Cincinnati Public School System. (Carleen actually began training many staff members in choice theory during the second semester of the 1993–94 school year.) This school of 600 regularly attending students (750 enrolled) has at least 300 students like John, who come to school almost every day. With the help of the principal, who was named best principal in Ohio in 1996, and a very good staff, we turned this school around.

By the end of the year, most of the regularly attending students who were capable of doing passable schoolwork were doing it.[3] Indeed, some of the work was much better than passable. None of the students like John were doing it when we arrived. Discipline problems that had led to 1,500 suspensions in the previous year slowly came under control and ceased to be a significant concern by the end of the school year.

By mid-February, after four months of preparation, we were able to start a special program in which we enrolled all the students (170) who had failed at least one grade and who also regularly attended school. Most had failed more than one grade, and some, now close to 17 years of age, had failed four times. Teachers from the regular school staff volunteered for this program. Our special program continued through summer school, by the end of which 147 of these 170 students were promoted to high school. The predicted number of students who would go to high school from this group had been near zero. Getting these students out of the "on-age" classes where they had been disruptive freed the regular teachers to teach more effectively, and almost all the "on-age" students began to learn. The "on-age" seventh-graders at Schwab had a 20% increase in their math test scores, another positive outcome of the program.

We were able to achieve these results because we taught almost all the teachers in the school enough choice theory to understand how students need to be treated if they are to put us into their quality worlds. Using these concepts, the teachers stopped almost all coercion—an approach that was radically different from the way most of these students had been treated since kindergarten. When we asked the students why they were no longer disruptive and why they were beginning to work in school, over and over they said, "You care about us." And sometimes they added, "And now you give us choices and work that we like to do."

What did we do that they liked so much? With the district's permission, we threw out the regular curriculum and allowed the students to work at their own pace. We assigned lessons that, when successfully completed,

proved that the students were ready for high school. The seven teachers in the special program (called the Cambridge Program)—spurred on by the challenge that this was their school and that they could do anything they believed necessary—worked day and night for almost two months to devise these lessons, in which the students had to demonstrate that they could read, write, solve problems, and learn the basics of social studies and science.

We told the students that they could not fail but that it was up to them to do the work. We said that we would help them learn as much as we could, and teachers from the "on-age" classes volunteered their free periods to help. Some of the students began to help one another. The fear began to dissipate as the staff saw the students begin to work. What we did was not so difficult that any school staff, with the leadership of its principal, could not do it as well. Because we had so little time, Carleen and I were co-leaders with the principal. A little extra money (about $20,000) from a state grant was also spent to equip the room for the Cambridge Program with furniture, carpeting, and computers, but it was not more than any school could raise if it could promise the results we achieved.

THESE Quality School ideas have also been put to work for several years in Huntington Woods Elementary School in Wyoming, Michigan. This nearly 300-student K–5 school is located in a small middle-class town and is the first school to be designated a Quality School. There were very few Johns in this school to begin with, so the task was much easier than at Schwab. Nonetheless, the outcomes at Huntington Woods have been impressive.

- All students are doing competent schoolwork, as measured by the Michigan Education Assessment Program (MEAP). The percentages of Huntington Woods students who score satisfactorily as measured against a state standard are 88% in reading and 85% in math (compared to state averages of 49% in reading and 60% in math).
- As measured by both themselves and their teachers, all students are doing some quality work, and many are doing a great deal of quality work.

- While there are occasional discipline incidents, there are no longer any discipline problems.
- The regular staff works very successfully with all students without labeling them learning disabled or emotionally impaired.
- Even more important than these measurable outcomes, the school is a source of joy for students, teachers, and parents.

I emphasize that no extra money was spent by the district to achieve these results. The school, however, did some fund raising to pay for staff training.

I CITE Schwab and Huntington Woods because I have worked in one of these schools myself and have had a great deal of contact with the other. They are both using the ideas in my books. Huntington Woods has changed from an SR-driven system, and Schwab has made a strong start toward doing so. Moreover, Schwab's start has produced the results described above. And more than 200 other schools are now working with me in an effort to become Quality Schools.

So far only Huntington Woods has evaluated itself and declared itself a Quality School. Even Schwab, as improved as it is, is far from being a Quality School. But, in terms of actual progress made from where we found it, what Schwab has achieved is proportionally greater than what Huntington Woods has achieved.

While many schools have shown interest in what has been achieved at Huntington Woods and at Schwab, very few of them have accepted the core idea: change the system from SR theory to choice theory. Indeed, there are many successful SR schools around the country that are not trying to change the fundamental system in which they operate, and I believe their success is based on two things.

First, for a school to be successful, the principal is the key. When an SR school succeeds, as many do, it is led by a principal whose charisma has inspired the staff and students to work harder than they would ordinarily work. This kind of success will last only as long as the principal remains. I am not saying that some charismatic principals do not embrace many of the ideas of the Quality School, or that the principal doesn't have to lead the systemic change that choice theory makes possible. However, once the system has been changed, it can sustain itself (with the principal's support, of course, but without a charismatic leader).

Second, the SR schools that are working well have strong parental support for good education and few Johns among their students. Where such support is already present or can be created by hard-working teachers and principals, schools have a very good chance of being successful without changing their core system. After all, it is these schools that have traditionally made the SR system seem to work. In such schools, Janet would be a very successful teacher.

While Huntington Woods had the kind of support that would have made it a good school without changing the system, the staff wanted it to become a Quality School and set about changing the system from the outset. With the backing of the superintendent, the staff members were given an empty building and the opportunity to recruit new staff members, all of whom were anxious to learn the choice theory needed to change the system. The fact that Huntington Woods has a charismatic leader is certainly a plus, but it is her dedication to the ideas of choice theory that has led to the school's great success. With very high test scores, no discipline problems, and no need for special programs, Huntington Woods has gone far beyond what I believe the typical SR school could achieve. Many educators who have visited the school have said that it is "a very different kind of school."[4]

Schwab today is also very different from the school it was. And what has been accomplished at Schwab has been done with almost no active parental support. The largest number of parents we could get to attend any meeting—even when we served food and told them to bring the whole family—was 20, and some of them were parents of the few students who live in the middle-class neighborhood where the school is located. Almost all the Schwab students who are like John are bused in from low-income communities far from the school, a fact that makes parents' participation more difficult.

At Schwab an effort was made to teach all the teachers choice theory. Then Carleen and I reminded them continually to use the theory as they worked to improve the school. At Huntington Woods, not only were the teachers and principal taught choice theory in much more depth than at Schwab and over much more time than we had at Schwab, but all the students and many parents were also involved in learning this theory and beginning to use it in theirlives.

Unfortunately, Janet has never taught in a school that uses choice theory. When she brings up her problems with John in the teachers' lounge, she is the beneficiary of a lot of SR advice: "Get tough!" "Show him right away who's boss." "Don't let him get away with anything." "Call his mother, and demand she do something about his behavior." "Send him to the principal." Similarly, like almost everyone whose marriage is in trouble, Janet has been the beneficiary of a lot of well-intended SR advice from family and friends—some of which, unfortunately, she took.

Her other serious problem is that she works in an SR system that is perfectly willing to settle for educating only those students who want to learn. The system's credo says, "It's a tough world out there. If they don't make an effort, they have to suffer the consequences." Since Janet is herself a successful product of such a system, she supports it. In doing so, she believes it is right to give students low grades for failing to do what she asks them to do. She further believes it is right to refuse to let them make up a low grade if they don't have a very good attitude—and sometimes even if they do.

In her personal life, she and her husband had seen so much marriage failure that, when they started to have trouble, it was easy for them to think of divorce as almost inevitable. This is bad information. It discourages both partners from doing the hard work necessary to learn what is needed to put their marriage back together. Life is hard enough without the continuing harangues of the doomsayers. In a world that uses choice theory, people would be more optimistic.

There has been no punishment in the Huntington Woods School for years. There is no such thing as a low grade that cannot be improved. Every student has access to a teacher or another student if he or she needs personal attention. Some students will always do better than others, but, as the MEAP scores show, all can do well. This is a Quality system, with an emphasis on continual improvement, and there is no settling for good enough.

Unfortunately for them, many Schwab students who experience success in school for the first time will fail in high school. The SR system in use there will kill them off educationally, just as certainly as if we shot them with a gun. They didn't have enough time with us and were too fragile when we sent them on. However, if by some miracle the high school pays attention to what we did at Schwab, many will succeed. There was some central office support for our efforts, and there is some indication that this support will continue.

The Huntington Woods students are less fragile. They will have had a good enough start with choice theory so that, given the much stronger psychological and financial support of their parents, they will probably do well in middle school. Indeed, data from the first semester of 1995–96 confirm that they are doing very well.

It is my hope that educators, none of whom are immune to marriage failure, will see the value of choice theory in their personal lives. If this happens, there is no doubt in my mind that they will begin to use it with their students.

---

1. William Glasser, *The Quality School* (New York: HarperCollins, 1990); and idem, *The Quality School Teacher* (New York: HarperCollins, 1994).
2. William Glasser, *Staying Together* (New York: HarperCollins, 1995).
3. The school also had about four classes of special education students who were in a special program led by capable teachers and were learning as much as they were capable of learning.
4. See Dave Winans, "This School Has Everything," *NEA Today*, December 1995, pp. 4–5.

A PARTNERSHIP FOR TEACHER DEVELOPMENT

NEA's Teacher Education Initiative: The First Year

Sylvia Seidel
Assistant Director
NEA Teacher Education Initiative

Imagine, all the key professional parties involved in quality education—local and state NEA affiliates, school boards, and schools of education working together to improve preK–12 schooling and teaching! It's exciting—and that's what the NEA Teacher Education Initiative is all about.

—Bob Chase, NEA President

Times have changed. Students attending America's public schools today are a more diverse population than ever before and are arriving at the schoolhouse door with greater learning needs. During the next decade, the two million plus new teachers entering the classrooms of our nation will face challenges and contexts significantly different from the experiences teachers confronted in the past.

Despite these new imperatives, traditional education programs have not changed dramatically from the past and often fail to provide preservice or practicing professionals with the necessary skills, knowledge, and support to meet the complex problems and demands of today's classrooms. The time has come to redesign teacher development for all professionals.

Teacher development must now be viewed as a continuum where the preparation of new teachers and the professional development of experienced teachers complement and reinforce one another. To ensure that every classroom has an effective teacher prepared to meet the challenges

From *Doubts & Certainties*, Spring 1997, pp. 1-7. © 1997 by the National Education Association. Reprinted by permission.

of contemporary schools, educational institutions across the nation are forming partnerships that offer quality professional development for new and experienced teachers. These school-university partnerships encourage all educators to try new ways of learning for themselves and for their students.

SCHOOL, UNIVERSITY, AND ASSOCIATION PARTNERSHIP

In 1994 the NEA established the Teacher Education Initiative (TEI). This innovative national program expands the concept of teacher training and retraining through a unique, equitable partnership among preK–12 schools, universities, and the Association. Its aims include: accelerating the pace of change and renewal in teacher preparation and practice; guiding, supporting, and facilitating significant improvement in the preparation and induction of new teachers and continuous professional growth of all educators; and fostering research and development of the teaching profession.

NEA's Teacher Education Initiative is organized around the principles listed, see box "TEI's Nine Guiding Principles." The nine TEI principles for systematic restructuring inspire a set of values, beliefs, assumptions, and preferred practices closely associated with best practice in teacher education.

TEI Restructuring Sites

George Mason University
(Fairfax, VA)
Montclair State University
(Upper Montclair, NJ)
Texas A&M University
(College Station, TX)
The University of Memphis
(Memphis, TN)
The University of South Carolina
(Columbia, SC)
The University of Southern Maine
(Gorham, ME)
The University of Wyoming
(Laramie, WY)

Application Process

To initiate the TEI program, the National Center for Innovation conducted a national application and selection process. Over 1,200 institutions expressed interest in the program. From these, ten "Exemplary" programs and seven "Restructuring" institutions were selected. Sites selected for the five-year Restructuring program form the core of TEI work. These sites demonstrated progress in the nine guiding principles and committed to yearly action plans and involvement in a

comprehensive research and evaluation design.

TEI Settings

TEI sites are real-life settings that represent the everyday world of most of America's teachers and are dedicated to advancing professionalism and student learning. TEI

School-university partnerships create cultures that transform the work in both institutions.

---

provides a model for collaboration. Participation in the partnership is based upon mutual trust, respect, and the valuing of the expertise provided by each member of the coalition. All partners have equal voice in decision making, planning and implementation. Decisions are grounded in the real needs and experiences of the individuals comprising the partnerships.

Professional Development Schools

The "laboratory" for TEI work is the professional development school (PDS). This concept, introduced more than a decade ago, emulates the medical profession's teaching hospital model. PDSs provide realistic field experience for preservice professionals, continuous professional development for current practitioners, and opportunities for all professionals to conduct research that contributes to the improvement of the quality of education offered to all students.

While some programs broadly interpret the concept of PDS, TEI adheres to specific parameters. For TEI, a professional development school is *a collaborative partnership to improve the quality of education offered to all students. Partners include preK–12 schools, institutions of higher education, teacher associations, parents, and communities. These partnerships seek simultaneous renewal of schools and universities by:*

➤*providing education and training to preservice and practicing teachers and higher education faculties;*

➤*sharing responsibility for improving teaching and learning for all students and adults;*

➤*improving teaching and learning through ongoing evaluation and research;*

➤*promoting policies, procedures, and resources that support teaching and learning;*

➤*providing quality education for diverse student populations;*

➤*preparing teachers in diverse settings.*

More than 100 PDSs, 17 universities, 7 community colleges, 25 school districts, and a state department of education are contributing to TEI partnership activities. Because reform is occurring in PDSs, TEI is continuing to expand its network of PDS models. This network enriches the work in TEI sites

and provides an opportunity for additional partners to join the effort. Participants in the PDS network include TEI core sites, foundation PDSs, and applicants from school-university partnerships nationwide. All will be linked electronically to TEI partner institutions.

Along with the PDS network, six additional work groups have evolved from the TEI program and are contributing to its development. They include: telecommunications networking, equity and diversity, TEI international, research, product development and dissemination, and Association staff.

NEA Roles

As part of his vision for reinventing the NEA, President Bob Chase is emphasizing "working partnerships with schools of education to transform teacher training and professional development." As the founder and a partner in the TEI venture, NEA plays an essential role. Along with bringing stakeholders together, the Association:

➤ provides support for research to advance systematic change at the university/college level and at the PDS sites;

➤ publishes and disseminates findings from its research;

➤ supports the seven restructuring partners with annual grants of $10,000, plus additional revenues to fund the comprehensive research study;

➤ facilitates communication among TEI participants, as well as other educators involved in school reform, through an electronic network.

Research Design and Documentation

A major commitment among the TEI restructuring partners is participation in a five-year comprehensive evaluation process. A longitudinal research design is being used by the seven core partners. Both statistical and anecdotal data are being gathered, including:

➤ teacher and principal focus groups,

➤ student intern observations and performance evaluations,

➤ case studies of TEI and traditional program interns,

➤ a school climate inventory, and

➤ follow-up of intern career patterns and achievements.

Prior to implementation of the project, staff from the Center for Research in Educational Policy at the University of Memphis and the NEA Research division assisted representatives from TEI sites in the development of the evaluation design and instruments. The five-year investigation is providing information about commonalities and differences within this diverse group of quality programs related to professional development procedures, staffing, training priorities, decision making, authentic evaluation and supervision, and diversity. Content, organization, and delivery of services are also being studied.

TEI's Nine Guiding Principles

Partnerships:

Collaborative relationships among preK–12 schools, institutions of higher education, and other stakeholders for the purposes of educational renewal.

Leadership Roles:

Expanded roles of school and university educators and other stakeholders, which might include: (a) the involvement of school-based educators as researchers, writers, adjunct faculty, and mentors; (b) the university-based educators taking on new and expanded roles within the schools; and (c) preparing preservice teachers as leaders and change agents.

Evaluation and Dissemination:

Ongoing reflection on practice, evaluation, action research, assessment, documentation, and contributions to the professional knowledge base.

Professional Preparation and Development:

Coherent program that includes extensive ongoing clinical experiences; strong curriculum base; mentoring and support for beginning teachers and professional development for school/university educators.

Systemic Change—External:

Involvement in programmatic and policy change at the local, state, and national level (participation in associations, organizations, coalitions, and networks).

Systemic Change—Internal:

Transforming teacher education programs and preK–12 schools to include changes such as: (a) a reward structure that includes clinical work, (b) reallocation of resources (time and money), (c) strong linkages with Arts and Science faculty, (d) innovative delivery of instruction, (e) stated mission and goals, and (f) continuous improvement through assessment.

Technology:

Using technology to enhance teaching, learning, and communication with linkages to external technological resources.

Equity and Diversity:

Reflected in curriculum, staff, and student populations; teaching and learning affirm and celebrate diversity and promote equity.

Teaching and Learning:

Linked to student outcomes, student needs, and authentic/alternative assessment.

The research questions guiding the evaluation design relate to the nine TEI principles—how they are defined and being implemented, what the effects are on the partner institutions (school, college, university), and how this restructuring effort affects the quality of teacher preparation as evidenced by efforts of candidates and graduates.

LESSONS FROM THE FIRST YEAR

Results from the first year's data collection are being used by the sites to guide their work. The first year's focus was on clarifying visions and goals, building relationships, and garnering resources. Preliminary data indicate that both preservice and experienced teachers benefited from the Initiative.

Future research will consider how TEI's work affects student achievement. Given the difficulty of gathering such information, a task force is exploring methods to capture the data.

Collaboration

Increased collaboration was cited as the most positive impact of the partnership during the first year. Collaboration among all stakeholders encouraged a shared vision, trust, and greater communication. Collaboration between schools and universities encouraged participants to assume new roles and leadership responsibilities. For example, some of the sites created a new position, school-university liaison. Usually the individual who volunteered for this bridging responsibility understood and felt comfortable functioning in both the school and the university.

While sites lauded the collaboration, they also cautioned that such interactions are fragile, labor and time intensive, and must be nurtured continuously by all stakeholders. Some preservice teachers said they felt accountable to many different people, which occasionally led to miscommunication, conflicting rules, and differing expectations.

Teacher Renewal

Mentor teachers reported a sense of empowerment and renewal in their teaching, particularly in their interactions with university faculty. As peers, they shared and received instructional models and teaching ideas. Mentor teachers' comments also re-

---

The "laboratory" for TEI work is the professional development school (PDS).

---

vealed increased confidence, professionalism, pride, and enthusiasm, and they credited these benefits to their interactions with the preservice teachers. Partnering with preservice teachers provided them an opportunity to reflect more on their own practice and articulate teaching behaviors. Additionally, the high visibility of this collaboration encouraged school administrators in several sites to pay more attention to teacher development.

The mentor teacher/preservice teacher interactions frequently were characterized as "team teaching." One mentor teacher described the interactions as follows: "Teacher and PDS students become a team . . . I am challenged by youth and energy and new technology . . . We are friends in education. We support each other."

Effective Preservice Teachers

The partnership also had a significant effect on preservice teachers. In this new culture, many of them were eager to try new instructional methods that emphasized teaching for higher order reasoning, technology, and use of alternative forms of assessment. Not only did these strategies reinforce good teaching practices for preservice teachers, they also improved student learning. Preservice teachers' enthusiasm and willingness to try new methods inspired mentor teachers to renew their own classroom and development efforts.

Approximately 70 percent of university faculty and mentor teachers who were surveyed stated that the new teachers educated in TEI sites were better prepared than other preservice professionals with whom they had worked. They reported that preservice teachers exhibited a greater comfort level in schools, were more confident, and behaved more like first-year teachers.

The preservice teacher's immersion in the school culture has many practical benefits. Superintendents, principals, and other school

---

Mentor teachers reported a sense of empowerment and renewal in their teaching.

---

leaders are giving hiring preferences to new teachers prepared in the partnerships. Confident in the quality of instruction preservice teachers provide, mentor teachers are requesting them when they need substitutes.

"I've worked with traditional student teachers for years," said one NEA member teacher, "and I was never ready to let them go. I knew they hadn't benefited from being immersed in the school culture," she explained. "This program significantly expands their learning and ultimately increases their comfort level and success in their first year of teaching."

A new teacher prepared in the program agreed: "It has enabled me to see teachers in action, develop opinions about methods, and have an opportunity to implement. The helpfulness of the teachers and the university faculty has enabled me to have confidence in my education and teaching abilities."

Additional Time

Mentor teachers, university faculty, and preservice teachers all noted an increase in time demands, but they generally viewed it as a positive experience. They saw the benefits to themselves and the students and were willing to invest the extra effort. To accommodate the additional time commitment, several school and university administrators introduced various reward systems, including monetary compensation and release time.

INTO THE SECOND YEAR

In September 1997, TEI held its annual symposium in Maine. Highlighting the agenda were site visits to the local schools and working sessions during which participants shared results and challenges. The most significant challenges included:

➤ attracting and retaining more minority students to teacher education programs,

➤ continuing efforts to advance the use of technology,

➤ maintaining parity among all project participants,

➤ collaborating on research to solve common problems,

➤ rewarding school and university faculty for clinical responsibilities,

➤ meeting data collection requirements,

➤ increasing participation of arts and science faculty members,

➤ increasing participation of NEA state and local affiliates,

➤ coping with leadership changes in schools/universities,

➤ securing adequate funding for a project of this magnitude,

➤ sustaining enthusiasm and support regardless of distances.

TEI invited Gary A. Griffin, professor at Teachers College, Columbia University and co-director of the National Center for Restructuring Education, Schools, and Teaching (NCREST), as a "provocateur" to challenge symposium participants.

Griffin's comments on TEI's strengths included the following:

➤ **TEI's nine principles:** The nine principles provide a solid platform for the Initiative's work. Depend on, refine, and hone them.

➤ **Collaboration and learning together:** TEI is demonstrating that expert practitioners and higher education faculty can learn together by collaborating in good faith.

➤ **Seriousness of purpose:** TEI's purpose and principled reasons for action are exemplars of collaborative work.

➤ **Broadened and deepened role definitions:** TEI is challenging 20-year-old mandates that have put limits on professionalism and blinders on policy makers.

➤ **Keeping track, keeping up, keeping score:** TEI is taking the important tasks of documentation, evaluation, and dissemination seriously.

Griffin challenged symposium participants to:

➤ **Consider how TEI's work affects students.** Make sure it provides better learning opportunities for students.

➤ **Develop a clinical model for teacher education based on TEI's experiences.** Teacher education is eager to learn from TEI.

➤ **Expand the field's understanding of what professional development schools can be.** Extend the influence of these new settings.

➤ **Beware of fixing existing organizations that are unsatisfactory.** Invent something brand new, in organizational terms.

➤ **Keep the enthusiasm going.** Support and sustain individuals within TEI who have worked hard and welcome newcomers to TEI.

As participants in the Teacher Education Initiative work to sustain this five-year, labor intensive, and costly reform effort, they must address many barriers. Both practicing and preservice professionals insist, however, that whatever difficulties these challenges pose, they can never return to traditional patterns of teaching and learning and teacher development. They are convinced this is the direction needed to ensure better prepared and more effective classroom teachers and higher achieving students for the next century.

Paying Attention to Relationships

Teachers' interpersonal skills are essential to creating a positive classroom climate. The Questionnaire for Teacher Interaction—developed in the Netherlands, the U.S., and Australia—provides a roadmap for professional improvement.

Theo Wubbels, Jack Levy, and Mieke Brekelmans

We've been searching for The Effective Teacher for more than a century (Borich 1988). In the 1800s, he or she was usually thought of as a good person, an honorable citizen, well educated, and hardworking. No special skills were necessary, other than being well organized, disciplined, authoritative, and dedicated to children. The search began in earnest at the beginning of this century and continued until the 1960s. During this period, thousands of studies tried to capture the special personality traits or attitudes that predicted teaching effectiveness (Getzels and Jackson 1963). Unfortunately, most of them came up empty.

The process-product research of the 1960s and 1970s identified teaching strategies that contributed to student achievement. These studies, which analyzed teaching primarily from a methods perspective, empirically explained how some teachers excel in asking questions, monitoring student progress, organizing and managing the classroom, and building appropriate lessons. Many educators today hold to the view that effective teaching can be defined in terms of a plethora of technical strategies, such as choice, organization, and presentation of teaching materials; motivational strategies; and assessment.

Our view of teaching effectiveness comes from a different—yet complementary—perspective. While instructional methodology is an important consideration, exceptional teaching can also be described in terms of teacher-student relationships. Our belief—based on 15 years of research with more than 50,000 students and teachers in The Netherlands, the United States, and Australia—is that a teacher's interpersonal skills are crucial to creating and maintaining a positive working climate. Essentially, effective teachers have to be excellent communicators as well as fine technicians.

We've developed a measurement process to determine how well teachers communicate with their students. Here we'll look at that process; describe what effective teachers do to solidify their relationships with students; look at how teachers' approaches to relationships evolve throughout their careers; and present some thoughts on professional development.

A Language for Interpersonal Relationships

Because teachers communicate in many ways, they naturally develop different types of relationships with their students. Some teachers are businesslike and others lenient. Some are dis-

tant and others friendly. To describe these characteristics more clearly, we adopted a communication model developed by clinical psychologist Timothy Leary (before LSD!) and modified for educational use at Utrecht University in The Netherlands (see Leary 1957; Wubbels and Levy 1993, chapter 2). Leary stated that people communicate according to two dimensions—a Dominance-Submission (or Influence) dimension (for example, who is controlling the communication) and a Cooperation-Opposition (or Proximity) dimension (how much cooperation is present between the people who are communicating). We can record the behavior of all parties in a discussion according to these dimensions on a graph like the one shown in Figure 1.

Let's imagine a dialogue between a mother and her young son on the subject of crossing the street. As the parent explains the process, she is engaging in dominant behavior because she is controlling the communication. If her explanation is presented in a patient, comfortable manner, her behavior would also be highly cooperative. Thus, she would be displaying high dominant/high cooperative behavior. This is indicated by an "A" in Figure 1. If, however, the child has just nearly been run over by a bus, the parent is likely to be agitated and possibly angry. She might even scream at the boy to be more careful. Her communication in this case would still be dominant but also highly oppositional, as indicated by a "B" in Figure 1.

We subsequently applied the model to the classroom by dividing Leary's original two dimensions into the eight behavior types shown in Figure 2. The eight sectors are labeled DC, CD, and so forth, much like the directions on a compass. For example, sectors DC and CD are both characterized by dominance and cooperation. In the DC sector, however, the dominance aspect prevails over cooperation. Thus, a teacher displaying DC behavior might be explaining something to the class, organizing groups, or making assignments. The adjacent CD sector includes behaviors of a more cooperative, less dominant character, and the teacher might be assisting students or acting friendly or considerate.

Teachers can exhibit acceptable behavior in each sector. In the course of a day, or a week, most teachers will encounter classroom situations in which it is appropriate to be dissatisfied, or uncertain, or admonishing (or any other category). In addition, one of the fundamental ideas behind the Leary model is that communication *behaviors* continually change. Communication *styles* emerge only after a great many behaviors have occurred and been observed.

Measuring Teacher Communication

Having created the language to describe the way teachers relate to students, we then developed the Questionnaire for Teacher Interaction (QTI), also based on Leary's model.[1] Teachers interested in measuring and improving classroom climate have found it easy to use and the feedback it provides reliable. As mentioned, more than 50,000 students and teachers have used the model. Versions are available in English, Dutch, Hebrew, Russian, Slovenian, Swedish, and Finnish.

Teachers normally wait a few months into the school year, until everyone gets to know one another, before administering the questionnaire. To receive feedback from the widest range of student groups, teachers usually select two classes that vary in age, learning ability, or some other characteristic. (Ironically, QTI scores from the different classes generally don't vary much, verifying the relative stability of teacher behavior [see Wubbels and Levy 1993, chapter 3].)

Each student answers the questionnaire items in terms of how he or she perceives the teacher. The teacher also completes the instrument. By gathering both perspectives, teachers can compare the results and gauge the quality of class atmosphere and how well they are communicating with students. We also ask teachers to describe their ideal behavior through the instrument, thereby providing them with a professional development roadmap for change.

Effective Teacher-Student Relationships

What interpersonal relationships should teachers strive for? To answer this question, we examined students' and teachers' descriptions of exceptional teachers, and the connections between teacher-student relationships and student achievement and attitudes.

We've had students complete the Questionnaire for Teacher Interaction for their best and worst teacher. Many teachers are surprised to learn that students and teachers agree on the characteristics of good teaching! According to students, the best teachers are strong classroom leaders who are friendlier and more understanding and less uncertain, dissatisfied, and critical than most teachers. Their best teachers also allow them more freedom than the norm. Further, when we asked students about their worst teachers, they described the opposite tendencies. Teachers visualize classroom quality in the same way. In general, then, good teachers are both highly dominant and highly cooperative.

A closer look at these perceptions reveals two distinct types of exceptional teachers. The first type, which we call Dominant, displays leadership and strictness, and a fair amount of cooperation. The second type, the Student-Oriented teacher, leans more toward allowing students greater

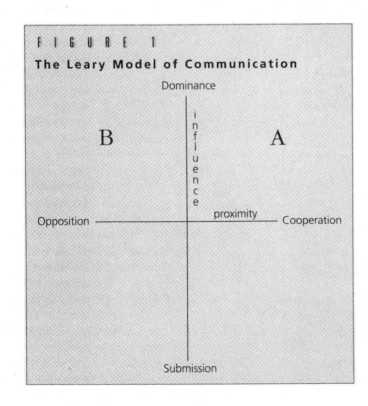

FIGURE 1
The Leary Model of Communication

responsibility in their learning. The two types characterize different teachers' opinions about the nature of an appropriate classroom atmosphere. For example, a Dominant teacher might say,

> Students won't learn if teachers don't control them and demand a lot. They are easily distracted, and allowing them too much freedom doesn't help at all.

In contrast, the Student-Oriented teacher might reply,

> Students have to enjoy the class before they learn anything. If the atmosphere is pleasant and stimulating, they'll be motivated to study, which is an important prerequisite for learning. Consequently, they'll thrive. It's more important to reward students for their efforts and

the things they do well than it is to correct their mistakes.

Student Achievement and Attitudes

Because effectiveness is generally associated with the quality and quantity of student learning, we didn't just accept students' and teachers' perceptions of good teaching. Rather, we measured them in terms of student achievement and attitudes. When kids are learning, and they're happy with the way things are going, what are their teachers like?

As we suspected, students' and teachers' ideas on exceptional teaching checked out quite well against measures of student achievement and attitudes. We analyzed the results

from three separate studies of 9th grade physics, 5th grade math, and 12th grade biology students (Brekelmans et al. 1990, Goh 1994, Fisher et al. 1995). The more dominant the teacher, the more his or her students achieve. Strict leadership and helpful/friendly behaviors are positively related to student achievement, whereas student responsibility and freedom and uncertain, dissatisfied behaviors are negatively related.

Similarly, the cooperation scales of the model (leadership, helpful/friendly, understanding, and student responsibility/freedom) are positively related to student attitudes. The more teachers emphasize these types of behaviors, the more their students respond positively. In contrast, the opposition scales (strict, admonishing, dissatisfied, and uncertain) are all negatively related to student attitudes. Thus, teachers who tend toward the right side and/or below average on the left side of the D-S axis of Figure 2 are viewed more positively by their students.

These results create a dilemma, however. If teachers want students to be both high-achieving and supportive, they may find themselves pulling in two directions: strictness correlates well with high achievement, while flexibility relates to positive attitudes. As a result, the dominant teacher who emphasizes strictness and leadership gets greater achievement out of a class, whereas his or her student-oriented counterpart enjoys a better affective atmosphere.

Remember, however, that an effective teacher's repertoire covers all eight sec-

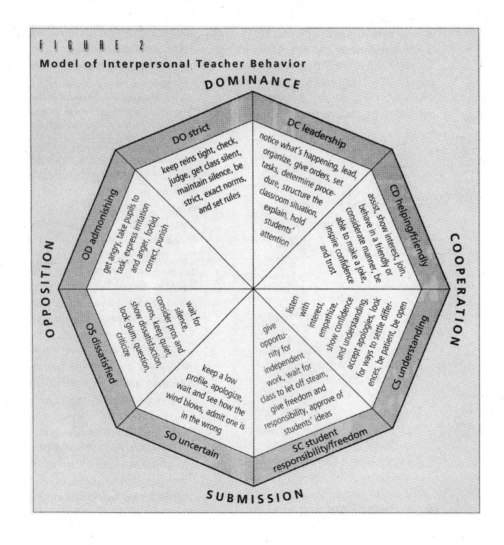

FIGURE 2
Model of Interpersonal Teacher Behavior

DOMINANCE

DO strict
keep reins tight, check, judge, get class silent, maintain silence, be strict, exact norms, and set rules

DC leadership
notice what's happening, lead, organize, give orders, set tasks, determine procedure, structure the classroom situation, explain, hold students' attention

OD admonishing
get angry, take pupils to task, express irritation and anger, forbid, correct, punish

CD helping/friendly
assist, show interest, join, behave in a friendly or considerate manner, be able to make a joke, inspire confidence and trust

OPPOSITION

COOPERATION

OS dissatisfied
wait for silence, consider pros and cons, keep quiet, show dissatisfaction, look glum, question, criticize

CS understanding
listen with interest, empathize, show confidence and understanding, accept apologies, look for ways to settle differences, be patient, be open

SO uncertain
keep a low profile, apologize, wait and see how the wind blows, admit one is in the wrong

SC student responsibility/freedom
give opportunity for independent work, wait for class to let off steam, give freedom and responsibility, approve of students' ideas

SUBMISSION

tors of the model. Instructional expertise requires a teacher to employ the most effective communication behavior called for by the situation. If oppositional behavior is appropriate at the moment (say a student is endangering the class), then the effective teacher must behave accordingly. Good teaching requires an interpersonal repertoire that is both broad and flexible.

Do Teachers Change?

Do teachers change their styles as they gain experience? Yes, they clearly do. As expected, beginning teachers experience some frustration as they grow into the job. For the first time in their lives, they are expected to assume an active teaching role, to take charge, to set standards, and to assess results. Their professional role and developmental stage are not yet in sync. Moreover, when they try to assert themselves, they often mistake opposition for dominance. We've frequently observed beginning teachers combine strictness with aggression. The announcement "No talking is allowed here" (DO) is almost always followed by the sanction "or you'll see what happens!" (OD). This combination of behaviors can easily escalate into an unproductive situation.

Beginning teachers do manage to adopt greater dominant behavior, and this increases for the first 6–10 years of their careers. They gradually feel more secure in the classroom, and exhibit increasing control over the proceedings. After the 10th year, things begin to level out in terms of dominance, though the teacher's cooperative behavior begins to decrease at this point.

Overall, then, teacher-student relationships steadily improve during the first 6–10 years of a teacher's career, leading to greater student achievement and more positive attitudes. Soon after, however, a change occurs that is both welcome and unwelcome. Teachers appear to decline in cooperation and increase in opposition, a change that negatively affects student atti-

tudes. They also become more strict, however, and this can heighten student achievement. (For more details on teacher-behavior over time, see Wubbels and Levy 1993, chapter 7.)

Issues for Professional Development

Our findings indicate that teacher education programs, both pre- and inservice, should encourage certain types of behaviors. In brief, good teachers are both dominant and cooperative. They should be able to empathize with students, understand their world, and listen to them. They should be able to set standards and maintain control while allowing students to have responsibility and freedom to learn.

Good teachers, moreover, know how they're being perceived by students. Their views of the way they are communicating in class match those of their students. As a result, they are better able to align their instruction with student needs and preferences. Conversely, average teachers see themselves differently (and usually better) than their students. This finding highlights the importance of reflectiveness through student feedback.

We've also noted how difficult it is to achieve stylistic flexibility. Dominant teachers will struggle during those moments that call for active listening and student initiative. They're great at providing structure, lecturing, handing out assignments, and staying on task. Switching to a more passive mode, however, presents problems. For example, when a student disagrees with the dominant teacher's position, this type of teacher may find it difficult to ascertain what the youngster is saying and feeling before reacting. These types of exchanges can easily invoke teacher uncertainty or aggression, a danger that points to the need to allow students the opportunity to explain and clarify. These teachers often confuse providing latitude with their own uncertainty and regard this as a weakness.

We've tried to describe a different side of effective teachers. In addition

to mastering the methodology necessary to design lessons and implement the curriculum, teachers must develop the communicative techniques that establish favorable relationships with learners. Both sets of skills are equally important. In fact, relationship-building is a prerequisite to a positive classroom climate. Without this piece of the repertoire, teachers cannot fully develop in their practice.

[1] For more information on the Questionnaire for Teacher Interaction, see Wubbels and Levy 1993, which includes a copy of it, or contact Jack Levy at the address below.

References

Borich, G. D. (1988). *Effective Teaching Methods*. Columbus, Ohio: Merill.

Brekelmans, M., T. Wubbels, and H. A. Creton. (1990). "A Study of Student Perceptions of Physics Teacher Behavior." *Journal of Research in Science Teaching* 27: 335–350.

Fisher, D., D. Henderson, and B. Fraser. (1995). "Interpersonal Behavior in Senior High School Biology Classes." *Research in Science Education* 25, 2: 125–133.

Getzels, J. W., and P. W. Jackson. (1963). "The Teacher's Personality and Characteristics." In *Handbook of Research on Teaching*, edited by N.L. Gage, pp. 506–582. Chicago: Rand McNally and Company.

Goh, S. C. (1994). "Interpersonal Teacher Behavior, Classroom Climate, and Student Outcomes in Primary Mathematics Classes in Singapore." Doctoral thesis. Curtin University, Perth, Australia.

Leary, T. (1957). *An Interpersonal Diagnosis of Personality*. New York: Ronald Press Company.

Wubbels, T., and J. Levy. (1993). *Do You Know What You Look Like? Interpersonal Relationships in Education*. London: The Falmer Press.

Theo Wubbels is Professor of Education, IVLOS Institute of Education, Utrecht University, P.O. Box 80127, 3508TC Utrecht, The Netherlands (e-mail: t.wubbels@ivlos.ruu.nl). **Jack Levy** is Professor, Graduate School of Education, George Mason University, MS 4B3, Fairfax, VA 22030-4444 (e-mail: jlevy@gmu.edu). **Mieke Brekelmans** is Associate Professor of Education, IVLOS Institute of Education, Utrecht University, P.O. Box 80127, 3508TC Utrecht, The Netherlands (e-mail: m.brekelmans@ivlos.ruu.nl).

A Look to the Future

As we prepare to soon move into the twenty-first century, we see the possibility of great change in how students learn in schools brought about by the revolution in computer-generated learning resources. The World Wide Web is here, and the electronic availability of massive knowledge bases at moderate or low cost is multiplying the possibilities of what teachers can do with their students. Making adequate computing equipment and educational software available to all teachers will be one of the economic challenges school systems will face in the near future.

Which education philosophy is most appropriate for our schools as we approach the year 2000? This is a complex question, and we will, as a free people, come up with alternative visions of what it will be. Let us explore what might be possible as more students go on the Internet, and the wonder of the cyberspace revolution opens to teachers and students. What challenges can we expect in using the technology of the cyberspace revolution in our schools? What blessings can we hope for? What sorts of changes need to occur in how people go to schools as well as in what they do when they get there?

The breakthroughs that are developing in new learning and communications technologies are really quite impressive. They will definitely affect how human beings learn in the very near-term future. While we look forward with considerable optimism and confidence to these future educational developments, there are still many controversies that will continue to be debated in the early years of the twentieth century; the "school choice" issue is one. We will not attain all the goals that were set for us for the year 2000 by the governors of the states and former president George Bush in 1989; but we will make significant progress toward them. Some very interesting new proposals for new forms of schooling, both in public schools and private schools, are under development. We can expect to see at least a few of these proposals tried in practice in the next few years.

Some of the demographic changes and challenges involving young people in the United States are staggering. Ten percent of all American teenage girls will become pregnant each year, the highest rate in the developed world. At least 100,000 American elementary school children get drunk once a week. Incidence of venereal disease has tripled among adolescents in the United States since 1965. The actual school dropout rate in the United States stands at 30 percent.

The student populations of North America reflect vital social and cultural forces at work to destroy our progress. In the United States, a massive secondary school dropout problem has been developing steadily through the past decade. The next decade will reveal how public school systems will address this and other unresolved problems brought about by dramatic upheavals in demographics. In the immediate future, we will be able to see if emergency or alternative certification measures adopted by states affect achievement of the objectives of our reforms.

At any given moment in a people's history, several alternative future directions are open to them. North American educational systems have been subjected to one wave after another of recommendations for programmatic change. Is it any wonder that change is a sensitive watchword for persons in teacher education on this continent? What specific directions it will take in the immediate future depend on which recommendations of the reform agenda are implemented, which agencies of government (local, state/provincial, and federal) will pay for the very high costs of reform, and which shifts in perceived national educational priorities by the public will occur that will affect fundamental realignments of our educational goals.

Basic changes in society's career patterns should also be considered. It is estimated that in the United States the average nonagricultural worker now makes a major job change about five times in his or her career. The schools will surely be affected, indirectly or directly, by this major social phenomenon. Changes in the social structure due to divorce, unemployment, and job retraining efforts will also have an impact. Educational systems are integral parts of the broader social systems that created them; if the larger social system experiences fundamental change, this is reflected in the educational system.

In the area of information science and computer technologies applicable for use in educational systems, the development of new products is so rapid that we cannot predict what technological capacities may be available to schools 20 years from now. In addition, basic computer literacy is becoming more and more widespread in the population. We are entering—indeed we are in—a period of human history when knowledgeable people can control far greater information (and have immediate access to it) than at any previous time. As new information command systems evolve, this phenomenon will become more and more meaningful to all of us.

The future of education will be determined by the current debate concerning what constitutes a just, national

tury. All of the social, economic, and educational institutions globally will be affected by these scientific breakthroughs. The basic issue is not whether schools can remain aloof from the needs of industry or the economic demands of society but how they can emphasize the noblest ideals of free persons in the face of inevitable technological and economic changes. Another concern is how to let go of predetermined visions of the future that limit our possibilities as free people. The schools, of course, will be called upon to face these issues. We need the most enlightened, insightful, and compassionate teachers ever educated by North American universities to prepare the youth of the future in a manner that will humanize the high-tech world in which they live.

All of the articles included in this unit can be related to discussions on the goals of education, the future of education, or curriculum development. They also reflect highly divergent perspectives in the philosophy of education.

Looking Ahead: Challenge Questions

What might be the shape of school curricula by the year 2020?

What changes in society are most likely to affect educational change?

Based on all of the commission reports of recent years, is it possible to identify any clear directions in which teacher education in North America is headed? How can we build a better future for teachers?

How can information about population demographics, potential discoveries in the basic sciences, and the rate and direction of technological change assist in planning for our educational future?

How can schools prepare students to live and work in an uncertain future? What knowledge bases are most important? What skills are most important?

Will privatized schools represent an expansion of educational opportunities for our children? Support your answer.

What is made possible in the classroom by the new learning and communications technologies that have been developed?

What can we expect to be the challenges confronting educators as more schools are enabled to go on the Internet and take advantage of the information technologies of the cyberspace age?

What should be the philosophical ideals for American schools in the fast-approaching twenty-first century?

response to human needs in a period of technological change. The history of technological change in all human societies since the beginning of industrial development clearly demonstrates that major advances in technology and breakthroughs in the basic sciences lead to more rapid rates of social change. Society is on the verge of discoveries that will lead to the creation of entirely new technologies in the dawning years of the twenty-first cen-

The Silicon Classroom

School districts are rushing to spend billions of dollars on computers. It's not clear they have a clue what to do with them.

DAVID A. KAPLAN
AND ADAM ROGERS

NEVER HEARD OF A COMPANY called MIPS? It'd like to change that. So this high-tech chipmaker decided to raise its profile outside Silicon Valley. And what better way to do that than join the bandwagon of companies giving away computer stuff and Internet access to schools? Late last year, MIPS solicited grant applications from needy institutions around the country that wanted free transportation onto the Information Superhighway. Lots of schools in rural communities and inner cities said they wanted to hook up. But MIPS gave its $55,600 award to John J. Pershing junior high in a tough Brooklyn neighborhood. Pershing had a different idea. "They didn't want our computers," says Steve Schick of MIPS. "They had a more urgent need—desks and chairs."

So much for technology revolutionizing American education. Since the late 1970s, billions of dollars—and perhaps even more words—have been spent to make your kid more wired than Bill Gates. In the current academic year alone, some estimates put technology spending in K–12 public schools at $4 billion, twice the amount spent on textbooks. Just as Herbert Hoover once promised a chicken in every pot, today politicians pledge a computer in every classroom. To show their commitment, the president and vice president of the United States even spent a recent Saturday running Internet wire through a California high school. But after years of hype and hope for electronic education, despite the best of intentions, the revolution isn't upon us.

A Guide for Parents

Your kid's school just got computers. But does anyone know what to do with them? Questions to ask:

• Can the teachers use the equipment?

Sounds obvious, but many educators don't have enough training. They need to be computer-literate and know how to integrate software into the curriculum.

• What are the computers used for?

Skip "drill-and-kill" applications. Look for problem-solving and exploration.

• Is there full access to the Internet?

A commercial online service like Prodigy isn't enough. Get unlimited service—and supervise it to keep kids off the Penthouse page.

• Is the technology up to date?

You need speed, memory and a CD-ROM. Old won't do.

The problem isn't computers themselves. "If a child can't read and do his math at the end of the year," asks Apple vice president Terry Crane, "would you blame the pencil?" Nobody except a Luddite doubts that age-appropriate technology can open new vistas, promote communication and even assist traditional rote learning. The Internet can give any student, even in the inner city, a digital field trip: access to explore a worldwide network of libraries and vast amounts of information presented in text, sound and graphics. The Net also can allow students and teachers to talk to their counterparts around the globe, maybe piping in the best physics teacher in the state for a demonstration. CD-ROMs and multimedia software offer "self-teaching" programs on reading, math, music and any subject a clever designer can dream up. Sure, some of this material can be learned with a book, but anyone who's ever played solitaire on a PC knows that digital interactivity is more engaging.

No, the crisis of computers and education isn't the lack of a millennial vision, but the good old 20th-century problems of lousy planning and bad management. For starters, many teachers don't know how to use the gadgets. "All over the country overhead projectors sit on shelves because a bulb burned out and nobody knew how to change it," says Richard White, technology administrator for Chicago's schools. "Teachers will have to get as comfortable with computers as blackboards, or it all will be a waste of money."

Best use: The larger difficulty is that both the sugar-daddy companies that make the equipment and the educators who want it usually have no clue about the best use of computers. They know that making students proficient players of "Doom" isn't the goal. But what is? Drill-and-kill memorization in arithmetic and spelling? Learning how to design a warm house in Antarctica? Or just making fourth graders more computer-literate entrants in the job market of 2010? And then how do you measure and quantify success? "A lot of people advocating the new technologies haven't thought real hard about the goals," insists Martha Stone Wiske, codirector of Harvard's Educational Technology Center. "They're well-meaning folks who simply think computers are a stepping stone to modernity."

At the Riviera Middle School in suburban Miami, for instance, one class of students devoted its 20 new Macintoshes not to gathering information but to designing cooler report covers. Term papers came in with gorgeous typefaces. But the writing stank. The teacher blamed herself. "If I don't say, 'Save graphics until the very end,' they'll spend the whole time playing with fonts," says teacher Roxanne Senders. Educators agree that computer literacy doesn't necessarily generate the traditional kind. Indeed the Internet may breed a kind of intellectual laziness. The Net's ability to find and list mountains of data, says Sherry Turkle of MIT, is no substitute for figuring out how to organize that information.

To show students how to exploit the computers, teachers need training. But they're not getting it. As Wiske reports, "Teachers say, 'Don't hand me the bare tool. I need curriculum to connect it to my life in the school—and I haven't got the time to invent that'." A 1995 federal study found that states put roughly 15 percent of their edutech budgets toward staff development, and recommend that the percentage be doubled. In West Virginia, the budget figure is 30 percent, and test scores have improved. But that statistic has a wrinkle: it's impossible to separate the effect of computers from the effect of better-trained teachers generally.

Obsolete equipment: Then there's the issue of what to buy. Neither the physical nor the administrative infrastructure exists to help the poor purchasing agents. One school gets Apple, another IBM. The technology changes so quickly that by the time the bureaucrats make a decision the equipment they buy is obsolete. And the schools' buildings themselves? Few were constructed with raised floors, dropped ceilings, optic fiber coursing through the walls, phone jacks and multiple outlets in every classroom, and other electronic accouterments of the 21st century.

That's not a problem at Du Sable High in one of the poorest sections of Chicago. High-tech is in full bloom. The school is the first in town to be fully wired, and every student has an Internet account. On a recent morning, the assignment was to write a report on a famous artist—something that could've been done with an encyclopedia. Students found themselves cruising sites like the Cline Fine Art Gallery in Santa Fe and the Arta Gallery in Jerusalem. One student was more curious. He wanted to find NBA standings on the Net and see how his Bulls were doing. The teacher, in keeping with the project, told him to explore on and find out who created the Bulls logo. It was a doable assignment. But the kid wasn't interested. That's not the computer's fault.

With TODD OPPENHEIMER *and* DOGEN HANNAH *in San Francisco,* PETER KATEL *in Miami and* STEVE RHODES *in Chicago*

Revisiting Tomorrow's Classrooms

Richard F. Bowman Jr.
Professor of Education
Winona State University
Winona, Minnesota

It is very difficult to make predictions, especially about the future.
—NIELS BOHR

In "Teaching in Tomorrow's Classrooms,"* I asserted that, "given what we know about the nature of the learner, our evolving cultural values and beliefs, our dawning technological capabilities, and the anticipated demands of our tomorrows upon us as citizens, consumers, producers, and spiritual beings, a compelling question emerges. What potential aims of education cry our for discussion, debate, and possible adoption in tomorrow's classrooms? In what ways, moreover, might such newly-christened aims be operationalized in the classrooms of the future?" (Bowman 1985, 296).

Despite Bohr's words of caution, I am delighted to revisit the "Six Aims for Tomorrow" that comprised the focus of "Teaching in Tomorrow's Classrooms." To what

---

*"Teaching in Tomorrow's Classrooms" originally appeared in *The Educational Forum*, Volume 49, Number 2, Winter 1985, pp. 296–300. In Volume 60, Summer 1996, *The Educational Forum* reprinted Bowman's 1985 essay; then it looked "at how events in classrooms and the world have impacted Bowman's aims for better student preparation" in an essay by Grant Mabie; finally, both articles were followed by this 1996 essay by Richard Bowman. **Ed.**

From *The Educational Forum*, Summer 1996, pp. 304–307. © 1996 by Kappa Delta Pi, an International Honor Society in Education. Reprinted by permission.

extent, then, have educators spliced the "Six Aims for Tomorrow" into the culture of contemporary classrooms?

In the first of the "Six Aims," I argued that students "experience relatively few opportunities for engaging in interdependent behaviors through collaborative problem solving and discovery" or by "psychologically connecting with others on issues of mutual concern" (Bowman 1985, 297). Today, corporate culture is awash in paradigm shifts: "from management to leadership," "from individuals to teams," and "in how we reward and recognize people for their efforts" (Tompkins 1995, 11). Yesterday's silos of organizational awareness have given way to team-based organizational structures intended to provide a framework for the unification of all employees' efforts. As Pascale (1996, 62) noted, "Modern corporations seek to bind people together in emotionally powerful ways to achieve excellence in certain kinds of activities. Cast in a very personal metaphor, the modern corporation must master the art of 'marrying' individuals to accomplish common goals." Team-based activities in today's K–12 classrooms require that students be more skilled, more adaptable, and more capable of working collaboratively, mirroring the interconnectivity of the '90s corporate culture. Ironically, what is reemerging is a communitarian dimension of learning that once served as the cultural centerpiece of the one-room school. Thus, the daunting task for educators today is to initiate and sustain in students a disposition to want to connect. As Manville and Foote (1996, 67) stated, "Interconnectivity begins with people who want to connect. After that, tools and technology can make the connection."

The second asserted that "educators need to develop rich opportunities for youth to confront, and cope with, the demands of global interdependence by immersing students in a diversity of thought, values, beliefs, and cultures" (Bowman 1985, 297). Gardner (1995, 7) recounted admiringly the efforts of Pope John XXIII to "reduce tensions between the superpowers, and build bridges that spanned many faiths, nations, and ideologies." Engagingly, Gardner argued that "travel in one's youth" (1995, 20), which Pope John XXIII did extensively, is one of the early markers of effective leadership. Multicultural education programs today assume that when majority and minority persons interact meaningfully, enlightened tolerance replaces prejudices and hostilities (D'Souza 1995).

Both collegiate and K–12 curricula reflect a resurgence of interest in meaningful cross-cultural encounters through travel, foreign-exchange students, and multicultural internships. At Moorhead State University, for example, over 2,000 education majors have participated in recent years in one of three supervised clinical-training experiences: Student Teaching Abroad, Sophomore Multicultural Internship in the Rio Grande Valley, and Student Teaching in South Texas. At the core of each of these programs is the belief that encountering diversity forces one to deconstruct and reconstruct one's view of the world and thus defines, in part, what it means to be an educated human being. Academically, each program provides structured practice for the dispositions and skills required for nurturing associational ties and consummating community and global life. Geopolitically, each functions as a poignant reminder that "peace is not an easy thing, but something that must be struggled for" (Norris 1996, 8).

In the third, I argued that, of the "attributes most central to survival in the decades ahead, none is more likely to be more critical than that of developing an evolving tolerance for ambiguity" (Bowman 1985, 297). Relatedly, it was noted that "learning to live with a sense of catastrophe may well circumscribe the curriculum of tomorrow" (Bowman 1985, 298). Recent downsizing, precipitated by quickly changing markets and technologies, has ushered in one of the most wrenching economic and social transitions in U.S. history. When coupled with a mushrooming concern over moral decline and an attending loss of confidence in government, the downsizing of more than 43 million jobs in the United States since 1979 is perceived widely as analogous to the trashing of our national soul. Uchitelle and Kleinfield (1996, 26) pointed to "diluting self-worth, splintering families, fragmenting communities, altering the chemistry of the workplace, and roiling political waters."

The outline of a narrative that attempts to make sense of an emergent, often alarming, economic and social reality is evolving in the classroom and the workplace. Many of today's students, for example, are being urged to embrace an ethos of self-reliance. Boldt (1996) argued that teachers should encourage students to wed talent and skill in an attempt to nourish their inner selves. Additionally, students of all ages are reminded daily that their career destiny rests in their own hands as never before. In workplace education, for example, Intel employees are responsible for gaining new skills so that they can continue to be employable either inside or outside the company. Again, one's career destiny is in one's own hands. Relatedly, we learn that, in the workplace and in the classroom, spending more time "focusing on the solution-after-next" as opposed to the "next solution" will sustain an evolving tolerance for ambiguity (Tompkins 1995, 19).

The fourth suggested that tomorrow's "students will engage in daily learning activities that invite the 'examination of sources and processes,'" so that meaning will become "the ultimate objective of learning" (Bowman 1985, 298; Foshay 1976, 145). In the postindustrial era, knowledge workers and students are being nudged beyond cognitive knowledge (know-what) and advanced skills (know-how) to systems understanding (know-why) and self-motivated creativity (care-why). Each must examine complex sources and processes to "anticipate subtle interactions and unintended consequences" and to cultivate the ultimate expression of systems understanding, "a highly trained intuition" (Quinn, Anderson, and Finkelstien 1996, 72). Educators in both the classroom and the workplace are also actively nurturing self-motivated creativity— the will, motivation, and adaptability—that will allow learners to thrive in the face of cascading change. Many contemporary classrooms exude a "demanding ecology of thought, imagination, decision, and action" (Philibert 1996, xiv).

The fifth focused on the concept of "fixability," in which "tomorrow's learners will begin to view themselves as manipulators of fractured knowledge" (Bowman 1985, 299). Interestingly, one of the major classroom themes today is the oft-expressed philosophy that "all students can learn." As a society, we are beginning to reject the "unconscious educational rule of thumb" that the function of the nation's schools and universities is to "weed out, not to cultivate, students for whom they have accepted responsibility" (Brock 1993, 1). Schools across the country have also embedded the concept of "fixability" in programs like "Conflict Management" and "Conflict Resolution."

In the last of the "Six Aims for Tomorrow," I predicted that a "new type of social structure will likely emerge: a network-based classroom" in which "computers will permit dialogues with diverse audiences on problems and hypotheses related to class activities" (Bowman 1985, 299). I asserted that the "dialogical dimensions of networked computing are likely to nourish a heightened reverence for multiple points of view, as well as an emergent awareness of learners' decreasing dependence on traditional authority figures" (Bowman 1985, 299). Today, access to the Internet allows faculty to teach and students to learn differently from just a decade ago. The exploding interest in distance learning and lifelong learning underscores how information technology is changing the expectations of faculty and students alike. A digital, networked, interactive, multimedia classroom, for example, fully operationalizes the related promise of "just-in-time learning." Additionally, many of today's students employ a full range of information technologies as "tools for manipulating ideas and images and for communicating effectively with other people" (McClure 1996, 29). The emergent environment is one in which students learn and assist others to learn with new tools and expanded information resources: literary and historic databases, simulations in the social sciences, digital imagery in art, theater, and architecture, and virtual laboratories in chemistry, physics, and biology" (Ringle 1996, 30).

Today, the key to success in the classroom and in the workplace is to discover "compelling reasons for finding others with knowledge to share, who in turn have compelling reasons to share their knowledge when asked" (Manville and Foote 1996, 67). The new-found connectivity also gives prominence to the notion of a genuine learning community in which informal groups of individuals use collective knowledge to solve problems and accomplish specific tasks. Ironically, in the classroom culture of the '90s, learning organizations will likely "leverage knowledge through networks of people who collaborate—not through networks of technology that interconnect" (Manville and Foote 1996, 66), suggesting a shift in authority, but not eliminating the human component in education.

REFERENCES

Boldt, L. 1996. *How to find the work that you love.* New York: Viking Penguin.

Bowman, R. 1985. Teaching in Tomorrow's Classrooms, *Forum* (Winter): 296–300.

Brock, W. 1993. *An American imperative: Higher expectations for higher education.* Racine, Wisc.: Johnson Foundation.

D'Souza, D. 1995. *The end of racism: Principles for a multiracial society.* New York: Free Press.

Foshay, A. W. 1976. Utilizing man's experience: The quest for meaning. In *Issues in secondary education,* ed. W. Van Til, 137–52. Chicago: National Society for the Study of Education.

Gardner, H. 1995. *Leading minds: An anatomy of leadership.* New York: Basic Books.

Manville, B., and N. Foote. 1996. Strategy as if knowledge mattered. *Fast Company* 2(1): 66–67.

McClure, P. 1996. Technology plans and measurable outcomes. *Educom Review* 31(3): 29–30.

Norris, K. 1996. *The cloister walk.* New York: Riverhead.

Pascale, R. 1996. The false security of 'employability.' *Fast Company* 2(1): 62, 64.

Philibert, P. 1996. Preface to *The cloister walk,* by K. Norris, xiv. New York: Riverhead.

Quinn, J., P. Anderson, and S. Finkelstien. 1996. Managing professional intellect: Making the most of the best. *Harvard Business Review* 74(2): 71–80.

Ringle, M. 1996. Technology plans and measurable outcomes. *Educom Review* 31(3): 30, 32.

Tompkins, J. 1995. *The genesis enterprise.* New York: McGraw-Hill.

Uchitelle, L., and N. R. Kleinfield. 1996. On the battlefields of business, millions of casualties. *New York Times,* 3 March, 1, 26, 28–29.

A Philosophy of Education for the Year 2000

A conception of school as a moral equivalent of home is as responsive to societal conditions at the end of the 20th century as the factory model of schooling is unresponsive to them, Ms. Martin points out.

Jane Roland Martin

JANE ROLAND MARTIN is a professor of philosophy emerita at the University of Massachusetts, Boston. Most of the material in this article is drawn from her book The Schoolhome: Rethinking Schools for Changing Families *(Harvard University Press, 1992).*

A T THE TURN of this century—in 1899, to be exact—John Dewey started off a series of lectures in Chicago with a description of the changes in American society wrought by the Industrial Revolution. "It is radical conditions which have changed, and only an equally radical change in education suffices," he said.[1] One of those radical conditions was the removal of manufacture from households into factories and shops. It was Dewey's genius to see that the work that in the relatively recent past had been done at home had offered genuine educational benefits, which had become endangered. It was his great insight that some other educational agent could and should take over what had previously been one of the responsibilities of the home.

I draw attention to Dewey's analysis because in the United States today home and family have once more been transformed. The critical factor now is the removal of parents from the household. With many households headed by a single parent, usually a mother, and most families in need of two salaries just to maintain a home, for many hours each day there is simply no one at home.

If nothing more were at stake than a child's misgivings about being home alone or a mother's exhaustion after working a double shift, educators might be justified in ignoring our changed reality.[2] But there are the three brothers, ages 12 to 15, in Lawrence, Massachusetts, who were arrested in February of 1994 for stealing their mother's jewelry to pay drug dealers for crack cocaine. "They looked like three little old men," said the police officer.[3] There are also the juveniles who were arrested two weeks before this incident for entering a roller rink in Boston and shooting seven children. "The police should have been there to take the gun away from my son before he went inside," said one mother.[4] And then there is the 4-year-old who, even as I was writing this, was discovered in unspeakable conditions in his own home. In tomorrow's newspaper, as on yesterday's television screen, there will be accounts of teenage shoot-outs, 5-year-olds toting guns, children in the drug trade.

I have no quarrel with those who point out that science and math and literacy education in the U.S. are not what they should be. I am as thoroughly convinced as anyone that the country's vocational education system needs overhauling. But this nation's political and educational leaders talk repeatedly about setting higher standards in the teaching of literacy, math, and science and about the schools' failure to develop a highly skilled work force—without ever seeming to notice that our changed social reality makes correspondingly radical changes in schools imperative. To put it starkly, there is now a great domestic vacuum in the lives of children from all walks of life. In light of this radical change in conditions, once again the pressing question has become, What radical changes in school will suffice?

Needed: A Moral Equivalent Of Home

In the U.S., as in other industrialized societies, home has traditionally been the agency responsible for turning infants who are "barely human and utterly unsocialized" into "full-fledged members of the culture."[5] Sherry Ortner's words bring to mind the "Wild Boy" of Aveyron. Until he emerged from the woods, Victor had no exposure to the curriculum that inducts our young into human culture—not even to wearing clothes, eating food other than nuts and potatoes, hearing sounds, sleeping in a bed, distinguishing between hot and cold, or

From *Phi Delta Kappan*, January 1995, pp. 355–359. © 1995 by Phi Delta Kappa International, Inc. Reprinted by permission.

walking rather than running.[6] He had to be taught the things that people—other than parents of the very young and teachers of differently abled children—assume human beings instinctively know.

Shattering the illusion that what is called "second nature" is innate, Victor's case dramatically illustrates that what we adults learned at home as young children is far more basic than the school studies we call the basics. Years ago, one of the research questions I was asking was, What entitles us to call some studies rather than others "the basics"?[7] My answer was that reading, writing, and arithmetic are considered essential—hence basic—components of education because of their roles in preparing young people for membership in the public world—specifically, for enabling them to be citizens in a democracy and to be economically self-sufficient individuals. In addition, we take the three R's to be fundamental because of the part they play in initiating our young into history, literature, philosophy, and the arts—"high" culture or Culture with a capital C. Bring the home's educational role into the picture, however, and one realizes that these three goals—achieving economic viability, becoming a good citizen, and acquiring high culture—make sense only for people who have already learned the basic mores of society.

Now there are some today who perceive the great domestic vacuum in children's lives, blame it on women, and would have us turn back the clock to a presumed golden age when mothers stayed home and took care of their young. These social analysts are simply oblivious to the present demands of economic necessity. They are also loath to acknowledge that it is not women's exodus from the private home each day that creates a vacuum in our children's lives. It is the exodus of *both* sexes. Had men not left the home when the Industrial Revolution removed work from that site—or had fathers not continued to leave the home each morning after their children were born—women's departure would not have the ramifications for children that it does.

The question is not, Whom can we blame? It is, What are we as a nation, a culture, a society going to do about our children?

In a widely read essay titled "A Moral Equivalent of War," written in 1910, William James introduced the concept of moral equivalency into our language. Given the great domestic vacuum in the U.S. today, the concept of a moral equivalent of home is as germane as James' moral equivalent of war ever was. Indeed, of the many things we can and should do for our children, perhaps the most important is to establish a moral equivalent of home for them.

To avoid misunderstanding, let me say that I am not proposing that home be abolished. When James spoke of a moral equivalent of war, he had in mind a *substitute* for war that would preserve those martial virtues that he considered the "higher" aspects of militarism.[8] When I speak of a moral equivalent of home, I have in mind the *sharing of responsibility* for those educative functions of home that are now at risk of extinction. Who or what will do the sharing? In accordance with Dewey's insight and in light of the universality, ubiquitousness, and claims on a child's time that characterize schooling, there is no institution so appropriate for this task as school. Yet there can be no doubt that school is an overburdened institution. How then in good conscience can I or anyone ask it to take on more responsibilities? Moreover, will school even *be* school if it shoulders the functions of the home?

If one learns nothing else from the study of educational history, one discovers that education in general and schooling in particular are as subject to change, as much a part of the societal flux, as everything else.[9] Thus to suppose that school has some immutable task or function that it and only it must carry out and that other tasks contradict or defile its nature is to attribute to school an essential nature it does not have. Yes, school can add new functions without losing its identity. It can also shed old ones, as well as share some of these—for instance, vocational education with industry, or science education and history education with museums. After all, those old functions were themselves once brand new.

History, then, teaches that school can be turned into a moral equivalent of home without its becoming hopelessly overextended. It teaches that, even as we assign the school some of the old educative functions of the home, we can ask the many other educational agents that now exist to share the educational work that our culture currently assigns to school.

The Schoolhome

Because they think of school as a special kind of production site—a factory that turns out workers for the nation's public and private sectors—government officials, business leaders, granting agencies, and educational administrators focus today on standards. As they see it, the products of our nation's classrooms, like the automobiles on a General Motors assembly line and the boxes of cereal in a Kellogg's plant, should be made according to specifications. When minimum requirements are not met, the obvious remedy is to tighten quality control. Colleges and universities are apt to respond to this demand by raising entrance requirements. Public schools will launch efforts to improve testing, to hold teachers accountable for student performance, and to standardize curriculum.

In an age when the lives of all too many children bring to mind Dickens' novels, it is perhaps to be expected that young children in school are pictured as raw material, teachers as workers who process their students before sending them on to the next station on the assembly line, and the curriculum as machinery that over the span of 12 or so years forges the nation's young into marketable products. However, this conception of schooling totally ignores the needs and conditions of children, their parents, and the nation itself at the end of the 20th century.

At the very least, children need to love and be loved. They need to feel safe, secure, and at ease with themselves and others. They need to experience intimacy and affection. They need to be perceived as unique individuals and to be treated as such. The factory model of schooling presupposes that such conditions have already been met when children arrive in school, that the school's raw materials—the children—have, so to speak, been "preprocessed." Resting on the unspoken assumption that home is the school's partner in the educational process, the model takes it for granted that it is home's job to fulfill these basic needs. Thus the production-line picture derives its plausibility from the premise that school does not have to be a loving place, that the classroom does not have to have an affectionate atmosphere, and that teachers do not have to treasure the individuality of students because the school's silent partner will take care of all of this.

One consequence of the great domestic vacuum that exists in children's lives today is that we can no longer depend on home to do the preprocessing. Speaking generally, the home cannot be counted on to transmit the love; the three C's of care, concern, and connection; and the knowledge, skills, attitudes, and values that enable each individual born into this society to become a member of human culture in the broadest sense of that term. If for no other reason, then, the factory model of schooling is untenable. To be sure, one can irrationally cling to it. Insisting that the school's raw materials are so defective that they cannot possibly be turned into acceptable end products, one can blame and penalize the victims of the latest transformation of the home instead of insisting that the school respond to their plight. The nation's children will be far better served, however, if we change our conception of school. The nation also stands to gain from a new idea of school, for its continued well-being ultimately depends on the well-being of the next generation and of its successors.

The recent transformation of home and family belies the very model of schooling that our political and educational leaders tacitly accept. A conception of school as a moral equivalent of home, on the other hand, is as responsive to conditions at the end of the 20th century as the factory model is insensible to them. Thus I propose that we as a nation set ourselves the goal of turning our school*houses* into school*homes*.

Instead of focusing our gaze on abstract norms, standardized tests, generalized rates of success, and uniform outcomes, the idea of the schoolhome directs attention to actual educational practice. Of course, a schoolhome will teach the three R's. But it will give equal emphasis to the three C's of care, concern, and connection—not by designating formal courses in these fundamentals but by being a domestic environment characterized by safety, security, nurturance, and love.

In a schoolhome, classroom climate, school routines and rituals, teachers' modes of teaching, and children's ways of learning are all guided by a spirit of familylike affection. And so are the relationships between teachers and students and between the students themselves. The inhabitants of a schoolhome will learn science and literature, history and math. But they will also learn to make domesticity their business. Feeling that they belong in the schoolhome and, at the same time, that the schoolhome belongs to them, the children will take pride in their physical environment while happily contributing their own labor to its upkeep. Perhaps even more important, with their teachers' help, the pupils in a schoolhome will countenance no violence, be it corporal punishment or teacher sarcasm, the bullying of one child by others or the

terrorization of an entire class, the use of hostile language about whole races or the denigration of one sex.

Now I realize that America's private homes were never idyllic sanctuaries and that at present they, like our streets, are sites of violence. When I propose that our schools be homelike, however, I have in mind *ideal* homes, not dysfunctional ones. Thus, in recommending that school be a moral equivalent of home, I assume a home that is warm and loving and a family that isneither physically nor psychologically abusive and that believes in and strives for the equality of the sexes.

Yet is home an appropriate metaphor for school in a nation whose population is as diverse as ours? It is, provided we recognize that, one century after Dewey's Chicago lecture, the question has become, How can we create a moral equivalent of home in which children of all races, classes, and ethnicities feel at home?

Needed: A New Curricular Paradigm

Surprisingly, those today who criticize this country's schools and make recommendations for their improvement pay little attention to the changed composition of the nation's population. I call them "restorationists" because, seemingly impervious to the pressing need our nation now has for a new inclusionary curriculum that will serve all our children, they want to restore the old outmoded one. Looking back with longing at the curriculum of their youth, they would reinstate a course of study designed for an earlier age and a different people.

It scarcely needs saying that a more inclusive curriculum is not necessarily a better one. Yet in a society in the process of changing color, can courses in African philosophy be considered frivolous? In a nation with a history of slavery and a continuing record of racial division and inequality, can the reading of slave narratives be irrelevant to the study of American history and literature? In a land in which rape is rampant, the victims of child sexual abuse are most often girls, and women are subjected to sexual harassment at home, at school, and at work, is it sensible to say that courses that represent and analyze women's history, lives, and experiences are parochial and take too subjective a point of view?

If all U.S. children are to feel at home in both school and society, then schools must reserve space in the cur-

riculum for the works, experiences, and societal practices of women as well as men, poor people as well as the middle classes, and ethnic, racial, and other minorities. But even more than this is required.

Protesting a school curriculum very like that which the restorationists would piece back together—one whose subjects of study represent abstract bodies of knowledge divorced from the activities of everyday life—Dewey called on us to educate "the whole child." I, in turn, ask that we educate *all* our children in our *whole* heritage so that they will learn to live in the world together.[10] Because that whole heritage includes ways of living as well as forms of knowing, societal activities and practices as well as literary and artistic achievements, we need more than a curriculum that honors diversity. We need a new curricular paradigm—one that does not ignore the disciplines of knowledge but assigns them their proper place in the general scheme of things as but one part of a person's education; one that integrates thought and action, reason and emotion, education and life; one that does not divorce persons from their social and natural contexts; one that embraces individual autonomy as but one of many values.[11]

Unfortunately, even when this nation's heritage is defined multiculturally, it is too easy for school to instruct children *about* it without ever teaching them to be active and constructive participants in living—let alone how to make the world a better place for themselves and their progeny. This is especially so when the school's business is thought to be the development of children's minds, not their bodies; their thinking and reasoning skills, not their emotional capacities or active propensities. Yet a nation that cannot count on home to perform its traditional educative functions dare not settle for so narrow a definition of the school's task.

We need to ask ourselves if turn-of-the-21st-century America is well-served by a population of onlookers. In 1989, in a letter to the *Boston Globe*, a schoolteacher wrote, "I used to wonder if my adolescent boys would remember my lessons once they left my classroom; now I wonder if they will live to remember them." At about that same time a Boston gang member was reminiscing: "When I was 12, I carried a .38 everywhere. I sold drugs in great balls. I was carryin' the gun just to be carryin' it. I wanted to be someone big. To me, a gun changes a person. It makes 'em brave. Sometimes I would go on the roof and shoot in the air. I felt like, let 'em come up on me. I'd be like Hercules. I even said, 'Let a cop come. I'll get 'em.' "[12]

Five years later the violence in the U.S. is all-pervasive, yet the school's critics and reformers seem as unaware of it as they are unconscious of the transformation of the home and of our changed population—or, if they are aware of the violence, they are quite confident that it is not education's concern. Mindless imitation is, however, the easiest path for someone to follow who has not been trained to bring intelligence to bear on living. In the best of cases, education for spectatorship teaches students to lead divided lives—to apply their intelligence when observing the world but to be unthinking doers. In the worst cases, it consigns them to the nasty, brutish, and short life that the philosopher Thomas Hobbes long ago attributed to the state of nature.

Choosing Integrative Activities of Living

It is sheer folly to expect our young to live and work together at home and in the world if they have never, ever learned to do so. Yet the restorationists would devote little or no curriculum space to the enormous range of ways of acting and forms of living that the young of any nation need to learn. In contrast, in the schoolhome, mind and body, thought and action, reason and emotion are all educated. Furthermore, if the occupations that children pursue there are well-chosen, they will integrate these elements in such a way that they in turn can be integrated into the lives those young people lead both in school and in the world.

When school is a surrogate home, children of all ages and both sexes not only engage in the domestic activities that ground their everyday lives there— e.g., planning, cooking, and serving meals and cleaning, maintaining, and repairing the physical plant—but they also participate in one or more of the integrative endeavors that stand at the very center of the curriculum.

Let me briefly list the integrative potential of two such activities—theater and newspaper. To begin with, theater and newspaper spin webs of theoretical knowledge in which students can be "caught." One thinks immediately of language, literature, and social studies, but serious ethical and legal questions also arise in the course of producing plays and publications.

Moreover, for those who engage in these activities, mathematical, scientific, and technical knowledge loom large. Furthermore, besides spinning webs of knowledge, theater and newspaper spin webs of skills, such as reading, writing, speaking, listening, drawing, designing, and building. In so doing, they connect mind and body, thought and action. By reaching out to every human emotion, they also join both head and hand to heart.

The webs of knowledge and skill that theater and newspaper weave and the integration of thought and action and of reason and emotion that they effect might in themselves justify placing these activities at the center of curriculum. Their integrative claims are enhanced, however, by the fact that social interdependence is built into them from the start. Through the demands of the shared task as well as the realization that everyone's efforts not only count but are vitally important, participants become bonded to one another. These two activities have the added integrative advantage that their products—the plays performed, the newspapers published—can be designed to speak to everyone's experience and to be seen or read by everyone. Tying together the shared emotions that derive from common experiences, the activities can weave young people of different races, classes, ethnicities, physical abilities, and sexual orientations into their own webs of connection.

The Objectives of the Schoolhome

Since there are numerous activities that can be integrative in these several different ways, the decision as to which ones to make the linchpins of any particular schoolhome curriculum must, I think, be based on local considerations, not the least of which are the interests and talents of both the teaching staff and the students. This, of course, means that, as local conditions change, so perhaps will the choice of integrative activities.

I also want to stress that, although theater and newspaper—or, for that matter, farming and building a historical museum—easily lend themselves to vocationalism and professionalism, these are not the interests that the schoolhome represents. Its concern is that the children in its care receive an education for living and working together in the world. Thus the schoolhome is not a training ground for

actors, architects, or journalists. Its students put on plays, raise crops, or put out a newspaper not to win competitions or add to their résumés. The best student actor by Broadway or Hollywood standards does not necessarily play the lead; the best feature writer or cartoonist does not necessarily get published. Rather, the schoolhome is a moral equivalent of home where this nation's children can develop into constructive, contributing members of culture and society—individuals who want to live in a world composed of people very different from themselves and who have practiced doing so. As I envision it, the schoolhome is also a place that possesses and projects a larger point of view; that of this nation itself—and ultimately the whole world of nations and the planet Earth— as a moral equivalent of home.

1. John Dewey, *The School and Society* (Chicago: University of Chicago Press, 1956), p. 12.
2. The material in this paragraph is drawn from Jane Roland Martin, "Fatal Inaction: Overcoming School's Reluctance to Become a Moral Equivalent of Home," paper presented at the American Montessori Society Seminar, Detroit, April 1994.
3. Kevin O'Leary, "Police: 3 Boys Dealing Cocaine," *Boston Globe*, 10 February 1994.
4. Mike Barnicle, "Dropping Our Eyes at True Evil," *Boston Globe*, 25 February 1994.
5. Sherry B. Ortner, "Is Female to Male as Nature Is to Culture?," in Michelle Zimbalist Rosaldo and Louise Lamphere, eds., *Women, Culture, and Society* (Stanford, Calif.: Stanford University Press, 1974), pp. 67–87.
6. Harlan Lane, *The Wild Boy of Aveyron* (Cambridge, Mass.: Harvard University Press, 1979).
7. Jane Roland Martin, "Two Dogmas of Curriculum," *Synthese*, vol. 51, 1982, pp. 5–20.
8. William James, "A Moral Equivalent of War," in Richard A. Wasserstrom, ed., *War and Morality* (Belmont, Calif.: Wadsworth, 1970), pp. 4–14.
9. See, for example, Bernard Bailyn, *Education in the Forming of American Society* (New York: Vintage, 1960); and Lawrence Cremin, *The Genius of American Education* (New York: Vintage, 1965).
10. There is an implicit value judgment in the notion of heritage as I use it. In the broad sense of the term, murder, rape, and so on are part of our heritage. I speak here, however, only of that portion of it that is worthwhile.
11. Jane Roland Martin, "Needed: A New Paradigm for Liberal Education," in Jonas P. Soltis, ed., *Philosophy and Education: 80th NSSE Yearbook, Part I* (Chicago: National Society for the Study of Education, University of Chicago Press, 1981).
12. Linda Ann Banks, letter to the editor, *Boston Globe*, 14 June 1989; and Sally Jacobs and Kevin Cullen, "Gang Rivalry on the Rise in Boston." *Boston Globe*, 16 March 1989.

Index

Credits/Acknowledgments

Cover design by Charles Vitelli.

1. How Others See Us and How We See Ourselves
Facing overview—Dushkin/McGraw-Hill photo by Richard Pawlikowski. 30, 32-33, 35, 37, 41-42, 44—Illustrations by Fred Bell.

2. Rethinking and Changing the Educative Effort
Facing overview—© 1998 by PhotoDisc, Inc. 50—Illustration by Jim Hummel.

3. Striving for Excellence: The Drive for Quality
Facing overview—© 1998 by Cleo Freelance Photography. 74—Illustration by Kay Salem. 82, 86, 88—Illustrations by Bill Dillon.

4. Morality and Values in Education
Facing overview—© 1998 by Cleo Freelance Photography. 100—Illustration by Bill Dillon.

5. Managing Life in Classrooms
Facing overview—© 1998 by Cleo Freelance Photography. 118—Illustration by Bill Dillon.

6. Equal Opportunity in Education
Facing overview—Dushkin/McGraw-Hill photo by Pamela Carley.

7. Serving Special Needs and Concerns
Facing overview—© 1998 by Cleo Freelance Photography. 214-217—Three In a Box, Inc. illustrations by Susan Todd.

8. The Profession of Teaching Today
Facing overview—© 1998 by Cleo Freelance Photography.

9. A Look to the Future
Facing overview—© 1998 by Cleo Freelance Photography.

ANNUAL EDITIONS ARTICLE REVIEW FORM

■ NAME: _____ DATE: _____

■ TITLE AND NUMBER OF ARTICLE: _____

■ BRIEFLY STATE THE MAIN IDEA OF THIS ARTICLE: _____

_____

■ LIST THREE IMPORTANT FACTS THAT THE AUTHOR USES TO SUPPORT THE MAIN IDEA:

_____

_____

_____

_____

■ WHAT INFORMATION OR IDEAS DISCUSSED IN THIS ARTICLE ARE ALSO DISCUSSED IN YOUR TEXTBOOK OR OTHER READINGS THAT YOU HAVE DONE? LIST THE TEXTBOOK CHAPTERS AND PAGE NUMBERS:

_____

_____

_____

_____

_____

■ LIST ANY EXAMPLES OF BIAS OR FAULTY REASONING THAT YOU FOUND IN THE ARTICLE:

_____

_____

_____

_____

■ LIST ANY NEW TERMS/CONCEPTS THAT WERE DISCUSSED IN THE ARTICLE, AND WRITE A SHORT DEFINITION:

_____

_____

_____

_____

*Your instructor may require you to use this ANNUAL EDITIONS Article Review Form in any number of ways: for articles that are assigned, for extra credit, as a tool to assist in developing assigned papers, or simply for your own reference. Even if it is not required, we encourage you to photocopy and use this page; you will find that reflecting on the articles will greatly enhance the information from your text.

We Want Your Advice

ANNUAL EDITIONS revisions depend on two major opinion sources: one is our Advisory Board, listed in the front of this volume, which works with us in scanning the thousands of articles published in the public press each year; the other is you—the person actually using the book. Please help us and the users of the next edition by completing the prepaid article rating form on this page and returning it to us. Thank you for your help!

ANNUAL EDITIONS: EDUCATION 98/99
Article Rating Form

Here is an opportunity for you to have direct input into the next revision of this volume. We would like you to rate each of the 46 articles listed below, using the following scale:

1. **Excellent: should definitely be retained**
2. **Above average: should probably be retained**
3. **Below average: should probably be deleted**
4. **Poor: should definitely be deleted**

Your ratings will play a vital part in the next revision. So please mail this prepaid form to us just as soon as you complete it.
Thanks for your help!

Rating	Article	Rating	Article
	1. Schools That Work		23. Changing the Way Kids Settle Conflicts
	2. Education: More Reform, Please		24. Six Surefire Strategies to Improve Classroom Discipline
	3. Can the Schools Be Saved?		25. Classroom Climate and First-Year Teachers
	4. Republicans and the Education Debate		26. The Challenge of Affirmative Action
	5. Voucher Advocates Step Up Attack		27. Social Class Issues in Family Life Education
	6. The 29th Annual Phi Delta Kappa/Gallup Poll of the Public's Attitudes toward the Public Schools		28. Accommodating Cultural Differences and Commonalities in Educational Practice
	7. Reforming the Wannabe Reformers: Why Education Reforms Almost Always End Up Making Things Worse		29. Children's Views of Poverty: A Review of Research and Implications for Teaching
	8. Sweeping Decentralization of Educational Decision-Making Authority: Lessons from England and New Zealand		30. Early Childhood Education: Issues of Ethnicity and Equity
	9. Teaching Teachers: Graduate Schools of Education Face Intense Scrutiny		31. Race and Class Consciousness among Lower- and Middle-Class Blacks
	10. Learning Curve		32. One Drop of Blood
	11. It Takes a School		33. Invincible Kids
	12. What Matters Most: A Competent Teacher for Every Child		34. Family and Cultural Context: A Writing Breakthrough?
	13. Using Standards to Make a Difference: Four Options		35. Pomp and Promises
	14. The Challenges of National Standards in a Multicultural Society		36. The Computer Delusion
	15. The Case for National Standards and Assessments		37. Columbus in the Curriculum: Shoring Up a Hero
	16. Teachers Favor Standards, Consequences . . . and a Helping Hand		38. When Is Work a Learning Experience?
	17. Professional Ethics and the Education of Professionals		39. Seventy-Five Years Later . . . Gender-Based Harassment in Schools
	18. The Last Freedom: Religion, the Constitution, and the School		40. The Quiet Revolution: Rethinking Teacher Development
	19. The Moral Dimensions of Schools		41. A New Look at School Failure and School Success
	20. Public Schools, Religion, and Public Responsibility		42. NEA's Teacher Education Initiative: The First Year
	21. Creating School and Classroom Cultures That Value Learning: The Role of National Standards		43. Paying Attention to Relationships
	22. Converting Peer Pressure		44. The Silicon Classroom
			45. Revisiting Tomorrow's Classrooms
			46. A Philosophy of Education for the Year 2000

(Continued on next page)

ABOUT YOU

Name _____ Date _____

Are you a teacher? ❑ Or a student? ❑

Your school name _____

Department _____

Address _____

City _____ State _____ Zip _____

School telephone # _____

YOUR COMMENTS ARE IMPORTANT TO US!

Please fill in the following information:

For which course did you use this book? _____

Did you use a text with this *ANNUAL EDITION*? ❑ yes ❑ no

What was the title of the text? _____

What are your general reactions to the *Annual Editions* concept?

Have you read any particular articles recently that you think should be included in the next edition?

Are there any articles you feel should be replaced in the next edition? Why?

Are there any World Wide Web sites you feel should be included in the next edition? Please annotate.

May we contact you for editorial input?

May we quote your comments?